WELFARE POLICY

WELFARE POLICY

[feminist critiques]

edited by Elizabeth M. Bounds,
Pamela K. Brubaker, and
Mary E. Hobgood

WIPF & STOCK · Eugene, Oregon

To all those who work to make this society
a better place for women and children

Wipf and Stock Publishers
199 W 8th Ave, Suite 3
Eugene, OR 97401

Welfare Policy
Feminist Critiques
By Bounds, Elizabeth M.
Copyright©1999 Pilgrim Press
ISBN 13: 978-1-60899-231-7
Publication date 1/8/2010
Previously published by Pilgrim Press, 1999

Contents

PART THREE
Analysis of Responses of Churches and Activists

Afterwords

Foreword

Beverly W. Harrison

THE PUBLICATION OF *Welfare Policy: Feminist Critiques* is for me an occasion for rejoicing. Grounded in the present public controversy over so-called welfare reform, the ten chapters published here, along with afterwords from noted womanist and *mujerista* theologians, model a genre of feminist ethics, informed normatively by radical reading of Christian or related religious traditions. However, the distinctiveness of this book lies in a theological perspective that is also profoundly and unapologetically political, rooted in advocacy for a policy that aims at women's well-being, a position situated outside the mainstream of current public policy debate.

Readers who do not follow the subtle shifts of academic theology and ethics in the academy may be surprised to hear me say that this wonderful collection of chapters is the first of its genre, but that it also could (if trends continue) be the last of the genre as well. Why is this so? Ours is a time when new and sometimes subtle forms of neoliberal theology and ethics are impacting every area of theological and religious studies, including feminist work in women's studies. While producing often-artful cultural criticism, much newer feminist theology is nevertheless dismissive of positive claims to religious or moral knowledge and is subtly antipolitical. Today's cultural critic (postmodernist jargon for any and all intellectuals who reread established intellectual traditions) frequently aims to deconstruct political, moral, and religious interpretations as such. Some recent feminist theology, and even some feminist religious ethics, rereads in ways remote from the actual dynamics of our historical situatedness in a political economy which, as never before, is restructuring the lives and life conditions of every man, woman, and child on little planet earth.

Such a retreat into apolitical feminist work follows a neoliberal enthusiasm for the erasure of politics and relegates cultural criticism to academic enclaves where the presumed rites of cultural radicalism go on. Much such academic work supposes that novel speech-acts uttered in classrooms or published in books are a sufficient politics of change. In this new neofeminist world, participation in public policy debate itself is often taken as a symptom that one has not understood the profundities of postmodernist critique. Imbibing the socially constructed right-wing attack on political correctness, enthusiasts for postmodernism often leave us without comprehension about this present world, where now everything is left to market forces. The current ideology of welfare reform itself is suffused with neoliberal moral and theological assumptions, including the deep and libelous assumption that private business can solve problems that the state heretofore has only mismanaged. Happily, the essays in this volume help unmask such welfare reform by locating these reforms in relation to global economic shifts that go unnoted in most of the public debate on the welfare question.

In their introduction, the volume editors provide a valuable account of the methodological assumptions that set these authors apart from ahistorical and antimaterialist genres of cultural criticism which I find so disturbing. As they note, the genre of feminist ethical work presented here is liberationist, not liberal. It seeks to address the concrete patterns of human suffering, not only to illumine gender injustice but to show how the interstructuring of racism as cultural supremacy and class/economic privilege, and labor exploitation interact with gender/sex oppression to shape ongoing public discourse.

Exposing the duplicity in welfare reform is not easy. It is central to the goal of this feminist ethical work to challenge the imposition of neoliberal ideology, so triumphant in the Reagan-Bush era and proceeding apace under President Clinton. The rhetoric of welfare reform aims to persuade us that serious efforts are being made at restructuring government spending. Welfare reform is a rhetorical concession that Clinton has tossed his right-wing critics to prove his fiscal caution and his commitment to less government.

The contention here—that the state should address more vigorously issues of justice and undertake new initiatives at distributive justice—has an almost quaint ring in this political climate. The media fill the airwaves with analyses that suggest that state-initiated efforts at solving social problems simply do not work. Welfare creates bureaucracy, it is said, and can do little else. Such arguments are merely propaganda, however, and they are wrong historically. The facts are that federal government initiatives can work and have done so consistently, reshaping society in a more democratic direction. Here and in every liberal western democracy where public policy has aimed at change, state programs have made important differences. Most justice-centered programs do what they were designed to do.

The problem is that the United States, unlike many European welfare democracies, never intended to do much for dependent children or poor women! It is a truism that the original Aid to Dependent Children in our now downsized welfare program was created intentionally to be bureaucratic. Our nation, with its fierce tooth-and-claw-like work ethic, creates all social programs with rigid standards for eligibility so as to require administration by experts to discern entitlement.

Because we believe that it is necessary to ferret out ruthlessly malingerers and the undeserving, public welfare American-style is an endless, tangled process of demonstrating and documenting need. Is it not "the American Way" to make the process of applying for public assistance so demeaning and so stigmatizing in itself that only the most desperate will ask for help? Needless to say, in the past, many welfare democracies (including Canada and most European nations) had programs in which moderate child-welfare subsidies were paid to each and every child born into the society. Such universal programs do not require costly administration and were the preferred pattern in most countries. Persons with disabilities, those receiving unemployment compensation or retirement benefits, can be benefited by programs that are designed to reduce administrative cost. By contrast, U.S. programs are created to search out and destroy unworthy claimants.

No one denies that there was an urgent need for reform in our former AFDC system. As the authors of these chapters make clear, however, the one thing that has never been tried is an approach that makes the survival and well-being of poor single mothers and their children a central value in the policy process itself. When the smoke clears from the present restructuring of AFDC, we may safely predict that this downsizing, said to be required by fiscal responsibility and the need for less government, will merely have further shifted the costs of bearing and raising children to poor and poorly educated women and to voluntary organizations such as churches and private agencies. The tiny savings in the federal budget garnered from ending federal programs will turn out to have been only an occasion to shift costs to state and local governments. Nor will these costs be accurately counted. Increased homelessness and poorer health and education will have a social cost that politicians will deny. Welfare reform is merely redistributing the cost of our social-moral contempt onto those already victimized by a death-dealing neoliberal theology that God rewards only those who help themselves.

So long as deeply racist, antidemocratic values prevail in this public debate, and so long as the debate is shaped by skepticism that political solutions can

Acknowledgments

ALL BOOKS REQUIRE NETWORKS IN ORDER to emerge. Much of the pleasure in creating this book came out of continuing connections. The original source of this work was our professional network, the American Academy of Religion, where some of these chapters were first presented at a session on welfare organized by Carol S. Robb for the Women and Religion Section, and others at a session sponsored by the Ethics Section. Our thanks go to the organizers, especially Carol.

The special network that brought the three of us together for this project comprises students, friends, and mentees of Beverly W. Harrison. Since Bev was the first one to tell us that our papers had to be a book, it gives us joy to acknowledge her support and to offer our work as one of the many honors for her retirement.

The actual production of this book required a network of contributors, helped by e-mail, mail, phone, and fax. Thanks to all of them. Thanks also to Timothy Staveteig of The Pilgrim Press, whose enthusiasm for this project has been a great support. And thanks to Michael T. Bradley Jr. for his editorial assistance at a very crucial point. We are also grateful to Sara Goldreich of the New England Welfare Reform Initiative for help with the resource list.

In addition, Liz would like to thank Candler School of Theology for providing resources (especially the help of Aimee Delevett and Tami S. Groves); Pam acknowledges gratefully California Lutheran University's help through grants and library assistance; and Mary thanks the College of the Holy Cross for a junior leave in the spring of 1997.

Contributors

Gloria H. Albrecht is associate professor of religious studies at the University of Detroit Mercy, Detroit, Michigan. She is the author of *The Character of Our Communities: Toward an Ethic of Liberation for the Church* (Abingdon, 1995).

Elizabeth M. Bounds is associate professor of Christian ethics at the Candler School of Theology, Emory University. She is the author of *Coming Together/Coming Apart: Religion, Community and Modernity* (Routledge, 1997).

Pamela K. Brubaker is associate professor of religious studies at California Lutheran University. Her publications include *Women Don't Count: The Challenge of Women's Poverty to Christian Ethics* (Scholars, 1994).

Beverly W. Harrison is the Caroline Williams Beard Professor of Christian Ethics at Union Theological Seminary in New York City. Her publications include *Our Right to Choose: Toward a New Ethic of Abortion* (Beacon, 1983) and *Making the Connections: Essays in Feminist Social Ethics* (Beacon, 1985).

Mary E. Hobgood is assistant professor of religious studies at the College of the Holy Cross, Worcester, Massachusetts. Her publications include *Catholic Social Teaching and Economic Theory: Paradigms in Conflict* (Temple University Press, 1991).

Ada María Isasi-Díaz is associate professor of ethics and theology at Drew University. Her publications include the edited volume *Hispanic/Latino Theology: Challenge and Promise,* with Fernando F. Segovia (Fortress, 1996). She is the author of *Hispanic Women, Prophetic Voice in the Church: Toward a Hispanic Women's Liberation Theology,* with Yolanda Tarango (1988; 2d ed., Fortress, 1993); *En La Lucha: Elaborating a Mujerista Theology* (Fortress, 1993); and *Mujerista Theology: A Theology for the 21st Century* (Orbis, 1996).

Janet R. Jakobsen is associate professor of religious studies and women's studies and co-coordinator of the Committee for Lesbian, Gay, and Bisexual Studies at the University of Arizona. Her publications include *Working Alliances and the Politics of Difference: Diversity and Complexity in Feminist Ethics* (Indiana University Press, 1998).

Ellen Ott Marshall is a doctoral candidate in religion, ethics, and society at Vanderbilt University.

Carol S. Robb is the Margaret Dollar Professor of Christian Social Ethics at San Francisco Theological Seminary. Her publications include *Equal Value: An Ethical Approach to Economics and Sex* (Beacon, 1995).

Joan Sakalas is a doctoral candidate in Christian social ethics at Union Theological Seminary, New York City, and works with welfare recipients.

Ruth L. Smith is associate professor of religion and philosophy at the Worcester Polytechnic Institute in Worcester, Massachusetts. Her publications include articles in *Cultural Critique* and the *Journal of Feminist Studies in Religion.*

Emilie M. Townes is professor of Christian social ethics at Saint Paul School of Theology in Kansas City, Missouri. Her publications include the edited volumes *A Troubling in My Soul: Womanist Perspectives on Evil and Suffering* (Orbis, 1993) and *Embracing the Spirit: Womanist Perspectives on Hope, Salvation, and Transformation* (Orbis, 1997). She is the author of *Womanist Justice: Womanist Hope* (Scholars, 1993), *In a Blaze of Glory: Womanist Spirituality as Social Witness* (Abingdon, 1995), and *Breaking the Fine Rain of Death: African-American Health Issues and a Womanist Ethic of Care* (Continuum, 1998).

Traci C. West is assistant professor of Christian ethics and African American studies at Drew University Theological School. Her publications include *Wounds of the Spirit: Black Women, Violence, and Resistance Ethics* (New York University Press, 1999).

Welfare "Reform": A War against the Poor

Elizabeth M. Bounds, Pamela K. Brubaker, Mary E. Hobgood

Digna Jimenez could not find new child care after her baby sitter slapped her daughter. When her welfare caseworker refused to help, Ms. Jimenez withdrew from workfare, preferring to reduce her welfare support by nearly 20 percent than risk her children's well-being.

RACHEL SWARNS, "MOTHERS POISED FOR WORKFARE FACE ACUTE LACK OF DAY CARE," *New York Times*, APRIL 14, 1998

A homeless woman in a workfare program filed a sexual harassment claim saying her supervisor continually made comments about her body and had once said he would help get her a job if she would go to a motel with him. "His conduct made me feel embarrassed and worthless, and affected my ability to do my job," she stated.

DAVID L. LEWIS, "WORKFARE WOMAN CLAIMS SEXUAL HARASSMENT," *New York Daily News*, MARCH 12, 1998

Keisha, a 28-year-old mother of two, was delighted to be accepted for nurse's training. But in order to qualify for childcare under the Ohio Work Program (a workfare program), she could not spend more than 10 hours a week in training while also working 20 hours a week at a job. Keisha may have to forgo training for a better job, and stay in a lower paying job to abide by the new welfare rules.

ARTHUR JONES, "NEW LAW MEANS MORE POVERTY," *National Catholic Reporter*, APRIL 17, 1998

1

Rosa Dolone goes by subway from food pantry to food bank in the Bronx, begging for groceries. As an immigrant, albeit legal, she has been dropped from the food stamp rolls. Even though one church food pantry won't accept her without a referral and another has run out of food, she keeps going, since "My children have to eat."

RACHEL L. SWARNS, "DENIED FOOD STAMPS, MANY LEGAL IMMIGRANTS SCRAPE FOR MEALS," *New York Times*, DECEMBER 9, 1997

These stories, women's stories, are the reason for this book. Recent welfare legislation has profoundly affected the lives of poor women in the United States. Feminist ethical work, accountable to promote the well-being of women, is required to respond to this situation. This accountability may even be greater for feminist Christian ethicists (the location of most of the contributors to this volume), since they also speak out of strands of Christian traditions that have called for justice for the poor and the most vulnerable members of our society.

The 1996 welfare legislation effectively dismantled the over-sixty-year legacy of federal responsibility for poor families in the United States. The Personal Responsibility and Work Opportunity Reconciliation Act (PRWORA) has initiated a historical restructuring of U.S. welfare policy by the federal government, states, and counties that is affecting the well-being of millions of women, children, and poor men. Our purpose is to expose critical assumptions that inform the welfare reform discussion and to explore some resources for shaping a policy discussion more accountable to the needs of women and children. Such work is urgent, we believe, as the current law will be reviewed by Congress in 2002.

In recent years, welfare dependency has emerged as a focus of public policy debate in a national economy that is booming but whose benefits accrue primarily to a small portion of the population. The majority suffers from economic insecurity, resulting from an increase in downsizing, low-wage work, underemployment, and the stagnation of real wages. Those at the bottom sectors of the economy, disproportionately women and people of color, suffer these effects with the greatest intensity. However, moral rhetoric about the poor is always careful to shift public attention away from critical analysis of the political economy, which has been radically restructured in the past quarter-century as capitalism becomes a global system. Public attention continues to be maintained now, as in the past, on the regulation of individual behavior, especially female sexual behavior, cast as "personal responsibility."

All of the chapters in this book resist this focus, insisting that ethical approaches to welfare policy must include critical feminist analysis of the political economy and of religious and other cultural ideologies that support the status quo. It is this perspective that distinguishes our work from that of some other recent work in Christian ethics, such as that done by the Center for Public Justice. While we share their Christian affirmation of human dignity, multifaceted responsibility, and a government called to establish public justice, we note the reluctance to identify the specific condition of poor women and the silence on the destructive impact of global capitalism.[1] We understand current welfare legislation in the United States to be part of the larger restructuring of late twentieth-century neoliberal corporate capitalism, which we will discuss in greater depth in the next section. In light of this understanding, we are especially concerned with the lack of attention to the economy in the welfare discussion. In this country, when we are electing presidents who can affect the well-being of the comfortable, we can cry "It's the economy, Stupid," but when we talk about welfare, the concern is economizing rather than the economy itself.

Thus, our purpose is to bring together in this volume progressive feminist religious voices that seek to make the economy and its complex effects more visible. While we highlight the exploitative power of economic forces, we simultaneously emphasize the complex interconnections with the historical forces of race and gender. Some authors focus more on macroanalysis—the big picture; others on microanalysis—details of the legislation. Some advocate major transformation of the political economy, others incremental change. While some are more focused on economic questions and others more on questions of race, sexuality, or ideological formation, all focus on the root causes of poverty.

We ourselves, the editors of this volume, speak specifically from materialist feminist Christian perspectives which draw on feminist and Christian traditions that are critical of the economy and on legacies of movements for social change.[2] Even though not all of the contributors would identify themselves in this way, we find each piece represented here makes a contribution toward the common goals of critiquing oppressive structures that thwart the well-being of poor women and their families and calling for new policies answerable to their needs.

In the remainder of this essay, we will offer some resources helpful for engaging the work of this volume by providing introductions to neoliberal economics, recent welfare legislation, and feminist Christian ethical approaches to public policy questions. Each of these sections will provide some basic information for readers new to these areas while further articulating the assumptions underlying our approach. They reflect the work of feminist Christian ethics, attentive to material realities while in dialogue with critical moral norms.

Welfare and Neoliberal Economic Policy

We understand welfare dismantling to be part of the larger system of neoliberal structural adjustment policies which are intensifying poverty for the majority of the world's population under the new conditions of the capitalist global economy. In the previous three decades, the post–World War II economic expansion by the United States has been replaced by fierce economic and financial competition among U.S.-, Japanese-, and Western European-based corporations. Although 85 percent of industrial output is still produced by national corporations, global production is increasingly dominated by relatively few corporations and mobile financial institutions. Investors no longer find themselves accountable to the communities and regions where they do business and can roam the planet for the best business deals (or, even more frequently, can threaten to do so). Class power has shifted with the "exit threat" of capital, which holds governments and workers hostage to its demands.[3]

These demands include nonrestrictive access to world markets, massive reductions in international and domestic labor costs, and increased state subsidies for the other costs of corporate profit making. This is accomplished through such neoliberal economic policies (often called economic "reforms") as free trade agreements, privatizing the public nonprofit sector, and "downsizing" the private sector. On a global scale, these policies promote the mechanization of higher-skilled work traditionally monopolized by men, the proliferation of low-wage labor increasingly dominated by women and children, and massive cuts in state spending for social welfare and environmental protection. They encourage foreign ownership of Two-Thirds World economies through short-term investments that can be pulled out abruptly at the first sign of lowering returns on profits. The economies cannot protect themselves against capital fluctuation, creating the need for massive bailouts and more severe adjustment policies as seen recently in Mexico and east Asia. Side effects of these polices include increased trafficking in armaments, which is profitable to countries like the United States, while also providing weaponry to repress resistance to the impact of these economic policies. Intensive and mobile industrial development has also severely impacted environments throughout the globe, from the depletion of rain forest resources to the dangerous pollution of many Two-Thirds World cities.

As a result of such policies which serve the profit-making interests of relatively few shareholders, income inequality is growing within as well as among nations. National and state legislatures find themselves competing with each other to subsidize jobs that may soon become lost altogether to technology, or are deskilled and devalued. Governments find themselves vulnerable to the demands of big business because it is often the only economic game in town and/or because they need relief from the escalating debt that plagues their economies.

The new so-called efficiency of neoliberal economic policy is, in large part, simply reflecting the shifting of costs from a paid labor force onto the invisible backs of women in the household. The theory of economic structural-adjustment policy is that an economy will be stronger if it is structured to serve a world market which makes profits for relatively few investors, with no consideration of social needs. States are supposed to assume that the experiences of belt-tightening due to higher prices for necessities, lower wages, and higher unemployment will be temporary until "trickle down" from long-term growth takes effect. Structural adjustment includes reducing the role of the state (by defunding environmental protection, education, and other social services) and increasing the role of the market. Such austerity plans have been initiated by the International Monetary Fund and the World Bank in the Two-Thirds World as a condition for refinancing a country's loans. In the United States, we have been experiencing deregulation, regressive tax policies, the dismantling of welfare, and moves to privatize increasing sectors of the economy like Social Security, Medicaid, public education, and transportation. We have seen a radical restructuring of the labor market, where 80 percent of workers have lost 20 percent of buying power over the last two decades and where over one-third of the work force (predominantly female) does contingent labor. The overall effect of these policies, in both the Two-Thirds World and the United States, has been a significant increase in women's work as they seek to "bridge the gap" between the needs of their families and the income available.

In a possible reversal of thirty years of small but measurable economic progress for women (as well as for many men), most women's overall situation has deteriorated since the onset of structural-adjustment policies. As governments cut education, health clinics, hospital stays, food subsidies, transportation, and other social services, household labor must increase to fill the gaps. Not only does unpaid domestic labor intensify as women care for the sick, educate the young, and try to grow more of their own food, but female employment increases exponentially. This is true not only in the United States but throughout the globe as women drop out of education and enter the expanding sectors of informal and low-wage labor, often in an effort to replace earnings from the better-paid jobs lost to men. As men migrate in search of employment, the number of female-headed households depending on their unstable and insufficient resources increases. As companies pressure one another to keep costs down in order to win the competitive game by making the highest profits, there is little doubt that women—especially poor women—have borne the brunt of neoliberal economic policy.

In this process of economic transformation, however, the neoliberal policies of late capitalism also threaten to erode other structures that historically have been important in maintaining the status quo in the United States. These include the male-dominant traditional family, the racially segregated labor market, and social expenditures in health, education, and welfare which historically have protected people from the worst fallout of the economic system. As female-headed families replace male-dominant ones, as whites join diverse peoples of color at the expanding lower rungs of labor markets, and as economic insecurity increases for larger sectors of the population, rising cultural anxieties and the need to protect relatively few shareholders at the top lead people to search for scapegoats to explain and justify these radical inequalities.

Welfare for poor families becomes a likely target, since historically it has provided the symbolic social space to assemble and reinforce racist, class-elitist, and gender-polarized religious and cultural values which have served to maintain the social order. If the behaviors of poor women, especially poor mothers of color, can be identified as the reasons for family instability, deepening poverty, and increasing economic insecurity for the majority, then the actual structural dynamics that systematically reproduce these outcomes remain invisible. Also escaping notice are the increases in women's unpaid domestic labor, which must remain unlimited and free in order for structural adjustments to "work."

As women throughout the globe underwrite its costs, neoliberal economic policy intensifies the inequalities promoted by class, race, and gender structures. It is these structures and the ideologies they promote that this book seeks to address and evaluate. In a time of escalating unmet domestic needs and increasing numbers of jobs that pay less than a living wage, welfare and other social services that provide people with some meager alternatives are being dismantled amidst intense attack. It is our contention that politicians, conservative think tanks, and the media use welfare issues as a foil for the economic interests they serve and the religious and cultural beliefs that maintain the status quo.[4]

Welfare Policy

Capitalism has always reproduced poverty and has struggled to contain its effects. During the Depression era, the Roosevelt administration realized that poverty could no longer be managed at the state level. The New Deal initiated a two-track federal welfare system. The first track, offered to those who were "independent" workers, included social insurance programs like unemployment and old-age insurance and offered aid as entitlements. Second-track public assistance programs like Aid to Dependent Children (ADC), which later became Aid to Families with Dependent Children (AFDC), were constructed as charity to those deemed "fit and proper"—at first, only white widows and their children. Welfare rights advocates organized in the 1960s to change the terms of welfare programs and to expand coverage. It was during this period that AFDC became a legal entitlement: if you met the financial criteria, you were entitled to assistance. As welfare beneficiaries came to be perceived as undeserving members of different racial and class groups, demands for "reform" began, which, in the context of increasing global economic pressures, have eventually developed into the current welfare legislation.

PRWORA, the Personal Responsibility and Work Opportunity Reconciliation Act of 1996 (Public Law 104-93) was a deliberate departure from the heritage of these policies. PRWORA dismantled welfare programs for poor families by, among other things, ending the federally mandated entitlement status, which ensured at least provisional benefits for anyone across the country who fell below a certain income level. It abolished AFDC, JOBS (the work and training program for welfare recipients), and Emergency Assistance to Families with Children (a program that provided emergency help to families with children).

All of these programs were replaced with Temporary Assistance for Needy Families (TANF), a block grant of federal funds distributed to the states. PRWORA requires states to operate welfare programs but gives them flexibility in allocating TANF funds—a percentage of which may be transferred into child care and development, community service jobs and employment incentives, or social service block grants. States were given increased authority to determine eligibility and to administer cash assistance, employment and training, and child-care funds in accordance with federal guidelines. These require that most parents must participate in work activities within two years and that individuals who have received aid for more than two months do "community service," unless a state opts out of this requirement. States were required to assess recipients' skills and could develop "personal responsibility plans" for individuals. Families were limited to a lifetime total of five years of cash assistance, although states may grant hardship exemptions to up to 20 percent of the average monthly caseload. States could deny cash benefits to children born to welfare recipients (the "family cap"). Food stamps for noncitizens were eliminated. Overall, cuts in federal funds for these welfare programs were projected to be a total of $54 billion over six years.

The Balanced Budget Act of 1997 made some adjustments to the 1996 legislation. Minimum-wage protection was to be applied to required jobs. A $1.5 billion "welfare-to-work" grant program was created to be distributed to the states in fiscal years 1998 and 1999, for use through 2001. Although further funds were added in the 1997 budget, the total is still not adequate to cover the cost of these programs. Recent increases in funds for child health and child care enacted by the federal government and some states are also insufficient to address needs.[5] The 1997 act and further 1998 legislation restored food stamps to certain categories of legal aliens, leaving many still without access to food relief.

One critical outcome of PRWORA was to change welfare from a program administered under common federal guidelines to programs that could vary widely according to different state mandates. Thus, assessing the impact of PRWORA requires a state-by-state analysis, which will take several years. The Children's Defense Fund issued a report in the fall of 1997 as an initial assessment of state programs developed in response to the federal legislation.[6] According to the report, twenty states have revised PRWORA's five-year maximum lifetime limit by allowing shorter stays over a longer period or by selecting various time limits of less than five years. The report indicated that advocates in some states have been successful in creating programs that are beneficial to poor children and help families go to work. States recognized for positive programs include Minnesota, Utah, Illinois, New York, and Ohio. Other states, however, are taking steps that will increase the severity of the new federal rules as they allow thousands of families to lose aid (fifteen states have implemented two-year time limits on welfare provision). Especially high termination rates have been observed for families in Mississippi, Massachusetts, Iowa, South Carolina, Virginia, and Wisconsin.[7]

The report noted that approximately one-third of families nationally (3.4 million out of 10.7 million) have been dropped from the rolls since 1993. It is estimated, however, that only 15 percent of these 3.4 million families left the roles because of increased parental earnings. It appears that most closings were due to a failure to comply with welfare rules, indicating that many families may be falling into increased immiseration. A New York state survey found that only 29 percent of those who went off New York welfare rolls from July 1996 through March 1997 found full-time or part-time work in the first several months without assistance. Between October 1997 and October 1998, the Wisconsin rolls fell by 70 percent. However, a University of Wisconsin study found that 75 percent of those who left for new jobs lost these jobs within nine months.[8]

It is not hard to be dropped from the system. The rules vary from state to state and may not even be uniform across a state. Often they are so confusing that welfare workers in the same state may often give clients different and contradictory information.[9] Minnesota case managers found that up to 75 percent of adults who had been sanctioned had at least one barrier to employment: either domestic violence, physical disability of parent or child, depression, or substance abuse.[10] A newspaper reporter accompanying a woman whose inability to find child care qualified her for exemption from the work requirement found that the social worker threatened her by stating falsely that the law had changed.[11]

Counties also have flexibility to develop their own programs within the bounds set by federal and state legislation. Los Angeles County in California has the largest welfare system of any county in the nation and is also larger than that of many states. In early 1998, more than 1.6 million county residents received some form of public assistance, with 768,000 enrolled in TANF, the largest cash-assistance program (which replaced AFDC). The Los Angeles County welfare program, adopted by county supervisors at this time, exempts mothers of children under one year old from work requirements, as permitted by state legislation. However, other single parents are required to participate in thirty-two hours of work or related activities per week to maintain their eligibility for a cash grant.[12] Los Angeles County's welfare-to-work program has received a national service excellence award. However, 85 percent of welfare recipients placed in employment remain on the welfare rolls because they cannot earn enough to provide their families with the minimum necessities.[13] A survey conducted by Diana Pearce for Wider Opportunities for Women found that mothers in urban California must earn two to three times the minimum wage to escape the need for government assistance and just to cover housing, child care, transportation, and medical needs. An adult with one infant would need $12.24 an hour, or with one infant and a preschooler, $16.24 an hour. In western Massachusetts, the Pearce study found that a woman with two children would have to earn $13.98 an hour, or almost $30,000 a year, in order not to have to choose between basic necessities, for example, between housing and health care.[14]

What will happen to these families when they reach the maximum five-year period for receiving benefits? The state of California did pass legislation that assures "continued but reduced assistance to children" once the family's time limit is reached (using state dollars since federal dollars cannot be used for this purpose).[15] But what will happen when this time actually comes, particularly if the state is in another period of recession?

Observers have already seen an increase in the numbers of the working poor seeking food aid. A survey by the U.S. Conference of Mayors reported that 86 percent of cities surveyed noted an increased demand for emergency food assistance, rising an average of 16 percent. And 38 percent of people seeking this assistance are actually employed, up from 23 percent in 1994. An increase in the number of working poor seeking food aid does not bode well for the success of welfare reform if our criteria for success is lifting people out of poverty. Nor does an increase in the number of women with children among the U.S.

homeless. An October 1998 survey by the International Union of Gospel Missions found a dramatic increase in the number of homeless women with children—from 46 percent of homeless families in 1991 to 66 percent in 1998. One-fifth of homeless families surveyed had lost AFDC and/or food stamps in the past year.[16]

While the purported major objective of PRWORA was making people "responsible" by bringing them into the waged work force, recent studies of workfare programs, which place welfare recipients in jobs, are extremely troubling. In an economy where thirty-year-old white, male high-school graduates have seen their real wages drop 35 percent in the last twenty years, workfare increases the competition for these low-wage jobs, potentially throwing even more workers into welfare poverty. According to the Children's Defense Fund, there are only enough new jobs nationwide to employ 54 percent of welfare recipients. The Midwest Job Gap Project discovered that in Ohio in 1997, there were four job-seekers for every low-skilled job; twenty-three potential workers for every low-skilled job that paid at least poverty-level wages ($12,278 annually); sixty-six for those that paid at least 150 percent of poverty level wages ($18,417); and one hundred for every one that paid what was estimated to be a living wage for families with children ($25,907).[17]

Nor can workfare jobs be seen as stepping stones to better-paying work. Restrictions on education and training enacted in the 1996 law were greatly tightened by the 1997 federal Balanced Budget Act, which makes it nearly impossible for adult welfare recipients to acquire the skills for decent-paying jobs. In contrast to prior welfare programs, TANF does not consider higher education to be work, only vocational education. And even if a woman pursues vocational education, work requirements permit only 30 percent of those on state rolls who are classified as working to be engaged in vocational education and only twelve months of support are allotted. Although women might try to attend college on their own time, there is little time left after work requirements and family needs are fulfilled. Indeed, there has been a dramatic decrease in the numbers of welfare recipients enrolled in community college, university, and adult education programs.[18] A *New York Times* report on the Work Experience Program, a New York City workfare program, remarks that "Much of the work is so menial that it offers few, if any, skills that employers demand," such as cleaning city offices and picking up trash in parks.[19] Further, workers are forced to do this unsanitary, sometimes dangerous, work under inhumane conditions, including lack of access to toilets and lack of basic equipment such as coats and boots for street sweepers.[20] It seems that work requirements are creating a "permanent underclass of workers that will be a source of slave labor for both public and private sectors."[21] A hopeful sign is efforts by some employers to work with job training programs, but these experiments are still rare.

Welfare reform may also make women more vulnerable to various forms of abuse and endangerment. Since many women enter welfare programs in order to leave abusive male partners, decreased access to benefits may compel them to remain. Strengthened paternity identification requirements, while encouraging paternal responsibility, can also force women to have greater contact with violent partners. Teenage mothers are required to live with their parents, which in some cases may expose them to further sexual abuse and also make their whereabouts known if they are in danger from violent partners. Women and their children may also be physically endangered if family cap rules discourage them from seeking prenatal care.

Since the 1996 welfare bill was not constructed with careful planning, foresight, or reasoned debate but rather was based on stereotypes, myth, and political ideology, no one has a handle on what may lie in store for poor families in the years ahead. Despite seven years of almost uninterrupted growth in the U.S. economy since 1989, the 13.7 percent official poverty rate for 1997 was higher than in 1989. Many analysts believe that these official figures would be much higher if they reflected the actual cost of living and after-tax income. In their 1986 pastoral letter on the economy, the U.S. Catholic bishops stated that perhaps one-fourth of the population was living below "any reasonable standard" of need.[22] Some studies estimate that 50 million Americans, or almost one-fifth of the population, live below the national poverty line, including one-fourth of U.S. children under the age of eighteen.[23] Yet while thousands of families are leaving the welfare rolls for greater immiseration and the poverty rate for children of workers is on the rise, experts on state fiscal affairs predict that at least one-half of the states will enact substantial tax cuts in 1998.[24] Even with the severe cuts in taxes for the wealthy (for example, the corporate share of tax revenue has decreased from 20 percent thirty years ago to 12.5 percent now),[25] most states are sitting on sizable tax surpluses. Such surpluses are unlikely to be redistributed to the poor and working class. For them, average weekly earnings have declined by almost one-fifth since 1973. The income gap is increasing everywhere in the nation. In New York state, for example, the gulf between the top fifth and bottom fifth of families has increased 127 percent since the 1970s.[26] Richard Freeman, a Harvard economist, fears that given these shifts and the elimination of the welfare safety net, any downturn in the economy will mean "that the bottom will literally fall out for Americans at the bottom of the income distribution."[27] In our future may be what Freeman has called the "apartheid economy," divided between the privileged "haves" and the destitute poor.

Feminist Ethics and Public Policy

Neoliberal economic policies and "reforms" such as welfare dismantling create social structures and systems that make the liberty of the market and profit for investors the unchallenged social priority. These structures channel funding from the bottom and middle sectors in the economy to those privileged at the top, and are unassailable in the media and dominant cultural ideology. Corporate and labor market structures, among other forces, systematically reproduce routinized inequality and injustice which fly in the face of principles of social ethics, especially feminist social ethics.

Feminist Christian ethics has something to say about welfare dismantling because it draws upon theological traditions and moral resources that are pertinent to the public policy debate. As Christian feminist ethicists, we find ourselves equipped with a rich set of resources as well as traditions that need to be challenged for considering questions of public policy such as welfare. We recognize, as Ruth Smith's discussion of Christian attitudes toward poverty shows, that Christian traditions have often used the poor as objects of charity, enabling the salvation of others through the economic and political perpetuation of poverty. And as both Janet Jakobsen's and Elizabeth Bounds's discussions of the Christian right demonstrate, contemporary conservative Christianity is actively engaged in constructing poor women (and men) as dangerous bodies, requiring moral regulation and rehabilitation. However, while acknowledging these oppressive strands, we also find that as we put feminism and Christianity into dialogue, transformative places emerge which strengthen the seeking of justice. We will point out a few of these transformative places in the formation of Christian feminist public ethics, noting their presence in the different chapters included in this volume:

Engagement and Accountability

Feminist ethics seeks not to be one more academic conversation but tries to follow the heritage of women's movements which have sought to change their communities. Christian ethics (although by now endowed with plenty of academic discussions), at heart, is also practical, seeking to discern the activities of Christian persons in the world. Such practical concerns mark every contribution in this volume from Ellen Marshall's suggestions for reforming Individual Responsibility Plans to Traci West's suggestions for antiracism work in the churches and Joan Sakalas's suggestions for developing a just, faith-based outreach support.

The practicality arises from a sense of accountability. Feminist policy proposals are not constructed while considering a generalized group of citizens but in engagement with the concrete struggles of women and of the men and children surrounding them. Feminists see themselves accountable to those within their own communities (evident particularly in the works of womanist and *mujerista* ethicists) and to women elsewhere in the nation and the world who struggle against exploitation and domination. Such accountability demands taking these women's experiences as central to the doing of ethics and considering their well-being as the focal point for policy making. It intersects with strands of Christian liberation theologies, which have sought to keep the poor at the center of moral and theological reflection.[28] This accountability is most vividly present in Joan Sakalas's reflection on a group of women in New York City, struggling to determine their lives. Her focus—to move, as she puts it, "from margin to center"—can be discerned in all the essays in this volume, which, regardless of the scope of their concerns, always keep at the center the present sufferings of women who are forced to rely on welfare.

Staying with the Concrete

Although feminist ethics may speak in a variety of voices, using many different theoretical modes, it is always attentive to the concrete, starting with the complexity of women's stories. As Beverly Harrison has explained, "A treatment of any moral problem is inadequate if it fails to analyze the morality of a given act in a way that represents the concrete experience of the agent who faces a decision with respect to that act."[29] The chapters in this volume construe the concrete in all of its multilayered complexity. Traci West, for example, looks at the ways in which the media and the government distorted the concrete realities of poor, black teenage mothers through inaccurate and unjust stereotypes. Gloria Albrecht uses women's experiences to reconstruct notions of dependency as she shows how the economy has had a profound effect on current family life. And Ada María Isasi-Díaz insists upon the centrality of *lo cotidiano* (the everyday) as the "first horizon" of *mujerista* ethics.

Complex Standpoints

Although it may seem paradoxical, careful attention to and analysis of the concrete requires, ultimately, complex and multifaceted theoretical frameworks. Close analysis of any particular moment leads to consideration of the contradictory and multiple forces that constitute that moment. This recognition has been slow in coming for white feminism, where pressure to shed a diverse consciousness encouraged a virtually unidimensional focus on gender.[30] However, challenges from women of color both within and outside of the United States, poor women of all races, lesbian women, disabled women have all shifted the single lens to a kaleidoscope which can encompass the multiple structures at work. As Nancy Fraser remarks, "The task facing feminists is formidable. If we are to have any hope of understanding just what it is we are up against, we need...frameworks that are sensitive to specificity, but that nevertheless permit us to grasp very large objects of inquiry, such as the global economy. We also need approaches that promote our ability to think relationally and contextually."[31]

While no single one of us can ever accomplish this task, the variety of lenses used here demonstrate a common understanding that only multidimensional theories are equal to the task. This complexity reveals itself in an acknowledged insistence on engagement with multiple dimensions of social reality—as when, for example, Traci West keeps race, class, and gender in tension in her analysis of the stigmatizing of black women or when Ada María Isasi-Díaz points to the intersecting social and economic forces constituting both Cuban and U.S. realities. It also reveals itself in a less-acknowledged assumption that feminist ethics is interdisciplinary, drawing on a variety of disciplines to get the fullest possible account of the problem at hand. For example, in order to comment on wage proposals for women, Carol Robb draws on both feminist moral theories and feminist economic theories to show that gender socialization shapes moral rationality in economic decision making. Janet Jakobsen's discussion of the regulation of sexual morality shaped by a restructuring postmodern capitalism uses both poststructuralist and postcolonialist theories. Mary Hobgood draws on class theory in her analysis of the intensification of poverty, racism, and sexism to evaluate the strengths and limitations of the U.S. Catholic bishops' response to the welfare reforms.

Critical Perspectives

While drawing on multiple perspectives and disciplines, feminist ethics does not content itself with a liberal pluralism but rather seeks to find vantage points that both illuminate and criticize. The possible location of such emancipatory criticism is a topic of debate in current feminist theory, as postmodern and poststructuralist theorists point out the ways in which criticism may avoid the exclusions and limitations of its own position.[32] While we recognize this problem of location, our concern here is to provide some perspectives other than those most widely heard in the welfare debates. All of our authors hope to provide insights into the mystification of economic and social power and the scapegoating of poor persons. Using differing theoretical frameworks, they subject welfare policies to sharp criticism, pointing to places for resistance to the status quo. Ruth Smith traces the limitations of approaches to the poor and poverty from early Christian history to contemporary social theory and liberation theologies that maintain spiritual and economic hierarchies. In Smith's discussion of poverty and Jakobsen's exploration of freedom, we see how ideologies weave a cloth of "common sense" that hides the seams of struggles and inconsistencies. Gloria Albrecht challenges assumptions of liberal and communitarian discussions of family and poverty. Mary Hobgood reveals the oppressive structures of current economic policies and the weaknesses of moral and theological statements that seek to alter them. Emilie Townes names the forces behind our "age of spectacle."

Relationality, Dignity, and Autonomy

There are a variety of moral norms shared by feminist and Christian ethics. First, there is both an ontological and a moral insistence on the relationality of all things. From Paul's image of the body of Christ to the U.S. Catholic bishops' statement that the human person is social and has obligations to all of society, Christianity has affirmed the relational nature of human life. Similarly, feminist work consistently stresses what Beverly Harrison calls "the centrality of relationship...the reality that our moral-selves are body-selves who touch and see and hear each other into life."[33] Emilie Townes insists upon the fundamental relationality of the African American community, "interactive and interdependent in a spirituality of wholeness."[34]

Such relationality seems little acknowledged in a welfare debate that defines individual responsibility as complete self-sufficiency, in ways antithetical to feminist and Christian thought. The autonomy of "personal responsibility" (a slogan of the welfare debate) is assessed in light of ideologies that ignore our basic interdependence. Elizabeth Bounds notes how women's dependence on men always has been the other side of male-defined self-sufficiency, which has enabled poor black women to be labeled as "improperly dependent." Gloria Albrecht points to the ways in which the economic well-being and status of affluent families have always been dependent on the unpaid labor of poor persons. Stepping outside of this dichotomy of independence/dependence, Pamela Brubaker tests current welfare reform in light of *inter*dependence, a theo-ethical norm derived from an acknowledgment of relationality. Joan Sakalas demonstrates a program that seeks empowerment through the strength of interdependence.

Yet feminist and Christian ethics do not reject autonomy when viewed within a context of responsible interdependency. Christian traditions have continually stressed the worth of the individual, created in God's image. In discussing reproductive rights, rape, and domestic violence, feminists have called for a women's right to body autonomy, to control what happens to her physical and emotional self. The valuing of the human—particularly here the female human—leads to assertion of the importance of enabling one to live with dignity and with the ability to shape as much as possible the circumstances of one's life. The question for feminists is how to balance the goods of autonomy and relationality. As one possibility, Ellen Marshall draws on Amartya Sen's notion of "freedom to achieve" as a form of autonomy that understands the individual as not isolated but as a person in society.

Connections of Public and Private

Both contemporary feminist and contemporary Christian ethics have struggled with a privatized location. In modern U.S. society, the church and women have been relegated to the feminized private sphere. In contrast, men are understood to inhabit a secular public sphere, conceptualized as a place where individual citizens make policy through the exercise of power. Over the past few decades, there has occurred a realignment of private and public. Persons and their issues from the "hidden" public of the black community and other marginalized racial/ethnic communities entered the public arena through civil rights legislation. Feminists brought into public discussion what were previously considered issues with few or no public moral dimensions: marriage, domestic violence, rape. Gay and lesbian persons continue to try to make sexual identity a public question involving rights and responsibilities.

For feminists, the public and private spheres must always be held in tension. From the early feminist insistence that "the personal is political" to Beverly Harrison's insistence that we connect "personal pains" to "the wider dynamics of the social system,"[35] feminists have examined the ways in which private and public intersect in the issues that concern us. Welfare, our subject here, is a wonderful example of the complexity of this interconnection. On one hand, it is clearly a public issue, subject to debate in the media and in the legislatures. On the other hand, what have been considered private issues—family, sexuality, race—have been very much part of the debate, as many of our contributors demonstrate. Janet Jakobsen, Gloria Albrecht, and Elizabeth Bounds all show how anxiety over the private world of family has been a central theme in welfare reform. Traci West shows how racialized and sexualized stereotypes profoundly affected public policy making.

Justice as Solidarity

Justice and love lie at the heart of Christian traditions. Feminism, which emerged around calls for justice for women, continues to have justice at its heart. Certainly in the welfare discussion *justice* was not a popular word. One key dimension of justice is the claiming of rights as part of the assertion of the dignity and well-being of persons. By removing the federal responsibility for welfare, the U.S. government removed the possibility of claiming welfare as a right. The emphasis instead was on "personal responsibility," a renunciation of collective obligations and a preoccupation with the morality of individual poor persons.

While we see rights as essential (since they are basic recognitions of the worth and dignity of persons), we do not, as both Christians and feminists, work with highly individualized notions of rights, preferring to see rights in the context of our basic relationality. As a norm, justice participates in many of the transformative places we have already discussed. It is a relational word, denoting accountabilities to others. Iris Young remarks that reflection on justice "begins in a hearing, in heeding a call,"[36]—that is, in response to the needs of others expressed through our relationship to them. In the welfare debates, this notion of justice as a mutual negotiation of needs was silenced in favor of an individualist model where, if one could not be "responsible" for providing for one's own needs, one should turn to charity. Yet charity, as Ruth Smith and Joan Sakalas point out, is preeminently a relationship among unequals, where the givers enhance their power and moral "goodness" and the receivers are considered dependent and morally inferior.

Justice as a relational category also requires attention to values of caring. Although no one in this volume draws upon the recent discussions concerning a distinctive feminine ethic of care,[37] we find that this discussion at its best highlights the importance of certain aspects of justice, such as mutuality and the creation and sustenance of positive human relationships. Attention to care also requires us to consider the realm of ordinary daily life where persons (primarily women) tend through caring labor to the daily needs of those around them. The degree of justice offered by any proposal for welfare policy must be measured in terms of its impact on the possibilities of providing care under conditions supporting the dignity and self-esteem of both the caregiver and the recipient.

Justice demands a full analysis of the social forces involved, so that we can understand just what needs to be changed and why. It is a norm of engagement rather than passivity. Such structural analysis, as found in these essays, is necessary, although not sufficient, for solidarity and coalition building. As Janet Jakobsen says, alliance politics is the very basis of an alternative possibility once we work to unearth the structural links among diverse oppressions. Speaking of Latinas, Ada María Isasi-Díaz writes, "Justice for us refers not only to what we receive but also to our active and effective participation in making justice a reality."[38] We find this a call to all of us to engage in the alliances necessary to transform unjust welfare policies.

Looking Ahead: Initial Policy Proposals

Whether stated or implicit, justice is perhaps the primary normative commitment uniting all of the contributors to this volume. While we acknowledge the ways a renewed language of "the common goal" may also orient people toward forms of mutual responsibility and common welfare, we insist that such language can perpetuate exclusion and domination if there is no attention to justice. The impetus behind this work is our hope that it will contribute, in at least some small way, to the realization of greater justice for poor women and their children than is possible under current welfare policies. We recognize the complexity of policy making, which is particularly evident in the post-PRWORA state-by-state variations in welfare law. Thus, we cannot pretend to advocate a clear set of specific policies, as these will have to emerge on a local basis.

What readers will find here are some base points, some fundamental moral considerations for constructing social policy for persons in poverty. What is morally at stake is the ability of women to achieve some measure of dignity and self-determination to provide for their own well-being and the well-being of those they love and for whom they are responsible. Proceeding from these feminist ethical values, we would like to enumerate, not a comprehensive program for social justice, but some components of what might comprise authentic welfare reform aimed at empowering poor women:

1. Our society needs to redefine work to include the socially necessary labor of caring for children, the sick, and the elderly, a task requiring the rethinking of the relationship of the public and private spheres. The mental, physical, and emotional caring labor that is absolutely necessary to maintain life and enhance its quality should secure for every household a tax-free income up to the actual cost of a decent standard of living. It should also include publicly subsidized high-quality child care. Public child care and the work of nurturing in the home can be remunerated out of public revenues secured through a more equitable tax code, including restoring more progressive corporate taxes and taxing household incomes above the decent standard of living level, regardless of their source, at progressively increasing rates.

2. Virtually full employment at above poverty wages and in conditions that support human dignity needs to be created to provide work for all who are able. Employment for all able to work can be achieved by shortening standard work time and creating additional work by publicly sponsored, socially necessary production. (Full employment does not exist now primarily because the competition for work among un-

employed people is necessary to decrease wages and increase profits.) Making work support human dignity means making work enhance self-respect, social recognition, and a sense of contributing to the commonweal. As work increasingly takes on these kinds of qualities, people do not have to be forced to do this work since it fulfills basic human needs for security and a sense of belonging to a community.

3. We need to provide a social context that sustains human communities. Such a context would include the publicly sponsored provision of socially necessary goods and services, such as affordable housing, universal health care, education, environmental protection, public transport, and infrastructure maintenance. Since these goods and services are considered "external costs" and unprofitable, they are not provided by our market-oriented, profit-making capitalist system. Policies preventing discrimination on the basis of race, gender, sexuality, age, and disability would also be a part of a supportive context.

4. We need a system of social security for all those not doing caretaking work in the home or attached to public labor. People unable to work include those involuntarily unemployed while searching for work, students, and people whose capacities for work are limited or nonexistent because of age, disabilities, and ill health.

5. We need to develop a policymaking system that draws upon the experience of past and present welfare recipients and includes them in program formation and policy evaluation. The formation of just policies requires the participation of all who are affected by their outcome.

Although we believe that only programs that include these five components can promote true "well fare," we also recognize that what may be offered instead are adjustments to basically unjust policy. Within this limited framework, we would call for the following:

- elimination of the five-year lifetime benefit limit or development of a more flexible exemption policy
- abolition of the family cap
- adoption of the family violence exemption as a federal mandate
- increase in the minimum wage to better approximate the wages required for adequate family provision
- more realistic work participation goals respecting the needs of adults to parent children
- provision of adequate health care and child care
- better evaluation of state performance to ensure that states are rewarded for promoting real self-sufficiency, not merely reducing welfare rolls

- promotion of education as an alternative to work, and more adequate job training
- monitoring of the health and safety of work conditions in workfare programs, including attention to any racial and sexual harassment[39]

We hope that the work in this volume, through its analysis of structural powers and its engagement in moral reflection upon welfare questions, will offer resources for evaluation and action for those both within and outside the Christian churches who work for a welfare system that ends rather than reproduces poverty. To seek authentic reform we need to engage in specific analyses as we forge alliances across boundaries of income level, gender, and race to create policy that will alter the welfare system and *stop this war against the poorest in our society.* We seek a world where no more Rosa Dolones travel the streets saying, "My children have to eat."

Notes

1. See "Appendix: A New Vision for Welfare Reform" in *Welfare in America: Christian Perspectives on a Policy in Crisis,* ed. Stanley W. Carlson-Thies and James W. Skillen (Grand Rapids, Mich.: Eerdmans, 1996), 551–79.
2. For an introductory discussion of materialist feminism, in relation to other forms of feminism, see the introduction to Rosemary Hennessy and Chrys Ingraham, *Materialist Feminism: A Reader in Class, Difference, and Women's Lives* (New York: Routledge, 1997), 1–14.
3. William Tabb, "Globalization Is an Issue, the Power of Capital Is the Issue," *Monthly Review* 49, no 2. (June 1997): 22; Frances Fox Piven and Richard A. Cloward, "Eras of Power," *Monthly Review* 50, no. 1 (January 1998): 20; Ellen Meiksins Wood, "Class Compacts, the Welfare State, and Epochal Shifts," *Monthly Review* 50, no. 1 (January 1998): 31, 41.
4. The argument in this section relies on M. Patricia Connelly, "Gender Matters: Global Restructuring and Adjustment," *Social Politics* 3, no. 1 (spring 1996): 12–31, and Pamela Sparr, ed., *Mortgaging Women's Lives: Feminist Critiques of Structural Adjustment* (London: Zed, 1994), 1–36, 183–201.
5. Children's Defense Fund, *Summary of the New Welfare Legislation,* Sept. 1996 (updated Oct. 22, 1997), 1–2.
6. Children's Defense Fund, *Special Report: Welfare to Work,* Oct. 1997.
7. Ibid., 5–9.
8. Raymond Hernandez, "Most Dropped from Welfare Don't Get Jobs," *New York Times,* March 23, 1998, A1; Jason DeParle, "Wisconsin Welfare Experiment: Easy to Say, Not So Easy to Do," *New York Times,* October 18, 1998, A1, A24.

9. *Survival News* 11, no. 1 (spring 1997): 34–36.

10. Children's Defense Fund, *The New Welfare Law: One Year Later,* March 1998.

11. Rachel L. Swarns, "Mothers Poised for Workfare Face Acute Lack of Day Care," *New York Times,* April 14, 1998, A20.

12. Carla Rivera, "County Supervisors Approve Bare-Bones Welfare Plan," *Los Angeles Times,* January 7, 1998, B8.

13. Leonard Schneiderman, "Perspective on Welfare," *Los Angeles Times,* January 9, 1998, B13. (Schneiderman is professor emeritus at the UCLA School of Public Policy and Social Research.)

14. Virginia Ellis, "Study Tracks Pay Women Need to Escape Welfare," *Los Angeles Times,* January 28, 1997, A3; Diana Pearce and Laura Russell, "The Self-Sufficiency Standard for Massachusetts," *Wider Opportunities for Women* (September 1998): 8.

15. Children's Defense Fund, *New Welfare Law,* 2.

16. Melissa Healy and Judy Pasternak, "New Face in Line at Soup Kitchen: Working Poor," *Los Angeles Times,* December 27, 1997, A14; *Religious News Service Digest,* November 23, 1998.

17. Children's Defense Fund, *New Welfare Law.*

18. "Welfare Reform and Post-Secondary Education: Research and Policy Update," *Welfare Reform Network News* 2, no. 1 (April 1998): 1–2.

19. Alan Finder, "Evidence Is Scant That Workfare Leads to Full-Time Jobs," *New York Times,* April 12, 1998, A8.

20. Ibid., A1.

21. *Western New York Peace Center Report* (Mar.–Apr. 1997): 4.

22. National Conference of Catholic Bishops, "Economic Justice for All: Catholic Social Teaching and the U.S. Economy," *Origins* 16, no. 24 (November 27, 1986): 411.

23. Holly Sklar, *Chaos or Community: Seeking Solutions Not Scapegoats for Bad Economics* (Boston: South End Press, 1995), 5, 12–13. See also Arloc Sherman et al., *Welfare to What: Early Findings on Family Hardship and Well-Being* (Washington, D.C.: Children's Defense Fund, 1998).

24. Kevin Sack, "Eager and Flush, Many States Plan Yet More Tax Cuts," *New York Times,* January 4, 1998, A1.

25. "Underground Economy," *The Nation,* January 12–19, 1998, 3–4.

26. Ibid.

27. Richard Freeman, "Unequal Incomes," *Harvard Magazine,* January–February 1998, 64.

28. For an introduction to Latin American liberation theologies, see Penny Lernoux, *Cry of the People* (New York: Doubleday, 1980), and Maria Pilar Aquino, *Our Cry for Life: Feminist Theology from Latin America* (Maryknoll, N.Y.: Orbis Books, 1993). For a focus on the liberation of Hispanic Ameri-

can women, see Ada María Isasi-Díaz, *En la lucha—In the Struggle: A Hispanic Women's Liberation Theology* (Minneapolis: Fortress, 1993).

29. Beverly Harrison, *Making the Connections: Essays in Feminist Social Ethics,* ed. Carol Robb (Boston: Beacon, 1985), 123.

30. Janet Jakobsen, *Working Alliances and the Politics of Difference* (Bloomington: Indiana University Press, 1998), 65.

31. Nancy Fraser, "Pragmatism, Feminism, and the Linguistic Turn," in *Feminist Contentions: A Philosophical Exchange,* ed. Seyla Benhabib et al. (New York: Routledge, 1995), 159.

32. For a good introduction to this debate, see the exchange in Benhabib et al., *Feminist Contentions.*

33. Harrison, *Connections,* 15.

34. Emilie Townes, *In a Blaze of Glory: Womanist Spirituality as Social Witness* (Nashville: Abingdon, 1995), 66.

35. Harrison, *Connections,* 247.

36. Iris M. Young, *Justice and the Politics of Difference* (Princeton, N.J.: Princeton University Press, 1990), 5.

37. Two key tests in this discussion are Carol Gilligan, *In a Different Voice: Psychological Theory and Women's Development* (Cambridge: Harvard University Press, 1987), and Nel Noddings, *Caring: A Feminine Approach to Ethics and Moral Education* (Berkeley: University of California Press, 1984). See also Barbara Andolsen, "Justice, Gender, and the Frail Elderly," *Journal of Feminist Studies in Religion* 9, nos. 1–2 (spring/fall 1998): 127–45, and Grace Clement, *Care, Autonomy, and Justice: Feminism and the Ethic of Care* (Boulder, Colo.: Westview Press, 1996).

38. Ada María Isasi-Díaz, "*Un poquito de justicia*—A Little Bit of Justice," in *Hispanic/Latino Theology: Challenge and Promise,* ed. Ada María Isasi-Díaz and Fernando E. Segovia (Minneapolis: Fortress, 1996), 237.

39. We are indebted to *Is It Reform? The 1998 Report of the Welfare and Human Rights Monitoring Project* (Boston: Unitarian Universalist Service Committee, 1998) and to David Gill of Brandeis University, "Toward Constructive Alternatives to the Welfare System," unpublished manuscript, 1997.

PART ONE

THEOLOGICAL AND PHILOSOPHICAL ETHICAL FRAMEWORKS

[1]

Making Women and Children Matter

A Feminist Theological Ethic
Confronts Welfare Policy

Pamela K. Brubaker

"We're already turning back people who need emergency food and it is going to get worse. I come from a poor family, and I know what it's like to not have food on a continuous basis—the feeling of not knowing where your next meal will come from. It's very disheartening, very frustrating. It's fearsome. It's scary. I've been tossing and turning in bed,... knowing there will be more poor people we can't help. But most people are not concerned because they have food security." —Herman Pena, manager of San Bernardino County Food Bank.

Los Angeles Times, MARCH 2, 1997

"The lowest you can get for rent is $450. I [have been] receiving $493. With the Pampers you have to get, the clothes you have to get, you're basically living on $20 a month. We are the guinea pigs of '97. They come out with these ideas to see if they're going to work and they try it out on us people without knowing what the result is going to be." —Yvonne Parris, twenty-six, living temporarily in a homeless shelter with her nine-month-old son because of eviction; monthly welfare payment reduced to $467 as result of federal welfare reform.

Los Angeles Times, JANUARY 1, 1997

One in five American children lives below the poverty line: 20.5 percent of children under eighteen years of age, 22.7 percent of children under six. Families with children under eighteen are three times more likely than families without children to be poor. This is particularly true of female-headed families. A majority of children (58.8 percent) under six living in female-householder families are poor.[1] Welfare programs such as Aid to Families with Dependent Children (AFDC), food stamps, and Medicaid, have been ways in which many poor children's basic needs are met. Without these programs, many children's life chances will be even more severely diminished. Thus, proposals for welfare reform must be evaluated from the perspective of these children and their families. Will their basic needs for food, shelter, clothing, education, and health care be adequately met?

Despite studies predicting that proposed legislation would throw more than 1 million more children into poverty,[2] Congress passed and President Clinton signed into law the Personal Responsibility and Work Opportunities Reconciliation Act (PRWORA) in August of 1996. This act dismantled AFDC and replaced it with Temporary Assistance to Needy Families (TANF). As of January 1, 1997, poor families are limited to a maximum of five years of federal cash assistance. Recipients are required to work within two years of signing up for welfare. No longer is there a guarantee of cash assistance to every eligible poor family with children. Cash welfare has been converted to block grants for states, which have more freedom to develop their own programs to move welfare recipients into jobs and are penalized if they do not.[3] With this federal legislation in place, the struggle has now moved to the state level.

Welfare reform is hotly contested terrain in the current political climate. Conservative critics charge that welfare programs erode the work ethic and traditional values and cause welfare dependency, rising rates of illegitimate births, teen pregnancy, and various social ills. It seems not to matter that there is little factual basis to the charges that welfare programs are the cause of these social ills.[4] Poor women and their children are convenient scapegoats for complex social and economic problems. Clearly, the well-being of children is not a central concern for conservative advocates of welfare "reform," for whom welfare is both a defense of traditional "family values" and an attack on government social spending. The lack of concern for families is evident in suggestions made by some conservatives that children whose parents cannot support them be taken away from them; equally evident is the lack of consideration by conservatives and liberals alike for the impact of cuts in benefits on children.

Why is it that poor children seem not to matter? Norton Grubb and Marvin Lazerson identify several factors in their book *Broken Promises: How Americans Fail Their Children*. Historically, family structure has changed from a predominance of extended families, with shared responsibility for children, to the nuclear family and the evolution of childrearing as a private responsibility. These developments have reinforced the tendency to differentiate sharply between one's own and other people's children. Structural inequalities along racial, class, and gender lines also affect and shape family relationships and children's opportunities, as well as public attitudes. "Class and racial biases harden the negative perception of other people's children." Grubb and Lazerson conclude that it is difficult to maintain a belief that children are a group deserving specific attention in a society with severe inequalities. When there are vast differences in income, advocacy of public responsibility for children seems to imply redistribution of resources from rich to poor, thus confirming the perception that "other people's children are costly liabilities."[5]

The gap between the wealthy and the poor in the United States continues to grow. Median family income showed the first statistically significant increase in six years in 1995, when it rose 2.7 percent. However, this was still below the median rate for 1989. In the period from 1974 to 1996, median income has increased just 1.6 percent, while in the period from 1947 to 1973, it doubled. Furthermore, the gap between the wealthy and the poor in the United States continues to grow and is the widest such gap in any industrialized country. By 1994, the top 1 percent controlled almost 40 percent of net worth. The top 10 percent owned 71 percent; the remaining 90 percent shared the other 29 percent.[6] This disparity in income and wealth, coupled with the stagnation in many families' incomes, is a factor in pressure for dismantling the welfare system.

A crucial factor in the calls for welfare reform, though, is political leaders' scapegoating of welfare recipients to deflect attention from the structural sources of economic inequality, such as the globalization of capital, changes in the labor market, and regressive taxation. Some citizens respond to stereotyping and scapegoating by asking why they should work and pay taxes to support people who are perceived to be irresponsible and lazy. However, polls show that children's issues—safety, health and education—are a top priority for voters, some of whom have expressed concern about the impact of welfare reform on poor children.[7]

The welfare debate is, among other things, a struggle over changing family structure, roles of women, caregiving, race, citizenship, and the state. At stake are different conceptions of the common good and the responsibility of the state for the general welfare. The term *welfare* at one time referred to the common good. The Preamble to the U.S. Constitution declares that the federal government was formed, among other reasons, "to promote the general welfare." I want to reappropriate this meaning of the term in order to develop an ethical conception of the common good in which poor women and children matter. I undertake this task in this chapter by presenting a theological ethic of compassion and solidarity, from which I develop criteria to evaluate conservative and liberal welfare reform proposals. Progressive public policy proposals grounded in conceptions of the common good in which women and children matter conclude the chapter.

A Feminist Ethic of Compassion and Solidarity

> To struggle against oppression, against alienation, is a matter of ongoing personal conversion that involves effective attempts to change alienating social structures. This personal conversion cannot happen apart from solidarity with the oppressed.... Who are the poor and oppressed for whom we must opt, with whom we must be in solidarity? They are the ones who are exploited, who suffer system violence, the victims of cultural imperialism. The poor and oppressed are those for whom the struggle to survive is a way of life.
>
> ADA MARÍA ISASI-DÍAZ, *Mujerista Theology*

A Theological Ethical Stance

My ethical stance is rooted in a Christian ethic of neighbor-love which has been deepened by the work of women of other racial/ethnic groups. I am a middle-strata, Anglo/white woman, the divorced mother of two grown sons. *Mujerista* theologian Ada María Isasi-Díaz teaches us that solidarity is a primary expression of love of neighbor. She calls those of us with some privilege to become friends of the oppressed, to join with them in the struggle for justice, liberation, and reconciliation.[8] I have found that compassion—the capacity to "feel with"—enables authentic solidarity. Through dialogue and friendship, compassion and solidarity are developed.

In a similar vein, womanist theologian Delores Williams challenges those who call themselves Christian to be in solidarity with suffering black people who struggle for survival/quality of life, including those "living in dire poverty, the poverty-stricken single parent trying to raise children."[9] Those like myself in positions of relative class, racial/ethnic, and/or gender privilege are summoned to see other people's children, as well as our own, as part of our community—or to speak theologically, to see them as part of the "kin-dom of God."[10] Isasi-Díaz's felicitous reimaging of the realm of God as an extended family is particularly appropriate to an ethic of compassion and solidarity. Additionally, it invokes Jesus' blessing of children, declaring that "it is to such as these that the [realm] of God belongs" (Mark 10:14), a blessing given despite the protests of the disciples, who wanted to keep the children out of the way.

Feminist biblical work also upholds an ethic of solidarity. The narrative of the Syro-Phoenician woman may be rhetorically invoked as a biblical metaphor for an ethical stance that embraces all children. This woman came from a different and despised ethnic group. She came to Jesus and begged him to cast the demon out of her daughter. Jesus said to her: "Let the children be fed first, for it is not fair to take the children's food and throw it to the dogs," emphasizing the distinction between the "chosen" children and "other" children. She responded, "Sir, even the dogs under the table eat the children's crumbs." In saying this, she disrupted sharp distinctions between children. Jesus told her, "For saying that, you may go—the demon has left your daughter" (Mark 7:24–30; also Matt. 15:21–28). Biblical scholar Laurel Schneider points out that the Syro-Phoenician woman "persisted in the face of overwhelming rejection." She suggests that although the woman seemed to accept Jesus' characterization of her people as dogs, by coming to Jesus she envisioned "the laying of a new table to which all are invited, under which none must grovel."[11] This narrative is a biblical remembrance of suffering, compassion, and solidarity.

Relevant Moral Principles

A feminist theological ethic may also articulate moral claims that are formulated in nontheological terms. These facilitate our ability to build alliances with nonreligious people in working for social justice. Two claims are particularly consequential for a more adequate conception of a common good in which women and children matter. These are: (1) the need to recognize interdependence as characteristic of our social relations and (2) the need to recognize the economic value of caregiving work. Both claims challenge androcentric and individualistic assumptions which undergird mainstream notions about dependency and economic value. In the following discussion, I will show that such assumptions do not adequately reflect our socioeconomic reality and are harmful to the well-being of poor women and children.

Interdependence

Assertions that social programs such as AFDC create welfare dependency have been a primary rationale in calls for welfare reform, which would end entitlement status for poor women and children. Empirically this claim is questionable: states with the lowest benefits tend to have the highest number of welfare recipients. Yet the claim is rhetorically effective in stigmatizing welfare recipients. Feminist social theorists Linda Gordon and Nancy Fraser charge that the term *dependency* "leaks a profusion of stigmatizing connotations—racial, sexual, misogynist, and more."[12] It is meant to conjure up an image of a "welfare queen"—a promiscuous, poor, black woman with several children sitting home and watching soap operas. (See the chapter by Traci West.) In the context of this debate, dependency is a morally reprehensible condition.

A careful examination of the meanings of dependency unsettles any such moral certainty. Historically, there has been a significant shift in the meaning of the word. Fraser and Gordon point out that at one time *dependency* meant gaining one's livelihood by working for someone—a situation in which many men were considered dependent. Today wage labor bestows independence, while counting on charity or welfare bestows dependency. These shifts reflect in part what Fraser and Gordon call "progressive differentiation of the official economy," the development of increasingly complex corporations (such as transnationals) and the expansion and segmentation of markets for commodities, labor, and capital.

> Before the rise of capitalism, any particular dependency was part of a net of dependencies, a single, continuous fabric of social hierarchies. Although women were subordinated and their labor often controlled by others, their labor was more visible, understood, and formally valued. With the emergence of religious and secular individualism, on the one hand, and industrial capitalism, on the other, a sharp, new dichotomy was constructed in which economic dependency and economic independence were opposed to one another. A crucial corollary of this dichotomy, and of the hegemony of wage labor in general, was the occlusion and devaluation of women's unpaid domestic and parenting labor.[13]

In other words, with the rise of capitalism, laborers who had been seen as economically dependent were now seen as independent. In the feudal system which predated capitalism, laborers were dependent on their masters, who in turn were dependent on someone above them in the social hierarchy. In this system, although women were subordinate, women's labor was visible and valued. With the development of wage labor under capitalism, women's household labor became invisible and devalued. While their wage-earning husbands were now perceived as "independent," they remained "dependent."

Diana Pearce, the activist and scholar who coined the term "feminization of poverty," also questions this valuation of dependent and independent. She rightfully argues that paid workers' perceived independence is possible because of "the hidden and unrecognized dependence the workers have on others," such as housewives and day care centers. Pearce suggests that we rehabilitate dependency as a valuable, even normal, human quality.[14]

Fraser and Gordon express caution about such an approach, noting that welfare recipients themselves saw the existing conditions of AFDC as wretched and damaging. They make a useful distinction between "socially necessary dependence,...the need for others' care that is an inescapable feature of the human condition," and "surplus dependence...rooted in unjust and potentially remediable social institutions." They further advocate transcending the dependence/independence opposition entirely, recognizing that in the contemporary world ever-higher relations of interdependence are created, based on ever-increasing divisions of labor. This necessitates a redefinition of work to include nonwage-earning labor, "such as housework and childcare, children's activity in attending school."[15] Our social reality is clearly one of interdependence.

Caregiving and Economic Value

Feminist social theorists Hilda Scott and Marilyn Waring pointed out over a decade ago that traditional women's work of caring is not given economic value unless it is commoditized—exchanged within the market. Even when commoditized, its value is low.[16] The devaluing of such work is questionable on both economic and ethical grounds. Economic theory is not value-free. It constructs reality, and, as now developed, theories of economic value do not value caregiving. Thus domestic labor such as food provision and preparation, child care, and family health maintenance are not counted as part of gross national product. This practice influences public policies and has a negative impact on women, children, and families, as was demonstrated by numerous studies during the United Nations Decade for Women (1975–85).[17]

Some feminist economists are now challenging reigning definitions of economic value, too. (See Carol Robb's chapter for a critical assessment.) Several members of the American Economic Association published a volume of essays, *Beyond Economic Man,* which its editors describe as the first of its kind, in the hope that it will lead to improving economic practice. Julie Nelson contends that economics has been too narrowly construed as the exchange of goods and services. She notes that Adam Smith, the founder of mainstream economics, understood economics to have a twofold focus: how society was organized by exchange and how society was provisioned. However, mainstream economics has focused solely on the organization of exchange—buying and selling. Nelson argues that economics should reclaim this concern for provisioning and engage itself "with the study of how humans, in interaction with each other and the environment, provide for their own survival and health."[18] Such a shift in focus would likely assure that unpaid caregiving activities are given economic value.

In this same volume, Diana Strassmann charges that limiting what counts as economics to buying and selling silences important objections to the "primacy of self-interested individualism and contractual exchange which reflect a male-centered and Western perspective on selfhood and individual agency." She cites Harvard economist Amartya Sen's questioning of the reliability of economic analyses based upon the story of the benevolent patriarch, a key component of mainstream economic theory. This story maintains that the male head of household makes choices that are in the best interest of his family, which is treated as an individual agent. Sen points out that the failure of many family patriarchs to act altruistically calls into question claims about the efficiency or optimal results associated with the workings of the market. Strassmann questions the "story of free choice," another key component of mainstream economic theory. She points out that there are constraints on choices—particularly for the young, women, and the elderly. She asks whether policy failures, "particularly the undue suffering of infants and children, may be partially attributable to the current thinking, of economics, which coheres with the American story of resources going to those who work for them and deserve them."[19] This belief is a corollary of the story of free choice, claiming that those who make good choices are rewarded and those who make poor choices suffer.

The insights of these feminist social theorists and economists on interdependence and the value of caregiving resonate with feminist theological criticisms of individualism and androcentrism. For instance, in her study of women's poverty, family policy, and practical theology, Pamela Couture critiques principles of personal responsibility and self-sufficiency as the basis for public policy. She offers instead the principle of shared responsibility, which she connects to interdependence and caregiving: "An ethic of care through shared responsibility allows room for the psychic empowerment of self-sufficiency by locating it within the larger context of interdependence." As a principle for public policy, shared responsibility would recognize that national policies "create conditions which impoverish women and children" rather than looking only to personal responsibility. With this recognition, policies would be developed to provide care for poor families and individuals on the basis of need to meet the basic needs of all for food, shelter, health care, and education.[20]

I draw on these principles of interdependence, valuing caregiving, and shared responsibility to develop criteria for evaluating current welfare reform proposals, the task of the next section. Are these proposals adequate in illuminating socioeconomic reality to account for sources of concrete suffering? Do they adequately meet basic needs and recognize the value of caregiving? Are they appropriate to our vision of a common good in which poor women and children matter?

Whose Welfare Matters? Analysis of Welfare Reform Proposals

"What's out there? McDonalds? Del Taco? I don't see how we're going to get off welfare and stay off welfare if we move on with no skills. We'll be right back where we started. We are scared our dreams might be taken away." —Luisa Ruiz, thirty-one-year-old community college student, high-school dropout, welfare recipient, and part-time worker.

Los Angeles Times, APRIL 13, 1997

Background

Since the New Deal in the 1930s, the United States has had a liberal form of welfare capitalism. Political scientist Gosta Esping-Anderson describes this as a residual welfare state which only reacts to what are perceived as market or family failures. Assistance is limited to marginal or especially deserving social groups.[21] As originally conceived, Aid for Dependent Children (ADC) was limited to dependent children of widows who maintained what was considered to be a proper middle-strata lifestyle. It was part of a two-track welfare system created during the New Deal.

The first track of the New Deal welfare system, according to Nancy Fraser and Linda Gordon, was social insurance programs, which included unemployment and old-age insurance. These programs offered aid as an entitlement to people with certain employment histories, "without stigma or supervision and hence without dependency." They were intended to replace temporarily the family wage. Few women and minorities were included in these programs, since domestic and agricultural workers (predominantly women and minorities) were exempted from them. Second-track public assistance programs like Aid to Dependent Children, which later became AFDC, were quite different from these first-track programs. They continued the practice of private charities which supported only those deemed "deserving." Because these programs were funded from general tax revenues instead of earmarked wage deductions, it seemed that recipients got "something for nothing." There were entirely different criteria for receiving aid: "means-testing, morals-testing, moral and household supervisions, home visits, extremely low stipends."[22]

Welfare rights advocates organized in the 1960s to change the terms of welfare programs and to expand coverage.[23] Beneficiaries came to be perceived as undeserving members of different racial and class groups. This was a significant factor in calls for welfare reform, which culminated in the dismantling of AFDC as of January 1, 1997. As states shape their own welfare programs, both conservative and liberal proposals are under consideration.

Conservative Proposals

Most of the policies supported by conservatives were incorporated into the adopted federal legislation (PRWORA). The most significant were ending the entitlement status of AFDC, putting a time limit on welfare benefits, and requiring recipients to work outside the home. Additional conservative proposals are not required by federal guidelines but may be instituted at the state level if conservatives have their way. Conservatives want now to abolish welfare altogether for unwed teen mothers. Also, states have the option to deny additional cash aid to welfare recipients who have children while receiving benefits. Some states have adopted these provisions.

States are also working out policies for meeting the federal work requirement, which mandates that states place at least 25 percent of cash welfare recipients in jobs or work programs by 1997, and 50 percent by 2002. Some conservative governors, such as Pete Wilson of California, have proposed that new mothers be required to go to work after only twelve weeks. He also proposed that recipients have twenty days for an up-front job search and that single parents must be in approved job activity thirty-two hours a week.[24]

Conservatives' proposals are based in a belief that poverty is a result of personal irresponsibility. This idea is a consistent theme in the debate on welfare reform in America, according to Joel F. Handler and Yeheskel Hasenfeld. They contend that "from the brief experiment with rehabilitation through social services (Eisenhower and Kennedy) to the concentration on the various work strategies, the focus has been on reforming the individual rather than on addressing the structural conditions of poverty."[25] This focus is consistent with conservative notions of the common good.

Conservatives generally envision the common good as being best served by a combination of an unregulated market, traditional families, and private charity. Each of these spheres is perceived as an autonomous, yet complementary, arena for the exercise of personal responsibility. In keeping with conservative views, there is no significant role for government in promoting the common good. Market efficiency, family discipline, and reform efforts of private charity are supposed to promote the common good. From this perspective, poverty is seen as a result of personal irresponsibility, not a failure in structural organization or institutional practice. At its crudest, this perspective is a form of social Darwinism: those who do not make it are considered unfit to survive.

This perspective does not adequately account for sources of concrete suffering. The separation of family and economic arenas from the political in conservative discourse biases this conception of the common good toward the advantaged. Nancy Fraser explains this dynamic in her discussion of the politics of needs interpretation. How do we decide what needs are legitimate and who has responsibility for meeting them? Needs are depoliticized when the political is separated from the domestic and the economic in social discourses about needs. Rather than recognizing that needs are interpreted and negotiated through political struggle, it is assumed that individuals identify and meet their own needs. In contemporary American society, this has the effect of advantaging dominant groups which have more political power to identify, legitimize, and fulfill their needs.[26] Thus, those in the capitalist, managerial, and entrepreneurial classes are understood to flourish because of the good choices they have made, not because of public policies such as mortgage interest deductions and corporate welfare, which benefit them. Likewise, poor single mothers, whether employed or not, are understood to suffer because of the poor choices they have made rather than public policies that make their needs invisible and provide no concrete opportunities to meet them. (See the chapter by Ellen Marshall.) Such an interpretation obscures rather than discloses the sources of concrete suffering.

Furthermore, market efficiency, family discipline, and private charity do not adequately redress the suffering of poor people. Unregulated market economies, particularly in a context of structural inequality such as exists in the United States, exacerbate poverty and economic injustice. For instance, poor people are not able to create sufficient demand for low-income housing, which is not as profitable for developers and the construction industry as other housing and real estate development. Nor are wages set by the low end of the labor market adequate to bring many poor people out of poverty.[27] Many poor people are employed, some full-time. The number of children in working poor families grew 30 percent, to 5.6 million, between 1989 and 1994. According to the Annie Casey Foundation, children in these families are "less likely to be fully immunized, less likely to enter school ready to learn, less likely to graduate and less likely to attend college."[28] Clearly, unregulated markets do not reduce poverty; they likely exacerbate it.

Nor do traditional families provide guarantees against poverty, as is evident from the number of two-parent families living below the poverty line.[29] Donald Hernandez found that although the overall poverty rates of children might have been 2 to 4 percentage points lower without the rise in mother-only families that has occurred since 1959, "more than 80 percent of children would still have been poor." Furthermore, Hernandez found that "economic insecurity and need also apparently contributed substantially to the rise in separation and divorce, at least after 1970."[30] Family stability is dependent in part on economic security. Social policies advocated by some conservatives that would threaten the poor with economic insecurity and coerce pregnant women into marriage or make divorce prohibitive for poor people are questionable as a means of reducing poverty. Social policies targeting fathers—such as tightening child-support enforcement and developing comprehensive programs for young fathers—may contribute to children's well-being, but research has shown that these programs alone do not remove the majority of families with young children from poverty.[31]

Although private charity has a place in a vision of the common good, it clearly is not capable of meeting the socioeconomic needs of poor and low-income people. When Congress began considering substituting private charity for welfare benefits, 115 charities jointly notified Congress that they would not be able to meet the needs of the poor if the government significantly cut benefits. Fred Kammer, president of Catholic Charities, said in Congressional testimony that religious charitable programs are primarily there during times of crisis when they drag small amounts of cash from limited funds to help people. He insisted that "What none of us [does] is to provide regular income to poor families. I speak here for everybody—Catholic, Protestant, Salvation Army, Jews, evangelicals. None of us [has] that kind of money." The bulk of the money for many of these programs comes from government funds—federal, state, and local. For example, Catholic Charities USA receives nearly two-thirds of its operating budget for its fourteen hundred programs from government funds.[32]

Public policy experts Handler and Hasenfeld charge that charity makes little real difference in alleviating poverty. "While specific acts of charity provide real benefits to some, charity is, by and large, myth and ceremony. It does little to relieve poverty; at the same time, it confirms the status of the donor and the recipient."[33] In other words, charity affirms the moral superiority of the donor, who is perceived as having funds to give because of individual choices and merit, and the moral inferiority of the recipient, who is "needy" because of some personal deficit, whether poor choice, ability, or luck. (See the chapter by Ruth Smith.)

The conservative vision of the common good—grounded in the market, traditional families, and private charity—and its attendant dismantling of the residual welfare state is actually a form of social Darwinism. Those with the most power, privilege, and resources thrive; the rest struggle to survive. Although a few do rise up the income ladder, as is to be expected in any Darwinian system, many more struggle to maintain a basic standard of living. Its assumptions are not congruent with the dynamics of socioeconomic reality, nor is its vision of the common good appropriate to a theological ethic of compassion and solidarity.

Liberal Proposals

More liberal proposals for welfare reform include education and job training as part of an effort to reform welfare. President Clinton's proposed 1994 Work and Responsibility Act included such provisions, but the act he signed into law in 1996 did not. It is up to states to include such provisions in their welfare legislation. Liberals see a positive role for government, both in providing a safety net for family and market failures and in providing what former Secretary of Labor Robert Reich calls a "springboard" to a better quality of life. While recognizing the appropriateness of notions of personal responsibility, liberals are aware of constraints on personal choice. Their proposals for welfare reform attempt some redress of inequalities in educational and economic opportunities.

Democrats in the California Assembly, for example, proposed a longer period for receiving benefits than Governor Wilson's proposed two-year limit: three years for those requiring training and five years for those requiring training and substance abuse, domestic violence, mental health, or other treatment. They also proposed that work training or treatment assignments could substitute for work requirements. Wilson's proposal makes no provision for training or treatment.[34]

Theoretically, such proposals have some merit, but to be effective, particular types of support, training, and reform are required. For instance, analysis of experimental job-training programs indicate that "you can, in fact, achieve very real gains if the programs permit AFDC recipients to invest in college education, which is the only reliable road to above-poverty wages for women."[35] A second caution in regard to education and training programs is that there must be sufficient jobs for those who complete such programs. Seldom, though, is this the case. Without a full-employment policy or a federal jobs program, the value of these programs is debatable. (See the chapter by Mary Hobgood.)

A primary purpose of training programs is to ensure that work pays a living wage, so that families are indeed lifted out of poverty. Another proposal for making work pay is increasing the Earned Income Tax Credit (EITC), so that low wages are supplemented by a sliding-scale tax credit. Some expansion of this program did take place during Clinton's first term. EITC has lifted some families out of poverty. However, the Institute for Women's Policy Research (IWPR) found that even proposed increases in the EITC do not necessarily bring women out of poverty. Using current recipients who combine work and welfare, they found that many would actually be worse off if EITC is substituted for their AFDC benefits. The average estimated annual EITC benefit would be $1,250, while the estimated loss of AFDC benefits would be $2,350. IWPR concluded that further increases in the EITC or a change in employment patterns would be necessary to make up for the loss. Their research shows that many women who receive AFDC during a two-year period do work in paid employment. This is particularly true of those with a high-school education, job training and work experience, no work-inhibiting disability, and who live in a state with a low unemployment rate. However, the jobs available to these women tend to be low-level service or clerical jobs, usually temporary.[36]

If the problem to be solved is not welfare dependency but *poverty*, additional strategies are needed. IWPR researcher Roberta Spalter-Roth concludes that it is quite unlikely that women will get out of poverty without additional sources of income support (from other family members or child support, which most do not receive) or without substantial reform of the low-wage labor market. To begin this reform, she advocates policies such as "raising the minimum wage, instituting pay equity, and enforcing anti-discrimination policies and unionization."[37] These strategies would also benefit working poor two-parent families. Obviously, the minimum-wage increase referred to would be significantly greater than the recent small increases from $4.25 to $4.75 to $5.15, which have not even restored the purchasing power that the minimum wage provided twenty years ago.

Welfare reform, whether from conservatives or Clinton's "New Democrats," has been promoted in the context of budgetary savings. The truth is that a comprehensive federal training and employment program would, in its initial years, necessarily burden the budget significantly rather than provide savings. Ignoring this reality means that the budget is to be balanced at great cost to our poorest citizens, as is the case with the balanced-budget agreement reached by President Clinton and Republicans in Congress in May of 1996.

Toward a Common Good in Which Women and Children Matter

"What is in the community interest is in our self-interest. The safety of children. The health of children. That's what we are advocating whether they're our children or somebody else's children. We will all suffer if they're not cared for. And we will all benefit when they are." —Sara Moores Campbell, minister and activist.

Los Angeles Times, FEBRUARY 9, 1997

Progressive Proposals

Proposals such as Spalter-Roth's, coupled with universal health care, affordable housing, and accessible and affordable quality child care, begin to move from a residual type of liberal welfare capitalism to what Esping-Anderson identifies as universalistic and egalitarian social democratic institutional states. Such states are proactive rather than reactive and intend to meet the welfare needs of all population groups.[38] These progressive proposals resonate with parts of the U.S. Catholic bishops' pastoral letter "Economic Justice for All," which advocates a new American experiment, through the guarantee of minimum conditions for human dignity economically for everyone.[39] These proposals are grounded in a more adequate analysis of the sources of concrete suffering and are more appropriate to a theological ethic of compassion and solidarity than either conservative or liberal proposals. Yet they do not yet fully address the needs of children for care or women's economic vulnerability grounded in their caretaking responsibilities.

The valuing of child care and other family labor is a critical element missing from conservative, liberal, and some progressive welfare reform proposals. This is an element crucial to the well-being of children and those who care for them. Although most mothers work in the paid labor market, many choose to work only part-time so that they have time to care for their children. Most women on welfare want employment. Part-time work outside the home should also be an option for them. Scholars and activists have made a variety of policy proposals that would give economic value to caretaking activities. These would benefit most children and their parents.

Economist Nancy Folbre advocates "public compensation for the value of family labor." These could be tax credits for family or community labor or some form of family allowances. Folbre proposes that "regardless of income level, or biological relationship, all those who devote time and energy to caring for children, the sick, or the elderly outside the market economy should receive some remuneration." Folbre supports her proposal by arguing that "children, like the environment, are a public good." She points out that parental decisions about child rearing and the resources they dedicate to it, although made individually, affect everyone economically. Many countries' social security programs are "based on transfers from the working to the retired population, which means that all the elderly depend on other people's children."[40]

Even when the elderly depend largely on private pensions and individual savings, Folbre contends that "the rate of return on savings and the prices of basic commodities... are strongly affected by the productivity of the working age generation." She points out that although it is appropriate to advocate a more equal sharing of responsibilities for child care and domestic labor between female and male kin, these efforts will not be sufficient given changing family and household structures. Given the potential benefit that older generations will receive from younger generations, shared responsibility for children is arguably in the best interest of all.

In our advocacy for the well-being of children, we must be careful not to limit women's role to that of mothering or to limit "mothering" to women. In her discussion of gender and social citizenship, Anna Shola Orloff criticizes paternalistic welfare policies that keep women subordinate and dependent. She offers criteria for evaluating the extent of paternalism in a welfare state: (1) "the extent to which the state has taken over the provision of welfare services," as it is more democratic and egalitarian than the market or the family; (2) "the relative treatment of paid and unpaid workers"; (3) "the bases of people's claims to social citizenship rights," which should be as citizens rather than as workers; (4) "women's access to paid work"; and (5) "women's capacities to form and maintain autonomous households," which are necessary to women's freedom from compulsion to enter or stay in marriages in order to obtain economic support.[41] These criteria are useful guidelines for a progressive vision of a common good in which women matter, too.

Progressives advocate translating justified basic-needs claims such as child care, health care, housing, education, income, and employment, into social or economic rights. This moves toward a proactive rather than reactive state, which recognizes not only civil and political rights and citizenship but also social and economic rights—social citizenship. This is a progressive vision of the general welfare, a common good which takes into account children's need for care and does not assume that a woman's life is necessarily like that of a man. I disagree with those communitarian and feminist critics who charge that rights-talk is inherently individualistic and androcentric. Rather, as Elizabeth M. Schneider contends, striving for rights can be both political process and an assertion of our identity and vision.[42] These are visionary goals, not currently on the political agenda. In fact, the recent welfare reform (PRWORA) was a significant move away from such a vision. Welfare benefits (meager as they were) are no longer an entitlement for people who fall into poverty, nor were they replaced with any universal social or economic rights. However, our task is, as ethicist Gary Dorrien says, "to uphold a long-term vision of the common good while working to achieve attainable goals toward that end."[43] Progressive religious and secular people can form alliances around such a vision.

As the damaging effects of welfare reform become better known, possible attainable goals toward this end are alternative income support programs through restructuring of unemployment insurance. The Institute for Women's Policy Research has proposed to decrease the work experience and earnings requirement, limit disqualifications for job-leaving that results from caregiving activities (childbirth or illness), and provide transitional unemployment benefits for those entering or returning to work.[44] These changes would make many more poor women eligible to receive unemployment insurance. Changes in unemployment insurance and temporary disability leave could gain support in the current political climate, as they are linked to direct contributions and thus may be more acceptable.

Scholar and activist Gwendolyn Mink advocates "reuniting all single and/or unemployed parents in a unitary program for social provision along the model of the survivors' insurance system."[45] This would be an expansion of current Social Security payments to dependent children of a deceased parent. Activist Theresa Funiciello supports this proposal, as it makes no distinction among children on the basis of their parents' status. Current congressional proposals to expand Medicare to provide health insurance for uninsured children are a model of an expansion of accepted social provision programs to include new beneficiaries. If a majority of voters become persuaded that children are indeed a "public good," expansion of social provision programs is possible.

Funiciello also supports providing a guaranteed annual income as another alternative.[46] One form this might take is a negative income tax. Economist Herman Daly and theologian John Cobb argue for this in their book *For the Common Good.* They note that the current system of social provision is inequitable, inefficient, and demeaning. "A preferred system should: (1) require that the truly basic needs of all be met, (2) be simple and inexpensive to implement, (3) require a minimum of information from recipients and impose a minimum of special conditions upon them, and (4) provide a strong incentive to work. One approach that meets all these requirements is the negative income tax."[47] Daly and Cobb note that no one claims that the market fairly distributes income or prevents poverty. Governmental action is necessary if the basic needs of all are to be met.

Although the idea of a guaranteed annual income seems unrealistic in the current political climate, continuing high levels of unemployment may lead to new ways of thinking about the connection between income and work. The current obsession with putting welfare mothers into the paid work force is inconsistent with our evolving technological society, in which there is and will continue to be a decreasing need for wage workers. Our future will necessarily focus less on how to put everyone to work and more on how to find work for all who need it. In this context, policies that recognize the economic and social value of nonmarket child care and other useful community labor are especially timely.

Conclusion

The well-being of many vulnerable children and their families is at stake in the ongoing experiments with welfare reform. Policy guidelines and proposals must move beyond punitive welfare reform toward social citizenship with effective programs to reduce poverty, share responsibility for children, and give economic value to caregiving, so that children in different kinds of families may flourish. Theresa Funiciello, once a homeless welfare mother, now an organizer, advocate, author, and policymaker, charges: "Justice requires us to be critical of the balance in our everyday lives. It requires us to reconcile what we do with what we ought to be. There will be justice only when the uninjured parties are as indignant as the injured parties."[48] Our theological ethic calls us to compassion and solidarity with the poor and oppressed. Progressive religious communities should advocate for justice with the injured parties. Let us struggle together for a common good that encompasses the welfare of all children and their families.

Notes

1. Leatha Lamison-White, "Poverty in the United States: 1996," *Current Population Reports,* Series P60-198, U.S. Department of Commerce, Bureau of the Census (Washington, D.C.: Government Printing Office, 1997), 7–8; "Poverty in the United States: 1992," *Current Population Reports,* Series P60-185, U.S. Department of Commerce, Bureau of the Census (Washington, D.C.: Government Printing Office, Sept. 1993), x.

2. According to an Urban Institute study, the legislation that was adopted could throw an additional 1.1 million children into poverty—a 10-percent increase in the number of children living below the poverty line. The Center on Budget and Policy Priorities reached similar conclusions. See Elizabeth Shogren, "Study Warns of Welfare Reform Impact," *Los Angeles Times,* July 26, 1996, A16. A prior study by the Department of Health and Human Services, which was suppressed by the administration, reached similar conclusions. See Ruth Sidel, *Keeping Women and Children Last: America's War on the Poor* (New York: Penguin Books, 1996), 103–4.

3. Elizabeth Shogren, "Historical Overhaul of Welfare," *Los Angeles Times,* Aug. 23, 1996, A1 ff., and Randy Albedla, "Farewell to Welfare, but Not to Poverty," *Dollars and Sense,* November–December 1996, 16–19.

4. For presentation of the conservative charges, see Robert Rector, "Welfare Reform, Dependency Reduction, and Labor Market Entry," *Journal of Labor Research* (1993): 283–97. For refutation of these claims, see, among others, Sanford M. Dornbusch and Kathryn D. Gray, "Single Parent Families," in *Feminism, Children, and the New Families,* ed. Sanford M. Dornbusch and Myra H. Strober (New York: Guilford, 1988), 274–96; Laurie J. Bassie, "Employment and Welfare Participation among Women," *Economic Inquiry* (1990): 222–38; Steven K. Wisensale, "A Commentary on 'The Welfare State and Family Breakup: The Mythical Connection,'" *Family Relations* (1991): 151–52; Richard K. Caputo, "Family Poverty, Unemployment Rates, and AFDC Payments," *Families in Society* (1993): 515–26; Mimi

Abramovitz, "Challenging the Myths of Welfare Reform from a Woman's Perspective," *Social Justice* (spring 1994): 17–21; and Gwendolyn Mink, "Welfare Reform in Historical Perspective," *Social Justice* (spring 1994): 114–31.

5. W. Norton Grubb and Marvin Lazerson, *Broken Promises: How Americans Fail Their Children* (New York: Basic Books, 1982), 78–79.

6. "Money Income in the United States: 1995," *Current Population Reports*, Series P60-193, U.S. Department of Commerce, Bureau of the Census (Washington, D.C.: Government Printing Office, 1996), vii; Faye Fiore and Ronald Brownstein, "Most in the U.S. Got Richer, Poor Got Poorer in 1996," *Los Angeles Times*, Sept. 30, 1997, A1, A14; Lawrence Mishel and Jared Berstein, *The State of Working America* (Washington, D.C.: Economic Policy Institute, 1994).

7. Lynn Smith, "Politics Aside, People Want What's Best for Children," *Los Angeles Times*, February 9, 1997, E2.

8. Ada María Isasi-Díaz, "Solidarity: Love of Neighbor in the 21st Century," in *Mujerista Theology* (Maryknoll, N.Y.: Orbis Books, 1996), 86–104.

9. Delores Williams, *Sisters in the Wilderness: The Challenge of Womanist God-Talk* (Maryknoll, N.Y.: Orbis Books, 1993), 201.

10. Isasi-Díaz, *Mujerista Theology*, 89, 103.

11. Laurel Schneider, quoted in Elisabeth Schüssler Fiorenza, *But She Said: Feminist Practices of Biblical Interpretation* (Boston: Beacon, 1992), 163.

12. Nancy Fraser and Linda Gordon, "'Dependency' Demystified: Inscriptions of Power in a Keyword of the Welfare State," *Social Politics* (1994): 21.

13. Ibid., 22.

14. Diana Pearce, "Welfare Is Not *for* Women: Why the War on Poverty Cannot Conquer the Feminization of Poverty," in *Women, the State and Welfare*, ed. Linda Gordon (Madison: University of Wisconsin Press, 1990), 275.

15. Fraser and Gordon, "'Dependency' Demystified," 23–25.

16. Hilda Scott, *Working Your Way to the Bottom: The Feminization of Poverty* (London: Pandora, 1984). Marilyn Waring, *If Women Counted: A New Feminist Economics* (New York: Harper & Row, 1988). Chapter 12 of Waring's book suggests a useful model for incorporating unpaid work into national economic statistics.

17. See Pamela Brubaker, *Women Don't Count: The Challenge of Women's Poverty to Christian Ethics* (Atlanta: Scholars Press, 1994), 34–42, for a discussion of studies of this issue and attempts to redress it at the international level.

18. Julie A. Nelson, "The Study of Choice or the Study of Provisioning? Gender and the Definition of Economics," *Beyond Economic Man: Feminist Theory and Economics*, ed. Marianne A. Ferber and Julie A. Nelson (Chicago: University of Chicago Press, 1993), 36. For my critique of neoclassical economics, see "Economic Justice for Whom: Women Enter the Dialogue" in *Reli-*

gion and Economic Justice, ed. Michael Zweig (Philadelphia: Temple University Press, 1991), 108–10.

19. Diana Strassmann, "Not a Free Market: The Rhetoric of Disciplinary Authority in Economics," in *Beyond Economic Man,* ed. Ferber and Nelson, 55, 63. See also Amartya Sen, *Resources, Values and Development* (Cambridge: Harvard University Press, 1984).

20. Pamela Couture, *Blessed Are the Poor? Women's Poverty, Family Policy, and Practical Theology* (Nashville: Abingdon, in cooperation with the Churches' Center for Theology and Public Policy, 1991), 169, 173. Couture draws on the ethics of Martin Luther and John Wesley to develop her own ethic of care and shared responsibility.

21. Gosta Esping-Anderson, *The Three Worlds of Welfare Capitalism* (Princeton, N.J.: Princeton University Press, 1990), 26–27.

22. Fraser and Gordon, "'Dependency' Demystified," 13. See also Virginia Sapiro, "The Gender Basis of American Social Policy," in *Women, the State, and Welfare,* ed. Gordon, 36–54.

23. See, for instance, Teresa L. Amott, "Black Women and AFDC: Making Entitlement Out of Necessity," in *Women, the State, and Welfare,* ed. Gordon, 280–98; and Frances Fox Piven, "Ideology and the State: Women, Power, and the Welfare State," in *Women, the State, and Welfare,* ed. Gordon, 250–64.

24. Virginia Ellis, "State Democrats Set Stage for Welfare Battle with Wilson," *Los Angeles Times,* May 8, 1997, A1, A40.

25. Joel F. Handler and Yeheskel Hasenfeld, *The Moral Construction of Poverty: Welfare Reform in America* (Newbury Park, Calif.: Sage, 1991), 164–65.

26. Nancy Fraser, "Women, Welfare, and the Politics of Needs Interpretation," in *Unruly Practices: Power, Discourse and Gender in Contemporary Social Theory* (Minneapolis: University of Minnesota Press, 1989), 168. For a lucid exploration of significant moral questions in regard to the "traditional family," see Susan Moller Okin, *Justice, Gender, and the Family* (New York: Basic Books, 1989).

27. A useful source for understanding the limits of the market in redressing poverty is Walter L. Owensby, *Economics for Prophets: A Primer on Concepts, Realities, and Values in Our Economic System* (Grand Rapids, Mich.: Eerdmans, 1988).

28. Jeff Leeds, "Study Fuels Debate over Welfare Reform," *Los Angeles Times,* June 3, 1996, B12.

29. "Even in families with two wage earners, a fifth remain poor" (Joel F. Handler, *The Poverty of Welfare Reform* [New Haven, Conn.: Yale University Press, 1995], 36).

30. Donald J. Hernandez, *America's Children: Resources from Family, Governments, and the Economy* (New York: Russell Sage Foundation, 1993), 435, 414, emphasis added.

31. Gina Adams, Karen Pittman, and Raymond O'Brien, "Adolescent and Young Adult Fathers: Problems and Solutions," in *The Politics of Pregnancy: Adolescent Sexuality and Public Policy,* ed. Annette Lawson and Deborah L. Rhode (New Haven, Conn.: Yale University Press, 1993), 216–37.

32. Laurie Goodstein, "Churches Can't Feed Many More Hungry," *Tampa Tribune,* February 26, 1995, A1.

33. Handler and Hasenfeld, *Moral Construction of Poverty,* 29.

34. Ellis, "State Democrats Set Stage," A40. The plan adopted by the legislature and signed by the governor was a compromise between the governor's and the Democrats' proposals. Wilson's two-year limit was adopted for current recipients, with only eighteen months for new ones. However, counties can extend this limit another six months. Able-bodied adult recipients must engage in work *or training* for twenty hours a week, thirty-two hours a week after Jan. 1, 2000. Mothers of newborns will be exempted from these requirements for six months, with counties having the option to reduce this to three months (Wilson's proposal) or extend it to a year (Virginia Ellis and Max Vanzi, "Legislature OKs Major Revamping of Welfare System," *Los Angeles Times,* August 5, 1997, A1, 14).

35. Teresa Amott, "Reforming Welfare or Reforming the Labor Market: Lessons from the Massachusetts Employment Training Experience," *Social Justice* (1994): 33–37. Participants in such a program at Cleveland State University, where I taught from 1990 to 1994, gave it high marks. They see it as a way to make a real difference in their own and their children's lives. Critical to the program's success, which has been documented by administrators and funders, are child-care provisions and a mentoring program.

36. Roberta Spalter-Roth and Heidi Hartmann, "AFDC Recipients as Caregivers and Workers: A Feminist Approach to Income Security Policy for American Women," *Social Politics* (summer 1994): 190–210.

37. Roberta Spalter-Roth, "The Real Employment Opportunities of Women Participating in AFDC: What the Market Can Provide," *Social Justice* (1994): 60–70.

38. Esping-Anderson, *Three Worlds,* 27–28. He also identifies another variation of the "institutional state" form of welfare capitalism, described as "conservative-corporatist regimes which preserve status and class differentials," as found in Italy, France, and Germany. This type resonates with organic conceptions of the common good in traditional Roman Catholic social teaching. Needless to say, the social-democratic form is found in the Nordic countries, but Esping-Anderson notes no single pure case.

39. U.S. Conference of Catholic Bishops, *Economic Justice for All: Catholic Social Teaching and the U.S. Economy* (Washington, D.C.: U.S. Catholic Conference, 1986). For a critical assessment of Roman Catholic social teaching in relation to women's reality, including this pastoral, see Brubaker, *Women Don't Count,* 59–99.

40. Nancy Folbre, *Who Pays for the Kids? Gender and the Structures of Constraint* (New York: Routledge, 1994), 258, 254.

41. Ibid., 258–59. Anna Shola Orloff, "Gender and the Social Rights of Citizenship," *American Sociological Review* 58 (June 1993): 323. Also see Barbara Hobson, "No Exit, No Voice: Women's Economic Dependency and the Welfare State," *Acta Sociologica* (1990): 235–50.

42. Fraser, *Unruly Practices,* 183. Schneider, "The Dialectic of Rights and Politics: Perspectives from the Women's Movement," in *Women, the State, and Welfare,* ed. Gordon, 226–49.

43. Gary J. Dorrien, *Reconstructing the Common Good: Theology and the Social Order* (Maryknoll, N.Y.: Orbis Books, 1990), 175.

44. Roberta M. Spalter-Roth and Heidi I. Hartmann, "AFDC Recipients as Care-givers," 190–210.

45. Mink, "Welfare Reform in Historical Perspective," 127.

46. *Tyranny of Kindness: Dismantling the Welfare System to End Poverty in America* (New York: Atlantic Monthly Press, 1993).

47. John Cobb and Herman Daly, *For the Common Good: Redirecting the Economy toward Community, the Environment, and a Sustainable Future,* rev. ed. (Boston: Beacon, 1994), 316. Their chapter "Income Policies and Taxes" (315–31) discusses the strengths and weaknesses of this proposal and other proposed tax changes. Christian ethicist Warren Copeland also supports a negative income tax. See his *And the Poor Get Welfare: The Ethics of Poverty in the United States* (Nashville: Abingdon, 1994), 183.

48. Theresa Funiciello, "The Fifth Estate: How and Why the Poverty Industry Distorts Welfare Issues and Displaces the Interests of People on Welfare," *Social Justice* (1994): 97.

[2]

Liberation from the Welfare Trap?

Ellen Ott Marshall

FOR THE FIRST TIME SINCE the creation of Aid to Families with Dependent Children in 1935, poor women and children are no longer guaranteed financial assistance from the federal government. Congress discontinued this entitlement on October 1, 1996, five weeks after the "Personal Responsibility and Work Opportunity Reconciliation Act" became law. One year later, two million fewer individuals received cash assistance.[1] For many, this statistic reflects the liberation of poor Americans from the welfare trap. But there is also an increase in the number of visitors to food pantries, emergency shelters, and soup kitchens, compounded by a shortage of available, low-skill jobs in many urban areas.[2] In one of the most promising states, only 29 percent of the cases closed in the first year were closed because the principal recipient secured employment. And, among this successful 29 percent, the average hourly wage was $5.82.[3] Even these few statistics prompt the question: Has the move from welfare to work been a liberating experience?

Proponents of the Personal Responsibility and Work Opportunity Reconciliation Act describe it as the path to liberation from the welfare trap because it emphasizes the "creation of opportunity" rather than the "distribution of benefits."[4] In other words, one of the fundamental assumptions underlying this approach is that providing the "means to achieve" is equivalent to providing freedom and opportunity. The most tangible vehicle for this provision of means is the Individual Responsibility Plan (IRP) in its various state forms.[5] In

47

order to continue to receive cash assistance in Tennessee, for example, welfare applicants must sign an IRP which details an employment strategy, sets forth obligations for the individual, and describes services to be provided by the state. Depending on the participant's age and background, the employment strategy may include further education, job training, or immediate job placement which the recipient must pursue forty hours per week.[6] The package of services made available to each participant may include various amounts of cash assistance, food stamps, transportation assistance, child care, and Medicaid.[7] At their best, therefore, IRPs are intended to provide participants with the means to achieve self-sufficiency.

As we shall see, however, the average long-term welfare recipient lives in a socioeconomic environment which inhibits her *freedom* to achieve.[8] In this environment, characterized by William Julius Wilson as "social isolation," the opportunities offered by a welfare-to-work plan are not real opportunities. Because IRPs do not take social isolation into account, they provide the means to achieve without addressing the web of factors which stifle an individual's freedom to achieve. Thus, there is a gap between the expectations of the program and the socioeconomic realities of its participants. The program assumes a context in which the opportunities it offers are real opportunities. In such a context, exiting the welfare rolls would truly signify economic independence. But for those participants circumscribed by social isolation, liberation from the welfare trap means destitution rather than freedom. Moreover, because this path to economic independence is laden with the language of personal responsibility, the woman who remains impoverished is held accountable for the failure of the program.

These are clearly public policy issues. But my concern is a moral one, rooted in two fundamental convictions. The first is the Christian mandate to care for the most vulnerable members of society. As followers of one who ministered to the marginalized, Christians have a responsibility to stand with and serve those in need. The second conviction is the theological claim that all individuals are created for freedom. Based on this claim, we are obligated to dismantle structures which suppress flourishing, such as social isolation. As Christians and as citizens, therefore, we have a responsibility to ensure that all individuals can flourish in our society, that all individuals have the chance to realize their full potential. To fulfill these mandates, we must not only open our hearts and behave charitably, but also educate ourselves so that we can make informed assessments of public policies and work to change them when they violate moral requirements. Thus, our first step as Christians, moral agents, and responsible citizens is to ask H. Richard Niebuhr's question: What's going on? My aim in this chapter is to provide an accurate description of one welfare initiative and its impact on women and children and to suggest an appropriate response. As summarized above, Individual Responsibility Plans do not take into account social isolation and therefore place women and their children in an increasingly vulnerable position. It is our responsibility, therefore, not only to work steadily to dismantle the structures which suppress flourishing, but also to ensure legislative and community-based supports as long as those structures persist.

One of the first things to clarify about this legislation is that, contrary to mainstream discourse, there is no crisis of expenditure and dependency. In 1992, AFDC expenditures amounted to a smaller proportion of the federal budget than they did in 1975.[9] In the 1990s, AFDC has consistently amounted to less than 1 percent of the federal budget.[10] Similarly, statistics about actual usage of public assistance reveal the concern over dependency to be unwarranted. Fifty percent of recipients exit AFDC in the first year, and 75 percent exit in the first two years. This means, for example, that although 5 percent of the U.S. population received cash assistance in 1995, only 2–3 percent are long-term welfare recipients.[11] A second point that contradicts mainstream assumptions is that there is no conclusive, promising evidence regarding welfare-to-work initiatives and job prospects for AFDC recipients. Despite nearly thirty years of welfare-to-work initiatives (since workfare was first legislated in 1967) and countless studies at the national and local levels, "no one program or course of action has been demonstrated as clearly better than another."[12] Moreover, as will be discussed later, there is little assurance that the average long-term welfare recipient (a single mother with small children, little education or work experience) will be able to secure a good job.

Given all of these factors—with a small percentage of federal dollars devoted to cash assistance, a relatively small percentage of the population impacted by this program, and with so little certainty as to how one might truly enable self-sufficiency—why reform now? Perhaps, as many observers suggest, welfare reform is prompted by what AFDC represents rather than by what it does.[13] In other words, this public assistance program is the target of so much attention because of the symbols, values, and stereotypes entwined with it rather than because of the actual administration, fiscal detail, and statistical impact of the programs. Some of these symbols appear in the following excerpt from President Clinton's speech announcing his decision to sign the bill.

> Today the Congress will vote on legislation that gives us a chance…to transform a broken system that traps too many people in a cycle of dependence to one that emphasizes work and independence, to give people on welfare a chance to draw a paycheck, not a welfare check. It gives us a better chance to give those on welfare what we want for all families in America, the opportunity to succeed at home and at work.[14]

Clinton draws on old, familiar symbols, the traditional family and the work ethic, and on a relatively new symbol, namely the welfare trap. The latter symbol has tremendous bipartisan appeal because it allows conservatives to denounce a program that has, in their opinion, outlived its purpose and allows liberals to acknowledge the problem without blaming the victim. Dismantling welfare becomes a venue for promoting the work ethic and other mainstream values. It is welfare that destroys initiative, motivation, and competitive impulses and therefore stands in the way of individual achievement and of market forces. Thus, both parties find common ground in the assertion that the current welfare system should be replaced with a program that gives individuals opportunities to live more responsibly, to hold together a marriage and family, to receive an education, and to work. And the Individual Responsibility Plans, ostensibly, provide the means for this more responsible and productive lifestyle to be realized. Or, more accurately, the IRPs move individuals off of welfare and into the free market where they can join the competitive race for a livelihood.

At their best, the Individual Responsibility Plans, in their various state forms, prepare an individual for economic independence, give her the education and training she needs to get a job, and provide for her in the transition period. The recipient's caseworker guides her through a comprehensive plan of action to which the recipient agrees. The state provides cash assistance, education, job training, and even transportation and child care when the individual becomes employed. The state also provides transitional assistance, food stamps and housing assistance if necessary.[15] In sum, the ideal Individual Responsibility Plan would offer a perfect balance of benefits and burdens, giving the individual what she needs to move toward economic independence.

Even in this best-case scenario, however, there is a federally legislated five-year lifetime maximum for receiving public assistance, a fixed block grant for the state's welfare budget, federally established percentage goals for work participation, and a reduction of $54 billion in spending for public assistance by 2002. My concern is that, even in this best-case scenario, the program assumes a certain social and economic context in which all of the opportunities afforded by IRPs are real opportunities. In such a context, the federally established time limits and budget constraints would not impinge upon the recipient's ability to acquire all of the services she needs. In other words, the Individual Responsibility Plans place tremendous faith in the symbol of individual success in the marketplace. Is this faith justified, or is the symbol of individual success in the marketplace in tension with the socioeconomic realities surrounding welfare recipients?

In his 1987 book *The Truly Disadvantaged*, William Julius Wilson defines social isolation as "the lack of contact or of sustained interaction with individuals and institutions that represent mainstream society."[16] Throughout his writing over the last ten years, Wilson describes neighborhoods of concentrated poverty, characterized by limited economic opportunities and multiple social restraints, ranging from the practice of redlining to weak school systems.[17] Expanding on the multiple constraints found in poverty settings, the authors of a recent book of essays, *The Work Alternative* (1995), explore the implications of social isolation on employment prospects for welfare recipients. The authors do not use Wilson's language, but they do describe a labor market in which the average AFDC recipient lacks the freedom to achieve and may well be trapped by social isolation. The authors agree that low-wage, low-skilled jobs are available, but argue consistently that these jobs will not move former welfare recipients toward economic independence even if they are able to work full time, year round. Gary Burtless, a senior fellow at the Brookings Institution, sums up this shared position by concluding that the research does "not show that job finding is impossible for women who receive AFDC. [But it does] show that many women who eventually find jobs will earn too little to support themselves and their children with any degree of comfort."[18] Moreover, as more low-skilled workers leave the welfare rolls and flood the market, wages and other job attributes will be driven down so that job seekers will continue to "face a labor market with low earnings and few advancement opportunities."[19]

The real opportunities for achievement are further diminished for women dealing with substance abuse or domestic violence, or who have little education and job experience, learning disabilities, or children with emotional or physical problems. Rebecca Blank, an economics professor at Northwestern and researcher in the university's Urban Policy Studies program, discusses these multiple burdens and criticizes the current legislation for not adopting the long-term approach these women need to move successfully from welfare to work. She writes, "given the limited funds and the very short time frame for public assistance, it may be impossible under this legislation to deal adequately with women who face multiple environmental and personal problems."[20] For women living in either isolated rural areas or urban areas of concentrated poverty, their own financial straits may be compounded by the impact of welfare cuts on the neighborhood. The journal of the Brookings Institution, *The Brookings Review*, devoted a recent issue to urban concerns, and several authors described the relationship between public assistance and social isolation. In her essay "Is Anybody Listening?" Margaret Weir, another Brookings research fellow in economics, makes a strong case for the extra burden placed on urban areas by this recent welfare legislation.

Big cities contain areas of concentrated poverty where cuts in welfare will have ripple effects likely to harm entire neighborhoods. As cuts endanger the ability of welfare recipients to pay rent and to patronize local businesses, whole neighborhoods face new instability. Abandoned housing and empty stores not only invite crime, but also pose a direct threat to the progress that neighborhood groups have made in recreating the social fabric of many poor neighborhoods once left for dead.[21]

The overarching theme in all of these economic and sociological assessments is that moving off of welfare is not solely a matter of personal responsibility. In other words, an individual's ability to become self-sufficient depends on a whole range of factors from personal health and well-being to a community's commitment and capacity to provide good jobs. Considering factors of social isolation that inhibit women and their families from joining mainstream society supports the claim that the symbolic goal of economic self-sufficiency in the free market is most definitely in tension with the socioeconomic realities of welfare recipients.

Like Wilson's concept of social isolation, Amartya Sen's notion of "capability to function" also helps us assess the adequacy of IRPs. In his 1992 book, *Inequality Reexamined*, Sen emphasizes the thoroughness of human diversity. We differ not only according to personal characteristics, but also by external situation.[22] Any measurement of inequality, then, must take all of these aspects into account: the individual, her resources, and her context. To that end, Sen suggests that inequality be measured not only in terms of goods and resources, but also in terms of capability to function.[23] Capability to function is a sweeping concept that includes the multiple aspects of a person's life which shape his or her real opportunities—personal *and* external characteristics, biographical sketch *and* socioeconomic context. Sen thus broadens the scope of his economic analysis to consider not just provision of means, but also the context in which the goods are received. Without this broad scope of consideration, we measure goods, but not freedom.

Sen understands freedom as the real choices an individual has. For example, is she free to choose one course of action, one way of living, one possible vocation over another?[24] In order to answer this, we have to evaluate the individual-in-society rather than just the individual. We must take into consideration the socioeconomic context in which she lives as well as her level of education, amount of work experience, and family responsibilities. Applying Sen's language to the issue at hand, we can say that a welfare recipient's capability to function is not determined solely by the skills she learns in a job-training session, but also by the real opportunities she has to secure and keep a job while caring for her family. In other words, her *real* opportunities are determined not by her IRP, but by the socioeconomic context in which she lives. And, as the research cited earlier shows, myriad forces inhibit an individual's freedom to achieve despite the various services provided to her. Sen's economic analysis, coupled with Wilson's sociological description, thus undermine a fundamental assumption behind IRPs, namely that providing the means to achieve is equivalent to providing freedom and opportunity.

Given these realities, Individual Responsibility Plans cannot ensure the freedom to achieve. As time limits approach, this fact takes on grave moral implications not only because many needy women and children will be denied further assistance, but also because these same women will be held personally responsible for remaining poor despite the state's best efforts. This situation demands a thoughtful and heartfelt moral response, as well as sociological and economic analysis. Because all persons deserve to realize their full potential, social welfare policy should aim to ensure conditions necessary to human flourishing. As we have seen, these conditions do not exist for many poor families, and the current welfare program, with its emphasis on individual responsibility, will make it very difficult for these families to prove themselves deserving of public assistance.[25] Those of us who are financially stable have a moral responsibility to care for these families, and we can begin to do this by advocating for fair appeals procedures and by creating supportive networks within the community. For example, MANNA, a local hunger relief organization in Nashville, Tennessee, hosts regular meetings to educate the community about the effects of welfare reform. Other nonprofit organizations and individuals have joined coalitions, such as the REAL Coalition for Welfare Reform and the Tennessee Commission on Social Welfare (TCSW), to increase their presence in state legislative committees. Indeed TCSW was instrumental in crafting and ensuring the inclusion of several important amendments to the Families First bill. And, as will be discussed shortly, many churches have partnered with a micro-lending organization to help welfare recipients build a savings account and acquire assets.

One of the most immediate concerns, however, is ensuring a fair appeals process. Each state is required by the federal government to "provide opportunities for recipients who have been adversely affected to be heard in a State administrative or appeal process."[26] The federal law also stipulates that the family of an individual who has been subject to physical, sexual, or mental abuse may continue to receive assistance for more than five years.[27] In addition to this "hardship exemption," states are to define "good cause exemptions" by which an individual may be excused from participating in work requirements or continue to receive assistance after a time limit has passed.[28] For example, in Tennessee, the caseworker may grant a good cause exemption if the recipient has complied with the Personal Responsibility Plan, has neither refused nor voluntarily quit a job (without good cause), earns less than the maximum grant for her family size, and would continue to receive support were it not for time limits. Regarding the work requirements, an individual will not be sanctioned for noncompliance if the work or the necessary services (child care and transportation) are no longer available, if she can prove that she is sick or caring for a sick relative, or if there is a temporary emergency. In Tennessee, the caseworker uses state guidelines to make these determinations but may also grant exemption for other reasons deemed appropriate.[29] In light of these provisions, we must acknowledge that recipients whose benefits are discontinued do have recourse to an appeals process and legislative stipulations which may serve as footholds for requesting further assistance.

Other aspects of these processes and their application, however, may prompt a less sanguine response. First, because state procedures vary, it will be extremely difficult to monitor the fairness of the appeals process. Thus far, states have made statistics about the decreasing welfare rolls much more readily available than statistics detailing the number of appeals and their outcomes.[30] Moreover, as of this writing, the appeals process has yet to be tested by those who reach their time limits and continue to need assistance. In Tennessee, the case managers will review each case before the eighteen-month or five-year time limit to determine whether good cause exists for extending the benefits. While a case manager may have the best intentions, she will probably not have the time to thoroughly review the situation for each of her eighty clients.[31] Moreover, if an individual appeals her case within ten days, she may continue to receive benefits until the judge makes a final determination. However, if the judge denies her appeal, she must repay "the excess benefits."[32]

One further reason for caution is that the political goal for welfare reform is to *reduce* the welfare rolls. It would be naive to think that the evaluation of appeals and the determination of good cause are immune to this goal and the rhetoric surrounding it. For instance, according to federal guidelines, a state is not allowed to provide hardship exemptions to more than 20 percent of its caseload.[33] However, studies on domestic violence, which is just one such good cause exemption, consistently reveal that 60 percent of welfare recipients suffer abuse.[34] Clearly, the political agenda of roll reduction rather than statistics like this established the 20 percent ceiling and will similarly impact the appeals process. Such examples highlight the tremendous imbalance of power that marks the agreement between the state and the welfare recipient. Indeed, for twenty-five years, the well-known social welfare historians Francis Fox Piven and Richard Cloward have pointed to this imbalance of power as the gateway to manipulative welfare legislation. In their words, "any institution that distributes the resources men and women depend upon for survival can readily exert control over them."[35] We must remember that any allowances by the state for an appeals process remain under the shadow of this fact: the state's primary interest is to reduce the welfare rolls. In other words, the case manager's decisions about her client's well-being are, unfortunately, not made in a neutral environment. Weighing in on each decision is the political goal to decrease spending for public assistance. And that fact necessarily calls into question the fairness of any appeals process or bureaucratic decision affecting the life of a poor woman and her children.

These larger political concerns, joined with the reality of social isolation and the legislative footholds for advocacy described above, set the agenda for those concerned about the plight of welfare recipients under this legislation. As citizens in a political process, we must advocate for a fair appeals procedure and monitor this procedure to ensure that the good cause and hardship exemptions are truly granted as needed. Without these legislative supports functioning truly and fairly, there will be no support for those "liberated" welfare recipients who remain destitute. Because IRPs do not address social isolation and fail to ensure the freedom to achieve, real and true back-up measures must be in place and functioning with the interests of poor women and children in mind.

In addition to advocating for a fair appeals process, we have a responsibility to create structures within the community to support those who cannot meet the expectations and time limits of the IRP. Across the country, civic and church organizations work either in conjunction with or in lieu of state programs to meet the needs of welfare recipients in their communities. Certainly, the burden for these efforts falls most heavily on those churches and organizations already serving the poor because of commitments which long precede this welfare legislation. And it is unfair and unrealistic to expect these same committed people to pick up the slack for an insufficient social welfare policy and for an unsympathetic majority. It is important, then, to stress that these efforts are examples to be followed rather than examples offered to quell concern. For instance, the Tennessee Network for Community Economic Development (or TNCED) organizes peer lending groups across the state for low-to-moderate income earners. The aim is to build assets which make the move off of welfare more feasible and long-lasting. Participants make deposits into an Individual Development Account (IDA), and a civic or church group contributes a two-to-one match to the savings account. The involvement of the church or civic group may be limited to this financial contribution or be expanded to host a peer lending group in which IDA savers participate in financial literacy training. Some Nashville area churches have further expanded their role to act as a sponsor for individual families.[36]

These community responses may not dismantle social isolation, but they do provide supportive structures so that welfare recipients are not further harmed by the unrealistic expectations of this public policy. Individual Responsibility Plans expect that participants will outgrow the need for public assistance if they engage their welfare-to-work program with diligence and commitment. But, as we have seen, the average long-term welfare recipient lives in a context which limits her real opportunities regardless of the effort she puts into her IRP. For these women and their families, these programs do not promise liberation, but threaten greater poverty and stigma. The gap between the program's expectation and its participants' real opportunities makes the need for a fair appeals process and community support even greater. These responses rest on a radically different assertion than that which undergirds IRPs, namely that economic independence is not solely a matter of personal responsibility. Rather, socioeconomic circumstances shape an individual's freedom to achieve. Therefore, it is up to the community to harness all of its resources, governmental and non-governmental, to create spaces in which every person may realize her full potential. It may be beyond the scope of this particular legislation to dismantle social isolation, but it is within its scope to jettison its participants into the labor market with or without support. Given the tenuous circumstances and multiple burdens of many poor women, social welfare programs must not only equip them to compete, but also support them if they (and their children) lose this competitive race.

Notes

1. Dept. of Health and Human Services Administration for Children and Families, Office of Public Affairs, "Change in Welfare Caseloads Since August 1996" (Washington, D.C., 1997); available from http://www.acf.dhhs.gov/news. As of July 1997, the number of recipients for cash assistance dropped to 10.2 million from 12.2 million in August 1996.

2. Paul Shepard, "Cities Survey Hints at Job Shortage," Associated Press, Nov. 21, 1997; available from http://www.washingtonpost.com. Thirty-four cities responded to a survey conducted by the National Conference of Mayors in which they were asked about job availability and social service usage since the implementation of the welfare law. Thirteen cities forecast tremendous job shortages ranging from 6,734 in St. Louis to 75,303 in Detroit. They also noted a sharp increase in requests for emergency food assistance from those who no longer qualify for food stamps.

3. Office of [Tennessee] Governor Don Sundquist, "Families First Is Working: Governor Cites University of Memphis Report as Program Celebrates First Anniversary," Sept. 2, 1997 (press release); Linda Rudolph, commissioner of the Dept. of Human Services in Tennessee, "Remarks of Commissioner Linda Rudolph: Open Cabinet Meeting" (Nashville, 1997). Regarding the remaining case closings: 18 percent were closed because the caretaker refused to sign the Personal Responsibility Plan; 21 percent were closed because the caretaker failed to comply with work requirements; the remaining 30 percent requested that their cases be closed "usually because they found jobs on their

own, they began receiving child support or they had some resources from family or friends," according to Commissioner Rudolph.

4. Tennessee Dept. of Human Services, "Families First: Summary Statement" (Nashville: TDHS, 1996), 1.

5. Personal Responsibility and Work Opportunity Reconciliation Act of 1996, H.R. 3734, section 408.b; available from http://thomas.loc.gov.

6. Tennessee Dept. of Human Services, "Variances between the Federal Law and the Tennessee State Plan" (Nashville: TDHS, 1996); Tennessee Dept. of Human Services, "Work Requirement" (Nashville: TDHS, 1996). In Tennessee, a participant may be exempt from the work requirement if s/he has a "medically verified disability," "is determined to be incapacitated," "proves that he/she is needed in the home full-time to care for a related disabled child or adult relative who lives in the home," "is age sixty (60) or older," or is "under 18 [and has] a child under 12 weeks old."

7. H.R. 3734, section 408.b.2.

8. The distinction between means and freedom to achieve is developed by Amartya Sen in his book *Inequality Reexamined* (New York: Russell Sage Foundation, 1992), which will be discussed later. Sen received the Nobel Prize for Economics in 1998.

9. Nathan Glazer, "Making Work Work," in *The Work Alternative,* ed. Deborah Smith Nightingale and Robert H. Haveman (Washington, D.C.: Urban Institute Press, 1995), 20. According to historical data from the Office of Management and Budget, the federal outlay for 1975 was roughly $332 billion. Glazer records AFDC expenditures that year as $5 billion, constituting 1.5 percent of the federal budget. (The 1996 legislation changed the name AFDC to Temporary Assistance for Needy Families (TANF). However, I intentionally refer to AFDC here because these comments describe statistics and sentiments that predate TANF).

10. Dept. of Health and Human Services, Administration for Children and Families, Office of Public Affairs, "Estimated FY 1997 State Family Assistance Grants Under P.L. 104-193" (Washington, D.C., 1997), available from http://www.acf.dhhs.gov/news; Office of Management and Budget, "Budget of the U.S. Government Fiscal Year 1997" (Washington, D.C., 1997), available from http://www.cher.eda.doc.gov/BudgetFY1997. According to the Department of Health and Human Services, the expected allotment for FY 1997 State Family Assistance Grants is $16.5 billion, still less than 1 percent of our federal budget. Moreover, this spending pales next to the amounts spent on Social Security ($368 billion) and national defense ($259 billion).

11. Joel Handler and Yeheskel Hasenfeld, "Introduction to Welfare" (New York: Twentieth Century Fund, 1996), available from http://www.epn.org/tcf/welfintro.html#q17; Dept. of Health and Human Services, Administration for Children and Families, Office of Public Affairs, "Percentage of the US

Population on Welfare since 1960" (Washington, D.C., 1997), available from http://www.acf.dhhs.gov/news.

12. Glazer, "Making Work Work," 30.

13. Ibid., 21. For further discussion of the symbols and ideology surrounding welfare reform historically, see Linda Gordon, *Pitied but Not Entitled: Single Mothers and the History of Welfare* (Cambridge: Harvard University Press, 1994); Joel F. Handler and Yeheskel Hasenfeld, *The Moral Construction of Poverty: Welfare Reform in America* (London: Sage, 1991); Michael B. Katz, *The Undeserving Poor: From the War on Poverty to the War on Welfare* (New York: Pantheon, 1989).

14. William J. Clinton, "Text of President Clinton's Announcement on Welfare Legislation," *New York Times*, August 1, 1996, A10.

15. These are all options for the state, described either in H.R. 3734 or in Tennessee's Families First summary.

16. William Julius Wilson, *The Truly Disadvantaged: The Inner City, the Underclass, and Public Policy* (Chicago: University of Chicago Press, 1987), 60.

17. For an overview of Wilson's sociological assessment and public policy recommendations for welfare reform, see chapter 8 of *When Work Disappears: The World of the New Urban Poor* (New York: Alfred A. Knopf, 1996).

18. Gary Burtless, "Employment Prospects of Welfare Recipients," in *The Work Alternative*, ed. Nightingale and Haveman, 86.

19. Rebecca M. Blank, "Outlook for the U.S. Labor Market and Prospects for Low-Wage Entry Jobs," in *The Work Alternative*, ed. Nightingale and Haveman, 33.

20. Rebecca M. Blank, "Policy Watch: The 1996 Welfare Reform," *Journal of Economic Perspectives* (winter 1997): 173.

21. Margaret Weir, "Is Anybody Listening?" *The Brookings Review* (winter 1997): 31.

22. Sen, *Inequality Reexamined*, 1–2.

23. I should note at the outset that I use Sen's capability approach differently with regards to welfare and poverty. In his chapters on these topics (6 and 7), he offers the capability approach as a measure of poverty. I use it here in order to assess a policy.

24. Sen, *Inequality Reexamined*, 39–40.

25. For further discussion of shifting definitions of the "deserving poor" through history, see Handler and Hasenfeld, *The Moral Construction of Poverty*; Katz, *The Undeserving Poor*.

26. H.R. 3734, section 402.1.A.i; section 402.1.B.iii.

27. H.R. 3734, section 408.7.C.i–iii.

28. H.R. 3734, section 408.10.B.

29. Tennessee Dept. of Human Services, *Case Managers' Families First Handbook* (Nashville: TDHS, 1996), 204, 234–35.

30. At the time of this writing, I have been unable to locate any statistics regarding appeals and outcomes for any state, including my own.

31. Tennessee caseworkers have an average of eighty Families First clients, but this number grows to three hundred when food-stamp clients are included.

32. Tennessee Dept. of Human Services, *Case Managers' Families First Handbook*, 268.

33. H.R. 3734, section 408.7.C.ii.

34. Jessica Pearson, Nancy Thoennes, and Esther Ann Griswold, "Colorado Model Project: Child Support and Domestic Violence: The Victims Speak Out" (Denver: Center for Policy Research, 1998). The authors of this study examine the gap between the percentage of welfare recipients who suffer domestic violence and the percentage who apply for a good cause exemption. It provides a helpful overview of the literature about domestic violence and welfare reform and reviews the current debate between advocates for victims of abuse and proponents of this welfare legislation. A copy of this report is available from the Web site of the Administration for Children and Families of the U.S. Department of Health and Human Services (http://www.acf.dhhs.gov/programs/cse/rpt/mofc/4victims.htm).

35. Frances Fox Piven and Richard A. Cloward, *Regulating the Poor: The Function of Public Welfare*, 2d ed. (New York: Pantheon, 1993), 22.

36. Tennessee Network for Community Economic Development, "Peer Lending Summary" (Nashville: TNCED, 1997); Gene TeSelle, "Responding to 'Welfare Reform' at the Community Level," *Southern Communities* (Oct. 1996): 1–2. TNCED bases its approach, in large part, on the work of Michael Sherraden; see *Assets and the Poor: A New American Welfare Policy* (Armonk, N.Y.: M. E. Sharpe, 1991).

[3]

Decentering Poverty

Ruth L. Smith

MY APPROACH TO CURRENT DEBATES about welfare reform is less direct than others in this volume but is equally concerned with the limitations of the terms of that debate and the serious consequences for those most immediately affected by it as well as for the larger society. I address my concern through examining the discourse of poverty in its relations with Christian beliefs and practices of salvation. Such an approach may appear far afield from public policy, but the discourse of poverty—that is, the habits of speech we use to identify, analyze, and describe poverty—constructs what we think poverty to be. In Christian traditions, the ethical-theological logics that link poverty with salvation decisively contribute to shaping experiences, relations, and ideals of poverty. It is tempting to consider that in this connection, the poor are the ones in need of the concerned Christian, but the Christian is also in need of the poor inasmuch as concern for the poor is believed to be the medium of salvation. I argue that in this complex relationship there is not only a demand for the alleviation of poverty but also a demand for the perpetuation of poverty.

The calls for voluntary agencies in the United States to increase their services as government agencies decrease theirs make this an opportune moment to consider religious assumptions about poverty which inform cultural and policy formulations of giving and receiving assistance. Societal notions of poverty still draw on these assumptions, despite the largely secular character of public life. Karl Marx makes the argument that Christianity legitimates existing social conditions to support the interests of the ruling classes, in part by spiritualizing poverty as a state of holiness and as a condition to be alleviated only in the next world.[1] I pursue a different angle by arguing that the ideals of voluntary poverty contribute to the assumption that involuntary poverty is a condition society cannot do without. While the configurations vary historically and with regard to class, gender, and race, they consistently reproduce narratives that connect goodness, poverty, and the ultimate fate of one's soul in religious and secular narratives about salvation and its consequences for individuals and societies.

To develop my argument and perspective, I identify the Christian idealizations of voluntary and involuntary poverty. Then follows an analysis of poverty in the medieval Roman Catholic Church which explicitly connects voluntary and involuntary poverty in a well-developed theological dynamic of renunciation, charity, and salvation. I then consider theoretical and theological arguments of the last two centuries that are critical of certain aspects of the Christian view of poverty and salvation but retain some of these same assumptions in their proposed notions of salvation. Finally, I consider associations of poverty, asceticism, and salvation in practices of authority. The discourse linking poverty, asceticism, and salvation bears the awkwardness of multiple perspectives, not all taking the same route but often loosely sharing the legacies of Christian referents. For that reason, it is important to outline the two primary Christian idealizations.

Idealizations of Poverty in Christianity

Christian traditions identify two clusters of moral/spiritual ideals about poverty. One is that of voluntary poverty, which in contemporary discussions of virtue can be identified as the attitude that goods should be fairly distributed or as the act of dispossessing oneself by goods by choice.[2] Voluntary poverty in this chapter refers to the ascetic tradition in which persons choose to sacrifice worldly goods for the sake of spiritual purification, union with God, and compassion for those who are suffering. The goods of food, clothing, and shelter, except for minimal requirements, are just the beginning of what is left behind in the turn from the world; voluntary poverty also traditionally involves relinquishing the worldly goods of security, power, and the ego-self. The other spiritual/moral ideal ensues from involuntary poverty, in which persons are poor because of political/economic circumstances. While these circumstances are worldly, the suffering they cause is understood to invite heightened divine concern for and heightened divine presence in the human being who so suffers. In this nexus of suffering and divinity, the involuntarily poor are often the special concern of the voluntarily poor, evident in monastic and other organized religious assistance. Christians who are not poor, by choice or circumstance, have historically venerated the voluntarily poor for their goodness and good works and attributed humility and innocence to the involuntarily poor on the basis of their vulnerability and need. In the history of these ideals in Christianity, poverty and eternity coalesce, in that to give to the poor in either position is to give toward one's own salvation.

In Christianity, the practices of voluntary asceticism are considered necessary to seek and express a more purely spiritual life than is available within what the ascetically oriented believe to be the compromised terms of ordinary morality. Voluntary poverty in Roman Catholic monastic discipline refers to one of the three vows, along with chastity and obedience, that men and women take as part of membership in religious orders. In Protestantism, voluntary poverty most distinctly takes the form of the "inner-worldly asceticism" of Calvinism (to use Max Weber's phrase), which entails disciplines of frugality and rejection of material display chosen in the context of engagement with the world instead of the monastery. Related versions of asceticism are evident in Lutheranism, Methodism, and other Protestant groups that initially define themselves in terms of the Reformation's idealization of the early church, including its mission to the poor, and are also part of Christian teachings of self-sacrifice and selfless compassion.

By contrast, involuntary poverty conventionally refers to those who are without sufficient economic means to provide food, clothing, and shelter for themselves and their households for reasons not of their own choosing or control. The factor of choice is complex, but for this argument it indicates the difference between those who willingly choose an ascetic life and those who do not. Christianity relies on both expressions of poverty to provide markers of spiritual hierarchy articulated in notions of innocence, humility, renunciation, sacrifice, charity, reward, and transcendence.

Renunciation, Charity, and Salvation

The development of Christian monastic orders encourages more-communal, less individualistic heroic models of renunciation than had been prevalent in earlier Eastern ascetic Christianity but continues the rejection of wealth as part of their ascetic practice. The orders are under the double injunction to live in poverty and to give to the poor; they especially are invested in poverty and giving as part of the sacrifice of self, exercise of spiritual discipline, and journey of spiritual development.

In emphasizing the two ideals of poverty, ascetics look to the life of Jesus, for whom poverty is one of several markers of the renunciation of this world and at the same time of concern for and identification with those considered societally outcast. Even monastic orders not founded exclusively for service, such as the Benedictines, are enjoined in numbers fourteen and fifteen of the seventy-two "Instruments of Good Works" in *The Rule of St. Benedict* to "comfort the poor" and to "clothe the Naked."[3] And throughout the Middle Ages, renewed vows of poverty and giving to the poor are common ways by which wayward orders attempt to relegitimate themselves after falling into corruption and disrepute.

Jesus' commandments first to love God and then to love one's neighbor— numbers one and two in the Benedictines' "Instruments"—have been taken to place love at the heart of Christianity. The interpretation of this love in a religion which looks both toward this world and away from it has been described as agape, or selfless love toward the other, which includes ascetic practices that combine self-sacrifice and pastoral-moral concern.[4] The qualities of love are also translated as "charity," the love which Paul recommends above all in the thirteenth chapter of 1 Corinthians. The extension of charity or love or agape toward the poor is often described as simple, associated with the adjectives "humble" and "innocent" as though this giving were a kind of natural, unmediated practice that erases itself of all social relations and their consequences. Yet giving is a social/religious relation of the exchange of need, the need for goods with the need for salvation: the ascetic needs the poor for his or her salvation, and the poor person needs the ascetic for his or her bread.

In giving to the poor, the great commandments to love and the great need for salvation come into spiritual alignment for the giver, yet the relationship between the voluntarily and involuntarily poor is not a reciprocity of equals. Christians make distinctions between the spiritual status of the two kinds of poverty by emphasizing the choice and selflessness through which the ascetic is more pure. Giving to the poor who are in need is an obligation the poor cannot meet, and the humility of these poor persons is assigned lower status than the humility of those voluntarily seeking poverty.

Problems between reciprocity and hierarchy are not only present in Christianity but also appear in other traditions that connect salvation with suffering. In the monastic practices of Buddhism, the poor are a consistent concern in injunctions and stories in popular and scholarly texts.[5] Historically, attention to the poor is not, however, as consistently a part of Buddhist ascetic practice, with its strong teaching of enlightenment through wisdom. In this case, the superiority that undercuts reciprocity is more likely to be that of wisdom over poverty. To an extent this also pertains to some Christian monastic orders, but Christian reciprocity is more likely to be undercut by the distinction between giver and recipient in charity. Awareness of this difference helps clarify the reliance of Christian notions of renunciation on giving to people in need and the intensity of the moral/spiritual tensions between voluntary and involuntary poverty.

The Christian focus on agency insists on a line between the activity of willing (that is to say, giving) and the passivity of not-willing (that is to say, receiving) that pervades even the ascetic's relinquishment of self in charity. Augustine's writings on charity and alms-giving became one of the central referents for Christian monastics and other believers of the Middle Ages.[6] In considering the qualities that should motivate giving to the needy, Augustine classifies ministering to hunger and thirst as a kind of "medicine"—medicine being those things that pertain to the body, in distinction from ministering to the soul, which is classified as "discipline." Augustine expresses two specific concerns as he struggles to formulate theological and administrative issues that poverty raises for himself and the church. One is that compassion be expressed from the motive of pure benevolence, not from the motive of empathy with those suffering, which would involve one's own interests and emotions. The other specific concern is that giving for bodily needs be accompanied by giving for the needs of the soul, because the soul is higher and, through discipline, should control all aspects of medicine.[7] The first identifies the notion of selflessness requisite for spiritual giving and the second identifies the tensions of body and soul with which all believers imputedly struggle and by implications identifies the poor as the vehicle with which to address this tension.

Because the health of the body is nothing without the health of the soul, Augustine counsels that the body not be ministered to as an end in itself. "[One], then, who loves his [or her] neighbor endeavors all he [or she] can to procure...safety in body and in soul, making the health of the mind the standard in...treatment of the body."[8] Augustine's worry, however, that the body as a body might be given too much attention is not first about hunger but about sex. In Augustine's view, it is sex that is the primary danger in the sensuality of the appetites and that pervades all other needs, despite the created goodness of the body. During the years following Augustine, church documents and visual arts translate bodily reference into sexuality to such an extent that any physical need is represented as at least implicitly erotic and therefore sinful. Everyone is a child of Adam and Eve, and everyone's clothing testifies to being caught consorting with the snake and picking the apple; every human body presents to others the knowledge that it is about sex covered up.[9]

While Christians, to varying extents, associate the body with the sinfulness of this world, they also develop traditions of caring for the body through hospitals and programs for food and clothing, at times in the most extreme circumstances of need, suffering, and danger. This care expresses, however, not the resolution but the tension between Christian activity in this world and its negation of this world, encapsulated in the body, which it would be dangerous to love. Historian Carter Lindberg finds that in the Middle Ages, Roman Catholics continued to emphasize the superiority of spiritual to merely corporal charity. This hierarchy is practiced by subordinating the value of physical care for the poor to the value of the self-mortification for the giver who touches the poor and to the value of converting the soul of the poor for God.[10] In the dichotomy and hierarchy of body and spirit, the involuntarily poor represent the body, and the voluntarily poor represent the spirit. This indicates that the state of the soul of the poor is negotiable according to the need of the ascetic practitioner, who from one stance needs contact with the humility of the poor whose spirit is already closer to heaven and from another stance needs contact with the impurity of the poor to express the ascetic's spiritual need for the physical punishment of self-sacrifice.

Nonetheless, to love the poor is safer than to love other persons or aspects of this world, because the poor are symbolically construed to be less of this world. The poor, then, are the privileged site of this-world denial and also the persons presumably in greatest need of worldly goods. This tension is resolved for the poor through the ascetic belief that, from a spiritual perspective, poverty is superior to wealth. The tension is resolved for those with wealth through the interpretation of poverty as poverty of the spirit only, and wealth as the means by which to finance ministry to the poor. In turn, religious institutions need the poor to attract the monetary gifts of the wealthy, as Lindberg observes in his analysis.[11] In the overall spiritual economy of poverty of the Middle Ages, the poor are counseled patience for well-founded hope for their souls in the next life, and the rich are counseled alms-giving for probable hope for theirs. "Poverty was good for everyone: the poor person was theoretically in an ideal state for salvation, and the rich person could secure the future by serving the poor."[12]

These theological arrangements articulate the static hierarchies of feudal society, and they also articulate the fluidities necessary to sustain the hierarchies. In a society in which people believe that salvation is theological, the poor are a means of securing everyone else's needs for salvation; poverty can be theologically elaborated according to whatever these needs are. For ascetics, the poor, as humble recipients of gifts, express the spiritual purity of the heavenly realm and express the impurity of the social/earthly realm as the suffering of bodily life, serving as a vehicle with which to separate the two realms. For the church and the wealthy, the poor mediate the heavenly and earthly realms by making it possible for wealth and power to coexist with salvation through giving to those whose bodies are in need. In this instance, hungry bodies are the route instead of the obstacle to spirit. Poverty is constructed in both cases to take whatever shape spiritual coherence requires, and this need overrides any problem of inconsistency in notions of poverty. What is consistent is that the poor are never theologically or politically equal to others, but always higher or lower.

Lindberg argues that the theological reading of poverty that persisted amidst the massive social upheaval of the shift from agrarian to urban societies in eleventh-century Europe prevented development of social policies to deal with major social and economic change. Thinking about poverty continued to find its reasoning from the older theological discourse, despite the gradual development of governmental and citizen-sponsored institutions for the poor. While there was a lack of political and economic discourse about poverty, in the face of changes and their anxieties (including the plague), religiosity increased and the theological interpretations of poverty shifted somewhat. The church sharpened the distinction between the voluntarily and the involuntarily poor—a distinction accompanied with greater hostility toward the involuntarily poor, who were as likely then to become beggars as to be ministered to through religious organizations. Chosen poverty increasingly was singled out as an ascetic virtue, embodied in the Franciscan and Dominican orders, while at the same time begging monks were often no longer accepted within city walls.[13] The church seemed to be indisputably in control of the older discourse of poverty and yet was struggling to adapt it to fit an urban, monetary political economy. In these shifts the voluntary and involuntary poor increase and overlap in new ways, and in the process poverty becomes simultaneously more problematic and more idealized in European societies.

Protestant reformers in the sixteenth century introduced new approaches to alleviate poverty, in part to enforce injunctions against religious and nonreligious begging (now read as disorderly) and in part to exercise new ideas of salvation as the given precondition of life instead of the goal to be hoped for only at the end of life. If only God gives salvation and if salvation is given as a presupposition of life and not its end reward, then, by Luther's argument, the theological economy of poverty and salvation crumbles because there are no requirements for salvation. Salvation lies in God's acceptance of the person just as the person is as a human being.[14] New ordinances and programs emphasizing public responsibility for the poor appear at this time, based not on poverty as an exalted spiritual condition but on notions of shared human dignity.[15] Luther's thinking about poverty itself narrows in scope as it becomes more embedded in his own hierarchical divisions, even as a Lutheran ethic of service emerges based on Christian concern for relations in this world instead of sacrifice and salvation.

Yet the association of the poor with salvation persisted, as did inattention to the causes of poverty and to the poor themselves on any extended basis. While giving to the poor had been central to the salvation narratives and practices of

Christianity, missing from the history of Christianity was a developed recognition of the agency of the poor themselves as givers. Further, the qualities of the souls of the involuntarily poor were constrained by a religious ideology not only about the problematic character of the body and bodily need but also about the superiority of the nonpoor giver who through a reversal could be understood to be the one who provided access to salvation with expressions of charity. The nonpoor represented the agency of the poor by determining how the poor were supposed to respond to being given to: with humility and gratitude. During the nineteenth century, this dynamic developed in philanthropic and mission movements—especially, though not exclusively, on the part of middle-class women who extended their own domestic ideals of self-sacrifice into ordering principles for those who were poor; this charity often entailed notions of religious and moral conversion.[16] Among such religious missions, concern for the salvation of the poor again expressed the need among the middle classes to save the poor in order to save themselves.

While the poor are still associated with salvation, they are also increasingly associated with sin and with resistance to the moral possibilities of the religious (as well as the political-economic) conversion opportunities offered by middle and even working classes. Nineteenth-century divisions between the deserving and the undeserving poor shift inconsistently in the ways institutions articulate the moral and economic conditions of the poor, elaborate their social significance, and design and implement policy.[17] There is no one way in which the terms deserving and undeserving are deployed. Nonetheless, amid their variations, the middle classes drive inequality into the poor themselves, so that neither the "deserving" nor the "undeserving" poor are considered equal to the citizen or even the proletariat. Referents such as "responsible" and "irresponsible," "hard-working" and "lazy," "chaste" and "promiscuous" are used increasingly to distinguish not only the nonpoor from the poor but also the working from the nonworking poor, and eventually the "good" poor from the "bad."[18] As with the eleventh century, it seems to be the case that the older ascetic language about poverty retains its authority as the terms of salvation, sacrifice, humility, and renunciation blend with new notions of society, individuality, and progress to help establish the moral spaces of the new bourgeois and the marginalization of the poor.

Social Transformation and the Idealizations of Poverty

Readers may argue that the problem I am wrestling with has already been resolved by social theorists and critical theologians over the last two centuries who have analyzed asceticism and poverty in Christianity. These thinkers identify poverty in relation to bourgeois authority structures in religion and political economy and call for change in these structures on behalf of those outside the bourgeois classes. At the same time, these analyses (even when arguing for the priority of the poor or the revolution of the oppressed) do not resolve the problem of the discourse of poverty that I am arguing—that of relying on poverty, asceticism, or a nonbourgeois class to mediate some kind of salvation. A look at the ambiguities these thinkers introduce in their imputed resolutions brings forward the gaps between the discourses of social change and the problems of poverty.

Karl Marx critically connected poverty and religion through his argument that religion is an aspect of class rule which gains its particular character from its claims beyond worldly to ultimate authority. Through religious claims (and Marx was thinking primarily of Christianity), the class which owns the means of economic production legitimates its cultural rule over the working class, in part by using Christianity to articulate a religious narrative of this world as a "veil of tears." This narrative renders action on the part of the working classes futile by encouraging suffering and acceptance in this world, with hopes for salvation postponed to the world to come. It is in this sense that religion is "the opium of the people."[19] The worship of God entails the worship of poverty, which masks and sustains the authority of the owner classes over the poor. From one perspective, Marx was transferring the logic of heaven to the logic of earth in order to make poverty a political and economic question. Drawing on his economic critique as well as his Jewish heritage, Marx argued that salvation is not a matter for the next world but for this one, and the poor need to benefit from it in the here and now if salvation is to have any appropriate authority. By connecting the proletariat with salvation, Marx in effect established the authority of the process of class struggle and reinforced the proletariat's dual social/economic role. As industrial workers, they were in a position to end their own oppression because they had a basis on which to organize against the control of the bourgeois and eventually to bring about the conditions for the freedom of all human beings.[20]

By the poor, however, Marx did not mean all poor people but only those "artificially impoverished," whom he identified as the proletariat. This group was impoverished by its place in the relations of capitalist production, in contrast with the "naturally arising poor" who may eventually come into the industrial working class.[21] For the most part, though, Marx and Engels associated the poor with nature and mechanical action, having no inner or outer potential for revolution in their constitution and position outside the entirety of class relations; this stood in contrast to the proletariat, whose organization and revolution were eventually to liberate all of humanity.[22] Two familiar, complementary logics of poverty are at work here: the elevated poor, whose suffering gives them special spiritual status, and the degraded poor, whose bodily condition renders their spirits intransigent to salvation. And in aligning the proletariat with the redemption of society, Marx, too, was reliant on one group of the poor to mediate salvation. The point is not to have caught Marx in a self-contradiction with his criticism of religion but to observe the persistence of the idealizations of poverty and their roles in salvation.

The earlier social gospel movements and contemporary liberation theologies have attempted to disconnect poverty from traditional theological discourse and connect poverty to a progressive democratic theological discourse. Both developments address poverty within a critical view of capitalism, with its economic classes, and of Christianity, with its hierarchical notions of sin and salvation. In defining the "Christian social order," Walter Rauschenbusch states that: "Modern humanity can never be saved until the working class is saved."[23] He argues that identification with the suffering of this class would help in the "rise" of this class from its difficult working and living conditions and would sensitize the rest of society about the contributions of the working class to the economy and general societal life.[24] This view is part of Rauschenbusch's reform-oriented notion of social sin in contrast to the view that sin is only an individual, private matter not subject to the scrutiny of other human beings.[25] The working class is the key both to understanding the injustices that make social sin a reality and to the kind of salvation that would bring justice and that merits hope. From this social gospel perspective, there is no salvation without economic and political justice goals, to be achieved through major economic and religious reform.

Gustavo Gutierrez and other liberation theologians of the later twentieth century have argued for a view of salvation much more aligned with the voices of the poor themselves—of those, largely Latin Americans, who fall outside of the working classes and therefore of traditional notions of revolution. The orientation is one of identification not with middle-class philanthropy and reform but with the actual lives and struggles of people in their communities. Such identification entails reciprocal relations, in contrast to the dominating, hierarchical relations that often characterize Christian traditions of charity. Faith is defined by one's solidarity with the poor, expressed most concretely by interacting in relations which presume that poor people are the authorities on formulating the terms of their life conditions, and by participating in their religious expressions of resistance, acceptance, and sanctification. The primary divide in this experience is between oppressed and oppressor, and faith requires the continuous process of separating oneself from the dominator.[26] Salvation is mediated through the ongoing struggle for liberation, a struggle which cannot be defined apart from its historical processes in this world.[27] There is no salvation without the liberation of the oppressed, which requires radical economic and religious change.

Despite significant differences between Rauschenbusch and Gutierrez, these two important critical notions of salvation are linked and tempered by claims that continue discursive practices of tying the salvation of everyone else to the poor and of making poverty the central interpretive image for theology, ethics, and economy. The concern for poverty could be affirmed as an achievement on behalf of the working classes and the poor that results in supporting social movements, addressing oppressive conditions, and shifting the consciousness and practice of some middle-class people. The association of the poor with salvation, however, is part of an older tradition that implicitly requires that the poor alleviate the moral and religious anguish of the privileged classes. Further, the notion of consciousness reproduces the dualistic/monistic assumption that one is either faithful or unfaithful, with the poor or against them, even though Gutierrez argues against the European metaphysical dualism of the two realities of a political world and a spiritual world, a difficulty Kathleen Sands discusses in her analysis of liberation theology.[28] As a consequence, dualisms of good and evil, power and powerlessness, social and natural, salvation and wealth, in which each term opposes and presupposes the other, reinstantiate the requirement of poverty in the terms of salvation.

These dualisms also emerge within asceticized notions of "social sin" in current liberation thinking inasmuch as it reproduces the emphasis on bodily self-renunciation. While "social sin" indicates a less personalized and more historicized notion of guilt and responsibility, it can remain oppressive in sanctions of suffering, self-sacrifice, and the rejection of all desire as a threat to spiritual worth. Delores Williams addresses this issue in her womanist theology of "social sin" and the African American community. Williams argues in disagreement with African American theologian of liberation James Cone and with spiritual songs and slave narratives that emphasize the denial of self in response to suffering and that devalue bodily experience in relation to spiritual experience.[29] For Williams, these views also place sin outside the African American community, implying that this community is without sin. A womanist perspective affirms the significance of bodily and sexual experience and therefore includes their abuse as part of social sin inside as well as outside of the African American community. Most significant in Williams's judgment is the need for a notion of "social sin" to face the abuse of black women's self-esteem as a result of oppression. "In the construction of a womanist notion of sin informed by the Black community's and Black theology's belief in social sin, it is quite legitimate to identify devaluation of Black women's humanity and the 'defilement' of their bodies as the social sin American patriarchy and demonarchy have committed against Black women and their children."[30]

In her analysis of liberation thinking, Williams locates another aspect of the requirement for emblems of self-sacrifice in salvation-liberation projects. Further, she describes social sins which cannot be named within the ascetic logic for which the body, on its own or in conjunction with the mind and soul, is a predetermined site of impurity. If the body is an emblem of sin, then the best it can do is become an emblem of self-sacrifice, and, as such, there is something right about a body that is hungry or otherwise abused. The problems of poverty cannot be addressed apart from the desires for health, identity, and well-being. But these aspects cannot be taken into account by simply adding them into older models of social change, such as those that may exhort adherents to freedom while retaining the authority patterns of ascetic ideals that sanction suffering, especially the bodily suffering of those whose spiritual representations vacillate between the ideal and the degraded—women and those who are poor. The gaps between these models and the issues of poverty indicate that the association of ascetic ideals with involuntary poverty is not a matter of ideals misapplied but of the construction of the ideal itself.

Authority Practices and Ascetic Requirements

Christianity is not the only tradition whose ascetic ideals rely on the poor as well as women for categories of impurity. For example, in the Hindu *Samnyasa Upanishads*, the impurity of the body is codified as the woman's body, which in turn represents all that is cast off as part of the detritus of society.[31] In contemporary Southeast Asian Buddhism, the patterns of male domination contribute to the persistent popularity of the story of Prince Vessantara, who decides to give up everything, including his wife and children, to take up the ascetic life.[32] In these representations, women and the poor are categories that share differentially shifting and hierarchical ambiguities that communicate authority relations as part of ascetic practice itself. Among these different traditions of renunciation, Christianity is distinct in the strenuousness of its demands on the poor because of the extent to which it holds them to both the higher spiritual standard of voluntary poverty and idealized involuntary poverty and the lower standard of those considered to be most degraded by their bodily existence.

The authority practices of Christian asceticism and salvation controlled by renunciation and self-sacrifice have been critiqued from several perspectives. Womanist thinking has been particularly critical of the ideas of suffering and servanthood tied into the traditions of sacrifice and obedience. For example, Emilie Townes argues that "suffering, and any discussion that accepts suffering as good, is susceptible to being shaped into a tool of oppression."[33] Ecologists have criticized the dualisms of asceticism that entail the devaluation of this world and of life itself.

White feminists have criticized the dualisms that devalue women and women's activities as antithetical to spiritual expression, as in Nel Noddings's argument that the virtues of asceticism extol suffering and moral heroism. In *Women and Evil,* Noddings criticizes William James's claim that poverty is the cornerstone of sainthood. In Noddings's analysis, poverty is part of the agonistic striving that James accords to sainthood; its stringencies indicate the achievement of a heroic status by heroic means.[34] In the morality of heroic asceticism, poverty is attached to manliness, masking the fear of femininity entailed in heroic asceticism, as Noddings notes. And I would add, heroic asceticism masks fear of nonvoluntary poverty itself, which in James's terms is constructed as a feminizing condition in its imputedly non-agential qualities of innocence and humility. Noddings identifies in James the problem of defining religion as asceticism and opens the way to considering a notion of religion in which relations of suffering and sacrifice demand critical attention but lose their authority to articulate the traditional narratives of salvation.

Noddings criticizes the polarities of moral condemnation and elevation deployed when people valorize the virtues of poverty and at the same time blame those who are poor for not overcoming poverty. Nevertheless, she reproduces the duality and hierarchy of giving and receiving by associating care with those helping the poor and helplessness with poverty. This unexamined move prevents her from recognizing narratives and activities that are more complex than the dualities of agency and the negation of agency, care, and helplessness. For example, Noddings has no way to account for the African American woman who can get no other work than that of caring for white people's homes and children in order to support her own children, whom she must leave on their own and yet still mother. The problem can be seen in the stories Katie Cannon tells of her own mother, who cleaned white women's houses, kept many additional odd jobs going, ensured that her family was active at church, and taught her children to live in a world without protection.[35] Cannon would push Noddings not to add another story to her notion of care but to consider more critically the authority and power relations of its root in the ascetic-charity practices of Christian compassion, especially as they come to us from nineteenth-century middle-class notions of virtue.

Gustavo Gutierrez struggles with questions of authority in his notion of a dialogue with the poor, but in his dialogue the poor remain the untouchable authority that governs everything else. There is a moment of truth in recognizing the authority that each person has over her or his own experience. However, to extend this moment into a theory of absolute knowledge erases its social character and its subjectivity. When a particular form of knowledge is assumed to be total and not partial, and to be immune from all interests and values deemed undesirable, the result is an asocial and ahistorical finished consciousness that mirrors the bourgeois view of its own moral consciousness as total, complete, and impermeable.

Marianne Janack's analysis of the feminist claim to women's epistemic priority is helpful here. Janack argues that we should shift from claims of epistemic privilege to critical questions about ways epistemic authority is "conferred" in practices and institutions. The authority of epistemic privilege, according to Janack, entails an unmediated, unambiguous view of experience, a kind of private revelation not submitted to public exchange or scrutiny.[36] To attribute epistemological privilege to the poor leads to attributing and requiring unambiguous goodness of the poor, whose consciousness is then imputedly innocent because it is free of societal interaction, or because it is only the result of external social forces, with no agency of its own. Such an attribute of privilege can further imply that the poor are a unitary and permanent group marked off by mind and body from everybody else. This perspective ignores the multiple kinds and experiences of poverty and the ease with which any person in this society can become poor. It also articulates a familiar claim that the poor are the vehicle of morality for everyone else and as such can represent only good or evil.

As a consequence, in Christianity the agencies of involuntary poverty are articulated as various alignments and valuations of lack and fullness.[37] In this cipher the voluntary and nonvoluntary are both merged and at odds: it is good to renounce material wealth, but it is bad not to participate in the freedom of the marketplace; it is good to be humble, and poor people should not make demands on society; the relinquishment of will is noble if pursued strenuously and is despicable if experienced out of powerlessness; it is worthy to give to the poor to entrust them with your soul, and the poor have nothing of spiritual worth to give; the poor are of value only if they can fulfill middle-class spiritual needs, and the middle classes are of value only if they can feel superior. The high demands on the discourse of poverty and on the poor themselves perpetuate all kinds of insidious superiorities and inferiorities whereby other people produce and reproduce their moral and spiritual status, preserving above all the authority of choice.

Without some notion of choice, voluntary poverty in Christianity would lose its spiritual authority. Granted, such choice is rarified since one is seen as succumbing to palpable spiritual pressure through practices leading to the ultimate surrender of one's will or ego. But this association of choice with ascetic practice is overridden in the case of the nonvoluntary poor. At the same time that people who are poor practice self-denial, the power of virtue is withdrawn from the poor so that their virtue, even if in compliance with these requirements, does not have the ultimate status of the virtues of chosen poverty. The virtues of the poor, inasmuch as the poor are seen to have them, are considered natural and therefore not an act of will. Yet the poor are also considered to be fully endowed with will, a reverse assumption evident in claims that everyone is an autonomous agent so that people are poor only because they choose to be. And one more perspective comes from Foucault's argument at its most strict, that all people in industrial societies submit to control from capitalism and from the legacy of Christian ascetic practices. The poor, like everyone else, only reinforce authority and order in their seemingly autonomous actions.[38]

The duality and hierarchy in Christian notions of renunciation do not simply express distinctions between body and soul, female and male, and receiver and giver. These distinctions articulate authority patterns in which the struggle for dominance entails the search for salvation and the search for salvation entails the struggle for dominance.

The blind alleys, double-binds, and circuitous routes produced in welfare policies are legion, with women and children often bearing the brunt of their worst consequences. Welfare policies are characterized by intractable contradictions: whether mixing prejudicial judgments of human behavior with rules about food stamps, or requiring that mothers on welfare find reasonably paying jobs while making it impossible for them to be educated for those jobs, or eliminating health care benefits while emphasizing women's responsibility for the well-being of themselves and their children.

Debates about welfare readily deploy notions of body and spirit in their regulations regarding food, work, and health care to articulate contemporary distinctions between the poor and the nonpoor and the deserving and the undeserving poor. As a society we rely on these markets of identity for economic and moral negotiation regarding who can be economically and morally saved. It is tempting to argue that the fraught character of the discourse of poverty simply indicates the desire to avoid confronting the conflicts of class. However, the continued presence of salvation stories, told in part and fragment here, with their referents of discipline, sacrifice, and bodily ambivalence, shows how such stories are required in order for our society to think morally as well as economically about goodness and evil, conflicts and their resolutions. To rely on poverty in these ways is to place it at the center of moral authority, a seemingly laudable move. However, to decenter poverty does not remove it from moral concern but fractures patterns of thinking and practice that require and reproduce poverty.

Notes

1. Karl Marx, "Introduction to a Contribution to the Critique of Hegel's 'Philosophy of Right,'" in *A Critique of Hegel's Philosophy of Right* (1844; Cambridge: Cambridge University Press, 1978), 131–42.

2. See John P. Reeder Jr., "Benevolence, Special Relations, and Voluntary Poverty: An Introduction," *Journal of Religious Ethics* 26, no. 1 (spring 1998): 5.

3. *The Rule of St. Benedict*, trans. and ed. Anthony C. Meisel and M. L. Del Mastro (Garden City, N.Y.: Doubleday, 1975), 52.

4. Gene Outka, "Universal Love and Impartiality," in *The Love Commandments*, ed. Edmund N. Santurri and William Werpehowski (Washington, D.C.: Georgetown University Press, 1992), 1–103.

5. Donald K. Swearer, "Buddhist Virtue, Voluntary Poverty, and Extensive Benevolence," *Journal of Religious Ethics* 26, no. 1 (spring 1998): 71–103.

6. Carter Lindberg, "Through a Glass Darkly: A History of the Church's Vision of the Poor and Poverty," *Ecumenical Review* 33 (Jan. 1991): 37–52, 39–40.

7. Augustine, "Of the Morals of the Catholic Church," in *The Basic Writings of St. Augustine, vol. 1*, ed. Whitney J. Oates (New York: Random House, 1948), see chaps. 26–28, pp. 342–46.

8. Ibid., 56.

9. Richard Leppert, *Art and the Committed Eye* (Boulder, Colo.: Westview Press, 1996), 216–23.

10. Lindberg, "Through a Glass Darkly," 48.

11. Ibid., 40–42.

12. Ibid., 41.

13. Ibid., 43–44.

14. Ibid., 46.

15. Pamela Couture, *Blessed Are the Poor?* (Nashville: Abingdon, 1991), 100–103.

16. Susan Thorne, "Suffer the Little Children: Victorian Evangelicals and Social Reform," paper presented at the Social Science History Association, New Orleans, October 11, 1996.

17. Karel Williams, *From Pauperism to Poverty* (London: Routledge & Kegan Paul, 1981), 95.

18. Michael B. Katz, *The Undeserving Poor* (New York: Pantheon, 1989), 14–15.

19. Marx, *Critique of Hegel's Philosophy*, 131.

20. Karl Marx and Fredrich Engels, "The Communist Manifesto," in *Essential Works of Marxism*, ed. Arthur P. Mendel (1848; New York: Bantam, 1971), 13–44.

21. Marx, *Critique of Hegel's Philosophy*, 142.

22. Ruth Smith and Deborah Valenze, "Mutuality and Marginality: Liberal Moral Theory and Working-Class Women in Nineteenth Century England," *Signs* 13 (winter 1988): 277–98.

23. Walter Rauschenbusch, *Christianizing the Social Order* (New York: Macmillan, 1912), 448.

24. Ibid., 450.

25. Walter Rauschenbusch, *A Theology for the Social Gospel* (New York: Macmillan, 1917).

26. Gustavo Gutierrez, *The Power of the Poor in History,* trans. Robert R. Barr (Maryknoll, N.Y.: Orbis, 1984), 90–94.

27. Ibid., 32–33.

28. Kathleen Sands, *Escape from Paradise: Evil and Tragedy in Feminist Theology* (Minneapolis: Fortress, 1994), 32.

29. Delores Williams, "A Womanist Perspective on Sin," in *A Troubling in My Soul: Womanist Perspectives on Evil and Suffering,* ed. Emilie Townes (Maryknoll, N.Y.: Orbis, 1993), 130–49, 138.

30. Ibid., 144.

31. Patrick Olivelle, *Samnyasa Upanishads: Hindu Scriptures on Asceticism and Renunciation* (New York: Oxford University Press, 1992), 76–77.

32. Margaret Cone and Richard Gombrich, *The Perfect Generosity of Prince Vessantara* (Oxford: Oxford University Press, 1977), xxi.

33. Emilie Townes, "Living in the New Jerusalem," in *Troubling in My Soul,* ed. Townes, 78–91, 85.

34. Nel Noddings, *Women and Evil* (Berkeley: University of California Press, 1989), 181–82.

35. Katie Cannon, *Katie's Canon* (New York: Continuum, 1995), 168–69.

36. Marianne Janack, "Standpoint Epistemology without the 'Standpoint'?: An Examination of Epistemic Privilege and Epistemic Authority," *Hypatia* 12 (spring 1997): 125–39, 133.

37. Ruth Smith, "Order and Disorder: The Naturalization of Poverty," *Cultural Critique* 14 (winter 1989–90): 209–29.

38. Michel Foucault, *Discipline and Punish,* trans. Alan Sheridan (New York: Vintage, 1979); and Michel Foucault, *The Use of Pleasure,* trans. Robert Hurley (New York: Vintage, 1990).

[4]

Rational Man and Feminist Economists on Welfare Reform

Carol S. Robb

WELFARE REFORM IS A WOMEN'S ISSUE, since women are the major clients of and jobholders in the welfare system. In each of the major means-tested programs in the United States, women and the children for whom they are responsible now comprise the overwhelming majority of clients.[1] Because women as a group are significantly poorer than men, and because women tend to live longer than men, significantly more women than men depend on the social welfare system as clients. Furthermore, women depend more on the social welfare system for jobs as paid human-service workers. When there are reductions in social spending, the jobs that are defunded are likely to be jobs that women have had.[2] So it is important that women have a voice about the shape of social welfare policies.

And yet it is very difficult to hear women's voices in the public debate about welfare reform. The loudest voices have been those of conservative males, who have argued that the AFDC program caused poverty by breeding dependency and promoting out-of-wedlock births.[3] While conservative white males have led the charge against public assistance programs, they are, I believe, simply using the reigning economic theory of what constitutes economic rationality. The main shape of "reform" has been to make public assistance grants smaller, attach more conditions and time limits to them, and thereby make them unattractive as a "choice" in the face of poverty. Beneath this reform are assumptions about what it means to act "rationally"; in economic language there is a

77

"simplifying assumption" that human beings in the economic realm act as *Homo economicus,* or "economic man."

In this chapter I want to describe what I understand to be the neoclassical view of economic man and "his" rationality. Then I will look at the literature being generated by some feminist economists to see whether they question or challenge the neoclassical view of economic rationality. Third, I will ask whether a revised view of rationality would have any bearing on different models of public assistance. Finally, I will summarize my own view of what constitutes an appropriate policy direction for addressing poverty.

Rational Man in Neoclassical Theory

Key to neoclassical understanding of *Homo economicus,* or economic man, is a particular theory of rational choice: people are perceived to be persons independent from one another (the separative self), making decisions on three bases:

First, it is not possible to establish whether my enjoyment of social goods is greater or less than your enjoyment of the same or other goods (utilities are interpersonally incommensurable). This assumption means we cannot know which of two persons gained more from a given exchange because there is no unit of measure. Gain or advantage comes from the satisfaction of a person's subjective desires. But we do not know how to compare subjectivities.[4] It is therefore not theoretically legitimate to assert that you are worse off than I am, whether as an individual or as a group. Applied to groups, this assumption deprives programs for alleviating poverty of any economic rationale, particularly if they involve redistributing resources from one group to another.[5] Who is to say that my enjoyment of a second, vacation, home is less, or less important, than your enjoyment of an annual visit for basic health care? "Pareto optimality" is the main criterion of economic efficiency. It describes a state of economic distribution in which no one's utility can be raised without reducing the utility of someone else, even if that someone else is living in gross luxury.[6]

Second, preferences or tastes are unchanging and created outside the market, and hence are unaffected by interactions that occur within the market. The market is thus an arena for people to choose which utilities (goods that provide satisfactions, well-being) they will exchange, given their limited resources. It is a clearinghouse, taking in information about what consumers desire (as measured by willingness to purchase), influencing the production of goods and services. Interference with the market will therefore inevitably lead to distortions which will create greater problems than what the interference is designed to correct. This is another simplifying assumption that leaves out too much of human experience. It obscures several ways in which people who work together influence each other's tastes (people in the job market), people who live in the neighborhood influence tastes (people in the housing market), and the way gender inequality or racial discrimination is perpetuated through generations and thus affects how those discriminated against change their tastes in job options.[7]

Third, my satisfaction does not depend on your happiness or unhappiness. Agents are self-interested. Utilities are interpersonally independent. Only commodities consumed by an individual contribute to that individual's satisfaction. Consumption may include the giving of gifts and taking pleasure in someone else's happiness. But what is excluded from *Homo economicus* are concerns for other people's satisfactions or sufferings that do not express themselves as one's market activities. This "economic man" is indifferent to relative position in society.[8]

Here we have it: economic man springs up fully formed, fully active and self-contained; he has no childhood or old age, no dependence on anyone. The ability to choose is the normal state of being. The environment has no effect on him, except as the passive material, the constraints over which his rationality will make decisions.[9] I do not perceive this view of economic man as a model held up for us to emulate; rather, it is purported by economists to be the best standard method of actually analyzing market decisions.[10] Since women trying to raise children alone, and facing poverty, are not generally described in these terms, could the effort to create new welfare legislation based on this economic man possibly be legitimate? I consulted the newly developing literature coming from people identifying themselves as feminist economists, most of them women, asking whether they turn a critical eye to this view of rationality and "rational man." I read this literature with these questions: Are there different ways of depicting rationality? Would a different view of rationality have any bearing on legislative reform of laws governing public assistance?

Feminist Economists on Rationality

There are several themes that emerge in this literature. To begin with, there is general acceptance of the usefulness of simplifying assumptions, as all models use them.[11] Accepting the legitimacy of modeling, Julie Nelson proposes *enlarging the model* to recognize that persons are socially and materially situated. Rather than focus solely on exchange as the stuff of economics, why not view economics as centrally concerned with provisioning, providing the necessaries of life? Economics as attempting to provision persons would include making distinctions among goods and services as to whether they support survival and health or tend more toward luxury. There is a place for "needs" in economic (and, I would add, moral) theory. Perhaps we can acknowledge that needs are not always clearly distinguishable from wants, and nevertheless admit that our human bodies are dependent upon the physical environment.[12] "Without such an understanding of material connection, we have the scandal of professional economists working out endless theoretical yarns about preferences while a majority of people in the world live in a state of neediness apparent to any observer who has not lost her or his humanity."[13] Thus, the neoclassical model must be enlarged.

If provisioning (in addition to choice) becomes the core of the discipline, the sustenance of life becomes the focus, to be aided and abetted by any of these means: the market, household, government action, exchange, gifts, or even coercion. Choice, scarcity, and rationality are potentially useful tools, but not necessarily the central ones.[14] In effect, the whole purpose of economics shifts when the simplifying assumptions related to the person as agent are enriched with greater attention to social, and conceivably the environmental, sciences. And yet there remains a place for some form of rational choice when the purpose of economics shifts to provisioning.

Some feminist economists suggest the need to *deepen our understanding of rationality* by acknowledging that economic behavior is not only self-interested, but can also be motivated by duty, loyalty, and good will—or morality. The assumption that tastes are unchanging and external to the market will not prepare us to understand the cultural embeddedness in many women's decisions about whether to go into the paid labor force or to seek public assistance so they can focus on domestic labor. Simon Duncan and Rosalind Edwards found clear differences in the United Kingdom between groups of low-skilled white single mothers' and black single mothers' reasoning on this matter. It is not just preferences about paid and unpaid work that vary, but also the rationalities about motherhood and morality.[15] In Duncan and Edwards's study, white mothers tended to see motherhood and employment as incompatible, feeling that good mothers put family and home first. Hence they were less likely to be in the paid labor force. Black mothers were more able to integrate the identities of "motherhood" and "worker" so that to be a good mother meant being in full-time work. Hence they are more likely to be in full-time paid work, even though the labor market is racially and sexually discriminatory.

Duncan and Edwards conclude,

> People are indeed highly rational (given the imperfect information they hold) and they do weigh up the costs and benefits of alternative courses of action— but both what is rational, and what constitutes a cost or a benefit, are defined in

collective moral and social terms, not simply in individual utility terms (which in economic work is very often reduced to monetary terms). Collective moral and social mores are of course highly gendered.[16]

Hence, "gendered moral rationalities" are primary factors in explaining single mothers' decisions about whether to be in the paid labor force. This research challenges the too-simple notion that "preferences" or "tastes" determine rationality. These preferences and tastes, say Duncan and Edwards, change according to the social context, where they are collectively negotiated, sustained, modified, and changed.[17] But rationalities so differently located are not all equal in import; some people have more power than others and are able to impose their tastes on those less powerful. Conservative politicians in some sense know "culture" is significant in the welfare reform discussion. They not only want to cut state benefits but also wish to reinforce culturally traditional values. Ironically, Duncan and Edwards's research indicates that women with traditional values are least likely to seek paid labor.

Here is a third illustration of how rational choice continues to pervade the literature of feminist economists, while the meaning of this rationality is changed. In this instance, a feminist economist has *shifted the question*. One question for policy makers is whether public assistance makes it "rational" to be sexually immoral (measured by out-of-wedlock childbearing) and economically dependent. Rebecca Blank researched this question and found that, indeed, the overall *number* of out-of-wedlock births has been rising, but the birthrate for single women (the probability that a single woman will have a child) has not changed much at all. Between 1960 and 1990, the probability of single white women giving birth increased from 0.9 percent to 3.3 percent. The probability that single black women would give birth decreased from 9.8 to 9.0 percent. However, since fewer women are marrying than in previous decades, there are more single women, and hence more babies born to single women.[18] Blank also notes the declining fertility among married couples, such that if there were no increase at all in the number of out-of-wedlock births, the out-of-wedlock birthrate would still go up.[19]

Blank asks, Why are there more single women? The rise in births among unmarried mothers is not limited to those who rely on AFDC for support. Fewer teens are marrying today, but probably not because the structure of welfare programs encourages teens not to marry. The monthly support levels available from AFDC and food stamps fell steadily from 1960 to 1996–98, when "welfare as we know it" was undone. Cross-cultural comparisons reveal government support for single mothers is much lower in the United States than elsewhere, yet the United States has one of the higher rates of single motherhood, and the highest rate of teen pregnancy. Blank did not observe, but might have, that the rate of abortion is also higher in the United States than among other industrialized countries. The highest rate of teen pregnancy plus the high abortion rate point to a deep ambivalence about sexuality among American youth. They like it, but don't think they should, and thus don't prepare for it to prevent pregnancy. In this respect, teen pregnancies are not a result of choosing but of failing to choose.

Fewer teens, fewer women are marrying because women's ability to find jobs and support themselves (if insecurely in the low-wage labor market) has increased. At the same time men's ability to support a family (particularly men with few formal job skills) has declined, making them less attractive as marriage partners. For both high-school dropouts and graduates, wage rates adjusted for inflation have declined substantially since the late 1970s, by 5 to 15 percent, depending on skill level. And further, the social stigma associated with unwed motherhood has declined.[20]

One could infer from Rebecca Blank's research that teens who do not marry are rationally calculating that their life chances are better not marrying, even if that means they will be dependent on public assistance. She reflects the significance of the social knowing of poor pregnant teens, challenging again the second assumption comprising *Homo economicus:* that preferences or tastes are unchanging and created outside the market. These teens have been affected by poor educational systems, poor job prospects, and racism or sexism in the job market and are acting out of class and racial moral rationalities. They are not acting individually so much as in communities that have historically experienced exclusion from work plans remunerated enough to support family life. In effect, Blank is showing it will do little good to trim welfare programs, and in fact will do much harm, since jobs above poverty wage, with benefits, are necessary to make it possible for teens to marry, and welfare reform may do nothing to encourage job formation. Since the marriage market for many teens has broken down, the job market, and welfare if jobs fail, represent the more rational choice.

Feminist Economics and Welfare Policy

What have feminist economists suggested should be the proper focus for alternatives to AFDC? They have responded to the wider literature on women's poverty which includes three general policy directions: marriage-market proposals, labor-market proposals, and remuneration of reproductive work.

Marriage-market proposals tend to focus on ways to encourage women to marry before giving birth. They are based on the notion that family income is raised by fostering "traditional" family structures and by enforcing child support. If there are two parents in a family, there are potentially two incomes, rather than the one of a single-parent household. As the description of Rebecca Blank's research indicates, this direction is futile without a concerted effort to create above-poverty-wage jobs with sufficient benefits. Because of the absence of such an effort on the part of Congress, none of the authors represented in the literature developed by feminist economists have taken this approach.

Labor-market proposals have at least two emphases: preparing welfare recipients for the labor market, and reforming the labor market to adequately support women responsible for children. The Welfare Reform Act has taken the direction of encouraging women to move into the paid labor force, "encouraging" being a euphemism for time limits on eligibility for public assistance. Some feminist economists have made contributions to labor-market proposals, based on the premise that paid employment is the most significant factor in securing income for women above poverty levels. But they caution that, unfortunately, movement from welfare to the labor market will not necessarily move women out of poverty for structural reasons, particularly occupational segregation by gender and women's overrepresentation in the low-wage labor market. However, the Institute for Women's Policy Research (IWPR) has recommended *packaging* AFDC together with wage labor to support women's being in the paid labor force.[21]

In addition, feminist economists Barbara Bergmann and Heidi Hartmann have made proposals that would help both women receiving assistance and low-income two-parent families who would not have to go on welfare to qualify. Their "Help for Working Parents," or HWP, would guarantee health insurance to all currently uninsured families with children; provide child care for preschool children and after-school care for older children at no cost to families in the bottom 20 percent, at sliding-scale fees to middle-class families; provide more housing assistance to families with children, especially in high rent areas; convert support for single parents not in jobs from a mostly cash benefit into a benefit consisting mostly of vouchers (charge account at the supermarket, rent and utility vouchers, transportation vouchers, plus $100 cash per month).[22] Since the vouchers make recipients more visible as stigmatized "welfare queens," the voucher component of this proposal drew consistent criticism from other feminist economists. Otherwise, this program received significant support.

The HWP proposal is based on survey findings that 60 percent of women who received AFDC would rather have worked if they could have afforded to work, given costs of health care and child care. It increases the ability of all low-income parents to participate in educational and training opportunities, providing full-time child care to parents, whether they work in or outside the home or both. It would require $86 billion additional to AFDC costs, not including the training component which they believe should be budgeted as an educational rather than welfare program. The HWP again uses rational-choice theory, proposing programs that they perceive would make entering the labor market a rational choice for people who until now could not have made income above the poverty level if they had been in paid labor, particularly given the high cost of child care and health care.

Another labor-market proposal, by Teresa Amott, is actually labor-market *reform*. Amott claims the only successful welfare reform will be a reform that takes as its target the labor-market barriers of job segregation and the wage gap. Comparable-worth policies would result in dramatic improvement in the economic status of women employed in service occupations and industries. Raising the minimum wage would also have a significant effect, since about 60 percent of all minimum-wage workers are women. But it would take a 96-cent increase (in 1995) in the national minimum wage to have the same poverty-reduction effect for women workers as a comparable-worth policy that excludes small employers with fewer than twenty-five employees. In 1996 the minimum wage was raised from $4.25 to $5.15 per hour in two increments. Although this increase raised the income of many low-wage women workers, it did not bring the minimum wage to its value of twenty years ago.[23] Comparable worth would reduce the incidence of poverty-level wages among women in administrative-support (including clerical) jobs by 74 percent. It would also result in dramatic improvement in the economic status of women employed in service occupations and industries.[24]

These feminist economists emphasize participating, albeit on fairer grounds, in the paid labor force as an alternative to, or perhaps in conjunction with, something like AFDC. This choice of strategy is most likely seen by these economists to be a way of dealing with the perception that unpaid and paid work confer unequal power, which plagues women in every economic system except nonmarket communal ones.

There is, however, a third approach: *remunerating reproductive labor*. Building on the observations that large-scale unemployment is a permanent feature of industrialized economies, that many European countries do not view single mothers as a "problem," and that taking care of children and the elderly is good and important work, this approach puts greater value on caretaking and wants to provide decent remuneration for it. The pieces needed for this approach are universal health insurance, perhaps universal day care, a guaranteed annual income or at the very least a universal family allowance. These programs should be universal and not means-tested.[25] One author suggests paying for it by dismantling the paternalistic welfare bureaucracy altogether.[26]

This third approach is not well developed in the literature of feminist economists. An allowance to care for children is not viewed by most as the vision for welfare reform, probably because, as mentioned previously, these economists desire to avoid the two-tiered labor system of productive work (with status) and reproductive work (without status). The efforts to confer status with family allowances and other policies in several European countries were motivated in part by nationalist desires to increase fertility rates. In no country have family policies had this result, because none of them can adequately compensate women for the conflict between productive and reproductive work in industrialized countries. But I would argue that increasing fertility rates is an inappropriate goal, given our awareness of the rate at which human populations are destroying the habitat of other species as a global phenomenon. Among the feminist economists I have surveyed, I have seen no indication that the preference for wage-labor strategies to address women's poverty is rooted in a concern for the effects of human reproductivity on other species.

A Feminist Ethical Perspective

It is with great appreciation that I view the effort of feminist economists to name the gender assumptions of *Homo economicus*. It is a good corrective to be reminded of the dependence of all of us on the material world, as we are nature also, in addition to being culture-makers. We are dependent upon others in several stages of our lives, and some people are for unique reasons dependent throughout their lives. We are interdependent with others, human and non-human, throughout our lives in any case. In addition, most of us are also choosers with varying degrees of autonomy and constraints in these choices. We are affected by our social location and social ties, including experiences of solidarity, and in addition have values of our own that may be uncharacteristic of our social support networks. Thus we need to think about models that go beyond those based on the assumptions of "rational man."

What are the consequences of correcting the picture of *Homo economicus* to include motivations of caring along with self-interest, to recognize the significance of dependency in addition to independence, to recognize our social natures in addition to our "choosing" behaviors? I do not believe that the point of these economists recognizing our dependency and interdependency is to promote an "ethic of care," distinguishable from a focus on legal rights to safety net programs. Quite the contrary. If Congress were to consider proposals that would obliterate all tax support for social programs or all wage support legislation, replacing them with appeals to citizens to voluntarily share from their resources out of a sense of *caring*, I and the economists I have cited would argue strongly that such a direction would replace justice with charity, unwisely. Tax-funded programs, minimum-wage laws, and comparable-worth policies are coercive, requiring compliance, and such coercion is justified by the demands of justice. People who have more than sufficiency owe something of their extra to those who do not have enough to live in community with dignity. Need makes claims on justice. To protect the dignity of the poor, tax-supported programs or wage-support policies should be administered through bureaucracies that are in large part impersonal. The corrective to poorly administered welfare systems is not interpersonal intimacy with charity workers who care. It is well-administered public policy whose reach includes all strata fairly.

The point of our dependency and interdependency is that caring for the vulnerable is a crucial part of a healthy community. Men should participate in this caring, too, at a level that goes far beyond "helping" women do reproductive work. Policy should be consistent with an economic ethic that puts a higher value on reciprocity, between labor and capital, between land and capital, and between the reproductive and productive spheres of our work. Such reciprocity will not count in economic terms until economists, with moralists and social scientists, develop modes of measuring value that goes beyond what *Homo economicus* values.

One possible way to implement such reciprocity between the reproductive and productive spheres of our work is to legislate and mandate what we might call "full-cost wages." Full-cost wages are modeled on full-cost pricing in the arena of environmental economics: acknowledging that fully legal production and consumption practices have resulted in the dumping of waste into the air, water, and soil, full-cost pricing involves putting an economic value on harm done (to real-estate value, to health, to recreation, as examples), which manufacturers pay through effluent taxes, resulting in higher prices for their products as they go onto the market. The higher prices result in either less consumption, which results in turn in less production (and therefore less pollution), or better research and development to identify less-polluting methods of manufacture. The effluent tax is politically derived and administered by a government agency (the Environmental Protection Agency), thus requiring a role for government. It depends not on the goodwill of either manufacturers or consumers, but on incentives (to avoid the tax) to stimulate more ecologically sensitive behavior. Yet such an approach cannot depend on self-interest narrowly conceived. The political will to mandate such effluent taxes depends on a vision of shared health and wholeness for ourselves, our children, and the biosphere, a vision we recognize will result in money coming out of our pockets. We will pay the higher prices because it is the right thing to do. To make such a vision possible, we acknowledge that all businesses have to play by the same rules, whether their persons in charge are capable of valuing such a shared vision or not.

Full-cost wages, I propose, could depend on a similar logic. First, acknowledge that productive institutions (manufacturing, construction, service) depend for their ability to function on reproductive activity. These activities include food preparation, cleanliness, provision of shelter, socialization, mental health, and at least a modicum of happiness of the labor force; plus childbearing and child rearing (future workers) and care of elders (people we care about). Then, acknowledge the tendency in the wage-labor market for wages to be bid down to low levels, such that even full-time wage earners cannot support themselves and their families above conditions of poverty. Finally, acknowledge the dependency of all productivity (whether private or public) on the health of the social fabric. Thus we can justifiably mandate (through political means) a minimum wage at a level, adjusted routinely and with a regional factor, such that all persons working thirty hours per week could support themselves and two (three? one? let's agree on the principle, then argue the details) other persons above the poverty level.

The thirty-hour paid work week will likely result in higher prices, and it will exacerbate tension caused by capital flight off-shore. So the political will necessary to pressure for full-cost waging will need to be internationalist in its scope. These are real difficulties.

However, full-cost waging will make less substitute child care necessary and thus make more feasible the expectation that every able adult, whether male or female, will be involved in the care and nurturance of their children and other domestic labor *and* involved in the paid labor force. This picture of the way to value reproductive labor seems fairer to me than the model of taxing wage earners (those in the paid labor force) to fund public assistance for adults not in paid labor to care for their children.

Full-cost waging plays a key role in my view of authentic welfare reform, because I see it as the most promising way to acknowledge and value reciprocity between the reproductive and productive spheres of our work. This approach is not remuneration of domestic labor through tax-funded public assistance. It emphasizes fairly remunerated work for both women and men, along with domestic labor for both women and men. I hope that girls will grow up expecting to be in the paid labor force most of their lives, and that boys will grow up expecting to take direct responsibility for children and elders for most of theirs.[27] Full-cost wages should, however, be one piece of a network of mutually reinforcing programs that, all together, include the following:

- *Social safety net:* There will always be a need for social safety nets that provide for people who simply cannot work, even if sufficient well-paying jobs were available. The injured, the chronically ill, the handicapped, and mothers of infants who do not have paid maternity leave deserve a level of support that sustains their dignity, regardless of the economic status of their families of origin.

- *Comparable-worth policies:* Within the paid labor force, the jobs associated as women's jobs tend to parallel the reproductive role in the home: nursing, food preparation, teaching and socialization, support work. Even when the content of a job category is not associated with the mothering or feminine role, when women predominate in that job the pay goes down relative to the same job category in another firm when it is filled mostly by men. Comparable-worth programs evaluate job descriptions in terms of skills needed, responsibilities entailed, risks involved. They help to counteract the gender bias in the wage structure.

- *Full-cost wages:* Raising the minimum wage and redefining full-time work so that thirty hours would constitute full-time work. Whatever increased costs would result from lowering the work week should be passed along to consumers, so that prices internalize the true cost of workers' time, needed as it is in nurturing self and others as well as in production.

- *Universal health care:* Any serious effort to replace public assistance as the main means of support for poor women and men with children recognizes that, in order for work to raise a family above poverty, a higher minimum wage, along with access to health insurance and child care, must be packaged.

- *National commitment to preschool and after-school programs:* Preschool education for children aged three and above, provided by educated teachers and staff, should be a part of the public school system. Caregivers and teachers should be certified to do this important work, and facilities should be appropriate to guarantee the emotional and physical safety of children, depending on their age. Preschool child care should also move in time to more reliance upon licensed centers, less reliance on unlicensed home-business care. The licensing procedure provides accountability to parents and to the public that facilities and programs are appropriate for little children. Likewise, after-school programs staffed by certified staff should be on the school campuses or very nearby, to provide back-up care for children. These educational and care programs can be paid for with a combination of sliding scale parent fees, and local and state subsidies. With the thirty-hour work week, and both parents (whether married or not) participating in child care, center care could conceivably be limited to twenty hours per week, which is recommended for young children, and perhaps for all children.

- *Insured child-support enforcement:* In the event of divorce or lack of marriage, absent parents should be held financially accountable, regardless of income level. All payments (a percentage of wage income) would be collected like taxes through automatic wage withholding by the employer. If the income from the custodial plus the absent parent is not sufficient to support the child, the government would make up the difference.

- *Parental leaves:* People would earn (by a specified number of months on the job) the right to parental leaves with full or semi-full pay plus benefits for periods (say up to six months) for childbirth or care of a sick family member or elderly parent. Men should be encouraged to take these leaves so that women are not viewed as liabilities in the labor force.

All together, these components of a "welfare program" constitute a wage-labor strategy, one that involves labor-market reform, but that nevertheless presumes that men and women with children will lean heavily on wage labor. This way of guaranteeing the economic support of children should be seen as the norm, a norm that makes provisions for exceptions.

We must continue to encourage church and other publics to break down rigid gender-role stereotyping so that men as well as women will see the rightness and opportunities for joy in being engaged in domestic work along with "productive" work. We must also persuade church and other publics to limit human impact on the earth's biosphere because it is right to do so. Full-cost pricing and full-cost wages are ways of implementing right-making directions. These are the tools at our disposal to show we care not only about the health of our homes, but also about the health of this planet, our home writ large.

Notes

1. According to Nancy Fraser, more than 81 percent of households receiving AFDC are headed by women. More than 60 percent of families receiving food stamps or Medicaid are headed by women. Seventy percent of all households in publicly owned or subsidized housing are headed by women. See Fraser's discussion in *Unruly Practices: Power, Discourse, and Gender in Contemporary Social Theory* (Minneapolis: University of Minnesota Press, 1989), 147.

2. Ibid., 148.

3. Randy Albelda, "Introduction: The Welfare Reform Debate You Wish Would Happen," *Feminist Economics* 1, no. 2 (summer 1995): 81.

4. Paula England, "The Separative Self: Androcentric Bias in Neoclassical Assumptions," in *Beyond Economic Man: Feminist Theory and Economics,* ed. Marianne A. Ferber and Julie A. Nelson (Chicago: University of Chicago, 1993), 42.

5. Ibid., 43.

6. Amartya Sen, *On Ethics and Economics* (New York: Basil Blackwell, 1987), 32.

7. England, "The Separative Self," 44.

8. Herman E. Daly and John B. Cobb Jr., *For the Common Good: Redirecting the*

Economy toward Community, the Environment, and a Sustainable Future (Boston: Beacon, 1989), 86.

9. Julie Nelson, *Feminism, Objectivity, and Economics* (New York: Routledge, 1996), 20. A similar discussion appears in Diana Strassman, "Not a Free Market: The Rhetoric of Disciplinary Authority in Economics," in *Beyond Economic Man,* ed. Ferber and Nelson, 62–63.

10. Simon Duncan and Rosalind Edwards, "Lone Mothers and Paid Work—Rational Economic Man or Gendered Moral Rationalities," *Feminist Economics* 3, no. 2 (summer 1997): 34.

11. Helen Longino, "Economics for Whom?" in *Beyond Economic Man,* ed. Ferber and Nelson, 167.

12. Nelson, *Feminism, Objectivity, and Economics,* 34.

13. Ibid., 35.

14. Ibid., 36.

15. Simon Duncan and Rosalind Edwards, "Lone Mothers and Paid Work—Rational Economic Man or Gendered Moral Rationalities?" *Feminist Economics* 3, no. 2 (summer 1997): 49–50.

16. Ibid., 56.

17. Ibid., 34.

18. Rebecca Blank, "Teen Pregnancy: Government Programs Are Not the Cause," *Feminist Economics* 1, no. 2 (summer 1995): 47–58. National Center for Health Statistics data from 1996 show that 3.9 percent of white teens have a child, and 9.2 percent of black teens do ("U.S. Teens Are Having Fewer Babies," *San Francisco Chronicle,* May 1, 1998, A2).

19. Ibid., 48.

20. Ibid., 50–51.

21. Heidi I. Hartmann and Roberta M. Spalter-Roth, *The Real Employment Opportunities of Women Participating in AFDC: What the Market Can Provide* (Washington, D.C.: Institute for Women's Policy Research, Oct. 1993), 1–10.

22. Barbara Bergmann and Heidi Hartmann, "A Welfare Reform Based on Help for Working Parents," *Feminist Economics* 1, no. 2 (summer 1995): 85–89.

23. Another increase has been proposed by Senator Edward Kennedy (D-Mass.), 50 cents a year in each of the next three years, bringing it to $6.65. This proposal has not been adopted as of this writing.

24. Teresa Amott, "Reforming Welfare or Reforming the Labor Market: Lessons from the Massachusetts Employment Training Experience," in *Women and Welfare Reform* (Washington, D.C.: Institute for Women's Policy Research, 1994), 35–40. A discussion of Amott's proposal is found in Deborah M. Figart and June Lapidus, "A Gender Analysis of U.S. Labor Market Policies for the Working Poor," *Feminist Economics* 1, no. 3 (fall 1995): 60–81.

25. Betty Reid Mandell, "Why Can't We Care for Our Own Children?" *Feminist Economics* 1, no. 2 (summer 1995): 99–104.

26. Theresa Funiciello, *Tyranny of Kindness: Dismantling the Welfare System to End Poverty in America* (New York: Atlantic Monthly Press, 1993).

27. For fuller discussion, see Carol S. Robb, *Equal Value: An Ethical Approach to Economics and Sex* (Boston: Beacon, 1995), esp. chaps. 2 and 7.

PART TWO

RACE, CLASS, AND FAMILY VALUES

[5]

The Production of Character

A Feminist Response to the Communitarian Focus on Family

Gloria H. Albrecht

PEOPLE NORMALLY DO NOT BOTHER to speak at length on that which is going well. Today, community claims the attention of U.S. society because many people live with the growing fear that our life together is becoming meaner, harsher, and more violent. Popular laments typically include references to teenage illegitimacy, fatherless homes, welfare dependency, urban violence, drug use, divorce rates, a cultural obsession with sex, a rejection of anything that limits one's freedom of choice (especially the constraints of marital and family responsibilities), a lack of morally responsible public role models, the frantic busyness of everyday life, an unlimited demand for entitlements, and the obsession with "making it." We have become, we fear, a nihilistic gathering of frenzied individuals.

Popular public descriptions are clearly dominated by those who see these issues as symptoms of a deeper problem: the loss of shared values which sustain a civil and ordered society. In his 1995 State of the Union address, President Clinton said that our civil life is suffering: "Citizens are working together less and shouting at each other more. . . . The common bonds of community which have been the great strength of our country from its very beginning are badly frayed."[1]

This description is not new. Twenty years ago Daniel Bell named our problem as the problem of community and located its origin within our culture.[2] According to Bell's description, wonderful energies are unleashed by the free, autonomous person pursuing self-interest in the marketplace. However, when such unlimited self-interest is pursued within our civil society, the result is a culture distorted by the chaos of hedonistic selves pursuing every impulse in an endless quest for personal fulfillment. What is needed, according to Bell, is a return to "the public household": a culture in which people are taught the limits of human finitude. In learning their interdependence with others, citizens accept restraints on their personal desires and acknowledge their moral obligations to others. What is needed, he writes, is the return to a sense of *civitas,* "a willingness to make sacrifices for some public good," a willingness that has been lost with the decline of family, synagogue, church, and community.[3]

More recently, the conversation has been entered by a group of self-described liberals and conservatives who call themselves the "new communitarians."[4] With Bell, they identify the problem of American society as an imbalance between the growing demand for individual rights and a reluctance to accept individual responsibility. Amitai Etzioni writes that between 1960 and 1990, American society "allowed children to be devalued, while the golden [calf] of 'making it' was put on a high pedestal."[5] The answer to this moral stagnation, he writes, lies in individuals making different choices...to choose to want less, to choose to buy less, to choose to work less, to choose to earn less. This requires a renewed commitment to the family. "The best place to start," the communitarian platform reads, "is where each new generation acquires its moral anchoring: at home, in the family. We must insist once again that bringing children into the world entails a moral responsibility to provide not only material necessities, but also moral education and character formation."[6] It is the family which teaches those values that form a responsible moral character: to respect others; that hard work pays even in an unjust world; that when you do what is right you feel better; and, most importantly, "to control one's impulses and to mobilize oneself for acts other than the satisfaction of biological needs and immediate desires."[7] The result will be a society of dependable workers and citizens who do not expect handouts.

The family is also the key to good community for Michael Novak. Novak describes humans as "social animals, shaped by the traditions and nourished by symbols, languages, and ideas acquired socially."[8] "More exactly than that," he writes, "each of us is a familial animal."[9] It is within families that individuals learn to accept human frailty in others and face their own foibles. It is within the family that one learns the duties of one's sex and one's social roles. In the family one learns courage, obedience, the just exercise of authority, the desire to earn one's rewards through merit, and the ability to delay self-gratification.[10] Thus, the good family transmits economic advantages to its children and motivates the individual economic agent to "herculean economic activities" by family-regarding self-interest.[11] Through the good family, an individual participates in an economic system which, over time and on the whole, rewards with economic success those families that teach these values.[12]

The differences between Bell, Novak, and Etzioni span the differences between neoconservative and neoliberal discourses. Yet they share a description of our society fragmenting under the assault of hedonistic individuals who are unfettered by any sense of moral responsibility for others. Their common response is to turn to the family as the original source of this moral crisis. As Allan Carlson, president of the Rockford Institute, has written, the family was "the social unit that reconciled liberty with order, that kept individual's interests in balance with the interests of community and posterity. We have already paid a huge price for forgetting that lesson, a price that ranges from high levels of crime to environmental degradation. The proper response, at both the policy and personal levels, is *a turn toward home.*"[13]

At this point it is necessary to caution that the way a problem is described reveals the often unnamed assumptions that are silently at work in the analysis. These assumptions include views of human needs and capacities and of appropriate political and economic orders. It is this underlying worldview that produces the description of the problem and then focuses the range of imaginable solutions. The contemporary communitarian description of our social problems and their focus on the family as the source of these problems is specifically based on unspoken assumptions rooted in certain basic tenets of classical liberal theory and the economic system of capitalism which embodies it:

1. That society consists of the separate and relatively independent spheres of government (the political), marketplace (the economic), and culture.
2. That the ethical climate of the society is produced by an amalgamation of the moral character of its individual members as displayed in individual choices.
3. That moral character is shaped or misshaped in the private sphere of culture where family, religion, and civic associations are located.
4. That the origin of our current social problems lies in the failure of families to form a moral character that sustains community (Bell's "hedonistic bourgeois society," Novak's "new class family of elites," and Etzioni's yuppie parents).
5. That the values which we once had and have now lost are a work ethic of self-restraint, the ability to delay self-gratification, and the control of

biological and emotional impulses (exemplified in the impact of the welfare system and its production of unwed mothers).

Unmasking and challenging these assumptions will help us untangle the ideologies behind the recent changes in the welfare system—changes that have endangered poor women and children in the name of preserving the work ethic and protecting families.

The Problem: A Redescription

A feminist liberative ethic analyzes such social descriptions in order to expose their underlying assumptions and to identify the social experiences from which such ideas make sense. In other words, analyzing how a discourse "sees" a problem reveals the "sense-making" assumptions out of which a group of people explain their society, shape themselves, and relate to others. As a Christian feminist using a liberative ethic of analysis, I offer a differing description of the problems facing our society, particularly our families. My differing description is a result of very different assumptions about society and the forces that shape it—assumptions resulting from different social experiences.

In *Moral Fragments and Moral Community,* Larry Rasmussen remembers reading Bell's book as "an epiphany." However, Rasmussen saw in Bell's description of the problem something Bell himself did not see. Rasmussen writes: "When Bell described modern culture and its moral ethos, I knew he was holding up to the light an X-ray of white, middle-strata psyches and society."[14] This insight points out that the communitarian account of lost community describes the experience of one community: "preponderantly middle-class white U.S. Americans heavily invested in the institutions and patterns of modernity."[15] It is a description of that community's sense of loss in a society where every aspect of successful life is modeled after the competitive, individualistic, self-interested, and instrumental relationships of a capitalist economy. This community now experiences itself as "autonomous creatures who, on the basis of their own wants and preferences, fashion their own world in a series of relationships they themselves make and unmake."[16]

In addition, Rasmussen's point reveals that the communitarian lament over their lost sense of community serves to deflect from view the experiences of those who have never shared equally in the "common" bonds of community. It ignores the history of the struggle of women, minority men, and the poor and working classes for participation in the decisions that shape social values and social institutions. "We" have not suddenly lost a sense of community or common values. Some of us were never meant to be a part of it—not if community implies mutuality and reciprocity in the cocreation of common well-being; not if shared values means a sharing in the processes that name values.

In the current debate about values and community now shaping secular culture and Christian ethics, therefore, it is important to distinguish among the views being produced from differing social locations based on differences of (at least) race, gender, and class. The demands of oppressed groups in our society for basic human needs, for economic security, and for equal voice in social decisions that effect them are ethically distinct from the self-interested demands of those who have had basic needs met and who traditionally have enjoyed such access.[17] Any ethical analysis that erases this difference (as these communitarian responses do) serves to maintain an unjust status quo.

For millions of Americans, the problems of our society are more accurately described as the problems of economic insecurity: declines in real wages; reduction of benefits and pensions; underemployment, unstable employment, and unemployment; the increase in part-time and temporary work; discrimination against women and men of color in the work force; the growing poverty among women who are the sole providers for children; the increasing disparity in income and wealth among sectors of the population; inadequate and unequal access to appropriate education and health care; exposure to pollution and toxic waste placed in one's neighborhood by others; and the unrelenting reduction of public support for families that lack access to sufficient income through employment. From the perspective of those who are marginalized in our society or whose labor is exploited by our society, injustice is the source of community destruction. It batters our civil associations, including the families which nurture us as social beings. From this contrasting description of our social problems, a liberative feminist analysis finds the unspoken assumptions of communitarians unacceptable.

Strong feminist analysis already has challenged the liberal myth of the separation of economic and domestic life.[18] The experiences of women's work makes this particularly clear. Capitalism (within patriarchy) has depended upon women to do the unpaid domestic and reproductive work that reproduces workers while serving (with minority men) as an expendable source of wage labor. At the same time, patriarchy (within capitalism) has depended on women's gendered identity to sustain the civilizing virtues of emotional intimacy, cooperation, regard for others, self-sacrifice, and so forth, because these virtues have no place in the economic sphere of competitive self-interest. These multiple roles have required some women—primarily single women, poor women, and women of color—to cross the boundaries of public and private spheres.

Crossing the boundaries provides a different perspective of society, one that Joan Kelly has called, "a unified, 'doubled' view of the social order."[19] It is a perspective formed by the experience of the interconnection between the so-called public/domestic and the so-called private/economic spheres. It exposes the false communitarian assumption of separate spheres that functions to hide both the realities of most women's lives and the power of the economy to continually reshape gender roles and family structures according to the needs of production.[20]

It is my contention that our current crisis is a crisis created by shifts in the requirements of economic production to which "the family" is responding in order to survive. In economic crises, a variety of family forms will result according to the concrete resources and explanatory worldviews available to families.[21]

Some examples from women's experiences of work will be illustrative. Historian Jeanne Boydston has shown how diverse forces in seventeenth-century colonial America caused shifts in productive relationships which created a new ideology of "economics."[22] While the household remained the center of seventeenth-century economic production, women's productive work there was dropped from the dominant concepts of "work" and "economics." By the mid-eighteenth century, one Jared Eliot concluded that the profit incentive was what separated activity that was "work" from indolence.[23] The nature and value of a woman's actual work did not change, but her position within the intersection of a "masculine" money economy and a "feminine" household made her "domestic" and her activities "not-work."[24]

Not until the nineteenth century did industrialization create an actual physical division between productive work and reproductive work to match the distinction that had already been accomplished ideologically. While this division between home and work primarily restricted the place of white, middle- and upper-class women, it cemented the myth of separate spheres into the social imagination and redefined the characteristics that society would require from each gender: the soft, nurturing, domestic "true woman," and the rational, competitive, aggressive, and public "economic man." Yet, as Stephanie Coontz argues, some women could be domestic "true women" only because the price of manufactured household goods was kept low by extracting surplus value from the slave labor of children, women, and men in the cotton fields; the industrial labor of women and children in the northern garment factories; and the domestic service labor of poor women.[25] The morality of "good" families (defined as those in which mothers could stay at home and teach their children the work ethic) required the "moral inadequacies" of "bad" families (defined as those in which mothers and children worked to support the family). Due to unpaid work (slavery) or poorly paid work (field, domestic, and factory work), the cash needs of poor and working-class families in the nineteenth century could not be met by the market labors of one person. Thus, wives and children transgressed the line between home and work. Rag pickers, scavengers, street vendors, daily domestics, taking-in work, and putting-out work contributed to the family's income. Women's unpaid domestic work also transformed the goods that came into the home into the instruments and products needed for family consumption.[26]

However, the dominant ideology of "the good family" in industrial capitalism had created a symbol system for good and failed families in which a married woman employed outside the home signaled an inadequate husband. Social-work agencies, addressing primarily white poverty in the early 1900s, denounced working mothers as the cause of husbands' abandonment of their responsibility to provide for their families.[27] Confronted with this worldview, poor families often gave up the middle-class ideal of nuclear family privacy for the shared economic resources of an extended family or for the income that could be gained by boarding strangers. It was the ideology of "the good family" that encouraged poor wives to work for extra income at home while poor, uneducated, young girls and their single older sisters flooded the mills for wages to supplement fathers' incomes. Stephanie Coontz's research shows that working-class families survived in the United States at the turn of the century only because the value of the work done at home by married women and very young children and the additional wages brought home by older child labor was added to the grossly insufficient wage of the adult male provider.[28]

One irony of this history is that the virtues currently identified by communitarian proposals as the necessary basis for communities of moral character and for the economic success of good families are the very virtues exemplified by these poor and working-class families. What communitarians fail to see is that survival itself has required the virtues of hard work, self-discipline, delayed gratification, and the ability to control biological and emotional impulses. However, as Jonathan Kozol has so well described in his book *Amazing Grace: The Lives of Children and the Conscience of a Nation*, these virtues are concretely different in the discourses that shape East Fifty-ninth Street in Manhattan and Brook Avenue in the South Bronx. Seven-year-old Cliffe lives in the South Bronx and knows God. Kozol asks him how he pictures God:

"He has long hair and He can walk on the deep water." To make sure I understand how unusual this is, he says, "Nobody else can."

He seems to take the lessons of religion literally. Speaking of a time his mother sent him to the store "to get a pizza"—"three slices, one for my mom, one for my dad, and one for me"—he says he saw a homeless man who told him he was hungry. "But he was too cold to move his mouth! He couldn't talk."

"How did you know he was hungry if he couldn't talk?"

"He pointed to my pizza."

"What did you do?"

"I gave him some!"

"Were your parents mad at you?"

He looks surprised at this. "Why would they be mad?" he asks. "God told us, 'Share!'"[29]

Cliffe (located in a different community) understands well the meaning of self-discipline and delayed gratification, but his meaning makes no sense within the market logic of our economy. It is not self-denial based on rational self-interest. At best it is the luxury of charity, which Cliffe and his family can ill afford. However, it is exactly this expression of hard work, self-discipline, delayed gratification, and belief in achievement through merit which history reveals among those whose lives and labor are being exploited by insufficient wages and the disappearance of work from neighborhoods. It is their values that should cast judgment upon those whose social privileges and "virtues" are dependent upon the products of cheap labor. The moral breakdown revealed by attention to the struggles of the poor can then be located in the unwillingness of the affluent to sustain work for others and to pay for it with living wages.

The end of the twentieth century presents another crisis for many U.S. families, one produced by the economic transitions toward a global and postindustrial economy: the shifting of economic sectors from manufacturing to service, geographic shifts of industries (from Rust Belt to Sun Belt and off-shore), and the increasing polarization of labor into high- or low-wage jobs. Today, families are threatened by the phenomenon of soaring corporate profits accompanied by stagnant wages, declining benefits, and increasing numbers of underemployed workers.[30] Recent attention to what is often referred to as an emerging black underclass belies the continuous history of poverty as a natural result of the capitalist system and an inadequate governmental response.[31] Looking at family changes among the so-called urban underclass, Maxine Baca Zinn concludes: "Families adapt to social and economic constraints by weaving together elements derived from their culture and the limited structural resources available to them. The results may be conceptualized as family strategies.... Family strategies can absorb many of the costs of race, class, and gender inequalities [but] still undermine family well-being. There may be a limit to what can be achieved by each line of adaptation."[32]

While these structural changes continue to disproportionately harm communities of color in the United States, they now also threaten middle-class white America. Finally, "we" have a crisis. Today white middle-class American families are clearly faced with the contradictions within patriarchal capitalism. In a postindustrial, global capitalism, the economy has an increasing need for workers who must tolerate bad work: lower pay, fewer or no benefits, part-time, low-skill work.[33] Under these economic pressures, real wages for men have declined, and more and more women have gone into the wage labor force to support their families. Karen Nussbaum, director of the Women's Bureau, concludes that "the last 10 years have been hard years for most working women and their families: the average working woman saw her real wages stagnate, her benefits contract, and the number of hours she worked grow longer. She is more likely than ever before to be working more than one job and with diminished job security.... The overwhelming majority of working women— 78 percent—earn less than $25,000 a year."[34] Thus, in different ways, at very different costs, middle- and upper-class families, as well as economically marginalized families of all colors, continue to resist, endure, and adapt in order to survive new economic pressures.

Conclusion

More of us are experiencing society as meaner, harsher, and more violent.[35] While the patriarchal assumptions of communitarianism provide no other place to turn for explanation than to the family (particularly the family in which a woman single-handedly functions as parent and provider), remembering the past struggles of oppressed groups within the United States exposes the falsehood of blaming families.[36] A feminist analysis of poor and working-class families requires that we redirect ethical attention from the communitarian focus on the family's (that is, women's) responsibility for public moral decay, and turn that attention toward the political economy. As the concrete place and set of relationships by which a society produces and distributes goods and services, the economy also participates in the material production of various types of family, gender identities, values, and, consequently, character. It produces a legitimating ideology by symbolically establishing a worldview through which people come to consciousness of themselves and others as "familied," as "gendered," as "worker," as "value-able" or "value-less."[37] I have argued for the necessity of analyzing this ideology as a socially produced description that gives us an explanation by which to understand ourselves and others. It provides values by which we learn to judge "good" and "bad" families. It shapes our capacity to see and name the social problem.[38]

I have argued that patriarchal capitalism is a description that explains and justifies both a sexist and racist division of labor and the removal of moral responsibility for social well-being from the political economy to family structures. While depending upon the strength of families, it calls us to ignore the economic demands that devastate some families. While praising family values, it requires values that actually work to destroy families. It requires values intended to reproduce human labor for a subordinate relationship to the demands of capital. For example, Etzioni tells us that hard work pays even in an unjust world and that we are not to be motivated by our biological needs.[39] Novak urges us not to expect our need for community to be part of our work life; delaying self-gratification and bettering oneself economically should be.[40] With historical examples, I have shown how patriarchal capitalism makes use of race, gender, and class to maintain conditions against which some people and families always have had to struggle. With statistics I have argued that the current economic transformations are threatening middle-class America and its ideal family with the same disregard for families and neighborhoods that poor people and people of color always have experienced in the United States. I contend that the erosion of community and the sense of social obligation that newly troubles middle- and upper-class Americans is a logical result of both the contradictions within patriarchal capitalism and of its stated values. Today more of us are feeling that threat.

From the perspective of women, and especially of poor and working class women, the basic assumptions of the new communitarianism render it unable to interrogate the political economy, to hold it accountable for the power it has to give life to families and neighborhoods, and to identify its abuse of that power. The communitarian myth of separate social spheres is particularly at work in welfare dismantling. By isolating the family as the primary originator of moral character, communitarianism participates in blaming the welfare system while ignoring the economic structures that provide both normative descriptions and material social options. Communitarianism ignores the larger web of social injustices which gives privileges and resources to those families defined as "good" while unjustly burdening those "welfare" families labeled "bad." In its refusal to see the material basis for the realities that families face in their responses to shifting economic demands, the new communitarianism merely perpetuates the cause of its own lament.

Notes

1. William Clinton, "The President's Address: We Heard America Shouting," *New York Times,* January 25, 1995, A17.
2. Daniel Bell, *The Cultural Contradictions of Capitalism* (New York: Basic Books, 1976). Bell defines culture as those aspects of a society in which the meaning of life (in response to the experiences of death, tragedy, limits, love, obligations, etc.) is explored symbolically, especially through literature, drama, rituals, and religion (see p. 12). The family is a primary social institution through which these meanings are transmitted.
3. Ibid., 25, 244f.

4. Amitai Etzioni, *The Spirit of Community: Rights, Responsibilities, and the Communitarian Agenda* (New York: Crown, 1993).

5. Ibid., 63.

6. Ibid., 256.

7. Ibid., 91.

8. Michael Novak, *The Spirit of Democratic Capitalism* (Lanham, Md.: Madison Books, 1982; reprint, 1991), 61.

9. Ibid., 161.

10. Ibid., 166–70.

11. Ibid., 163.

12. Ibid., 85. See also George Gilder, *Wealth and Poverty* (New York: Bantam, 1981), esp. chap. 6.

13. Allan Carlson, "The Family and the Constitution," *The Family in America* 3 (1989): 8 (emphasis in the original).

14. Larry Rasmussen, *Moral Fragments and Moral Community* (Minneapolis: Fortress, 1993), 86–87.

15. Ibid., 21, n. 1.

16. Ibid., 37.

17. I use the term *oppressed* informed by the definition provided by Iris Marion Young in *Justice and the Politics of Difference* (Princeton, N.J.: Princeton University Press, 1990), chap. 2.

18. See, for example, Stephanie Coontz, *The Social Origins of Private Life* (New York: Verso, 1988); Jean Bethke Elshtain, *The Family in Political Thought* (Amherst: University of Massachusetts Press, 1982); Susan Okin, *Justice, Gender, and the Family* (New York: Basic Books, 1989); Carol Pateman, *The Problem of Political Obligation* (New York: Wiley, 1979).

19. Joan Kelly, "The Double Vision of Feminist Theory: A Postscript to the 'Women and Power' Conference," *Feminist Studies* 5, no. 1 (spring 1979): 216. Paradoxically, women's capacity to transgress these boundaries was rooted in industrial capitalism's patriarchal construction of the "feminine," specifically in the "feminine" virtue of sacrifice for family. In the United States, some women's work in field, factory, office, and home for wages or barter is justified as a "sacrifice for family" while other women's isolation at home doing unpaid domestic labor (a different form of economic vulnerability) is also justified as a "sacrifice for family." What links together these contradictory social locations is this ideology of the feminine—that is, the appropriateness of women's self-sacrifice for the well-being of the family.

20. See Linda Kerber, "Separate Sphere, Female Worlds, Woman's Place: The Rhetoric of Women's History," *Journal of American History* 75, no. 1 (June 1988): 9–39. For an account of how particular forms of labor exploitation led to creative and adaptive forms of family among African American, Chinese, and Chicano communities in the United States, see Bonnie Thornton

Dill, "Fictive Kin, Paper Sons, and Compadrazgo: Women of Color and the Struggle for Family Survival," in *Women of Color in U.S. Society*, ed. Bonnie Thornton Dill and Maxine Baca Zinn (Philadelphia: Temple University Press, 1994), 149–69.

21. For an analysis of the relationship between the economy and family patterns in the urban underclass, see Maxine Baca Zinn, "Structural Transformation and Minority Families," in *Women, Households, and the Economy*, ed. Lourdes Beneria and Catharine Stimpson (New Brunswick, N.J.: Rutgers University Press, 1987), 155–71.

22. Jeanne Boydston, *Home and Work: Housework, Wages, and the Ideology of Labor in the Early Republic* (New York: Oxford University Press, 1990).

23. Ibid., 28.

24. Julie Matthaei, *An Economic History of Women in America: Women's Work, the Sexual Division of Labor, and the Development of Capitalism* (New York: Schocken, 1982), 33–34.

25. Stephanie Coontz, *The Way We Never Were: American Families and the Nostalgia Trap* (New York: Basic Books, 1992), 11. In 1840, 40 percent of the industrial labor force comprised women and children. See Claudia Goldin, *Understanding the Gender Gap: An Economic History of American Women* (New York: Oxford University Press, 1990), 50.

26. Boydston, *Home and Work*, 88–90.

27. Matthaei, *Economic History of Women*, 130.

28. Coontz, *The Way We Never Were*, 111, 235. A 1923 study of poverty-level families showed a labor force participation rate of 96.3 percent for fathers, 96.6 percent for sons, 95 percent for daughters, and 25.9 percent for wives. See Matthaei, *Economic History of Women*, 127.

29. Jonathan Kozol, *Amazing Grace: The Lives of Children and the Conscience of a Nation* (New York: Crown, 1995), 8.

30. For example, see Floyd Norris, "Paradox of '92: Weak Economy, Strong Profits," *New York Times*, August 30, 1992, section 3, p. 1. Norris reports the new highs reached by corporate earnings in the midst of a recession by laying off workers and reducing payrolls. He writes, "America is not doing very well, but its corporations are doing just fine." Where technology once replaced human muscle, it now replaces human brains. Today, the service industry faces the kind of technological upheaval that has reduced agricultural and manufacturing jobs. The big boom in employment in the 1990s is in temporary work and part-time jobs. See Teresa Amott, *Caught in the Crisis: Women and the U.S. Economy Today* (New York: Monthly Review Press, 1993), 36–37, 61–64.

31. Several recent studies have concluded that between one-third and one-half of the increase in poverty among families with children in the 1980s was due not to changes in family structure but to the decline in antipoverty impact of government programs (Coontz, *The Way We Never Were*, 260).

32. Baca Zinn, "Structural Transformation," 168. Similarly, Jeremy Rifkin, citing Sidney Willhelm's warning in 1970 that the racial outcome of the technological revolution would be to move black Americans "from exploitation to uselessness," concludes that "the commodity value of Black labor has been rendered virtually useless by the new automated technologies." See James Weinstein, "Worked Over," *In These Times* 26 (June 1995): 29.

33. The Women's Bureau of the U.S. Department of Labor reports that the majority of jobs created between 1975 and 1990 and the majority (nearly 94 percent) of new jobs which will be created between 1990 and 2005 will be in the service-producing industries. Twenty-two percent of all new jobs will be in the retail trade division, where many of the jobs will be part-time, offer low pay, require little training or skill, demand little work experience, offer limited advancement, and be extremely sensitive to shifts in the economy (U.S. Department of Labor, Women's Bureau, *1993 Handbook on Women Workers: Trends and Issues* [Washington, D.C., 1993], 232–33).

34. Ibid., iii. In 1986, the Joint Economic Committee of the U.S. Congress estimated that if large numbers of women (primarily married white women) had not entered the wage labor force in the past two decades, real family income would have dropped 18 percent between 1980 and 1986. See the Taskforce on Issues of Vocation and Problems of Work in the U.S., *Challenges in the Workplace* (Louisville, Ky.: Publication Service, Presbyterian Church [U.S.A.], 1990), 19. The shift to service work and corporate efforts to reduce the cost of labor (including downsizing, the off-shoring of jobs, greater use of part-time and contract workers, and reductions in benefits) continue to depress family income. In 1988, it took two wage earners in two-thirds of white and three-fourths of black households to earn a middle-class income (between $25,000 and $50,000). See Marvin L. Oliver and Thomas M. Shapiro, *Black Wealth/White Wealth: A New Perspective on Racial Inequality* (New York: Routledge, 1995), 96. Coontz estimates that if both parents were not working, more than one-third of all two-parent families would be counted as officially poor. (See Coontz, *The Way We Never Were,* 260.) In 1992, more than one-half of those mothers with children under the age of three were in the wage labor force; more than three-fourths of those mothers with children between the ages of six and thirteen were in the labor force. It should be noted, however, that there is still a large difference between the participation rates of black women and white women with preschool children. In 1990, black mothers of preschoolers had a labor force participation rate of 73.1 percent, compared to 57.8 percent of white mothers. (See *1993 Handbook on Women Workers: Trends and Issues,* 5, 12.)

35. For example, the poverty rate for all children has increased from 14 percent in 1969 to 21.8 percent in 1991, with much higher rates for children of color. (See James Newton Poling, *Deliver Us from Evil* [Minneapolis: Fortress Press, 1996], 86.) The United States now ranks twenty-first in the world in infant mortality. (See Coontz, *The Way We Never Were,* 2.)

36. We need to remember that in 1920, one-fifth of all American children lived in orphanages because living parents could not afford to care for them; that in 1960, one-third of all American children lived in poverty despite low divorce rates. (See Coontz, *The Way We Never Were*, 4–5.)

37. See, for example, Samuel Bowles and Herbert Gintis, "The Economy Produces People: An Introduction to Post-Liberal Democracy," in *Religion and Economic Justice*, ed. Michael Zweig (Philadelphia: Temple University Press, 1991), 221–44.

38. See Mary McClintock Fulkerson, "Feminist Theology and the Subjecting of the Feminist Theologian," presentation to the American Academy of Religion, Nov. 1993.

39. Etzioni, *Spirit of Community*, 91.

40. Novak, *Spirit of Democratic Capitalism*, 137, 93–94.

[6]

Family Values and Working Alliances

The Question of Hatred and Public Policy

Janet R. Jakobsen

THE CONTEMPORARY DISCOURSE OF "family values" has become so omnipresent within U.S. political culture that it is invoked by representatives of both mainstream political parties. In the 1996 presidential election, there was apparently no disagreement about the necessity of family values for America, despite the question of whether it takes a village or just a 1950s-style nuclear family, conjoined with "values." This bipartisan agreement is perhaps not so surprising given the ever-more-minute product differentiation between the two parties, but it is noteworthy given the fact that this bipartisanship was enacted legislatively in the 1996 welfare "reform" bill. This legislation (perhaps the largest social change yet of the post-Reagan era), passed by a Republican Congress but signed by the Democratic president, was funded in part by the bipartisan talk of family values that it materialized.

Talk of family values has become so omnipresent because it condenses an entire series of social relations. When enacted, "family values" is the sexualization of race, gender, and poverty, that authorized welfare reform. The complexity of relations condensed within family values is belied by the apparent obviousness of the invocation. In contemporary U.S. politics, the meaning of "family values" is so obvious, so commonsensical, that one doesn't have to say what is meant by either "family" or "values" or the conjunction. And yet, this naturalization of the term is precisely what allows it to operate in such a powerful fashion, allowing its invocation to cover over a series of incoherencies that it condenses.

What, after all, does "family values" mean? I have to admit a certain (and willful) bafflement. The documents that have codified its meaning, particularly the Contract with the American Family and its sibling, the Contract with America, which was used so successfully in the 1994 Congressional elections, might promise the possibility of, if not diminishing, at least articulating this bafflement, but these documents just do not make sense. To cite just one example, one point in the Contract with the American Family urges an end to, or privatization of (whichever comes first?), the Public Broadcasting System. Given the political right's frequent condemnation of the "filth" produced in Hollywood and on the internet and its relation to children, it seems just a little odd that the one source of consistent, "clean" (and nonviolent) children's programming would be targeted as evil in a document focused on the family. Similarly, welfare reform as a specifically "family" value can be read as contradictory. Certainly, the primary program to be cut—Aid to Families with Dependent Children—was conceived to provide support specifically for families in difficult financial situations. Only a very specific set of assumptions can make *cutting* support for families seem like a coherent expression of valuing the family.

Simply pointing out these inconsistencies, however, has not necessarily proved to be an effective strategy in resisting the power of the invocation or its political effects. When, for example, opponents of the 1996 "Defense of Marriage Act" (DOMA) pointed out that many of its proponents, while appealing to the language of family values, had themselves been married multiple times, the obvious contradiction had no effective impact on the vote itself. Similarly, with regard to debate over welfare policy, it is not enough to point out the inconsistencies in the rhetoric of welfare reform: to point out that the budget deficit could be addressed by cuts in other areas; to show that the stereotypes on which this rhetoric depends are precisely stereotypes (and in particular that they are racist stereotypes); to demonstrate the importance of reliable, affordable child care and health care; or to point out that an economy dependent on ongoing un- and underemployment has its costs. Naming these facts will not, in and of itself, counter the prevailing rhetoric, because the enumeration of facts does not address the complex of relations that are being reworked through talk of family values, nor does it address the ways in which the apparently obvious meaning of "family values" both pulls together and covers over the contradictions within this complex of relations. Simply to point out a contradiction does not intervene in the management of contradiction that makes for common sense and that makes talk of family values such a powerful discourse in the contemporary United States.

Unfortunately, however, the claims of those social movements which have opposed the right-wing uses of family values can also take on this supposedly self-evident but nonsensical quality. Take, for example, the popular slogan found on bumper stickers and T-shirts "Hate Is Not a Family Value." It seems quite possible that "hate" *is* a family value, and if the Defense of Marriage Act and the welfare reform bill are any indication, it may be central to family values. Apparently, if gay people get married (a relatively conservative act that affirms social structure), America's families will fall apart. Given the nonsensical nature of this argument (it makes sense to "defend" heterosexual marriage against gay marriage only if one believes that, given the option, the majority of people would choose gay marriage), something more than logic must be motivating DOMA. Somehow the denigration of homosexuality in relation to heterosexuality is necessary to hold families together.

The question is, what is the specific relationship between the moral discourse of family values and the affective invocation of hatred? There is certainly a distinction between hate groups and movements and the widespread sites of family values, including those middle Americans who experience themselves as not hateful and, in fact, as tolerant of "others." The political spectrum in the United States is not, however, merely a line-up of individual and distinct positions. It is, rather, a moral economy of positions that have meaning only in relation to one another.[1] Moreover, it is important to ask the specific question of the relationship between ongoing domination and hate. Why is it that America has been unable to eradicate various forms of domination, given that the American public thinks of itself as liberal in the sense of being fully democratic and understands its public affect to be a tolerance correlative to that liberalism?

Welfare reform has a complex relation to hate in that it both depends on the affective motivations for dominations and on the denial that hate is in any way part of the policy process. Thus, policies that are substantially draconian can be represented as not only *not* motivated by hatred, but as somehow beneficial to participants in government programs: welfare reform will "free" them from the "cycle of dependency." I will argue that these two facts—the distinction between hate groups and family values and the passage of legislation that does the work of hate—indicate the working of a complex economy in which the moderate disavowal of hatred can work to extend rather than extinguish its effects.

"Family values," thus, is part of a Christian-right discourse that serves as a connector between groups, movements, and discourses which might explicitly be referred to as "hate groups" and a moderate, Christian-identified public which remains invested in relations of domination but wishes to disavow connection to the affective dimension of domination—that is, hatred. The simultaneous disavowal and enactment of hatred works together to such an extent that even members of explicitly white-supremacist groups like the Ku Klux Klan might disavow hatred.[2] While the national offices of an organization like the Christian Coalition certainly would deny such outright hatred, the connector provided by Christian homophobia allows the disavowal to enable the functioning of the hate. Once the disavowal is made, there need be no responsibility taken for the connections between outright hatred named Christian and moderate homophobia traveling under the same name (Christian). Thus, the strong emotion and even violence linked to hate can remain part of explicitly Christian discourses. For example, at a political rally in Atlanta in 1993, a Christian minister proclaimed that he wouldn't be satisfied "until all of them [homosexuals] are carried out in body bags."[3] Similarly, bumper stickers like "I'm Pro-Life and I Shoot" or "Army of God and Atlanta Bomb Squad" (a reference to the bombings in Atlanta at a clinic that provides abortions and at a lesbian bar in 1997), remain part of the right-wing Christian activist culture.[4] This question of relation is so important because it points out how complicated it is to intervene in the rhetoric of the right. If denying that you hate anyone is one of the tools that enable hatred, if the right is happy to disavow hatred and to claim moderation and even tolerance, then simply opposing hatred will not be effective.

If a straightforward counterdiscourse will not provide effective intervention in the litany of claims made in the name of family values, how should activism and advocacy be framed and undertaken? A crucial starting point is to ask, why sexual regulation? Why is the containment of sexuality within the confines of "family" the most visible articulation of "values" in the current moment? Why is a major social change like welfare reform undertaken through a rhetoric focused on young poor women and their sexuality? The prevailing discourse simply takes for granted that American politics should be conducted through talk of sexuality. Is there, after all, anything more "American" than an obsession with sexuality *and* its regulation? In particular, is it not the primary concern of American "religion" to regulate sexuality? How did values about sexuality, rather than, for example, social justice become the primary purview of religion in America? The political centrality of sexuality and the connections between sexual regulation and religion often seem assumed, despite the fact that it is not the case that sexual regulation has taken this particular form (family values) at all times and places. It is not the case that all religions have been invested in this type of family values. It is not even the case that Christianity has always been invested in the particular types of sexual regulation currently trumpeted.[5]

Once again, however, the counterdiscourse can depend on these same as-sumptions. For example, the explanation for family values, within a radical field like lesbian, gay, and bisexual studies, often depends on some version of the naturalization of religion as sexual regulation, along the lines of "Oh, of course, they hate us, they're religious." And, yet, this very logic of reduction is precisely the claim the right wants to make, "Of course, we hate them, we're religious, and to be religious is to have values and to have values is to be con-servative." In accepting the "of course they hate us," story (a story which pro-duces a naturalized set of connections from religion through Christianity to sexual regulation), progressive politics can come to articulate the very claims that it would contest. This naturalization is not useful politically. In fact, it plays into one of the central claims of the right: that to be religious or Christ-ian is to be invested in the particular set of values named "family," and that if you don't agree with these particular values, you don't have any values and can't be truly religious. This move not only hides the complexities of something we might call "religion," and undercuts those sites from within religious history and practice where resistance might be undertaken, it sets up an oppositional dynamic between sexual deviants and Christians that works not only to the ad-vantage of the right, but which also constructs a "tolerant," middle-of-the-road, middle-class that tolerates hatred along with the hated.

"Family values" addresses a fear that political liberalism has evacuated all values, so the move to religiously inflected family values is a means of reassert-ing values of any kind. The condensed understanding of values makes it seem like the choice is family values or no values. Thus, the Democrats have taken up this language because to fail to do so would leave them open to the charge of valuelessness. By connecting values to something so supposedly common as family (after all, doesn't everyone have a family?), it is possible to assert values without the middle class's sense of itself as tolerant being challenged. Thus, the conjunction of family and values allows for a position that asserts sexual regu-lation under the continuing guise of tolerance.

Politics and Common Sense

The question faced by activists is how the assertion of something so common-sensical, so seemingly benign and even positive as ascribing a value to "family," can work as an ideology that allows for policies like welfare reform which actu-ally have such detrimental effects on some families. Common sense is con-structed through a network of binaries that organize conceptual categories and possibilities, that organize what can make "sense" in a given moment. And in the contemporary situation, these binaries enable sexual regulation through the invocation of family values. This network of binaries, like that between moral and immoral or hetero- and homosexual, is the discursive fabric that makes family values into common sense, into words that can be invoked to great effect without having to state their specific meanings. Catherine Bell theorizes the workings of such networks, arguing that the complex interrelations of the binaries are what allow the network to provide a (common) sense of "a loosely knit and loosely coherent totality."[6] Within such a network, the binaries both line up (she uses the example of light/dark, good/evil, culture/nature, male/female)[7] and don't precisely line up, so that in the process of shifting among binaries a series of claims are articulated with one another, but they can be defended on the grounds of the single binary that makes the most sense in a given moment or argument.[8] The oppositions are treated as homologies: light is to dark as good to evil, culture to nature, and male to female; but there is also slippage among the terms so that they are not precisely homologous. This slippage, rather than undermining the network, can actually reinforce it, however, by providing a shifting site of reference in the face of counterevidence. Thus, if men empirically show themselves to be not necessarily good, the terms can slip to the culture/nature binary and whatever "evil" men do—wars, for example—is now placed in the context of the (necessary and) good production of culture. The slippage to the culture/nature binary shifts the meaning of the good/evil binary so as to return male to its homologous relation to good. "Culture" becomes a node that articulates in two directions—to good and to male—and as such, it also stabilizes the meaning of "good" in relation to "male." The possible incoherence sparked by empirical counterexample is, thus, averted. Rather, the network of binaries allows precisely for the management of incoherencies. When one binary is challenged, threatened, insufficient, problematic, or itself incoherent, it is possible to discursively slip to another, thus protecting the network as a whole.[9]

The network of binaries invoked by and condensed into family values works to regulate a number of social relations which are not named directly, because invoking one opposition can invoke the network as a whole. Thus, for example, moral/immoral can be mapped onto social locations, like man and woman in Bell's example or hetero- and homosexual in the Defense of Marriage Act. The image of family can, in the case of the Defense of Marriage Act, be invoked to police homosexuality. But in the case of welfare reform, family values works to regulate heterosexuality, and by tying the regulation of sexuality to black/white and middle-class/poor binaries, it can work to regulate the (hetero)sexuality of poor young women of color. Through this regulation, discourses of race, class, and gender relations are elaborated even as they are invoked in condensed form.

If the image of appropriate family relations is restricted to the supposedly traditional but historically specific (even unusual) postwar American nuclear family, then sexuality, and in particular sexual "respectability," is made the marker for middle-class propriety to which all Americans should aspire.[10] The American dream of class mobility is here tied to sexual respectability. All Americans should aspire to the middle class, and the best means of doing so, regardless of economic resources, is to emulate the middle-class family. Therefore, all Americans should act as if they are living in middle-class families. The moralistic underpinnings of this mobility narrative imply that a personal and moral failing can be ascribed to those who are not mobile. This narrative has been further racialized, such that the empirical fact of race hierarchies in the United States is narratively explained not by reference to the historic and ongoing operations of racial domination, but to the supposedly unfortunate, but necessary results of a refusal by or an inability of people of color to adopt and enact middle-class family values.[11] As Patricia Hill Collins states, "The advice to the poor seems to be that the sole requirement to lift oneself out of poverty is to think and behave like white, middle-class men and women."[12]

These family values are strongly gendered such that both "family" and "values" should read through gender hierarchy. "Family" means only a patriarchal family with "appropriate" gender hierarchy in which caring for children is women's work but work that can only be accomplished successfully if supervised by a man.[13] The onslaught of talk about the apparently unavoidably negative consequences of raising children without fathers (itself a gendered discourse where single mothers supposedly produce girls who become single mothers and boys who become criminals) makes women's work to care for their children when single a moral failing rather than an accomplishment. This assumption plays into a history of descriptions of mothering in which women are both designated as the guardians of culture and mistrusted in their ability to carry out this task without supervision, a mistrust that is indicative of a cultural anxiety about women's autonomy more generally.[14] Thus, "values," when conjoined with "family" is an assertion against women's claims to moral autonomy. The slashing of Aid to Families with Dependent Children works to materially enforce the denial of women's autonomy by limiting the economic and hence relational possibilities for women to negotiate in or leave heterosexual relationships.

As a condensation of this complex matrix, the invocation of family values articulates in two directions. Through sexual regulation, race, gender, and class relations are also regulated as moral discourse about sexuality reinforces social hierarchies and dominations. Welfare reform enacts the economic and political changes of budget-cutting and shifting the role of government through a moralistic discourse focused on out-of-control sexuality and inappropriate familial form. These shifts in government reinforce class hierarchies as the elites benefit from shifts in tax policy while middle-class entitlements are protected and the poor pay the costs of reducing government. In the other direction, sexuality itself is regulated. Yet these economic and government shifts are accomplished through a discourse dependent on a racialized set of images of welfare mothers, images invoked in order to control the sexuality of young, single women of color and the number of children they have by limiting already severely constrained economic choices. The Defense of Marriage Act similarly constricts the options for any form of sexual relation that is not defined by heterosexual marriage by restricting the form under which a whole series of social benefits, from health care to citizenship, are available. Ultimately, welfare reform works to reinforce a racialized and patriarchal heterosexuality, naturalized as the (white, middle-class) "family."

In the case of family values, the network of binaries is quite extensive. In addition to the ties among moral/immoral, white/black, middle class/poor, and hetero-/homosexual, which are tied to the structure of "family," a set of binaries is condensed into the conjunction with "values." These binaries connect a set of structural issues by tying together terms like: religious/secular, moral values/economic value, Christian/non-Christian, and American/un-American, with moral/immoral, hetero-/homosexual, black/white, and middle class/poor. This complex network invoked through the claim for values accomplishes a number of things for the right. If, for example, to be American is to be Christian in a certain way, then non-Christians, or even those who are Christian in another way, will always be minorities that can only be tolerated within the broader American public. Moreover, members of religious minorities are American only insofar as they agree with dominant American (that is, Christian) values. So the points of similarity or overlap in values, not the differences among traditions, become the publicly acceptable articulation of all religions. These claims also pose the Christian-identified radical right as the site of the intersection between religion and values, such that any alternative configurations of these relationships (values, for example, that are not necessarily Christian) are erased. Thus, "family values" allows a reference to values that are effectively marked as religious and Christian without the need to name them directly as such.

This move is at once universalizing and specifying, or, more accurately, it enacts the universalization of a specific set of values, such that all values that travel under other names can be conflated with Christian values and further condensed into family values. All those that cannot be so condensed are simply placed outside the realm of recognizable values. They simply are not values. So, for example, Katie Cannon argues that black womanist ethics are often not recognized as moral, are labeled immoral or amoral, precisely because they are in resistance to capitalism, rather than enacting the dominant U.S. Protestant ethic that supports capitalist endeavor.[15] In other words, even Protestant Christian values if not in line with the secular-market version of Christianity are unrecognizable as values. The Christian Coalition has, in fact, had difficulty in its attempts to form Catholic and Jewish alliances precisely because the values that the Christian Coalition names as "Christian" or as "religious" are a particular version of Protestantism.[16]

An opposition is then established between the religious as the site of values and another nonreligious site supposedly free of values which could be termed the "secular."[17] The split between the secular and the religious, as it developed in the modern period, was often articulated as being about establishing a site of "freedom" from religious dogma. This freedom from religion included economic freedom from ecclesiastical authority, instituting the market as a site of economic activity outside of the oversight of the church.[18] Thus, the secular is the site of capitalism, where the market operates freely, driven only by economic value, not moral values. While individuals are expected to bring their own (Protestant) work ethic to their actions in the market, the market itself responds only to economic, not moral, incentive. The fear induced by this structural asymmetry is that the market, because value-free, will not recognize and may not reward hard work. This disconnection between economic and moral value can open the space for a moral discourse critical of capitalism, but I will argue that moral values can also be invoked as the buffer to the market. Specifically, the desire for family values is, in part, the expression of a desire to buffer the effects on the middle classes of the expansion of the market. The fear that a value-free market has evacuated all possible moral value is countered by the location of a nonmarket site of values named "family." This allows for a discourse of values that in being distinct from capitalism nonetheless does not challenge but rather works with that economic system.

Why Welfare? Why Now?

The notion of family values thus lays the groundwork for various forms of social retrenchment. In this sense, the fact that talk of "family values" is ubiquitous indicates that the field of contemporary American politics is predisposed in favor of intensifying social regulation. Regulation on social (but not economic) issues is the likely outcome of political struggles. Regulation is not, however, the necessary outcome. As activists, we need to ask both how to intervene effectively and why regulation takes the particular forms it does in the current moment. We cannot assume that the particular battles engaged by the right are the necessary outcome of social conditions. Rather, they are constructed *as if* necessary in order to make it seem only natural that politicians are talking about cutting the social safety net, thereby setting the terms of debate in favor of regulation before the debate is even engaged. For example, one of the central questions about welfare reform is how welfare has become the site for budget-cutting. Why are social programs that address poverty paradoxically treated as "luxuries" when budget-cutting is proposed as necessary? And why is the response to the economic changes that supposedly motivate budget-cutting not one of social solidarity? Why was there a language of social solidarity that could be meaningful, if not fully effective in terms of justice, during the hard economic times that led to the establishment of social programs? And why is such language apparently so unavailable in U.S. public discourse today? How is it that the moral language of "social" and "justice" has been transfigured into one of "family" and "values"? And how does the move to make family values coextensive with morality allow the work of hatred to be conducted under the auspices of the moral?

The rhetorical effectiveness of family values provides part of the answer. Talk that conjoins family and values not only serves to condense social relations, it also constructs the relationship between economic value and moral values. In particular, it works to manage a particular set of contradictions created by recent economic shifts—shifts which David Harvey has theorized as the move from the modern to the postmodern.[19] Harvey argues that the economic shifts through deindustrialization from an economy organized around industrial production to one in which capital is much more mobile are so fundamental as to be indicative of an epochal shift: from industrial capitalism to postindustrial capitalism and from modernity to postmodernity. In particular, Harvey argues that in the United States, the shift toward the "condition of postmodernity" has been a shift away from the Fordist compromise(s) between U.S. corporations, government, labor, and the "public" which connected U.S. national interest to the welfare of U.S. corporations. Fordism for Harvey is the relatively stable economic arrangement which enabled industrial production.[20] Thus, under Fordism it made sense to say "As goes GM, so goes the nation." The contemporary movement toward transnationalism as the mark of (U.S.) corporate structure has also prompted a reworking of the relationship(s) among the economy, the state, and the American "nation." Now, GM is more of a transnational, than an "American" company. These economic shifts have created a number of dislocations in the nation, most dramatically the deindustrialization of much of the United States, particularly in the Northeast and Midwest (traditionally sites of extensive labor movement and union activity), but also including a decrease in job security and an increasing disparity between economic classes. Moreover, the presumed tie between U.S. corporations and the welfare of the American nation has been undercut by transnationalization.

In reference to the modern period, it is common to speak of the "nation-state" as a single term. Because the nation-state developed in some conjunction with capitalism, the function of the state is usually understood as mediating between the market and persons subjected to the market embodied as the "public" or "nation." In the post–World War II Fordist compromise, this was certainly the case: the role of the state was both to mediate the compromise between corporations and organized labor and to constitute a single nation which this compromise sustained. Thus, the welfare state, particularly through its federal programs, was supposed to create a nation in which everyone had some sense of investment in the success of corporate America. Even as the terms of the agreement stabilized corporate power, they also opened up a discursive space in which checks on corporate "interests" could be articulated when corporations did not serve the "national interest." Thus, corporations in this period were the primary site of reference in the invocation of the term "special interests." This rhetoric of corporate special interests was not to say that corporations (or capitalism) were themselves problematic, but rather that they needed to operate within the terms of the national interest—the terms set by the "public," which supposedly included everyone and which supported families. Social movements of the 1950s and 1960s succeeded in accomplishing what they did, in part, by showing that not all "Americans" were included in the well-being of the nation. The terms of the agreement provided the discursive space to challenge through new social movements the all-too-real ways in which many Americans continued to be shut out of the supposed benefits of Americanness and to challenge corporations as sources of, if not oppression or domination, at least problems of constraint and danger, which needed to be addressed.[21]

Now, however, in the move to the postmodern period,[22] two major shifts have taken place: transnationalization and the shift in the relationship between the financial markets and industrial production, such that financial markets dominate industrial production in a new way, as indicated, for example, by the 1980s' mania for leveraged buyouts and the breakup and sale of corporate assets. These two shifts—transnationalism and the extension of the supremacy of finance—indicate changes in the way that the state works for the market, specifically the ways in which the state works now in the service of the financial markets as relatively autonomous in relation to the market for goods which drives industrial production.

What the combination of these two shifts implies is that the job of the state in relation to American business has shifted and the nation must in some sense be constructed separately from the state's relation to transnational corporations. Both of these tasks may still take place at the site of the government, but the restructuring of government that we currently see under way is reflective of the differentiation of these two tasks. As Harvey points out, the state's traditional job of working for capitalism and serving as a site for the constitution of the nation is now a contradictory one:

> Arenas of conflict between the nation state and trans-national capital have, however, opened up, undermining the easy accommodation between big capital and big government so typical of the Fordist era. The state is now in a much more problematic position. It is called upon to regulate the activities of corporate capital in the national interest at the same time as it is forced, also in the national interest, to create a "good business climate" to act as an inducement to trans-national and global finance capital, and to deter (by means other than exchange controls) capital flight to greener and more profitable pastures.[23]

These shifts are accompanied by a shift in the labor market that intensifies both class and race divisions in the United States as the sense of threat in relation to the loss of capital and industrial production overseas is articulated for and by middle America as a threat of: "Don't complain or *we* may soon all be out of a job." The effectiveness of this threat has been an apparently paradoxical embrace of corporate America just as it becomes even less socially responsible. Thus, we no longer can speak of corporations as enacting special interests, but rather those who would challenge corporate policy or the boundaries of middle America become the transposed site of threat and are now named "special interests."

Enter Reagan's America, where this fear on the part of middle America conjoined with the corporate interest in union-busting to cut back on the "high" cost of labor under Fordism can be used to slash federal programs. If, because of the loss of jobs tied to industrial production and the destabilization of job security, middle America no longer has access to the proceeds of U.S. industry, it is certainly not going to stand by while poor Americans receive any kind of support from the federal government. Thus, for example, just as low-income housing became more necessary because of deindustrialization in the late 1970s and early 1980s, it was slashed drastically by Reagan's policy, and we see the rise in homelessness that now seems inevitable and irreversible but that is in fact the result of policy decisions.

These shifts are also connected to a whole set of retrenchments around the social issues of 1960s' and 1970s' movement, so that we see through the 1980s not just the white flight to the suburbs that marked the post–civil rights retrenchment in major cities, but a flight of both whites and capital to the South and West as a means of reworking the social relations changed by the sixties. It is not a mistake that we now have all kinds of automakers, both "American"

(Saturn) and "foreign" (Honda, Nissan, etc.), setting up manufacturing in the less unionized, more white "rural" areas of states like Kentucky and Tennessee.

The question is why have these retrenchments worked in this way at this time? Why does it no longer matter if large segments of the American population have any stake in the nation? First, the threat of corporate movement, of jobs or of the corporation itself, is effective. Were it not, we would not see bidding wars between states over corporate location where any positive effects for "the community" are given back in the tax, zoning, and regulatory structure of the agreements.

Second, and perhaps more importantly, talk of family values provides one means of managing the dislocations caused by the shift to transnationalization and mobile finance capital by shifting the site of the nation away from the state and toward the family. In order for the state (the U.S. government) to continue to work on behalf of (now) transnational capital, it must now embody a transnational form of Americanness: American only insofar as transnational corporations are also U.S. corporations.

This contradictory task is managed, in part, by reducing the size of government to allow for the greater mobility of capital, yet there is also a need to constitute the nation at another site so as to manage reaction against transnationalization articulated as the loss of Americanness. In this climate, the primary site of Americanness is being shifted from the state to the family, which can come to embody the nation precisely because, under the discourse of family values, it embodies American values.

The shift that we see is a shift in primacy. Family values can be spoken of so self-evidently as a site of nationalism because of the long history of association between "family" and "nation." Now, however, moral values (named family) rather than economic value become the primary site of nationalism, because economic value, even "American" economic value, is fundamentally transnational.

The heightened discourse of Americanness indicated in moves against flag-burning, indecent (un-American) art, or protection of the military from infiltration by gays is all a means of reasserting the nationhood of America. If the "one nation under God" sanctified for public schoolchildren in the Pledge of Allegiance now occurs within the family rather than the state, then the investment in social control of familial form increases. If the slogan "as goes GM, so goes the nation," has now been replaced by "as goes the family, so goes the nation," then a high level of intervention in familial form is justified to protect the "nation."

This shift explains how we have (paradoxically?) moved into a period of smaller government that is also more, rather than less, invested in social control. Thus, we see a shift in regulation similar to the shift in primacy between moral and economic value(s): less regulation of corporations and an extension of regulation of familial form.

Efforts to "reform" welfare insofar as they are also attempts to enforce nuclear family structure, then, are also efforts to re-form the American nation. Re-forming both federal and state budgets by cutting welfare seems to make sense in this climate because it shifts governmental budget priorities toward subsidizing economic value, as embodied in transnational corporations, while enforcing nationalism through the proclamation of American values, as embodied in the nuclear family. Thus, the tension between American economic value and moral values that is raised by a shift to postmodernity in which economic and national interests no longer mesh, is managed by making national interests the subject of (family) values, thus allowing the state to support the transnational interests of economic value. Controlling both federal and state budgets by reforming welfare means that the state will continue to regulate this re-formed nation, while simultaneously leaving open the state's ability to subsidize corporations.

Yet why is the answer to the problem of transnationalization one of retrenchment rather than social solidarity? Why does the destabilization of the American middle class lead to a decrease, rather than increase, in the resources available to families through the social safety net? Harvey's story tells us something of the economic conditions that have prompted shifts in social policy over the past quarter-century, the ways in which shifts in the relations that produce economic value have opened the door to a (re)new(ed) discourse of moral values in the service of nation-building. It can also indicate how these shifts in the relations of production of both economic value and moral values lead to policy changes like welfare reform. What Harvey's story can't tell us is why the work of distinguishing Americanness takes the form that it does. Why do American (family) values also have to be the values that structure American domination?

Is Hate a Family Value?

To ask this question is also to pose the fundamental question of the relationship between economic (value-free) exploitation and (value-laden) domination. Economic exploitation is supposed to be free of determination by cultural values. It is supposedly based only on the profit motive and the operation of the market. Social domination, on the other hand, is value laden. It enacts the values of a given society.

For example, the race, class, and gender dominations enabled through the policy of welfare reform enact the value that men should be heads of households within a nuclear family structure. While it may seem natural to assume that exploitation leads to domination, that exploitation is the basis of social domination, if moral values can operate as primary to economic values, then the relationship between the two is much more complicated. Domination can structure economic value, just as economic value can structure domination.

If the terms are conflated, then the complexity of the relationship between economic value and social values is made invisible. Recognizing the constitutive role that domination plays in relation to exploitation, as well as the ways in which domination is the product of exploitation, points to the constitutive role that values play in relation to the production of value, the ways in which cultural values establish both what is produced and the relations of production—the social arrangements within which production takes place.

As Gayatri Spivak points out in "Scattered Speculations on the Question of Value," to understand how exploitation works, we must understand not only how a body that labors is exploited but how that body is produced.[24] If labor is not so denaturalized, we lose sight of the process by which bodies are made into labor power—bodies, in Mary Poovey's terms, "simply disappear into labor power,"[25] thus, reenacting the very disappearing act by which human beings become their labor that Marx would incite us to critique. Spivak rethinks domination and exploitation by reading domination as a tool of exploitation, in which the need to exploit bodies leads to social domination, and by reading domination as in some sense preceding exploitation, indicating the ways in which the exploitation of labor power is an effect of cultural values. She argues that cultural values contribute to the construction of bodies that labor through "desire," both the desire for consumption and the desire of the body disciplined in Weberian or Protestant terms to labor, to (in Spivak's terms) "consume the (affect of) work itself."[26] These desires make for "affectively necessary labor," such that the production of bodies that are both dominated and exploited "can no longer be seen as the excess of surplus labor over *socially* necessary labor."[27] Exploitation is never itself value free, because it is *both* dependent upon *and* structured by the values carried by the normatively inscribed—the dominated—body.

Spivak's argument demonstrates not only the importance of maintaining a complicated understanding of the relationship between exploitation and domination, it also points to the work that affect does in relation to social issues. It is on this basis that we need to inquire into the role that the affect of hate plays in relation to family values. If exploitation alone determined domination, if domination were only about the requirements of the market, there would be no need for hatred, but if domination also precedes and constitutes exploitation, then the affect necessary to the work of domination must itself be produced.

Talk of family values enables the particular forms of exploitation required by transnational capital by mediating between a liberal "tolerance" which is the public sphere corollary to (value-free) capitalism and the affect accompanying (value-laden) American domination. Thus, there is a chain of affect which moves from hate through family values to tolerance. Just as the relationship between exploitation and domination is often ideologically obfuscated so as to mask the interdependence of the terms, so also the affective stance of liberal tolerance works by being able to claim a distinction from the type of affect tied to domination that is named by "hate." The political discourse of a republic of freedom and democracy articulates with a sense that the U.S. public is not structured by either domination or exploitation but by tolerance of and even solicitude toward "others."

Family values provides the circuitry that enables policies like welfare reform (which might be seen as hateful) to be represented not only as impartial, but as somehow benevolent to those whose lives are affected. Family values accomplishes this particular task by taking up a middle—and, in this case, privileged—third position between tolerance and hate, and in so doing it materializes the tolerance of hatred. Thus, hate is simultaneously distinguished from and connected to tolerance. Middle Americans (the group which understands itself to be "tolerant" in the sense that it represents the "we" who tolerates a "they") can claim that "we" don't hate anyone, and yet support policies that effect domination—domination motivated not simply by the functionalist requirements of exploitation, but by the necessary affect of domination.

In sum, hate is part of a circuit of value(s) that runs from exploitation to domination and back again. Values serve not only as a cultural control on the market, the stable discourse of regulation to be appealed to in times of change, they also serve the socially constructive function of making crucial distinctions[28]—distinctions that signify Americanness even in an increasingly global society and distinctions that enable both domination and exploitation. The values of Americanness, for example, serve to distinguish between those persons whose lives are inscribed only in economic value, who are simply the subjects of exploitation, and those persons who have values, and so are empowered to be agents in relation to the market and economic value.

Domination works for America not (only) because it is functional in providing reserve supplies of labor and a consistent level of unemployment—in other words, not simply as a direct tool of exploitation. Domination works for America because it promises a site separate from exploitation in which some will be visibly marked as the exploitable and others will not; the circuitry that both separates domination from exploitation and still connects the two is currently called family values.

So, if "hate is not a family value," the two are connected in such a way that we can say that family values does the work of hate. Thus, welfare reform is empowered precisely because those persons who participate in Aid to Families with Dependent Children can be marked as lacking values. They themselves, rather than the social structure, are in need of reform.

In the current political climate, the connections among groups on the far right that might be specifically labeled "hate" groups, Christian-identified right-wing political organizations, conservative mainstream political actors, and "middle America" must be taken seriously, although not as part of a conspiracy theory. While there are conscious links among these sites, they also form a working economy in which persons and groups who would actively disidentify with one another may nonetheless take up positions that work together.

In the set of relationships that distinguishes and connects hate and tolerance, the middle is materialized as that social space between hate groups and the hated, who of necessity in this binary discourse must also be an "extreme." The middle, then, is the site of tolerance that disidentifies with both extremes and in so doing maintains the power to hold the extremes in place as marginalized in relation to the middle. The discourse of tolerance, by not openly naming the power of the middle, makes it seem natural, but the position it establishes is also unstable precisely because it does not openly proclaim its power or the values that are enacted through tolerance.

The work of the Christian right in relation to hate groups, hated groups, and the tolerant middle is to contrast the discourse of (family) values to tolerance as the absence of values. Establishing a position for values in contrast to both tolerance and hate expands the middle position to include both values and tolerance, and although it excludes hate, it opens the door to the work of hate under the name of values. To "defend" marriage against homosexuals or to "reform" welfare is not to hate anyone. It is simply to have values.

The Christian right stands between, is a connector for, middle America and hate. A chain is, then, established that runs from hate through values to tolerance to the hated. The investment of middle America in making this connection is incited as the desire for values. Middle America needs the right because it materializes something that is recognizable as values, and it does so under the name "Christian," thus protecting middle America from the fear that in a secularized context there are no values left.

Middle America needs values because without them all that is left is the market, and there is no cultural protection (for middle America) from its exigencies. Thus, even if hate is not a family value, "family values" materializes the connection between hate and public policy. Americanness constructs itself through this connection with, but difference from, "hate" per se.

Working Alliances

This network of differentiated but connected positions is precisely the social matrix that enables the contradictory alliances of the contemporary political right in the United States. The set of networked conceptual binaries—religious/ secular, moral values/economic value, Christian/non-Christian, white/ black, hetero-/homosexual, moral/immoral—forms the effective worldview of a network of political alliances that are internally contradictory but nonetheless "work." In particular, the alliance on the political right between fiscal and social conservatives has enabled a series of claims which might otherwise have broken down through their incoherence. The potentially libertarian interpretation of fiscal conservatism might counter the regulatory impulses of social conservatism, but instead fiscal and social conservatives came together to make the alliance that formed the "Reagan Revolution."

In this alliance, fiscal conservatism carries a double meaning that allows it to operate as the node at which the network is articulated, the connection that allows the alliance to work. Fiscal conservatism articulates in two directions. When articulated with/as libertarianism, fiscal conservatism enables the claim that the government should not be funding social welfare programs, because the government is always a site of regulation or control. Fiscal conservatism, however, also can be (and, in fact, often is) articulated in very socially conservative terms. Fiscal conservatism, even in its libertarian form, can fund a certain punitive impulse toward those who might receive government aid in the form of "welfare" (as opposed to middle-class "entitlements"), because those who accept government assistance are not participating in the freedom of the market.

Programs that assist the middle class are acceptable, because the middle class is acting out market freedom, and government assistance helps them continue to do so. Cutting off benefits will help welfare recipients because it will make them "free" persons. The libertarian sense of market freedom is easily articulated with a socially conservative (Protestant) ethic that recipients of government aid are undisciplined and greedy, in the sense of desiring to consume too much without having sacrificed in advance for the privilege of so doing. Interestingly, through this double articulation, fiscal conservatism connects and stabilizes the relation between libertarianism and social regulation.

This connection between libertarianism and social regulation effectively manages the contradictions of U.S. public discourse by allowing for the type of slippage among terms that Bell refers to in describing networked binaries. When faced, for example, with the question of welfare reform, the fiscal conservative can defend his or her position by focusing on only the libertarian side of the articulation: "I don't believe in sexual regulation," or "I'm not a racist. I just don't believe in big government. So, I'm willing to vote for a welfare reform bill that enacts racism, sexism, and sexual regulation for my own reasons: to be free of government control. The fact that social conservatives also want this bill—that's just politics." The alliance works in the other direction as well, in that social conservatives can enact their agenda through the language of fiscal conservatism and budget-cutting which formed the basis for welfare reform.[29]

The distinction between fiscal and social conservatives remains important for social conservatives as well, because social conservatives cannot fully embrace the market ideology of freedom. Thus, keeping the two forms of conservatism distinct allows the socially conservative side of the alliance to attack Hollywood for the loss of values implied in simply being driven by market value to produce the sex and violence that "sells."

Switching among binaries manages the potential contradictions of connecting the two positions. If, for example, the contradiction of promarket policymakers not following through on their own ideology when working for regulation of the internet is pointed out, then a switch is made from the freedom/regulation binary to the values/valuelessness binary. The need for values is asserted, and opponents are accused of promoting valuelessness. If, on the other hand, the value of social justice is asserted over against an ideology focused solely on the market, then freedom becomes the most salient term for conservatives, and justice is lined up with the binary oppositions on the side of "unfreedom." By asserting either values or freedom in a given situation, it is possible to take up a coherent position in each case despite the contradiction between cases. Thus, even though there may be persons/movements that are fiscally but not socially conservative, it is also possible for the same person/movement (and the same politician) to hold both positions, despite contradiction, by switching among binaries. In addition, each assertion lines up counterpositions of valuelessness and unfreedom, making counterdiscourse virtually untenable. If claims for social justice are always lined up as the opposite of freedom, then it is particularly difficult to sustain such claims.

The explanation, then, for the fiscal and social conservative alliance is not that they are the same, but that they work together. In fact, the disjunction between them is precisely why they work. To be allied is not to come to a consensus, to agree, but to work in and through and to depend upon differences. If fiscal conservatives had to identify actively with the socially conservative aspect of the right's agenda, or vice versa, then the contradictions of their positions would be brought to the fore. The libertarian argument, thus, is not simply a cover for social conservatism. Individuals and movements really are fiscally and not socially conservative. Others are socially conservative and willing to vote for tight fiscal policy because they see it as part of a socially conservative agenda. There are tensions among the positions—as, for example, James

Dobson threatens to undermine the Republican party for not maintaining a position that is conservative enough on social issues.[30] The distinction between the two positions can, however, work to manage the contradiction, and thus far it has done so. The separation among conservative positions enables them to speak to different sites in the political landscape, while their connection enables conservative dominance.

The network of binaries, thus, enables a network of conservative political positions that forms the working alliance that is the contemporary right. Talk of family values can condense a set of regulatory issues and social relations because it invokes not a single issue but the entire network. Once such a network is established, it is particularly difficult to intervene, because pointing to the contradictions of any given position will not be effective. The response will be to switch ground to the libertarian/big government, freedom/unfreedom binary, which alone doesn't contain the contradiction.

It is important to note that this particular articulation is overdetermined but not determined (not necessary), and, thus, it could be disarticulated. This alliance was not always so. In fact, the former post–New Deal Democratic alliance articulated precisely the same contradiction between fiscal and social conservatism in the other direction—socially conservative (white, southern) Democrats were willing to participate in the party of social programs in part because these programs were value-related: we will enact the Great Society, where "great" is the node that can be articulated with/as social "values" and economic or political (not really justice but) amelioration. The articulations, the connections or links, that make such alliances also make for political effectiveness. It is not necessary that issues be articulated in a conservative network. They could be articulated in another fashion.

Can We Work (in) Alliances?

The fact that family values represent the condensation of a complex matrix of social relations gives power to their invocation, but it also makes them vulnerable to intervention. If family values must carry the weight of multiple, contradictory relations, it opens the opportunity (albeit difficult to realize) of intervention; yet a particular type of intervention is required—an intervention in the network, not in a specific position or in the contradiction per se. The interventions need themselves to be networked in ways that not only can challenge the binaries, but take apart, rearticulate, and reposition the various aspects of the (dominant) network.

If the meaning of a particular term is fixed not by its own logic or commonsensical meaning but by its relationships to other terms—to its opposite and to the other terms in the network—then meaning can be shifted by shifting these relationships. For example, tying social justice to positive values rather than appealing to or depending on tolerance opens the possibility of shifting political discourse away from the binaries that fuel the right. The power to enact such a shift comes from the materialization of connections among positions and movements.

All too often, however, progressive advocates address sexual regulation, not as the condensation of a series of social relations but as a single issue. The battle against DOMA, for example, was frequently conducted as being simply about the regulation of homosexuality over against the assertion of a right to gay marriage. In this single issue formulation, gays should have access to the same benefits, such as access to employee health insurance plans, that accrue to married couples.

Yet there are other ways to formulate the issue triggered by the unequal distribution of benefits. Obviously, for example, a health-care system that made health care and/or insurance available to the entire public would shift the debate dramatically. But even if the issue of benefits were framed in the relatively conservative terms of access through employment, gay rights movements could focus on benefits that were designed so that a working person could include another person, not necessarily his or her spousal-equivalent. Then, these movements would, for example, address working people who are responsible for elder care in circumstances where their elders do not have health insurance, as well as gay domestic partners.

This type of strategy could articulate with feminist critiques of marriage as an institution which constitutes family values as patriarchal values in support of the state. Such a move lays the groundwork for connecting campaigns against sexual regulation. Gay rights activists, for example, need to become involved in the set of issues around race, poverty, and sexuality that are implicated in welfare "reform," not out of an altruism or correctness but because the interventions necessary to disrupt heterosexism and homophobia can only be effective if they are part of an alternative network of claims that can provide counterweight to the condensed network that is family values.

Similarly, welfare rights activists must recognize the ways in which sexual regulation perpetuates welfare policy. If "family values" works by making distinctions between those people who have sexual "values" and hence who deserve the benefits of citizenship and those who do not have values, then attacks on homosexuality in the name of family values work not only against homosexuals. They also work to create a structure of binary opposition between those who have values and those who do not, a structure that obfuscates all of the complexities of life choices in relation to social structures, in favor of a moralistic schematization of the world.

"Family values" works because it can connect various forms of sexual regulation under the banner of values. Supporting a radical politics of sexuality which makes room for various forms of social bonding, including but not limited to various forms of families, is a crucial component of an effective move to intervene in the discourse that has made welfare reform acceptable to the U.S. public. Alliance politics, thus, becomes not some future goal to be accomplished in the utopian moment of relating across differences, but the very basis of alternative possibility.

Notes

1. For the concept of "moral economy" and the argument about the interrelation of positions, see chapter 1 of Janet R. Jakobsen, *Working Alliances and the Politics of Difference: Diversity and Feminist Ethics* (Bloomington: Indiana University Press, 1998).

2. See, for example, Kathleen Blee's interviews with women who participate in hate movements (Kathleen Blee, "Reading Racism: Women in the Modern Hate Movement," in *No Middle Ground: Women and Radical Protest,* ed. Kathleen M. Blee [New York: New York University Press, 1998], 180–98).

3. Personal communication, Juliana Kubala.

4. *RESIST Newsletter,* June 1997.

5. See, for example, Carolyn Walker Bynum's work on the import of food symbolism in medieval Christianity and Beverly Harrison's history of Christian perspectives on abortion (Carolyn Walker Bynum, *Holy Feast and Holy Fast: The Religious Significance of Food to Medieval Women* [Berkeley: University of California Press, 1987]; Beverly Harrison, *Our Right to Choose: Toward a New Ethic of Abortion* [Boston: Beacon, 1983]).

6. Catherine Bell, *Ritual Theory, Ritual Practice* (New York: Oxford University Press, 1992), 106.

7. Ibid., 104.

8. Bell's analysis draws on the work of Pierre Bourdieu. For example, in the first seven pages of *Distinction,* Bourdieu offers the following set of binaries: sacred/profane, beautiful/ugly, tasteful/vulgar, quality/quantity, form/substance, liberty/necessity, upper-/lower-class (Pierre Bourdieu, *Distinction: A Social Critique of the Judgement of Taste,* trans. Richard Nice [Cambridge: Harvard University Press, 1984]).

9. My reading of Bell's concept of networked binaries and common sense is first worked out in relation to possibilities for specifically queer resistance to domination in my article, "Queer Is? Queer Does?: Normativity and Resistance" (*GLQ: A Journal of Lesbian and Gay Studies* 4, no. 4 [1998]: 511–36).

10. For an extensive consideration of sexual "respectability" and middle-class morality in relation to the history of nationalism, see George Mosse, *Nationalism and Sexuality: Middle-Class Morality and Sexual Norms in Modern Europe* (Madison: University of Wisconsin Press, 1985).

11. Probably the most effective articulation of this narrative has been its circulation in the form of the "Moynihan Report," the basic tenets of which have been repeatedly recirculated despite repeated interventions on the part of activists, particularly African American women activists, that demonstrate the problems with the narrative (Office of Policy Planning and Research, United States Department of Labor [Daniel Patrick Moynihan], *The Negro Family: The Case for National Action* [Washington, D.C., 1965]). Such interventions can be found as early as 1970, when many of the contributors to the anthology *The Black Woman* criticized the "myth of the Black matriarchy" (Toni Cade, *The Black Woman: An Anthology* [New York: New American Library, 1970]). Patricia Hill Collins, however, is responding to a television version of the Moynihan narrative presented two decades later by Bill Moyers in "The Vanishing Family: Crisis in Black America" (Patricia Hill Collins, "A Comparison of Two Works on Black Family Life," *Signs* 14, no. 4 [summer 1989]: 875–84; Bill Moyers, "The Vanishing Family: Crisis in Black America," CBS News Special Report, 1986).

12. Collins, "Comparison of Two Works," 878.

13. For example, one of the films produced by conservative Christian James Dobson and his organization, Focus on the Family, entitled *Where's Dad?*, encourages men to participate in their families. In an article that includes a description of this film, its "profound effect" on U.S. Representative Frank Wolf is reported to have made him choose to stay home on Sundays, thus indicating that caring for the children the rest of the week is not his responsibility ("A Righteous Indignation," *U.S. News & World Report*, May 4, 1998, 20–29).

14. See, for example, Linda Gordon, ed., *Women, Welfare, and the State* (Madison: University of Wisconsin Press, 1990), for histories of how moral narratives about women and family were incorporated in the formation of the welfare state. For discussions of anxieties over women's moral autonomy in the context of debates over reproductive freedom, see Harrison, *Our Right to Choose;* Faye Ginsburg, *Contested Lives: The Abortion Debate in an American Community* (Berkeley: University of California Press, 1989); and Janet R. Jakobsen, "Struggles for Women's Bodily Integrity in the United States and the Limits of Liberal Legal Theory," *Journal of Feminist Studies in Religion* 11, no. 2 (fall 1995): 5–26.

15. Katie Cannon, *Black Womanist Ethics* (Atlanta: Scholars Press, 1988).

16. In fact, the Catholic Alliance, auxiliary to the Christian Coalition, took up positions with which the Catholic bishops actually disagree on a number of issues (*New York Times*, November 5, 1995, A16).

17. These connections between the specific nature of reformed-Protestant values and the value-free market are also worked out in the context of a reading of the relationship between the Contract with America and the Contract with the American Family in Janet R. Jakobsen, "Family Values: Social Movements and Sexual Regulation," in *Religion and Sex in American Public Life*, ed. Kathleen Sands (New York: Oxford University Press, forthcoming).

18. John Guillory, *Cultural Capital: The Problem of Literary Canon Formation* (Chicago: University of Chicago Press, 1993), 328.

19. David Harvey, *The Condition of Postmodernity: An Enquiry into the Origins of Cultural Change* (Cambridge, Mass.: Blackwell, 1990).

20. See chap. 8, on "Fordism," in Harvey, *Condition of Postmodernity*.

21. So, for example, the late 1960s and early 1970s saw the growth of occupational health-and-safety issues as promoted by labor unions and countercultural movements against the constraining aspects of working for "the man" (Harvey, *Condition of Postmodernity*, 125–40).

22. See Harvey, *Condition of Postmodernity*, chap. 3, "Postmodernism"; chap. 9, "From Fordism to Flexible Accumulation"; and chap. 10, "Theorizing the Transition."

23. Harvey, *Condition of Postmodernity*, 170.

24. Gayatri Spivak, "Scattered Speculations on the Question of Value," in *In Other Worlds: Essays in Cultural Politics* (New York: Methuen, 1987), 154–75. I consider Spivak's argument in more depth in Janet R. Jakobsen, "Can Homosexuality End Western Civilization As We Know It?" in *Queer Globalization/Local Homosexualities*, ed. Arnaldo Cruz-Malavé and Martin Manalansan (New York: New York University Press, forthcoming).

25. Mary Poovey, *Making a Social Body: British Cultural Formation, 1830–1864* (Chicago: University of Chicago Press, 1995), 31.

26. Spivak, "Scattered Speculations," 162.

27. Ibid., emphasis in original.

28. Bourdieu, *Distinction*.

29. The shifts in controversies over arts-funding in the 1990s demonstrate how the alliance works in both directions. Arguments to cut public funding for the arts initially were made in the socially conservative terms of decency and preventing funding for obscenity, and are now made in the fiscal terms of the budget deficit (Laurel George, "Culture and Commerce in the New National Endowment for the Arts," Center for the Humanities Lecture Series, Wesleyan University, 1996).

30. See "A Righteous Indignation."

[7]

Agenda for the Churches

Uprooting a National Policy of Morally Stigmatizing Poor Single Black Moms

Traci C. West

IT CAN BE HEARD IN CASUAL CONVERSATIONS among friends and neighbors. There are sometimes references to it in comments that pass between strangers who share an airplane ride or who sit together waiting for their clothes to dry in the laundromat. We certainly hear it in the claims of elected officials and political analysts in the media. In a variety of public contexts, single black moms who receive welfare benefits are commonly depicted as a vile moral contagion destroying this society.[1]

This labeling of poor black women and girls as morally inferior not only demeans and objectifies them. It also helps to justify government regulations that experiment with withholding from these moms access to food and money needed for the physical and material survival of their families. The brutal measures are considered treatment that "welfare mothers" deserve. How can we bring to a halt, or at least vehemently protest, both the stigmatizing "welfare mother" rhetoric reinforced by the media and the sadistic material assaults that are institutionalized in public policy? In particular, religious ideas and leaders traditionally have contributed to shaping the moral agenda of this country. How might churches play a role in challenging this intense national drive to morally castigate poor black single moms?

133

Creating the needed change involves recognizing and uprooting the prejudices that are woven into the ways that "the welfare problem" is publicly formulated. There are especially resilient forms of sexism and racism that make the dehumanizing treatment of poor black women and girls seem rational and normal. Fed by a variety of cultural cues, we learn to view poor black single moms as objects rather than people. We learn to discount each mom as some thing that is shameful and that fits a category other than our own good, hardworking, deserving selves. Thus, a poor single black mom who receives welfare benefits is too often dismissed as simply a shameful other who resides over there, amidst a host of shameful activities and elements. Instead of accepting and perpetuating these false and debasing depictions of "welfare mothers," we must awaken our capacity to renounce them. We need to identify the specific ways that racial stereotypes and gender biases infuse common beliefs about the innate moral degeneracy of these individuals. The work of exposing and rejecting the rampant, devaluing myths about women and girls who receive welfare benefits furthers the likelihood of dismantling the cruel policies that are based on these distorted images.

Depending upon their racial and economic makeup, churches bear differing responsibilities in this effort. In white church communities, the members benefit directly from the continued disparagement of those labeled "the shameful other," because it reinforces the myth of their superior white racial status. Members of another community might internalize the embarrassment of being racially linked to the shameful other, as middle-class blacks often do. Alternatively, some live each day with all of the consequences of actually being the ones relegated to the position of the shameful other, as poor black single moms must. Each of these represents a wholly distinct vantage point. Hence, it varies greatly by context which strategies are required for impacting the attitudes internally among church members and for providing broader community leadership on issues of race, gender, and welfare policy. Nonetheless, all churches ought to share the common goal of leading a retreat from the popular consensus on maligning and inflicting limitless suffering on some of the economically poorest and socially most marginalized members of our society.

Confront the Blackening of Welfare

An incident that a friend of mine recounted vividly reminded me of the common racial associations that "the welfare problem" conjures up for most Americans. He described an encounter that took place just after President Clinton signed the purported welfare reform law, the 1996 Personal Responsibility and

Work Opportunity Reconciliation Act. My friend stopped at a self-service gasoline station located in a medium-sized southeastern town. When he went to the counter to pay for the gasoline that he had pumped, the comments of the white attendant took my friend completely by surprise. While handing back the change, the white male gas station attendant looked up at my black friend, and, in a sympathetic voice, he queried: "What the colored gonna do now that the welfare is ended?" This white man naturally assumed that welfare subsidies are a factor in the lives of all "colored" people, probably also supposing this to be the case for my friend. The attendant had additionally acknowledged, with some pity, that this new legislation would destructively impact the lives of the "colored." As the straightforward question of this man illustrates, "the welfare problem" is generally perceived as an issue that chiefly affects "the colored" people, and welfare reform is understood as a punitive measure against them.

Images of "Welfare Mothers"

The automatic racial assignment of "the welfare problem" to the exclusive domain of the black community is culturally reinforced in myriad ways. One method involves utilizing black women as public symbols. For, as titles of federal welfare legislation such as the 1995 Personal Responsibility Act strikingly demonstrate, our political leaders have decided to locate the problems that welfare policy seeks to address within the moral behavior of certain individuals. In other words, welfare policy no longer seeks to eliminate social problems such as poverty but rather targets the personal inadequacy of one sector of the population.[2]

On certain public occasions, politicians use black women as principle icons for what needs reforming and who needs to exercise personal responsibility. When President Clinton signed the 1996 Personal Responsibility and Work Opportunity Reconciliation Act, he was flanked by two black women who were former welfare recipients, Penelope Howard and Janet Farrell. They literally functioned as exhibits personifying the societal problem that this legislation was meant to reduce. Clinton pointed out the women in his speech at the signing ceremony, notifying his audience that such women are, in fact, capable of personal responsibility and of actually working.

The governor of New Jersey orchestrated the same type of exhibition during her televised 1997 State of the State speech. As Governor Christine Whitman discussed her welfare reform achievements and proposals, she pointed to Monica Jones, a black female former welfare recipient, who then stood up to serve as a live display. For political leaders of this nation to persuade the public that economic problems related to poverty are merely matters of deficient moral fiber among welfare recipients, the visual identification of a black woman serves as one of the most potent tools available.

In addition to these instances of public objectification, media-generated images can help teach the same lesson. Media images can instill the idea that the term "welfare recipient" refers to an individual with a moral problem, and that "welfare recipient with a moral problem" (hear the redundancy) equals black woman.

For instance, a degrading caricature of a black woman was presented in the *Boston Globe* to depict the "welfare mother" problem. A drawing of several blackened figures grabbing for cash appeared on the editorial page of the *Globe* beside an article written by Ellen Goodman entitled "Welfare Mothers with an Attitude."[3] The most prominent silhouette in the center of the illustration was a female with an Afro hairstyle, a wide nose, and a baby on her hip, who was also reaching up to get some of the cash. In this instance, the public is literally drawn an object lesson on "the welfare problem" and taught to focus on black women. The news consumer viewing this page is led to believe that "the welfare problem" is mainly embodied in black, big-nosed females who are greedy for cash like this one, and who sexually reproduce similarly greedy offspring.

Goodman's accompanying written editorial was probably supposed to be sympathetic to "AFDC mothers." However, much of the article provides examples of the kind of objectifying messages about poor women who receive welfare benefits that are typically found in the media. Furthermore, trying to unravel the details of these messages is an essential step in arousing our sensitivity to the public disparagement of these moms. In all likelihood, Goodman intended to dispel stereotypes with comments such as "Welfare mothers do not have more children than other mothers."

Yet the terminology "welfare mothers" and "AFDC mothers," which she uses here and throughout the piece, reinforces the idea of an interdependent relationship between mothering and welfare benefits. It fosters the perception that for individuals who wear this title, "AFDC mother," welfare is central to *why* and *what* they mother. It is as if when the women give birth, they see, instead of a baby, only the guarantee of welfare checks. The terminology builds a distinction between these mothers who are focused on "welfare" and normal, good mothers whose attention is on the children whom they have brought into the world. Thus, the name "welfare mothers" suggests that poor women and girls are implicitly guilty of the charge of procreating in order to receive welfare benefits.

The power of this suggestion is bolstered by the accompanying illustration of the silhouettes grabbing for cash and by Goodman's later discussion of the values these mothers lack. Yes, mistaken notions about the disproportionate number of children that "welfare mothers" produce are being corrected by Goodman. But, by calling them "welfare mothers," the status of these women as deviant, bad mothers is also maintained. So when examined closely, what seemed at first to simply be a debunking of myths about welfare mothers turns out also to implant reassurance in the consciousness of the reader that these deviant mothers are not producing more children than (normal?) mothers.

In addition, after we are convinced through the repetition of this language that there exists such a phenomenon as "welfare mothers," does that fact mean that there are also "welfare children"? The question is visually answered in the affirmative by the black silhouette of the baby who stretches out a tiny hand trying to grab some cash like its woolly-headed mother. Again, the written editorial reassures the public that children of (normal?) mothers will not be outnumbered by welfare children like the one that is pictured.

Later in the article, Goodman asserts the need to teach "middle-class values" to welfare mothers. She proclaims the importance of telling "AFDC mothers" that "No, we won't pay more for more children born onto the welfare rolls." This contention emphasizes the assumption that "AFDC mothers" are morally flawed in a manner that "middle-class" people are not. Again, without offering any proof, this argument about the need to tell them "no, we won't pay," presupposes that these mothers are instinctively concerned with gaining welfare benefits when they have children.

How do we know that they are using pregnancy for cash? Why isn't some proof of this accusation necessary? In the logic used here, since the women are poor, they are also condemned as inherently immoral (without "middle-class values"), which leads one to deduce that by their very natures, they are greedily focused on birthing children to gain welfare money. It is a circular argument that traps poor mothers inside of a degrading stereotype. They can never be seen as innocent mothers struggling to care for their children, since they are believed to be guilty of immorality the moment that they are born poor and black.

The tone of such analysis patronizingly treats these moms like children, who can perhaps be taught to do better. We—the good people, presumably the middle-class people, who are repeatedly juxtaposed to the welfare mothers— can try to teach them better values by saying "no" to them. Stripping "AFDC mothers" of the same human proclivities that "we" have in relation to mothering and morality in the ways noted above, solidifies their inferior status. Therefore, it is taken for granted that the rights and privileges of our superiority to welfare mothers include exerting control over them. We have the right and even the responsibility to tell them how to behave. Who is this we? It is those who have "middle-class values" to teach, those who in no way resemble that black silhouette with the Afro hairstyle and wide nose.

When any of us actively or silently agree to these assumptions about the innate human inferiority of poor black moms who receive welfare benefits, *whose* morality is clearly perverted? How do we who profess Christian faith deliberately inoculate ourselves with a gospel-based definition of innate human worth when we are surrounded by so many persuasive sources that alter that valuation for "welfare mothers"? How do we maintain an unwavering allegiance to the gospel notion of human worth, which never varies according to one's racial grouping, economic status, or any other category we construct in the societies of our human world?

Defining "Welfare"

Racialized messages about moral inferiority are not only conveyed by the concrete images of welfare mothers presented by politicians and the mass media for public consumption. The very term "welfare" has come to be generally understood as a description of a social problem that is primarily located in the black community. Welfare is usually included in a list of antisocial behaviors that certain people choose. These lists are so routinely invoked that, to the casual observer, this newly acquired definition of "welfare" no longer appears odd. For example, in a September 1996 speech, Gayle Wilson, the First Lady of the state of California, gave a speech on teenage pregnancy in which she listed "the attendant pathologies that accompany teen pregnancy," such as "homelessness, welfare, abused and neglected children."[4] In Wilson's analysis, welfare is viewed as a social malady that is comparable to the abuse of children!

These kinds of issues are regularly grouped together as a type of shorthand reference to urban black and Hispanic communities. And, when applied to these communities, there seems to be almost no limits on the pejorative use of the "welfare" label. In New York City, in April 1989, a white woman jogger was viciously beaten and gang-raped in Central Park by a group of black and Hispanic teenage boys. In the aftermath, one local newspaper printed an article castigating the entire community where these youths grew up, using this now almost standard practice of reeling off a list of community pathologies including welfare. *New York Post* columnist Pete Hamill asserted: "these kids... were coming downtown from a world of crack, welfare, guns, knives, indifference and ignorance. They were coming from a land of no fathers."[5] In Hamill's formulation of the social ills that he believes characterize poor black and Hispanic communities, he likens single moms and welfare to drugs and weapons. He does so to show how understandable it is that such "a world" produces such heinous behavior as gang-rape. There is no necessity for this reporter to offer justification for his utterly absurd claim that welfare is a contributing factor leading to certain young men carrying out a gang-rape. The combination of welfare and poor black and Hispanic single moms is simply presumed to nurture sociopathic behavior.

Welfare was also used as a handy target for blame when violence erupted in black and Hispanic communities in Los Angeles in 1992. In California, after jurors acquitted four white police officers of wrongdoing in beating black motorist Rodney King, tremendous civil disorder ensued, which included some loss of life, many physical injuries, and significant property damage. The top leadership of this nation seemed both unaffected by the videotaped brutality of the police beating (fifty-six blows to King were recorded in eighty-one seconds) and immune to the shock of the full acquittal of the officers. President Bush's press secretary, Marlin Fitzwater, and Vice President Dan Quayle assigned blame for the outraged response in Los Angeles which boiled over into tragic disorder in the spring of 1992 to the failure of welfare programs.[6]

As evidenced by these examples, when media and political leadership characterize welfare as a potent harmful force, it is almost always linked to race. In a major speech on Affirmative Action in July 1995, President Clinton decried the fact that too many children "are clearly exposed to poverty and welfare, violence and drugs."[7] President Clinton presents poverty, welfare, violence, and drugs as interlocking, equivalent forms of antisocial behavior. Apparently, we are to conclude that one goes out and applies for welfare just like someone decides to go out and sell drugs or commit violent acts. According to this usage of the term, welfare has evolved away from being a program established and conducted by the government, and, like others, aimed at helping to address the economic needs facing a particular sector of the citizenry. President Clinton probably would never bemoan the fact that children are "exposed to" unemployment compensation or Social Security. Welfare is considered a type of criminal behavior in which poor people choose to engage or which infects them with its deleterious power.

Moreover, why is this point about welfare included in a presidential speech about Affirmative Action? The subject of Affirmative Action has become a euphemistic way of talking about racial minorities. Of course in actuality, Affirmative Action programs redress discrimination against white women as well as people of color. However, the reality that white women have disproportionately been the beneficiaries of Affirmative Action programs seems to be readily ignored. So, too, the fact that whites have represented the majority of recipients of federal welfare benefits, is easily forgotten.[8] Therefore, it seems fitting that President Clinton would place a point about welfare within a speech on Affirmative Action: both topics have now become a means of identifying and discussing the problems of racial minority groups. In everyday parlance, discussions about race are synonymous with discussions about blacks. And public discussions about blacks often consist of discussions about "What's wrong with them? Why don't they try to better themselves?" (for conservatives) or "What can be done about all *their* problems?" (for liberals). These formulations rule out whites as the problem. That is, they rule out an understanding that views whites as the ones who possess the problems that we need to focus upon in order to eliminate racial inequities.

Therefore, as the issue of racial discrimination is most often raised in relation to Affirmative Action, the problem to be solved is more closely identified with racial minority groups than with the whites who perpetuate the discriminatory acts. It becomes even more evident in the context of a speech on Affirmative Action that a discussion of welfare is not only a thinly disguised reference to the subject of racial issues but also a reference to racial/ethnic minority groups. The behavior of whites as a racial grouping is seldom if ever the obvious focus of conversations about "the welfare problem." The invoking of welfare can cover over white actions as perpetrators of police brutality (referred to above) or hide a sizable white presence among recipients of the same programs. No, the term "welfare" is used to isolate black and Hispanic racial groups and particularly to label poor single moms of those groups as tainted with pathology.

To depict welfare as bad behavior tremendously distorts reality. No matter how many times this notion is repeated by newspaper columnists or by the president of the United States, in actuality, "welfare" simply does not refer to any type of antisocial behavior. Welfare benefits are government subsidies, like Medicare or corporate tax deductions. Just as elderly people, regardless of their income, apply for Medicare benefits to pay for their health care needs, people who do not have enough money to feed themselves and their children must go through an elaborate process to qualify for welfare benefits. To insist that poor people are behaving pathologically or criminally when they apply for and receive welfare benefits is to promote a mean-spirited falsehood.

Exposing some of the racial prejudices built into the terminology and framing of welfare policy is only a first, partial step toward undermining some of the vicious and dishonest claims that are made about welfare. The receptivity of American audiences to believe and be politically guided by those prejudices also has to be confronted.

Challenge the Barrier of White Prejudices

The depth of white prejudices, in particular, needs to be acknowledged and "unpacked" for there to be any chance of effectively shifting the moral agenda of welfare policy from attacks on poor moms toward the elimination of the poverty conditions with which these moms must contend. Deeply held, pervasive stereotypes about blacks and Hispanics represent a key obstacle to this shift. Many studies reveal the extent to which whites believe that a desire to be dependent on welfare benefits is an innate character flaw which blacks and Hispanics possess.

A 1991 general social survey conducted by the National Opinion Center at the University of Chicago reflects the salience of white stereotypes about the relationship between welfare and racial minorities. When white respondents in the study were asked to evaluate whites in comparison to blacks on whether each group preferred living on welfare assistance or being self-supporting, over half of the white respondents ranked blacks and Hispanics toward the end of the spectrum indicating a preference for welfare. Of whites surveyed, 78 percent thought blacks were more likely to prefer living on welfare over being self-supporting, and 74 percent thought Hispanics were more likely to prefer living on welfare. In a 1992 Anti-Defamation League national survey of white attitudes toward blacks, 76 percent of those surveyed agreed with one or more antiblack stereotypes.[9] The eight categories that respondents were given included such descriptions as "more prone to violence," "prefer to accept welfare," "having less native intelligence," "less ambitious." Fifty-five percent of whites agreed with two or more of the categories, and 30 percent agreed with four or more.

Such prejudices grant whites permission to be indifferent to the dire survival struggles of poor black single moms who rely on welfare funding. The stereotypes justify the dismissal of the women's full humanity and their right to dignity and respect. When one starts with the presupposition that "these people" desire welfare because they are lazy and dumb, the discussion of welfare policy has been poisoned with pernicious lies before it has even begun.

Negative racial attitudes can powerfully impede white people's ability to think clearly about political and economic policy, including consideration of their own self-interests. Yale political science professor Martin Gilens conducted a study of "race coding" and white opposition to welfare.[10] He found that the racial attitudes of whites are the single most important influence on their welfare views. He discovered a specific correlation between negative views of black welfare mothers and substantial opposition to welfare funding. According to this study, whites' impassioned negative beliefs about black welfare mothers generated greater opposition to welfare spending than comparable views of white welfare mothers. Negative views of blacks in general forcefully shape whites' beliefs about "welfare mothers." One of his most important findings was that white perceptions of blacks as lazy have a larger effect on their welfare policy preferences than does economic self-interest, beliefs about individualism, or views about the poor in general.[11] The judgment of whites about how to construct national policy is fundamentally distorted by their racist views.

Moreover, it is crucial to understand the function of these stereotypes and prejudices by whites in relation to their own white identity. In their study of white racism, sociologists Joe Feagin and Hernàn Vera emphasize the fact that whites do not merely create negative myths about blacks, they also simultaneously invent positive myths about themselves. Remember, prejudice is a prejudgment on insufficient grounds which can either be in favor or opposed to someone or something. As whites make negative assessments of "others," they cling to positive images of themselves. Feagin and Vera explain that white individuals usually see themselves as "not racist," as "good people," even while they think and act in antiblack ways.

Sincere fictions are both about the other (those fictions are usually called "prejudice") and about one's group and oneself.[12] Hence, a reference to single black moms as "those lazy welfare mothers" is not just a slur against the women, it is also an implicit assertion about whiteness. The statement may demonstrate a personal-identity need by a white individual to feel good about her/his own whiteness. Unfortunately, the goodness of whiteness is understood as possible only in converse relationship to the badness of blackness. A statement by a white educator offered in the Feagin and Vera study illustrates the creation of white "fictions." When asked her opinion of programs that compensate black Americans for discrimination, the white respondent changed the subject to the "welfare system," saying:

> There is this welfare system that enables young mothers...who can't support their children anyway. I see that system intact. And a lot of ways [it] encourages poor people to have children, and they don't have to work. And I see public housing, and Headstart...and free daycare, and free services, and free medical.... I guess this is my prejudice; it's toward education: I don't think you need to have money so much, just have some values towards certain types of things, like education or intellect, or something like that. Instead of, you know, just loafing, and watching TV, and getting welfare.... And you know, getting fat, and being angry, and taking your anger out on robbing people, and killing people.[13]

While this woman depicts black mothers as sitting around doing nothing but watching TV and obtaining almost every basic family need for free, she also asserts a self-description. She represents herself as "having values" directed toward education and an intellect. This teacher was asked a question about discrimination against black Americans, and, in response, she launched into a speech about their moral weaknesses and simultaneously pointed out her own moral virtues. She apparently has a need to affirm the value of her white racial identity, which, for her, comprises the same category as moral identity. In other words, in this woman's frame of reference, one's race determines one's morals. She affirms her own moral/racial identity by underscoring its superiority to black, lazy, fat, robbing, killing identity.

Even white women who are recipients of welfare benefits may find some comfort in asserting their inherent superiority to (black) "welfare mothers." The topic of racial dynamics among women welfare recipients once surfaced during a class session that I was teaching. During this session, a white woman student admitted that she had received welfare benefits at an earlier point in her life. She then testified to conversations with other white female welfare recipients in which they characterized most black women who also collect welfare benefits as lazy. Though she was now not at all proud of these sentiments, the student explained that this group of white women felt "Yes, we are on welfare, but at least we are not like the black women." These white poor single mothers found affirmation of their moral value in their whiteness.

Similarly, in a report on poor single mothers, a white female welfare recipient is quoted as conceding that she "probably" benefited from prejudice against (black) "welfare mothers," but sees justifiable reasons in that occurrence. For "Lori," it was "humiliating" and "horrible" just to find herself at the welfare office surrounded by "these people." She says, "I'm a snob and I'm sitting among the homeless filling out these forms."[14] In one comment, she marvels at how "these people" are able to fill out all of the forms, since "I think it takes a high IQ" to figure them out. "Lori" described one incident in which a rule was waived for her that would have barred her from child care benefits. She explained that the social service official was willing to ignore the regulation, most likely because "I was a well-dressed white woman that didn't talk slang and wasn't missing my teeth, and I looked like I was serious—and I said I really need help."[15] Even as she violates regulations so that she may fraudulently receive welfare funds, this woman offers a derogatory caricature of those "other" welfare recipients, whose race, dress, and manner do not merit the same treatment.

The rampant prejudice accounted for in these studies and examples is especially significant for the work of predominantly white faith communities involved in constructing a church-sponsored agenda on welfare policy. Since negative images of blacks are often the single most important driving force shaping white opinions of this government policy, intensive antiracism work has to be an *ongoing*, nonnegotiable aspect of the community's work. Deep issues involving the way that white racial identity needs are encrusted with prejudice have to be confronted forthrightly in white communities across the spectrum of economic groupings. The welfare issue is not only insidiously formulated as a black social problem in our country. It is also specifically culturally loaded with intense biases against blacks, which must be confessed and dismantled before any relevant policy issues can be authentically addressed.

Interrogate the Call to Moral(?) Action by Political Leaders

One of the more confusing aspects of trying to decide what kind of welfare policy is right and good is the constant use of the term "morality." Especially for those who place a high priority on their commitment to practicing a religious faith, just the mention by public officials of the need to promote moral behavior in America commands immediate attention and agreement. Moreover, few political issues have been couched in more references to morality than public discussions of welfare policy. This concept has become a handy political tool for many popular welfare reform advocates. They employ varied and sophisticated strategies to manipulate public audiences. More precisely, elaborate myths about the immorality of poor black mothers are devised by political leaders to create a sense of urgency about the need for action against these women and girls.

Even federal legislation can sound almost like an altar call for people of good conscience to recognize this supposed spreading blight and seek to control it. For example, the 1995 Personal Responsibility Act utilizes statistics to blame poor black single moms for violent crime.[16] These statistics are cited in the section of the act called "Reducing Illegitimacy." This introductory section explains that "it is the sense of the Congress" that the sexual reproduction of single poor women and girls and the related list of "negative consequences" the act offers represent "a crisis in our nation" which this welfare policy seeks to remedy. The legislation specifically asserts that "the greater the incidence of single parent families in a neighborhood, the higher the incidence of violent crime and burglary."[17] In an even more explicit reference targeting black single moms, the act states: "the likelihood that a young black man will engage in criminal activities doubles if he is raised without a father and triples if he lives in a neighborhood with a high concentration of single parent families."[18] Thus, the Congress of the United States promotes the absurd claim that the mere presence of black single moms in high concentrations within a neighborhood causes crime to skyrocket. There is no reasoning given for how these mothers induce high crime rates other than their mere identities and presence as single black mothers. Why is it tolerable for federal policy to be based on such a dehumanizing, prejudiced belief? Why is it so comfortable for our national leaders to single out this one population of American citizens to objectify and insult? In short, where can one find a rationale for federal policy, written into Congressional legislation, that refers to the impact on communities and on the nation of a high concentration of white males in a given vicinity?

Furthermore, creating statistics that link violent crime to single moms is obviously an arbitrary decision. Crime statistics could also be linked with the degree to which people in a neighborhood suffer from hunger, with the quality of schools, or with the quality of housing conditions, for example. Formulating a correlation between single moms and crime serves the particular agenda of stigmatizing and targeting poor black single moms as blameworthy for social ills. The strategy is to further a political agenda through frightening statistics that urgently announce a moral crisis descending upon the whole nation via these poor single moms.

In other types of justifications for welfare reform, poor black single moms are widely caricatured as a group of horribly deficient parents. In this strategy, the cause of "welfare reform" is advanced by convincing the public that poor black single moms are all sadistically abusive parents who produce sociopathic children and that welfare benefits for these families function primarily to perpetuate this cycle. For instance, Newt Gingrich based his call for welfare reform, in part, on the notion that mothers who receive welfare benefits are such awful parents that their children would be better off in orphanages.[19] Gingrich used horrendous examples to represent to the public the welfare problem that he sought to remedy legislatively. Defending his orphanage idea, he explained:

> The little four-year-old who was thrown off the balcony in Chicago would have been a heck of a lot better off in Boys' Town; that 11-year-old who was killed after he killed a 14-year-old might have had a chance.... The children you see in DC killed every weekend might be better off in a group home or a foster home.... We say to a 13-year-old drug addict who's pregnant, you know, "Put your baby in the Dumpster, that's OK." ... Now wouldn't it have been better for that girl, instead of dumping her baby in a Dumpster, to have had a place she could go to and say, "I'm not prepared to raise a child."[20]

The Speaker of the House of Representatives offers appalling images of mothers and children as typical lifestyles of those who receive welfare benefits. Like the instances I noted earlier, this serves as another method of defining "welfare" as intrinsically linked to violent behavior. The public is led to understand that not only do these adolescent monsters try to kill their own children, but the mothering of any and all poor inner-city women and girls who depend on welfare benefits to help their families naturally spawns the killing of youngsters by others in their neighborhoods. Based on these examples, Gingrich argues, "wouldn't it have been better" if his "reform" proposals had been implemented. The political agenda is openly presented as a moral choice: which do you want—homicidal mothers producing homicidal children or welfare reform?

Presidents Ronald Reagan and Bill Clinton offer yet another version of this strategy from the highest level of political leadership in our nation. Instead of listing multiple reprehensible examples as Gingrich did, presidents Reagan and Clinton preferred the tactic of offering one archetypal, distorting image of a poor urban (black?)[21] woman, which they liked to repeat over and over again in their speeches.

President Reagan chose to cite a story about a welfare "chiseler," guilty of illegal and unethical behavior who was prosecuted for her crimes. Reagan invoked "a woman in Chicago" who "has 80 names, 30 addresses, 12 social security cards.... She's got Medicaid, getting food stamps, and is collecting welfare under each of her names. Her tax-free cash income alone is over $150,000."[22] Would as many Americans be persuaded by an argument for legislatively eliminating the presidency on the basis of Richard Nixon's lies and criminality as were swayed by Reagan's "welfare queen" argument? I don't think so.

President Clinton's version of this tactic differs in that he depicts a (black?) "welfare mother" with an attitude of repentance. He shares with his audiences a story of a former welfare recipient who witnesses to reforming herself and "now has a job." President Clinton likes to relate a personal conversation with a former welfare recipient who tells him that she wants the president to set up job-placement programs for people like her. According to this Clinton narrative, the woman says, "If you don't make us do it, we'll just lay up and watch the soaps."[23] She also tells him that what makes her proudest of having a job is that "when my boy goes to school and they ask him what does your mama do for a living, he can have an answer." First, Clinton cleverly achieves his political aims through citing a welfare recipient's *own* admission that she will only abandon her preferred lazy lifestyle if forced to do so by the government. She asserts the need for the government to reform her seemingly natural slovenly tendencies. Second, the woman indicates how her own child previously suffered because of his mother's shamefulness (prior to the government intervention forcing her to do something for a living). In short, she names herself as shameful and innately lazy, albeit through the mouth of the president of the United States, who was attempting "to end welfare as we know it" when he recounted "her" story. In both the Reagan and Clinton strategies, one woman is considered to stand for an entire group.[24] The presupposition is that if we understand this one case, we understand all of "them." The recipients of welfare benefits are easily lumped together under one umbrella of inherently deficient character.

The citizen listening to these arguments is compelled to become a partner in the struggle against the immorality. She or he may be most persuaded by the statistical verification of a spreading crime wave due to the presence of these mothers in neighborhoods, or the threat of homicidal maniacs embodied and incited by the mothers, or a confession and personal plea by one of them to be protected from her own indolent proclivities. Any aspect of this picture of immense depravity spurs one toward immediate action against the population identified as the problem. Unfortunately, these depictions of poor black single moms are at best grossly overstated generalizations of the most negative behavior, which very few have the capacity to carry out. Most importantly, the terms of morality have been appropriated by political leaders who sway the nation by offering large quantities of misleading information and by attaching some of the most vicious stereotypes that can be concocted.

We need to reclaim the idea of morality, demanding that truthfulness become a requisite element built into public presentations of moral issues. However, such a reclaiming process means overcoming the temptation to retreat into cynicism about political leaders, the media, and the possibilities for changed priorities in our local communities. Such cynicism is chiefly upheld by a misguided view that lies that are publicly advanced about certain poor women do not have a direct, negative impact upon one's own selfhood and cannot be overturned by deliberate, joint efforts of those interested in doing so. Such cynicism is truly a threat to our collective moral health.

Question, Embrace Inclusive Community, Protest . . .

Our ability to recognize politically popular falsehoods masquerading as moral claims can be developed by posing thoughtful questions of ourselves. The goal of the questioning is to activate one's conscience for critically evaluating the view of reality that is presented by political leaders in order to provoke and nurture less-distorted, alternative views. This process of moral formation should occur in a collaborative manner that allows both individual and corporate conscience to emerge. For example, we need to learn to challenge the disparaging terms used in discussions of welfare. We might probe the assumptions that underlie the terms we consume through questions like those that follow.

WHAT LABELS, IMAGES, AND STEREOTYPES? What labels, images, stereotypes, terms, jargon, or adjectives describing personal traits or characteristics are applied to those directly involved with welfare policy? List all of the labels that you can think of that are attached to the following person(s) because of their direct connection to welfare policy: (1) welfare recipients, (2) legislators, (3) the president, and (4) members of the press. It might be helpful to close your eyes and picture the persons that belong to each category within the particular setting that most directly connects them to welfare policy, and then freely associate the identifying labels that come to mind.

From what sources did you learn these labels? Which categories were harder to find labels for? Why? What language should be used to describe the traits of each? When should a reference to the morality of the person be invoked? Why? For example, should the morality of a legislator who wants to cut food benefits to poor mothers and children be part of the terminology used to identify him or her publicly? Why or why not?

For each category, how are the labels and images that you have listed related to race? For example, discuss why and how the racial/ethnic background of a president who makes welfare reform a major priority, matters? Even if it is not openly discussed in the newspaper, what difference does the president's race/ethnicity make to the public, to the way he or she shapes the issue, to the president's political effectiveness in achieving "reform"?

For each category, what aspects of your religious faith and practice might be a helpful resource for evaluating the labels that you use and hear others use for persons directly involved in welfare policy? Give specific examples.

WHO IS LABELED, IMAGED, STEREOTYPED? Which racial/ethnic communities and economic groupings are labeled in relation to welfare? List them. Then, make a second list of the racial/ethnic communities and economic groupings that are not labeled in relation to welfare. For both lists, how and why are the family structures and moral values of members of these groups labeled? Which labels are appropriate? Why?

Exactly where do your criteria for making the judgments and assumptions about the morality of persons and families who do not receive welfare benefits come from? Make a detailed list of the sources that help you to form your opinions about this group of people.

What aspects of your religious faith and practice might be helpful in deciding how you should make these judgments?

The Larger Myth-Making Agenda

Discerning which labels we use and which ones we take for granted comprises only a small fraction of the myth-making process that leads to punitive welfare policies against single poor black moms. Nevertheless, the practice of interrogating the morally loaded terms and images constructed about both those considered "welfare" people and those considered to be nonwelfare, "normal" people, should be fostered. Especially when this practice is developed in a group setting such as an open community forum, an adult Sunday-school class, or a youth group, there is a strong potential for cultivating the needed resistance to the brutal policies.

Alongside of this effort of insistently posing questions, we must also work to transform divisive definitions of community. We need to put on "eyeglasses of faith" that evoke in us a commitment to building a just and inclusive community ethos. This must be a commitment that, as Christian ethicist Larry Rasmussen describes, "sets in motion those dynamics that draw us into webs of association that bind us together, sensitize us to needs beyond our own, and call forth active response to and with others."[25] In order to participate in this kind of embracing, engaging mode of relating to one another, we must openly confront the alienating, rigid barriers of racism and vast socioeconomic disparities that exist between us. Ultimately, in stepping fully into this kind of commitment, we come to recognize any assault on poor single black moms as constituting an assault on *our* community.

To achieve this, there is a need to continually resist popular notions like "*We* have to teach *them* values so *they* don't continue to receive so many of *our* tax dollars." We are bombarded with ideas like this one which discourage acknowledgment of the breadth of claims made on communal resources by the nonpoor. Feminist legal theorist Martha Fineman explains that "the public nature of perceived inadequacies of single mothers justifies their regulation, supervision and control. Private families, by contrast, are protected."[26] Middle-class families have access to government entitlement programs such as FHA or VA loans at below-market mortgage rates. Since these families live up to "normal" social expectations, they are considered to have earned the right of privacy from state supervision and control which "deviant" families are subject to.[27] All families with children who file federal income tax returns receive government financial assistance. A tax credit deduction is given by the government to these families simply because they have children they claim as dependents.[28] A poor woman applying for welfare benefits should be as entitled to tax moneys as those mothers of any economic background who file for tax-deduction benefits.

Out of this appreciation for how a variety of moms financially benefits from our shared base of community resources, we come to realize that "welfare mothers" exist to the same extent that "tax-deduction mothers" do. Making this acknowledgment might be a starting point for dialogue among mothers across socioeconomic barriers and might create possibilities for building coalitions. Mothers might unite actively against the way that entitlement to community resources has been rescinded for certain moms in the enactment of welfare reform legislation. This kind of dialogue could plant the seeds for solidarity and advocacy of radical change to increase economically just and respectful treatment of poor moms as well as nonpoor ones.

In predominantly black communities, racial and economic forces combine to create special pressures to view the interests of poor single black moms who collect welfare benefits as distant from or opposed to those of members of the community who do not rely upon those resources. Paying attention to divisive community dynamics prompted by economic disparities, Christian ethicist Cheryl Sanders calls for a remoralization process in African American communities that is centrally sponsored by black churches. Among other key issues that will demand response in this remoralization, Sanders identifies the following dilemma: "if the tendency of those with wealth is to distance themselves from poor neighborhoods, churches, and people, how does one teach, preach, and promote reconciliation in between the affluent and the poor within the African American community?"[29]

For blacks, the particularly potent nature of white racism against those who receive welfare can intensify antagonism toward the poor by those in middle- and upper-class income brackets. Pursuit of the illusive goal of white acceptance, which one needs in order to be considered successful in this country, provides incentive for blacks to disassociate themselves from those "tainted" poor single moms.

Black community antagonism against the poor rooted in class biases can also join with peculiarly gendered dynamics, in which black single moms are blamed for the troubles that poor black males face. In particular, the emphasis on black males as an "endangered species" in the media and by several black community leaders has led to theories blaming the deficiencies of single black moms in the raising of their sons for this crisis.[30] For African Americans, internal depictions of "our" community must not echo popular views of these moms as the problem population. Unfortunately, whether through programs that paternalistically try to "fix" the welfare recipient or by sponsoring economic development plans with the stated aim "to rid our community of welfare dependency," black churches can also perpetuate the falsehood that black moms have committed some shameful wrong in using government benefits to help support their families.

An authentically inclusive community ethos is one in which poor single black moms hold leadership and shape policy discussions about day care, education, welfare benefits and other aspects of communal life. Because of the formidable amount of hard work demanded of them as they struggle to take care of their families, most of these women have developed keen skills in navigating bureaucratic social agencies and have demonstrated courageous perseverance against scornful public opinion and vicious attacks by political leaders. Poor black single mothers have something to teach us all.[31] Community practices that honor, celebrate, and build on the costly lessons of that experience are imperative.

Finally, we must raise our voices in protest. In 1995, Nicholas Politan, a federal judge in New Jersey, cleared the way for New Jersey's law denying benefits for children born after a mom initially applies for benefits (a precursor for like provisions in the 1996 federal law). He explained how his ruling was consistent with what "the nation is crying out for."[32] We must make our unqualified dissent with the punishment and stigmatizing of black single moms heard by speaking up in our informal conversations with friends or strangers, as well as in the formal religious or civic public gatherings we attend. We must raise our voices in protest using any internet sources, print, radio, or television media to which we have access. Inflicting further suffering on moms and children in our communities who have the least resources is not what everyone in this "nation is crying out for." Is it?

Notes

1. I would like to express my appreciation to Jody Caldwell, Kyung-in Kim, and Pauline Wardell-Sankoh for their research assistance and to Jerry Watts, who served as an invaluable dialogue partner on this project.

2. In analyzing the "war on welfare" that has emerged since the 1970s, Nancy Ellen Rose notes the deliberate decision by Clinton-administration advisers to choose to focus on eliminating welfare dependency rather than poverty as the administration's main objective. This decision was made by David Ellwood and the White House Working Group early in the process of devising the Clinton approach to welfare policy (*Workfare or Fair Work? Women, Welfare and Government Work Programs* [New Brunswick, N.J.: Rutgers University Press, 1995], 172).

3. Ellen Goodman, "Welfare Mothers with an Attitude," illus. Barrie Maguire, *Boston Globe,* April 16, 1992, 19.

4. Gayle Wilson, "Looking at the Nineties through the Eyes of the Fifties," speech given at Radisson Hotel, Sacramento, Calif., May 29, 1996, sponsored by the Comstock Club, Sacramento, Calif.

5. Pete Hamill, "A Savage Disease Called New York," *New York Post,* April 23, 1989, 4.

6. Michael Wines, "White House Links Riots to Welfare," *New York Times,* May 5, 1992, A1, A26; Seth Sutel, "Quayle: Welfare to Blame," *Boston Globe,* May 14, 1992, 13.

7. "Remarks of President Bill Clinton Regarding Affirmative Action," White House briefing, Washington, D.C., July 19, 1995, [database online] *Dialog File 660: Federal News Service,* Washington, D.C.

8. U.S. House of Representatives, *Background Material and Data on Programs within the Jurisdiction of the Committee on Ways and Means* (Washington, D.C.: U.S. Government Printing Office, 1994).

9. Anti-Defamation League, *Highlights from an Anti-Defamation League Survey on Racial Attitudes in America* (New York: Anti-Defamation League, 1993).

10. Martin Gilens, "'Race Coding' and White Opposition to Welfare," *American Political Science Review* 90, no. 3 (Sept. 1996): 593–604.

11. Ibid., 593. See also Martin Gilens, "Racial Attitudes and Opposition to Welfare," *Journal of Politics* 57 (Nov. 1995): 994–1014.

12. Joe R. Feagin and Hernàn Vera, *White Racism: The Basics* (New York: Routledge, 1995), 135.

13. Ibid., 151.

14. Valerie Polakow, *Lives on the Edge: Single Mothers and Their Children in the Other America* (Chicago: University of Chicago Press, 1993), 82.

15. Ibid., 83.

16. *Personal Responsibility Act of 1995*, 104th Congress, 1st Session, H.R. 4.

17. Title I, Sec. 100, Para. 3(P).

18. Title I, Sec. 100, Para. 3(O).

19. This suggestion does not represent a new public policy idea. In devising welfare policy in the 1960s, the morality of welfare recipients was a focal issue. A 1967 Senate Finance Committee report noted that "some children now receiving AFDC would be better off in foster care homes or institutions than they are in their own homes. This situation arises because of poor home environment for child upbringing in homes with low standards, including multiple instances of births out of wedlock" (*Senate Report No. 744, 90th Cong., 1st sess., [1967]*, quoted in Lucy A. Williams, "Race, Rat Bites and Unfit Mothers: How Media Discourse Informs Welfare Legislation Debate," *Fordham Urban Law Journal* 22, no. 4 [summer 1995]: 1159–96, 1180).

20. *Meet the Press*, NBC, December 4, 1994.

21. I have already noted above the way in which language about welfare is racially coded so that a Gingrich, Reagan, or Clinton example of a welfare recipient's immorality is popularly understood as a reference to African Americans. The politicians and the public mutually reinforce this prejudiced perception.

22. "'Welfare Queen' Becomes Issue in Reagan Campaign," *New York Times*, February 15, 1976, 51.

23. Remarks by President Bill Clinton at the National Legislative Association of Counties Legislative Conference, Washington, D.C., March 7, 1995 [database online], *Dialog File 660: Federal News Service*, Washington, D.C.

24. The use of the Ventura case in Massachusetts by the governor represents another example of how one story about one family comes to stand for all persons receiving welfare benefits, and most importantly comes to directly influence policy. Governor William Weld (R-Mass.) sent copies of a newspaper story to legislators during debate about welfare reform. The story was about a Hispanic mother of five who was accused of abusing her four-year-old son by putting his hands in boiling water and then leaving him for days without medical treatment (Don Aucoin and Scot Lehigh, "Weld Using Story on Welfare Reform to Aid His Case on Need for Welfare Reform," *Boston Globe*, February 25, 1994, 14). With the use of this story by Weld and other legislators, a two-year time limit was placed on the receipt of welfare benefits for persons over the age of eighteen, by a vote of twenty-five to one in the Mass-

achusetts Senate. For a detailed study of this example and how media informs welfare policy, see Williams, "Race, Rat Bites and Unfit Mothers."

25. Larry Rasmussen, *Moral Fragments and Moral Community: A Proposal for Church in Society* (Minneapolis: Fortress, 1993), 105.

26. Martha Albertson Fineman, *The Neutered Mother, The Sexual Family and Other Twentieth Century Tragedies* (New York: Routledge, 1995), 190–91. For a historical discussion of how issues of motherhood and race have been translated in welfare policy, see Jill Quadagno, *The Color of Welfare: How Racism Undermined the War on Poverty* (New York: Oxford University Press, 1994), esp. chap. 5, "The Politics of Motherhood."

27. Fineman, *Neutered Mother,* 191.

28. This analogy was offered by Lucy A. Williams in her opinion editorial "Welfare: Save a Dollar, Lose a Child," *Boston Globe,* May 12, 1994, 15.

29. Cheryl J. Sanders, *Empowerment Ethics For a Liberated People: A Path to African American Social Transformation* (Minneapolis: Fortress, 1995), 108.

30. Afrocentric psychiatrist Frances Cress Welsing exemplifies this trend in *The Isis Papers: The Keys to the Colors* (Chicago: Third World Press, 1991). As she describes in a vehemently homophobic argument about the feminizing of black males, "[A]s Black females are left to rear Black male children alone, the alienation, hate and disgust felt towards adult males are visited upon their sons subtly" (88). Welsing works with black mothers of black male children so that they will learn to raise strong men and stop "making babies of their sons and husbands" (92). For a refutation of multiple racist/sexist arguments that are used to scapegoat black women, see bell hooks, *Killing Rage: Ending Racism* (New York: Henry Holt, 1995), esp. 77–85.

31. This idea is developed more extensively in Barbara Omolade, *The Rising Song of African American Women* (New York: Routledge, 1994), esp. 67–78.

32. Robert Rudolph, "Aid Limits Upheld for Moms in New Jersey Welfare Program," *Star-Ledger* (Newark), May 5, 1995, 1.

PART THREE

ANALYSIS OF RESPONSES OF CHURCHES AND ACTIVISTS

[8]

Welfare as a Family Value

Conflicting Notions of Family in Protestant Welfare Responses

Elizabeth M. Bounds

FROM THE EARLIEST POORHOUSE ARRANGEMENTS, welfare provisions in this country have been about everything *except* enabling poor people to have access to adequate work, food, clothing, and shelter. As Joel Handler, a welfare policy scholar and advocate, explains, "Welfare policy...is not addressed to the poor—it is addressed to us. It is an affirmation of majoritarian values through the creation of deviants."[1] The recent welfare debates have amply proved Handler's point: few of the dominant voices paid any attention to one of the most fundamental requirements of poor women and men, access to a decent job at a living wage. Instead, the promised "end to welfare as we have known it" was conducted as an intense moral crusade.

Yet, although these debates have played out some old themes, there have been new emphases and intensities. The most potent image has been of black teenage nonmarried mothers who have moved from being Reagan's "welfare queens" to being dehumanized in Congressional debates as "crocodiles" or "wolves" who bring up children "unfit for the company of cats."[2] The notion of unfit mothers had always been present in welfare policy, since one of the most important "majoritarian values" it has reinforced from its inception has been the white bourgeois family. However, the symbolic force of these images takes on a new intensity. The behavior of these paradigmatic women has been credited as the source of the dissolution of the family, the work ethic, and the moral heritage of the Founding Fathers. And the solutions demand a cleansing punitive morality, necessary, it is claimed, for our national survival.

Such intensity, I would like to suggest, is a response to shifts in social and economic structures in ways that have undermined the consensus underlying the welfare state. Globalization has made it impossible for the national welfare state to provide the employment and the protections that were part of the consensus over its formation and legitimation.[3] The loss of consensus over the welfare state opens up a possibility for positive change, since the welfare state institutionalized many forms of gender and racial domination. However, as the recent welfare debates have demonstrated, it also has enabled the loss of an assumed minimal provision and protection of the poorest members of our society. In this chapter, I will suggest some of the ways these tensions have focused on a key institution: the family.

I have chosen this particular focus because during the welfare debates I was struck by the relative silence and invisibility of the old-line liberal Protestantism which is my context. In contrast to the hypervisibility of conservative Protestants, liberal Protestants seemed to be sidelined and shy. While this contrast is partially due to the declining public role and overall numbers of the liberal Protestant denominations,[4] I would also argue that conservative Protestants were able to best articulate the meld of race, gender, and economic anxieties that come together in the evocative appeal to the "family."

From their inception, welfare policies were constructed to support particular notions of work linked to the model of the white bourgeois family, while stigmatizing different family forms. However, changes in the relationship of the public and private spheres, in the economy, in racial formations, in women's roles, have all created insurmountable difficulties for continuing to maintain the white bourgeois family as the model of the "proper" family against which all families could be morally evaluated. The conservative emphasis on the family reasserts the security of the bourgeois family form, which they claim can be reconstituted simply through "personal moral responsibility." This turn to morality allows the illusion of control and the possibility of blaming "others," while masking the economic forces at work.

To explain this hypothesis, I first will describe the ways in which the main welfare program, Aid to Families with Dependent Children (AFDC), was established on the basis of certain assumptions about women, families, and citizenship. Then I will discuss how changing social and economic circumstances have dissolved such legitimation, leading to the current attacks on welfare as undermining, rather than strengthening, bourgeois family forms.

Such analyses will enable me to consider the particular problems facing Protestant Christian churches as they engage in the welfare debates. Following the political right, the conservative Protestant campaign for welfare reform has come to attack welfare policy as government interference that has endangered the bourgeois family. By contrast, the less audible liberal Protestant public voices have deemphasized the family questions and focused on social and governmental responsibility to the poor. While I find this an important corrective to conservative views, my analysis will suggest that the liberal churches need to engage questions of the family and its role as part of their concern to support positive welfare reform.

Christian churches in this country invested and continue to invest heavily in the bourgeois family form, which was vital to the Protestant ethic. Nineteenth-century Christian teaching often stressed the important interrelation of family/religion/nation: as one Protestant wrote in 1858, a disordered home "brutalizes human nature, dishonors God, subverts the principles of constitutional society...and overthrows both church and state."[5] The "family pew" continues to symbolize for Protestants "the dream of a loving, happy, churchgoing family as the hope of a Christian nation,"[6] an ideal implicit in the life of most liberal Protestant congregations and explicit in most conservative Protestant churches.

The welfare state emerged from a period in the late nineteenth and early twentieth centuries in which responsibility for provision for the poor was transferred from religious social reformers operating on the basis of charity, purity, and moral reform to the state, where some of these shaping motives remained but were transformed into state bureaucratic apparatuses. These transfers to the state, although marking the diminishing public status of religion, also encoded some of the basic Protestant values of family and charity as part of the state welfare framework. Part of the renegotiation of the welfare consensus is thus linked to recognition of the eroding cultural authority of the Protestant ethic, which necessarily requires Christian communities to renegotiate aspects of their identity.

From Virtuous Widows to Welfare Queens

To understand the ways in which models of the family undergird the current welfare arguments, it is important to look back at two key developments in nineteenth- and twentieth-century American history. The first is the emergence of citizenship on the basis of a society divided between public and private spheres. The public sphere, the arena of citizenship, was a place of "free" men, unencumbered of the dependency that would endanger the autonomous use of reason in decision making. The private sphere, the world of the family, was, by contrast, a "world of particularity, natural subjection, ties of blood, emotion, love and sexual passion"—the world of women and of motherhood.[7] Women whose economic or sexual activities did not conform to this world were morally stigmatized as "bad" women and/or "unfit" mothers. And men whose economic and sexual activities did not conform to the corresponding public world of autonomous, independent men were feminized—and thus stigmatized—as dependent and inferior. Thus, the two spheres not only determined social gender roles but structured two forms of citizenship. Although both were understood as essential to national strength and survival, one form included formal access to the civil and political rights of citizenship while the other was a female citizenship-as-dependence.

The family wage system, the second key development and an underlying assumption of all welfare provision, emerged from these divisions. The independence deemed necessary for citizenship required a reconceptualization of wage labor from a mark of dependency (on the employer) to independence. Through working-class struggle, economic independence became defined as the ability to receive the family wage, which would maintain not only the male worker but a household of dependent women and children.[8] Middle-class Protestant women reformers joined the working class in seeking protective legislation for women and a family wage for men, which appeared to bring economic structures in line with domestic ideology. Men would be able to be the sole family breadwinners, freeing women to be the angels of the home, or, in other words, providing essential unpaid reproductive and moral tasks such as childrearing and household maintenance while dependent upon male income. This combination represented the "American way," the embodiment of the Protestant ethic, and it demonstrates the way in which this ethic was gendered. Since, however, wages for many men were never "family"-sized and since many women had no men to support them, this domestic model was never available for a large part of U.S. society, allowing it to serve as a punitive badge of race and class status, demonstrating the way the Protestant ethic was *race*d and *class*ed.

The symbolic family wage and its accompanying domestic ideology were crucial in the initial formation of the U.S. welfare system. The welfare consensus assumed a model of work which entailed a family wage and a bourgeois family form. As feminist historian Linda Gordon has put it, "assumptions that . . . women would marry, remain domestic, and be supported by their husbands imbued virtually all...welfare programs."[9] From the earliest poorhouse provisions, the fear has been that too-generous welfare provision would undermine the work ethic necessary for male citizenship and participation in U.S. society (which included responsibility for dependent women and children). Even when changing attitudes suggested that dependent mothers and children should be helped by the state, it was understood that such help must strengthen, not undermine, "proper" families supported by their male breadwinners. In the 1920s and 1930s, the mostly Protestant middle-class white women behind the Aid to Dependent Children (the predecessor of today's AFDC) understood themselves as helping "deviant" immigrant families achieve, or at least not threaten, the family model and family wage. They argued that this type of welfare provision by the state would not provide incentives for immoral single motherhood and that these dependent women ought to be able to stay at home to fulfill their domestic role.

This vision of dependent mothers shaped by white, middle-class ideology lies behind our two-tier welfare system, in which one track has enabled those categorized as independent male breadwinner-husbands to claim entitlements based on rights, while the other track has permitted those categorized as dependent female mother-wives to experience state intervention to help their needs only if the breadwinner is unavailable. The ideology of this system, promoted by the New Deal government, continues to enable many Americans to view Social Security payments as "entitlements," which are "deserved," while welfare is a charitable handout, even though both systems draw from a common tax fund.[10]

From its inception, the privatized family model assumed by the welfare system created contradictions for its intended recipients. The professional arguments against mothers' employment, although aimed "to win support for mother's aid," resulted in the "stigmatization of mothers who worked," who seemed "less deserving of support," which reinforced prejudice against poor and nonwhite women whose circumstances forced them to do waged work.[11] As Gordon sums it up, "Already victimized by the failure of the family wage system, the charity of public assistance system added to [single mothers'] disadvantages—such as low wages and responsibility for children—by emphasizing domesticity as their only maternal virtue."[12] Single mothers were doubly stigmatized since they were both dependent (that is, poor) and *improperly* dependent, since their dependency could not be relieved "naturally" through the family system but required action by society or the state. This deviant dependency became linked with ideas of laziness, greed, and female sexual immorality, carried out by "morals testing" to determine if the single mother was able to provide a "suitable home."[13]

Tension around the notion of the virtuous welfare mother became even more evident as more women from families outside the white bourgeois world entered into the welfare system. For the first decades of ADC, African American women basically had no access to these programs, since part of the political compromise that enabled the Social Security Act was a virtual exclusion of the southern black work force.[14] States were permitted to use "suitable home" or "man-in-the-house" rules, which were generally enforced against African American women.[15] With the postwar migrations from the rural South to the urban North and the civil rights legislation of the 1960s, greater numbers of African American women were admitted to the welfare rolls. In 1931, 96 percent of ADC families were white and 3 percent African American; by 1975, 40 percent of AFDC recipients were white, 44 percent African American, and 12 percent Hispanic.[16] Differing African American and Hispanic American family structures, with greater reliance on extended family for child raising and an extended work history for women, were at odds with the family model assumed in AFDC policy. The model of the dependent mother was also challenged by welfare activism in the 1960s, chiefly through the National Welfare Rights Organization, which made the new suggestion that welfare provision, rather than charity, might be an entitlement or a right, claimed on the basis of the family nurture provided by women. Simultaneously with entrance of these new populations and new claims, came a series of five changes that have affected U.S. families profoundly.

First, women (especially married women) were an increasing presence in the work force, which was now publicly acknowledged. In 1950, three-fifths of U.S. households had a male breadwinner and female homemaker; by 1990 more than three-fifths of all married women with dependent children were no longer homemakers but fellow breadwinners.[17]

Second, the number of single-parent households began to rise, due to both divorce and reduced rates of marriage. Rising rates of divorce resulted in a 37 percent increase in the number of woman-headed white families between 1960 and 1970, and a 40-percent increase between 1970 and 1980. Declining opportunities for black male employment meant an increase of 37 percent and 35 percent, respectively, in black female single-headed households during those same two decades.[18]

Third, "male" high-wage blue-collar jobs began to be replaced by "female" low-wage service-sector jobs (a shift most devastating to African American workers). The availability of high-wage blue-collar jobs and semi–white-collar jobs, generally held by white men, began to decline and to be replaced by low-skilled service jobs, more likely to be held by white women and minority persons.[19]

Fourth, due to shifts in birth rates and immigration patterns, the percentage of the white population began to decline while that of blacks, Asians, and Hispanics began to rise. In this decade, the non-Hispanic white population decreased by 3.0 percent while the black population rose by 0.3 percent, the Asian by 0.8 percent, and the Hispanic population by 2.0 percent.[20] While these numbers may seem small within the given number of years, this is a steady trend and has already been exaggerated by persons who fear these changes.

Fifth, shifts in economic production and distribution have meant that the share of income going to the top one-fifth of the U.S. population rose by 13 percent between 1979 and 1996, while the share going to the bottom one-fifth fell by 22 percent. The result contributes to what economist Richard Freeman has termed the "apartheid economy," where there are increasing geographic divisions between the haves and have-nots.[21]

These changes, wrapped up in the complex phenomenon of globalization, leave us, in Anthony Giddens's phrase, living lives in contexts of "manufactured uncertainty," affected at all levels by a variety of global forces. David Harvey speaks of the increased flexibility of capitalism, which can rapidly put new technologies into use and which can move capital increasingly rapidly around the globe. These changes have privileged certain groups whose technological expertise is required and enabled the displacement of other groups whose work is expendable. They have also required the increasing use of female labor throughout the globe.[22] The presence of women in the work force and the connected shifts in family forms have made the notion of a stable heterosexual two-parent unit supported by the man and nurtured by the woman at home increasingly difficult to maintain and justify. The traditional forms of family are being restructured in the face of reshaped relations and social contexts. No longer are marriage and family assumed but, for vast numbers of our population, are decisions or choices. As a recent study of religion and family has put it, cultural and economic structures have been "pushing families toward a democratization of intimacy, work, value formation, and parenting."[23] Thus, it is harder to preserve the assumption of a certain form of family, the white two-parent heterosexual isolated unit, as "natural." Direct ideological work is required to mobilize emotional allegiance to a form contradictory to economic and social structures. Appeals to family values help people negotiate a postindustrial economy that demands a flexible work force by maintaining belief in the protection of the family as a haven in what has become an even more heartless world.[24] This belief must be supported through moralizing divisions that divide the good insiders from the bad outsiders. As has historically been the case, the "deviancy" of the poor is the fault line of this divide, a deviancy loaded with race and gender connections.

These demographic, economic, and social changes have shifted the terrain for the welfare conversation. Kathy Rudy suggests that from the 1950s, "anxiety over the loss of separate spheres and the integration of sexes and races was articulated in the celebration of whiteness and traditional domestic feminism...staving off the claims of those who had been excluded."[25] Starting in the late 1960s, new arguments against welfare have emerged which preserve traditional concepts of poverty as a moral failing but now cast state welfare provision as the destroyer of the bourgeois family. As welfare analyst Lucy Williams puts it, there has been "a powerful coincidence of two events: the growth of the Right's attack on welfare, and the arrival of African Americans and other people of color on the welfare roles,"[26] a coincidence, I have argued, embedded in the sharp economic and social changes in capitalism over the last decades.

Welfare policy has become located in the midst of a series of contradictions. The demand for low-cost labor creates pressures to push persons, including mothers of young children, into the kinds of unskilled menial jobs that are the bulk of those provided by workfare. Middle-class fears about the stability of their own work and economic situation in this world of "manufactured uncertainty" reduce notions of charity and reinforce the always available sense that welfare is a handout to the shiftless and lazy funded by the hard working and respectable. Yet, over against these forces pressing for increased welfare-to-(any)work programs, which necessarily separate women from their children, are claims for family values that promote the traditional presence of women at home. While the ideological world of early ADC policy stigmatized women for going to work and not being "good mothers," the current ideological climate around welfare reform doubly stigmatizes them for not being good mothers (the common attack on poor women) *and* for being lazy—that is, not good workers (an attack traditionally made on poor men). The legitimation or compromise underlying both the power of the Protestant ethic and the legitimacy of the welfare system is being pulled apart.

Family Values or Poor People?

These current contradictions have been visible in Protestant participation in the welfare debates. The historical, theological, institutional connections between Christianity and the care of the poor bring churches into the welfare debates. Yet their perspectives on provision for the poor are also marked by their investment in traditional family forms, their role as nongovernmental providers, and (in the case of the Christian right and the mainline Protestant churches) a dominantly Euro-American culture. The two examples discussed here, statements by the Family Research Council (FRC) and the Evangelical

Lutheran Church in America (ELCA), negotiate the contradictions and interests in quite different ways. The FRC, a voice on the religious right, supports
conservative economic and family forms but must mediate between promoting what the economy demands and the FRC's family ideology. The ELCA,
one of the historically mainline liberal Protestant denominations, raises some
questions about the economy but tends not to talk about family at all. It raises,
rather, a different set of problems as it cannot speak to the lived tensions of the
experiences of many of its middle-class and working-class members or, possibly, challenge some of their assumptions concerning the nature of the family.

Let me turn first to the family-values campaigns of the Family Research
Council, which was formed in the early 1980s to represent the conservative
Christian perspective on Capitol Hill. While it is a division of the evangelical
Focus on the Family (run by James Dobson), its lobbying and research work is
done in the language of national politics, without explicit theological or religious references.[27] Thus, it provides a particularly good perspective on the social and moral views underlying conservative Christian approaches to welfare,
which was a central focus of the FRC's work during the welfare reform debates.

For the FRC, welfare is a subset of its primary concern, the current "crisis"
of the family. Reading through their literature,[28] the family crisis appears to
be, at bottom, a crisis of morality. What is at stake is the central value of U.S.
society—freedom. This is not a freedom of pluralized values and self-fulfill-
ment, but a freedom based on personal responsibility and self-restraint. It is, in
fact, the freedom of the Protestant ethic, where self-denial leads to both prosperity and virtuous behavior and counters the innate human tendency towards
pleasure ("the individual preference for pleasure over pain, privilege over
duty").[29] In order to uphold the Protestant ethic, the FRC supports a free-
market (rather than a globalized) version of the capitalist economy, in which
the freedom of the market promotes prosperity and morality, guaranteed by a
bourgeois family structure.

The welfare crisis, in the eyes of the FRC, arises from two related social
problems. One is the loss of what FRC calls the "natural married-couple family" through divorce, single parenthood, and "disappearing fathers."[30] The
FRC is somewhat cautious about explicitly stating the gendered nature of this
natural family, putting a heavier emphasis on common parental responsibilities. Yet it is clear that the "natural" behavior of young men is toward "irresponsible sexual behavior" unless "socialized into responsible adult behavior"
and "self-restraint," while the "natural" behavior of young women seems
headed toward marriage unless prevented by the "unnatural" intervention of
the government welfare check.[31]

This sexual ethic is evidently (if only implicitly) class- and race-biased. Jennifer E. Marshall, the welfare policy expert for FRC, writes of the dangerous

weakening of a universal reliance on "bourgeois virtues," including the virtue of the family form. While she insists these virtues are "available to all, regardless of race and class," she invokes Mary Ellen Richmond, a social worker who argued that "The way to integrate the deviant into society... is to educate and indeed direct them toward the shared values of the mainstream culture."[32] It is significant that in the 1920s Richmond opposed the original plans for "mother's aid" because she feared that such aid would promote family forms deviating from the Anglo-Saxon bourgeois norm.

The family is understood as the place for moral education, an education that can only be provided by the "natural" pair of married heterosexual parents operating as a self-sufficient unit. As Ralph Reed, the former head of the Christian Coalition, puts it, "The intact family is the most effective department of health, education, and welfare ever conceived." There is no mention, of course, of who has traditionally done most of the healing, educating, and caring. In the FRC's words, "The role of the traditional two-parent family is essential in sustaining the institutions of a free society precisely because it is the vehicle by which values are transmitted from generation to generation."[33] Since we now live in a "culture that values sexual liberty over the marital bond,"[34] these values cannot be transmitted, which jeopardizes American (Christian) civilization.

The second social problem that the FRC recognizes as leading to the welfare crisis is the damaging relationship of government and family, particularly through the welfare system. The council argues that the government undermines the institution of the family through bureaucracy and regulation. It opposes government intervention on a range of moral issues; for example, advocacy of parental rights over compulsory government-provided education, particularly provision of sex education. In the FRC's model, government stands over against institutions of family and community, politics over against morality. It is silent, however, on certain forms of government provision, such as Social Security, which evidently pose no moral problems.

The FRC's understanding of the two problems affecting formation of poor families shapes its two-fronted attack on welfare, one prong focusing on family structure, the other on the overall communal context. The most prominent argument is that government welfare provision promotes what the FRC calls "a culture of illegitimacy" within family life. Illegitimacy used to be controlled by "natural economic consequences," however the provision of government benefits regardless of marital status of recipients "subsidizes illegitimacy." The current welfare system encourages family disintegration and discourages personal responsibility by guaranteeing a right to cash benefits regardless of behavior and "perpetuate[s] a welfare system that makes it harder for men and women to pursue virtuous living."[35]

The attack on illegitimacy highlights the gendered nature of the FRC's moral analysis. The moral disorder caused by welfare lies in the way it removes the limits on naturally unrestrained male sexuality and misdirects the natural or appropriate dependency of women. Without constraint, men's sexuality can never be responsible: "If society does not stress the importance of marriage, what father will not have his pleasure now and avoid the pain and pressure that lie between him and rewards he only dimly grasps?"[36] Indeed, "If not socialized into responsible adult behavior and, as it turns out, into responsible sexual behavior, young men are dangerous."[37] This last comment not only genders but races morality, since it is linked to a quote from James Q. Wilson about the ways the "underclass" (generally a reference to urban African American teenage men) reproduces itself. For men, there must be the "deferred gratification" of the Protestant ethic, which socializes them not only into family responsibilities but also into work.

"Women on welfare," on the other hand, "should have equal opportunity to follow the playbook that for centuries has been surest guarantor of human happiness," "the traditional anti-poverty program called 'marriage.'"[38] What is wrong with young women on welfare is not so much that they are sexual or even that they are mothers, but that they are *improper* mothers—that is, their motherhood is not carried out within a bourgeois family structure, including, in particular, economic dependence upon men. The model of motherhood is the same white bourgeois model underlying the original formation of ADC, which condemns women for work or sexuality carried out apart from male economic control. The policy focus of FRC is not, however, to limit welfare payments to "good" women who are not to blame for their manless condition, but to reduce or eliminate benefits through family caps, reducing pregnancies, and promoting reliance on men. Women are not exempt from work since the FRC has supported workfare provisions for "older mothers," along with men.

The FRC's second argument against welfare is an expansion of the problem of the culture of illegitimacy. Welfare provisions not only distort the primary institution of the family but affect individual autonomy and the communal nature of the social order. The welfare system makes it impossible to raise free people, because it interferes in the "natural" family form and the "natural economic consequences" of moral behavior by "suppress[ing] a sense of personal responsibility" and creating a "culture of dependency" that deprives individuals of freedom and the personal moral responsibility necessary for economic responsibility.[39] Government provision is "tribute" money which creates alienated relationships through bureaucracies that have "eroded community cooperation and displaced the 'one-on-one practice of compassion.'"[40] Further, liberal government policy is "political salvationism," which has preempted "traditional morals" in communities.[41] Private charity enables relationships "as fellow human beings" and forms part of the community which fosters good families and "right habits of the heart."[42] The FRC says transformation of welfare will restore individual freedom and vitality of community, restoring functions of community and church.

For the FRC, there is a linked set of equivalencies which form their moral framework. Throughout its work, it emphasizes the central role of "family, virtue, and freedom," which can be seen as "natural" = "moral" = "freedom." A biologically based bourgeois family, a conservative morality of responsibility, and an economy of free-market capitalism all come to seem "natural" in contrast to the "unnatural" formation of the liberal welfare state. This natural/unnatural division is also written as a moral/political division so that any historical and social reconstruction becomes impossible. Appeals are made to nature and common sense, neither of which needs to be questioned: "The family we seek to rebuild must be the one that nature and commonsense tell us is best for children: a father and mother, joined in marriage, striving to the best of their ability, with the reinforcement of tradition and public policy, to remain together for life."[43]

The welfare problem is not a problem of poverty but a problem of morality. The history of the welfare state as an effort to patch up some of the side effects of capitalism is occluded, as is any understanding of the current forms of mobile global capital which undermine the strong national community the FRC celebrates.

The FRC's proposals allow it to be both cheap and moral: cheap because it supports the deep cuts in welfare and the overall use of workfare; moral because it argues for combining these cuts with targeted restrictions, such as family caps, that would punish nonmarital sexual behavior and "renew the ethic of individual responsibility and personal compassion that will restore moral authority to the Founders' notion of liberty."[44] The council's proposals also allow for the support of capitalism by limiting the cost of the unemployed, while still endorsing the bourgeois family form.

In "Working Principles for Welfare Reform," affirmed in March 1994 by the Board of the Division for Church in Society of the Evangelical Lutheran Church in America,[45] there is a quite different placement of poverty, family, work, and government. Instead of making welfare a moral problem, the ELCA states at the beginning of the document that "Poverty is the underlying problem welfare programs seek to alleviate," which stands in contrast to the FRC's insistence that the real problem is morality. This different starting point enables the ELCA to point to at least some of the structural constraints involved in the welfare issue.

While both the ELCA and the FRC stress the reality of human interdependence, they have very different understandings of the implications of this reality for the role of government. The FRC believes that government must stand apart from the practice of human compassion within the sphere of civil society, leaving this to private charity. The ELCA insists that "government has the responsibility to help meet the needs and uphold the rights of those who are at the margins of the economic system." They also suggest that the common good is created both through government policies and private or civil activities.

The ELCA avoids any suggestion of moral inadequacy in its discussion of the poor, remarking that "none of us are truly 'self-sufficient,' 'deserving,' or autonomous" and stating that "Welfare policies that make distinctions between persons who are 'deserving' and those who are 'undeserving' need to be questioned." The ELCA's emphasis on the positive sense of dependency and its repudiation of self-sufficiency as an overriding moral good moves away from the traditional emphases of the Protestant ethic. In sharp contrast to the FRC, the ELCA states that there is a right to basic provision: "All human beings are entitled to the basic necessities of a dignified, humane existence and/or to the means of securing such." While agreeing with the need for policies that encourage responsibility ("Welfare policies should nurture the power to act responsibly"), the ELCA envisions policies based on incentives rather than restrictions ("Coercive or punitive measures should not be used to compel human action"). The importance of work is stressed, but in the context of a critique of workfare in light of the reality of a low-wage job market and the necessity for job training. While the FRC implies that any kind of work is morally beneficial, the ELCA sees the need to consider the ways in which demeaning work can affect people's lives.

Support of families is part of the ELCA proposal, since they "are the basic communities in which personhood is fostered." However, this is one point among several, rather than the focus of concern. Instead of emphasizing the moral necessity of marriage, the ELCA states that "Policies that require or encourage parents to remain unmarried or to separate in order to qualify for welfare programs must be changed." In this light, it insists that single parents of young children should not be required to work "if they decide that the good of their children, and thus the social good, is best served in their circumstances through the work of nurturing their family, rather than through efforts to become economically self-sufficient." Like the FRC, the ELCA is criticizing the ways in which welfare policy can hurt families, but unlike the FRC it does not connect such criticism to any explicit defense of the bourgeois family form. Further, it calls for "Quality, affordable child care," a demand that is invisible in the FRC program.

The ELCA positions the church and Christianity quite differently from the FRC. It envisions a society where government has responsibility to the poor, where work must enable dignity and self-support. While also concerned with social morality, it does not locate the source of this morality solely in the "personal responsibility" of individuals. Nor does it make the bourgeois family responsible for the moral well-being of the nation. Instead, it sees personal and social responsibility in dialogue and finds that the government can play a positive moral role, rather than just operating as a moral check.

Although it has moved away from the Protestant ethical emphasis on individual work and a "good" family, the ELCA still does not confront some of the issues at stake. In spite of its awareness of the broader context of the welfare issue, the ELCA backs away from naming economic exploitation, the loss of good work, the stigmatization of those on welfare, and the reality of different family forms.

Conclusion

The family is (or, in the words of the Christian right, "family values" are) a fault line in a struggle over adjustment to pressures of globalizing economy, where companies are mobile and jobs ephemeral. The tension becomes particularly clear in the intersection of welfare issues and family values where the pressures of the economy on the poorest are repackaged as moral faults in their family life. The fears of the middle class and working class about their own economic security and their own family transformations are projected on those who have no political power—women on welfare. Welfare is not about "personal responsibility" but about changes in the status of the welfare state. The dismantling of welfare, especially through attacks on "deviant" families, is a way of mopping up the effects of capitalism by blaming them on the poor.

As I suggested at the beginning of this chapter, a focus on the family raises particular issues for Protestant Christian churches, which have historically been invested in the bourgeois family form as part of the legitimation of their own moral authority. The erosion of this authority requires renegotiation of their position. For conservative Protestants, this means strongly reasserting their moral authority, refashioning the Protestant ethic over against any governmental authority, and turning back to traditional family forms. Yet this form in its historical origins was partnered with the family wage, which no longer exists. Thus the FRC champions the moral form of family, insisting that women be dependent on men in an economy that no longer supports this; the practical effect is denying support to single poor women. It and other conservative Protestant groups manage this contradiction by insisting on the "natural" or "commonsense" connection of bourgeois family, morality, and economic "self-reliance." One price of this management has been the FRC's attack on any form of government support. Another price has been the intense attack on the moral character of poor people.

While the ELCA supports the continued role of government in protecting the poor, it does not directly engage with any of these undercurrents, keeping silent about just what family or what poor people are being discussed. Because of power of the "natural" or "commonsense" connection, it is necessary to intervene more directly in the debate. There is a need to revisit the presuppositions of the Protestant ethic, which was a particular combination of work, family, morality, Christianity, and nationhood that still is an implicit assumption in much liberal Protestant thought. There is a particular need to rethink the dynamic of dependence and independence present in this ethic. Nancy Fraser and Linda Gordon remark on the ways in which dependency has become increasingly stigmatized in our postindustrial society. "Everyone," they say, "is expected to 'work' and be 'self-supporting.'"[46] Equality of opportunity can be claimed in ways that rewrite the ongoing structural inequalities as personal failures. The family becomes the only place where we can be "dependent," yet that "good" dependency is tied into the bourgeois family form, which can be used punitively against women—especially poor women of color.

For liberal Protestants to contribute to welfare debate, we need to name the moral, economic, and social forces at work as part of a reconstruction of the Protestant ethic. We need to affirm flexible family forms and condemn the stigmatization of poor people of color. We have permitted conservative Christianity to monopolize public moral discussion with its notion of family and its notion of economy, and thus we are debating notions of morality devoid of acknowledgment of the effects of the economy, politics, race, class, and gender. We need to name a morality that takes these forces into account, that names the shifting relations of government/civil society/economy. There is no doubt that poor families need support: any engagement with the lives of poor women brings one into contact with women who struggle valiantly to ensure the minimal conditions of well-being for their families. But an exclusive emphasis on punitive morality will not build an economic and social context where these women can realize their hopes. And a punitive definition of dependence falsifies our common interdependence (on families, friends, social structures, governments).

Churches must take a lead in naming kinds of truly "family friendly" welfare policies that involve the work of government, business, and civil society in the interdependent business of our lives. We need to be part of a conversation that insists there can be no *personal* responsibility without renewed *social* responsibility.

Notes

1. Joel Handler, *The Poverty of Welfare Reform* (New Haven, Conn.: Yale University Press, 1995), 8–9.
2. Mary McGrory, "Wolves, Studs, and Nazis," *Washington Post,* April 2, 1995, C4.
3. Anthony Giddens, *Beyond Left and Right: The Future of Radical Politics* (Stanford, Calif.: Stanford University Press, 1994), 135–40.
4. For an account of the shifting fortunes of oldline Protestantism, see Wade Clark Roof and William McKinney, *American Mainline Religion: Its Changing Shape and Future* (New Brunswick, N.J.: Rutgers University Press, 1987). For discussion of the shifting relations of liberal and conservative Protestantism, see James Davison Hunter, *Culture Wars: The Struggle to Define America* (New York: Basic Books, 1991), and Robert Wuthnow, *The Struggle of America's Soul: Evangelicalism, Liberalism, and Secularism* (Grand Rapids, Mich.: Eerdmans, 1989).
5. Quoted in Colleen McDannell, *The Christian Home in Victorian America* (Bloomington: Indiana University Press, 1986), 113.
6. Janet Fishburn, *Confronting the Idolatry of the Family: A New Vision for the Household of God* (Nashville: Abingdon, 1991), 20.
7. Carole Pateman, *The Disorder of Women: Democracy, Feminism, and Political Theory* (Stanford, Calif.: Stanford University Press, 1989), 43.
8. Nancy Fraser and Linda Gordon, "'Dependency' Demystified: Inscriptions of Power in a Keyword of the Welfare State," *Social Politics* 1, no. 1 (spring 1994): 11.
9. Linda Gordon, *Pitied but Not Entitled: Single Mothers and the History of Welfare* (Cambridge: Harvard University Press, 1994), 3.
10. Ibid., 31.
11. Ibid.
12. Ibid., 291.
13. See ibid., 282. It is important, however, to recognize that poor women have never simply accepted the role of deserving or undeserving poor. In their actual negotiations with the welfare framework, they did and continue to demonstrate creative agency in using the system to enable them to escape domestic abuse, to help them support their children, to try to move ahead with their lives. See, for example, Mimi Abramovitz, *Regulating the Lives of Women: Social Welfare Policy from Colonial Times to the Present* (Boston: South End, 1988).
14. Abramovitz, *Regulating,* 226–27, 318–27.
15. Lucy Williams, *Decades of Distortion: The Right's 30-Year Assault on Welfare* (Somerville, Mass.: Political Research Associates, 1997), 3.

16. Joel F. Handler and Yeheskel Hasenfeld, *The Moral Construction of Poverty: Welfare Reform in America* (Newbury Park, Calif.: Sage, 1991), 70, 113.

17. Judith Stacey, *In the Name of the Family* (Boston: Beacon, 1996), 6. See also, Handler and Hasenfeld, *Moral Construction,* 136.

18. Handler and Hasenfeld, *Moral Construction,* 114.

19. The real wages of low-income workers have fallen 20–25 percent over the last twenty-five years, and the starting salaries of college graduates have also declined (Richard Freeman, "Unequal Incomes," *Harvard Magazine,* January–February 1998, 64).

20. The U.S. Bureau of the Census, Population Division, release PPL-91, "United States Population Estimates, by Age, Sex, Race, and Hispanic Origin, 1990 to 1997."

21. Freeman, "Unequal Incomes," 62, 64.

22. David Harvey, *The Condition of Postmodernity* (Cambridge, Mass.: Blackwell, 1989), 189–97.

23. Don S. Browning, Bonnie J. Miller-McLemore, Pamela D. Couture, K. Brynolf Lyon, and Robert M. Franklin, *From Culture Wars to Common Ground: Religion and the American Family Debate* (Louisville, Ky.: Westminster John Knox, 1997), 65.

24. I have been helped in forming these ideas through the draft dissertation work of Ann Burlein and earlier drafts of the essay by Janet Jakobsen appearing in this volume.

25. Kathy Rudy, *Sex and the Church: Gender, Homosexuality, and the Transformation of Christian Ethics* (Boston: Beacon, 1997), 28.

26. Williams, *Decades of Distortion,* 1.

27. See Matthew Moen, *The Transformation of the Christian Right* (Tuscaloosa: University of Alabama Press, 1992), 132.

28. All of the FRC literature cited below (notes 29–44) is found on their Web site, available at http://www.frc.org. The material is divided into different series, which are cited as appropriate.

29. Charles A. Donovan, "First Comes the Baby Carriage," *Perspectives.*

30. "Why Does the FRC Exist and What Do They Stand For?"

31. Jennifer E. Marshall, "Observations about America's Welfare Crisis," *At the Podium.*

32. Jennifer E. Marshall, "Sanctioning Illegitimacy: Our National Character Is at Stake," *Insight.*

33. Jennifer E. Marshall, "Illegitimacy: Compassion's Offspring," *Perspectives.*

34. Donovan, "Baby Carriage."

35. Marshall, "Observations."

36. Donovan, "Baby Carriage."

37. Marshall, "Observations."

38. Jennifer E. Marshall, "The Legacy of the New Jersey Family Cap," *At the Podium*, and "Capping Welfare Payments: Subsidizing Illegitimacy Isn't Pro-Life." The second article attempts to answer the charge that family caps would promote abortions by arguing that only marriage and compassionate charity will ultimately prevent abortions.

39. Marshall, "Legacy" and "Observations."

40. Marshall, "Capping."

41. Ibid.

42. Marshall, "Observations," "Legacy."

43. Donovan, "Baby Carriage."

44. Marshall, "Legacy."

45. Evangelical Lutheran Church in America, "Working Principles for Welfare Reform" (Chicago: Division for Church in Society of the ELCA, 1994); available from http://elcasco.elca.org/des/welfare.html. All subsequent citations in this section are from this document.

46. Fraser and Gordon, "'Dependency,'" 15.

[9]

Poor Women, Work, and the U.S. Catholic Bishops

Discerning Myth from Reality in Welfare Reform

Mary E. Hobgood

THE 1995 U.S. CATHOLIC BISHOPS' STATEMENT entitled "Moral Principles and Policy Priorities on Welfare Reform" makes an important contribution to the welfare policy discussion and the development of welfare ethics. This discussion continues to be of crucial importance as the Personal Responsibility and Work Opportunity Reconciliation Act of August 1996 becomes implemented at the state level throughout the nation.

In an ·effort to continue the work of developing welfare ethics, I argue in this chapter that a critical analysis of political economy challenges the central assumption driving U.S. welfare reform and has the potential to enhance Catholic welfare ethics. By examining the radical restructuring of work, rising corporate subsidies, and the ideological function of welfare, I support the bishops' policy goals while I expand the moral principles at stake and redefine the scope of the problem. I also identify the political challenges the bishops' proposals will actually pose.

Bishops' Letter on Welfare Policy

The bishops claim that "poverty has national dimensions and consequences" and that private and religious efforts to address poverty, while important, are inadequate.[1] Therefore, the bishops advocate strengthening the federal social safety net for poor children and their families. The bishops believe that the proper goal for welfare reform is to promote productive work that enables families to leave poverty behind. To achieve this goal, they support such new investments as a children's tax credit, a strengthened earned-income tax credit, education, training, and other concrete forms of assistance. The heart of the bishops' welfare policy consists of decent jobs with health and child-care benefits that permit families to live and work in dignity.[2]

Since welfare restructuring is significantly impacting the poor, especially women and children, it is a moral issue that the bishops do well to address. Indeed, the Urban Institute, an eminent research group studying poverty, predicts that the 1996 federal welfare bill will push 2.6 million people into poverty, including 1.1 million children. Moreover, the bishops' proposals, which affirm full employment, above-poverty wages, and a strengthened social safety net, are laudable and necessary social justice goals that can provide grounds for moral criticism of the new legislation.

Unfortunately, the bishops' proposals for dignified jobs and benefits are not informed by an analysis that probes the structural causes of poverty. Such analysis is essential not only if we are to identify wider economic policies pertinent to authentic welfare reform but also if we are to identify successful strategies needed to achieve such reform. Thus, while their 1995 statement—like the earlier pastoral letter "Economic Justice for All"—provides a moral beacon for Christians concerned about economic injustice, the bishops are not successful in orienting Christian moral thinking amid the treacherous currents of global markets and ideological maneuvering.

In the pages that follow, I will offer such an analysis, drawing attention to what I take to be its four principal benefits. First, I will use such analysis to show that the heart of the problem is deeper than welfare costs and the desirability of making people self-sufficient by putting them to work (although both the federal legislation and the bishops' letter cast the issues in these terms). Rather, the government is dismantling welfare as a response to the restructuring of social relations by advanced global capitalism. In particular, welfare dismantling responds to the more fundamental problem of work and the destruction of better-paying jobs in a global economy that is hostile to workers.[3]

Second, an analysis that probes the structural causes of poverty will enlarge the number of moral principles that are pertinent to welfare ethics. To those already identified by the bishops, such as the right to meet one's basic survival needs and the duty of government to protect the poor, structural analysis adds the principle of restitution, or returning to the poor what has been stolen from them.

Third, a structural reading of welfare not only unmasks the dynamics of increasing economic misery and the moral principles that these dynamics violate but also corrects stereotypes or myths about poor women. This is especially relevant to poor women of color, who have suffered twice over: once by always being made to shoulder a disproportionate share of the worst work in this economy, and then, a second time, by being held morally blameworthy for their economic misery—misery that is actually the result of unjust economic policy. Rather than simply lament the temptation to view the poor as "easy scapegoats of our society's social and economic difficulties,"[4] Catholic welfare ethics needs to unmask these myths so as to offer Christians a welfare story that reflects a more complex and accurate view of social relations.

Finally, an analysis of the specific mechanisms, organizational patterns, and mythology that support poverty and keep people in bondage helps Christian ethics to develop better-informed strategies concerning what we ought to do to achieve the bishops' policy goals, especially given the current legislation. By offering an explanation of how welfare functions within late twentieth-century global capitalism, we can begin to identify the extent of the ethical and political challenges that morally principled, woman-friendly welfare reform will actually pose.

Labor, Work, and Welfare: A Social Analysis

Dominant political discourse claims that the root of social problems—from crime to high taxes—is welfare, and the solution is forcing people to work by shredding the social safety net, which has been in place for the past six decades. To enact this goal, the first part of the August 1996 welfare legislation (a set of federal guidelines to the states) mandates cutting $55 billion over the next six years in programs that primarily will affect poor legal immigrants, low-income children with disabilities, working poor families, and the elderly poor. But, as former assistant secretary for Health and Human Services Peter Edelman says, as a way of putting people to work, these cuts, which mainly affect working families, are "wildly inconsistent with the stated purposes of the overall bill... [and] are just mean, with no good policy justification."[5]

The second part of the new welfare bill converts the Aid to Families with Dependent Children (AFDC) program into Temporary Assistance to Needy Families (TANF). Federal money (a total of $16.4 billion to fiscal year 2003) will be given to the states in fixed block grants that will be decreased if people are not moved off the rolls. This new law mandates a five-year lifetime limit on welfare benefits, and, because states can define "the needy" in any way they wish, they can decline to give any cash assistance at all. States must impose a work requirement of twenty hours of community service per week after two years and thirty hours by the year 2000. Severe penalties are put on out-of-wedlock births, and participation in higher education is no longer considered legitimate work. Finally, there is no requirement that states document the effects of the programs they will enact according to their individual interpretations of these federal guidelines.

In this chapter, I wish to challenge the central assumption of both the new welfare legislation and the bishops' proposals that the problem is welfare and the solution is putting people to work. Rather, I wish to argue that the real problem is *work,* and the social relations that are being restructured by advanced global capitalism. Only from a more critical perspective can we see why current capitalist interests are "reforming" or dismantling welfare as a "solution" to the larger problem of work and economic crisis.

Welfare comes into public discourse as a "social problem" in order to reinforce prevailing ideology that affirms dominant values and social arrangements when advanced global capitalism is eroding them. As a prelude to exploring the history and ideology of welfare, I will examine the radical restructuring of the labor market that has been underway for the past twenty years, as well as simultaneous increases in government support of corporations. Together these provide the background for further arguing that the shaming of poor unmarried mothers (especially young, poor mothers of color) is essential to maintain cultural norms in an economy that is eroding work and the material basis for the work ethic, male-dominant marriage, and the racially segregated work force.

The Restructured Labor Market

Driven by the engine of profit seeking, capitalism is a revolutionary force in world history that continually reshapes the world into new configurations. Capitalism is also a historical institution that promotes commonly held expectations or rules of behavior (social roles) which human agents decide to fulfill or obey.[6] Capitalism is an institutional "mask," if you will, that human agents wear so that a few can own and control production and investment and can produce for profit rather than for what the larger society might decide is useful and sustainable. The agents who fulfill capitalist social roles include producers and consumers, investors and money managers, and those who direct global finance and trade, like the members of the World Bank, the International

Monetary Fund, and the World Trade Organization. Capitalism also requires a state apparatus that will absorb the resistance to the negative fallout from capitalist operations and maintain a social environment favorable to business.

In the drive for increasing profits, those who control the institutions of transnational capital restructure the workplace and the composition of the global working class. The creation of new decentralized technologies and the ability of investors to move capital around the globe instantaneously have transformed the appearance of capitalism since the early 1970s. The human agents in charge of mobile and highly technologized capital have created policies to enact deindustrialization, relocate industrial plants, segment labor markets, establish alternative systems of labor control, and automate production—all of which have seriously weakened the position of workers.[7]

During the last two decades, the fallout for workers from the new situation of global capital has been hidden by political rhetoric in the United States. The dominant discourse, shaped by former Labor secretary Robert Reich, among others, has promoted the "skills-mismatch rationale" for the lack of better-paying jobs with good benefits.[8] We are told, in accord with traditional neoclassical economic theory, that if workers were more highly skilled or had the right kind of new skills, the market would provide better jobs in order to take advantage of them. In reality, while the labor market is requiring a smaller sector of very highly trained workers, global capital is generating increasing amounts of low-wage work. As workers within and between nations are forced to compete against others to do this low-wage work, the United States is rapidly resembling other Two-Thirds World nations in becoming a cheap labor haven for corporations.

For example, a recent study by the U.S. Labor Department found that retraining for better-paid high-tech jobs under the Trade Adjustment Assistance Act failed to raise wages. In fact, more than three-fourths of the retrained workers earned less after three years than in their pre-layoff jobs.[9] This may be a consequence of the fact that more than three-fourths of all new jobs created between 1979 and 1989 were in low-paying retail trade and service industries.[10] One-half of total projected job growth through 2005 is expected to be in occupations that do not require more than a high-school education.[11]

Because mass production is often not as profitable as smaller units of diversified production with quick turnover potential, corporate leaders find that long-term commitments to workers are counterproductive. The Bureau of Labor Statistics reports that dislocated workers in the mid-1990s numbered over 3 million per year.[12] While 30 percent of all college graduates march straight into unemployment or underemployment, the United States General Accounting Office reports that the number of illegally employed children under the age of fourteen has nearly tripled since 1983.[13]

As educated workers are laid off and children's unskilled labor is illegally exploited, the public is misled regarding the number of adults without work. While the official unemployment rate in 1994 was just over 6 percent, the actual jobless rate, according to MIT economist Lester Thurow, was 15 percent.[14] Lance Morrow of *Time* magazine says that corporations want high unemployment to keep wages down and a work force that is "fluid, flexible and disposable."[15]

This restructured labor market—now resembling a pyramid rather than a ladder—is built around a core of better-paid, high-benefit, and often overworked employees who manage a much larger web of full-time, part-time, and contingent low-wage workers. Thus we have increasing overwork, underwork, and unemployment existing simultaneously. Overtime is rising such that the average United States full-time worker puts in an extra month of work compared to workers twenty years ago, while the fraction of the labor force working part-time but desiring full-time work has increased more than sevenfold.[16]

How these trends are reflected in the double shift for women is receiving increased attention from researchers. Harvard economist Juliet Schor cites a Boston study which showed that employed mothers averaged over 80 hours of housework, child care, and employment per week. Her own studies show that gaining a husband adds 4.2 hours of domestic work per week to a woman's schedule.[17] Sociologist Arlie Hochschild studies mothers employed outside the home who are fixated on the topic of sleep like hungry people are fixated on food.[18]

In this restructured labor market, the poverty rate is increasing not only for the lowest strata but also for many families that in previous generations could count on some level of economic security. While productivity is up 15 percent since 1990 and corporations are experiencing record profits, 80 percent of United States workers have endured a 20 percent drop in wages since 1973.[19] Dollars that should be going into wages and salaries for the people who produce the products and services are going instead to the richest 10 percent, who own 90 percent of outstanding corporate stock and have seen their dividends increase since 1980 by over 250 percent.[20] According to a Children's Defense Fund study, since 1973 the earnings of U.S. men aged twenty to twenty-four have fallen over 30 percent, and their marriage rate has declined by 50 percent. This study documents that poverty rates more than doubled in one generation for three groups: young white families with children, families headed by married couples, and families headed by high-school graduates.[21]

The deep erosion in earnings since 1973 also affects the approximately 30 million people who do the full-time, year-round jobs that no one else wants, such as those in fast food, janitorial service, and the lowest rungs of hospital labor. Working full-time for their poverty, they cannot afford decent housing, adequate nutrition, health care, and child care. Deeply intertwined with the welfare poor, they often live with them and rely on their food stamps and subsidized housing to survive.[22] Like the working poor, studies show that the overwhelming majority of AFDC receivers have desired not increased benefits, but jobs that pay more.[23]

For those who "choose" welfare, the average benefit in 1993 ($4,476 annually) was less than 40 percent of the poverty threshold for a family of three in the United States.[24] Both AFDC and food-stamp funding ($32.2 billion in 1991) reach fewer than two-thirds of all poor children in the United States.[25] Medicaid ($52.5 billion in 1991) has been a bit more protected since it uses the poor to fund hospitals and doctors.[26] Nevertheless, even before the new legislation, more than 25 percent of those who officially qualified as poor received no government assistance of any kind.[27]

Given such meager benefits, it is not surprising that although only 20 percent have reported non-AFDC income, between 40 and 50 percent of welfare recipients have been working outside the home.[28] One study found that 40 percent of recipients combine welfare with half-time employment, the same amount of employment on average as nonpoor mothers of small children. This is especially the case for women receiving welfare who are not disabled or caring for a disabled relative, and who are living in an area where the local unemployment rate is low.[29]

These statistics shed light on many issues pertinent to the bishops' discussion of welfare. An exploration of the radical restructuring of the labor market explains why poverty has deepened significantly in the United States over the last twenty years. It also helps to resolve the moral ambiguity of poverty.

In their effort to "lift up the moral dimensions and human consequences" of welfare,[30] the bishops try, in liberal fashion, to balance the need for greater personal responsibility on the part of the poor with the need for greater social supports from state and federal government. However, as my analysis of the political economy makes clear, poverty is not primarily a matter of lacking the personal values of work and independence. Women on welfare want decent work like everyone else. Whenever possible, they are active agents who, in the face of a discriminatory low-wage labor market, combine employment and welfare for the survival of their families. Mandatory work policies, a central feature of the government's welfare "reform," insult the poor who are already working very hard under heavier economic and cultural burdens than other workers endure.

The bishops rightly lament the temptation to view the poor as "easy scapegoats of our society's social and economic difficulties."[31] Yet without a systemic analysis of the function scapegoating serves, the bishops are reduced to individual moral exhortation. This does not help the ever-larger numbers of economically at-risk people who lack a social analysis to decipher what is really going on in the economy and who are ready to blame those groups targeted by politicians and the corporate-controlled media as the reason for their own economic vulnerability. At a time when increasing numbers are enduring overwork or low-wage work and when at least 40 percent of workers fear loosing their jobs, people often need to engage in the arduous task of justifying a system that is detrimental to their own well-being.[32] Influenced by the dominant analysis that is designed to punish those in subordinate positions, people experience understandable rage toward those who are presented as not pulling their own weight.[33]

This analysis also points to some of the difficulties that will be involved in implementing the bishops' proposal for full employment, which flies in the face of downsizing trends. Investors make more money with fewer workers, especially fewer workers who make above-poverty wages. It would seem, therefore, that assumptions that the poor lack motivation to work, or that the poverty problem can be solved by simply putting people to work, need serious reassessment. Also in need of reassessment (as I will show in the following section) is the assumption that the present government will provide the supports needed by the poor.

The Problem of Corporate Subsidy

In addition to the radical restructuring of the labor market, another factor pertinent to the current shaming of the welfare poor is the significant increase in public "aid to dependent corporations." The phenomenon of rising corporate welfare during the last half of this century has its roots both in capital mobility and in the increasing competition among capitalist firms facing the problems of overproduction and sustaining effective demand in a world with increasing inequalities of income.

Roaming the planet for the best business deals, those with capital to invest can hold nations and their workers hostage to their demands. Investors who can destroy massive amounts of above-poverty-wage work in the search for profits are increasing the gap between those at the bottom and in the eroding middle strata, and those at the top of the global economy. However, their drive to cut costs by decreasing wages seems to imperil the system itself. Who will buy the products that make the profits if potential customers keep losing economic ground?

Consequently, corporate investors are replacing mass production with highly diversified, smaller units of production that have the potential for rapid turnover. They hope that the rising income of those few at the top levels of the economy will make up for the loss in income of increasing numbers of dispos-able workers. This means that competition is ever more keenly felt as global businesses vie for the lion's share of potentially saturated global markets. Hence, the relentless push for "free-trade" agreements and the assumption by United States policymakers (who get elected through corporate-financed cam-paigns) that taxpayers should subsidize the profits and socialize the costs of do-ing business.[34]

Statistics on corporate welfare reveal the deepening dependency of big busi-ness on the public dole. The tax shifts during the Reagan and Bush adminis-trations transferred the costs of state activities from big firms to low- and mid-dle-strata households. Corporate contributions to total income-tax collections have steadily decreased since the 1950s. Once comprising 39 percent of total tax revenues, corporations in the 1980s paid only 17 percent of total taxes col-lected, and their projected share by the year 2000 is 11.1 percent.[35] During the 1980s, corporations would have contributed $130 billion more every year (enough to wipe out the annual federal deficit) if their taxes had not decreased from the previous decade.[36] In 1991, nearly 60 percent of U.S.-controlled cor-porations, and 74 percent of foreign firms doing business in the Unites States, paid no federal taxes.[37]

In the early 1990s, all money spent each year on AFDC and food stamps (under $40 billion), combined with that spent each year on Medicaid (just over $50 billion), amounted to less than the yearly subsidies enjoyed by corpo-rations. As of this writing, progressive legislators have put the Corporate Re-sponsibility Act before the 105th Congress; this act addresses the over $100 billion in annual corporate welfare, specifically targeting $800 billion over the next seven-year period.[38]

An even larger aspect of corporate welfare is the increased appropriation by the business elite of more-hidden forms of the economic surplus belonging to workers. Especially since 1970, when the post–World War II business boom ended, corporations have had to rely on external financing for their operations. As a result, major sources of the investment capital of British, U.S., and Cana-dian firms, for example, have come from their control over the pension plans, savings accounts, insurance policies, and the interest on credit-card debt of or-dinary workers.[39] It is clear that the entire economy is hostage to the profits of a few.

As low- and middle-income wage earners pay for rising profits to corporate investors through their higher taxes, decreasing wages, and lack of control over their own pensions and other economic surplus, the corporate-controlled me-dia focus on the welfare poor as the cause of their impoverishment. An alter-native social analysis reveals, however, that the ethical concern is not a parasitic poor stratum but those with power in the political economy who profit at the expense of the majority. A structural analysis of the political economy demonstrates that the overwork, enforced leisure, and increasing economic vulnerability of the majority is primarily financing not welfare for the poor but the increasing shares in income and wealth enjoyed by the relatively few at the top of the economy.

The Ideological "Solution" of Welfare

Given that AFDC constituted less than 1 percent of the U.S. federal budget and less than 3 percent of state outlays, and given that the average benefit has been 40 percent of the poverty threshold, welfare policy is not primarily about meeting the needs of the poor.[40] Welfare, and rhetoric about welfare "reform" now at the state level, try to legitimize a political economy that is both destroying higher-wage work and rewarding the business activities of the rich with extensive subsidies.

Historically, welfare has provided inadequately for poor women and their children, since its purpose has been to promote the male-breadwinner family (a social arrangement that now prevails in fewer than 15 percent of U.S. families).[41] Welfare was designed to partially compensate for the supposedly temporary loss of the male family wage among those who were accustomed to upper-working-class or middle-strata incomes.[42] Consequently, welfare rhetoric is primarily about the public production of symbols that affirm dominant values and social arrangements—especially the entire social system of class, race, and gender subordination. Revitalizing welfare rhetoric is especially necessary when the economy is eroding the material base for sustaining these values and arrangements, including women's economic dependence on men, and men's dependence on employers and the unpaid labor of women.[43]

From its inception in the 1930s, welfare has served a twofold function: to control and stigmatize deviant behavior as it legitimized the male-dominant family, the work ethic, and the proliferation of people of color at the bottom of the economy. The specific ways in which welfare functions ideologically, however, change as the needs of capitalism change, as a historical review will demonstrate.

The system of "mothers' pensions," the precursor to AFDC, supported male dominance, racism, and class elitism by awarding pensions only to those mothers who were widowed from husbands who had worked. In this way, widows who were predominately white and from the middle strata were rewarded but also kept out of better-paying jobs in a shrinking Depression labor market.

At the same time, this system refused pensions to poor mothers who were divorced or had never married—a group disproportionately comprising women of color. Gwendolyn Mink observes that the origins of the American welfare state lie in a racist response to the perceived lack of moral fitness of those women who did not conform to white, middle-strata maternal values.[44] These women were needed to do the work that no one else wanted in the low-wage agricultural, mining, and domestic-labor markets, which were also removed from coverage under Social Security or unemployment compensation.[45] The labor of poor women of color was readily exploited while they simultaneously were blamed for violating the patriarchal domestic code.[46]

The proportion of women of color receiving AFDC rose dramatically in the 1950s and 1960s, primarily for two reasons: One was the massive displacement of sharecroppers forced off the land due to the mechanization of southern agriculture. They entered northern cities just as jobs and low-cost housing were disappearing due to automation, capital flight and "urban renewal." The second reason women of color—especially African American women—gained access to AFDC was due to their political mobilization in the civil rights and national welfare rights movements, which made it harder to discriminate against them and their children.[47] Since that time, even though more AFDC mothers have been white than African American, racism dictates that the public face of welfare is an African American woman.[48]

Now that labor market needs have changed drastically, what is socially sanctioned must also change to serve the needs of corporate investors. We cannot understand the national obsession of the last two decades with so-called welfare reform and workfare unless we see the confluence of these three realities: the enormous proliferation of low-wage work; a relatively expanded AFDC system dating from the 1960s; and the changed labor patterns of middle-strata women, whose work is no longer exclusively childrearing.

The decades following the 1960s saw the expansion of AFDC into communities of color with the simultaneous massive entry of white, middle-strata women into the labor force. Since it now took two or more middle-strata incomes to do what one used to accomplish, caring for children was no longer the only culturally sanctioned work relegated to these women.[49] As a consequence, lower-strata women (who historically were denied earlier forms of welfare because they *were* in the work force) cannot expect the state to fund them for work in the home. In other words, poor women used to be shamed and penalized because they didn't stay home like middle-strata women. Now their social safety net is being removed when they stay home with their children and do not have middle-income jobs like middle-strata women! Here we see the classist and racist subtext of so-called family values. Social conservatives insist on children's needs for a mother's care, but not if the mother is a poor woman of color.[50]

The current focus on the welfare poor, however, serves different purposes from what appears on the surface. A primary function served by welfare "reform" is not to move people out of poverty through work but to make welfare so meager and so despised as to increase the incentive of those at the bottom of the economy to endure work that denies conditions of human dignity.

Despite the political rhetoric, about 70 percent of recipients traditionally have moved off welfare in two years, although increasing numbers (currently about 22 percent) have been cycling on and off welfare because of unstable employment, poverty-level wages, lack of benefits like health care or social supports like child care.[51] In addition, many women cannot enter the work force, either because they have children under the age of six or because they themselves have disabilities or are caring for a disabled child or relative. There is a second reason why these women will not work their way out of poverty: if they do find work in a highly depressed labor market, the work they are most likely to get will pay poverty wages, and most states will find it too costly to subsidize this work by paying for child care.

To the extent that programs do force people to work outside the home for their poverty, the programs exacerbate the crisis for workers in myriad ways. For example, critics of the newly passed Wisconsin Works (W-2) program (which forces mothers of children as young as twelve weeks to work in any available job) argue that it is detrimental not only to the mothers and children immediately involved but to all workers and their children. Such programs subvert the minimum wage and jeopardize the jobs of minimum-wage workers, make the public subsidize low-wage employers, increase the pressure for substandard day care, and create incentives for workers to collude with employers to keep wages low, since earning more may mean losing what benefits are left.[52] If the conditions of work continue to erode and if low-wage, low-skill work expands even further, it is more than likely that programs like W-2 will increase as welfare is all but eliminated in order to force the most vulnerable into these jobs.

The current effort to dismantle welfare is a solution that the corporate elite and the politicians who work for them require in order to maintain social order when so many people who are currently working are living in misery. Shaming poor unmarried mothers, particularly those of color, and targeting them as public enemies eroding civic order and undeserving of a social safety net accomplishes at least three things for corporate interests.

First, it increases the incentive to work at poverty wages in an economy that is generating a disproportionate amount of low-wage, part-time, and contingent work.

Second, by targeting the unmarried poor in an economy that is rapidly reducing the pool of marriageable men (that is, men who earn above-poverty wages), policymakers affirm marriage and the patriarchal family. Dominant discourse on welfare supports not only any job under any circumstances but any marriage under any circumstances. If the unmarried can be targeted for their personal sexual immorality, then the basic dynamics of an economic system that is destroying the material basis for family life remain invisible and unchallenged, and marriage remains the main route out of welfare.[53] The social vulnerability of women and children escalates when what little alternative women have had to exploitative and abusive employers and husbands is dismantled.

Third, by targeting despised racial groups, dominant discourse promotes racial hostility to counteract the potential solidarity of people across racial/ethnic lines who find themselves sharing a common class position at the expanding bottom of the economy.

In short, the deep hostility toward the female-headed household in poverty uses racism and sexism to focus attention away from the problem of class elitism in the political economy, a problem that is manifested in the deteriorating labor-market structure and the increasing flow of wealth to people at the top of the economy. Poor unmarried mothers of color serve as the symbolic repositories of all that is a threat to individualistic, competitive, workaholic, sexually repressed (and obsessed) capitalist culture. They are the shock absorbers whose despised status helps to maintain discipline in the deteriorating capitalist workplace. The shaming of poor unmarried mothers of color is necessary to affirm dominant class, race, and gender arrangements in a political economy that cannot provide better jobs, higher wages, and universal health care, even to increasing numbers of white men, without jeopardizing the profits accruing to those at the top of the U.S. class structure.

Social Analysis and Ethical Principles

This kind of critical social analysis is needed to augment the laudable welfare policy goals of the U.S. Catholic bishops. The concrete study of the structural dynamics of contemporary economic arrangements does more than uncover important factual information that ethicists and policymakers must take into account; it also alters the theoretical matrix within which the debate about justice and welfare is carried on. Social analysis enhances the search for welfare justice by helping us sort out what belongs to whom. But more importantly, it enables us to see that restitution of stolen resources is an ethical principle that is highly relevant to this debate.

The bishops operate from three assumptions pertinent to welfare policy: (1) people deserve to have their survival needs met; (2) people deserve to have access to dignified work in order to participate in economic life, and (3) government has a duty to protect the poor. As Carol Robb has pointed out, these principles are rooted in the notion that "private property cannot be amassed or used in ways that are contrary to distributive justice and the dignity of all persons."[54]

The assumption that surplus should not be enjoyed when others' basic needs are unmet has a long history in Christian ethical tradition. One finds it in the work of Thomas Aquinas, who taught that "in cases of need all things are common property."[55] One finds it in Catholic social teaching in the principles of the accountability of private property to the common good and of capital to just, productive relations. One finds it, as well, in much recent work in Christian economic ethics, such as *Toward a Christian Economic Ethic*, by Prentice Pemberton and Daniel Rush Finn,[56] and Carol Robb's *Equal Value: An Ethical Approach to Economics and Sex*.[57] Christian ethicist Beverly Harrison sharpens this principle when she says that "no one has a right to luxury or even less essential 'enhancement needs' if those needs are satisfied at the price of others' basic dignity or physical survival."[58]

A structural analysis of political economy, however, expands the principle of just distribution to show that the poor are deserving not only because they are poor in the midst of affluence but because they themselves have created the wealth in the society. That is, as long as profit and "return on investment" are the basic operating principles of the economy, the overwork, underemployment, and unemployment of the majority will serve the profits of shareholders and the corporate elite. Those who have in excess of what they need have no right to it, not only because those who have more should share with those who have less but because what they are sharing rightfully belongs to those whose exploitation and marginalization have served to create it in the first place.

However, without a social analysis that uncovers the structural relationships between wealthy persons, social institutions, and the various sectors of the economically vulnerable and the poor, a moral evaluation of how property or capital is amassed at the expense of others cannot be articulated. We remain ignorant about how the generation of wealth for a minority requires the overwork of some, the enforced leisure of others, and the economic vulnerability of the many. People in need have a justice claim on others because the affluence of the few is being built on their collective backs and stolen from them.

Even though managerial capitalist culture promotes contempt for weakness and a need to punish and control others (phenomena beyond the scope of this chapter), I do not think that conspiracy against workers and poor people is the issue here. Making the highest possible profits for investors is the issue, as well as sustaining a self-justifying analysis of capitalism that makes people fear that any alternative would be worse than what we already have. Indeed, studies show that neither the highest-income population nor the most highly educated are knowledgeable about the structural causes of poverty.[59] More-explicit

structural analysis by Christian social ethicists not only would address this ignorance but also would disclose more clearly what justice demands of us.

As scripture scholar Walter Brueggemann reminds us, biblical justice entails
a right reading of social reality, of who has the power and who has the goods,
so that we can sort out what belongs to whom and return it to them. This is especially pertinent to those who have controlled what belongs to others for so
long that they mistakenly believe it belongs to them. If doing justice is the primary expectation of the biblical God, we need critical analysis to help us do it.
The work of ethics uses social analysis to sort out what belongs to whom; the
work of justice is "giving things back," enacting the restoration.[60]

Discerning the Myths in Welfare Rhetoric

As I suggested above, rhetorical complaints about the irresponsible poor often
have a very precise (if unrecognized) ideological function in deflecting blame
for economic misery; the resources of social analysis can help Catholic welfare
ethics expose the myths that function as deceptive moral justifications of violations of justice. Three such myths focus on mothers as a group and on teen
mothers and African American unmarried mothers in particular.

The first myth is that the only work is paid work. Critical economic analysis shows how wealth for the few is maintained in part by rapidly deteriorating
public work, but also by the completely invisible domestic work of caring for
children, the sick, and the elderly. This work encompasses perhaps one-fourth
to one-third of all economic activity.[61] The myth is that this "women's
work"—not even measured by mainstream economic theory—is not *real* work
and so is denied social status and remuneration. Vandana Shiva says we must
unmask the myth that mothers, who raise the next generation of workers and
taxpayers, are economic parasites and do not deserve a share of social wealth.[62]
Philosopher Nancy Fraser agrees when she observes that "the real free-riders in
the current system are not poor solo mothers who shirk employment. Instead
they are men of all classes who shirk carework and domestic labor, as well as
corporations who free-ride on the labor of working people, both underpaid
and unpaid."[63] The responsibility to make women's work visible and to honor
their claim to a fair share of economic resources cannot be divorced from the
responsibility to support all families and to restructure "women's work" so that
it is no longer relegated to women alone and to poor women of color more
than any others.

The myth of the African American welfare queen—another myth central to
the dominant discussion on welfare—illustrates how those who are economi-

cally exploited are then paradoxically and perversely blamed for situations and behaviors that only express their oppression and exploitation by the powerful. This myth, relentlessly promulgated by politicians and the media, is particularly unjust since black women have shouldered a disproportionate share of social labor in this country. First they were enslaved workers and forced breeders of slaves for over two centuries. Then the only work open to them was on the lowest rungs of agricultural, factory, and mining labor, which no other workers would do. More recently, they have been domestics who have had to spend more time raising white people's children than their own. As a group, black women continue to bear a disproportionate share of low wages and poverty today.[64] In her history of black women, work, and the family, Jacqueline Jones documents black women's struggle over the centuries for the freedom to care for their own families without interference from slaveholders, welfare bureaucrats, or workfare-minded politicians.[65] What should be learned from this resistance?

Also in need of unmasking is the myth of the irresponsible teen who is having multiple babies in order to increase her welfare payments. Contrary to the dominant view, the percentage of total births to teen mothers (all races) was *less* in 1990 than in 1980, and this decline has been steady since the 1970s.[66] In addition, research has found consistently that over two-thirds of teen mothers have children by men who are over twenty-one years of age, and the younger the mother, the wider the age gap. While dominant ideology waged by powerful white men is blaming teen mothers for being economic parasites and for destroying family values, thousands of teenagers are suffering sexual abuse in the home.[67]

This analysis makes clear that poverty is essentially a form of structural violence sustained by economic, political, and cultural institutions that violate a wide range of Christian ethical principles and thrive on stereotypes that mask the true nature of social relations. Those involved in an ethical evaluation of welfare need to educate people as to how the political economy mediates the violence of poverty and unjust social relations, upheld (and concealed) in this process by destructive social myths.

Social Analysis and Liberating Praxis

In addition to expanding the moral principles at stake in welfare ethics and critiquing the cultural myths that support poverty, a critical economic analysis reveals the scale of transformation, both immediate and long-term, required for authentic reform and social transformation. The struggle for welfare justice will require enormous effort, even though we know what is needed and even though we already have the resources to afford all people in the United States an above-poverty standard of living. Critical analysis not only reveals the extent of the challenges we face, it also gives people an alternative story about our collective situation, a story that is essential if we are to sustain the moral passion necessary for the costly social changes recommended by the Catholic bishops.

False Consciousness, False Problems, False Solutions

The problem of addressing welfare and poverty in the short-term is neither lack of knowledge about what to do nor lack of resources to do it. For example, in 1991, the U.S. Census Bureau determined that about $70 billion ($37 billion in addition to the $32.2 billion of AFDC and food stamps) would have raised the income of all poor families with children to the poverty line that year.[68] A similar estimate of $86 billion was proposed for a 1996 program by the Institute for Women's Policy Research. This program would provide all low-wage workers and parents who do not work outside the home with the health insurance, child care, housing assistance, and other supports necessary to attain an above-poverty standard of living. These necessities could be financed by shifting funds from programs that support those at the top of the economy, like programs for the Pentagon, the CIA, and agricultural subsidies to wealthy farmers.[69]

The problem is, rather, ideological and political. It is ideological because the lie that "nothing works" or the mantra that "money is no solution to being poor" supports an economic system that requires poverty, unemployment, and low-wage work to keep profits up.

The problem is also political, as evidenced by the particular shape of current programs that, like the bishops' proposals, advocate putting the poor to work. These workfare programs—such as the federally enacted Work Incentive Program (WIN), and state programs such as the Employment and Training Program (ET) in Massachusetts and the Greater Avenues for Independence Program (GAIN) in California—have had occasionally modest but usually dismal results. Such programs only begin to work if they operate within a relatively tight local labor market, if expensive support services like child care are actually funded, and if participants have at least some college education and can be placed in administrative and professional jobs.[70] Scholars who have studied pre-1996 experimental workfare observe that while these welfare reform programs have demanded that AFDC mothers work outside the home, they (like the economy itself) are structured so that most will fail to escape poverty through employment. The successes that a few will experience will appear to validate hard work, and the many failures will appear to confirm dominant ideology about the depth of the degeneracy of the poor who, despite the supposed opportunities offered by these programs, still fail to leave poverty.[71]

It seems, therefore, that workfare persists in the new welfare legislation not because it reduces welfare rolls significantly but because the able-bodied unemployed are a threat to current assumptions. They threaten not only the work ethic but the perception that the capitalist market economy can provide work for all its citizens so that they can escape poverty. Given the uncritical support of work programs, which are expensive even when they (usually) fail, it would seem that they serve primarily a symbolic purpose to uphold cultural norms, the economic status quo, and continued belief in a deeply flawed system.[72]

Moreover, it is quite likely that the future of welfare will be dependent not on the adequacy of workfare but on the state of the economy. More draconian measures like the previously mentioned Wisconsin Works program (W-2) which reduce benefits to almost nothing and "force low-skilled mothers of small children into full-time sub-minimum wage jobs with warehouse care for their kids" will be the face of the future.[73] As Sister Noel Doyle, SND, a religious working at Project Hope in Dorchester, Massachusetts, has said: "What we are seeing is nothing less than institutionalized domestic violence" at the national level.[74] Such violence will escalate if hostility to workers persists and investors increase their dependency on the public subsidies, low-wage work, and enforced leisure afforded by the masses. How these programs affect the hopes, dreams, aspirations, and basic survival of poor parents and their children is a matter that does not have to be documented according to the new legislation. It is largely ignored because the current consensus has us believe that the poor have forfeited their right to the free exchange of their own labor by accepting welfare.[75]

If the bishops do not wish their program to be, at best, merely symbolic or, at worst, supportive of forms of wage slavery and increasing public irresponsibility for children, they need to be cognizant of these realities as they respond to welfare reform and the struggles that are increasingly in store as states interpret the new federal guidelines. It is unlikely that a just welfare reform will result from policy prescriptions that are not grounded in a systemic understanding of poverty and the need for disciplined, sustained political strategies to exert mass pressure on policymakers.

Building a New Order

Policies that address the violence of poverty and build genuine welfare reform will require the creation of a new postindustrial welfare state that gives poor women and their children an alternative to abusive spouses, employers, and state officials.[76] It will necessitate significant public control over corporations, macroeconomic policies aimed at creating high-quality permanent jobs, shorter work weeks, universal child and health care, a social security system for all children and adults who work in the home, lower military spending, and more-progressive tax policies. Many of these are identified in the bishops' proposals. They are not only the minimum required to establish basic justice in the land, they are essential for the long-term well-being of the society as a whole and the economy itself.

However, getting these measures passed and implemented will require more fundamental change than the bishops and traditional liberal political groups admit. It will require especially the enactment of democratic forms of decision making about economic priorities. This is essential in an economy where rising stock prices, productivity rates, and corporate profits are in fundamental opposition to the increased wages, improved working conditions, and better integration of work and family life that mean real economic improvement for the majority.

Welfare reform that adequately addresses the low-wage labor market and the high levels of aid to dependent corporations has to be part of a larger national struggle for social change. Enacting such social and labor policies will require, for a start, passing a campaign-finance reform bill that reduces the influence of corporations on lawmakers. It will also require organizing people at the local, state, regional, national, and international levels to keep politicians accountable once elected. Until the state represents a wider sector of political opinion, it will support those who monopolize economic power and put national governments and their citizens in competition with one another in order to make the highest profits for corporate investors. Until the state becomes accountable to a wider economic spectrum, it will not raise the revenues needed to restructure the labor market and provide authentic national security in a postindustrial world.

The struggle for genuine welfare reform in the United States must be part of a larger international struggle to protect jobs, communities, democracy, and the planet itself against the imperatives of global economic expansion. Until the few who run the international corporate and financial institutions that are destroying national and regional economies and the environment are challenged, the vast majority of people on the globe will become landless and homeless, fighting one another for increasingly fewer jobs as we are poisoned by a ravaged planet. National and international networks and coalitions engaged in disciplined, sustained mass pressure against the status quo are necessary to reshape the structures of political economy so that they embody such goals as ecologically sustainable development and community control over land, jobs, resources, and cultural institutions.

While as yet there are no massive social movements to achieve these goals, there are increasing numbers of ordinary people who believe in their right to a better life and who struggle to create structures for keeping government accountable to people rather than profits. The seeds of such movements may be found in the revitalization going on in labor unions and community organizing across the country and in various feminist, environmental, consumer, human-rights, antiracist, and economic justice organizations. The best of these are developing forms of gender, race, and class analyses that are international in scope. When these groups and organizations create national and international alliances with one another, hope is kept alive in the power of courageous collective action to challenge the status quo of white supremacist, male-dominant, global corporate feudalism.[77]

What Can Churches Do?

At its best, ethics is a discernment process which is done in the context of communities doing liberating praxis, communities that are enacting the restoration. While many of the churches are a long way from engagement in such liberating praxis, those of us involved in the construction of welfare ethics can at least pay attention to three things.

First, as a necessary prelude to becoming their allies, we need to listen to what the poor are up against, and portray people on welfare as they describe themselves. Moreover, a just welfare policy requires that poor women be active participants in the political project of defining what they need. As struggles over the interpretation of the new federal legislation are waged at the state level, the Catholic bishops are needed as allies of local welfare groups who represent these women. The voice and authority of the bishops can support these and other social justice organizations as they put pressure on state legislatures to enact better welfare policy.

In addition, the churches might do what states are not required to do: document the success or failure of such programs from the point of view of the women, children, and other poor people that they are intended to serve.[78] By gathering and publishing information of this kind, the bishops would give ongoing support to their own 1995 welfare policy proposals. Such activity would also confirm continuing commitment to the central concern of their 1986 letter on the economy, "Economic Justice for All," which asked about the impact of economic policy on people, especially the people at the bottom.[79]

Finally, if we are to actualize religious values of justice and mercy, Christian social ethicists must begin to use more boldly and more consistently the resources of critical social analysis to identify the power relations at work in the political economy. Only then will we be able to clarify the ethical principles at stake in the structural violence of poverty and increasing economic insecurity for the majority. This insistence, that accurate analysis of the socioeconomic arena is an indispensable requirement to responsible theological ethics, is also a mandate of the bishops' 1986 letter.[80] We must deepen our understanding of the material relations that intimately (though invisibly) bind us together, or more to the point, allow some to enjoy privilege out of the sacrifice of others. That knowledge must not stop with church leadership but must find its way into the parishes and congregations. Only the churches can offer the necessary resistance to the deceptive and myth-ridden public story of the blameworthy poor.

However much the bishops protest blaming those on welfare, people will continue to do so if they are not offered a new and better welfare story, a story that tells what welfare looks like from the point of view of women struggling for survival and dignity at the bottom of the economy. Without a story that is more faithful, not only to the poor but also to the experiences of those who suffer increasing economic insecurity, Christians will lack altogether the necessary theoretical base for a liberating social praxis. Without an alternative story, the faithful are not able to understand their own collective vulnerability in an economy hostile to workers.

Christian social ethics and social policy formation need to challenge the dominant view of welfare; identify its historical, political, and economic distortions; and offer people a more complex and accurate view of social relations. The renewal of Christian identity through critical awareness of the society in which we live is no substitute for moral agency and the hard work involved in collective political action for genuine welfare reform. But justice in this area, as in all others, will not be done without it.

Notes

1. United States Catholic Conference Administrative Board (USCC), "Moral Principles and Policy Priorities on Welfare Reform," *Origins* 24, no. 41 (1995): 667–77.

2. Ibid., 675–77.

3. There are also other agendas fueling welfare reform, such as deficit reduction, and as I discuss below, the need to punish women who have children without husbands.

4. USCC, "Moral Principles," 677.

5. Peter Edelman, "The Worst Thing Bill Clinton Has Done," *The Atlantic Monthly,* March 1997, 48.

6. Michael Albert and Robin Hahnel, *Quiet Revolution in Welfare Economics* (Princeton, N.J.: Princeton University Press, 1990), 128.

7. David Harvey, *The Condition of Postmodernity* (Cambridge, Mass.: Blackwell, 1989), 141–239.

8. Holly Sklar, *Chaos or Community: Seeking Solutions Not Scapegoats for Bad Economics* (Boston: South End, 1995), 26.

9. Ibid., 26–27.

10. Ibid., 32.

11. Ibid., 26.

12. Between January 1993 and December 1995, 9.4 million workers over the age of twenty lost or left jobs because their position or shift was abolished or because their plant or company closed or moved (U.S. Dept. of Labor, Bureau of Labor Statistics [BLS], "Worker Displacement during Mid-1990s," *Displaced Workers Summary*, USDL 96-446: 1–2).

13. Sklar, *Chaos or Community*, 26, 51.

14. Herbert J. Gans, *The War against the Poor* (New York: Basic Books, 1995), 107; Sklar, *Chaos or Community*, 60–64.

15. Sklar, *Chaos or Community*, 31.

16. Juliet B. Schor, *The Overworked American* (New York: Basic Books, 1991), 17–41.

17. Ibid., 21, 38.

18. Ibid., 20. Nancy Fraser, *Justice Interruptus: Critical Reflections on the Postsocialist Condition* (New York: Routledge, 1997), 47–48.

19. For the top United States corporations, profits increased by 19 percent in 1992, 20 percent in 1993, and 40 percent in 1994 (Council on International and Public Affairs [CIPA], "Why Today's Big Profits Mean Big Trouble," *Too Much* [fall 1995]: 1).

20. Ibid.

21. Sklar, *Chaos or Community*, 69.

22. Katherine Newman, "Working Poor, Working Hard," *The Nation* 263, no. 4 (1996): 20–23.

23. Coalition on Human Needs, *How the Poor Would Remedy Poverty* (Washington, D.C.: Ford Foundation, 1986–87), 12.

24. Randy Albelda, "The Welfare Reform Debate You Wish Would Happen," *Feminist Economics* 1, no. 2 (summer 1995): 82.

25. Ibid.

26. Warren R. Copeland, *And the Poor Get Welfare: The Ethics of Poverty in the United States* (Nashville: Abingdon, 1994), 56.

27. Sklar, *Chaos or Community*, 14.

28. Barbara Bergmann and Heidi Hartmann, "Get Real! Look to the Future, Not to the Past," *Feminist Economics* 1, no. 2 (summer 1995): 111. Gans, *War against the Poor*, 70.

29. Roberta Spalter-Roth and Heidi Hartmann, "Small Happiness: The Feminist Struggle to Integrate Social Research and Social Activism," in *Feminism and Social Change: Bridging Theory and Practice,* ed. Heidi Gottfried (Urbana: University of Illinois Press, 1996).

30. USCC, "Moral Principles and Policy Priorities," 675.

31. Ibid., 667.

32. Gans, *War against the Poor,* 107, 129.

33. It is not only the corporate elite and the national politicians and think tanks funded by the elite who support an agenda that is hostile to the welfare state and the environment. The organized right in the churches and in state and local politics harnesses the collective energy of hundreds of thousands of ordinary people who use legitimate tactics to implement regressive policies (Sara Diamond, *Facing the Wrath: Confronting the Right in Dangerous Times* [Monroe, Me.: Common Courage Press, 1996]).

34. Sklar, *Chaos or Community,* 41.

35. Donald L. Bartlett and James B. Steele, *America: What Went Wrong?* (Kansas City, Mo.: Andrews & McMeel, 1992), 47. Charles M. Sennott, "The $150 Billion Welfare Recipients: U.S. Corporations," *Boston Sunday Globe,* July 7, 1996, A1.

36. Sklar, *Chaos or Community,* 144.

37. Aaron Zitner, "Tax Codes Give Companies a Lift," *Boston Globe,* July 8, 1996, A6.

38. Marc Bayard, conversation with the author, January 30, 1997. Bayard is an organizer with Share the Wealth, a nonprofit organization in Boston; Gans, *War against the Poor,* 82.

39. Richard Deaton argues that pension reform could gradually socialize key sectors of advanced market economics in the public interest if corporate control over inadequate pensions were replaced by adequate pensions and public control over capital formation (Richard Lee Deaton, *The Political Economy of Pensions: Power, Politics and Social Change in Canada, Britain and the United States* [Vancouver: University of British Columbia Press, 1989], 306–51).

40. Albelda, "Welfare Reform Debate," 82.

41. Nancy Fraser, *Unruly Practices: Power, Discourse and Gender in Contemporary Social Theory* (Minneapolis: University of Minnesota Press, 1989), 149.

42. Linda Gordon, "The New Feminist Scholarship on the Welfare State," in *Women, the State, and Welfare,* ed. Linda Gordon (Madison: University of Wisconsin Press, 1990), 12–13.

43. Joel F. Handler and Yeheskel Hasenfeld, *The Moral Construction of Poverty: Welfare Reform in America* (Newbury Park, Calif.: Sage, 1991), 12–13, 20–22.

44. Gwendolyn Mink, "Gender, Race and the Origins of the American Welfare State," in *Women, the State, and Welfare,* ed. Gordon, 102–4.

45. Teresa L. Amott, "Black Women and AFDC: Making Entitlement Out of Necessity," in *Women, the State, and Welfare,* ed. Gordon, 288.

46. Handler and Hasenfeld, *Moral Construction,* 15–43.

47. Sklar, *Chaos or Community,* 94.

48. About 39 percent of families receiving AFDC have been white, 37 percent black, 18 percent Latino, 3 percent Asian, and 1 percent Native American. Ibid.

49. Lise Vogel, *Marxism and the Oppression of Women* (New Brunswick, N.J.: Rutgers University Press, 1983), 150.

50. Fraser, *Unruly Practices,* 161.

51. Gans, *War against the Poor,* 70; Sklar, *Chaos or Community,* 99.

52. Katherine Sciacchitano, "Wageless in Wisconsin," *In These Times,* May 27, 1996, 14–17.

53. The increasing economic instability experienced by men is only one reason for the increase in black female-headed families from 18 percent in 1950 to 44 percent in 1985. Other reasons include the lower ratio of black men to black women due to higher disease rates and accidents on the (dangerous) job; the racism of criminal justice system, which removes a disproportionate number of men of color (especially black and Latino) from the community; black women's higher (relative to white women) labor-force participation; and women's choices to live independently or with other women (Amott, "Black Women and AFDC," 284–87).

54. Carol S. Robb, *Equal Value: An Ethical Approach to Economics and Sex* (Boston: Beacon, 1995), 144.

55. Thomas Aquinas, *Summa Theologiae,* IIaIIae 66.7, trans. Fathers of the English Dominican Province (Westminster, Md.: Christian Classics, 1981), 3:1256–72.

56. Prentice L. Pemberton and Daniel Rush Finn, *Toward a Christian Economic Ethic* (Minneapolis: Winston, 1985), 36–40.

57. Robb, *Equal Value,* 142–59.

58. Beverly W. Harrison, "Theological Reflection in the Struggle for Liberation," in *Making the Connections: Essays in Feminist Social Ethics,* ed. Carol S. Robb (Boston: Beacon, 1985), 255. For an ethical assessment of "needs," including enhancement needs and luxuries, see Dennis Goulet, *The Cruel Choice: A New Concept in the Theory of Development* (New York: Atheneum, 1973); Agnes Heller, *The Theory of Need in Marx* (London: Allison & Busby, 1978). For the politics of need interpretation, see Fraser, *Unruly Practices,* 144–60.

59. Gans, *War against the Poor,* 89.

60. Walter Brueggemann, "Voices of the Night—Against Justice," in *To Act Justly, Love Tenderly, Walk Humbly,* ed. Walter Brueggemann, Sharon Parks, and Thomas H. Groome (New York: Paulist Press, 1986), 5–6.

61. Robb, *Equal Value,* 136–37.

62. Ibid., 137.

63. Fraser, *Justice Interruptus,* 62.

64. Teresa L. Amott and Julie A. Matthaei, *Race, Gender, and Work: A Multicul-*

tural Economic History of Women in the United States (Boston: South End, 1991), 183–91.

65. Jacqueline Jones, *Labor of Love, Labor of Sorrow* (New York: Basic Books, 1985).

66. What has risen is the proportion of black children born to unmarried mothers (most of whom are not teens). This reflects the dramatic decline (for reasons made evident in this chapter) in the proportion of married black women. However, throughout the United States population, out-of-wedlock birth rates are rising because of a decline in childbearing among married women and an increase in the number of unmarried women in the population (Rebecca Blank, "Teen Pregnancy: Government Programs Are Not the Cause," *Feminist Economics* 1, no. 2 [summer 1995]: 47–48; Amott, "Black Women and AFDC," 284; Sklar, *Chaos or Community,* 90).

67. Joe Klein, "The Predator Problem," *Newsweek,* Apr. 29, 1996, 32; Mike Males, "Poor Logic," *In These Times,* January 1995, 12–15.

68. Gans, *War against the Poor,* 117; Copeland, *And the Poor Get Welfare,* 56.

69. Barbara Bergmann and Heidi Hartmann, "A Welfare Reform Based on Help for Working Parents," *Feminist Economics* 1, no. 2 (summer 1995): 85–89.

70. Handler and Hasenfeld, *Moral Construction,* 132–200.

71. Ibid., 42.

72. Ibid., 198–99.

73. Katha Pollitt, "Village Idiot," *The Nation,* February 5, 1996, 9.

74. Susan Jhirad, "Ready for the Long Haul," *The Women's Review of Books* 14, no. 5 (Feb. 1997): 21.

75. The belief that lack of participation in public work forfeits one's right to participate in the economy contradicts the notion in neoclassical economic theory that work is a private commodity that one is free to exchange or not in the marketplace.

76. Fraser, *Justice Interruptus,* 46.

77. John Anner, *Beyond Identity Politics: Emerging Social Justice Movements in Communities of Color* (Boston: South End, 1996); Joel Bleifuss, "Reforming the Beast: Campaign Finance Reform," *In These Times,* June 24–July 7, 1996, 12–15; Jeremy Breecher, John Brown Childs, and Jill Cutler, *Global Visions: Beyond the New World Order* (Boston: South End, 1993); Kevin Danaher, ed., *Fifty Years Is Enough: The Case against the World Bank* (Boston: South End, 1994); Gary Delgado, *Organizing the Movement: The Roots and Growth of Acorn* (Philadelphia: Temple University Press, 1986); Paulo Friere and Myles Horton, *We Make the Road by Walking: Conversations in Education and Social Change* (Philadelphia: Temple University Press, 1990); Gottfried, ed., *Feminism and Social Change;* Mary Ann Hinsdale, Helen M. Lewis, and S. Maxine Waller, *It Comes from the People: Community Development and Local Theology*

(Philadelphia: Temple University Press, 1995); Biorn Maybury-Lewis, *The Politics of the Possible: The Brazilian Workers' Trade Union Movement* (Philadelphia: Temple University Press, 1994); David Moberg, "State of the Unions: AFL-CIO's Aggressive New Strategies," *In These Times*, April 1–13, 1996, 22–23; John Nichols, "Labor Gets It Together," *The Progressive*, August 1996, 22–24; Mary Beth Rogers, *Cold Anger: A Story of Faith and Power Politics* (Denton: University of North Texas Press, 1990).

78. Between March 1994 and February 1997, welfare caseloads dropped by 18 percent nationwide. However, none of the states knows the economic status of the families that are no longer on the welfare rolls (Jason DaParle, "A Sharp Decrease in Welfare Cases Is Gathering Speed," *New York Times*, February 2, 1997, 1, 18).

79. National Conference of Catholic Bishops (NCCB), "Economic Justice for All" (Washington, D.C.: United States Catholic Conference, 1986), 130, 319.

80. Ibid., 134.

[10]

Face to Face

Transforming Faith-Based Outreach

Joan Sakalas

"IF I WERE A WELFARE RECIPIENT, what would I ask of the church?"[1] Would I trust that people know or even care about my life when they have not asked what I need? Would men and women in congregations welcome me at worship even though my clothes come from the Goodwill box? Do they want to help me so that I will stay away from their neighborhood, their church? As a woman, I am troubled by these questions. As a feminist, I believe that women must speak for themselves—especially women whose voices have been missing from public discourse. Church congregations have tried to address poor mothers' problems by imagining what might be needed and generally by making goods available. Communities and churches, in particular, have directly impacted families lacking basic resources. The many church-run shelters, soup kitchens, and pantries in New York City attest to the effectiveness of this grassroots approach. However, even faith-based groups with the best of charitable intentions often neglect to involve recipients directly in decision making, in the process of articulating their needs, and in program design. One obstacle to this involvement, Thomas Szasz argues, is our tendency to portray recipients of public assistance as morally inferior.[2] We need to ask ourselves whom this kind of image serves. Do we excuse ourselves from effective redress and direct contact by accepting images of mothers receiving public assistance as hopelessly impaired?

From these questions, two related themes emerge. First, how can we structure outreach programs in ways that empower poor mothers? And second, how can churches support such empowerment? With these questions in mind, in the summer of 1997 I began to design a program that would create a different paradigm for outreach to poor mothers. With Mothers Together I created a model that shifts the power to make decisions, set the pace, and define content to the women involved. The model engages a feminist methodology placing the participants, mothers receiving public assistance, at the center and assumes that they know their aspirations and needs best. By involving women in a cooperative entrepreneurial business, Mothers Together rejects stereotypical images of mothers receiving public assistance and suggests that the broad entrepreneurial possibilities available to middle-class women could be appropriate for poor women as well. By providing the opportunity to create and market their own goods, participants prove to themselves that they can enter an economic and social realm generally unavailable to them. In this case, a successful business experience moves women toward greater economic and social stability by expanding their vision of possible work and of themselves as creative, successful women.

The program creates a team effort enlisting the support of metropolitan faith-based congregations and business people to expose mothers receiving public assistance to the world of work and entrepreneurship. Further, it creates coalitions with other business, child care, training, and educational programs and resources in each community, maximizing opportunities for participating women to connect upon completion of the program with further training, education, or work.

The business cooperative offers hands-on experience in textile design and product production, in basic business accounting, and desktop publishing as they design and create the program newsletter. Mothers Together assumes that one size does not fit all women. Instead it begins with each woman's perception of her own needs, interests, and talents. To this end the training seeks to help women discern their needs, build confidence, and develop communications skills necessary to work effectively toward their goals. For many women this is their first positive experience of working cooperatively with other women. Participants are recruited through metropolitan churches, tenants' associations, neighborhood shelters, and social service agencies. Graduates of the program also make referrals. Working together, the women create and implement a business plan, develop a sales plan, design and produce their goods, and share the profits of their work.

I use this program as a case study for several reasons: first, I am intimately in touch with its genesis and development; second, the program represents an effort to engage congregational goodwill and resources in practical measures to prepare poor women to move toward increased economic and social stability; third, the program provides an example of a paradigm shift from "charity" to outreach.

In this chapter, I place the stories and testimonies of women enrolled in Mothers Together at the center, allowing their words to suggest a different vision of responsive and relevant outreach for faith-based communities.[3] The women's stories serve three purposes. First, they illustrate the problematic dimensions of welfare charity. Second, they articulate the mothers' needs as they see them. Third, they demonstrate the insights of mothers struggling to be independent of public assistance when their own agency is affirmed.

Finally, in order for the reader to understand the difference between a charity and a neighbor model of outreach, I include three composite stories of congregations making the decision to support Mothers Together. I define neighbors as people with whom we expect to come in contact frequently, people who will impact our lives and whose lives we expect to impact. They are people for whom we take some responsibility and whom we expect to take some responsibility for us. Neighbors are not anonymous; they have faces and names, problems and passions. Although we may not like all of our neighbors, we cannot ignore them and may indeed view them as an extended family. The stories that follow illustrate how our sense of relationship to the objects of our outreach defines the quality of our involvement.[4]

Content and Structure—Seven Vignettes

The following vignettes are based on my experience facilitating weekly leadership training groups and coordinating the business workday at the shelter-based site of Mothers Together. The vignettes raise issues regarding the content and structure of outreach and demonstrate the wealth of participating mothers' insight in their own words.

Monday—Leadership Training

SACRED SPACE—IS THIS A HOLY PLACE? We arrived at the shelter early. This week Mary was to lead the opening ritual. At Mothers Together, meetings begin with a simple ritual, the creation of a circle, to recognize that this is a special time and place for the women gathered. The circle metaphorically represents a space of safety, a space where we have deliberately gathered to spend special time together. All materials used in the ritual must be free, found, or of special significance to the woman beginning the ritual. By placing a higher value on found objects, we are agreeing that many of the most meaningful resources have no price and are already held by us.

As Mary entered, Ashley, the facilitator, asked whether she was ready with the opening. Mary responded, "No, I can't think of any way to begin." Ashley asked if she had any item in her room that might become the focus of the opening ritual. She asked whether she could use two photos of Cherokee chiefs that were very important to her. None of us knew that Mary was part Cherokee.

When she returned carrying the photos, Mary told Ashley, "They remind me that my people were once free and happy." Ashley asked if Mary felt free in the shelter. Mary replied, "No." Ashley pursued the issue of freedom, asking, "Do you feel free anywhere?" Mary's answer surprised both of us. "Yes, I feel free in this room when we meet." When Ashley asked why, Mary replied, "Because when we gather here we say what we think and what we feel. Here I am free."

By now the other women had arrived. Following the circle-ritual custom, Mary prepared to pass the photos around. Today to open she asked each woman to say what she saw as they looked at the photos.

THE CIRCLE CONTINUES—THIS IS NOT JUST A BASEBALL GLOVE. The creation of the circle became an integral part of our Monday leadership groups. When the women planned their graduation ceremony, they decided to begin with the circle. They wanted to set a tone and show their guests how we do things. At graduation, Carmen volunteered to plan the ritual. As we settled in our chairs, she held out a baseball glove and ball. She told us that they were Christmas gifts she had bought for her five-year-old daughter with the money she earned in the Mothers Together business. Before she passed them around she told us that she gave a glove and ball to her daughter because as a little girl she never had one. Carmen wanted these gifts to say to her daughter that anything is possible.

THE WHAT-IF GAME. How will you sell your hats? That was the question for our role-play exercise today. The challenge was to imagine approaching a minister of a neighborhood church to ask whether a group of mothers could sell hats after the Sunday service. Shawna drew the slip this time. She read it and looked distressed. In response she said she couldn't do it. She would not speak to a minister. Half of the women in the group agreed. When asked why, Shawna said she would not feel comfortable. "Ministers judge you; he will look at my clothes and think they aren't good enough." Alice added, "Yes, he wouldn't like us. He'd say, 'You don't belong here.'" When I asked whether the other women agreed, they said, "No." Helen said, "I'd talk with a minister. After all they're just like the rest of us. They're not really perfect; they make mistakes. I'd feel comfortable."

BARBARA'S COLLAGE.   Ashley wanted action this week, not words. We were continuing our Monday exploration of how women would move toward their goals. Her choice, a collage that shows our journey toward our dreams, created from magazines, newspapers, and catalogs.

The floor was strewn with the raw materials and the tools: scissors, glue sticks, paper. The shelter had left no tables for us today, so we worked on chairs, the floor, and the broad windowsills. Sometimes a woman asked for a picture. "Does anyone have a picture of a baby? Anyone found animals?" Otherwise we worked silently.

After about one hour, we were ready. Each woman in turn interpreted her combination of words and pictures, describing how they represented her vocational journey. For some like myself, the journey was very immediate, for some like Teresa, long-term.

We had completed our stories, except for one, Mary. She said, "I don't want to show you mine." Thinking that she was embarrassed, we encouraged her, reminding her that we all had shown ours. Her response, however, took us by surprise. "I don't want to show you my collage because it is very important to me. I'm going to put it up in my room. I'm not ready to share it yet." At her graduation she reiterated that she still had the collage on her wall and that it represented the beginning of her realization that she could do something.

Thursday—Business Day

I CAN'T SEW.   There were three tables. At one, two women pinned and cut the patterns for the children's hats. At another, three others were carefully assembling and sewing. At the third, two discussed the flyer they were designing to advertise their work. In the midst of all this busyness, Carmen sat unoccupied. Her attendance in the program was 100 percent and her enthusiasm clear, yet she sat unoccupied. Martha, the volunteer who created the patterns, noticed Carmen and asked if she wouldn't like to help with a new hat design. Carmen said, "No, I'm afraid of the machine. I've never sewn. You don't want to work with me. I'll just mess up." Martha said, "Sit down. We'll work through it together. Then you'll make your own."

Forty-five minutes later, as the women put the fabric away and set tables for lunch and their business meeting, Carmen was still at her machine. Martha asked her whether she was ready to stop and eat lunch. As she cleaned up, Carmen held up two hats, "I made these by myself. You know, sewing isn't that hard. I think I like it."

MOTHERS' STORIES. It was the first week of the program. The women agreed that although they might feel more comfortable cutting or hand-sewing or keeping the books, they would all try every job. As they circulated around the room, two women showed particular skill at machine sewing. Speaking as she sewed, Teresa told us, "My mother was a seamstress. She died a long time ago but always supported us with her sewing. I forgot how much I learned from her."

Carla, who sat at the next machine, was smiling. She said, "Yes, me too, I forgot how much fun I had with my mother. When I was a little girl, she taught me to sew. We don't get along anymore. I forgot that we did have fun."

Postscript: Three weeks later Teresa announced that she asked her husband to buy her a sewing machine for Christmas this year. We talked about brands, about new or used, about business possibilities.

GETTING DOWN TO BUSINESS. At the business meeting Carla asked, "How will we describe the goal of our business? That's the question." Mary answered, "We'll tell them that we are trying to establish a work record. We are building a sense that we can do something successfully. And we are learning to work together and help each other."

"Presence is everything. We need to know what we want to accomplish, and we need to stand tall so people will see that we are proud of what we do. That's what's important when we meet people who might buy our hats," Carmen added. Carmen was the organizer, the woman with a sense of how to structure the business to make it work. "But how will we organize ourselves when it comes time to sell our hats?" she asked. Teresa had a plan. "Each of us will have a job. One will carry and show the hats, one will carry and distribute the flyer, and one will carry the clipboard and speak about the business. The clipboard should have a list of things we want to accomplish so we don't forget what we need to do."

"Yes, a group, that makes sense." agreed Mary. "After all, we are Mothers Together."

Neighbors and Others

A Story of Three Congregations

In order to understand the proposed shift in how we develop outreach, it is helpful to look at examples. This is a story of the responses of three groups— in reality, three modes of faith-based outreach. The first describes a refusal to help. In one conversation I had with the director of a church-sponsored shelter, I was told that she would not refer any women to Mothers Together because the women in her shelter were incapable of following through with a program lasting for four months. I wondered how this director could make this judgment about every resident in her shelter. What message did her judgment give to her residents? Certainly it was not one of hope and empowerment.

A hierarchical model that presumes that the staff of programs and shelters or members of congregations know best has not worked and is not respectful of either the recipients or the providers of services. The approach is a dead end for both parties in that it encourages arrogance on the part of the provider and belligerence, helplessness, or hopelessness on the part of the recipient. We need to pay more attention to what nourishes those of us who are economically and socially more secure. Those nourishing experiences need to become commonplace and frequent for shelter residents as well as for mothers on welfare.

For instance, in Mothers Together, although we use sewing as a vehicle for a business, the goal of the program is not necessarily to produce significant numbers of seamstresses. For a small number, sewing and textile design may open a career path. However, for most, the sewing machines serve as a vehicle for successful mastery of a skill. When mothers learn to sew and create marketable items, that accomplishment proves to them that they can do something well. For women who have no work history or an interrupted one, they need experiences that build or rebuild their confidence in themselves and their capabilities. Integral to the work is reflection on insights and concerns that rise from the work. The specific context of a sewing business provides a vehicle for airing and addressing fears and dreams together. The wisdom of the staff is not privileged. The assumption is that all women present know a great deal from their own life experience and that through the act of sharing we grow and support one another.

In the second and third encounters, I made appointments to speak to the appropriate parish committees, forwarding a proposal, budget, and timetable for the Mothers Together program to each. My hope was that the congregations would make a commitment to offer both material and volunteer support to the program. Realistically, however, I knew that finances were often tight and that jobs and family obligations made volunteer work difficult. The women the program was proposing to serve were not members of the congregation, and in fact, though they were a part of the neighborhood surrounding these churches, they never participated in church activities.

At the second group, a wealthy congregation, representatives had a clear sense of their financial resources. They spoke of how wonderful it would be to do something together and how authorization of financial support was quite probable in that this was clearly the kind of "mission work" they wanted to encourage. They also saw it as a possible vehicle for creating a link with the neighborhood. Initially they provided seed money, and their sense of solidarity with the developing project became evident as members of the congregation regularly inquired about its progress.

Eventually, several women decided that they wanted to accompany their charitable gifts with direct involvement. They wanted to visit Mothers Together to help out with the program as volunteers. However, their resolve gave rise to another practical problem. How could their involvement become more than a voyeuristic exercise where they were either doing good for the needy or attending the program as charitable tourists? Even when the resolve is there to meet face to face, how we construct that meeting is critical.

First the churchwomen were asked what they had to offer the program. Could they sew? Did they have business skills? After discussion, they agreed that their strength lay in fundraising. The challenge then was to structure a meeting in which Mothers Together participants and the women with fundraising skills could develop a strategic plan together. In fact, the participants are the experts on the program, its strong points and its processes. Participating mothers could learn from the churchwomen just how a fundraising event is planned. Both groups of women could speak to one another from their own experience. Thus the meeting held the possibility of both groups becoming neighbors, of moving beyond recipients and donors.

In another community not very far from the second, the third committee gathered. This time several congregations were represented. They asked me to describe the program and made it clear that they were looking for a project through which they might revitalize their neighborhood and respective congregations. As they discussed the program, they described their congregations as aging and with little money. Once they were told that participants in Mothers Together would be sewing hats as their first business, they began to name specific members of the community who were retired seamstresses. They suggested that the seamstresses might be interested in working as mentors and might benefit from the new relationship as well. They named sources such as local shelters and welfare offices where we could recruit participants. One woman expressed concern that poor women would feel uncomfortable entering their church. They asked that we consider holding a workshop where they could consider ways to make women feel welcome. Their answer to my request was a commitment to recruit, provide space, and interact with the participants regularly.

In fact, the financial support of the second church and other individuals made possible the purchase of needed materials, and the support of a small staff. However, this financial support needed to be combined with the direct involvement of the third group of congregations for the program to thrive.

The questions asked at the third church illustrated the difference in their sense of relationship to potential participants. Why would mothers who don't know us feel welcome here? How can we make women feel welcome? What should we say when they walk in the door? All of these questions speak to the congregation's desire to make a positive connection with the mothers involved. Until the participants of Mothers Together become neighbors, become mothers with faces and hopes and aspirations, both parties, the donors and the participants, remain "others." The third group reached toward the women; they committed themselves to listen and trust the dreams and wishes of the mothers. Without active contact, outreach remains something we do for others. With active contact, we begin to create the possibility of transformation, of both parties becoming neighbors, of both parties being transformed.

The Process of Becoming Neighbors

Proposing how church congregations can address poor mothers' problems is a difficult challenge marked often by a focus on service delivery rather than process. Although it may sound outrageous, I find that what congregations do as outreach is not really as important as how the outreach is done. My stories are intended to demonstrate that though the problems to be addressed are complex, attention to process in conjunction with attention to the needs and insights of the subjects of our outreach is as important as the nature of our outreach.

When addressing issues of welfare in the United States, faith-based communities must set empowerment, employment, and economic security as goals for outreach programming, not just service delivery. We need to reframe our focus from welfare to *well fare*. To fare well includes economic, social, and spiritual well-being. It means that congregations must come in contact with one another to be neighbors. Reaching out cannot simply involve mailing a check accompanied by an encouraging letter. Many people are aware of the poor from reading or watching news and videos that graphically portray stories of poverty, but again, that is at a distance. In order to become neighbors, we must meet face to face. And we must be willing to walk in one another's neighborhoods to speak and hear one another directly. Jesus did not minister from a distance; he ministered face to face.

If we believe that congregations must be responsive to our neighbors' needs, then one of the few ways we can know what those needs are is by direct contact with our neighbors, including mothers receiving public assistance. Further, we must trust what we hear and not dismiss their perceptions as any more distorted than our own. Programming which honors the competency of our neighbors is essential if transformation is to take place. For too long, social service, governmental, and faith-based agencies have offered assistance and programs that presume the recipients of services are incompetent or infantile. For instance, some congregations speak of "adopting" a poor family. Yet in the United States we do not adopt adults; we adopt children. We need then to examine whether, by using a term generally applied to children, we are infantilizing the families we wish to help. Perhaps the word "mentoring" is a more accurate representation of the assistance we wish to offer. Even our choice of words makes a difference.

The suggestions listed below are offered as a framework for developing faith-based outreach support.

Suggestions—Outreach

First, congregations must move toward being neighbors as well as benefactors. This means that men and women such as the mothers enrolled in Mothers Together must be made to feel welcome in our churches *as they are.* Although we hope people will arrive at church looking their best, Christianity is not about wealth or expensive clothing. Shawna's concern that her clothes would not be appropriate for church needs to be overcome.

Second, the subjects of outreach must be participants and definers of the shape and substance of that outreach. Once poor men and women feel welcome in our churches, they must be invited to participate on boards and committees and recognized as integral to the effectiveness of any outreach. This does not mean that they must officially join the congregation. Our churches cannot hold our neighbors hostage to the requirement of membership.

Third, once our neighbors feel welcome, their suggestions for modifications to program design must receive serious consideration. Actually, maybe we should rename Christian outreach as "Christian inreach." In other words, we embrace our neighbors, bringing them into our homes, into our churches, so that we can build together better, more effective ways of life for our whole community.

Fourth, privileged negative myths about poor men and women must be replaced with more complex understanding of factors and forces in their lives. As Christians we cannot give in to the popular myths which hold injustice in place. We need to understand why Mary felt free in our room at the shelter. We need to hear what makes poor women feel welcome in a church. We do not know the answer without their insight.

Fifth, in the delivery of faith-based outreach programs we must understand work as an exchange of learning and growth. Although the financial gift of the first congregation in the story, "Neighbors and others," offered critical support, more valuable for both the congregation and the objects of the outreach is a direct encounter where neighbors become people whose faces we know. And it was the exchange of information between the churchwomen and mothers about the program and fundraising in the second story that leveled the playing field, making it possible for the women to appreciate one another as neighbors.

Sixth, congregations need to abandon programs that recreate an authoritarian model where participants are told what to do by presumed experts. Volunteers and staff must model leadership and mutuality. For instance, in Mothers Together it was critical that Ashley and I create and share a collage along with participants. Only as we were willing to participate could we deepen the level of trust. As Christians we expect transformation in our lives. Our outreach must be structured to encourage mutual transformation.

Seventh, men and women can move forward when given freedom to be honest about fears and needs. Mary described a sense of freedom in the leadership group that hinged on a sense of being able to say and think what she felt. An atmosphere in which she was not judged and where her experience was valued created an environment where change and growth were possible. Space for work can be sacred space, and the sacred is everywhere we do our work. Without imposing a particular faith tradition on programs, we can still acknowledge values central to our faiths. The stories of the opening ritual offer one example of the use of simple ritual to acknowledge the sacredness of the world and the places where we work and grow. At the first Mothers Together graduation, participants all placed God and God's work in their lives at the center of their success.

Eighth, skills are taught best when the gifts of wisdom, dignity, and leadership of the women involved are respected. When Carmen voiced her fear of sewing, she was not excused from the work. Instead, Martha worked with her. This respectful cooperation is critical to success in overcoming obstacles to the new experiences of learning.

Face to Face

"If I were a welfare recipient, what would I ask of the church?"[5] The designers of faith-based outreach need help in order to answer this question. The elimination of long-term public assistance programs in the United States heightens the needs of mothers receiving public assistance. As we consider how we can effectively respond to these new, less secure, less responsive social, political, and economic circumstances, we must pay particular attention to how we design and implement responses.

Our congregations must be places where judgment and a sense of superiority are not the salient attitude driving outreach, where our outreach is given to "others." As Christians, we are called to live in relation to the world, to minister to one another, and to love one another. That means that we need to remove ourselves from our own eyeballs and admit that we cannot claim to love men and women with whom we are unwilling to talk. We need to hear the wisdom of the men and women who understand that ministers "make mistakes" and are human like them. We need to be neighbors who "make mistakes" and who are willing to share our gifts, wisdom, and expertise with our neighbors who also bring gifts, wisdom, expertise, and dreams. *Well fare* must become the central concern of our outreach, and a sharing of gifts our methodology.

Notes

1. Teresa Amott, as quoted by Julian Shipp in "Economist Says U.S. Churches Must Brace for the Impact of Welfare Reform," *PCUSA News,* November 5, 1997, 1.

2. Szasz sets poverty relief in historical context, arguing that in the twentieth century, poverty has been criminalized and addressed in a "quasi-therapeutic" manner, which reinforces the vision of the poor as criminal, morally depraved, or insane (Thomas Szasz, *Cruel Compassion: Psychiatric Control of Society's Unwanted* [New York: Wiley, 1994], 21).

3. The Mothers Together program is currently housed in a transitional shelter for homeless families, a Methodist church in Harlem and in a Protective Services suite in a housing project. Besides producing hats and storage bags for sale, participating women develop basic business, computer, and leadership skills. The program is supported by one Union Theological Seminary field intern, Garen Murray, who edits the newsletter; two skilled volunteers, Margaret Watt and Dorothy Lashley; and six trained coordinators (five are graduates of the program). For purposes of this chapter, the names of participants have been changed. The statements they make, however, are based on actual conversations in the leadership and work sessions.

4. Shipp, "Economist Says U.S. Churches Must Brace," 1.

5. The stories are, in fact, aggregates, composites of experiences that shape the outreach of faith-based groups and represent two distinct modes of engagement of congregations with their neighborhoods.

AFTERWORDS

Economics, Ethics, and the Everyday

Reflections from Another Shore

Ada María Isasi-Díaz

In Cuba

I was standing in line for twenty minutes waiting to get into this small grocery shop surprisingly set up, not as the old *bodegas,* with a long counter and all the goods in a storage area behind it, but as a tiny supermarket with the goods on open shelves.[1] I waited outside because there was no room for anyone else inside. As I waited, I watched the waves crashing over the wall of El Malecón, the graceful avenue that borders the sea along much of La Habana. Car traffic on this main road of the capital of Cuba is minimal, and the cars are so old that one wonders time and again how those motors still propel the scarred metal bodies which the paint seems to be holding together.

My melancholic reminiscence was interrupted continuously by what I was able to see—much of it happening under the cover of a surprisingly quiet surface. There was a man holding a couple of pairs of gym shorts in such a casual way that it made the conspicuous inconspicuous as he softly said, pronouncing it in Spanish, "Nike, Nike." There was a woman who looked down at her hands as folks went by and whispered "chocolate balls," calling attention to the candy she was selling. A man came up to the woman behind me and very softly asked her to buy something. She said she had to wait and see if she had enough dollars. Yes, this was a small *bodega* where you could pay only in dollars.

There were all kinds of people in line: some were dressed better than others, and I took that to mean that they were economically better off than the others. There were young people who bought beer and snacks. There was a grandmother with her grandson who bought a couple of pieces of bread and a liter of milk. In line waiting to get to the modern register to pay, the talk from all sides had to do with whether they had enough money to pay for what they had taken from the shelves. The two times I visited this *bodega*, I was the only one who paid with five-dollar bills. Everyone else I saw had only one-dollar bills and the coins the Cuban government has minted that inside Cuba are worth the same as U.S. coins.

Pepe, whom I had contracted to drive me around La Habana, like the owners of the dollar *bodega*, is a *cuentapropista*, a person who works on his own. The owners of the *bodega* have to pay taxes on the income from their business; Pepe does not pay taxes because he is part of the vast underground economy in the island. If he held a regular job, he would have taxes to pay. Cristóbal sells secondhand books and magazines in a park in La Habana. I asked him if he makes enough money to survive. Well, he explained, he has a small radio program for which he gets the equivalent of six dollars a month. (An economist who is a member of the Communist party had told me that one needs at least the equivalent of twenty dollars a month to make ends meet.) Cristóbal assured me that he does get the rest that he needs by selling books, which he buys mostly from elderly people. Since part of the small amounts of books he sells are paid for in dollars, and since there are some things that one can get only with U.S. dollars, Cristóbal seemed to be happy with this little business he has on the side.

Though in 1998 I have noticed an increase in buying and selling, Cuba seems to remain more a direct-exchange-of-goods economy than a money economy, *permutar* (to exchange) instead of *comprar* (to buy) is what you hear about when it comes to durable goods. I stayed in La Habana in the apartment of a friend. I asked him how he had gotten that apartment. "Well," he told me, "I exchanged it for a car!" Another friend of mine wanted to *conseguir* (to get) a small, rather dilapidated house occupied by more than one family. My friend had access to dollars, but the people she was buying from did not want money. They did not want to continue living together, so what they asked for in exchange for the house was two separate places in which to live. Another friend lives in a small house in La Habana with her daughter and grandchild. "I exchanged this house for my daughter's apartment plus the one I used to live in."

Housing is a great problem in Cuba. Houses are dilapidated, and many are being kept standing by wood "crutches," scaffolding that holds them up; the need for paint is very obvious. Everywhere you can see the sign, *se permuta* (for exchange). I called a friend, and a man answered the phone. When my friend called me back, I asked her who had answered the phone. "That is my ex-husband." Though divorced, they live in the same household simply because there is no place for him to move.

Much has been said in the United States about the *jineteras,* the numerous young sex workers that are so visible around the hotels. These women do not want to be called prostitutes for they insist that what they do is not a way of life they have opted for but what they need to do to *resolver*—the ever-present Spanish word that means to solve the situation at hand. Yes, at the personal as well as at the national level, the economy in Cuba is not a matter of planning but of fixing, solving, handling, as well as one can.

Three conversations I had about the economy in Cuba were very illuminating. One economist was furious with me for pointing out that any and all systems have to pay attention to *lo cotidiano* (the daily life of the people). If *lo cotidiano* is unbearable, if people have to spend several hours a day obtaining what they need to survive, then the system has to take a look at itself and it has to change. The economist was angry because, as he blurted out at one point, "*lo cotidiano* is destroying our socialist project." I had the sense that he was not willing to take into consideration the heavy burden people shoulder to solve their needs day in and day out, and what this says about the project of the government. I understood him to be insisting on some sort of abstract idea of a socialist project, which is very far from the reality of the Cuban people in the closing years of the twentieth century.

The other economist recognized that the ad hoc nature of the economy at present is a great danger for the socialist project. But instead of blaming the people as the previous economist had done, he understood the need for the socialist project to respond to what was happening. "Many of our ills can be blamed on the embargo; but we also made mistakes by adopting a model that was foreign to us," he said, referring to the centralization and the bureaucratization of the economy that Castro's government copied from the Soviet model. He was very open about the fact that there is no way of keeping a market economy out of Cuba. "The challenge for us is how to introduce the market in a rational way so it does not destroy our project," he explained.

He told me that there are two main concerns for them right now. One is how to introduce some agility into the economy. This they are doing by decentralizing the economy and by putting business people in charge instead of government functionaries. "Business people know that they have to be effective, and government bureaucrats do not know that," he said. Their other problem is how to get capital, which is where the embargo has such a negative effect.

From many different people I heard that this attempt to allow a market economy to develop carries many dangers. In 1997 and now in 1998, I saw differences in economic status that I certainly had not seen during my previous visit in 1987. The person who explained this to me perhaps most clearly was a worker in a hotel where people who come to Cuba for medical treatment stay. He recognizes that there is a need for free elections in Cuba. "The problem is that if Fidel opens his iron fist, the Americans will swallow us whole," he said worriedly. "The Americans will allow no other system but theirs," he continued, "and we do not want to be subservient to them."

To emphasize the will of many Cubans to resist American control, a friend told me the following story. "Several years ago I had the opportunity of being in Chile and was having a conversation with miners. This man approached me and gave me a one-dollar U.S. bill. Since this is not the currency that is used in Chile, he had to go out of his way to get it. As he gave it to me, he told me this was for me to give to the Cuban government so Cuba could continue to maintain its independence from the United States. This is why we keep trying to survive against such great odds: we do not want to be controlled by the United States."

Tourism in Cuba today is the second source of hard currency, the first one being the dollars the Cuban exiles send to their relatives and friends on the island.[2] However, as long as the U.S.-imposed and -monitored embargo is not rescinded, "all that we get is cheap tourism, which buys a cheap package deal and spends little outside what that purchases for them," an accountant explained. "When the embargo is lifted, we know that expensive tourism— American tourism—will come," he concluded. Everybody dislikes the apartheid that has developed in Cuba: a two-tier system in which all kinds of goods are available for the tourists but not for the Cubans. This system extends to all aspects and levels, and separates those who have access to U.S. dollars from those who do not. My friend the economist told me that 50 percent of the population is believed to have access to between twenty and one hundred dollars a month. How do Cubans get U.S. dollars? Many receive them from their families who live abroad; others work in an industry where incentives are paid to the workers in dollars. According to my friend, construction workers, those who work in the sugar industry, in communications, in oil industries, and in tourism receive U.S. dollars from the government as incentives.[3]

A man whose observation skills I came to value enormously, and whose analyses I respect, knowing that they are not meant to paint a false picture, told me he believes that one-half of the people have no jobs or do not go to work. Another friend told me that she thought that was a bit high, but she did not offer any other number. "The fact is that many people can do better hustling than working at a steady job." A man who tried to sell me alligator steaks as I walked through the less-touristy areas of famous Varadero Beach confirmed this. He insisted that he fared better economically hustling a few dollars here and there from tourists than working very hard as a construction worker. What do they mean by "hustling"? Well, for this construction worker, it meant somehow getting alligator meat and then trying to sell it; he also tries to recruit tourists for a boat ride that is not licensed by the government. Then there was the man on a bicycle who offered to sell me towels. I was sitting with a friend in her house, and since it was warm, we had the door open. I saw the bicycle rider go by. He backtracked when he saw us, to try to sell us towels. When I asked where he had gotten the towels, my friend said that "most probably he stole them."

After fourteen days of keen observation and asking everyone I could every question possible, I used the last three days to test one of my hypotheses. Somewhat afraid that I would be chided for rash judgment, I said to a friend, "I have the sense that every Cuban commits ten illegal acts a day." "No," he replied quickly, "most probably, we commit fifteen illegal acts a day." This led me to a conversation with two pastors. One told me about how difficult it is to preach given this situation. According to him, people come to church in search of some sort of transcendence that allows them to escape the situation at hand. "It is very difficult to preach about anything concrete," he said. "They do not want to hear it, and we do not know what to say." Another pastor explained, "I do not know how to tell the people in my church that, as Christians, they have to be honest. I know that to survive one has to do illegal things such as not go to work, work on your own, underground, so you do not have to pay taxes, take anything you can from the workplace so you can sell it and get some needed cash."

"What about the church's responsibility to denounce injustice?" I asked. These two pastors certainly acknowledged that the situation is not without injustices, but at the same time they think that the government is doing the best it can, given the situation. But, should they not change the system? For these pastors, that is not a solution, for they support the socialist project and believe that if the political system were changed, unbridled capitalism would come into the island and undo much of what the social projects have been able to achieve.

When one comments that the only time the socialist projects worked better was when Cuba was depending on the Soviet Union, and that to rely on the United States is the same as relying on the Soviet Union, the response is that Cuba was not that dependent on the Soviets. Cubans insist that if they had been that dependent, the present Cuban government would have fallen when the Soviet Union fell, and it did not. But then, they also tell you that Cuba was able to survive for so long because it traded sugar for oil and many other goods with the USSR and the Soviet bloc—sugar always being valued in such a way that there was no trade deficit. They also agree that the present economic situation is undoing the socialist project.

Some Reflections on the U.S. Economy Using the Cuban Reality as a Starting Point

I have attempted to structure this chapter in a way that decentralizes the United States while realistically accepting the fact that everything that happens in the economy of the United States has an effect on Cuba and all other Two-Thirds countries. What follows, then, are some reflections about the economy prompted by the chapters in this book and using the Cuban reality I have described above as the starting point.

First, as an ethicist, I must insist on the fact that we are responsible as individual U.S. citizens for immediate and foreseeable-future effects of the policy decisions that are taken and implemented at present in this country. The promotion of economic value as the only value that guides this nation's policies negatively affects Cuba and many other places, and we cannot but denounce the lack of human values that rules the U.S. government, U.S. and U.S.-controlled economic organizations, and U.S. and U.S.-controlled businesses. Therefore, we cannot judge what happens elsewhere if we do not understand how it is driven by what the United States has done and does all around the world. I am in no way absolving Cuba or any other nation of its responsibilities, but those responsibilities are ameliorated, I believe, by the lack of control that Two-Thirds World countries have over the situation they face.

This leads me to my second point. We in the United States have a moral responsibility to realize and act according to the fact that the economic situation we enjoy and the privileges it gives us are at the expense of two-thirds of the people of the world. Our world has finite resources, and what we have is related to the fact that the majority of people do not have enough. The neoliberal economic policy of the United States hides this reality from the majority of its citizens. And those of us who do see the way our country exploits other people are incapable of bringing about change. Perhaps what Cuba and other Two-Thirds World countries challenge us to do is to see the broader picture and build solidarity with them across geographic frontiers so our struggle against economic exploitation can become effective. Maybe the cry "economically exploited people of the world, unite" will gather enough of us to shake the present world order. Cubans see very clearly that the struggle against neoliberal policies will be long and arduous. "The United States will never allow us to have a system different from theirs because that would change theirs," a woman who supports the socialist project in Cuba told me. She insists that with the economic changes that have taken place on the island lately, Cuba is ready to take off economically, "and this will show the rest of Latin America that there is a different model than the one of the United States. This is why there is so much opposition to removing the embargo," she concludes.

Third, it is painfully poignant to realize that whether governmental cuts are due to structural-adjustment policies required by neoliberal economic policies or whether they are imposed because of failed governmental economic policies and the U.S. embargo, women in the United States as well as Cuba are the ones who bear the brunt. This is so because the cuts affect mostly the essentials of life—food, shelter, health, education—essentials for which women have been made responsible through the ages. In Cuba, according to professors in the Women's Studies program of the University of La Habana, the division of roles and tasks between women and men continues to be quite traditional. They indicate, however, that changes are noticeable when it comes to attributing human qualities such as tenderness, caring, assertiveness, firmness of character. So, though one finds endearing men, figuring out how to make do with the very limited amount of groceries that are available falls still mainly on women.

The issue of the youth in Cuba came up repeatedly. Two remarks were central for me. One was made by a man supportive of the regime who believes that "the nation is in peril because the young think there is a need for annexation to the United States. They do not see any other way out of the present economic situation." The friendly economist from whom I learned much made the other remark. "The young people have aspirations that cannot be fulfilled in the present situation of our society. What the youth does not understand is that they have those aspirations because of what this socialist society has given them." I then engaged him in a discussion about motivations and finished by saying to him that the regime in Cuba has the same problem the churches have everywhere—how to motivate people to follow a vision that does not necessarily lead to accumulation of material goods.

Also important to point out when talking about youth in Cuba is the relationship between autonomy and interdependence, between the social and the personal. Usually, in the United States it is the exaggerated emphasis on individualism that leads to ignoring or rejecting social responsibility and interdependence. In Cuba one also notices, especially among the youth, a rejection of social responsibility and interdependence. There, however, it seems to be a reaction to the obliteration of the personal, to the collapse of individual thought, aspirations, and projects. In other words, there is no space for individual expression, because the people, the concept of nation, and the government all are spoken for by the Cuban Communist party.

For me, solidarity continues to be the main expression of justice. I believe that we have great need to continue to insist on the commonality of interests that exists across frontiers in our world today. For me, this commonality of interests, based on a healthy self-love, is central to all the struggles for justice in our world today. Negative understandings such as spiritual poverty or ascribing positive value to destructive self-sacrifice and self-abnegation contribute, I believe, to keeping the poor oppressed and to devaluing a Christian sense of solidarity which really can promote justice in our world.

It is from this perspective that I think we need to indict the U.S. Congress and the Clinton administration for the undoing of the welfare laws. I saw the welfare laws as the only effective means within the present system that could question and, in a tiny but real way, modulate the unbridled capitalism which is bringing so much misery to so many in this country and abroad. The welfare laws were also a different kind of system, in which economic value was not the only value, in which there was a sense of moral responsibility that extended to all in society and not only to those who can contribute to the riches of the few. These were the laws that made the government work for the whole of society and not just for those who can turn a profit. Many in the United States now criticize the present regime in Cuba for turning to the churches for help, especially with the elderly. I believe that the Cuban regime needs to look for effective ways to change its political and economic system so that it can take care of the elderly. But I also realize that this is precisely the same thing that the U.S. Congress did when it suggested that private charities could take care of the needy in the U.S. society. Even if they could, which they cannot, it is immoral for the government to attempt to relieve itself of this responsibility. At least the Cuban regime does so begrudgingly after insisting for decades that taking care of the poor and weak in society was the responsibility of the government.[4]

I find that we have to work avidly at highlighting the importance of *lo cotidiano;* we have to emphasize the intrinsic connections between structural changes and *lo cotidiano*. The undoing of welfare policies points precisely to the opposite. Most welfare policies have been understood to deal with the private sphere, and their undoing has been given little importance, I would like to suggest, because it is seen as relating mainly to *lo cotidiano*. However, *lo cotidiano* is precisely the first horizon of our lives, of the materiality of life. It is in *lo cotidiano* that we first meet and deal with the ethical world, that we form, uphold, and live out our morality. The relegation of *lo cotidiano* to the private sphere is one of the main reasons why the world of women is considered unimportant. The relevance of this is not difficult to guess when one realizes that women constitute more than one-half of the world's population and yet we receive less than 10 percent of the world's income.

Years ago when I was studying in college, one of the professors said that the reason why the United States was willing to drop a bomb on Hiroshima and not, let's say, on Mississippi is because the latter was part of this nation and the former was not. What this rather simplistic example taught me when I had just arrived in the United States is that almost all issues are, in the long run, issues of inclusion or exclusion. I think that this is applicable to the relationship of the United States with Cuba as well as to the undoing of welfare policies. Basically, what the embargo and aggressive policies against Cuba mean is that Cuba is excluded because it is not willing to follow the lead of the United States, to be a pawn in U.S. hands, to sacrifice autonomy and the welfare of the Cuban people so that less than 20 percent of the world can consume over 80 percent of the world's goods. What the undoing of welfare policies points to is the exclusion of women from the common good, from the world that matters. This is why our women's perspectives as ethicists, as Christian ethicists, are so important.

Notes

1. No matter how many parenthetical remarks I introduce in this article, what I say will be read whichever way the reader chooses, greatly determined by her or his ideology, whether she or he is aware of it or not. But, regardless, I need to state my perspective. I am in many ways a social democrat, which means that I support many of the social projects promoted by the Cuban government, such as education and health care. I adamantly oppose, however, the political measures that the Cuban government has used and continues to use to implement these and other social projects. I oppose the lack of free elections, the lack of freedom of speech and information (which go hand in hand with not allowing a free press), and the violation of human rights of anyone who dares to oppose the government. I understand perfectly how vulnerable Cuba is to being swallowed by the United States, and I will always energetically denounce any such attempts. I do not believe that capitalism and democracy are the same thing—a myth that is as much alive in Cuba as it is in the United States, read in each of these countries from two different sides. Furthermore, I do not believe that true justice can exist within capitalism, though I do see the need for some sort of market economy.

2. I know that this is also true of several nations in Central America and most probably in other parts of the world. Those with least resources continue to be the ones who help the poor throughout the world. Though there are a noticeable number of Cubans living in the United States who are not poor, in the majority of those cases, their families and friends also left Cuba. The Cubans who live in the United States who have family and friends back in the

island to whom they send money are mostly those of us with the least economic resources.

3. Freedom of speech is very limited in Cuba, but the jokes weave a deeply insightful narrative. The jokes are funny, but since many are a critique of society, they are also extremely sad. Here is one of them: The police arrested a drunk, whose only answer to all questions was "I am a bellboy at the Riviera Hotel." Finally, in the early hours of the morning, the police were able to get him to tell them the name of his wife. When she came to pick him up, the police asked her why he was so fixated on being a bellboy at the Riviera. Her answer, which points to the need for access to U.S. dollars, was, "When he gets drunk, he gets delusions of grandeur. In reality, he's a neurosurgeon."

4. I believe also, however, that the Cuban government has not allowed the churches to help until now because this gives them a space and importance in civil society that the government has not been willing to give them. I believe that only because it is faced with the desperation of the present situation has the Castro government allowed the churches to begin performing some social action, acting beyond their own doors.

Welfare in the Age of Spectacles

Emilie M. Townes

IT WAS EARLY 1981. NANCY REAGAN wanted new china for the White House. The cost of the Lennox pattern with a raised gold presidential seal was $209,508 for 220 place settings. Ronald Reagan was talking about cutting welfare eligibility as the misery index (inflation plus unemployment) was more than 20 percent.

Our culture has developed a fascination and admiration for power and status. Nothing is more important to this culture than its symbols. Reagan inherited an America in shock from a decade of humiliation. We had lost the longest war in our history as a nation. A president had resigned in disgrace. Our economy was in shambles. Only one-fourth of the voting-age population felt that they could trust government to do what was right most of the time. Jimmy Carter had talked about malaise; Ronald Reagan's response was to talk about power and status. The 1960s spawned the civil rights movement, the antiwar movement, and Woodstock. Reagan talked about the magic of the marketplace—with trickle-down and tax cuts.

Money words, "yuppie," "buppie," "upscale," "privatization," "takeover," became the key language of the 1980s. In the culture of power and status, the past was modern because it held the key to the future. Getting rich was justified because it left the nation better off. Cutting aid to the poor was humane because welfare hurt initiative. The Reagan administration cut personal taxes and established Justice Department guidelines that all but ended antitrust activity.

On Wall Street, we created a paper economy in which the buying and selling of companies were more profitable than running them. Leveraged buyouts and junk bonds made the hostile takeover possible. "Greenmail" was paid to avoid takeovers. Companies were attacked by "raiders" and saved by "white knights." Fired executives floated into retirement on "golden parachutes." While Ronald Reagan spoke of "welfare queens," national attention was diverted away from the looting of the nation's savings and loans by wealthy white men.

In our foreign policy, there was a revival of the Imperial America. We became committed to showing our power. From 1980 to 1987, the military budget more than doubled, to $282 billion annually. Reagan called for us to abandon our "Vietnam syndrome."

The 1983 Grenada invasion came less than seventy-two hours after Lebanese terrorists killed 241 Marines in their barracks. It refocused our attention on a part of the world that has been an American sore spot since the 1979 Nicaraguan revolution. The fighting was over in days. Casualties (as wars go) were light: 19 killed; 115 wounded; 8,612 medals awarded. Many in the land experienced an enormous sense of release of tension: we were no longer a helpless giant.

Yuppies and buppies became dream consumers. The Laffer curve was tailor made for this group, and a new bootstrap was invented: All we have to do is lower tax rates at the upper level, and the rich will try to get richer. In so doing, they would improve the economy and government revenues through their investments and business activities. Jokes abounded about the materialism of yuppies and their passion for brand names. But many of us would only buy Louis Vuitton, Gucci, Mercedes, Liz Claiborne—or at least we wished we could.

The essence of who we were as a nation was image—the extravaganza (grand cultural/master narratives writ large). Reagan's first inauguration cost $8 million for four days (an $800,000 fireworks display at the Lincoln Memorial, two nights of show-business performances, nine inaugural balls). But these extravaganzas were not concerned with the work ethic of small-town America; they were advertisements for America the Grand. The beautiful was the expensive; the good was the costly.

The 1984 Olympics in Los Angeles saw the new patriotism evidenced in the crowds chanting "U.S.A." every time a U.S. athlete competed. The resurgence of national pride Reagan advocated was captured in the $6 million opening and closing ceremonies directed by Hollywood producer David Wolper.

The two hundredth anniversary of the Statue of Liberty saw an opening night in which the faces of the president and his wife were superimposed on the relit statue. Later, Reagan spoke of his tax bill putting a smile on Liberty. Wolper was the director again, this time with a $30 million budget.

And of all the various messages that we, as a nation, drew from this, at least one message was clear: to be an American was to be powerful and to be powerful was to be rich. Reagan assured us that the social safety net for the elderly, needy, disabled, and unemployed would be left intact in this new culture of power and status. However, the crucial point was that the safety net was to be kept out of sight. The problem, it seems, was that our concern for the poor actually crippled them.

Charles Murray, in *Losing Ground* (a 1984 book that was mandatory reading in the Reagan administration), told us that because of relaxed welfare standards and liberal court rulings, the 1960s made it easier for the poor to get along without jobs and to get away with crimes. Murray's methodology was—and is—a conservative individualistic analysis of poverty and welfare policy. For him, the only impulse that is dependable is self-interest. Therefore, he argues for individual freedom unrestrained by government intervention. Murray understood poverty as a personal failure compounded by government-created bad incentives. For him, the only welfare program is one that does not exist at all, as individuals should be left alone to make their own way in life or depend on the charity of their families or neighbors.

Murray's view of poverty offered Reagan the perfect reason to cut back on aiding the poor. The denial of compassion became respectable as the standard of living for the people living in the bottom one-fifth of the economic strata dropped by 8 percent while the top one-fifth rose 16 percent. All this while, Irangate, the 1987 stock market crash, EPA scandals, influence-peddling trials of White House aides (something that remains a feature in the Clinton administration) had little or no effect on the culture of power and states.

In the 1970s, we jogged our way to health. By the 1980s, we powered our way to health with the Nautilus machine or liposuction. The point of this new elegance was to make it clear that what lay beneath all the surface luxury was raw power.

What happened to us is a classic shell game. If the past could be appropriated, it is a powerful weapon for discrediting anyone who opposes the culture of power and status—and, what is more important, all its traditions and values. Make no mistake, those who voted for Reagan and Bush in the 1980s were not voting out of simple self-interest. In 1984, the Reagan-Bush voting bloc comprised 54 percent of blue-collar workers, 59 percent of white-collar workers, and 57 percent of those with incomes between $12,500 and $24,999. They were voting for a culture they saw as hopeful and with which they identified—even though it did not benefit them directly. Part of the cost of that identification was a $2 trillion federal debt and a $500 billion-plus savings-and-loan scandal.

The 1990s have been no better. The current drive for tax cuts and spending reductions is due, in some measure, to Bill Clinton's attempt to shift the balance slightly in 1992. The wealthy paid 16 percent more in taxes the following year as a result, and the antiwelfare rhetoric began in earnest once again. As the dust settles from the Personal Responsibility and Work Opportunity Reconciliation Act of 1996, it is becoming increasingly clear that low-income and poor people are the ones who must bear the weight of balancing the budget. The only deep and/or multiyear budget cuts that were actually enacted as a part of the tax reform of 1996 affect poor and low-income folks.

The moralization of poverty in the age of spectacle is a gruesome and death-dealing pageant for poor and low-income women, men, and children. The poor in U.S. culture and society are often ignored, rendered faceless, or labeled "undeserving"; they are considered an eyesore, their own worst enemy, or simply down on their luck. The recent welfare reforms were crafted with these negative images playing a tremendous (sub)conscious role. These degrading images tell us that poverty is an aberration of the grand narrative of progress and success which fuels much of our culture, or it is an end produced by the poor themselves—they have simply brought this on themselves. In a rather curious circular logic, media portrayals of poverty point out the ways in which the poor suffer from forms of deprivation and then loop back to define those differences as the cause of poverty itself.

The results are all too predictable: there is something fundamentally wrong with the victims. Pundits point to biology, psychology, family environment, community, race, or, more often, to combinations of these in order to map out the reasons for poverty. They also point to these influences in plotting strategies to deal with the gross assumption (which turns into conviction) that the poor are failures because they have not lifted themselves out of poverty. This cesspool of ideologies ignores the fact that poverty in the United States is systematic and the direct result of political and economic policies that deprive people of jobs, subsistence wages, and access to health care.

To speak of "the poor" in U.S. society is to attempt to synthesize a variety of highly diverse people who need different kinds of help. This has, can be, and will continue to be disastrous as governmental policies continually seek to formulate a single policy to deal with the poor through welfare reforms. Welfare is a complex and interlocking set of dynamics that combine (at bare minimum) education, jobs, housing and homelessness, crime, addictions, race, gender, class, health care, and geography.

The war on welfare recipients is, I believe, a strategy being employed by political leaders—both Democrat and Republican—to shift the attention away from the government's redistribution of wealth to the wealthy. We have become an economically stratified industrial nation. The richest 1 percent of U.S. households (those with a minimum net worth of $2.3 million) nearly equals the wealth of the bottom 95 percent of U.S. households.

What does it mean when more than 93 percent of the budget reductions in entitlements have come from programs for low-income people? When the 104th Congress finished its work in 1996, it had reduced entitlement programs by $65.6 billion in the period from 1996 to 2002. Within this amount, almost $61 billion comes from low-income entitlement programs such as food stamps and the Supplemental Security Income program (SSI) for the elderly and disabled poor, and assistance to legal immigrants. One frustrating reality in this is that although entitlement programs for low-income folks accounted for 93 percent of the reduction in entitlement programs, these same programs accounted for only 37 percent of total expenditures for entitlement programs other than Social Security and only 23 percent of all entitlement spending.

Even those programs for low-income folks that are not entitlements experienced a disproportionate reduction in funding in the 1996 budget cuts that ushered in welfare reform. Although these programs represented 21 percent of overall funding for nondefense discretionary programs, they bore more than one and one-half times their share of the nondefense discretionary cuts. From 1994 to 1996 alone, funding for discretionary programs for low-income households was reduced more than 10 percent while funding for other nondefense discretionary programs shrank 5 percent.

There is something dreadfully wrong here.

The chapters in this book begin to show us the nature and the texture of what is wrong with a welfare policy that has at its core the demonization of poor women, children, and men. This policy sees poverty (and those who endure it) as the problem rather than a socioeconomic system structured to insure inequality while touting its openness to all: one must simply work harder to reap the benefits that are there for the taking.

From a clear and abiding stance of justice and justice-making, the authors point to the very real and concrete public policy issues spawned by neoliberal economic policies that demonize poverty. The result becomes a deadly economic funnel that sucks the lifeblood and life chances out of those of us who live in the bottom and middle tiers of economic life while sanctioning corporate welfare.

They pinpoint the ways in which feminist, *mujerista*, and womanist ethics wed theory and practice. Because the authors have, at the very foundation of their work, a sense of accountability to concrete individuals *and* communities, a moral insistence on the relationality of all things, each offers astute analysis *and* practical suggestions and insights on the nature of welfare and its impact on the lives of children, women, and men. In short, the authors are grounded in the concrete experiences of people and not in distracting abstractions that serve to obscure the real-life suffering and triumphs in living and surviving.

Such attention to concrete living necessitates an interstructured analysis that can balance competing and contradictory claims with ones that are in concert with each other. Such an analysis, as the authors note, can clarify the complexity of our humanness and give us more helpful and liberatory analytical tools. Monocausal and monolithic theoretical or practical frameworks are insufficient and may, in fact, serve to reinscribe patterns of domination and subordination that sanction the moralization of poverty in new and more deadly forms.

Seeking to do a feminist or womanist analysis of the nature of the transformation necessary to deliver us from the fears and hatreds and absolute ignorance that often fuel our understanding of welfare policy, the lives of those who need welfare assistance, and the policies we then shape is much like searching for paradise in a world of theme parks. This can be a maddening search through the maze of socioeconomic inequalities that are spawning theoethical debates that are not anchored in the realities of poverty in the United States. Rather than factor in the cost of dead-end jobs and disposable workers in the social order, welfare reform ignored the fact that real wages for average workers are plummeting to levels below those of 1967: 16 percent between 1973 and 1993. That this is happening in the midst of rising productivity represents irony and obscenity combined. Meanwhile, the average CEO of a major corporation earned as much as 41 factory workers in 1960 and 149 factory workers in 1993.

This age of spectacle, our postmodern culture, suffers from the enormous impact of market forces on everyday life. Everyday life has become commodified as corporate profits shoot through the roof in an ironic but deadly gambol. In 1994 alone, the profits of the Fortune 500 companies shot up 54 percent while growth in sales was only 8 percent. This disjuncture was made possible by slashing payrolls, investing in technology, overhauling assembly lines, and reducing fringe benefits. Companies reduced their work force and became more efficient in creating greater profits. Union jobs, which provide better wages and benefits, are disappearing. The downsizing of corporate America has meant the downsizing of the poor.

This tumbledown economic reality has also ushered in the age of racist, sexist, and classist ideologies which mask the realities of an increasingly morally bankrupt economic climate in the United States. These deadly ideologies function to mask the fact that the majority of the poor and those on welfare are white. Inner-city neighborhoods are viewed as sites of pathology and hopelessness. Rural areas are ignored or painted with the pastoral gloss of rugged individualism as the last vestige of true Americana.

Our views of welfare and welfare reform are rimmed with these inadequate and specious views of life in America. We have created (and now are maintaining) a society that simply refuses to care beyond our narrow self-interests. The 1996 welfare reforms are the institutionalization of this callousness. And worse, we have tied these reforms to the hope that our economy will remain strong and provide the jobs needed to give the reforms enacted a chance to work. This is a dangerous assumption and may prove to be a deadly one. If the conditions in Hawaii in 1998 are any indication, the reforms of 1996 may find a most inhospitable economic climate in which to work. Although most of the country has seen dramatic declines in welfare in our current economic boom, Hawaii is experiencing the opposite because its economy is more closely tied to faltering Japanese markets. Welfare rolls are climbing, and Hawaii may be the test case to see if welfare reform can work in a bad economy. Conservatives and liberals have differing interpretations and predictions of (and prescriptions for) what is happening and what needs to happen in Hawaii. But the bottom line will be: Can these reforms—built on mean-spiritedness, self-interest, stereotypes, and political expediency—work to enhance the lives of those who are living in whirlpools of catastrophe in postmodern America? I think not.

The old welfare law needed reforms because it did not adequately require or provide opportunities for work and parental responsibility to help families to get off the roles. Indeed, it often locked families into dependency that had the potential for becoming generational (although this potential was not necessarily fulfilled). However, the crafting of the recent reforms was built in an atmosphere in which the commodification of lives through spectacle, extravaganza, and political-rhetorical absolutes polarized and obscured lives. For conservatives, federal entitlements were equivalent to irresponsibility and lifelong dependency. For liberals, the replacement of entitlements with block grants was equivalent to work requirements. Left in the middle, as political fodder, are poor children and their families. This is truly obscene.

Resources

Abramovitz, Mimi. *Regulating the Lives of Women: Social Welfare Policy from Colonial Times to the Present.* Boston: South End, 1996.

Albelda, Randy, and Chris Tilly. *Glass Ceilings and Bottomless Pits: Women's Work, Women's Poverty.* Boston: South End, 1997.

Albelda, Randy, Nancy Folbre, and the Center for Popular Economics. *The War on the Poor: A Defense Manual.* New York: New Press, 1996.

Amott, Teresa. *Caught in the Crisis: Women and the U.S. Economy Today.* New York: Monthly Review Press, 1993.

Amott, Teresa, and Julie Matthaei. *Race, Gender and Work: A Multicultural Economic History of Women in the United States.* Boston: South End, 1991.

Browning, Don S., Bonnie J. Miller-McLemore, Pamela D. Couture, K. Brynolf Lyon, and Robert M. Franklin. *From Culture Wars to Common Ground: Religion and the American Family Debate.* Louisville, Ky.: Westminster John Knox, 1997.

Cobb, John, and Herman Daly. *For the Common Good: Redirecting the Economy Toward Community, the Environment, and a Sustainable Future.* Rev. ed. Boston: Beacon, 1994.

Coontz, Stephanie. *The Way We Never Were: American Families and the Nostalgia Trap.* New York: Basic Books, 1992.

Copeland, Warren. *And the Poor Get Welfare: The Ethics of Poverty in the United States.* Nashville: Abingdon, 1994.

Couture, Pamela. *Blessed Are the Poor? Women's Poverty, Family Policy, and Practical Theology.* Nashville: Abingdon, 1991.

Dill, Bonnie Thornton, and Maxine Baca Zinn, eds. *Women of Color in U.S. Society.* Philadelphia: Temple University Press, 1994.

Edin, Kathryn, and Laura Lein. *Making Ends Meet: How Single Mothers Survive Welfare and Low-Wage Work.* New York: Russell Sage Foundation, 1997.

Ferber, Marianne A., and Julie A. Nelson, eds. *Beyond Economic Man: Feminist Theory and Economics.* Chicago: University of Chicago Press, 1993.

Fineman, Martha Albertson. *The Neutered Mother, the Sexual Family, and Other Twentieth Century Tragedies.* New York: Routledge, 1995.

Folbre, Nancy. *Who Pays for the Kids? Gender and the Structures of Constraint.* New York: Routledge, 1994.

233

Funiciello, Theresa. *Tyranny of Kindness: Dismantling the Welfare System to End Poverty in America.* New York: Atlantic Monthly Press, 1993.

Gans, Herbert. *The War against the Poor.* New York: Basic Books, 1995.

Goldin, Claudia. *Understanding the Gender Gap: An Economic History of American Women.* New York: Oxford University Press, 1990.

Gordon, Linda. *Pitied but Not Entitled: Single Mothers and the History of Welfare.* Cambridge: Harvard University Press, 1994.

———, ed. *Women, the State, and Welfare.* Madison: University of Wisconsin Press, 1990.

Handler, Joel F. *The Poverty of Welfare Reform.* New Haven, Conn.: Yale University Press, 1995.

Handler, Joel F., and Yeheskel Hasenfeld. *The Moral Construction of Poverty: Welfare Reform in America.* Newbury Park, Calif.: Sage, 1991.

Harrison, Beverly W. *Making the Connections: Essays in Feminist Social Ethics,* ed. Carol Robb. Boston: Beacon, 1985.

Hernandez, Donald. *America's Children: Resources from Family, Governments, and the Economy.* New York: Russell Sage Foundation, 1993.

Katz, Michael B. *The Undeserving Poor: From the War on Poverty to the War on Welfare.* New York: Pantheon, 1989.

Kozol, Jonathan. *Amazing Grace: The Lives of Children and the Conscience of a Nation.* New York: Crown, 1995.

Mink, Gwendolyn. *Welfare's End.* Ithaca, N.Y.: Cornell University Press, 1998.

Okin, Susan Moller. *Justice, Gender, and the Family.* New York: Basic Books, 1989.

Oliver, Marvin L., and Thomas M. Shapiro. *Black Wealth/White Wealth: A New Perspective on Racial Inequality.* New York: Routledge, 1995.

Omolade, Barbara. *The Rising Song of African American Women.* New York: Routledge, 1994.

Owensby, Walter L. *Economics for Prophets: A Primer on Concepts, Realities, and Values in Our Economic System.* Grand Rapids, Mich.: Eerdmans, 1988.

Piven, Frances Fox, and Richard A. Cloward. *Regulating the Poor: The Function of Public Welfare.* 2d ed. New York: Pantheon, 1993.

Polakow, Valerie. *Lives on the Edge: Single Mothers and Their Children in the Other America.* Chicago: University of Chicago Press, 1993.

Quadagno, Jill. *The Color of Welfare: How Racism Undermined the War on Poverty.* New York: Oxford University Press, 1994.

Rasmussen, Larry. *Moral Fragments and Moral Community: A Proposal for Church in Society.* Minneapolis: Fortress, 1993.

Robb, Carol S. *Equal Value: An Ethical Approach to Economics and Sex.* Boston: Beacon, 1995.

Rose, Nancy Ellen. *Workfare or Fair Work? Women, Welfare, and Government Work Programs.* New Brunswick, N.J.: Rutgers University Press, 1995.

Sanders, Cheryl J. *Empowerment Ethics for a Liberated People: A Path to African American Social Transformation.* Minneapolis: Fortress, 1995.

Sherman, Arloc. *Poverty Matters: The Cost of Child Poverty in America.* Washington, D.C.: Children's Defense Fund, 1997.

Sidel, Ruth. *Keeping Women and Children Last: America's War on the Poor.* New York: Penguin Books, 1996.

Sklar, Holly. *Chaos or Community: Seeking Solutions Not Scapegoats for Bad Economics.* Boston: South End, 1995.

Sparr, Pamela, ed. *Mortgaging Women's Lives: Feminist Critiques of Structural Adjustment.* London: Zed, 1994.

The Twentieth Century Fund. *Welfare Reform: A Twentieth Century Fund Guide to the Issues.* New York: Twentieth Century Fund Press, 1995.

Williams, Lucy. *Decades of Distortion: The Right's 30-Year Assault on Welfare.* Somerville, Mass.: Political Research Associates, 1997.

Withorn, Ann, and Diane Dujon. *For Crying Out Loud: Women's Poverty in the United States.* Boston: South End, 1997.

Zweig, Michael, ed. *Religion and Economic Justice.* Philadelphia: Temple University Press, 1991.

National Organizations Working on Welfare Reform

Activist/Policy Focus

Catholic Charities USA
National Service Center
1731 King Street, Suite 200
Alexandria, VA 22314
(703) 549-1390
http://www.catholiccharitiesusa.org

Center for Community Change
Rich Stolz
1000 Wisconsin Avenue, NW
Washington, DC 20007
(202) 342-0519

Center for Law and Social Policy
1616 P Street NW, Suite 150
Washington, DC 20036
info@clasp.org

Children's Defense Fund
25 E Street, NW
Washington, DC 20001
(202) 628-8787
http://www.childrensdefensefund.org

National Association of Social Workers
15 Park Row, 20th Floor
New York, NY 10038
(212) 577-5000

National Coalition for the Education of Welfare Recipients
Contact: Pam Bayless (212) 794-5581

Welfare Reform Watch Project
c/o NETWORK Education Program
801 Pennsylvania Avenue, SE, Suite 460
Washington, DC 20003
(202) 547-5556
network@igc.apc.org

Welfare Law Center
275 Seventh Avenue, Suite 1205
New York, NY 10001-6708
(212) 633-6967
wlc@welfarelaw.org
http://www.welfarelaw.org

Wider Opportunities for Women
815 Fifteenth Street, NW, Suite 916
Washington, DC 20005
(202) 638-3143

Research/Monitoring Implementation

AFSCME Information on Welfare Reform
http://www.afscme.org//pol-leg/welftc.htm

American Public Welfare Association
810 First Street, NE, Suite 500
Washington, DC 20002-4267
(202) 682-0100
http://www.apwa.org/index.htm

Business Partnerships: W-t-W
http://www.welfaretowork.org

Idea Central
http://epn.org/idea/welf-bkm.html

Institute for Global Communication
http://www.igc.org

Institute for Women's Policy Research
1400 Twentieth Street, NW, Suite 104
Washington, DC 20036
(202) 833-4362
http://www.ipr.org

National Immigration Law Center
Los Angeles, CA
(213) 964-7930

Political Research Associates
120 Beacon Street, Suite 202
Somerville, MA 02143
(617) 661-9313

The Twentieth Century Fund
41 East 70th Street
New York, NY 10022
(212) 535-4441

Urban Institute
2100 M Street, NW
Washington, DC 20037
(202) 833-7200
http://www.urban.org

Welfare Information Network
http://www.welfareinfo.org

Welfare Mom Homepage
http://www.geocities.com/CapitolHill/1064

Welfare Watch
http://www.welfarewatch.org

SOURCES
of the

JESUS
TRADITION

EDITED BY R. JOSEPH HOFFMANN

SOURCES *of the*

JESUS
TRADITION

SEPARATING
HISTORY FROM MYTH

Prometheus Books
59 John Glenn Drive
Amherst, New York 14228–2119

Published 2010 by Prometheus Books

Inquiries should be addressed to
Prometheus Books
59 John Glenn Drive
Amherst, New York 14228–2119
VOICE: 716–691–0133
FAX: 716–691–0137
WWW.PROMETHEUSBOOKS.COM

14 13 12 11 10   5 4 3 2 1

Library of Congress Cataloging-in-Publication Data

Sources of the Jesus tradition : separating history from myth / edited by R. Joseph Hoffmann.
    p.   cm.
Includes bibliographical references.
ISBN 978–1–61614–189–9 (cloth : alk. paper)
1. Jesus Christ—Historicity I. Hoffmann, R. Joseph.
BT303.2.S66 2010
232.9—dc22

2010016614

Printed in the United States of America on acid-free paper

CONTRIBUTORS

R. Joseph Hoffmann (DPhil, Oxford), author of *Marcion on the Restitution of Christianity*, translator of *Celsus on the True Doctrine*, and distinguished scholar in residence at Goddard College, teaches history at Geneseo College.

Dennis R. MacDonald (PhD, Harvard) is Professor of Religion at Claremont Graduate School, an expert in Christian origins, and the author of *Does the New Testament Imitate Homer?*

Justin Meggitt (PhD, Cambridge) is University Senior Lecturer in the Study of Religion and the Origins of Christianity at Cambridge University, Fellow and Tutor at Wolfson College, and the author of *The Madness of King Jesus*.

Richard C. Carrier (PhD, Columbia) is a classical historian and the author of *Not the Impossible Faith*. He contributes regularly to professional and popular journals on the subject of historiography and the philosophy of religion.

Robert M. Price (PhD, Drew), a member of Jesus Seminar, has published extensively in the field of New Testament Studies, including *The Incredible Shrinking Son of Man* and *Jesus Christ Superstar: The Making of a Modern Gospel*.

Bruce Chilton (PhD, Cambridge) is Bell Professor of Religion at Bard College and was Claus Professor of New Testament at Yale University. His many works include *A Galilean Rabbi and His Bible* and *The Temple of Jesus*. He is the editor of the *Cambridge Companion to the Bible*.

CONTRIBUTORS

David Trobisch (DrPhil, Heidelberg), Throckmorton-Hayes Professor of New Testament Language and Literature at Bangor Theological Seminary, is the author of several important studies of the origins of the New Testament including *The First Edition of the New Testament*.

Frank R. Zindler is a former professor of geology and neurobiology (SUNY) and is the managing editor of American Atheist Press. He is the author of over one hundred technical and popular articles relating to science and religion. He is the author of *The Jesus the Jews Never Knew: Sepher Toldoth Yeshu and the Quest of the Historical Jesus in Jewish Sources*.

Robert Eisenman (PhD, Columbia) is an American archaeologist and biblical scholar. He has been Senior Visiting Member at Linacre College Oxford and the director of the Institute for the Study of Judeo-Christian Origins at CSU Long Beach. Among his many works on Christian origins is *James: The Brother of Jesus*.

Ronald A. Lindsay (PhD, Georgetown; JD, University of Virginia) is a philosopher, practicing attorney, and the author of *Future Bioethics: Overcoming Taboos, Myths, and Dogma*. He is the president of the Center for Inquiry in Buffalo, New York.

Gerd Lüdemann (Dr Theol, Goettingen) is the director of the Institute for Early Christian studies and a professor at the University of Goettingen. His most recent book is *The First Three Years of Christianity*.

J. Harold Ellens, a licensed psychologist, is a retired university professor of philosophy and psychology, a US Army colonel, Presbyterian pastor, and theologian. His books include *Sex in the Bible* and *The Destructive Power of Religion*.

CONTENTS

CONTENTS

OF ROCKS, HARD PLACES, AND JESUS FATIGUE

R. Joseph Hoffmann

Crouching somewhere between esthetic sound byte and historical detail is Michelangelo's famous statement about sculpture. "The job of the sculptor," Vasari attributes to *il Divino*, "is to set free the forms that are within the stone." It's a lovely thought—poetic, in fact. If you accept the theory of Renaissance Platonism, as Michelangelo embodies it, you also have to believe that Moses and David were encased in stone, yearning to be released—as the soul yearns to be set free from the flesh in the theology of salvation.

You will, however, be left wondering why such a theory required human models with strong arms and firm thighs, and why the finished product bears no more resemblance to real or imagined historical figures than a drawing that any one of us could produce. We may lack Michelangelo's skill and his deft way with a rasp and chisel, but we can easily imagine more probable first millennium BCE heroes—in form, stature, skin tone, and body type—than the Italian beauties he released from their marble prisons. In fact, the more we know about the first millennium BCE, the more likely we are to be right. And alas, Michelangelo didn't know very much about history at all. And what's more, it made no difference to his art, his success, or to his reputation. That is why idealism and imagination are sometimes at odds with history, or put bluntly, why history acts as a control on our ability to imagine or idealize anything, often profoundly wrong things.

If we apply the same logic to the New Testament, we stumble over what I have once or twice called the Platonic Fallacy in Jesus research. Like it or not, the New Testament is still the primary artifact of the literature that permits us to understand the origins of Christianity. It's the stone, if not the only stone. If we possessed only Gnostic and apocryphal sources as documentary curiosities and no movement that preserved them, we would be hard pressed to say anything other than that at some time in the first and second century a short-lived and highly incoherent religious movement fluoresced and faded (many did) in the night sky of Hellenistic antiquity. The Jesus we would know from these sources would be an odd co-mixture of insufferable infant *à la* the *Infancy Gospel of Thomas*, a hell-robber, like the liberator of the *Gospel of Nicodemus*, a mysterious cipher, like the unnamed hero of the *Hymn of the Pearl*, or an impenetrable guru, like the Jesus of the gnostic *Gospel of Thomas*. Despite the now-yellowed axiom we all learned as first-year divinity students (of a certain generation) and later in graduate school (the one where we are taught that "no picture of early Christianity is complete without availing ourselves of *all* the sources"), I will climb out on a limb to say that these sources are not so much integral to a coherent picture of early Christianity as they are pebbles in orbit around the gravitational center we call the canon. They are interesting—fascinating even—in showing us how uniformity of opinion and belief can wriggle out of a chaos of alternative visions, but they are not the stone that the most familiar form of Christianity was made from. That recognition is as important as it is increasingly irrelevant to modern New Testament discussion.

So, how do we approach the New Testament? What kind of rock is it? We know (to stay with the analogy) that it's "metamorphic"—made of bits and pieces formed under pressure—in the case of the New Testament, doctrinal and political pressure to define the difference between majority and minority views and impressions, once but now unfashionably called "orthodoxy" and "heresy."

Whatever the root causes of canon formation, canon we have. The Platonic Fallacy comes into play when New Testament scholarship labors under assumptions that emanated from the literary praxis of Renaissance humanists and then (in methodized form) fueled the theological faculties of Germany well into the twentieth century (before a staggering retreat from "higher criticism" by neo-orthodox, and then existentialist, postmodern, and correctness theologians). The sequence of Jesus-quests that began before Schweitzer (who thought he was writing a retrospective!) and the succession of theories they produced were honest in their understanding of the metamorphic nature of the canon and the textual complexity of the individual books that composed it. The legacy, at least a legacy of method, of the early quests was a healthy skepticism that sometimes spilled over into Hegelianism, as with F. C. Baur, or mischievous ingenuity, as with Bruno Bauer. But what Left and Right Hegelians and their successors—from Harnack to Bultmann to the most radical of their pupils—had in common was a strong disposition to approach the canon with a chisel, assuming that if the historical accretions, misrepresentations, and conscious embellishment could be stripped away, beneath it all lay the figure of a comprehensible Galilean prophet whose life and message could be used to understand the "essence" (the nineteenth-century buzzword) of Christianity.

Whether the program was demythologizing, politico-liberationist, or poststructuralist, the methods seemed to chase forgone conclusions about what the Gospels were and what the protagonist must "really" have been like. Judged by the standards of the chisel bearers of the Tübingen school, Schweitzer's caution that the Jesus of history would remain a mystery ("He comes to us as one unknown") was both prophetic and merely an interlude in the effort to excavate the historical Jesus. If it was meant to be dissuasive, it was instead a battle cry for better chisels and more theorists. In the latter part of the twentieth century, it has involved a demand for more sources as well—not to mention cycles of translations, each purporting to be "definitive" and thus able to shed light on a historical puzzle that the previous translation did not touch or failed to express. Judas, Philip, and Mary Magdalene have achieved a star status far out of proportion to anything they can tell us about the historical Jesus, let alone considerations of literary merit or influence on tradition. When I say this, I am not asking modern scholarship to embrace the opinions of "dead orthodox bishops" or "winners," but to acknowledge and investigate the choices the church's first intellectuals made and their reasons for making them. The politicization of sources, the uninformative vivisection of historically important theological disputes into a discussion of outcomes (winners, losers) may make great stuff for the Discovery channel or the Easter edition of *Time*, but it is shamelessly Hollywood and depends on a culture of like-minded footnotes and a troubling disingenuousness with regard to what scholars know to be true and what they claim to be true.

Moreover, it is one of the reasons why a hundred years after the heyday of the Radical School of New Testament scholarship—which certainly had its warts—the questions of "total spuriousness" (as of Paul's letters) and the "nonhistoricity of Jesus" are still considered risible or taboo. They are taboo because of the working postulate that has dominated New Testament scholarship for two centuries and more: that conclusions depend on the uncovering of a kernel of truth at the center of a religious movement, a historical center, and, desirably, a historical person resembling, if not in every detail, the protagonist described in the Gospels. This working postulate is formed by scholars perfectly aware that no similar imperative exists to corroborate the existence (or sayings) of the "historical" Adam, the historical Abraham, or Moses, or David—or indeed the prophets—or any equivalent effort to explain the evolution of Judaism on the basis of such inquiry. We are prone to think that the Jesus we excavate with literary tools is more historical than the religious icons Michelangelo released through his sculpting. But why?

The Platonic Fallacy depends on the "true story" being revealed through the disaggregation of traditions: dismantle the canon, factor and multiply the sources of the Gospels, marginalize the orthodox settlement as one among dozens of possible outcomes affecting the growth of the church, incorporate all the materials the church fathers sent to the bin or caused to be hidden away. Now we're getting somewhere. It shuns the possibility that the aggregation of traditions begins with something historical, but not with a historical individual—which even if it turns out to be false, is a real possibility. Even the most ardent historicists of the twentieth century anticipated a "revelation" available through historical research. Thus Harnack could dismiss most of the miracles of the Gospels, argue for absolute freedom of inquiry in Gospels research (a theme Bultmann would take up), and insist that "historical knowledge is necessary for every Christian and not just for the historian"—all, however, in order to winnow "the timeless nucleus of Christianity from its various time bound trappings."[1]

The so-called Jesus Seminar of the last century was perhaps the last gasp of the Platonic Fallacy in action. Formed to "get at" the authentic sayings of Jesus, it suffered from the conventional hammer and chisel approach to the sources that has characterized every similar venture since the nineteenth century, missing only the idealistic and theological motives for sweeping up afterward. It will remain famous primarily for its eccentricity, its claim to be a kind of Jesus-vetting jury and to establish through a consensus (never reached) what has evaded lonelier scholarship for centuries.

The Seminar was happy with a miracle-free Jesus, a fictional resurrection, a Jesus whose sayings were as remarkable as "And how are you today, Mrs. Jones?" It used and disused standard forms of biblical criticism selectively and often inexplicably to offer readers a "Jesus they never knew": a Galilean peasant, a cynic, a de-eschatologized prophet, a craftsman whose dad was a day laborer in nearby Sepphoris (never mind the Nazareth issue, or the Joseph issue). These purportedly "historical" Jesuses were meant to be more plausible than the Jesus whose DNA lived on in the fantasies of Dan Brown and Nikos Kazantzakis. But, in fact, they began to blur. It betimes took sources too literally and not literally enough, and when it became clear that the star system it evoked was resulting in something like a Catherine wheel rather than a conclusion, it changed the subject.

As long ago as 1993, it became clear that the Jesus Seminar was yet another attempt to break open the tomb where once Jesus lay. It was then that I commented in a popular journal, "The Jesus of the Westar Project is a talking doll with a questionable repertoire of thirty-one sayings. Pull a string and he blesses the poor." I was anticipated in this by none other than John Dominic Crossan (a Seminar founder) who wrote in 1991, having produced his own minority opinion concerning Jesus, "It seems we can have as many Jesuses as there are exegetes... exhibiting a stunning diversity that is an academic embarrassment." And Crossan's caveat had been expressed more trenchantly a hundred years before by the German scholar Martin Kaehler: "The entire life of the Jesus movement," he argued, was based on misperceptions "and is bound to end in a blind alley.... Christian faith and the history of Jesus repel each other like oil and water."[2]

If we add to the work of the Jesus Seminar the "extra-Seminar Jesuses," magicians, insurgents, and bandits, we end up with a multiplicity that "makes the prospect that Jesus never existed a welcome relief."[3]

Some contributors to this volume are chastened expatriates from that experience, wary of further projects and either "minimally" hopeful of further results, or at least realistic in making claims for what can be known for sure about Jesus. Others are quite openly skeptical of the sources and the story they tell, and alert us to the contextual possibility that the Gospels are the products of the Christian imagination. All, I believe, think that the era of breaking rocks and piecing them back together to create plausible Jesuses, as Michelangelo created a plausible Moses for the Italians of the sixteenth century, is over. In fact, one of the benefits we inherit from the Jesus Seminar is a record of success and failure. It raised the question of methodology in a way that can no longer be ignored, without, however, providing a map for further study. Its legacy is primarily a cautionary tale concerning the limits of "doing" history collectively, and sometimes theologically—a caution that must taken seriously. For that reason, the reader of this volume will find no consensus but an anthology of ideas, no finality but an interesting batch of possibilities.

Jesus research—biblical research in general—through the end of the twentieth century was exciting stuff. The death of one of the great Albright students in 2008, and a former boss of mine at the University of Michigan, David Noel Freedman, reminds us that we may be at the end of the road. Albright's scholarship and research, and his general refusal to shy away from the "results" of archaeology, were accompanied by optimism in terms of how archaeology could be used to "prove" the Bible. In its general outline, he felt, the Bible was true; there was no reason (for example) to doubt the essential biographical details of the story of Abraham in Genesis. A "biblical archaeologist's" job was not to test the Bible against the evidence but to test the evidence against the Bible.

Albright's pupils were less confident of the biblical record, and as William Dever observed in a 1995 article in *The Biblical Archaeologist*, "His central theses have all been overturned, partly by further advances in Biblical criticism, but mostly by the continuing archaeological research of younger Americans and Israelis to whom he himself gave encouragement and momentum. . . . The irony is that, in the long run, it will have been the newer 'secular' archaeology that contributed the most to Biblical studies, not 'Biblical archaeology.'[4]

New Testament archaeology is a different house, built with different stones. It is even more susceptible to the hazards, however, than the house of Albright. Every story about lost tombs and the discovery of the house of next door to the house of the Holy Family in Nazareth is a sad reminder of how piety fogs the brain and muddies conclusions. To be perfectly fair, the biblical appendix—the New Testament—lacks the geographical markers and vivid information that suffuse the Hebrew Bible. If the Old Testament landscape is real geography populated by mythical heroes, the New Testament trends in the opposite direction. For that reason, New Testament scholars in my opinion have tried to develop an ersatz "archaeology of sources" to match the more impressive gains in Old Testament studies. We learn more with each passing decade about the contexts of the so-called New Testament period. We have not learned correspondingly more about the inhabitants of the story.

The reasons for the "new sources" trend in New Testament research are multiple, but the one I fear the most is Jesus fatigue. There is a sense that prior to 1980, New Testament scholarship was stuck in the mire of post-Bultmannian ennui. Jesus Seminars and Jesus Projects have been in part a response to a particular historical situation. Five Gospels are better than four. The more sources we have, the more we know about Jesus. Q (a) did exist, (b) did not exist, or (c) is far more layered and interesting than used to be thought. Judas was actually the primary apostle. No, it was Mary Magdalene. The scholarship of whimsy, of course, is not unique to the study of this ancient source, but in the study of no other ancient material are scholars able to get by with more that is plainly absurd.

As a Christian origins scholar by training, I am not even sure how one would go about the task, if it is a necessary task, of "proving" that Jesus existed. The fact that the majority of sayings attributed to him were not his is not an encouraging beginning to determining the status of a man who is otherwise known chiefly for his miraculous deeds. I am not certain that such a task can be taken seriously, even if it were worth performing, because the evidence continually recedes in front of us. We have established an enviable science of sourceology, but without visible improvement in our knowledge of its purposes.

Yet the possibility that Christianity arose from causes that have little to do with a historical founder is one among many other questions investigators should take seriously. The demon crouching at the door is not criticism of its intent nor skepticism about its outcome, but the sense that biblical scholarship in the twentieth century will not be greeted with the same excitement as it was in Albright's day. Outside America, where the landscape is also changing, fewer people have any interest in the outcomes of biblical research, whether it involves Jericho or Jesus. Most of us were trained in a generation that believed certain questions were inherently interesting. But fewer and fewer people do. Jesus fatigue—the sort of despair that can only be compared to a police investigation gone cold—is the result of a certain resignation to the unimportance of historical conclusions.

Gazing at the stars and looking back into history have in common the fact that their objects are distant and sometimes unimaginably hard to see. As an offering to current scholarship, the aggregate effect of these essays I hope is to discourage rock breaking, and model making and learning to train our lens in the right direction. Part of that process is to respond to the challenge: Why is this important? And I have the sense that in trying to answer that question, we will be answering bigger questions as well.

AN ALTERNATIVE Q AND THE QUEST OF THE EARTHLY JESUS

Dennis R. MacDonald

The quest for the historical Jesus to a large extent is a literary enterprise, at the heart of which is the so-called Synoptic Problem and cognate intertextual considerations, such as the relationship of the Gospels of John, Thomas, and Peter to the Synoptics. I hold to an alternative solution to the Synoptic Problem, namely, the Q+/Papias Hypothesis. In the following diagram you will note that I refer to Q by its likely original title, the *Logoi of Jesus.*

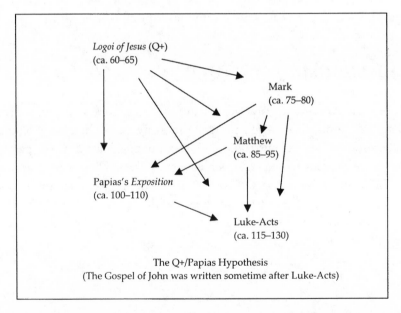

Logoi of Jesus (Q+)
(ca. 60–65)

Mark
(ca. 75–80)

Matthew
(ca. 85–95)

Papias's *Exposition*
(ca. 100–110)

Luke-Acts
(ca. 115–130)

The Q+/Papias Hypothesis
(The Gospel of John was written sometime after Luke-Acts)

Here I should also confess that, in my view, the author of the Gospel of Mark, in addition to redacting *Logoi*, heavily imitated the *Iliad* and the *Odyssey* for characterizations, plot devices, and type-scenes, as I have argued in *The Homeric Epics and the Gospel of Mark.*[1] Matthew composed a hybrid Gospel from *Logoi* and Mark without the benefit of much additional information about Jesus; Papias, for his part, tried to make sense of the sequential differences between Mark, on the one hand, and *Logoi* and Matthew on the other, both of which he thought were flawed translations of a Hebrew Gospel of Matthew. Luke, who, like Mark, frequently imitated classical Greek poetry, sought to improve on the hybrids that he found in Matthew and Papias's *Exegesis of Dominical Logia*, in part by extending his combination of *Logoi* and Mark to Paul's Roman imprisonment.

For the purposes of this article, I restrict my comments to the implications of this model and reconstruction of the *Logoi of Jesus* for understanding the historical Jesus. Let me lead off with my conclusions. I see no compelling reason to doubt the existence of Jesus of Nazareth, but I also see no compelling reason to attribute any individual saying to him, including the Golden Rule or the Lord's Prayer. At stake is not the recovery of Jesus' words but of his distinctive voice. This conclusion, of course, is not new; what is new is my description of that voice.

THE *LOGOI OF JESUS* (Q+)

Here is an overview of my reconstruction of the lost Synoptic source. (The first numbers for each pericope indicate the sequential chapter-verse order in my reconstruction. The numbers that follow in parentheses are the Luke-based chapter-verse numbers. These verses appear in *The Critical Edition of Q* [Robinson, Hoffmann, and Kloppenborg; *CEQ*]. Those that did not are preceded with a plus sign [+]. After the rubric one often will find an indented line indicating the influences of a text from the Jewish Bible.

1. John the Prophet

1:1–5 (+3:2–4, [M] 3:4–5). The Introduction of John
  The logoi of Moses in the wilderness (Deut 1:1)
1:6–8 (3:7–9). John's Denunciations of Abraham's Children
  Trees that do not produce fruit (Deut 20:20)

The day of God's vengeance (Deut 32:32–33 and 35)
1:9–10 (3:16–17). John and the One to Come
    The promised prophet like Moses (Deut 34:10–12)

2. Jesus' Empowerment and Testing

2:1–2 (3:21–22). Baptism

2:3–15 (4:1–4, 9–12, 5–8, 13). Temptations in the Wilderness
    Israel's temptations in the wilderness (Deut 8:2–5)
    Moses does not eat for forty days (Deut 9:9)
    Moses sees the Promised Land (Deut 34:1–4)

3. Jesus Acquires Disciples and Alienates Pharisees

3:1 (4:16). Return to Nazara

3:2–7 (9:57–60, +61–62). Acquiring Disciples
    The calling of Elisha (1 Kgs 19:19–21)

3:8–13 (+5:27–32). Eating with Tax Collectors and Sinners

3:14–19 (+5:33–38). Not Fasting

3:20–24 (+6:1–5). Gleaning on the Sabbath
    Death to the one who violates the Sabbath (Ex 31:12–15)

3:25–28 (+6:6–7, 9–10). Healing on the Sabbath
    The healing of King Jeroboam (1 Kgs 13:3–6)

3:29–33 (+6:12–16). The List of the Twelve
    Moses' ascent of Horeb with one man from each tribe
    (Deut 1:23–24 and 10:3)

4. The Inaugural Sermon

4:1–4 (6:20–23). Beatitudes
    Moses' final beatitude on Israel (Deut 33:29)

4:5–7 (+6:24–26). Woes

4:8–9 (14:34–35). Insipid Salt

4:10–11 (16:16–17). Since John the Kingdom of God

4:12 (+[M] 5:19). Observing the Commandments

4:13 (16:18). Divorce Leading to Adultery
    Moses' permission of divorce (Deut 24:1–4)

4:14–16 (+[M] 5:22–24). Reconciling before Sacrificing
    Bringing one's gift to the altar (Lv 4:22–35)

4:17–18 (12:58–59). Settling out of Court

4:19–21 (+[M] 5:34–35, 37). Against Swearing Oaths
    On oaths (Lv 19:12)

4:22–24 (6:29, [M] 5:41, 6:30). Renouncing One's Own Rights
    On lending (Deut 23:14–15)

4:25–27 (6:27–28, 35). Love Your Enemies
    On loving God, who will curse one's enemies (Deut 30:6–7)

4:28–29 (6:32, 34). Impartial Love
    On lending (Lv 25:37)

4:30 (6:36). Being Full of Compassion Like Your Father

On being holy as God is holy (Lv 19:2)

4:31–32 (6:37–38). Not Judging
On just weights and measures (Lv 19:35)

4:33 (6:31). The Golden Rule
An eye for an eye (Lv 24:19–20)

4:34 (6:39). The Blind Leading the Blind

4:35 (6:40). The Disciple and the Teacher

4:36–37 (6:41–42). The Speck and the Beam

4:38–40 (6:43–45). The Tree Is Known by Its Fruit

4:41 (6:46). Not Just Saying Lord, Lord

4:42–44 (6:47–49). Houses Built on Rock or Sand
Moses' blessings and curses (Deut 30:15–18)

5. The Centurion's Faith

5:1–7 (7:1, 3, 6–9, +10). The Centurion's Faith
Moses slays the children of Gentile kings (Deut 2:31–34, 3:3–6, and 31:1–4)

6. Jesus' Praise of John

6:1–4 (7:18–19, 22–23). Signs That Jesus Is the One to Come
The promise of a prophet like Moses (Deut 34:10–12)

6:5–9 (7:24–28). John—More Than a Prophet

6:10–11 (7:29–30). For and Against John

6:12–16 (7:31–35). This Generation and Wisdom's Children
Moses' wicked generation (Deut 32:5)

6:17–23 (+7:37–41, 49–50). The Woman Caught in Adultery
God's finger writes on stone (Deut 9:10)

7. The Mysteries of the Kingdom of God

7:1–6 (+8:5–10). The Sower and the Reason for Parables

8. More Controversies

8:1–5 (+20:21–25). Tribute to Caesar

8:6–17 (+20:29–38). Marriage and the Resurrection
Levirate marriage (Deut 25:5–6)

8:18–21 (+10:25–28). The Great Commandment
On loving God (Deut 6:5)
On loving one's neighbor (Lv 19:18)
Keeping the commandments (Lv 18:5)
"I am the God of your father" (Ex 3:6)

8:22–29 (11:14–15, 17–22). The Beelzebul Accusation
Death to the false prophet who produces signs (Deut 13:2–4 and 6)

8:30–33 (11:23–26). The Return of the Unclean Spirit

8:34–35 (+11:27–28). Blessed Are Those Who Keep God's Word
Moses' blessing of the womb (Deut 28:1–2 and 4)

8:36–40 (11:16, 29–32). The Sign of Jonah for This Generation
Pharaoh's demand for a sign (Ex 7:9)
The miracle-working finger of God (Ex 8:15)

8:41–51 (+[M] 15:1–11). Unwashed Hands
    Honoring father and mother (Ex 20:12 and 21:16)

8:52 (11:33). The Light on the Lampstand

8:53–54 (11:34–35). The Evil Eye

9. Woes Against Religious Leaders

9:1–3 (11:46, 43, 52). Woes Against Religious Leaders I: On Exploitation

9:4–10 (+[M] 23:16–22). Woes Against Religious Leaders II: On Oaths

9:11–16 (11:42, 39, 41, 44, 47–48). Woes Against Religious Leaders III:
    On Purity

9:17–19 (11:49–51). Wisdom's Judgment on this Generation

9:20–21 (13:34–35). Judgment over Jerusalem
    As an eagle protects his brood (Deut 32:11)

9:22 (+[Mk] 14:58). Jesus Will Destroy the Sanctuary

10. The Discipleship Discourse

10:1 (+12:1). Keep Yourselves from the Leaven of the Pharisees

10:2–3 (12:2–3). What Was Whispered Will Be Known

10:4–7 (12:4–7). Not Fearing the Body's Death

10:8–9 (12:8–9). Confessing or Denying

10:10 (12:10). Speaking Against the Holy Spirit

10:11–12 (12:11–12). Hearings before Synagogues

10:13–16 (+12:35–38). Preparing for the Return of the Master
"Tie up your loose clothing" (Ex 12:11)

10:17–23 (12:39–40, 42–46). The Faithful or Unfaithful Slave

10:24–27 (12:49, 51, 53, +52). Children Against Parents
The coming wrath of God (Deut 32:20–25)

11. The Coming of the Kingdom of God

11:1–3 (12:54–56). Judging the Time

11:4–5 (13:18–19). The Mustard Seed

11:6–7 (13:20–21). The Yeast

11:8–11 (13:24–27). I Do Not Know You

11:12–13 (13:29–28). Many Shall Come from Sunrise and Sunset

11:14 (13:30). The Reversal of the Last and the First

11:15 (14:11). The Exalted Humbled and the Humble Exalted

11:16–22 (14:16–18, +19–20, 21, 23). The Great Supper

11:23–25 (14:26–27, 17:33). Hating One's Family and Taking One's Cross
Obedience to God above family (Deut 33:9)

12. On Entering the Kingdom of God

12:1–2 (17:1–2). Against Enticing Little Ones

12:3–5 (+[M] 5:30, 29). Cutting Off Offending Limbs

12:6 (+18:24–25). The Camel and the Eye of the Needle

12:7–9 (15:4–5, 7). The Lost Sheep

12:10–12 (15:8–10). The Lost Coin

12:13–16 (+[M] 21:28–31). The Two Sons

12:17–18 (17:3–4). Forgiving a Sinning Brother Repeatedly
   On reproving a brother (Lv 19:17)

12:19–30 (+16:1–12). The Unjust Manager

12:31 (16:13). God or Mammon

13. The Eschatological Discourse

13:1–2 (17:23–24). The Son of Man Like Lightning

13:3–8 (17:37, 26–27, +28–29, 30). As in the Days of Noah
   Coming punishment like that inflicted on Sodom
   (Deut 29:21–22 [MT 29:22–23])

13:9–10 (17:34–35). One Taken, One Left

13:11–24 (19:12–13, 15–24, 26). The Entrusted Money
   Gathering where one did not sow (Deut 6:10–12)

14. The Mission Speech

14:1–6 (+8:1, 9:1–2, [M] 10:5–6, 23). Do Not Go to the Gentiles
   Convening the twelve tribes for final instructions (Deut 29:1)

14:7–8 (10:2, 3). Workers for the Harvest

14:9–14 (10:4–9). Instructions for the Mission

14:15–17 (10:10–12). Response to a Town's Rejection

14:18–20 (10:13–15). Woes Against Galilean Towns

14:21 (10:16). Whoever Takes You in Takes Me in
     Response to a town's rejection (Deut 20:10–14)

14:22–23 (+10:18–19). The Fall of Satan

14:24–27 (10:21–24). Jesus' Prayer

14:28–30 (11:2–4). The Disciples' Prayer

14:31–34 (+11:5–8). The Generous Friend

14:35 (17:6). Faith like a Mustard Seed

14:36–40 (11:9–13). The Certainty of the Answer to Prayer

14:41–42 (12:33–34). Storing up Treasures in Heaven

14:43–48 (+12:16–21). The Rich Fool

14:49–58 (12:22–31). Free from Anxiety like Ravens and Lilies
     God's provisions in the wilderness (Deut 8)

14:59–61 (22:28, +29, 30). Judging the Twelve Tribes of Israel
     Moses' blessing of the twelve tribes of Israel (Deut 33)

THE APPLICATION OF HISTORICAL CRITERIA

Because my model places the *Logoi of Jesus* at the beginning of the Synoptic literary tradition and proposes that the bulk of didactic content in later Gospels ultimately derived from it, I would maintain that the most important task for scholars interested in recovering the teachings of Jesus is to apply historical criteria to this document. I will adopt those criteria favored by John P. Meier in *A Marginal Jew*, and show how they apply to the text that I propose.[2]

Meier rightly disregards several potential criteria, such as "traces of Aramaic," "Palestinian environment," "vividness of narration," "tendencies of the developing Synoptic tradition," and "historical presumption." In other words, to say that a pericope contains Aramaic words or syntax or that it issues from a Palestinian environment says nothing necessarily about Jesus, who was but one of many in the movement he founded who spoke Aramaic and lived in Palestine. "Vividness of narration" could suggest an eyewitness account, but it more likely suggests literary art. The criterion of "tendencies of the developing Synoptic tradition," once favored by form critics who wanted to write histories of various pericopae (as implied by the word *Formsgeschichte*), has run afoul of the plasticity and unpredictability of the transmission of oral traditions. By "historical presumption," Meier refers to the challenge often made by Christian apologists that anyone who would doubt the authenticity of information in the Gospels must prove it to be false, but as he sagely notes, "the burden of proof is simply on anyone who tries to prove anything."[3]

These caveats about dubious criteria pertain as well to my reconstruction of the *Logoi of Jesus*. Even though one finds many transliterated Aramaic words and evidence of a Palestinian provenance in this reconstruction, these data need not point to Jesus. Claims about vividness and tendencies in the tradition must be put to the side, and there is no special burden of proof for doubting its historical unreliability. In fact, because one must deal first and foremost with a work of literature, if there is a burden of proof, it lies heavier on those who would push the content back to an oral-traditional stage, not to mention the historical Jesus.

Meier's five preferred criteria are "multiple attestation," "embarrassment," "discontinuity," "coherence," and "rejection and execution"; each of these is relevant to my reconstruction. The criterion of *multiple attestation* "focuses on those sayings or deeds of Jesus that are attested in more than one independent literary source (e.g., Mark, Q, Paul,

John)."[4] According to the Q+/Papias Hypothesis, Mark and the Synoptic source are not independent; they are intimately connected. Furthermore, I am convinced that the author of the Gospel of John knew at least two of the Synoptics.

Here are the parallels between my reconstruction of *Logoi* and Mark. (Numbers appearing in the *Logoi* column in parenthesis seem to have inspired free redactions by Mark.)

Logoi	Mark	Pericope Title	
Luke-based	sequential		
7:27	6:8	1:2	Citation of Ex 23:20 and Mal 3:1
+3:2–4, (M) 3:4–5	1:1–5	1:3–6	The introduction of John
3:16	1:9	1:7–8	John and the one to come
3:21–22	2:1–2	1:9–11	Baptism
4:1–2, 10–11	2:3–4, 8–9	1:12–13	Temptations in the wilderness
"John arrested."		cf. 1:14a	John arrested
4:16	3:1	1:14–15	Jesus returns to Galilee
"Jesus performs miracles."		cf. 1:23–2:12	Jesus performs miracles
(9:57–60)	(3:2–5)	1:16–20	Jesus calls fishermen

For the next pericope Mark transformed a healing story from *Logoi* into a controversy and relocated it to introduce four other controversies, where Mark follows the sequence of his source precisely.

(7:1, 3, 6–9, +10)	(5:1–7)	2:1–12	The sinful paralytic
+5:27–32	3:8–13	2:13–17	Eating with tax collectors and sinners
+5:33–38	3:14–19	2:18–22	Not fasting
+6:1–5	3:20–24	2:23–28	Gleaning on the Sabbath
+6–7, 9–10	3:25–28	3:1–6	Healing on the Sabbath
+6:12–16	3:29–33	3:13–19	The list of the Twelve

Mark relocated the Beezebul controversy and *Logoi* 3:31–35 to augment these controversies, and thus emphasized Jewish hostility to Jesus earlier in the Gospel. Between these two units he inserted another saying from the Synoptic source to recruit it for a battle with Pharisees.

11:14–15, 17–18, 21–22	8:22–25, 28–29	3:20–27	The Beelzebul controversy
(12:10)	(10:10)	3:28–29	Speaking against the Holy Spirit
(+11:27–28)	(8:34–35)	3:31–35	Jesus' true family

He created the parable speech in chapter 4 as an alternative to *Logoi*'s Inaugural Sermon by collecting and redacting parables that were scattered throughout his source.

+8:5–10	7:1–6	4:1–12	The sower and the reason for parables
11:33	8:52	4:21	The light on the lampstand
12:2, 3	10:2–3	4:22–23	What is hidden will be known
6:38	4:32	4:24	Measure for measure
19:26	13:23	4:25	Whoever has, it will be given to him
(13:20–21)	(11:6–7)	4:26–29	The seed growing secretly
13:18–19	11:4–5	4:30–34	The mustard seed
(7:1, 3, 6–9, +10)	(5:1–7)	5:21–43	Jairus's daughter and the hemorrhaging woman

The Mission Speech apparently came at the end of *Logoi*. Mark mined it for content in three sections earlier in his Gospel: chapters 9–10 for teachings on discipleship, chapter 11 for teachings on prayer, and here in chapter 6 for his own version of the Mission Speech. By relocating the discourse here, he provided reason for Herod Antipas's awareness of Jesus' activities.

+8:1, 9:1–2, (M) 10:5	14:1–4	6:6b-8b	Calling the disciples for their mission

10:4–9	14:9–14	6:8–10	Instructions for the mission
10:10–12	14:15–17	6:11–13	Response to a town's rejection
+(M) 15:1–11	8:41–51	7:1–17	Unwashed hands
(11:39, 41)	(9:12–13)	7:18–23	Nothing outside a person can defile
(7:1, 3, 6–9, +10)	(5:1–7)	7:24–30	The Syrophoenician woman
(11:16, 29–30)	(8:36–38)	8:10–12	No sign for this generation (narrativized)
(+12:1)	(10:1)	8:13–21	Keep yourselves from the leaven of the Pharisees (narrativized)

He constructed the subsequent discourse on discipleship from various chapters of *Logoi*, but especially 10–12.

(14:26–27, 17:33)	(11:23–25)	8:34–37	The cost of discipleship
12:8–9	10:8–9	8:38	Confessing or denying
(+[M] 10:23)	(14:6)	9:1	Some standing here will not taste death
(10:16)	(14:21)	9:33–37	Taking in children (narrativized)
(11:23)	(8:30)	9:40–41	Whoever is not against us is for us
17:1–2	12:1–2	9:42	Against enticing little ones
+(M) 5:29–30	12:3–4	9:43–48	Cutting off offending limbs
14:34–35	4:8–9	9:49–50	Insipid salt
(16:18)	(4:13)	10:1–12	Divorce leading to adultery (narrativized)
(12:33–34)	(14:41–42)	10:21–22	Storing up treasures in heaven
+18:24–25	12:5–6	10:23–28	The camel and the eye of the needle
(14:26–27, 17:33)	(11:23–25)	10:29–30	The rewards of discipleship
(13:30)	(11:14)	10:31	The reversal of the first and the last
(14:11)	(11:15)	10:41–45	The greatest is the slave
13:35	9:21	11:9–11	Blessed is the one who comes in the name of the Lord (narrativized)

The evangelist next relocated pericopae from the Mission Speech into instructions on prayer after his destruction of the fig tree.

17:6	14:35	11:22b–23	Faith like a mustard seed
11:9–10	14:36–37	11:24b	Certainty of the answer to prayer
(+[M] 5:23–24a)	(4:12–13a)	11:25	Forgiving before praying
(11:2–4)	(14:28–30)	11:25	Forgiving before praying
(14:16–18, +19–21, 23)	(11:16–22)	12:1–12	The murderous vinedressers

Mark apparently relocated the following controversies to intensify the hostilities between Jesus and the Jewish authorities before his prediction of the destruction of Jerusalem. Once again, he seems to follow *Logoi*'s order.

+20:21–25	8:1–5	12:13–17	Tribute to Caesar
+20:27–38	8:6–17	12:18–27	Marriage and the resurrection
+10:25–28	8:18–21	12:28–34	The great commandment
11:43	9:2	12:38–40	Front seats in synagogues
(+[M] 23:16–20)	(9:4–10)	12:41–44	The widow's penny (narrativized)
(+[Mk] 14:58)	(9:22)	13:1–2	Not one stone left on another (narrativized)

The evangelist created chapter 13 in part by collecting *Logoi*'s predictions of the future.

(12:11, 12)	(10:11–12)	13:9–11	Hearings before authorities
12:49, 51, 53 +52	10:24–27	13:12–13	Children against parents
(+11:27)	(8:34)	13:14–20	The War: woe to those who nurse
17:23–24	13:1–2	13:21–23	The Son of Man like lightning
(17:23–24)	(13:1–2)	13:24–27	"The stars will fall from the sky"
(+[M] 10:23)	(14:6)	13:30	This generation will not pass away

(16:17)	(12:33)	13:31–32	Jesus' words will not pass away
(12:39–40)	(10:17–18)	13:33–37	The uncertainty of the hour

From this point to the end of the Gospel one will find no primary redactions of *Logoi*, though Mark seems to have narrativized several sayings from it.

(17:1–2)	(12:1–2)	14:21	Woe to the betrayer
(4:1–4, 9–12, 5–8)	(2:3–14)	14:32–42	Gethsemane
(11:2–4)	(14:28–30)	14:35–42	Jesus' prayer at Gethsemane (narrativized)
(+[Mk] 14:58)	(9:22)	14:58–64	We heard him say, "I will destroy this sanctuary" (narrativized)
(6:29)	(4:22)	14:65	Jesus' slapped on the face
([M] 5:41)	(4:23)	15:21	Simon of Cyrene carries Jesus' cross (narrativized)
(+[Mk] 14:58)	(9:22)	15:28–32	"Destroyer of the sanctuary,... rescue yourself" (narrativized)

I am aware that knowledgeable readers most likely hold to some version of the two dominant Synoptic solutions: the Two-Document Hypothesis (2DH) or the Marcan-Priority-without-Q Hypothesis (Mw/oQH). Both camps may well view this list as outrageous. Advocates of 2DH generally insist that Mark knew nothing of Q; advocates of Mw/oQH deny the existence of a lost source altogether.

Furthermore, advocates of both positions will recognize in my assessment the loss of independent testimony to the historical Jesus. Partisans of the 2DH insist that Mark and Q represent independent channels of tradition, and advocates of the Mw/oQH similarly assume that Matthew had access to traditions about Jesus independent of Mark, even without Q. But I would argue that similarities between Q (or Matthew's tradition) and Mark usually issue from Mark's redaction of the *Logoi of Jesus*. Thus, the only significant textual deposit of teachings ascribed to Jesus is the lost Synoptic source. If the Gospels are indeed so literarily related, the number of possible multiple attestations shrivels.

But it does not shrivel to nothing. Three passages in Josephus largely square with the depictions of John the Baptist and Jesus in the Synoptic source and thus independently attest to them:

> To some of the Jews the destruction of Herod's army seemed to be divine vengeance, and certainly a just vengeance, for his treatment of John, surnamed the Baptist. For Herod had put him to death, though he was a good man and had exhorted the Jews to lead righteous lives, to practice justice towards their fellows and piety towards God, and so doing to join in baptism. In his view this was a necessary preliminary if baptism was to be acceptable to God.... When others too joined the crowds about him, because they were aroused to the highest degree by his sermons, Herod became alarmed. Eloquence that had so great an effect on mankind might lead to some form of sedition, for it looked as if they would be guided by John in everything that they did. Herod decided therefore that it would be much better to strike first and be rid of him before his work led to an uprising, than to wait for an upheaval, get involved in a difficult situation, and see his mistake. Though John, because of Herod's suspicions, was brought in chains to Machaerus... and there put to death. (*A.J.* 18.118–19 [LCL])[5]

The opening pericopae of the *Logoi of Jesus* present John in a similar light: he was a popular and controversial preacher of moral exhortation to crowds who thronged to be baptized in the Jordan River. I also propose that John had been imprisoned early in the document, which would explain why he had to send his disciples to ask if Jesus were the one to come (6:1–2 [7:18–19]). Josephus does not say what in John's message Antipas found seditious, but the Baptist's preaching of impending wrath and apocalyptic intervention, as in *Logoi*, may well have been part of the story.

The second passage in Josephus is the most controversial of the three, because it was heavily interpolated by a Christian hand. Fortunately, one can rather confidently excise these clumsy interpolations while leaving some of the original elements intact. The following is Meier's translation of the truncated Greek text, but one must use it with caution: it is a reasonable but nonetheless hypothetical reconstruction:

At this time there appeared Jesus, a wise man.... He gained a following both among many Jews and among many of Greek origin. And when Pilate, because of an accusation made by the leading men among us, condemned him to the cross, those who had loved him previously did not cease to do so. And up until this very day the tribe of Christians (named after him) has not died out. (reconstructed from *A.J.* 18.63–64)[6]

Much of this summary applies to the Jesus of *Logoi*, where he is admired by Gentiles as well as Jews. Religious authorities considered him guilty of a capital crime, but it was Romans who crucified him. After his death his followers continued their devotion to him.[7]

The third and final citation in Josephus concerns Jesus obliquely. *A.J.* 20 narrates the death of his brother James at the hands of Ananus the high priest, a Sadducee, who illegally

convened the judges of the Sanhedrin and brought before them a man named James, the brother of Jesus who was called the Christ [another Christian interpolation?], and certain others. He accused them of having transgressed the law and delivered them up to be stoned. Those of the inhabitants of the city who were considered the most fair-minded and who were strict in observance of the law were offended at this. They therefore secretly sent to King Agrippa urging him... to order Ananus to desist from any further such actions. (*A.J.* 20.200–201 [LCL])

This fascinating passage suggests that Torah-observant Jews in Jerusalem not long before the Jewish War were divided about whether apparent violations of Torah by James and "certain others"—almost certainly other followers of Jesus—merited stoning. Only the intervention of those "who were strict in observance of the law" prevented the Sanhedrin from executing others who had similarly transgressed.[8]

The depiction of Jesus throughout *Logoi* as challenging Mosaic laws and establishing alternative rules of conduct squares with Josephus's statement that the Jerusalem Sanhedrin condemned James and other followers of Jesus as scorning sacred norms. It also is worth noting that, according to the Synoptic source, Jesus, though critical of aspects of the law and the management of the temple, reaffirmed traditional customs, including the offering of gifts and sacrifices at the temple. In other words, Josephus's depiction of polarized attitudes toward James among the Jerusalem religious elite is consistent with Jesus' complex relationship to Torah in the *Logoi of Jesus*.

Other promising examples of multiple attestation are overlaps between the Synoptic source and the authentic epistles of Paul, the majority of which are unmarked, that is, not directly attributed to Jesus.

	Paul	*Logoi of Jesus*
Bless those who persecute	Rom 12:14; 1 Cor 4:12	4:25–26 (6:27–28)
Do not return evil for evil	Rom 12:17, 21 1 Thes 5:5	4:33 (6:31)
Be kind to one's enemies	Rom 12:19	4:25 (6:27)
Give tribute to Caesar	Rom 13:6–7	8:5 (+20:25)
The love command	Rom 13:8–10	8:18–21 (+10:25–28)
Do not judge others	Rom 14:10, 13	4:31 (6:37)
Do not entice others to sin	Rom 14:13	12:2 (7:2)
Nothing is unclean in itself	Rom 14:14	8:51 (+[M] 15:11)
Faith can move mountains	1 Cor 13:2	14:35 (7:6)
Give away one's possessions	1 Cor 13:3	14:41 (12:33)
Jesus will return as a thief	1 Thes 5:2	10:17 (12:39)
When people say peace, then destruction	1 Thes 5:3	13:5 (17:27)

In four invaluable cases, Paul attributes to Jesus teachings similar to those found in the Synoptic source. The first appears in 1 Thessalonians:

> For we tell you this by a word of the Lord, that those of us who are alive and remain until the coming of the Lord will by no means precede those who slept [viz. died]; the Lord himself, with a command, with the sound of an archangel, and with a trumpet of God, will descend from heaven, and the dead in Christ will arise first. Then we, the living and the remaining, together with them, will be snatched up in clouds to meet the Lord in the air, and thus we will always be with the Lord. (1 Thes 4:15–17)

The *Logoi of Jesus* often speaks of the return of Jesus as the Son of Man to rescue the faithful, but no passage precisely matches this passage in Paul.[9] Its value lies in its witness to traditions attributed to Jesus in which he predicts his return, but there remains a long leap between such traditions and the historical Jesus.

Romans 14:9 provides the second example: "I know and am persuaded in the Lord Jesus that nothing is defiling in itself." I take the reference to "the Lord Jesus" to imply that Paul knew a tradition that attributed this claim to the historical Jesus. *Logoi* 8:51 (+[M] 15:11) reads: "What goes into a person does not defile him, but what comes out of a person defiles him."

The third example of Paul's attribution of a tradition to Jesus is his prohibition of divorce: "I command those who are married—not I but the Lord—that a woman not separate from her husband (but if she does separate, let her stay unmarried or let her be reconciled to her husband), and that a man not leave his wife" (1 Cor 7:10–11). Unlike a similar command in *Logoi* 4:13 (16:18), Paul applies the dominical prohibition first and primarily to a woman's separation from her husband, whereas *Logoi* addresses only the husband's divorce of his wife. What makes this Pauline reference most significant for understanding the historical Jesus is the attribution to Jesus of legislation that contradicts Deuteronomy 24:1–4, apparently to protect a woman from arbitrary dismissal by her husband.

No less important is the final example, also from 1 Corinthians, in which Paul says that he chose not to abide by a command of "the Lord," namely, that "those who proclaim the gospel should live by the gospel" (9:14); earlier in the chapter he stated that he, like "the other apostles and brothers of the Lord and Cephas," had "the right to eat and drink" at the expense of others and be exempt from other labor (9:4–6). One recalls Jesus' command to the Twelve in *Logoi* 14:12 (10:7): "And at that house remain, eating and drinking whatever they provide, for the worker is worthy of one's reward." This parallel is significant not simply because of similar wording; Paul knows that Jesus demanded a pattern of apostolic support that other missionaries followed; he also was aware that the Corinthians faulted Paul for violating the demand by working with his own hands. The author of *Logoi* knew this same institution; in other words, this overlap between Paul and the Synoptic source beautifully satisfies the criterion of "multiple attestation," but one cannot immediately assume that Paul or the author of *Logoi* was correct in attributing to Jesus either the command to live by the gospel or the command against divorce.

It also is important to note that both Paul and the *Logoi of Jesus* use of the metaphor ἡ βασιλεία τοῦ θεοῦ, "the kingdom of God." This expression is surprisingly rare in writings demonstrably earlier than the New Testament, but it appears seven times in authentic Pauline epistles (Rom 14:17; 1 Cor 4:20, 6:9 and 10, and 15:24 and 50; Gal 5:21), and nineteen times in my reconstruction of *Logoi*. These points of contact between Paul and *Logoi* are important, but one must recognize that multiple attestation can only prove that the two authors, neither of whom knew the other's work, received such material as traditions. To determine if Jesus himself was the origin of these traditions, one must apply other criteria.

Meier describes his criterion of *embarrassment* like this: "The early Church would hardly have gone out of its way to create material that only embarrassed its creator or weakened its position in arguments with opponents."[10] The author of *Logoi* probably did not create Jesus' submission to John's "baptism of repentance"; surely he did not create the fasting of the followers of John the Baptist and the absence of the practice among the Twelve, for the text acknowledges that after Jesus' death, the Twelve regularly did fast; presumably he did not create the objection that some of Jesus' opponents accused him of being "a glutton and drunkard, a chum of tax collectors and sinners!" (6:15 [7:34]).[11]

"Closely allied to the criterion of embarrassment, the criterion of discontinuity...focuses on words or deeds of Jesus that cannot be derived from Judaism at the time of Jesus or from the early Church after

SOURCES OF THE JESUS TRADITION

him."[12] I would modestly adjust Meier here by replacing the words "cannot be derived" with "most likely were not derived." The Synoptic source contains neutral or apparently unfreighted details, adiaphora, that seem not to have been generated either from Judaism or the Christian movement. I see no reason to suspect the accuracy of the following information: Jesus' home was in Nazareth of Galilee; he traveled to Judea, was baptized by John (an apocalyptic and ascetic preacher of repentance who was scorned by the religious establishment), returned to Galilee, conducted a ministry in towns and villages there (e.g., Chorazin, Bethsaida, and Capernaum), and traveled with several male disciples; he was considered a teacher, exorcist, and wonder worker (regardless of what we now might believe about demons or miracles), met hostility from Torah-observant Jews, and was crucified by the Romans with the encouragement of the Jewish authorities in Jerusalem. Although the number of the disciples, twelve, surely is significant, their names are not, and at least the names John and Peter (Cephas) are attested independently in Pauline Epistles. This summary of adiaphora in *Logoi* says little about Jesus' proclamation, and for that very reason, because it is not religiously weighted, it probably reflects reliable traditions about him.

This summary, however, says virtually nothing about Jesus' teachings. Meier gives several examples of teachings that he would qualify on the basis of discontinuity, including Jesus' "sweeping prohibition of all oaths" (4:19–21 [+(M) 5:34–35, 37]) and his "total prohibition of divorce" (4:13 [16:18]).[13] Both of these appear in my reconstruction.

I would argue, however, that the literary concerns of the author of the *Logoi of Jesus* render this criterion of discontinuity somewhat less compelling than Meier might have one believe. The author of the lost Synoptic source apparently composed it as an imitation of the book of Deuteronomy to depict Jesus as the prophet like Moses promised in Deut 18:18–19 and 34:10–12. Here I will include only the beginnings of the two works.

Deut 1:1	*Logoi* title, 1:1 and 5 (+3:2 and +[M] 3:5)
These are the logo that Moses	The Logoi of Jesus
spoke to all of Israel beyond the Jordan	1:1 It happened that John the Baptist was
in the wilderness	in the wilderness

> preaching a baptism of repentance....
>
> 5 And all the region of the Jordan went out to him, and were baptized in the Jordan river].

Jesus' temptations in the wilderness after his baptism both imitate and quote Deuteronomy 8; he clearly plays a role similar to Moses when he takes twelve chosen disciples up a mountain where he presents his Inaugural Sermon; and the book ends with blessings on Jesus' disciples if they remain faithful to him after his departure, much as Moses blessed the twelve tribes before his death at the end of Deuteronomy. The author sustains this presentation of Jesus as the prophet like Moses throughout much of the book.

Not only is Jesus a prophet *like* Moses, he is the Son of God and therefore *superior* to him. In other words, Jesus' teachings in *Logoi* are discontinuous with Judaism because the author wanted to display Jesus in competition with Moses. The criterion of discontinuity, therefore, is most compelling when Jesus' teachings are discontinuous not only from Judaism but also from the perspectives of the Jesus movement represented by *Logoi*. I would suggest at least two examples that satisfy this more rigorous test. The author knew that after Jesus' death his disciples fasted, but he retained information that they did not fast during Jesus' lifetime, unlike the disciples of John and the Pharisees (3:14–19 [+5:33–38]). Jesus in the Synoptic source claims that God had forsaken the Jerusalem temple, yet the author seems to retain Jesus' commands to his followers about how to give proper sacrifices there (4:15–16 [+(M) 5:23–24]).

As we have seen, both Paul and *Logoi* speak of "the kingdom of God," a rather rare expression in ancient Judaism. The author of *Logoi* distinguishes between God's kingdom, "the kingdoms of the world" (2:11 [4:5]), and the kingdom of Satan (8:25 [11:18]). John the Baptist was the last prophet before the advent of the kingdom. "The law and the prophets were in force until John. From then on the kingdom of God is in force" (4:10 [16:16]). "The least significant in God's kingdom is more than" John the Baptist (6:9 [7:28]). Jesus' exorcisms witness to the advent of the kingdom. "If it is by the finger of God that I cast out demons, then there has come upon you the kingdom of God" (8:27 [11:20]).[14]

Empowered by the Spirit, aware that he is the Son of God, and unsuccessfully tempted by the devil, Jesus returns to Galilee and preaches "Repent! The kingdom of God has arrived" (3:1 [4:16]; cf. 14:1 [+8:1]). This was also to be the message of Jesus' disciples after his death: "And cure the sick there, and say to them, 'The kingdom of God has reached unto you'" (14:14 [10:9]). To be "fit for the kingdom of God" requires one not to look back to one's birth family (3:7 [+9:62]). God prepared it for Jesus' poor disciples (4:1 [6:20]), where those who hunger will eat, and those who mourn will be consoled (4:2 [6:21]). "How difficult it is for those who have wealth to enter into the kingdom of God. It is easier for a camel to go through the eye of a needle than for a rich person to enter the kingdom of God" (12:5–6 [+18:24–25]).

The kingdom also has a mysterious quality. The Twelve were "given to know the mysteries of the kingdom of God, but to the rest it is given in parables" (7:6 [+8:10]).

11:4	And he said, *"What is the kingdom of God like,* *and with what am I to compare it?*	13:18
11:5	*It is like a seed of mustard,* *which a person took and threw onto the earth.* *And it grew and became a tree."*	13:19
11:6	And again, *"With what am I to compare the kingdom of God?*	13:20
11:7	*It is like yeast,* *which a woman took and hid in three measures of flour* *until it was fully fermented."*	13:21

Although the kingdom already is present in the world, it will not come to fruition until the end of history, as is implied in the Lord's Prayer.

14:28	*"When you pray, say:* *Father—may your name be kept holy!—* *let your kingdom come."*	11:2

God will reward with bounty those who suffer hardships in following Jesus.

14:58 *"But seek his kingdom,*	12:31
and all these shall be granted to you."	

The kingdom of God was for the children of Abraham, "the sons of the kingdom," but it will be Gentiles who will dine in the future kingdom.

11:12 *"And many shall come from sunrise and sunset and recline*	13:29
11:13 *with Abraham and Isaac and Jacob in the kingdom of God,*	13:28
but the sons of the kingdom will be thrown out into the outer	
darkness, where there will be wailing and grinding of teeth."	

The parable of the great supper illustrates this insofar as those who were invited to the dinner ultimately do not attend, because of their attachments to family or possessions. The house is filled instead with those who had not originally been invited (11:16–22 [14:16–17, 18, +19–20, 21, 23]).

The "exegetes of the law" neither go into "the kingdom of God" nor let others enter it (9:3 [11:52]). "Truly I tell you that tax collectors and prostitutes will precede the Pharisees into the kingdom of God" (12:16 [+(M) 21:31]). "The last will be first, and the first last" (11:14 [13:30]).[15]

14:59 *"Truly I tell you that you are the ones who followed me;*	22:28
14:60 *my Father will give you the kingdom,*	+22:29
and when the Son of Man sits on the throne of his glory,	
14:61 *you too will sit on twelve thrones judging the twelve tribes of Israel."*	22:30

Furthermore, the *Logoi of Jesus* presents him, the announcer of God's kingdom, violating traditional Jewish law with respect to Sabbath observance, table purity, divorce, association with sinners, and the stoning of adulterers. In other words, his disputes with Pharisees and his actions match his view that God's kingdom introduces a new regime that replaces "the law and the prophets," which culminated in John the Baptist.

The kingdom of God is a profound, coherent, and alternative moral vision that attempts to redefine fidelity to the God of Israel. This understanding of God's rule probably reflects the historical Jesus and not merely the commitments of the author of the lost Synoptic source or his tradition. I would suggest that the metaphor of the kingdom of God implies an alternative to traditional Judaism, which might explain Jesus' selection of twelve men to be his most intimate disciples (a tradition known also to Paul). For the author of *Logoi*, Jesus was a prophet like Moses.

I am unwilling to defend the authenticity of any of these sayings; indeed, I am confident that most of them cannot have come from the historical Jesus. On the other hand, many of the elements of this portrayal of the kingdom of God are coherent with another of Meier's criteria.

"The criterion of coherence holds that other sayings and deeds of Jesus that fit well with the preliminary data base established by using our first three criteria have a good chance of being historical (e.g., sayings concerning the coming of the kingdom of God or disputes with adversaries over legal observance)."[16] Here it will be useful to review the data base about Jesus' teaching that I have argued for from the first three criteria.

Criterion 1: Multiple Attestation to Content in *Logoi*

Antipas arrested John the Baptist, a popular moral preacher (Josephus).

Jesus apparently had twelve male followers, two of whom were named John and Peter or Cephas (Paul).

His followers claimed that he prohibited divorce (Paul).

His followers believed that he said that food of itself did not render one defiled (Paul).

His followers used the utopian metaphor "the kingdom of God" (Paul).

He had followers among both Jews and Gentiles (Josephus).

His followers claimed that he had issued a command that "those who proclaim the gospel should live by the gospel" (Paul).

Pilate crucified him, but his cause did not die out (Josephus; cf. Paul).

Torah-observant Jews disagreed among themselves about the righteousness of his followers (Josephus).

His followers claimed that he predicted (before or perhaps after his death) that he would descend from heaven and rescue his followers (Paul).

Criterion 2: Embarrassing Features in *Logoi*

He was baptized by John.

He rejected fasting.

Criterion 3: Content in *Logoi* Discontinuous with the Jesus Tradition

He did not fast.

He instructed his followers about how to offer sacrifices at the temple.

Armed with such information, one could comb through the reconstructed Synoptic source and argue for the authenticity of related passages, including many directly related to the kingdom of God. The result would also satisfy Meier's final criterion.

"The criterion of Jesus' rejection and execution ... does not directly indicate whether an individual saying or deed of Jesus is authentic. Rather, it directs attention to the historical fact that Jesus met a violent end at the hands of Jewish and Roman officials and then asks us what historical words and deeds of Jesus can explain his trial and crucifixion."[17] Surely Jesus' proclamation of the kingdom of God whose ethics ran counter to prevailing Judaism and with political implications for Rome would have been sufficient to get him into enough hot water to get him crucified.

CONCLUSION

This essay has argued that the most pressing issue facing scholars invested in understanding the earthly Jesus is not historical but literary, namely, the proper assessment of the intertextual connections among the Gospels. Advocates of the Two-Document Hypothesis are correct in insisting that Matthew-Luke overlaps against Mark point to a missing source, namely, Q, but they are wrong in concluding that Mark was ignorant of this document. Advocates of Marcan-Priority-without-

Q are correct in insisting that Luke knew Matthew, but this need not compromise the existence of Q. I have attempted to reconstruct the missing Synoptic source by taking Mark seriously as a third witness to it, and the resulting text is about twice the size of other reconstructions (Q+, which I prefer to call the *Logoi of Jesus*).

Furthermore, I would insist that Q is not the only Synoptic source that has disappeared, for Luke seems to have known Papias's five-volume *Exegesis of Dominical Logia*, which has survived only in a score of fragments. I thus hold to the Q+/Papias solution to the Synoptic Problem.

Armed with this new model for Synoptic intertextuality and a new reconstruction of the *Logoi of Jesus*, I have attempted to apply historical criteria to my reconstruction with the following results. Even though the lost Synoptic source is a sophisticated Greek rewriting of the book of Deuteronomy to portray Jesus as the promised eschatological prophet like Moses, the author had access to much traditional information about Jesus. Not only did an earthly Jesus exist, he provided his followers a coherent moral vision in his teaching on the kingdom of God, a moral vision that apparently shaped his conduct and that of his first followers.

JESUS AND THE BROTHERS
The Theology of the Imperfect Union

R. Joseph Hoffmann

I n a book written in 1994, New Testament scholar Marcus Borg suggests that the Jesus of the Gospels, a shadowy figure if ever there was one, can be seen as a social reformer who stretched the interpretation of the Jewish purity code to its limits.[1] "Purity code" is shorthand for a section of the book of Leviticus (18–27) that lists various prohibitions against certain kinds of social and sexual behavior. The code forbids fathers to sleep with daughters, donkeys to be used as surrogates for males, men to sleep with menstruating women, and men to "sleep with a man as with a woman" under pain of death (Lv 20:13). The code is too early to envisage "a man sleeping with a man as with a man," and says nothing, given the androcentric nature of the advice, to prohibit the unthinkable crime of a "woman sleeping with a woman as with a woman."

Whether or not Jesus himself said anything about specific sexual taboos listed in the code is unknown: he certainly is reported as saying a few things about purity and clean thoughts in the so-called Sermon on the Mount (Mt 5–7)—but whatever the case, it is beside the point. As a Jew living in the Mediterranean world, he was a social outcast and a religious pariah for failing to find a suitable *kallah*, settle down, and raise a family. It is only when this historical reality is laid aside—for example, in the belief that as the son of God it is unthinkable for him to have had children (after the manner of Zeus?)—that the question of his specialized and unusual sexual existence becomes insignificant. And so it was until the last century—insignificant.

In Jesus' day, he was pricking at the goads of a system that equated homosexuality with the sacrifice of children to Molech (an "abomination, against nature," Lv 18:21), and in his longest disquisition on an aspect of the purity code (adultery: Mt 5:27–30; cf. Lv 20:9), he has no word to say on the subject of "healthy" sexual relationships.

This is more amazing when one considers that, in the same discourse, Jesus is given to define anger, murder, lust, and adultery (equating lust with adultery [5:28] in a notoriously austere fashion that probably reflects the thinking of a married but sexually austere second-century bishop) but has nothing to say about πορνεια, a word that can mean simply "fornication" but more often means homosexuality. A majority of biblical scholars would meet this silence with a shrug, as if to say, "Why should he talk about something that didn't come up?" I have a different question: Why doesn't he?

The answer should embarrass the knowledgeable as much as it stuns the unaware: Jesus doesn't think of marriage as Christian. Nor does he think of it as "normative," as his own preference for all-male companionship proves. "Marriage" is an immeasurably old social institution by his time, mythically ordained in the Garden of Eden as part of a fertility agreement, and he does nothing to challenge it.

* * *

Because Jesus, as far as we know, never married, one can wonder why his expert advice is sought on a subject on which he cannot have been an expert. But the common view of New Testament scholarship is that the subject of "defining" marriage does not arise in Jesus' own lifetime and that the various contradictory pronouncements on marriage (Mt 19:9; Mt 5:31–32; Mk 10:11–12; Lk 16:18) we find in the Gospels come from a later period, a time when divorce was the burning issue for Christians looking for a way out of "mixed" marriages, Christian-to-Jew and pagan-to-Christian. The early Christians could ill afford divorces: their numbers were too few and increasing at rates that varied widely from region to region and, with persecution always a threat, from decade to decade. Procreation within the sect, a form of endogamy, was a surer way to expand than conversion—though both options were tried. Ultimately, the Jewish strategy of cultic endogamy as a mode of increase guaranteed the survival of the struggling sect.

This perception—the idea of the "utility" of marriage—took a while to take hold. It cannot be projected into the time of Jesus and his followers. The earliest Christians didn't like marriage at all and tried to avoid it, probably in memory or imitation of Jesus and his ostensibly celibate community. The earliest literature is a tale of wandering charismatics and neglected widows, with the only prominent married couple—Ananias and Sapphira—being slain by God for their selfishness (Acts 5:1–12), in contrast to the generosity of the all-male apostles. That community was, we assume, celibate, or at least single-sex, for a reason: the world was ending—if not immediately, then pretty soon—and, if soon, why bother to cooperate in the thankless task of propagating sinners?

The "Essene" Jews of Qumran (the "Dead Sea community"), to the extent they can be identified, held equivalent sentiments, and despite theories being disseminated by the revisers of apocalyptic theory, the best way to see Jesus is still, in my opinion, as an end-time preacher with resemblances if not connections to other world-denying apocalyptic sects.

In such a community, any form of marriage—Jewish, pagan, and mixed—becomes an issue, an encumbrance, and a distraction. Why buy land (or hold back part of the sale-price of it, as Ananias did) when the land will burn? "Console each other with these words," Paul advises the Christians at Thessaloniki in our earliest bit of Christian literature: "The day of the Lord is coming like a thief in the night" (1 Thes 5:2). And simply to amplify Paul's encouraging words, the unknown author of 2 Peter, early in the second century, writes, "On that day the heavens will disappear in flames and the earth will be laid bare...and the heavens will blaze until they fall apart, and will melt the elements in flames" (2 Pt 3:10–13). Since Jewish marriage custom comes under the guidelines of property law, and since acquisition of property is to be discouraged in all apocalyptic systems, taking ("acquiring") a wife was contrary to the faith of the Christian community at least to the extent the eschatological framework is taken seriously by converts. To the extent the church developed a stratified system of ministers and laity, with slightly different disciplines for each, a theology of marriage could begin to develop.

But prior to this delineation we cannot assume the popularity of marriage. Even normal human companionship becomes "lust" in this context, "carousal [with the opposite sex] in broad daylight, seeking pleasure, sitting at table, chatting away, reveling in their own ignorance and wantonness" (2 Pt 2:12–13).

* * *

The Talmud specifies that a woman is "acquired" (i.e., becomes a wife) in three ways: through money, through contract, and through sexual intercourse (Mishnah Kiddushin 1:1). Ordinarily, all three of these conditions are satisfied in rapid and predictable succession, although only one is necessary to enter into a binding marriage. In all cases, the Talmud specifies that a woman can be acquired only with her consent and not without it (Kiddushin 2a–b). For the early Christians, the terms of the contract were problematical: though divorce was possible, contracts were not made to be broken. Though bride price could be small or great (usually small—a *perutah* or copper coin sufficed) according to circumstances, Christians were poor. And while sexual intercourse was considered (eventually) the "binder" rather than the modus of the contract, in the Hellenistic world, as much later in the history of sexual relationships, having sex often led to marriage as a consequence. Christians were hemmed in by apocalyptic logic, poverty, and the strong urge to chastity that emerges from the models of Jesus and his male and female followers—whether Jesus was the source of this discipline or not. Marriage, in short, was a source of some conceptual and doubtless also social stress.

A "Christian" as opposed to a Jewish conception of marriage develops against an essentially world-negating background, Jewish marriage being understood as an arrangement designed to fulfill the mandate of Genesis 1:22, "Be fruitful, multiply"—a creation-friendly rather than destruction-friendly view of conjugal life. As John Crossan has said, we can notionally separate the "ethical eschatology" of Jesus, replete with its sexual corollaries, from the apocalyptic eschatology of his followers and interpreters, with its images of violent destruction.[2] Yet in the social life of the community, and especially in the case of marriage and divorce, these two strains are combined.

Bluntly put, there is no such thing as "normative" marriage—or indeed "normal" sexual behavior—in times thought to be extraordinary and final. The strange, disapproving tones of 2 Peter suggest that even adolescent conversation has become "lewdness." The early Christian conception can only look weird by modern standards: Paul advises that marriage is permissible because the end time has not yet arrived, and temptations to sexual lust must be controlled in the meantime: "So, in a time of stress like the present, this is the best way for a man to live: it is best for a man to be as he is. I mean, are you in a marriage? Don't seek to be divorced. Have you been divorced? Don't seek another wife. If you do marry, you have done no wrong... except those who marry will have pain and grief in this bodily life and I would spare you that.... But the time we live in will not last long; and while it lasts, married men should act as though they had no wives" (1 Cor 7:26–30).

It seems fairly clear that this text does not form the background for the sacramental understanding of Christian marriage that develops in the Middle Ages, and not formally (ecclesiastically) until the twelfth century. The view is pessimistic, eschatological, and expedient—marriage is good because it gives people a place to release their passions (1 Cor 7:2–6). If it did not exist "in these times of stress," heaven knows what people might do.

Although Jesus never said a word about marriage, as distinct from divorce, the early community did, or rather gave him the words to say. By the time the Gospels were written, circumstances had changed. Paul was dead; so too, we think, was Peter. Christianity was no longer primarily a Jewish religious sect, and its marriage laws, though based on Jewish rather than Greek precedent, had already gone through the period of eschatological refashioning. The Temple had been destroyed, rabbinical Judaism was a welter of nitpicking debates over every aspect of the Torah (codified in the Talmud), and, to make matters worse, neither Jews nor pagans saw the Christians as a legitimate religious sect. More important, a generation of Christians had grown up and old waiting for the second coming—a long time of abstinence for a sect that did not find its model of sexual purity among the hive-dwelling Jews of the Dead Sea.

What could be done? The mythical encounter between some Pharisees and Jesus in Mark 10:1–12 is transparently an attempt to fix a problem. It casts Jesus in the role of Moses, the ancient lawgiver whose authority exceeds the opinion of the rabbis, in a controversy centering on the permissibility of divorce and not the sanctity of marriage. Given the parlous state of the community in the year 70 (?) CE, the Jesuine toughening of Paul's advice ("If you are married, stay that way: it won't be for long") is predictable.

To the Pharisees' question, Jesus says, "If a man divorces his wife and marries another, he commits adultery against her; if she divorces her husband and marries another, she commits adultery" (Mk 10:10). The statement is curious, because in Jewish law (the context where the controversy is supposed to occur) a woman cannot divorce her husband. Moreover, the Christian cult's view of divorce as adultery is unsupported in Jewish tradition, excepting cases where a valid *get* or certificate of divorce has not been delivered by the male. The rabbinical opinion of first-century Jerusalem was fully centered on Deuteronomy 24:1—a man who has married "a woman who fails to please him" can break the contract unilaterally, that is to say, "free her" to marry another man. If the second husband also rejects her, she is not free to return to her first husband "as she has become to him unclean." The penalty for adultery was clearly spelled out in the purity code and elsewhere. If a man "commits adultery," both the man and the woman shall be put to death (Lv 20:10). By simple inference then, Jesus' words concerning the indissolubility of marriage should entail that all divorced Christians, as adulterers, should be subjected to the penalty provided by the code: stoning. But this situation does not seem to be the object of the discourse.

It is no accident that the medieval way around the immediate biblical context was to insist on the sanctity of marriage as an indissoluble contract of a man and a woman—a prescription that arises from the propagative and missionary needs of the early church. Furthermore, in arriving at the idea of the "sanctity" (later the sacrament) of marriage, there is the added element that adultery is no longer defined as an act against marriage (sleeping with the neighbor's wife); it is now defined as the act of divorcing a partner for any reason except adultery.

The Lord (as Moses) had spoken. The bishops spoke later, but loudly. Jesus' editors' defense of the marriage act, however, doesn't make marriage Christian: it specifically leaves it *Jewish* (and in Hellenistic context, conventual) in a contractual sense but now an all-but-unbreakable contract between "a man and a woman." The possibility of any divorce, as the Catholic Church would stubbornly insist later, is excluded if the saying of Jesus is applied as a rule. But the existence of marriage as a Christian sacrament, as Luther and the Protestants rightly recognized, is also excluded as marriage is pre-Christian and Jesus does not reinvent it. And as the English Church (but the Spanish Catholics first) recognized, there is that bit about "except for adultery." That may not apply to peasants, but surely kings must have both rules and exceptions. Jesus does not reinvent marriage. He describes divorce within a strange socioreligious environment. He does not suggest that marriage is a "sacrament," whatever that might have meant, only that the "union" of a man and a woman—which can only mean sexual union in his day—represents an agreement to reproduce, one that (according to the rather unrabbinical gloss of Genesis 2:24) should not be broken.

In one sense, it does not get less Jewish or more incoherent than this gloss, since an "adulterating wife" brings shame on a husband and under the purity code must be punished to save the household from disgrace. Knowing this—that indissolubility could not be absolute—the Jewish writer known as Matthew inserts "except for unchastity" after the prohibition in 5:32 and 19:9, probably finding Mark's simple equation of divorce and adultery intriguing but incomprehensible.

*　　*　　*

How can we make sense of this tangle of witnesses? What was Jesus doing with the purity code, marriage, divorce—or, more precisely, what was the early church doing with Jesus?

Answering that question is difficult: Once you start fiddling with purity codes and marriage law, as Jesus seems to have been doing, according to Borg, can you end it? In little more than thirty years, marriage went from being the lesser of lifestyle evils (celibacy and virginity remaining the higher lifestyle choice in the Gnostic, Marcionite, Augustinian, and early monastic traditions, surviving anomalously in the discipline of priestly celibacy) to being an indissoluble union of opposites dictated by the celibate Lord.

On the one hand, this tells us something about the progress of "thinking about" marriage and the competing motives involved in giving it first grudging and then canonical approval. At the same time, it tells us something about how divorce and nonmarriage were initially endorsed: the former made taboo and the latter only rarely available except to a religious elite. There is no inkling in any of this that Jesus was promarriage (as opposed to antidivorce) or interested in the concept of "family." Living so long after the canonization of marriage and pious interpretations of the birth narratives and Jesus' empathy with "little children" (Mt 19.14, doubtless a moralia built on a lost parable), we find it difficult to accept that Jesus shows absolutely no interest or concern for families in any gospel. But that is the case.

In its long history, the church has had repeatedly to invent stratagems around the assertion—a very early part of the Jesus tradition—that his message is designed intentionally to create divisions in families (Mt 10:37) and that he rejected his biological family for its rejection of him (Mk 3:31 ff.), with later pious amendments made in the interest of covering over his contempt for the value of marriage and family life. But the question must be asked: What would Jesus do? What did he do?

The answer is obscure, but a hint of it may be found in one of the most puzzling passages of the New Testament, coming in Matthew's Gospel just after the question of the Pharisees to Jesus about divorce (Mt 19:10–12). Mark does not record this little drama; it does not (seem to) belong to Q—the hypothetical sayings source, if it existed—and Luke is mysteriously silent on the issue. Here is a literal rendering of the passage:

> His disciples then say to him, "If this [marriage] is the way it is for a man and woman, then [surely] it is best not to marry [at all]." And Jesus said to them, "*But not all men can understand this teaching: only those who have been prepared [to receive it]. For there are eunuchs who are that way from their mother's womb; and there are 'eunuchs' who are made this way because of men, and men who become 'eunuchs' by their own hand, for the [sake of the] kingdom of God.*"

It does not matter whether Jesus is equating "sexless" (*eunochos*) with celibacy, castration, or (as I think) male bonding—an exclusive brotherhood—in this passage. The meaning is clear in any event: following a discourse on marriage, the celibate teacher is asked directly about the "case" of the all-male community. The apostles reckon that, given the complexity of heterosexual contracts, not marrying at all would be the best solution. Jesus agrees. His advice is for *hoi polloi*, the "average." The dialogue is presented in a style more familiar from Mark's salon-style conversations between Jesus and his closest followers, always in a venue beyond earshot of the uncomprehending and slightly dimwitted multitudes (cf. Mk 4:10–12; Mt 13:10–15).

This gospel-within-the-Gospel tradition includes other mysteries with decided same-sex overtones, notably the famous encounter with the "rich young man" (Mk 10:17–22), the youth's later and puzzling re-emergence as a naked runaway in Mark 14:51, and, most suggestive of all, the youth's presence in the tomb of Jesus (having regained his white robe) on Easter morning (Mk 16:16). The tradition fits broadly into the pattern of the "secret gospel of Mark," the controversial fragment that seems to include a more elaborate tradition concerning Jesus' encounters with the young man, possibly a homosexual baptismal or marriage rite undergone by early ministers of the tradition.

It seems entirely possible that Matthew's continuation of the marriage discourse with the Pharisees belonged to Mark, his source, but was eliminated from Mark along with other elements of the "private" tradition because of its same-sex motif. In any case, the tradition is there; Jesus agrees—in language reminiscent of Paul's dissuasion: "Yes, it would be better to be the way we are—but not everyone is, or can be. Some know from birth the way we are, some know from experience, some choose to live the way we do. Try to understand that everyone is not like us." Jesus did not define marriage as the "union" of "a man and a woman" but defines the man-woman union as the (optional) form of contract that has child rearing as its purpose. It is a lesser estate, a ritual that seems to be associated with "the crowd."

The cult would not be spread by the priestly elite with their secret oaths to eunuchy or celibacy or same-sex partnering. It would be spread by the lesser union: the union of opposites, symbolically expressed by slurring reference to "the sons of this age [who] marry and are given in marriage" (Lk 20:34) that results not in spiritual perfection but in the seed of the church. This recognition will dominate the canonical thinking about marriage from 1208 (when it is defined by Pope Innocent IV) onward. But the "sons of the resurrection," also called by Luke "the sons of God," do not marry. Jesus the Lord, the teacher of eunuchs, like Paul the apostle, seems to have seen marriage differently: with his band of spiritual brothers, he sees the homosexual union (whether also homoerotic we cannot know) as less strenuous, more perfect, and more in keeping with the times. Bluntly put: the Jesus community did not engage in marriage. They did not regard it as a sacrament, as later Christian piety would make it. Like the Gnostics—or perhaps because of them—they regarded it as a moral expedient for the spiritually weak.

POPULAR MYTHOLOGY IN THE EARLY EMPIRE AND THE MULTIPLICITY OF JESUS TRADITIONS

Justin Meggitt

The purpose of this essay is to examine the implications for our evaluation of traditions about Jesus of the dynamics of myth-making (or *mythopoesis*) in the early Roman Empire. When the popular cultural contexts within which stories about Jesus were first told or retold are taken into account, it becomes apparent that they are likely to be characterized by far more creativity, improvisation, idiosyncrasy, and inconsistency than has hitherto been assumed by most New Testament scholars. Far from being careful and cautious in their handling of such traditions, the earliest Christians appear to have been largely indiscriminate or partisan in their judgments and, for the most part, show little concern about questions of historicity that so preoccupy current scholarship. This does not render any attempt to study the historical Jesus impossible, but it does demand a high level of historical agnosticism on many matters that is rarely conceded by current authors.

The period between the origins of traditions about Jesus and the composition of written texts referring to him has been poorly conceived in much New Testament scholarship. Most scholars have tended to underestimate or pass over the potential for mythmaking in the initial years of movements that made claims, of one kind or another, about the figure of Jesus. It is usually argued that such activity is only evident in later traditions about Jesus, and largely restricted to noncanonical sources, visible in such details as, for example, the speaking cross of the *Gospel of Peter* or the petulant miracles of the child Jesus in the *Infancy Gospel of Thomas*. Where present in the canonical accounts, it is usually thought to be largely confined to either the beginning or the end of narratives about Jesus' life—the points at which, for example, the synoptic Gospels most obviously and significantly diverge and conflict (one needs only compare the birth narratives of Luke and Matthew).[1] Invention within the main body of traditions about Jesus is often presumed to be limited to imaginative embellishments of a discernible historical tradition transmitted by his first followers—accretions that can be removed through the application of appropriate criteria (though there is, of course, much dispute as to what these criteria might be).[2] There are two common assumptions that lead most scholars to have faith in the notion of a recoverable, underlying core that contains authentic data about the historical Jesus that is not fundamentally indistinguishable and inseparable from myth:

(i)   First, it is assumed that the central traditions about Jesus originated with, and were somehow determined by, the teachings and actions of the historical Jesus himself.

(ii) Second, it is assumed that core traditions were transmitted and controlled by communities of believers in Jesus that either corporately or through the ongoing authority given to eyewitnesses guarded against significant innovation.

As we shall see, both these assumptions are questionable. In fact, the license and creativity of those who relayed stories about Jesus is likely to have been so great that the association between many traditions and specific historical events that may have been their original genesis is largely unrecoverable.

POPULAR MYTHOLOGY
AND THE EARLY ROMAN EMPIRE

Definition of "Popular"

It is important to begin with some brief remarks about the use of the term *popular* in the context of this essay. By using this term I want to draw attention to the understandings and experiences of myth that were prevalent in the early empire and to note that these do not necessarily equate with ideas and concerns of the literary elite that tend to dominate our interpretations. I use the term *popular* here, as I have elsewhere in studies of method in the analysis of the church at Corinth,[3] early Christian attitudes towards magic and healing,[4] illness,[5] the imperial cult,[6] and economics,[7] to draw attention to practices and beliefs that appear to be widespread and common in the empire but are generally neglected by those whom I believe do not take time to establish a plausible context of interpretation; those who eschew the difficult questions about not just the *presence* but also the *prevalence* of practices and beliefs when establishing the "background" of early Christianity. In short, I am keen that we recognize what E. P. Thompson has called (albeit in a different context) "the enormous condescension of posterity"[8] that has left most people in history without a history, something that has adversely affected our understanding of the context with which the earliest Christians lived. I am not alone in this desire to take the popular cultures of the early empire seriously,[9] but it still remains an underdeveloped perspective.

I must emphasize that in using the word *popular* I do not necessarily assume a homogeneity amongst the non-elite of the early empire (as though the non-elite of the empire were a lumpen, undifferentiated mass without ethnic, religious, gendered, economic, or other differences, many of which were important to them and should be to us). Nor do I rule out the possibility that there are areas where popular cultures and elite cultures intersect and overlap. For example, Aesop's *Fables* are often taken as evidence, par excellence, of popular culture in the Roman empire,[10] but we know that they were also the subject of expensive art in the empire too (Philostratus the Elder, *Imagines*, 1.3) and attracted the attention of the highly educated—indeed, according to one tradition Socrates spent the last night of his life versifying some of these fables (Plato, *Phaedo*, 61b).

Indeed, in the area of mythology, traditions could be in some sense shared across most population groups. This is perhaps most obvious with literary traditions. Homer's poems were, for example, the formative and most widely known texts in the empire. Their cultural significance is visible in numerous ways. For example, the Borysthenes on the Black Sea, originally Greek colonists,[11] allegedly continued to know them by heart although they lost the ability to speak Greek (Dio Chrysostom, *Orationes,* 36.9). They were sufficiently prominent that the poems were even the subject of discussion in rabbinic literature.[12] Heraclitus, a first-century commentator on Homer, could say:

> From the earliest age, children beginning their studies are nursed on Homer's teaching. One might say that while we were still in swathing bands we sucked from his epics as from fresh milk. He assists the beginner and later the adult in his print. In no stage of life, from boyhood to old age, do we ever cease to drink from him. (*Quaestiones Homericae,* 1.5–6)[13]

Such a picture was not limited to the educated and wealthy but is confirmed in a wide range of literary and material remains that tell us of the enduring and popular reception of Homer amongst all classes within the empire.[14] Knowledge of his work is evident everywhere, including in material of a peculiarly popular provenance, such as amulets[15] and do-it-yourself oracles.[16] There is also evidence that literary mythologies or recastings of traditional myth that were of a more recent origin, by the likes of Ovid and Virgil, could similarly be rapidly and enthusiastically embraced by the wider populace.[17]

Nonetheless, the term *popular* should remind us that our concern does not begin and end with literature of this kind if we want to understand myth and mythopoesis in the early empire. We need to cast our net rather more widely. It is important to examine literary remains that tell us both directly and indirectly about popular conceptions of myth. The works of Strabo, Pausanias, or Julius Hyginus should attract most attention, as they give us our most detailed knowledge about local myths, but there is much also to learn from ideas about gods and heroes implicit, for example, in other forms of writing, such as the popular slave biography, the *Vita Aesopi*; the book of dream interpretations produced by Artemidorus; or paradoxographical literature (a popular genre that recounted marvels, see Aulus Gellius, *Noctae Atticae,* 9.4.9ff).[18] Even graffiti can, on occasion, tell us something.[19] It is also vital to take account of the material culture of the empire. The archaeological record of the eastern Mediterranean should remind us that people inhabited a world full of myths. As Rüpke, for example, has noted, this is visible in the decorations of temples—from the cult statues or their miniatures, figure ensembles on temple pediments, the contents of the friezes that decorated the entablature that ran along the outside of a temple, the acroteria (terracotta decorations on the four corners of the roof of a temple, and on the gable ends) that often depicted mythological scenes or the attributes of gods, and the antefixes, often decorated with the faces of gods.[20] In addition we should add formal paintings that depicted scenes from myths also adorned temples and other public spaces and were regularly commented upon, for example, by Pausanias (e.g., *Periegesis,* 1.3; 1.15) but have left little trace today, although the wall paintings of houses in Pompeii, especially the House of the Tragic Poet, may give us some intimations of their character.[21] Such visual representations were clearly very influential on the ways that stories were known and interpreted ("poets and painters make equal contribution to our knowledge of the deeds and the looks of heroes," Philostratus the Elder, *Imagines,* 1.1). Indeed, we should also not overlook private or semipublic material culture too, from paintings (on plaster, boards, or canvas), to the plethora of domestic artifacts, the precious "small things" that Deetz has reminded us are so central to the ways that past people constructed their lives and allow us to get an insight into the character and content of ideas that were significant and widespread: we can learn much, for example, from the mythical iconography evident or evoked in such things as cooking utensils, brick stamps, oil lamps, figurines, vase paintings, coins, bath tokens, jewelry, amulets, and grave markers.[22]

Of course, it is not always easy to make sense of some of this data and to gauge how typical or representative it might be. The renderings of myth are also sometimes perplexing. For example, what should we make of the scrap of a second-century CE Homer hypothesis found at Oxyrhynchus that omits any reference to the activity of the gods?[23] Many of the visual representations of myths or artifacts associated with them are not just hard for us to interpret but appear to have left the ancient viewer confused or undecided too (e.g., Pausanias, *Periegesis,* 5.18.6–7; see also *Periegesis,* 1.35.7–8).[24]

A number of key modes of transmission of popular mythology are also now largely unrecoverable. Songs and oral traditions about the gods and heroes, which were probably the main ways that myths were transmitted, are largely lost to us, with occasional exceptions recoverable from the pages of Strabo or Pausanias.[25] We hear only indirectly about the visual representations of myths that accompanied festivals (e.g., Apuleius, *Metamorphoses*, 11) or public games (what Coleman refers to as the "fatal charades" that are familiar from some martyrdom accounts where Christians and others were dressed up as gods and made to enact famous mythical scenes).[26] We know virtually nothing about the most popular form of theatrical entertainment in the first-century Roman Empire, the mime (see Cicero, *Pro Rabirio Postumo*, 35; Athenaeus *Deipnosophistai*, 1.20d; Philo, *In Flaccum*, 34, 38, 72; 75),[27] even though these functioned to give popular form to myth, both ancient and modern (the mimes were not silent but accompanied by songs and dialogue; see Lucian, *De Saltatione* 29–30, 63, 68). Mime artists were capable of rapidly forging new myths, when events required it, that could provoke powerful, even violent, reactions in their audience (not least through their roles at funerals; see *Cassius Dio*, 56.29.1).[28]

However, problems of evidence and interpretation aside, the attempt to focus upon popular mythology is one worth undertaking. Nonetheless, we should note that negative judgments on the value of the cognate, though distinct, business of studying popular religion in the empire might make our subject matter somewhat contentious. Peter Brown dismissed the notion of popular religion in his influential *The Cult of the Saints*, describing it as a two-tier approach derived from the prejudices of commentators.[29] Elsner is quite right to note that

> there is much that was right about Brown's position, especially his criticism of the lazy thinking that blamed anything a scholar disapproved of on the vulgar habits of the masses. But one of the problems of the abandonment of two tiers is that the whole of popular religion becomes merely that which is sanctioned and tolerated by the elite, liable to change through a "slow but sure pressure from on top."[30]

The revisiting of popular religion in the early Roman Empire is long overdue, although important work, such as Frankfurter's seminal study of religion in Roman Egypt,[31] is indicative of what can be gained by such a focus, alerting us to the ways in which worshipers sustained, innovated, and appropriated meanings through their own rituals and interpretations unsanctioned by elite and priestly classes intent on trying to control the forms of practice and tradition that should predominate.

Definitions of Myth

It is also important, at this stage, to define what is meant in this essay by *myth*. Definitions of myth are numerous[32] but few bear much resemblance to the meaning of the Greek term *mythos* that will be the focus of this essay. Although the meaning of this word changed over time, it can be usefully thought of as referring to a story, or more precisely, a popular story of a god or hero.[33] As Dowden notes, by the first century BCE it seems to have been common to think of myths as including matters that were neither true nor probable (*Rhetorica ad Herennium*, 1.13).[34] Wiseman remarks, "Such a story may be (in our terms) historical, pseudo-historical or totally fictitious, but if it matters enough to be retold, it can count as a myth."[35]

This conception of myth might, to some, seem rather anemic. As Fritz Graf has noted, an enormous semantic gap has arisen between what was meant by *mythos* (or the Latin *fabula*) and modern meanings of myth as a consequence of processes begun in the eighteenth century.[36] Most definitions today assume that myth can be described rather more precisely and are predicated on the notion that the term should be limited to hoary old tales about a time long before or apart from the world of the teller, involving nonhuman beings and extraordinary events. Myths are assumed to be bearers or generators of significant meanings about, for example, society, morality, psychology, ontology, cosmology, history, or ritual life. "They are more than stories that lack empirical validation; they serve as symbolic statements about the meaning and purpose of life in this world."[37]

The question of the definition of myth has been even more confused by the unhelpful distinction between *myth* and *legend* so ingrained in the thinking of New Testament scholars (largely, as a result of the ongoing legacy of form criticism, and notably Martin Dibelius and Rudolph Bultmann).[38] As Graf says, such attempts at categorization are "irrelevant at best, misleading at worst: it is a matter of our own categories and there is no scholarly consensus as to what these categories mean."[39] It has also been complicated by fact that many of those studying the historical Jesus have preferred, in the last few decades, to use the terms *narrative* or *story* in preference to *myth*, because these words are less emotionally charged and allow critics to sidestep questions of historicity implicit in the latter.[40]

Although I think that Mack is quite right to complain that contemporary scholarship concerned with Christian origins has suffered as a consequence of its failure to engage with what he terms "modern myth theory,"[41] and outputs of the Society of Biblical Literature's Seminar on Ancient Myths and Modern Theories of Christian Origins demonstrate what can be gained by attending to just such approaches,[42] for the purposes of this essay, a narrower, rather more prosaic understanding of myth as *a story about a popular figure that includes material that is neither true nor probable* will be used without any theoretical assumptions about the function or meaning of such material.

THE CHARACTER OF MYTH
IN THE EARLY ROMAN EMPIRE

So, having explored what we mean by popular mythology in the early empire, we need now to say something of its fundamental character before briefly elucidating some of its central features. Gould's remarks are particularly apposite:

> The...absence of finality is characteristic of Greek myth. Greek myth is open-ended; a traditional story can be re-told, told with new meanings, new incidents, new persons, even with a formal reversal of old meaning.... The improvisatory character of Greek myths is not just a literary fact.... It is not bound to forms hardened and stiffened by canonical authority, but mobile, fluent and free to respond to a changing experience of the world.[43]

Of course, what Gould says here refers predominantly to Greek myth, and some might feel that it is therefore of little consequence for understanding the way myth could be conceived in other cultural contexts, primarily in the eastern Mediterranean, in which we know the earliest Christians lived. However, a tendency towards mythmaking was an inextricable characteristic of popular Hellenism (still a valid concept, though one requiring substantial critical reflection),[44] and Hellenism was a dynamic, component part, in some manner, of all cultures within the eastern empire (indeed, in many ways, it was constituted by these cultures, taking different forms in different locations, through processes of fusion and hybridization). While in no way wishing to downplay the differences between, for example, Roman and Greek cultures and religion, differences that preoccupied writers such as Plutarch in his *Questiones Romanae* and *Questiones Graecae*, we should not assume, for example, that Romans and those influenced by Roman culture did not approach myth in the same way and have the same capacity for mythmaking. As Wiseman has shown, the notion that the Romans did not have their own myths is really a legacy of Romanticism and does not reflect the evidence: "The Romans were not a people without myths. They too had stories to tell about their gods, their forefathers and the achievements of their city."[45] We need to rid ourselves of some age-old prejudices about Roman culture that continue to shape interpretations today; Kurt Latte's description of the Romans as "an unspeculative and unimaginative people" who simply borrowed and left undeveloped the myths of the Greeks is not accurate as we can see from a cursory examination of, for example, Ovid's *Fasti*, the poem about the Roman sacred calendar.[46] Elsewhere in the empire, Frankfurter's work on Roman Egypt shows just such mythic dynamism as characteristic of religion there,[47] and we can see something similar in the cult of Magna Mater (Cybele) that continued to develop in Phrygia and throughout the empire, amongst the Anatolian diaspora and others in Greece and Rome long after the formal importation of the Goddess into Rome in 204 BCE.[48]

Nor should it be thought that Jews were somehow exceptions, uninfluenced by the prevailing cultural forces that shaped the lives of others in the region, and with which they had lived for centuries.[49] As has been recently argued, we need a revised analytical paradigm for understanding the relationship between Hellenism and Judaism, and Alexander might well be right that this should now be "always in favour of similarity rather than dissimilarity."[50] One only needs to look at the tendencies in traditions about such key first-century figures as Yohanan ben Zakkai[51] or the unhistorical and fantastical narratives that found their way into the Talmud[52] or Philo's *De Vita Mosis* to see that myth-making was as common among Jews as anyone else in the early empire (and such an attitude to myth is not in any way dependent upon syncretism or Jewish involvement in religious practices of Hellenism).

So, having established the open-ended nature of mythmaking in the early empire, let us now make a few further remarks about its character before returning to the question of the early Christian traditions about Jesus.

The Fecundity of Myth

Myth in the early empire was *not* conservative. Pausanias at times despaired because of its constant mutations. He complained, "Those who like to listen to the miraculous are themselves apt to add to the marvel, and so they ruin truth by mixing it with falsehood." He did not restrict this practice to those who recounted tales about the past, noting that even events in his own day "have been generally discredited because of the lies built up on a foundation of fact" (*Periegesis*, 8.2.6–7).

Even when knowledge of written, canonical versions of a myth became widespread, as was the case with Virgil and Homer, further mythmaking could continue apace, often involving the deliberate rewriting and reordering of the written accounts. Tertullian's complaints about how heretics used Christian scripture contain a passing reference to just such widespread practices:

> In profane writings also an example comes ready to hand of a similar facility. You see in our own day, composed out of Virgil, a story of a wholly different character, the subject-matter being arranged according to the verse, and the verse according to the subject-matter. In short, Hosidius Geta has most completely pilfered his tragedy of Medea from Virgil. A near relative of my own, among some leisure productions of his pen, has composed out of the same poet The Table of Cebes. On the same principle, those poetasters are commonly called Homerocentones, "collectors of Homeric odds and ends," who stitch into one piece, patchwork fashion, works of their own from the

lines of Homer, out of many scraps put together from this passage and from that (in miscellaneous confusion). Now, unquestionably, the Divine Scriptures are more fruitful in resources of all kinds for this sort of facility. Nor do I risk contradiction in saying that the very Scriptures were even arranged by the will of God in such a manner as to furnish materials for heretics, inasmuch as I read that "there must be heresies," [1 Corinthians 11:19] which there cannot be without the Scriptures. (*De Praescriptione*, 39.)

Written material and the oral traditions could be combined in a myriad of new configurations to create yet further myths. This, for example, is evident from the remarks of Philo, who begins his *De Vita Mosis* with the following words:

I shall proceed to narrate the events which befell him, having learnt them both from those sacred scriptures which he has left as marvellous memorials of his wisdom, and having also heard many things from the elders of my nation, for I have continually connected together what I have heard with what I have read, and in this way I look upon it that I am acquainted with the history of his life more accurately than other people. (*De Vita Mosis*, 1.1.4)

From what we can tell, specifically oral renderings of myth within the empire appear to have been a particularly creative undertaking, characterized by improvisation. With the possible exception of some distinctive groups, such as the Pythagoreans, "verbatim transmission of memorized traditions does not appear to apply to the vast majority of oral traditions in the Greco-Roman world."[53]

The Pluriform Nature of Myth

It is perhaps unsurprising that mythmaking does not appear to have been overburdened with a concern for coherence and consistency. For most people there were no significant problems caused by the persistence of multiple versions of the same myth, even when they flatly contradicted one another, and no particular reason to chose between them. Even Pausanias, for example, is often content merely to recount different versions of a story without indicating which he considers the more plausible (e.g., Oedipus in *Periegesis* 1.28.6). Artemidorus similarly advises that one should not seek to distinguish between contradictory versions of a tradition (although he considers nonmiraculous accounts are more likely to be accurate; *Oneirocritica* 4.47; see also Plutarch, *Vitae parallelae*, 2.3–6). Even the existence of the tomb of Zeus in Crete and the local tradition that the king of the gods was in fact dead, does not seem to have bothered most people in the empire until it became part of the arsenal of arguments used by Christian apologists against paganism (see Athenagoras, *Apologia*, 30; Origen, *Contra Celsus*, 3.43; *Pseudo-Clementine Homilies*, 5.23, 6.21).

As Pausanias complained, for most of those who lived within the Roman Empire, the kinds of myths they believed did not need to be coherent or require rational scrutiny: "Most people tell and believe untruths, including whatever they picked up as children from tragedies and oratorios" (*Periegesis*, 1.3.3). Although there were educated students of myth, such as Plutarch, who tried "to purify the mythic, making it yield to reason" (*Vita Thesei*, 1.5), to remove the wheat from the chaff, standing in a rational tradition of criticism of classical myth that went back at least as far as Hecataeus of Miletus in the sixth century BCE (Pausanias, *Periegesis*, 3.25.5), they were conscious that neither they nor those who tried to overcome such problems through the alternative strategy of allegorization[54] represented the prevailing attitude within the popular cultures of the empire. Others were content to allow a profusion of alternative versions of myths to stand, without judging between them.

The inconsistencies in myth were, of course, something of which nonpagan critics could make much. Josephus, for example, ridiculed the claims of Greeks about the accuracy of their knowledge of their past history, noting the incongruities in their myths—something that he ascribed, in part, to the oral nature of the earliest accounts (notably in relation to Homer; *Contra Apionem*, 1.2–3). He contrasted them unfavorably with the antiquity and accuracy of the Jewish written canon (*Contra Apionem*, 1.37–43), although we also know from adverse comments of Philo that other educated Jews saw similar problems with the biblical texts that they too treated as myths ripe for criticism (*De Abrahamo*, 33.178–34; see also *De Confusione linguarum*, 2.2–4, 9).[55]

The Limited Knowledge of Myth

This incoherence came about, in part, because most people were not expected to know the myths in any particular detail. With some exceptions, paganism of the early empire was not a textual religion, and what texts did possess some kind of authority—notably the Sibylline Oracles (or rather, what could be reconstructed of them after a devastating fire of 83 BCE)—do not seem to have contained much in the way of myth and could only be consulted by a few specialists. Although the contents of myth did form part of most people's education, both formal and informal, at an early age, "only those who had attended school knew the fine points.... The essence of a myth is not that everyone knows it but that it is supposed to be known and is worthy of being known by all."[56] Literary evidence indicates just such partial and somewhat confused knowledge on the part of many in the early empire. Petronius, for example, portrays the freedman Trimalchio self-consciously and inaccurately referencing Homer (*Satyricon*, 39.3–4, 48.7, 52.1–2). Interestingly, as Noy has suggested, those who were enslaved were often prevented from having anything but the most limited knowledge of the cults of their homeland, something that may well have hastened the creation of alternative renderings of myth and tolerance of diversity of myth in the empire.[57]

Various Modalities of Belief and Myth

The nature of belief in myths varied. As Veyne notes "modalities of belief are related to the ways in which truth is possessed"[58] and there was no formal expectation of belief in the literal "truth" of myth as the religions of the Greeks and Romans were, within limits, religions of orthopraxy rather than orthodoxy. However, when we ask:

> Did the Greeks believe in their mythology? The answer is difficult, for "believe" means so many things. Not everyone believed that Minor, after his death, continued being a judge in Hell, or that Theseus fought the Minotaur, and they knew that poets "lie." However, their way of not believing the things is disturbing to us. For in the minds of the Greeks, Theseus had, nonetheless, existed. It was neces-

sary only to "purify Myth by Reason" and refine the biography of Heracles' companion to its historic nugget.[59]

One of the perhaps surprising cultural assumptions that seems to emerge from examining mythology in antiquity is the paradox that "there were people who did not believe in the existence of the gods, but never did anyone doubt the existence of the heroes."[60] Indeed,

> during the period . . . from the fifth century B.C. to the fourth century A.D., absolutely no one, Christians included, ever expressed the slightest doubt concerning the historicity of Aeneas, Romulus, Theseus, Heracles, Achilles, or even Dionysus; rather, everyone asserted this historicity.[61]

Euhemerism, the belief that the gods were really humans about whom legends had grown, did not function to undermine the subjects of myth, but rather to give people a reason to believe in them.

The Informal Transmission of Myth and the Process of Mythmaking

There were a number of ways in which myth could be learned and relearned throughout a person's life in the empire. Although it is hard to know, as Aune has noted,[62] exactly what narratives accompanied many festivals or were expressed in hymns as we have so little information about the liturgical life of paganism in the early empire, nonetheless *aretalogoi*, professional tellers of the activities of gods and heroes, seem to have functioned around temples[63] and were possibly employed in richer households (e.g., Suetonius, *Octavius*, 78.2). Freelance, professional recounters of myths seem to have been common and plied their wares, alongside jugglers and musicians, in crowds (Dio Chrysostom, *Orationes*, 20.9–10). Those visiting famous religious sites seem to have been plagued by guides keen to interpret the stories evidenced in the paintings, sculptures, or inscriptions, or to provide local traditions, for a small fee, even if, much as today, such information was not easy to believe—as we can see in remarks by Lucian (*Amores*, 8), Pausanias (*Periegesis*, 1.19.2; 1.31.5; 2.9.7), and Plutarch (*De Pythiae oraculis*, 395a).[64] As Horsfall has reminded us in his recent study of the culture of the Roman plebs, most of the inhabitants of the empire acquired their culture without formal schooling, through the theater, or buskers or other leisure pursuits.[65]

Although education in the content and criticism of myth, particularly as found in Homer, would form part of any formal education[66]—indeed, Homer was at the core of primary education throughout the empire[67]—one recurring feature of descriptions of myth in antiquity is that most initially learned myths in a domestic context, from the women directly involved in their early upbringing. Women in antiquity were, perhaps unsurprisingly, "a fundamental instrument of the transmission of a culture."[68] As Philostratus the Elder remarked to an inquisitive ten-year-old:

> That Theseus treated Ariadne unjustly... when he abandoned her while asleep on the island of Dia, you must have heard from your nurse; for these women are skilled in telling such tales and they weep over them whenever they will. (*Imagines*, 1.14)

The extent of information transmitted in this manner clearly varied. Veyne, for example, questions whether children were taught the great mythic cycles early in their lives, querying whether they had to wait until they were "under the grammarian's authority to learn the great legends?"[69]—assuming they were sufficiently privileged to gain a formal education of that kind. However, from what we can determine, the telling of myths, or parts of them, by these women, educating and entertaining their charges, involved improvisation and innovation. Philostratus the Younger, for example, recalls how his nurse "entertained me with these tales, which she accompanied with a pretty song; some of them even used to make her cry" (*Heroicus*, 136–37).

There were no particular controls on how a myth was presented within this context and our data emphasizes that the retellings often focused upon events of a miraculous nature (indeed, for some elite males, reflecting their own notions about rationality and gender, belief in the miraculous was a peculiarly female characteristic—Polybius, *Historiae*, 12. 24. 5). In the words of Tacitus, young children were exposed to "idle tales and gross absurdities" (*Dialogus de oratoribus*, 29)—though most treated these "absurdities" as fact, as Sextus Empiricus complained (*Pyrrhonean Outlines*, 1.147; see also Aretmidorus, *Oneirocitica*, 4.47).

Despite the evidence of the prominence of women as transmitters of myth within a domestic context, this has largely been ignored in studies of oral tradition in the Roman Empire.[70] Although this has merited mention by some,[71] it has also been passed over in major contributions of New Testament scholars on the role of the oral tradition in the origins of Christianity, and is not discussed in works such as those by Gerhardsson, Kelber, Dunn, and Bauckham.[72] This neglect is perhaps all the more surprising given a possible clue of the importance of this process within the churches in the words addressed to "Timothy" by "Paul": "I am reminded of your sincere faith, a faith that lived first in your grandmother Lois and your mother Eunice and now, I am sure, lives in you" (2 Tim 1:5).

Evidence of Concern about Myth in the New Testament

Having now sketched something of the place and character of popular myth within the early empire, let us now turn to its significance for our evaluation of the early traditions about Jesus.

First, it is clear that the production of myth, the spinning of stories about Jesus, was a concern in some early communities. In a number of places in the New Testament, the authors are keen to distinguish themselves from those whom they complained purveyed myths about Jesus. For example, in 2 Peter: "For we did not follow cleverly devised myths when we made known to you the power and coming of our Lord Jesus Christ, but we had been eyewitnesses of his majesty" (2 Pt 1:16). Although this passage probably implies that the author believed that the "cleverly devised myths" were being proclaimed by others, as for example, Kelly maintains,[73] it is also possible, as Neyrey has argued, that the author is actually defending himself from others who judged that the traditions that the author himself proclaimed were myths.[74]

In 1 Timothy we find a clear warning that members of the church should avoid myths (with the obvious implication that myths were, in fact, something that appealed to many early believers):

I urge you, as I did when I was on my way to Macedonia, to remain in Ephesus so that you may instruct certain people not to teach any different doctrine, and not to occupy themselves with myths and endless genealogies that promote speculations. (1 Tim 1:3–4)

And, perhaps unsurprisingly, given our previous discussion, the author of this epistle makes a direct association of dangerous myths with women: "Have nothing to do with profane myths and old wives' tales" (1 Tim 4:7).

Indeed, the process of mythmaking in Christian churches seemed, to the author of 2 Timothy, unavoidable:

For the time is coming when people will not put up with sound doctrine, but having itching ears, they will accumulate for themselves teachers to suit their own desires, and will turn away from listening to the truth and wander away to myths. (2 Tim 4:3–4)

It is important to note here that the myths in question need not be, as is often assumed, the complex, cosmological and etiological myths associated with most forms of Gnosticism—if we accept, for a moment, the analytical value of the term *Gnosticism*, first coined in the seventeenth century.[75] Myths of this kind are classically represented by the myth found in the *Apocryphon of John* and Irenaeus, *Adversus Haereses*, 1.29 (and which seems to be present in rudimentary form in traditions about such early Gnostic groups as the Simonians; Irenaeus, *Adversus Haereses*, 1.23). Such an interpretation of the meaning of *mythos* in the Pastoral epistles owes itself, to a great extent, to the use of the word *gnosis* by the author of 1 Timothy when describing the content of the "profane chatter" of which he so strongly disapproved (1 Tim 6:20). But *gnosis* is a common, nontechnical Greek term, and it seems far more likely that the knowledge consisted of myths about Jesus and others, probably biblical characters (indeed, this would better explain the association of such myths specifically with Jews in Titus 1:14).

It is also important to note that the term *myth* here is clearly pejoratively contrasted with the "truth" of the traditions that the respective authors claim to have received (2 Tim 4:4; Titus 1:14; 2 Pt 3:16) and to pass on (1 Tim 6:20, 2 Tim 1:12, 14). However, the traditions about Jesus that were sanctioned and promoted by the author of an epistle such as 1 Timothy would have looked suspiciously like myth to most inhabitants of the empire. No specific dominical traditions about Jesus are appealed to in the letter, and the kerygmatic summary of his life by the author sounds suspiciously mythic according to our initial definition:

> Without any doubt, the mystery of our religion is great: He was revealed in flesh, vindicated in spirit, seen by angels, proclaimed among Gentiles, believed in throughout the world, taken up in glory. (1 Tim 3:16)

So, it appears from the evidence of the Pastoral and Petrine epistles, the early Christians were indeed concerned with mythmaking, both sanctioned and unsanctioned, within their communities.

From Monogenesis to Polygenesis, from Arboriforms to Rhizomes

However, the significance of mythmaking for evaluating the earliest traditions about Jesus is particularly apparent when it is married to a more plausible model of the origins of Christianity than that which currently is in the ascendant. The dominant model remains a rather conservative one that reflects, more or less, the pattern presented in the two earliest histories of the church—Luke–Acts and Eusebius's *Historia Ecclesiae*—in which the life, death, and resurrection of Jesus are taken as the originating and determinative events that explain what follows. Such a model allows little room for the creation and proliferation of different traditions about Jesus and their consequences, as it assumes an ongoing coherence and consistency in the development of the faith, with the Jerusalem church functioning, in the early years, as arbiters of tradition and authority among all those who propagated a message about Jesus. Such a model presupposes monogenesis.

This model has, of course, had its critics. Although there have been dissenting voices for centuries, some of whom, such as the seventeenth-century deist Henry Stubbe, deserve to be somewhat better known, following Walter Bauer's *Orthodoxy and Heresy in Earliest Christianity* (first published in 1934) scholars have been especially aware of the diversity of forms of earliest Christianity, and alternative versions of the faith that subsequently lost out to "orthodoxy" may well have been the first, dominant, and indeed the only form of Christianity in many areas. Particularly since Helmut Koester pushed Bauer's historical schema back into the apostolic age,[76] it has been common to talk, even in quite conservative circles, about the diversity of theological perspectives in the New Testament, as evidenced by, for example, James Dunn's *Unity and Diversity in the New Testament.*[77]

However, in recent years, the argument for diversity has been pushed yet further. Some, such as Crossan and Mack,[78] have suggested multiple, distinct forms of the Christian movement from the earliest period, which had little or no common ground other than a reverence for Jesus, which only gradually merged and assimilated with one another.[79] For example, it is often noted that Q and the *Gospel of Thomas* seem to have little interest in the death of Jesus, mentioning it at best only obliquely (Q 14:27; GThom 55),[80] and preferring, instead, to focus upon Jesus as a teacher of wisdom. Yet the death of Jesus is a key datum in other forms of early Christianity (e.g., Rom 10:9, 1 Cor 2:1–2, etc.), some of which, such as that propagated by Paul, conversely show a similar level of indifference to the sayings traditions of Jesus that Q so cherishes. It is hard to see how the life and death of one particular historical figure could account for such diversity of both tradition and interpretation, and so Price can even say, with some justification, having surveyed the variety of Jesuses evident in the earliest forms of Christianity, that "it is an open question whether a historical Jesus had anything to do with any of these Jesuses, much less the Jesuses of the Gospels."[81]

There are, however, good reasons to have reservations about the grounds on which such radical diversity is argued by some. It is unwise, for example, to assume that each text making mention of Jesus was written by and for a community with a distinct understanding of the figure of Jesus. Such texts may be indicative of separate communities but are hardly conclusive proof of them. They often assume knowledge of traditions external to the text that may well be shared with other forms of the faith (for example, the brief reference to John the Baptist in logion 46 and James the Just in logion 12 of the *Gospel of Thomas* assumes the readership knows much more about these figures than is evident from the text). The existence of some of the texts on which models of radical diversity are dependent is also far from as assured as some scholars presume. For example, it is often forgotten that Q is a *hypothetical* construct and there are good grounds for doubting its validity[82] and serious questions are now raised other than the authenticity of *Secret Gospel of Mark*.[83]

Nonetheless, it seems far more reasonable to envisage the origins of Christianity as polygenic rather than monogenic. Indeed, the canonical New Testament itself, on closer inspection, seems to indicate as much. For example, Apollos, a key figure in the early propagation of faith in Christ in the eastern Mediterranean, who was equal to both Paul and Peter in the eyes of the Corinthian congregation (1 Cor 1:12; 3:4–6, 22; 4:6) and who operated independently of both (1 Cor 16:12), appears to have become a committed advocate of Jesus in Alexandria (Acts 18:24). Whatever version of the new religion he obtained there, and we have absolutely no idea who first took ideas about Jesus to Alexandria, it is clear that for the author of Acts of the Apostles it was inadequate ("he only knew the baptism of John"; Acts 18:25) and it was necessary for him to have the "Way of God" (a shorthand for the particular understanding of Christianity approved by the author) explained to him more accurately by Priscilla and Aquila (Acts 18:26). Although we know little about Apollos, he is representative of this fundamental diversity present at the outset and his story illustrates the mutual ignorance of different forms of Christianity. Similarly, Acts also tells us of a group of "disciples" in Ephesus who again seem to know only about John's baptism (Acts 19:1–7) and to be ignorant of the role of the holy spirit in the new faith—something so aberrant in the eyes of the author of Luke–Acts that, unlike Apollos, it required their rebaptism.

The notion that earliest Christianity, from the outset, took numerous forms is something that seems not to have caused any particular concern among the orthodox apologists themselves. Origen, for example, refuted Celsus's accusation that as Christianity had attracted more and more followers, the self-interest of its leaders led to divisions, by saying that even when the apostles were preaching and eyewitnesses were alive "from the very beginning, when, as Celsus imagines, believers were few in number, there were certain doctrines interpreted in different ways" (Origen, *Contra Celsus*, 3.10ff).

Indeed, unlike many modern scholars, who are reluctant to posit really significant theological diversity in the earliest period and as a consequence deny the influence of Gnosticism in understanding the development of Christianity until the second century, early Christian writers had no difficulty in seeing it present in the initial decades of the religion's existence, as we can see in what they tell us of, for example, the formative roles of Simon Magus (Justin, *Apologia*, 1.26; Irenaeus, *Adversus Haereses*, 1.23.1–4; *Pseudo-Clementine Homilies*, 2.22–26; Epiphanius, *Panarion*, 21.2.5; *Acts of Peter*, 31–32; Hippolytus, *Refutationes*, 6.9.4–18.7; see Acts 8:9–24) and Cerinthus (Irenaeus, *Adversus Haereses*, 3.3.4).

There is a great deal that we do not know about the emergence of Christianity in this early period, and which we shall never know. However, it seems that the polygenic character of early Christianity allowed individuals and groups to innovate quite dramatically with little recourse to anyone else. Acts, for example, tells of some followers from Cyprus and Cyrene making the crucial step of converting Gentiles in Antioch to what had previously been a Jewish sect. They did this, apparently, without consulting followers of Jesus elsewhere (11:20) nor even informing them (11:22), something that indicates that the Jerusalem church did not function as arbiters of tradition and authority among all those who propagated faith in Jesus in the empire, despite its ideological significance in early Christian historiography.[84] Such developments are unsurprising given the preeminence of direct religious experience that not only legitimated but also provided the content of the faith of many early Christians. Paul, for example, could famously claim that his Gospel was not of human origin "for I did not receive it from a human source, nor was I taught it, but I received it through a revelation of Jesus Christ" (Gal 1:12). However, it is clear that he was not alone in claiming direct revelations from Jesus about the true character of the faith that was to be proclaimed. John of Patmos, for example, could publish letters to the seven churches in Asia purporting to be from the exalted Jesus decades after the latter's death (Rev 2–3) and that castigated other Christian leaders and groups (Rev 2:14–15, 20–25).

The inability of much scholarship to conceptualize the multiplicity, fluidity, and heterogeneity of forms of earliest Christianity is partly accounted for by the influence of predominant metaphors that have been used to describe the movement. Too often accounts speak in terms of roots, trunks, and branches, yet, as Wright puts it: "Arborescent metaphors go hand-in-hand with hierarchical structure, extreme stratification, and linear thinking"[85]—notions that seem to do violence to the data that we possess. It might be more helpful to utilize a metaphor made popular by Gilles Deleuze and Félix Guattari and to think of early Christianity as fundamentally rhizomorphous (a rhizome is a horizontal stem of a plant, normally subterranean, that often sends out roots and shots from nodes, which can themselves break off and survive independently, beginning yet further networks).[86] Although it is pushing the evidence too far to say that early Christian groups "at first had nothing to do with each other,"[87] such a metaphor allows for the possibility of only distant or tenuous relationships between some of the groups that emerged and the coexistence of complementary and competing conceptualizations of their origins. When such a polygenic model of the origins of Christianity is taken seriously, the likelihood of endemic mythmaking amongst the first believers becomes all the more plausible.

The Myth of Control in the Creation and Preservation of Oral Traditions about Jesus

It could be objected that my analysis does not take seriously the evidence that Christian communities, collectively or as a consequence of the ongoing presence of credible eyewitnesses, controlled and delimited the traditions so that innovations of a fundamental kind were impossible. In models presented by, for example, Bailey, Bauckham, Boman, Byrskog, Dunn, Gerhardsson, and Kelber,[88] Christian communities, or individuals of standing within communities, exerted some authority over the transmission of oral material. Such scholars argue that we should speak of "preservation" or "survival" of the Jesus tradition, albeit in rather different ways.

So, for example, Gerhardsson thinks in terms of the handing on of a tradition that was formally memorized, and was initially explicitly taught by a teacher to his disciples before finding its way into the Gospels, whereas Bauckham argues that

> the period between the "historical" Jesus and the Gospels was actually spanned, not by anonymous community transmission, but by the

continuing presence and testimony of the eyewitnesses, who remained the authoritative sources of their traditions until their deaths.[89]

Dunn speaks of "oral traditioning," imagining, for example, that when a Christian wished to hear again a particular story in the life of Jesus,

> a senior disciple would tell again the appropriate story or teaching in whatever variant words and detail he or she judged appropriate for the occasion, with sufficient corporate memory ready to protest if one of the key elements was missed out or varied too much.[90]

However, such models seem improbable. Nowhere can we find any explicit statements about communities or representatives of communities making collective judgments on oral traditions in this or any other manner in early Christian sources. From what we know about how early Christians went about sifting the wheat from the chaff when judging the traditions about Jesus, it seems that this was not a collective activity nor one that particularly concerned communities, but rather an initiative of particular individuals within the churches. This is evident from the preface to Luke's Gospel (Lk 1:3) and in what we know of Papias's collection of the traditions that went into the now lost *Expositions of Oracles of the Lord* (Eusebius, *Historia Ecclesiae*, 3.39). Indeed, Papias's account is all the more telling as he contrasts his attempts to discover authentic traditions with the undiscerning "multitude" who "take pleasure in those that speak much" (Eusebius, *Historia Ecclesiae*, 3.39.3) and yet Papias himself not only seems extremely haphazard in his approach, questioning those who just happened to be visiting to his church (Eusebius, *Historia Ecclesiae*, 3.39.4) but, for all his protestations, he appears to have been as drawn to sensational *paradoxa* (marvelous tales; 3.39.8f) as anyone else, and his judgments about the veracity of traditions were disturbing to later Christians. Eusebius complains that the collection of oral traditions that Papias compiled in the five books of *Expositions of Oracles of the Lord* contained "strange parables and teachings of the Savior, and some other more mythical things" (*Historia Ecclesiae*, 3.39.11). Indeed, it is clear from the Gospel of John that tradi-

tions about Jesus were legion and most early Christians had no difficulty with this: "But there are also many other things that Jesus did; if
every one of them were written down, I suppose that the world itself
could not contain the books that would be written" (John 21:25). The
author makes it clear that he has selected only a few traditions for
inclusion in his Gospel, but the criteria for selection are expressly theological. He does not show any concern about the authenticity of the
much larger body of traditions he does not include:

> Now Jesus did many other signs in the presence of his disciples,
> which are not written in this book. But these are written so that you
> may come to believe that Jesus is the Messiah, the Son of God, and
> that through believing you may have life in his name (John 20:30–31).

John nowhere shows any evidence of either doubting other traditions nor some collective process in authenticating the material he
includes. Indeed, John's apparent indiscriminate attitude towards traditions about Jesus appears to share much with the popular genre of paradoxography, which was characterized by "acceptance without question
of any available information; the problem of the truth or credibility of
the phenomena or facts, which were presented, was simply not raised."[91]

Nor can it be contended that our knowledge of the apparently conservative manner in which the early Christians handled written sources
about Jesus, evident from examining the relationships between the synoptic Gospels, should lead us to question such widespread credulity on
the part of most early Christians when faced with traditions about Jesus
(approximately 89 percent of Mark is preserved verbatim or near verbatim in Matthew, and 72 percent in Luke).[92] Whatever tendencies may
be evident in the handling of *written* sources by early Christian authors
is irrelevant for assessing the oral traditions that may lie behind them
with which this paper is concerned. Indeed, there is nothing particularly
conservative about the way in which early Christian writers made use of
textual sources. Matthew's use of Mark is, for example, characterized by
the widespread abbreviation, addition, omission, conflation, elaboration,
and reordering of material, and displays a degree of license indistinguishable from that apparent in the way that Greek, Roman, and Jewish
writers of the time made use of their written sources.[93]

CONCLUSION

When properly conceived, it is apparent that myth and mythmaking were dynamic components of popular cultures of the early Roman Empire and, as we can see from the complaints of the Pastoral and Petrine epistles, were a characteristic of early Christian communities. In the light of this, any evaluation of traditions about Jesus must take seriously the likelihood that they could have had little or no direct connection with the historical Jesus himself. Leaving aside the birth and resurrection narratives, all traditions about the earthly Jesus, not just those that might strike the modern reader as overtly *mythic*, such as the baptismal miracle (Mt 3:13–17; Mk 1:9–11; Lk 3:21–22), the temptations (Mt 4:1–11; Mk 1:13; Lk 4:1–13), and the transfiguration (Mt 17:1–8; Mk 9:2–8; Lk 9:28–36), were potentially the product of or affected by mythmaking, and should be treated with caution.

Indeed, this mythmaking need not have even originated solely with followers of Jesus. For example, the healing narratives, which are present in the earliest Jesus traditions[94] are likely to have been attractive to those who were not part of any particular Jesus movement but sought out healing and may well have originated with them.[95] Figures such as the seven sons of Sceva (Acts 19:13–20) or the unnamed exorcist (Mk 9:38), who exorcised in the name of Jesus, are evidence of the circulation of traditions about Jesus among those unconnected with any followers of Jesus and such people might also have developed further traditions.

In the earliest period it is also quite possible that some myths about the figure of Jesus continued to be preserved and developed by those who had left the churches, or perhaps believed that the churches had left them. For example, on seeing the risen Jesus, Matthew's Gospel notes that some of his followers worshipped him but it also adds "but some doubted" (Mt 28:17). Elsewhere in the Gospels *doubt* seems to be mentioned in order to be resolved, whether in the famous example of Thomas in John (20:24–29), the appearance of the risen Jesus on the road to Emmaus (Lk 24:13–27) or to the disciples in Jerusalem (Lk 24:36–49). However, in this incident there is no such resolution and the implication is that among those Jews who did not believe in the resurrection of Jesus (Mt 28: 15) were followers of Jesus.

I would like to conclude by noting that I do believe that it is historically probable that some material within canonical and noncanonical sources might well bear some relation to the sayings and parables taught by a first-century Jew, and reflect the reputation he acquired in his lifetime as an effective healer and exorcist.[96] I have elsewhere argued that it is likely that this figure met his death on a Roman cross.[97] However, if anything much can be determined with relative certainty about the historical Jesus from the records we possess, it can only be data of a very general kind, akin to the most abbreviated of the skeletal lists of Sanders.[98] The capacity for, and character of, popular mythopoesis within the early empire, and the concomitant lack of concern and mechanisms for the control and transmission of traditions about Jesus among his multifarious followers in the decades following his death, despite the optimistic claims of the likes of Gerhardsson, Dunn, and Bauckham, makes such a conclusion unavoidable.

BAYES'S THEOREM FOR BEGINNERS
Formal Logic and Its Relevance
to Historical Method

Richard C. Carrier

In the latest quest for the historical Jesus, many attempts were made to develop a method for determining what could be known about the historical Jesus. The only popular procedure was to try to develop criteria by which genuine historical facts could be sorted from mythical or other accretions. The basic idea was that the more criteria any particular detail met, the more likely it was to be historical, although some criteria were asserted as decisive in themselves (anything that met even one of them was considered historical). Or so it was proposed.[1] As with every prior quest, initial hopes were dashed in the end, as analysis led to serious doubts about the utility or even validity of any of the criteria proposed.

Stanley Porter demonstrated this in his complete survey of all the "historicity criteria" anyone had so far developed.[2] He then attempted to solve the problem by developing three new criteria of his own, but they, too, are fatally flawed,[3] only establishing a certain plausibility, incapable even by his own admission of determining whether any particular conclusion about Jesus was probably true.[4] The growing consensus in the field is that this entire quest for criteria has failed.[5] In their final analysis of the problem, Gerd Theissen and Dagmar Winter all but threw up their hands in despair, concluding that some sort of holistic methodology is needed.[6] They confess to not knowing what exactly it could be, but what they call for as the road to a solution sounds exactly like Bayes's Theorem. Theissen and Winter were evidently unaware of this, but that's no surprise, as historians tend to shun formal logics and mathematical reasoning, and thus aren't generally informed about them. Consequently, very little has been done to promote and adapt Bayes's Theorem to what historians do—even in general,[7] much less in the specific field of Jesus studies.

HISTORICITY CRITERIA

The number of historicity criteria developed so far is hard to pin down, as they often overlap or appear under different names. By some counts, there have been two or three dozen. Some are positive (what fulfills the criterion is more likely true), and some are negative (what fails to fulfill the criterion is more likely false, i.e., a detail must meet that criterion to be true, but is not thereby true). The following seventeen are representative:

- Dissimilarity: If dissimilar to Judaism or the early church, it is probably true.
- Embarrassment: If it was embarrassing, it must be true.
- Coherence: If it coheres with other confirmed data, it is likely true.
- Multiple Attestation: If attested in more than one source, it is more likely true.
- Explanatory Credibility: If its being true better explains later traditions, it is true.
- Contextual Plausibility: It must be plausible in Judeo-Greco-Roman context.
- Historical Plausibility: It must cohere with a plausible historical reconstruction.
- Natural Probability: It must cohere with natural science (etc.).
- Oral Preservability: It must be capable of surviving oral transmission.
- Crucifixion: It must explain (or make sense of) why Jesus was crucified.
- Fabricatory Trend: It must not match trends in fabrication or embellishment.
- Least Distinctiveness: The simpler version is the more historical.
- Vividness of Narration: The more vivid, the more historical.
- Textual Variance: The more invariable a tradition, the more historical.
- Greek Context: Credible if context suggests parties speaking Greek.
- Aramaic Context: Credible if context suggests parties speaking Aramaic.

- Discourse Features: Credible if Jesus' speeches cohere in a unique style.

Analyzing the failure of these criteria, Porter and others have found that either a given criterion is invalidly applied (e.g., the text actually fails to fulfill the criterion, contrary to a scholar's assertion or misapprehension) or the criterion itself is invalid (e.g., the criterion depends upon a rule of inference that is inherently fallacious, contrary to a scholar's intuition), or both. The only solution is twofold: scholars are obligated to establish with clear certainty that a particular item actually fulfills any stated criterion (which requires establishing what exactly that criterion is), and scholars are obligated to establish the formal logical validity of any stated criterion (especially if establishing its validity requires adopting for it a set of qualifications or conditions previously overlooked). But meeting the latter requirement always produces such restrictions on meeting the former requirement as to make any criterion largely useless in practice, especially in the study of Jesus, where the evidence is very scarce and problematic. Hence the growing consensus is, "There are no reliable criteria for separating authentic from inauthentic Jesus tradition."[8]

Yet even solving those problems won't be enough. As Theissen and Winter conclusively demonstrate, all criteria-based methods suffer the same fatal flaw, which I call the *Threshold Problem*: at what point does meeting any number of criteria warrant the conclusion that some detail is probably historical? Is meeting one enough? Or two? Or three? Do all the criteria carry the same weight? Does every instance of meeting the same criterion carry the same weight? And what do we do when there is evidence both for and against the same conclusion? In other words, insofar as meeting certain criteria increases the likelihood of some detail being true, when does that likelihood increase to the point of being effectively certain or at least highly probable? No discussions of historicity criteria have made any headway in answering this question.

Another problem, largely overlooked, is the *Fallacy of Diminishing Probabilities*. The probability of a conclusion being true is the product of the probabilities of all its premises being true. But since you need a separate premise to establish each item of evidence, and the products of probabilities always diminish, the more evidence you have, the less probable the conclusion is. Clearly that's wrong. But how is this fallacy avoided? This problem is typically overlooked because a proper logical analysis of historical arguments is rarely attempted, but when it is, the issue arises (as will be demonstrated below). Both the Threshold Problem and the Fallacy of Diminishing Probabilities belie something fundamentally wrong with the usual assumptions of historical reasoning. As I will argue, it's no accident that Bayes's Theorem simultaneously solves both. In fact, as far as I know, it's the only form of logical-empirical argument that does.

MAKING PROGRESS WITH LOGICAL ANALYSIS

Formal logical analysis of historical reasoning is the key to flushing out fallacies and unwarranted assumptions. We can then revise our assertions and rules of inference to achieve logical validity. Usually we learn a great deal in the process. Logic is a rich and diverse field from which a lot can be learned and which historians should study more than they do. Here, I will only offer the simplest of examples to illustrate the utility of formal logical analysis and why it is important for us to perform this analysis on our own reasoning in order to understand our methods and assumptions, check them for error, and correct them if needed.

The most basic syllogism of interest to historians has the following general form:

Major Premise:	[Some general rule.]
Minor Premise:	[Some specific fact satisfying the general rule.]
Conclusion:	[That which follows necessarily from the major and minor premise.]

For example:

Major Premise:	All working wagons had wheels.
Minor Premise:	Jacob owned a working wagon.
Conclusion:	Therefore, Jacob owned a wheel.

This is true by virtue of the definition of "working wagon," which renders the conclusion rather trivial. But now consider a less trivial example:

Major Premise: All major cities in antiquity had sewers.
Minor Premise: Jerusalem was a major city in antiquity.
Conclusion: Therefore, Jerusalem had sewers.

This will be true to a very high degree of probability if there is abundant background evidence, including archaeological and textual, that is uncontestable for its scope and degree—even without direct archaeological evidence of Jerusalem's sewers (unless, of course, archaeology confirms there were none). But the above argument conceals a key assumption: that probabilities can be assumed to be certainties. For though the above argument is valid as written (the conclusion does follow from the premises), it is not sound, since neither premise is literally true. Even assuming that abundant evidence supports both premises, they will still only be true to some degree of probability. So:

Major Premise: [Very probably] all major cities in antiquity had sewers.
Minor Premise: [Very probably] Jerusalem was a major city in antiquity.
Conclusion: Therefore, [very probably] Jerusalem had sewers.

In other words, there may yet be some major cities without sewers. Even if we have ample evidence that every excavated example did, we can't excavate every ancient city. Likewise, though we're almost certainly right to classify Jerusalem as a major city (assuming we define "major city" in an explicit way, such as housing a population of a certain size—whatever size would render the major premise true), there is always some probability, however small, that we are wrong about that. In most cases, these probabilities are so securely on one side that we don't trouble ourselves over them. But when we start dealing with increasingly uncertain facts and generalizations, we can no longer pretend probability equals certainty. Then problems arise. (We will revisit this fact later.)

When a historical argument is formulated as a simple syllogism or system of syllogisms, it is easy to determine if the argument is valid: just observe if the conclusion strictly follows from the premises (as we will eventually see, this still generates the fallacy of diminishing probabilities, but we will address that problem later). It is harder to determine if the argument is also sound, however, and in logic a conclusion must be both sound and valid in order to be true. A sound conclusion requires all the requisite premises to be true (as a conclusion cannot be truer than its weakest premise). Formal analysis must be used to ascertain the merits of our premises by ascertaining what assumptions and evidence they are based on and whether this foundation is sufficient to formally entail the truth of a premise (however stated). To accomplish this, just build out the required syllogisms supporting each premise, nesting one set of syllogisms within the other. For example:

Major Premise 1a:	All major cities in antiquity had public libraries.
Minor Premise 1b:	Jerusalem was a major city in antiquity.
Conclusion:	Therefore, Jerusalem had a public library.

This argument is formally valid. But is it sound? Few would likely contest the minor premise. Though that is not a good excuse to assume that it is true (we should always question anyone's assumptions and examine on what evidence and inferences they are based), for brevity we will test the major premise instead (which some may find more dubious). A sound premise must be the conclusion of another (at least conceivable) syllogism that is itself both sound and valid. For example:

Major Premise 2a:	If archaeologists and historians (a) find that a large number of major cities in antiquity had public libraries and (b) have insufficient data to confirm there was any major city that lacked a public library, then (c) all major cities in antiquity had public libraries.

Minor Premise 2b: Archaeologists and historians have found that a large number of major cities in antiquity had public libraries and have insufficient data to confirm any major city lacked a public library.

Conclusion: Therefore, **Major Premise 1a:** all major cities in antiquity had public libraries.

The conclusion validly follows. But is it sound? Again, assume here that the new minor premise is uncontested. What then of the new major premise? That, too must be the conclusion of a sound and valid syllogism. For example:

Major Premise 3a: If {Minor Premise 3b} is true, then {Major Premise 2a} is true.

Minor Premise 3b: If a large number of representatives of a class have property p, and there is insufficient data to confirm any members of that class lack p, then all members of that class have p.

Conclusion: Therefore, **Major Premise 2a:** if archaeologists and historians find that a large number of major cities in antiquity had public libraries and have insufficient data to confirm there was any major city that lacked a public library, then all major cities in antiquity had public libraries.

This time, the major premise is less contestable than the minor premise (here both are general rules of inference, but Major Premise 3a is more general than Minor Premise 3b and is therefore the Major Premise in this case). Assume we continue the analysis for Major Premise 3a and find it to be sound. Minor Premise 3b may still be dubious. So we go one level further:

Major Premise 4a: If there can be no exceptions to a rule {if A, then B} then it is always the case that {if A, then B}.

Minor Premise 4b: There can be no exceptions to the rule {if a large number of representatives of a class have property p, and there is insufficient data to confirm any members of that class lack p, then all members of that class have p}.

Conclusion: Therefore, **Minor Premise 3b**: if a large number of representatives of a class have property p, and there is insufficient data to confirm any members of that class lack p, then all members of that class have p.

Now we've gotten to the bottom of our general rules of inference, as Major Premise 4a is necessarily true (and therefore needs no further analysis to confirm it is sound). But we've also gotten to the root of our assumptions and exposed a flaw in our reasoning: contrary to Minor Premise 4b, there can be exceptions to the rule {if a large number of representatives of a class have property p, and there is insufficient data to confirm any members of that class lack p, then all members of that class have p}. Therefore, Minor Premise 4b is false. Therefore, Minor Premise 3b is unsound. Therefore, Major Premise 2a is unsound. Therefore, Major Premise 1a is unsound. Therefore, our original Conclusion is unsound.

We can fix this collapsing house of cards by revising Minor Premise 4b so that it is true, and then our original Conclusion will also be true (once suitably modified). For example:

Minor Premise 4$_{\text{TRUE}}$: There can be no exceptions to the rule {if a large number of representatives of a class have property p, and those members were effectively selected at random from among all members of that class, and there is insufficient data to confirm any member of that class lacks p (and it is probable we would have such data in at least one instance if many members of that class lacked p), then it is at least somewhat probable that any given member of that class has p}.

This version of Minor Premise 4b is necessarily true. But this entails modifications of the nested syllogisms all the way back up the line. So we have located the underlying rule, discovered its flaw, and when we correct that flaw, we discover the necessary qualifications and analyses that we overlooked before.

In this case: (a) we now know we should qualify our premises (and thus our conclusion) as a matter of probability, and a probability less than what we would consider a historical certainty; (b) we now know to ask whether we should even expect evidence of major cities lacking public libraries, if any did in fact lack them; and (c) we now know to ask whether the sample of major cities for which we have confirmed public libraries is effectively a random sample of all major cities—and if not, will the known bias in sampling affect our generalization about libraries? As to (a), instead of "all major cities in antiquity had public libraries," we should say "most major cities in antiquity had public libraries" (which entails "somewhat probably a major city in antiquity had a public library"). As to (b), we might be able to say that if there were many such deprived cities, we should have evidence of at least one case by now, whereas if there were only a few, we might not have evidence of that (so we must allow there could have been at least a few). As to (c), we might observe that the bias now is in fact against having evidence for the largest of cities (since modern cities often stand on top of the most successful ancient cities, making archaeological surveys spotty at best), and since it is highly improbable that numerous lesser cities would have public libraries while yet greater cities lacked them, the bias is actually in favor of our conclusion that all major cities had public libraries.

Therefore, logical analysis like this can be a useful tool in history: to identify or check against possible errors by identifying underlying assumptions regarding rules of inference and trends and generalizations in the evidence, and to discover new avenues of analysis, qualification, and inquiry that could improve our methods, our results, and our understanding.

LOGICAL ANALYSIS OF HISTORICITY CRITERIA

Now apply this general lesson to the specific case of arguing from historicity criteria. For example:

> **The Criterion of Dissimilarity**: "If a saying attributed to Jesus is dissimilar to the views of Judaism and to the views of the early church, then it can confidently be ascribed to the historical Jesus."

This analyzes to:

Major Premise 1c: If any saying s attributed to Jesus is dissimilar to the views of Judaism and to the views of the early church, then Jesus said s.

Minor Premise 1d: Saying s [= Jesus directly addressed God as his Father] is dissimilar to the views of Judaism and to the views of the early church.

Conclusion: Therefore, Jesus said s [= Jesus directly addressed God as his Father].

The minor premise analyzes to:

Major Premise 2c: If we have no evidence of saying s [directly addressing God as one's Father] from Jews (prior to or contemporary with Jesus) or the early church (without attribution to Jesus), then saying s [Jesus directly addressing God as his Father] is dissimilar to the views of Judaism and to the views of the early church.

Minor Premise 2d: We have no evidence of saying s [directly addressing God as one's Father] from Jews (prior to or contemporary with Jesus) or the early church (without attribution to Jesus).

Conclusion: Therefore, **Minor Premise 1d**: Saying *s* [Jesus directly addressing God as his Father] is dissimilar to the views of Judaism and to the views of the early church.

If we continued this nesting analysis, we would find both Major Premise 2c and Minor Premise 2d insupportable, because we do have evidence of early Jews directly addressing God as one's Father,[9] and it is not the case that if we have no evidence of a practice that it did not exist. The Criterion of Dissimilarity thus reduces to an *Argumentum ad Ignorantiam*, a textbook fallacy. Applying the criterion to produce a conclusion of any confidence requires just as much confidence that the practice did not exist, which is very difficult to establish. One must thoroughly survey all relevant evidence and scholarship, no simple task (e.g., D'Angelo's paper is not easy to find and publishes research you are unlikely to have completed yourself). In fact, it is often impossible to establish, since we know for a fact there was a great deal more diversity in Jewish beliefs and practice than we presently know any specifics of;[10] there was a great deal going on in the early church that we know nothing about (e.g., how and when did Apollos become an Apostle, and exactly what Gospel was he preaching?); and since the survival of sources is so spotty, no valid conclusion can be reached about what no Jews or early Christians ever thought, said, or did.

That invalidates the Minor Premise on which the Criterion of Dissimilarity relies. But even the Major Premise here will be found indefensible on a thorough nesting analysis. "If any saying *s* attributed to Jesus is dissimilar to the views of Judaism and to the views of the early church, then Jesus said *s*" assumes an invalid rule of inference: that only Jesus could innovate. But if Jesus could innovate a saying, then so could anyone, including an actual Gospel author (or other intermediary source). Paul, for example, innovated a law-free Gentile mission, and if Paul could do that, so could anyone innovate anything. We know too little about the many Christians and Jews who lived prior to the Gospels to rule any of them out as originators of any seemingly unique saying, yet we would have to rule them all out in order to isolate Jesus as the only available innovator we can credit for the innovation.

For instance, any saying s_1 we think we can isolate as being unique to Jesus may in fact be unique to Peter instead (or Paul or anyone else who uniquely imagined, hallucinated, dreamed, or invented Jesus saying s_1. There is no more reason to assume the innovation was of Jesus' own making than of Peter's (or Paul's or anyone else's)—whether consciously, for a specific innovative purpose, or unconsciously, as a construct of what Peter (etc.) took to be visions or revelations but were actually the product of his subconscious mind creatively responding to the problems and ambitions of his time. So how are we to tell the difference? The Criterion of Dissimilarity cannot. Therefore, it is methodologically invalid.

The same procedure will similarly invalidate every historicity criterion. The Criterion of Multiple Attestation, for example, runs into the problem of establishing whether we even have independent sources of a tradition (or whether they are all dependent on each other), as well as the problem of determining a valid rule of inference. For even a false claim can be multiply attested to in independent sources (e.g., multiple independent sources attest to the labors of Hercules), and folklorists have documented that this can occur very rapidly (there is no relevant limit to how rapidly multiple sources can transform and transmit the same story). So mere multiple attestation is not enough. This criterion also runs into the Threshold Problem: When do we have enough independent witnesses to believe what they say? Similarly, the Criterion of Embarrassment requires establishing that some detail was in fact embarrassing to the author who records it (this cannot merely be assumed, especially for a sect that was so internally diverse and rooted in open rejection of elite norms) and that this author did not have an overriding reason to include such a detail anyway (such as to convey a lesson or shame his audience into action). This criterion also assumes a rule of inference that is demonstrably invalid unless somehow plausibly qualified. For instance, the castration of Attis and his priests was widely regarded by the literary elite as disgusting and shameful and thus was a definite cause of embarrassment for the cult, though the claim and the practice continued unabated. Yet no one would now argue that the god Attis must therefore have actually been castrated.

In all these cases, there is a common lesson: we must always ask what other reasons there might have been to invent or tell an "embarrassing" story (or for "independent" witnesses to repeat a false story, or for something "innovative" to appear in the record, etc.). Criteria-based methods ignore the crucial importance of alternative theories of the evidence and their relative merits. The importance of avoiding invalid rules of inference, overcoming the Threshold Problem, and comparing our theory with alternatives all point toward Bayes's Theorem as the correct model of proper method. For Bayes's Theorem is specifically constructed from valid rules of inference and solves the Threshold Problem by taking alternative theories into account. In the same way, it also solves another problem.

THE FALLACY OF DIMINISHING PROBABILITIES

Earlier, I mentioned that the premises in a historical argument are only true to some degree of probability, and I said that when these probabilities are not so high as to be practically 100 percent, problems arise. For example:

Major Premise: All major cities in antiquity had public libraries.
Minor Premise: Jerusalem was a major city in antiquity.
Conclusion: Therefore, Jerusalem had a public library.

Which earlier I demonstrated should be revised to:

Major Premise: [Somewhat probably] a major city in antiquity had a public library.
Minor Premise: [Very probably] Jerusalem was a major city in antiquity.
Conclusion: Therefore, [somewhat probably] Jerusalem had a public library.

The major premise here is entailed by the more accurate statement, "Most major cities in antiquity had public libraries" (since we cannot confirm they all did), and the strength of the conclusion cannot exceed the strength of the weakest premise. But even this version is not formally accurate, since the language of probability here is misleadingly vague. Due to the Law of Conditional Probability, the probability of the conclusion (or $P_{LIBRARY}$) cannot equal the probability of the weakest premise but must equal the probability of both premises being true, which is the product of their probabilities ($P_{MAJOR} \times P_{MINOR}$). So although the conclusion here says "somewhat probably Jerusalem had a public library," this "somewhat probably" must be slightly less than the "somewhat probably" in the major premise. For instance, if the major premise has a probability of 60 percent (i.e., we are confident at least 60 percent of major cities had public libraries) and the minor premise a probability of 90 percent (i.e., we are at least 90 percent certain Jerusalem was a "major city" in the same sense employed in the major premise), then $P_{LIBRARY} = 0.60 \times 0.90 = 0.54$, which is 54 percent, not 60 percent.

Now consider what happens when we add more evidence (the following probabilities are again invented here solely for the sake of argument):

Major Premise 1: 60 percent of all major cities in antiquity had public libraries.

Major Premise 2: 80 percent of the time, when the surviving text of something written by an ancient author mentions consulting books in a city's public library, then that city had a public library.

Minor Premise 1: We are 90 percent certain that Jerusalem was a major city in antiquity.

Minor Premise 2: We are 95 percent certain that the author of an ancient papyrus mentions consulting a public library in Jerusalem.

Conclusion: Therefore, Jerusalem [probably] had a public library.

The probability that Jerusalem had a public library should be increased by our having two kinds of evidence mutually supporting the same conclusion—and if more evidence were added, it should raise the probability of the conclusion even more. But the Law of Conditional

Probability produces the opposite result. Since P_{LIBRARY} must equal the product of the probabilities of all the premises being true, with the given probabilities we would get a result of $P_{\text{LIBRARY}} = P_{\text{MAJOR-1}} \times P_{\text{MAJOR-2}} \times P_{\text{MINOR-1}} \times P_{\text{MINOR-2}} = 60\% \times 80\% \times 90\% \times 95\% = 0.60 \times 0.80 \times 0.90 \times 0.95 = 0.41$ (rounding off) $= 41$ percent. We have added evidence and yet dropped from 54 percent to 41 percent, from "probably" to "probably not." Adding more evidence would clearly lower this result even further. Thus the conclusion appears to be less probable when we get more evidence, which cannot be correct.

There is no obvious way around this, which means historical reasoning cannot be validly represented by simple syllogistic logic. Though syllogistic analysis can still be useful to identify flaws in our reasoning and correct them, it does not accurately model historical reasoning. So what does? What logical formula allows the accumulation of evidence without diminishing the probability of the conclusion or violating the Law of Conditional Probability? The answer is Bayes's Theorem.

GETTING STARTED WITH BAYES'S THEOREM

The literature on Bayes's Theorem is vast and usually technical to the point of unintelligibility for historians. But Yudkowsky provides a very good introduction to the theorem, how to use it, and why it is so important,[11] and Hunter provides an extended example of how to employ Bayesian reasoning to history.[12] Yudkowsky's focus is the sciences, but he covers all the basics and is a good place to start. Likewise, though Hunter was a Central Intelligence Agency analyst and writes about using Bayes's Theorem to assess political situations, the similarities with historical problems are strong, and his presentation is intelligible to beginners. Wikipedia also provides an excellent article on Bayes's Theorem (though often untrustworthy in other areas, Wikipedia's content in math and science tends to surpass even print encyclopedias). If you want to advance to more technical issues of the application and importance of Bayes's Theorem, see Jaynes and Bretthorst, Bovens and Hartmann, and Swinburne, while McGrew provides a more extensive bibliography on Bayesian reasoning specifically directed at beginners.[13]

These sources will help with many details. Here I can only cover the rudiments. Bayes's Theorem is represented in a mathematical equation, which has a longer and a shorter form. Its longer (complete) form is:

$$P(h|e.b) = \frac{P(h|b) \times P(e|h.b)}{\left[\,P(h|b) \times P(e|h.b)\,\right] + \left[\,P(\sim h|b) \times P(e|\sim h.b)\,\right]}$$

Its shorter form is:

$$P(h|e.b) = \frac{P(h|b) \times P(e|h.b)}{P(e|b)}$$

The shorter form is simply abbreviated from the longer, and as the long form is more useful to historians, I recommend it. The first thing to recognize about this theorem is that its form is:

$$P = \frac{A}{A + B}$$

In other words, the complete value of the numerator appears again in the denominator, which means there are really only four distinct numbers involved, $P(h|b)$, $P(\sim h|b)$, $P(e|h.b)$, and $P(e|\sim h.b)$, two of which are simply repeated. And since $P(\sim h|b)$ is always the converse of $P(h|b)$, i.e., $P(\sim h|b) = 1 - P(h|b)$, there are really only three values to determine, each of which is the formal equivalent of a premise in an argument, representing a particular estimate of likelihood.

Though in science there are usually precise data from which to derive these values, this is not required by the logic of the argument. Though the equation looks scary, even "too mathematical" for use in solving historical problems, the math merely represents a logic. Though the equation looks complicated, the logic of historical reasoning is that complicated. In fact, this equation models all correct historical reasoning. Whenever we reason correctly about empirical matters (whether in science, history, or everyday life), we are adhering to Bayes's Theorem—and if we're not, we are not reasoning correctly. It is therefore the key to understanding and analyzing all historical thinking and checking and correcting it. As historians, we should all understand the underlying logic of our own methods. And this is it.

The complete Bayesian equation has four basic components. The term to the far left is the probability that some theory we have (or some claim we are making) is true. This is our conclusion. Everything then to the right is what we must solve to produce our conclusion. The equation in the numerator measures how likely our hypothesis is. Then there are two equations in the denominator, connected by a plus sign. As noted, the first of these equations is identical to the equation in the numerator (so you just repeat the same numbers in both places). That leaves the second equation in the denominator, which measures how likely the alternative hypotheses are. Put all this together and you have an exact representation of sound historical reasoning. And that means historical reasoning is only sound when it fully takes into account alternative explanations of the evidence and takes seriously our intuited estimates of likelihood (which we also call plausibility, probability, credibility, believability, etc.).

Since this is (as advertised) "Bayes's Theorem for Beginners," I'll explain every symbol in the equation (other than common mathematical symbols, which I hope all educated readers are familiar with):

P = Probability (which means epistemic probability = the probability that something stated is true)

h = the hypothesis being tested

~h = "not-*h*" = all other hypotheses that could explain the same evidence if *h* is false

e = all the evidence directly relevant to the truth of *h* (*e* includes both what is observed and what is not observed despite adequate looking)

b = total background knowledge (all available personal and human knowledge about anything and everything, from physics to history—in other words, everything else we know, about the world, people, time, and place in question, etc.)

The upright bars separating the terms inside the parentheses indicate conditional probability, that is, the probability that the term on the left of a bar would be true, if all the terms on the right of that bar are true. Put all these together and we get all the combined terms in the equation, now starting to the left of the equals sign:

P(h | e.b) = the probability that a hypothesis (*h*) is true given all the available evidence (*e*) and all our background knowledge (*b*)

This is our conclusion: How likely is it that what we are saying is actually what happened or how things actually were? To reach this result, we need to decide how likely the other terms to the right of the equals sign are:

P(h | b) = **the prior probability that *h* is true** = the probability that our hypothesis would be true given only our background knowledge (i.e., if we knew nothing about *e*); this is a measure of what was typical in that time and place, or in the universe generally, representing what we would usually expect to happen.

P(e | h.b) = **the posterior probability of the evidence (given *h* and *b*)** = the probability that all the evidence we have would exist (or something comparable to it would exist) if the hypothesis *h* (and background knowledge *b*) is true.

P(~h | b) = 1 − **P(h | b)** = **the prior probability that *h* is false** = the sum of the prior probabilities of all alternative explanations of the same evidence, which is always the mathematical converse of the prior probability that *h* is true (so P(~h | b) and P(h | b) must always sum to 1).

There are different ways to deal with more than two competing theories at the same time. One way or another, all possible explanations of the evidence must be represented in the equation (which means prior probability is always a relative probability, i.e., relative to all other possible explanations of the evidence). If there is only one viable alternative, this would mean the prior probability of all other possible theories is vanishingly small (i.e., substantially less than 1 percent), in which case $P(\sim h \mid b)$ is the prior probability of the one viable competing hypothesis. If there are many viable competing hypotheses, they can be subsumed under this as a group category ($\sim h$) or treated independently by expanding the equation, for example, for three competing hypotheses the denominator expands from:

$$\left[P(h|b) \times P(e|h.b) \right] + \left[P(\sim h|b) \times P(e|\sim h.b) \right]$$

to the more elaborate:

$$\left[P(h_1|b) \times P(e|h_1.b) \right] + \left[P(h_2|b) \times P(e|h_2.b) \right] + \left[P(h_3|b) \times P(e|h_3.b) \right]$$

in which all three priors must sum to 1, that is, $P(h1 \mid b) + P(h2 \mid b) + P(h3 \mid b) = 1$.

$P(e \mid \sim h.b)$ = **the posterior probability of the evidence if b is true but h is false** = the probability that all the evidence we have would exist (or something comparable to it would exist) if the hypothesis we are testing is false, but all our background knowledge is still true. In other words, this is the posterior probability of the evidence if some hypothesis other than h is true (and if there is more than one viable contender, you can represent this fact in either fashion noted previously).

Here's the gist: prior probability is a measure of how typical what we are proposing is or how typical it was in that time and place (or how atypical it was, as the case may be), while posterior probability is a measure of how well the evidence fits with what we would expect if our hypothesis were true, and how well the evidence fits with what we would expect if our hypothesis were false.

Even allowing for a large margin of error, we all have some idea of what was typical or atypical, and we can make a case for either from the available evidence. If we cannot, then we must admit that we don't know what was typical, in which case we cannot say one theory is initially more likely than another (their prior probabilities are then equal). Either way, we can represent the relative likelihood of the options with rough figures. Since we already do this anyway, only with vague language about relative likelihoods, Bayes's Theorem forces us to put numbers to our estimates, which forces us to examine how sound or defensible our judgments really are. If we cannot defend our number assignments, then we need to lower or raise them until we can defend them. And if we cannot defend any value, then we cannot claim to know whether the evidence supports or weakens our hypothesis (or any other). All this goes for both the prior and the posterior probabilities.

Since we already make these probability judgments in every argument that we make as historians (only in vaguer language or with unstated assumptions), Bayes's Theorem does not ask us to do anything we shouldn't already be doing. Hence, the theorem simply represents the reasoning we are already engaging in and relying upon. But it does so in a formally valid structure that allows us to check whether we are reasoning correctly or not, and it helps us discover what we need to be looking for or thinking about in order to justify our arguments and assumptions. It thus helps us do what syllogistic analysis does, with the singular difference that it correctly models historical reasoning.

In an adjunct document online,[14] I provide more discussion and examples of both logical and Bayesian analysis, along with summaries, applications, and a tutorial in using Bayes's Theorem. I further discuss historical methods (in general), including references to other books on the subject, in my *Sense and Goodness without God*,[15] with supporting examples and remarks in my "The Spiritual Body of Christ and the Legend of the Empty Tomb."[16] But I will provide a much more detailed example of a real-world application of Bayes's Theorem, with extensive methodological discussion, in my forthcoming book, *On the Historicity of Jesus Christ* (especially in chapters 2 and 6).

WHY BAYES'S THEOREM?

There are six reasons we should learn Bayes's Theorem well enough to understand its logic and apply it, especially if we want to test possible claims regarding what is and is not historical about Jesus (or anything else in history).

First, Bayes's Theorem solves the Threshold Problem. In other words, it provides the means to tell if your theory is probably true rather than merely possibly true. It achieves this, first, by forcing you to compare the relative likelihood of different theories of the same evidence (so you must think of other reasons the evidence we have might exist, besides the reason you intuitively think is most likely), and, second, by forcing you to examine what exactly you mean when you say something is "likely" or "unlikely," "more likely" or "less likely," "plausible" or "implausible," "somewhat implausible" or "very plausible," and so on. It also forces you to examine why you think such terms are justified and how you intend to justify them. As long as historians go on ignoring these questions, no progress can be made, and we will end up with a different historical Jesus (and a different mythical Jesus) for every scholar who looks and no way to assess whose conclusions are the more probable. Though Bayesian analysis does not make this assessment easy, it is the only known method that makes it possible.

Second, Bayes's Theorem will inspire a closer examination of your background knowledge and of the corresponding objectivity of your estimates of initial likelihood. Whether you are aware of it or not, all your thinking relies on estimations of prior probability. So making these estimations explicit will expose them to closer examination and testing. For example, whenever you say some claim is implausible or unlikely because "that's not how things were done then" or "that's not how people would likely behave" or "that wasn't typical" or "other things happened more often instead," you are making estimates of the prior probability of what is being claimed. And when you make this reasoning explicit, unexpected discoveries can be made. For example, as Porter as well as Theissen and Winter observed, it is inherently unlikely that any Christian author would include anything embarrassing in his Gospel account, since he could choose to include or omit whatever he wanted (and as we can plainly see, all the Gospel authors picked and chose and altered whatever suited them). In contrast, it is inherently likely that anything a Christian author included in his account was done for a deliberate reason—to accomplish something he wanted to accomplish, since that is how all authors behave, especially those with a specific aim of persuasion. Therefore, already the prior probability that a seemingly embarrassing detail in a Christian text is in there because it is true is low, whereas the prior probability that it is in there for a specific reason regardless of its truth is high—the exact opposite of what is assumed by the Criterion of Embarrassment.

Third, as already noted, Bayes's Theorem will force you to examine the likelihood of the evidence on competing theories, rather than only your own. So you have to take alternative theories seriously before dismissing them. This is one of the most common errors in historical reasoning: defending your own pet theory in isolation and ignoring or downplaying all the alternatives. If you start with a theory and then try to solve how the evidence supports it, you may be able to make the evidence fit almost any theory. But if you take seriously all other attempts to do the same thing, you will be forced to ask why your theory's fit-to-evidence is more credible than any other, and the answer will always lead you back to the logic of Bayes's Theorem, whether you are aware of it or not.

Fourth, Bayes's Theorem eliminates the Fallacy of Diminishing Probabilities. It is therefore the only correct way to weigh a combined array of evidence. That means it is the only correct description of sound empirical reasoning. So its underlying logic ought to be well understood by anyone making empirical arguments (as historians do).

Fifth, Bayes's Theorem has been proven to be formally valid. Any argument that violates a valid form of argument is itself invalid. Therefore, any argument that violates Bayes's Theorem is invalid. All valid historical arguments are described by Bayes's Theorem. Therefore, any historical argument that cannot be described by a correct application of Bayes's Theorem is invalid. That means Bayes's Theorem provides a useful method for testing any historical argument for validity.

Sixth, you can use Bayesian reasoning without attempting any math, but I recommend the math. Doing the math keeps you honest. It forces you to ask the right questions, to test your assumptions and intuitions, and to actually give relative weights to hypotheses and evidence that are not all equally likely. But either way, using Bayes's Theorem exposes all our assumptions to examination and criticism and thus allows progress to be made. For, once all our assumptions are exposed in this way, we will be able to continually revise our arguments in light of the flaws detected in our reasoning, as well as our mistakes (as there will inevitably be) in attempting to apply Bayes's Theorem to any given problem.

THREE COMMON ERRORS

There are many mistakes one can make in employing Bayes's Theorem. I will describe three of the most common before concluding.

The first is the Fallacy of False Precision: mistaking the fact that we are using numbers and math as somehow indicating we are generating mathematically precise conclusions. Since we do not have scientifically precise or abundant data as historians, any numbers we plug into a Bayesian equation will only be rough estimates—and, therefore, so will our conclusions. But this is already true of historical reasoning generally. Hence this fallacy will be avoided if we recognize that the numbers we use represent the limits of wide margins of error and then aim to generate conclusions a fortiori or with significant levels of uncertainty. In probability theory (as reflected in scientific polls, drug efficacy studies, etc.), the wider the margin of error, the higher the confidence level (and vice versa). So if you widen your margin of error as far as you can reasonably believe it possible for that margin to be (given the evidence available to you and all other expert observers at the time), then your confidence level will be such that you cannot reasonably believe the conclusion is false. That is the highest state of objective certainty possible in historical inquiry.

For instance, you may see a poll result that says 20 percent of teens smoke, but in a footnote you see "97% at +/-3%." This means the data entail there is a 97 percent chance that the percentage of teens who smoke falls between 17 and 23 percent (and therefore a 3 percent chance it is either less or more than that). The first number (97%) is the confidence level, the second (+/-3%) is the margin of error. Given any set of data, raising the confidence level widens the margin of error (and vice versa) according to a strict mathematical formula. So if you lack scientifically precise data, you can compensate by setting your margins of error as wide as you can reasonably believe them to be. For instance, if you lacked scientific data on teen smoking and had to estimate without it, you may think it unreasonable from your own personal knowledge and consultation with others that the percentage of teen smokers could be anything above 33 percent, which is in effect saying you are highly confident, at least 99 percent certain, that the percentage can be no more than 33 but could easily be much less than that. You can similarly derive a lowest rate of teen smoking that you can reasonably believe exists and then run the math for both numbers, which will in turn generate a conclusion that is also a range between a lowest and highest number. Following that procedure, you cannot reasonably believe the conclusion falls outside that range (you will be highly confident that it does not), but you might not be sure exactly where it falls within that range (unless you lower your confidence in the conclusion).

An a fortiori argument thus results if your theory is still confirmed as probable even when using the most unfavorable probability estimates you can reasonably believe. And an argument of uncertainty results if your theory ends up with a Bayesian probability like 40 to 70 percent, a range of values that actually crosses into improbability, thus leaving you only somewhat confident that your conclusion is true. Accordingly, if you recognize the relationship between margins of error and confidence level, the fallacy of false precision can be avoided, and Bayes's Theorem can still be used effectively without scientific data. Used thus, it will always generate conclusions that correctly match what you can honestly have confidence in.

The second common mistake is the Fallacy of Confusing Evidence with Theories. For example, Christian apologists will often insist we have to explain the "fact" of the empty tomb. But in a Bayesian equation, the evidence is not the discovery of an empty tomb but the existence of a story about the discovery of an empty tomb. That there was an actual empty tomb is only a theory (a hypothesis, h) to explain the production of the story (which is an element of e). But this theory must be compared with other possible explanations of how and why that story came to exist ($\sim h$, or h_2, h_3, etc.), and these must be compared on a total examination of the evidence (all elements of e, in conjunction with b and the resulting prior probabilities). Hence, a common mistake is to confuse hypotheses about the evidence with the actual evidence itself. This mistake can be avoided by limiting "evidence" (e) to tangible physical facts (i.e., actual surviving artifacts, documents, etc., and straightforward generalizations therefrom). Though hypotheses can in fact be included in e (as well as b), this is mathematically problematic unless those hypotheses are so well confirmed as to be nearly as certain as the existence of the evidence that confirms them (in fact, almost all "facts" are ultimately hypotheses of just such a sort).[17] Otherwise, without mathematically accounting for a hypothesis's level of uncertainty, the fallacy results of wrongly assuming it is as certain as any other facts. It is easier to just leave everything out of e and b that is not effectively certain and treat the rest as elements of h and $\sim h$.

The third common mistake is the Fallacy of Confusing Assumptions with Knowledge. Assumptions in, assumptions out, so mere "assumptions" should have no place in Bayesian argument, as its conclusions will only be as strong as their weakest premise, and an assumption is a very weak premise indeed. In Bayes's Theorem, the term b establishes that all the probabilities in the equation are conditional probabilities—conditional on the truth of our background knowledge. Therefore, only background knowledge should be included in b and thus considered in assigning probabilities, not background assumptions or mere beliefs. Indeed, the very difference between professional and unprofessional history is the acceptance in b of only what has been accepted by peer review as an established fact (or an established uncertainty of some degree, as the case may be). So the contents of b should be limited to the confirmed consensus of expert knowledge.

Committing this fallacy leads to a common misapprehension that, for example, prior probabilities in Bayes's Theorem are worldview dependent. They are not. For example, it doesn't matter whether you are a naturalist and believe no miracles exist or a Christian and believe that they do. Either way, if you are behaving professionally, you both must agree that so far as is objectively known, most miracle claims in history have turned out to be bogus, and none so far have been confirmed to be genuine. Therefore, the prior probability that a miracle claim is genuine must reflect the fact that most miracle claims are not—and that is a fact even if genuine miracles exist. In other words, the naturalist must allow that he could be wrong (so he must grant some probability that there might still be a genuine miracle somewhere, whatever that probability must be), and the Christian must allow that most miracle claims are false (not only because investigated claims overwhelmingly trend that way, and even Christians admit that most of the miracle claims even within their own tradition are not credible, but also because the Christian must grant that most miracle claims validate other religious traditions and therefore must be false if Christianity is true). If most miracle claims are false, then the prior probability that any particular miracle claim is false is therefore high regardless of whether miracles exist or whether Christianity is true.

Therefore, although worldview considerations can be allowed into b, Bayes's Theorem does not require this. When such considerations are brought into b, that only produces conditional probabilities that follow when the adopted worldview is true. But if a certain worldview is already assumed to be true, most arguments do not even have to be made, as the conclusion is already foregone. Therefore, b should only include objectively agreed knowledge (and probabilities then assessed accordingly), unless arguing solely to audiences within a single worldview community.

CONCLUSION

If you avoid these and other mistakes, and treat each probability you assign in the Bayesian equation as if it were a premise in an argument and defend each such premise as sound (as you would for any ordinary syllogism), Bayes's Theorem will solve all the problems that have left Theissen and others confounded when trying to assess questions of historicity. There really is no other method on the table, since all the historicity criteria so far proposed have been shown to be flawed to the point of being in effect (or in fact) entirely useless. The task now falls on historians to practice and develop procedures for adapting Bayes's Theorem to solve specific problems in the quest for the historical Jesus, as I will soon in *On the Historicity of Jesus Christ.*

*   *   *

The chart on the following page represents the complete logic of Bayes's Theorem (for two competing hypotheses), which can be used with non-numerical declarations of relative likelihood at each step. To use the chart, the term "Low" means lower than 50 percent (< 0.50), and "High" higher than 50 percent (> 0.50), although when $P(e|h.b) = 50$ percent, then treat it as "High" if $P(h|b)$ is "High," and "Low" if $P(\sim h|b)$ is "Low," accordingly. "Sufficiently lower" (or "Sufficiently higher") means $P(e|\sim h.b)$ is lower (or higher) than $P(e|h.b)$ by enough to overcome the prior probability (and thus produce a conclusion contrary to what the prior probability alone would predict), though there is hardly any principled way to determine this without returning to the math. To read the results, a high $P(h|e.b)$ means your hypothesis is more likely true; a low $P(h|e.b)$, more likely false (and the higher or lower, the more likely either way). When $P(h|b) = 50$ percent (and therefore is neither "High" nor "Low"), then the hypothesis with the higher $P(e|b)$ is more likely true.

Bayesian Flowchart

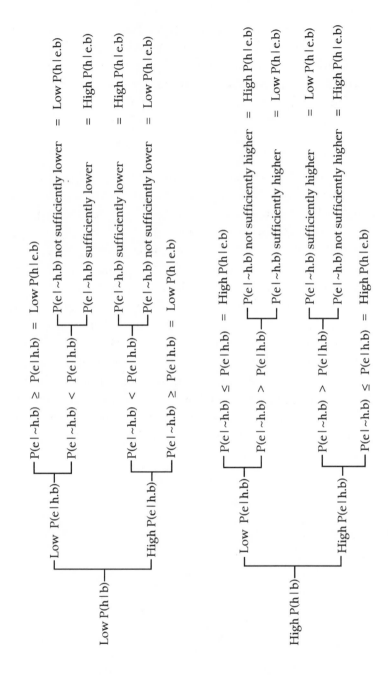

Low P(h|b)

Low P(e|h.b) ⎧ P(e|~h.b) ≥ P(e|h.b) = Low P(h|e.b)

⎩ P(e|~h.b) < P(e|h.b) ⎧ P(e|~h.b) not sufficiently lower = Low P(h|e.b)

⎩ P(e|~h.b) sufficiently lower = High P(h|e.b)

High P(e|h.b) ⎧ P(e|~h.b) < P(e|h.b) ⎧ P(e|~h.b) sufficiently lower = High P(h|e.b)

⎩ P(e|~h.b) not sufficiently lower = Low P(h|e.b)

⎩ P(e|~h.b) ≥ P(e|h.b) = Low P(h|e.b)

High P(h|b)

Low P(e|h.b) ⎧ P(e|~h.b) ≤ P(e|h.b) = High P(h|e.b)

⎩ P(e|~h.b) > P(e|h.b) ⎧ P(e|~h.b) not sufficiently higher = High P(h|e.b)

⎩ P(e|~h.b) sufficiently higher = Low P(h|e.b)

High P(e|h.b) ⎧ P(e|~h.b) > P(e|h.b) ⎧ P(e|~h.b) sufficiently higher = Low P(h|e.b)

⎩ P(e|~h.b) not sufficiently higher = High P(h|e.b)

⎩ P(e|~h.b) ≤ P(e|h.b) = High P(h|e.b)

THE ABHORRENT VOID
The Rapid Attribution of Fictive Sayings and Stories to a Mythic Jesus

Robert M. Price

Nature abhors a vacuum.
—Jesus Christ (You can't prove that he *didn't* say it!)

OUT OF NOTHING SOMETHING COMES

I t seems to conservative scholars, apologists, and rank-and-file Gospel readers quite implausible, indeed outlandish, when critics write off the majority of sayings and stories of Jesus in the Gospels as secondary and inauthentic. Even if one grants the likelihood that false attribution and secondary embellishments may occasionally have occurred, does it not seem like skeptical ax grinding for scholars to dismiss most of the tradition as spurious? C. H. Dodd, no fundamentalist, sought to rein in such skepticism.

> When Mark was writing, there must have been many people about who were in their prime under Pontius Pilate, and they must have remembered the stirring and tragic events of that time at least as vividly as we [in 1949] remember 1914. If anyone had tried to put over an entirely imaginary or fictitious account of them, there would have been middle-aged or elderly people who would have said (as you or I might say) "You are wasting your breath: I remember it as if it were yesterday!"[1]

Is it my imagination, or is this argument not hopelessly circular? It makes a lot of sense if we know in advance that the events involving Jesus and Pilate were indeed as the grumpy old-timers claimed to remember them. Otherwise, we cannot know whose version of the story is imaginary and fictitious. Dodd already sides with the old hecklers and assumes we do, too. It behooves us to observe, too, that Dodd's appeal to a solid historical bottom against which traditions may be sounded is gratuitous if we do not take for granted that a historical Jesus was born when the Gospels imply, between 4 and 6 BCE. If, as some of us think, such dating is insecure, as is the very existence of a single historical founder of Christianity, then spurious traditions (myths, legends, rumors) will have had all the time in the world to grow and evolve.

Everett F. Harrison, more of a conservative than Dodd, still seems to utter only common sense when he voices his skepticism about skepticism:

> All will agree that, according to the gospels, teaching was one of the major activities of the Master and that His teaching made a profound impression on those who heard it (Mark 1:22; cf. John 7:46). To have a tradition *that* Jesus taught, without a tradition of *what* he taught, would be strange indeed and quite incomprehensible, since the tradition *that* he taught includes the report of the impact of his words. It would be strange also, on the assumption that the Church rather than Jesus had authored or doctored the greater part of the corpus of instruction in the Gospels, that the statement of his uniqueness in this area should be retained, "You are not to be called rabbi, for you have one teacher" (Matt. 23:8, RSV; cf. Mark 1:27).[2]

Harrison had not yet grasped the full extent of the insidious character of the critical mind. Should it not be obvious that, if there had been no teacher, no Rabbi Jesus (Paul knows of no such character, nor of a thaumaturgic Jesus), the subsequent attempt to claim his divine authority for one's own teachings would make it advisable to posit that Jesus had been a great teacher? One is thus feathering one's own nest, providing increased clout for whatever one intends to ascribe to Jesus. It is not strange at all. It would be like claiming Jesus had been a carpenter so one could sell off one's own bedroom and dining-room sets as Jesus' work![3]

We have three models, proposed analogies, to help us understand the plausibility of positing a wholesale and rapid growth of a vast body of inauthentic Jesus traditions and even that it might have been expected. This will be the case whether we believe in a Jesus who was, like fellow messiah Sabbatai Sevi, not much of a teacher or whether we think there was no Jesus Christ at all. In other words, such things as "skeptical" critics posit in the case of the Gospel traditions have famously happened in other historically analogous cases.

KID STUFF

First, we may recall that many or most early Christians came to believe that Jesus had initially appeared (or been adopted) as a deity in adult form. Picture it either way you prefer. The historical Jesus grew up in obscurity, entering public life only once he received John's baptism. When this happened, many early Christians, presumably including Mark the evangelist, believed Jesus had been divinely anointed as God's son. He could not have laid claim to that honor at any previous time. Others held, as Marcion did, that this Jesus deity appeared out of thin air upon our earth one day, but in adult form, like Adam created as an adult—with a belly button he had never needed. In either case, stories of Jesus would have depicted him as an adult gifted with divine power. Later on, Christians came to believe that Jesus, having been born from a miraculous conception, was the son of God from day one. Christian curiosity rapidly went to work filling the newly apparent gap. What would an infant or a child god have been doing in the years before tradition made him appear on the public scene? There was an immediate flood of stories. The ample results are contained in the Infancy Gospels of Thomas, Matthew, and James and the Arabic Infancy Gospel. The canonical Gospels of Luke and John each contain one example of such stories: Lk 2:41–51 and Jn 2:1–10. As Raymond E. Brown[4] argued, the Cana story must have had a prehistory as a story of Jesus the divine prodigy. As in practically all such stories, Jesus' miracles and precocious insights are magnified against the stupidity and incompetence of adults. Same here: they have run out of wine. And, contra the redactional frame, where the water-into-wine miracle is explicitly said to be his first, mother Mary knows Jesus will give in and bail out the adults with a handy miracle as he always does. ("Do whatever he tells you.")

In precisely the same way, the Christ-myth theory reasons that, once an adult, mortal-seeming Jesus was said to have come to earth in recent history, Christian imagination went to work supplying what he must have been doing and saying. These stories and sayings now fill the familiar Gospels. It does not sound so odd that, e.g., the Jesus Seminar was able to authenticate only 18 percent of the material. I consider that figure way too optimistic.

Some might dispute the aptness of the analogy, pointing out that the Infancy Gospel stories are comical compared to the stories of the adult Jesus, which, despite their miraculous extravagance, do not seem ridiculous. But I would suggest the reason for the difference is simply the comedy inherent in stories of a child prodigy with miraculous powers. Jesus the Menace. I am not saying the idea is not silly; indeed it is. But can one take all the canonical stories completely seriously? Cursing the fig tree? Sending demoniac pigs into a lake? Healing Peter's mother-in-law so she can cook dinner for Jesus? My point is simply that fictions featuring Jesus the god-man as an adult might be equally extravagant as stories featuring him as a child but less comical since they would not involve the inevitably comedic element of a child displaying adult behavior.

THE (GROWING) BEARD OF THE PROPHET

The second analogy/model for a rapid accretion of spurious Jesus traditions lies at hand in the explosion of (universally spurious) hadith, traditions of what the Prophet Muhammad said and did, providing precedents and teachings for devout Muslims, thus supplementing the Qur'an. Just as some Muslim hadith reflect rabbinical and New Testament sources,[5] it is no surprise that the Gospels should be filled to the brim with echoes of rabbinical, Cynic, and Stoic materials, as well as maxims first offered in the Epistles with no claim that they originated with a historical Jesus.[6]

Consider how the reasons for the fabrication of "traditional" stories and sayings of Muhammad correspond precisely to those suggested for Gospel traditions by the form critics:

> The Prophet's authority was invoked by every group for every idea it evolved: for legal precepts couched in the form of tradition, as well as

for maxims and teachings of an ethical or simply edificatory nature. Through solid chains of tradition, all such matters acquired an unbroken tie to the "Companions" who had heard these pronouncements and statutes from the Prophet or had seen him act in pertinent ways. It took no extraordinary discernment on the part of Muslim critics to suspect the authenticity of much of this material: some reports were betrayed by anachronisms or other dubious features, some contradicted others. Moreover, certain people are named outright who fabricated and spread abroad traditions to support one trend or another. Not a few pious persons admitted, as the end of life neared, how great their contribution to the body of fictive hadiths had been. To fabricate hadith was hardly considered dishonorable if the resulting fictions served the cause of the good. A man honorable in all other respects could be discredited as a traditionist without having his religious reputation tarnished or his honor as a member of society called into question. It was, of course, possible to assert, on the Prophet's authority, that the bottomless pit awaited those who fraudulently ascribed to Muhammad utterances that he never made. But one could also try to save the situation by vindicatory maxims, in which the Prophet had supposedly recognized such fictions in advance as his own spiritual property: "After my death more and more sayings will be ascribed to me, just as many sayings have been ascribed to previous prophets (without their having really said them). When a saying is reported and attributed to me, compare it with God's book. Whatever is in accordance with that book is from me, whether I really said it or no."[7] Further: "Whatever is rightly spoken was spoken by me."[8]

The fabricators of tradition, as we see, laid their cards on the table. "Muhammad said" in such cases merely means "it is right, it is religiously unassailable, it is even desirable, and the Prophet himself would applaud it."[9]

Even if one prefers to reckon according to a historical Jesus who was born in Herod the Great's reign and perished in that of Pontius Pilate,[10] there is plenty of time available in which to picture the eruption of false Jesus hadith. It certainly seems not to have taken very long in the case of Islam.

All the Islamic authorities agree that an enormous amount of forgery was committed in the *hadith* literature. The Victorian writer William Muir thought that it began during the caliphate of Uthman. It is more likely, however, that it originated during the lifetime of the Prophet himself. His opponents would not have missed the opportunity to forge and attribute words and deeds to him for which he was not responsible, in order to rouse the Arab tribes against his teaching.[11] During the caliphate of Abu Bakr, too, when apostasy had raised its head, it is not unlikely that some of the apostates should have forged such traditions as suited their purpose. During the caliphate of Uthman, this kind of dishonesty became more common. Some members of the factions into which the community was then divided forged traditions in order to advance their faction's interests.[12] During the first century of Islam, and also thereafter, the various political parties, the heretics, the professional preachers, and even a number of sincere Muslims, all made their contributions to the growing rubbish-heap of false traditions.[13]

Sectarian leaders as well as popular edifying story-tellers forged plenty as they addressed the people following morning and evening prayers.[14] Compared to the volume of hadith generated in the name of Muhammad by interested and imaginative parties, the scope of invention when it comes to Jesus is quite modest.

Spurious traditions were coming into being, drowning the genuine ones. There were motives at play behind this development. Some of these new traditions were merely pious frauds, worked up in order to promote what the fabricators thought were elements of a pious life,[15] or what they thought were the right theological views.[16] Spurious traditions also arose in order to promote factional interests. Soon after Muhammad's death, there were cutthroat struggles for power between several factions, particularly the Alids, the Ummayads, and later on the Abassides. In this struggle, great passions were generated, and under their influence, new traditions were concocted, and old ones usefully edited. The pious and hero-worshipping mind also added many miracles around the life of Muhammad, so that the man tended to be lost in the myth.

Under these circumstances, a serious effort was made to collect and sift all the current traditions, rejecting the spurious ones and committing the correct ones to writing. [The need for this work was recognized about a century after the Prophet's death, but it took another century for the process to get started.]

[Muhammad Ismail al-]Bukhari [810–870 CE] laid down elaborate canons of authenticity and applied them with a ruthless hand. It is said that he collected 600,000 traditions but accepted only 7,000 of them as authentic.[17]

But even the remainder of Muhammadan hadith seems excessive. Apparently, what Bukhari and the others did was merely to catalogue those hadith that were not debunked by their criteria, not that this vindicated them. The same error attaches to the decisions of New Testament critics who nominate as authentically dominical the sayings that are not obviously disqualified by their criteria of dissimilarity, multiple attestation, coherence, etc. Any or all of them still might be spurious; they just haven't been "caught in the act." ("I know of nothing against myself, but I am not thereby acquitted" [1 Cor 4:4].] Just so, there is no particular reason to regard any of the hadith of Muhammad as definitely authentic.

We must abandon the gratuitous assumptions that there existed originally an authentic core of information going back to the time of the Prophet, that spurious and tendentious additions were made to it in every generation, that many of these were eliminated by the criticism of *isnads* (chains of attestors) as practiced by the Muhammadan scholars, that other spurious traditions escaped rejection, but that the genuine core was not completely overlaid by later accretions. If we shed these prejudices, we become free to consider the Islamic traditions objectively in their historical context, within the framework of the development of the problems to which they refer, and this enables us to find a number of criteria for establishing the relative and even the absolute chronology of a great many traditions.[18]

Indeed, why not consider the Qur'an itself as hadith? It appears to be a collection of contradictory and redundant materials on various topics, all ascribed to Muhammad (and thence to Gabriel) in order to secure prophetic authority.

When I see how conservatives[19] flock to the suggestion of Harald

Riesenfeld and Birger Gerhardsson[20] (admittedly very great scholars) that the canonical Gospel traditions be read on analogy with strictly memorized, authorized Rabbinical traditions simply because conceivably the early disciples *might possibly* have followed such practices, it becomes clear to me we are dealing again with apologetics. Why not consider the analogy of the Muhammadan hadith? The diversity, anachronism, and tendentiousness of the Gospel material would seem to me to make the hadith analogy the better fit. (However, we ought to keep in mind Jacob Neusner's demonstration[21] that rabbinical sayings-ascriptions are no likelier to be authentic anyway!)

FROM MUHAMMAD TO NAG HAMMADI

In her fascinating treatise *Jesus in the Nag Hammadi Writings*,[22] Majella Franzmann points out the theological agenda that has excluded the Egyptian Gnostic texts from serious consideration as possible sources for the historical Jesus and for early Christology. She does not argue, as does Margaret Barker,[23] that the Nag Hammadi texts provide substantial material for a reconstruction of the Jesus of history. No, her point is rather that few bother even to look—outside the canon. The same blind spot occurs among the apologists.

> Indeed, the evidence is that the early Christians were careful to distinguish between sayings of Jesus and their own inferences and judgments. Paul, for example, when discussing the vexed questions of marriage and divorce in 1 Corinthians 7, is careful to make this distinction between his own advice on the subject and the Lord's decisive ruling: "I, not the Lord," and again, "Not I, but the Lord" (F. F. Bruce).[24]

On the one hand, it is far from clear that, in these instances, Paul means to say he has on record a quoted statement from Jesus of Nazareth. In light of 1 Corinthians 14:37, it seems much more likely that he merely distinguishes between his own sage advice and revelations he has received in a mantic state ("prophesying"). On the other, it is obvious to us, as it was not to the orthodox Bruce, great scholar though he was, that "the evidence" is not to be found only in the canon. (He doesn't even seem to consider the letters to the seven churches in Revelation 1–3.) I should say the evidence as to whether "the early Christians were careful to distinguish between sayings of Jesus and their own inferences and judgments" must include the voluminous, if deadly boring, Gnostic texts (Nag Hammadi and Berlin Codices) and the Epistle of the Apostles. Granted, Ron Cameron and others have sought to dredge up some authentic words of Jesus from the Dialogue of the Savior and the Apocryphon of James, and Thomas's gospel is a special case. But most of these attempts to find a needle in a haystack are exceptions that amply prove the rule: the early Christians who composed these texts had no thought of segregating their own words from those of a historical Jesus Christ. Indeed, they did not even think it was a good idea. The very existence of works like Pistis Sophia, the Books of Jeu, the Dialogue of the Savior, the Gospel of Mary, the Sophia of Jesus Christ, and so on makes it simply ridiculous to urge that early Christians would never have dared put Jesus' name on their own fabrications, just as Elizabeth Claire Prophet[25] and Helen Schucman[26] do today. Why does anyone fail to see this? Because, for most, the "real" early Christians are New Testament characters. Whoever wrote Pistis Sophia was one of those Gnostic heretics, in short, spurious "early Christians" who weren't really Christians at all, any more than today's Protestant fundamentalist is willing to admit that Roman Catholics are genuine Christians. But this is not a judgment fit for historians. It is no judgment at all, but only a prejudice. And the same prejudice makes it falsely obvious to conservatives that the canonical Gospels could not be the result of wholesale fabrication by well-meaning Christians. There is just no reason Christian writers could not have composed the Sermon on the Mount if they created the Dialogue of the Savior. If they could have fabricated Pistis Sophia, they could much more easily have fabricated the Gospel of John. Whether they did is another matter, the discussion of which starts here, not stops.

JESUS' DISPUTE IN THE TEMPLE AND THE ORIGIN OF THE EUCHARIST

Bruce Chilton

Critical discussion of Jesus throughout the modern period has been thwarted by a single, crucial question. Anyone who has read the Gospels knows that Jesus was a skilled teacher, a rabbi in the language of early Judaism.[1] He composed a portrait of God as divine ruler ("the kingdom of God," in his words) and wove it together with an appeal to people to behave as God's children (by loving both their divine father and their neighbor).[2] At the same time, it is plain that Jesus appeared to be a threat both to the Jewish and to the Roman authorities in Jerusalem. He would not have been crucified otherwise. The question that has nagged critical discussion concerns the relationship between Jesus the rabbi and Jesus the criminal: how does a teacher of God's ways and God's love find himself on a cross?

Scholarly pictures of Jesus that have been developed during the past two hundred years typically portray him as either an appealing, gifted teacher or as a vehement, political revolutionary. Both kinds of portrait are wanting. If Jesus' teaching was purely abstract, a matter of defining God's nature and the appropriate human response to God, it is hard to see why he would have risked his life in Jerusalem and why the local aristocracy there turned against him. On the other hand, if Jesus' purpose was to encourage some sort of terrorist rebellion against Rome, why should he have devoted so much of his ministry to telling memorable parables in Galilee? It is easy enough to imagine Jesus the rabbi or Jesus the revolutionary. But how can we do justice to both aspects and discover Jesus, the revolutionary rabbi of the first century?

Although appeals to the portrait of Jesus as a terrorist are still found today, current fashion is much more inclined to view him as a philosophical figure, even as a Jewish version of the peripatetic teachers of the Hellenistic world. But the more abstract Jesus' teaching is held to be—and the more we conceive of him simply as uttering timeless maxims and communing with God—the more difficulty there is in understanding the resistance to him. For that reason, a degree of anti-Semitism is the logical result of trying to imagine Jesus as a purely non-violent and speculative teacher. A surprising number of scholars (no doubt inadvertently) have aided and abetted the caricature of a philosophical Jesus persecuted by irrationally violent Jews.

The Gospels all relate an incident that, critically analyzed, resolves the problem of what we might call the two historical natures of Jesus. The passage is traditionally called "The Cleansing of the Temple" (see Mt 21:12–16; Mk 11:15–18; Jn 2:14–22; Lk 19:45–48). Jesus boldly enters the holy place where sacrifice was conducted and throws out the people who were converting the currency of Rome into money that was acceptable to the priestly authorities. He even expels vendors and their animals from the Temple, bringing the routine of sacrifice to a halt.

Such an action would indeed have aroused opposition from both the Roman authorities and the priests. The priests would be threatened because an important source of revenue was jeopardized, as well as the arrangements they themselves had condoned. The Romans would be concerned because they wished for political reasons to protect the operation of the Temple. They saw sacrifice there as a symbol of their tolerant acceptance of Jews as loyal subjects, and they even arranged to pay for some of the offerings.[3] The same Temple that was for the priestly class a divine privilege was for the Romans the seal of imperial hegemony.

The conventional picture of Jesus as preventing commercial activity in God's house is appealing but oversimplified. It enables us to conceive of Jesus as opposing worship in the Temple, and that is the intention of the Gospels. They are all written with hindsight, in the period after the Temple was destroyed (in 70 CE), when Christianity was emerging as a largely non-Jewish movement. From the early Fathers of Christianity to the most modern commentaries, the alluring simplicity of the righteous, philosophical Jesus casting out the "money-changers" has proven itself attractive again and again.

As is often the case, the conventional picture of Jesus may be sustained only by ignoring the social realities of early Judaism. Jesus in fact worshiped in the Temple and encouraged others to do so (see, for example, his instructions to the "leper" in Mt 8:4, Mk 1:44, Lk 5:14). In addition, the picture of Jesus simply throwing the money-changers out of the Temple seems implausible. There were indeed "money-changers" associated with the Temple, whose activities are set down in the Mishnah and recorded by Josephus. Every year, the changing of money—in order to collect the tax of a half-shekel for every adult male—went on publicly throughout Israel. The process commenced a full month before Passover with a proclamation concerning the tax,[4] and exchanges were set up outside Jerusalem ten days before they were set up in the Temple. The tax was not limited to those resident in the land of Israel, but was collected from Jews far and wide. An awareness of those simple facts brings us to an equally simple conclusion: the Gospels' picture of Jesus is distorted. It is clear that he could not have stopped the collection of the half-shekel by overturning some tables in the Temple.

A generation after Jesus' death, by the time the Gospels were written, the Temple in Jerusalem had been destroyed, and the most influential centers of Christianity were cities of the Mediterranean world such as Alexandria, Antioch, Corinth, Damascus, Ephesus, and Rome. There were still large numbers of Jews who were also followers of Jesus, but non-Jews came to predominate in the early church. They had control over how the Gospels were written after 70 CE and how the texts were interpreted. The Gospels were composed by one group of teachers after another by a process of oral and written transmission during the period between Jesus' death and 100 CE. There is a reasonable degree of consensus that Mark was the first of the Gospels to be written, around 73 CE in the environs of Rome. As convention has it, Matthew was subsequently composed, near 80 CE, perhaps in Damascus (or elsewhere in Syria), while Luke came later, say in 90 CE, perhaps in Antioch. Some of the earliest teachers who shaped the Gospels shared the cultural milieu of Jesus, but others had never seen him; they lived far from his land at a later period and were not practicing Jews. John's Gospel was composed in Ephesus around 100 CE and is a reflection upon the significance of Jesus for Christians who had the benefit of the sort of teaching that the synoptic Gospels represent.

The growth of Christianity involved a rapid transition from culture to culture and, within each culture, from subculture to subculture. A basic prerequisite for understanding any text of the Gospels, therefore, is to define the cultural context of a given statement. The cultural context of the picture of Jesus throwing money-changers out of the Temple is that of the predominantly non-Jewish audience of the Gospels, who regarded Judaism as a thing of the past and its worship as corrupt. The attempt to imagine Jesus behaving in that fashion only distorts our understanding of his purposes and encourages the anti-Semitism of Christians. Insensitivity to the cultural milieus of the Gospels goes hand in hand with a prejudicial treatment of cultures other than our own.

Jesus probably did object to the tax of a half-shekel, as Mt 17:24–27 indicates.[5] For him, being a child of God (a "son," as he put it) implied that one was free of any imposed payment for worship in the Temple. But a single onslaught of the sort described in the Gospels would not have amounted to an effective protest against the payment. To stop the collection would have required an assault involving the central treasuries of the Temple, as well as local treasuries in Israel and beyond. There is no indication that Jesus and his followers did anything of the kind, and an action approaching such dimensions would have invited immediate and forceful repression by both Jewish and Roman authorities. There is no evidence that they reacted in that manner to Jesus and his followers.

But Jesus' action in the Temple as attested in the Gospels is not simply a matter of preventing the collection of the half-shekel. In fact, Lk 19:45–46 says nothing whatever about "money-changers"; because Luke's Gospel is in some ways the most sensitive of all the Gospels to historical concerns, the omission seems significant. Luke joins the other Gospels in portraying Jesus' act in the Temple as an occupation designed to prevent the sacrifice of animals that were acquired on the site. The trading involved commerce within the Temple, and the Jesus of the canonical Gospels, like the Jesus of the Gospel according to Thomas, held that "traders and merchants shall not enter the places of my father" (Thomas saying 64), a stance that coincides with the book of Zechariah (chapter 14).

Jesus' action in the Temple, understood as a means of protecting the sanctity of the Temple, is comparable to the actions of other Jewish teachers of his period. Josephus reports that the Pharisees made known their displeasure at a high priest (and a king at that, Alexander Jannaeus) by inciting a crowd to pelt him with lemons (at hand for a festal procession) at the time he should have been offering sacrifice.[6] Josephus also recounts the execution of the rabbis who were implicated in a plot to dismantle the eagle Herod had erected over a gate of the Temple.[7] By comparison, Jesus' action seems almost tame; after all, what he did was expel some vendors, an act less directly threatening to priestly and secular authorities than what some earlier Pharisees had done.

Once it is appreciated that Jesus' maneuver in the Temple was in the nature of a claim upon territory in order to eject those performing an activity he obviously disapproved of, it seems more straightforward to characterize it as an occupation or a raid; the traditional "cleansing" is obviously an apologetic designation. The purpose of Jesus' activity makes good sense within the context of what we know of the activities of other early rabbinic teachers.

Hillel was an older contemporary of Jesus who taught (according to the Babylonian Talmud, Shabbath 31) a form of what is known in Christian circles as the Golden Rule taught by Jesus, that we should do to others as we would have them do to us. Hillel is also reported to have taught that offerings brought to the Temple should have hands laid on them by their owners and then be given over to priests for slaughter. Recent studies of the anthropology of sacrifice show why such stipulations were held to be important.[8] Hillel was insisting that, when the people of Israel came to worship, they should offer of their own property. Putting one's hands on the animal that was about to be sacrificed was a statement of ownership.

The followers of a rabbi named Shammai are typically depicted in rabbinic literature as resisting the teachings of Hillel. Here, too, they take the part of the opposition. They insist that animals for sacrifice might be given directly to priests for slaughter; Hillel's requirement of laying hands on the sacrifice is considered dispensable. But one of Shammai's followers was so struck by the rectitude of Hillel's position, he had some three thousand animals brought into the Temple and gave them to those who were willing to lay hands on them in advance of sacrifice.[9]

In one sense, the tradition concerning Hillel envisages the opposite movement from what is represented in the tradition concerning Jesus: animals are driven into the Temple rather than their traders expelled. Yet the purpose of the action by Hillel's partisan is to enforce a certain understanding of correct offering, one that accords with a standard feature of sacrifice in the anthropological literature. Hillel's teaching, in effect, insists upon the participation of the offerer by virtue of his ownership of what is offered, while most of the followers of Shammai are portrayed as sanctioning sacrifice more as a self-contained, priestly action.

Jesus' occupation of the Temple is best seen—along lines similar to those involved in the provision of animals to support Hillel's position—as an attempt to insist that the offerer's actual ownership of what is offered is a vital aspect of sacrifice. Jesus, as we will see, did not oppose sacrifice as such by what he did. His concern was with how Israelites acquired and then offered their own sacrifices.

Jesus' occupation of the Temple took place within the context of a particular dispute in which the Pharisees took part, a controversy over where the act of acquiring animals for sacrifice was to occur. In that the dispute was intimately involved with the issue of how animals were to be procured, it manifests a focus upon purity that is akin to that attributed to Hillel.

The nature and intensity of the dispute are only comprehensible when the significance of the Temple, as well as its sacrificial functioning, is kept in mind. Within the holy of holies, enclosed in a house and beyond a veil, the God of Israel was held to be enthroned in a virtually empty room. Only the high priest could enter that space and then only once a year, on the Day of Atonement; at the autumnal equinox the rays of the sun could enter the earthly chamber whence the sun's ruler exercised dominion, because the whole of the edifice faced east. Outside the inner veil (still within the house) the table of the bread of the presence, the menorah, and the altar for incense were arranged. The house of God was just that: the place where he dwelled and where he might meet his people.

Immediately outside the house and down some steps, the altar itself, of unhewn stones and accessible by ramps and steps, was arranged. Priests regularly tended to the sacrifices, and male Israelites were also admitted into the court structure that surrounded the altar. Various specialized structures accommodated the needs of the priests, and chambers were built into the interior of the court (and, indeed, within the house) to serve as stores, treasuries, and the like. The bronze gate of Nicanor led eastward again, down steps to the court of the women, where female Israelites in a state of purity were admitted. Priests and Israelites might enter the complex of house and courts by means of gates along the north and south walls; priests and Levites who were actively engaged in the service of the sanctuary regularly used the north side.

The complex we have so far described, which is commonly known as the sanctuary proper, circumscribed the God, the people, and the offerings of Israel. Within the boundaries of the sanctuary, what was known to be pure was offered by personnel chosen for the purpose, in the presence of the people of God and of God himself. Nothing foreign, no one with a serious defect or impurity, nothing unclean was permitted. Here God's presence was marked as much by order as by the pillar of cloud that was the flag of the Temple by day and the embers that glowed at night. God was present to the people with the things he had made and chosen for his own, and the people's presence brought them into the benefits of the covenantal compact with God. The practice of the Temple and its sacrificial worship was centered upon the demarcation and the consumption of purity in its place, with the result that God's holiness could be safely enjoyed within his four walls and the walls of male and female Israel. In no other place on earth was Israel more Israel or God more God than in the sanctuary. A balustrade surrounded the sanctuary, and steps led down to the exterior court: non-Israelites who entered were threatened with death. Physically and socially, the sanctuary belonged to no one but God and what and whom God chose (and then, only in their places).

The sanctuary was enclosed by a larger court, and the edifice as a whole is referred to as the Temple. On the north side, the pure, sacrificial animals were slain and butchered, and stone pillars and tables, chains and rings and ropes, and vessels and bushels were arranged to enable the process to go on smoothly and with visible, deliberate rectitude. The north side of the sanctuary, then, was essentially devoted to the preparation of what could be offered, under the ministration of those who were charged with the offering itself. The south side was the most readily accessible area in the Temple. Although Israelites outnumbered any other group of people there, and pious Jews entered only unshod, without staff or purse (cf. Berakhoth 9:5 in the Mishnah), others might enter through monumental gates on the south wall of the mount of the Temple. The elaborate system of pools, cisterns, and conduits to the south of the mount, visible today, is evidence of the practice of ritual purity, probably by all entrants into the Temple, whether Jewish or Gentile.

Basically, then, the south side of the outer court was devoted to people, and the north side to animals; together, the entire area of the outer court might be described as potentially chosen, while the sanctuary defined what actually had been chosen. The outer court was itself held in the highest regard, as is attested architecturally by the elaborate gates around the mount.

The Gospels describe the southern side of the outer court as the place where Jesus expelled the traders, and that is what brings us to the question of a dispute in which Pharisees were involved. The exterior court was unquestionably well suited for trade since it was surrounded by porticoes on the inside, in conformity to Herod's architectural preferences. But the assumption of Rabbinic literature and Josephus is that the market for the sale of sacrificial beasts was not located in the Temple at all but in a place called Chanuth (meaning "market" in Aramaic) on the Mount of Olives, across the Kidron Valley. According to the Babylonian Talmud,[10] some forty years before the destruction of the Temple, the principal council of Jerusalem was removed from the place in the Temple called the Chamber of Hewn Stone to Chanuth. Caiaphas both expelled the Sanhedrin and introduced the traders into the Temple, in both ways centralizing power in his own hands.

From the point of view of Pharisaism generally, trade in the southern side of the outer court was anathema. Purses were not permitted in the Temple according to the Pharisees' teaching, and the introduction of trade into the Temple rendered impracticable the ideal of not bringing into the Temple more than would be consumed there.

Incidentally, the installation of traders in the porticoes would also involve the removal of those teachers, Pharisaic and otherwise, who taught and observed in the Temple itself.

From the point of view of the smooth conduct of sacrifice, of course, Caiaphas's innovation was sensible. One could know at the moment of purchase that one's sacrifice was acceptable and not run the risk of harm befalling the animal on its way to be slaughtered. But when we look at the installation of the traders from the point of view of Hillel's teaching, Jesus' objection becomes understandable. Hillel had taught that one's sacrifice had to be shown to be one's own by the imposition of hands; part of the necessary preparation was not just of people to the south and beasts to the north but the connection between the two by appropriation. Caiaphas's innovation was sensible on the understanding that sacrifice was simply a matter of offering pure, unblemished animals. But it failed in Pharisaic terms, not only in its introduction of the necessity for commerce into the Temple but in its breach of the link between worshiper and offering in the sacrificial action.

The animals were correct in Caiaphas's system, and the priests were regular, but the understanding of the offering as by the chosen people appeared—to some at least—profoundly defective. The essential component of Jesus' occupation of the Temple is perfectly explicable within the context of contemporary Pharisaism, in which purity was more than a question of animals for sacrifice being intact. For Jesus, the issue of sacrifice also—crucially—concerned the action of Israel, as in the teaching of Hillel. Jesus' action, of course, upset financial arrangements for the sale of such animals, and it is interesting that John 2:15 speaks of his sweeping away the "coins" (in Greek, *kermata*) involved in the trade. But such incidental disturbance is to be distinguished from a deliberate attempt to prevent the collection of the half-shekel, which would have required coordinated activity throughout Israel (and beyond) and which typically involved larger units of currency than the term *coins* would suggest.

Jesus shared Hillel's concern that what was offered by Israel in the Temple should truly belong to Israel. His vehemence in opposition to Caiaphas's reform was a function of his deep commitment to the notion that Israel was pure and should offer of its own, even if others thought one unclean (see Mt 8:2–4; Mk 1:40–44; Lk 5:12–14), on the grounds that it is not what goes into a person that defiles but what comes out (see Mt 15:11; Mk 7:15). Israelites are properly understood as pure, so that what extends from a person, what one is and does and has, manifests that purity. According to the book of Zechariah, evidently the prophetic inspiration of Jesus' act, once sacrifice was offered without commercial mediation in the Temple, God would reorder all the powers of the earth and open worship to non-Israelites. That focused, generative vision was the force behind Jesus' occupation of the Temple; only those after 70 CE who no longer treasured the Temple in Jerusalem as God's house could (mis)take Jesus' position to be a prophecy of doom or an objection to sacrifice.

Neither Hillel nor Jesus needs to be understood as acting upon any symbolic agenda other than his conception of acceptable sacrifice or as appearing to his contemporaries to be anything other than a typical Pharisee, impassioned with purity in the Temple to the point of forceful intervention, although Jesus' prophetic motivation eventually became transparent. Neither of their positions may be understood as a concern with the physical acceptability of the animals at issue. In each case, the question of purity is: what is to be done with what is taken to be clean?

Jesus' interference in the ordinary worship of the Temple might have been sufficient by itself to bring about his execution. After all, the Temple was the center of Judaism for as long as it stood. Roman officials were so interested in its smooth functioning at the hands of the priests they appointed that they were known to sanction the penalty of death for gross sacrilege.[11] Yet there is no indication that Jesus was immediately arrested. Instead, he remained at liberty for some time and was finally taken into custody just after one of his meals, the Last Supper (Mt 26:47–56; Mk 14:43–52; Lk 22:47–53; Jn 18:3–11). The decision of the authorities of the Temple to move against Jesus when they did is what made it the final supper.

Why did the authorities wait, and why did they act when they did? The Gospels portray them as fearful of the popular backing that Jesus enjoyed (Mt 26:5; Mk 14:2; Lk 22:2; Jn 11:47–48), and his inclusive teaching of purity probably did bring enthusiastic followers into the

Temple with him. But there was another factor: Jesus could not simply be dispatched as a cultic criminal. He was not attempting an onslaught upon the Temple as such; his dispute with the authorities concerned purity within the Temple. Other rabbis of his period also engaged in physical demonstrations of the purity they required in the conduct of worship, as we have seen. Jesus' action was extreme but not totally without precedent, even in the use of force. Most crucially, Jesus could claim the support of tradition in objecting to siting vendors within the Temple, and Caiaphas's innovation in fact did not stand. That is the reason for which rabbinic sources assume that Chanuth was the site of the vendors.

The delay of the authorities, then, was understandable. We could also say it was commendable, reflecting continued controversy over the merits of Jesus' teaching and whether his occupation of the great court should be condemned out of hand. But why did they finally arrest Jesus? The Last Supper provides the key: something about Jesus' meals after his occupation of the Temple caused Judas to inform on Jesus. Of course, "Judas" is the only name that the traditions of the New Testament have left us. We cannot say who or how many of the disciples became disaffected by Jesus' behavior after his occupation of the Temple.

However they learned of Jesus' new interpretation of his meals of fellowship, the authorities arrested him just after the Last Supper. Jesus continued to celebrate fellowship at table as a foretaste of the kingdom, just as he had before. As before, the promise of drinking new wine in the kingdom of God joined his followers in an anticipatory celebration of that kingdom (see Mt 26:29; Mk 14:25; Lk 22:18). But he also added a new and scandalous dimension of meaning. His occupation of the Temple having failed, Jesus said over the wine, "This is my blood," and over the bread, "This is my flesh" (Mt 26:26, 28; Mk 14:22, 24; Lk 22:19–20; 1 Cor 11:24–25; Justin, *Apology* I.66.3).

In Jesus' context, the context of his confrontation with the authorities of the Temple, his words can have had only one meaning. He cannot have meant, "Here are my personal body and blood"; that is an interpretation that only makes sense at a later stage in the development of Christianity.[12] Jesus' point was rather that, in the absence of a Temple that permitted his view of purity to be practiced, wine was his blood of sacrifice and bread was his flesh of sacrifice. In Aramaic, blood (*dema*) and flesh (*bisra*, which may also be rendered as "body") can carry such a sacrificial meaning, and in Jesus' context, that is the most natural meaning.

The meaning of "the Last Supper," then, actually evolved over a series of meals after Jesus' occupation of the Temple. During that period, Jesus claimed that wine and bread were a better sacrifice than what was offered in the Temple, a foretaste of new wine in the kingdom of God. At least wine and bread were Israel's own, not tokens of priestly dominance. No wonder the opposition to him, even among the twelve (in the shape of Judas, according to the Gospels), became deadly. In essence, Jesus made his meals into a rival altar.

That final gesture of protest gave Caiaphas what he needed. Jesus could be charged with blasphemy before those with an interest in the Temple. The issue now was not simply Jesus' opposition to the siting of vendors of animals but his creation of an alternative sacrifice. He blasphemed the Law of Moses. The accusation concerned the Temple, in which Rome also had a vested interest.

Pilate had no regard for issues of purity; Acts 18:14–16 reflects the attitude of an official in a similar position, and Josephus shows that Pilate was without sympathy for Judaism. But the Temple in Jerusalem had come to symbolize Roman power as well as the devotion of Israel. Rome guarded jealously the sacrifices that the emperor financed in Jerusalem; when they were spurned in the year 66, the act was seen as a declaration of war.[13] Jesus stood accused of creating a disturbance in that Temple (during his occupation) and of fomenting disloyalty to it and therefore to Caesar. Pilate did what he had to do. Jesus' persistent reference to a "kingdom" that Caesar did not rule and his repute among some as Messiah or prophet only made Pilate's order more likely. It all was probably done without a hearing; Jesus was not a Roman citizen. He was a nuisance dispensed with under a military jurisdiction.[14]

At last, then, at the end of his life, Jesus discovered the public center of the kingdom: the point from which the light of God's rule would radiate and triumph. His initial intention was that the Temple would conform to his vision of the purity of the kingdom, that all Israel would be invited there, forgiven and forgiving, to offer of their own in divine fellowship in the confidence that what they produced was pure (see Mt 15:11; Mk 7:15). The innovation of Caiaphas prevented that by erecting what Jesus (as well as other rabbis) saw as an unacceptable barrier between Israel and what Israel offered.

The last public act of Jesus before his crucifixion was to declare that his meals were the center of the kingdom. God's rule, near and immanent and final and pure, was now understood to radiate from a public place, an open manifestation of the divine kingdom in human fellowship. The authorities in the Temple rejected Jesus much as Herod Antipas in Galilee already had done, but the power and influence of those in Jerusalem made their opposition deadly. Just as those in the north could be condemned as a new Sodom (see Lk 10:12), so Jesus could deny that offerings co-opted by priests were acceptable sacrifices. His meals replaced the Temple; those in the Temple sought to displace him. It is no coincidence that the typical setting of appearances of the risen Jesus is while disciples were taking meals together. The conviction that the light of the kingdom radiated from that practice went hand in hand with the conviction that the true master of the table, the rabbi who began it all, remained within their fellowship.

THE AUTHORIZED VERSION
OF HIS BIRTH AND DEATH

David Trobisch

T he term *New Testament* is used today to specify a closed collection of twenty-seven specific writings. The manuscript tradition demonstrates that this collection was transmitted in four volumes: The Four-Gospel-Book, Acts and General Letters, Letters of Paul, and Revelation of John. The dates of the oldest manuscripts and the evidence from the first documented readers of the New Testament (Irenaeus, Tatian, Tertullian, Clement of Alexandria, Origen) further indicate that the first edition was in existence by the second half of the second century.[1] What would a second-century person, reading the New Testament at face value and without the benefit of scholarly historical research, have gleaned from this collection of writings about the birth and the Resurrection of Jesus of Nazareth? The following passages are quoted from the New Revised Standard Version.

The first sentence of the Letters of Paul offers a definition of the contents of the "Gospel" (ευαγγελιον, *eu-angelion*, good news), God's central message:

> Paul, a servant of Jesus Christ, called to be an apostle, set apart for the Gospel of God, which he promised beforehand through his prophets in the holy scriptures, the Gospel concerning his Son, who was descended from David according to the flesh and was declared to be Son of God with power according to the spirit of holiness by resurrection from the dead, Jesus Christ our Lord, through whom we have received grace and apostleship to bring about the obedience of faith among all the Gentiles for the sake of his name, including yourselves who are called to belong to Jesus Christ. (Rom 1:1–6)

According to Paul, the Gospel as it was foretold by the prophets of the Holy Scriptures identifies Jesus as the Christ for two reasons. The first reason is that Jesus was a descendant of the royal house of David, and the second reason is that Jesus' Resurrection clearly demonstrates that he was Son of God with exceptional spiritual powers. Paul finishes by stating that his apostleship is dedicated to promoting the obedience of faith in Jesus Christ among the nations, i.e., among people living outside of Judea.

Although the very first information readers of Romans receive about Jesus is that Jesus is from the royal family of David, Paul, the implied author of all fourteen canonical letters of Paul, does not elaborate much on this point. In 1 Timothy, literary Paul orders Timothy, a pastor in training, to charge "certain people" not to "occupy themselves with myths and endless genealogies that promote speculations rather than the divine training that is known by faith" (1 Tm 1:4). A reader of the New Testament will quickly discover that the Gospels offer two contradicting genealogies of Jesus (Mt 1:1–17 and Lk 3:23–38) and may rightly assume that Paul in 1 Timothy warns his followers not to waste their time with useless speculations on how to reconcile them. Other than that, canonical Paul is silent about Jesus' relation to the royal house of David. When it comes to Jesus' Resurrection, however, Paul is more eloquent:

> For I handed on to you as of first importance what I in turn had received: that Christ died for our sins in accordance with the scriptures, and that he was buried, and that he was raised on the third day in accordance with the scriptures. (1 Cor 15:3–4)

Paul gives an outline of the events following Jesus' death as they had been passed on to him. The context suggests that Paul is defending himself against accusations of being uninformed about the historical Jesus, and therefore takes the utmost care to represent the tradition he had received accurately (1 Cor 15:1–3).

Paul was told that Christ died, was buried, and raised the third day according to the scriptures. The reference to the scriptures provides the readers with a link to Paul's statement in Romans 1:1 that the Gospel was promised beforehand in the writings of the prophets. To this point Paul's statements conform nicely with the traditions of the canonical Gospels. But the text continues with a series of six events, all of which are unparalleled:

and that he appeared to Cephas, then to the twelve. Then he appeared to more than five hundred brothers and sisters at one time, most of whom are still alive, though some have died. Then he appeared to James, then to all the apostles. Last of all, as to one untimely born, he appeared also to me. (1 Cor 15:3–8)

Paul states that Christ first appeared to Cephas (Peter). One of the few traditions all four Gospels share is that women were the first to discover the empty tomb (Mt 28:1–8; Mk 16:1–8; Lk 24:1–11; Jn 20:1). This tradition is curiously absent in Paul. Except for an obscure note in Luke 24:34, there is no hint that Jesus appeared to Peter separately.

Paul continues that Christ then appeared to the twelve. But according to Matthew and Luke (Mt 27:3–10; cf. Acts 1:18–19), Judas committed suicide even before Jesus died on the cross and therefore Jesus could only have appeared to the eleven (Mt 28:16; Lk 24:9.33; cf. Mk 16:14), not the twelve. Paul seems unfamiliar with the tradition of Judas's suicide. Then Christ appeared to more than five hundred. There is no such story in the Gospels, and the statement is even more surprising as Paul gives living proof: some witnesses are still alive and ready to testify.

The differences continue. Christ, Paul insists, then appeared to his brother James. This story, sorely missing from the Gospel accounts, nicely explains why the Lord's brother received the high recognition among the Early Christian community, which Paul attests to him in Galatians (Gal 1:19; 2:9.12).

Paul insists that Christ then appeared to "all the apostles." This statement is confusing. What exactly is an "apostle" in this context? Are the twelve not "all" the apostles? Is Cephas who is mentioned separate from the twelve not an apostle (cf. 1 Cor 9:5)? And isn't Paul an apostle as well? Or is the term *apostle* defined as someone who "sees" the resurrected Christ (cf. 1 Cor 9:1)? However Paul's language is explained, this statement is difficult to reconcile with the Gospel accounts. Paul's last remark is more compromising than all the others put together. Paul writes: "Last of all he appeared also to me" (1 Cor 15:8).

When Paul talks about his experiences of Christ, he calls them revelations (Gal 1:12) or visions (12:1). Like dreams, these visions are subjective and irrelevant to any other person than the one who experiences them. Paul describes his revelations as an out-of-body experience in 2

Cor 12:1–10: "whether in the body or out of the body I do not know; God knows" (12:3.4).

For Paul, all Resurrection accounts of 1 Corinthians 15 are "appearance" stories. The term ωφθη (he appeared) is used for each of the six events. Revelation is a spiritual experience, a vision, a dream. For Paul, Christ is not a "real" person. The notion that the resurrected Jesus existed physically, that he would eat (Lk 24:43), that his wounds could be touched (Jn 20:27), is not what Paul had been taught.

Paul's statements sharply contrast what the Gospel According to Mark has to offer to its readers:

> They came to Jericho. As he and his disciples and a large crowd were leaving Jericho, Bartimaeus son of Timaeus, a blind beggar, was sitting by the roadside.
>
> When he heard that it was Jesus of Nazareth, he began to shout out and say, "Jesus, Son of David, have mercy on me!" Many sternly ordered him to be quiet, but he cried out even more loudly, "Son of David, have mercy on me!" (Mk 10:46–52)

The only time Mark makes an allusion to Jesus being from the royal family of David is in the story of blind beggar Bartimaeus, who cries out "Son of David" (Mark 10:46f). His shouting is a public embarrassment, and he is ordered to be quiet. Readers will hardly see the scene as an endorsement of Jesus' ancestry.

And when it comes to providing an account of Jesus' Resurrection, Mark is silent:

> As they entered the tomb, they saw a young man, dressed in a white robe, sitting on the right side; and they were alarmed.
>
> But he said to them, "Do not be alarmed; you are looking for Jesus of Nazareth, who was crucified. He has been raised; he is not here. Look, there is the place they laid him. But go, tell his disciples and Peter that he is going ahead of you to Galilee; there you will see him, just as he told you." (Mk 16:5–7)

The women encounter a nameless young man in a white gown at the empty tomb who tells them that Jesus was raised from the dead and that they should tell the disciples and Peter to go ahead to Galilee, where he will meet them. But what do the women do?

> So they went out and fled from the tomb, for terror and amazement had seized them; and they said nothing to anyone, for they were afraid. (Mk 16:8)

They said nothing to anyone, for they were afraid (εφοβουντο γαρ). This is the last sentence of Mark's Gospel. The resurrected Christ has not appeared and the first witnesses "say nothing to anyone." This is the worst imaginable ending for a Gospel.

Measured against Paul's definition of what the Gospel of God is about, Mark fails on both accounts. Jesus is not portrayed as a son of David, and there is no Resurrection story of Jesus. The readers are left with allusions to Jesus' Resurrection provided by an unidentified young man in a white robe.

But only the oldest manuscripts of Mark end with verse 8. The vast majority of manuscripts provide the so-called long ending. The long ending of Mark gives us a rare window into the struggles of early editors of the New Testament as they attempt to provide an authoritative version of the Resurrection accounts:

> Now after he rose early on the first day of the week, he appeared first to Mary Magdalene, from whom he had cast out seven demons. She went out and told those who had been with him, while they were mourning and weeping. But when they heard that he was alive and had been seen by her, they would not believe it. (Mk 16:9–11)

The appearance of the resurrected Christ to Mary is taken from John 20:

> After this he appeared in another form to two of them, as they were walking into the country. And they went back and told the rest, but they did not believe them.
>
> Later he appeared to the eleven themselves as they were sitting at the table; and he upbraided them for their lack of faith and stubbornness, because they had not believed those who saw him after he had risen.

And he said to them, "*Go into all the world and proclaim the good news to the whole creation. The one who believes and is baptized will be saved; but the one who does not believe will be condemned.*" (Mk 16:12–16)

The story of the two disciples walking into the country is taken from Luke 24. The dinner of the disciples on Easter Sunday is told in Luke 24 and John 20. Both stories mention a lack of faith (Lk 24:38; Jn 20:24–28). And finally, which reader of the New Testament would not immediately relate Jesus' commission "To go into the world" and "baptize" to the last scene of Matthew's Gospel, the so-called Great Commission (Mt 28:16–20)?

So the long ending in Mark compensates for the unsatisfying and abrupt end of Mark by combining the accounts of Matthew, Luke, and John. There is more to come:

"*And these signs will accompany those who believe: by using my name they will cast out demons; they will speak in new tongues; they will pick up snakes in their hands, and if they drink any deadly thing, it will not hurt them; they will lay their hands on the sick, and they will recover.*"

So then the Lord Jesus, after he had spoken to them, was taken up into heaven and sat down at the right hand of God.

And they went out and proclaimed the good news everywhere, while the Lord worked with them and confirmed the message by the signs that accompanied it. (Mk 16:17–20)

Narratives about speaking in foreign languages (Acts 2:6–8), about surviving snakebites (Acts 28:5), and about the ascension of Jesus (Acts 1:9) are found in Acts. The last sentence of the long ending: "And they went out and proclaimed the good news everywhere," reads like a summary of the plot of Acts.

The long ending of Mark combines all four Gospels and adds the testimony of Acts. It can be read as an early attempt to harmonize the accounts of the events following Jesus' Resurrection. But—and this needs to be stated clearly—the New Testament is not a harmony. It provides four distinct Gospels with four distinct accounts.

The Gospel According to Matthew, as title of this book is transmitted in the manuscripts of the Four-Gospel-Book, begins with a genealogy of Jesus:

Jesse was the father of King David. And David was the father of Solomon by the wife of Uriah, and Solomon the father of Rehoboam, and Rehoboam the father of Abijah, [the line is continued from here to Joseph, father of Jesus]. (Mt 1:6–7)

The implied author, Matthew the tax-collector (Mt 9:9), is perceived by readers as someone who professionally deals with official records. He states that Jesus is related to King David through David's son Solomon. Furthermore, Matthew insists that Joseph and Mary have been living all their lives, like their ancestors, in Bethlehem (cf. Mt 2:1).

The difficulty Matthew and any other Gospel writer face, is to explain how someone called Jesus of Nazareth could be linked to David. By making Jesus' parents citizens of Bethlehem the narrative solves part of the problem. But why did Jesus move to Nazareth? Why did he not stay in Bethlehem?

There he made his home in a town called Nazareth, so that what had been spoken through the prophets might be fulfilled, "He will be called a Nazorean." [οτι Ναζωραιος κληθησεται] (Mt 2:23)

The narrator solves the mystery by insisting that the scriptures predicted the Messiah to be called a "Ναζωραιος." The narrative context (cf. Mt 4:13; 21:11; 26:71) suggests beyond reasonable doubt that the term is used to designate a "Nazarene," a citizen of Nazareth. But no such scripture exists. Nazareth is not mentioned in the Jewish Bible.

In the Gospel According to Luke, the readers are presented with a genealogy of Jesus that differs from Matthew's records. Instead of relating Jesus through Solomon to David as Matthew does, the implied author, the physician Luke, relates Jesus to David through another son, Nathan. The discrepancy could not be bolder.

[Jesus...] son of Melea, son of Menna, son of Mattatha, son of Nathan, son of David, son of Jesse, son of Obed, son of Boaz, son of Sala, son of Nahshon, [... son of Adam, the son of God.] (Lk 3:31–32)

And when it comes to the Gospel According to John, the readers are confronted with the notion that Jesus was present at the creation of the world, long before King David was born. The question whether Jesus was actually related by blood to the royal family suddenly seems irrelevant:

> In the beginning was the Word, and the Word was with God, and the Word was God. He was in the beginning with God. All things came into being through him, and without him not one thing came into being. What has come into being in him was life, and the life was the light of all people.... And the Word became flesh and lived among us, and we have seen his glory, the glory as of a father's only son, full of grace and truth. (John 1:1–4:14)

"What good can come from Nazareth?" Nathanael asks a few lines down in this Gospel (Jn 1:46), and Philip gives him an answer that feels true for many evangelicals, mysticists, Pentecostals, Mormons, Isa Muslims, and anyone who bases religious convictions on the spiritual experience of Christ: "Come and see!" They may not have a solution that is intellectually satisfying, but they promise that anyone who joins their group will make spiritual experiences that back up the claim that Jesus is the Christ.

A second-century reader of the New Testament, who followed Paul's outline of what the Gospel is about, would have been confronted with the following information.

Concerning Jesus as the Son of David, Matthew and Luke provide different genealogies of Jesus—something that is biologically impossible. Mark makes no statement about it, and John insists that the question is irrelevant.

When it comes to the Resurrection events, Matthew and Luke do not agree where Christ appeared to his disciples. Matthew places the event on a mountain in Galilee, Luke in Jerusalem. Mark suggests Galilee but lacks a story, and John combines both traditions, providing stories in Jerusalem and Galilee. And Paul, the maverick apostle, disagrees with each of these accounts.

What is the version of Jesus' ancestry and Resurrection promoted in the New Testament and regarded as authoritative by the Christian movement for almost two millennia? The answer is rather simple. The New Testament does not provide an authorized version of the birth and Resurrection accounts of Jesus of Nazareth.

Editors, translators, and commentators of the New Testament have struggled and will always struggle with the apparent diversity of voices. The title of the first volume of the New Testament that contains the four canonical Gospels is preserved in many manuscripts as τετραευαγγελιον (*tetra-euangelion*), and the uniform transmission and lack of variants for this title suggest that it was part of the archetype from which all manuscripts of the New Testament derive. *Tetra* signifies the number four, but *euangelion* (Gospel) is used in the singular. The title is impossible to translate into English but its intention is easy to grasp: as far back as the earliest edition of the New Testament, editors were aware of the significant discrepancies in the accounts of the four Gospels, and yet they insist that in this choir of witnesses there is a shared message.

And Paul, as was demonstrated above, follows a completely different narrative tradition.

PROLEGOMENON TO A
SCIENCE OF CHRISTIAN ORIGINS

Frank R. Zindler

W e are all aware of the fact that this meeting of the Jesus Project [in 2008] is being sponsored by the Committee for the Scientific Examination of Religion. By my reckoning, that means that it not only behooves us to be as scientific as possible in our inquiry into the historicity of Jesus of Nazareth, it absolutely *requires* us to create a science of Christian origins.

Fortunately, the science of religion and religiosity is already a burgeoning field of research. Anthropology has always investigated religions and examined them under its microscope. The sociology of religions is also a developed science, and many important insights into the nature of religiosity have been attained in psychology and psychiatry. In recent years, neuroscience (one of my own areas of expertise) has contributed astonishing understanding of the physiological basis for prayer, meditation, and so-called transcendent experiences. Archaeology, as long as it has been studying "other" religions, has been invaluable for gaining objective knowledge of Amerindian religions in particular. Unfortunately, so-called biblical archaeology until quite recently was really not a science. Rather, it has largely been a special branch of Christian apologetics. That no longer can be tolerated. *All* archaeological investigations, of *all* religions, must be fitted to the Procrustean requirements of genuine science.

What has not yet developed to a satisfactory degree is a science dedicated to the investigation of the historical dimensions of religions in general and of Christianity in particular. It is often supposed that history is not amenable to scientific methods because, it is alleged, science can only deal with the spatial dimensions in the here and now. Of course this is not true. Astronomy has long trained its instruments upon the history of our entire universe. Archaeology, geology, and paleontology all are scientific enterprises that study the past. In my lifetime, molecular and evolutionary genetics (another one of my areas of expertise) has created a panoramic picture of the history of *Homo sapiens* itself. The human genome is being read today like a lengthy and frequently interpolated biblical palimpsest.

RULES OF SCIENCE

As we resolve to develop a truly scientific approach to the study of Christian origins, we must remind ourselves of some of the logical and philosophical rules of science that have so often been stumbling blocks for students of religion—especially for those who are themselves religious.

First of all: science can only deal with propositions that are *meaningful*, in the sense that they must in principle be *falsifiable*. That is, one must be able at least in the imagination to think of possible tests that could conceivably prove the proposition wrong. A proposition that cannot be tested even theoretically is not wrong: it is *scientifically meaningless*. It cannot even be wrong.

It is helpful to distinguish between *theoretical falsifiability* (testability) from *practical falsifiability*. To understand the distinction, let us suppose that in the year 1611 someone made the claim, "The moon is made of green cheese." At that time it would have been impossible in practice to test the proposition, as neither space-flight nor spectroscopic analysis were yet available. Even so, anyone living at that time could imagine being transported to the moon and proceeding to check whether or not the "soil" worked well in salad dressing. Thus, the green-cheese proposition—although now known to be false—was still scientifically meaningful even though not being *practically* testable at the time.

What if, however, in the year 1611 or 2010, someone claims, "Undetectable gremlins inhabit the rings of Saturn"? We cannot even imagine a way to test for undetectable entities. Such a claim could not even be false. It would be scientifically meaningless.

Often, when I point out the significance of the fact that there are no eyewitness reports or accounts of Jesus of Nazareth, it is argued that

Jesus was too ordinary and obscure a person to attract attention. He didn't *really* walk on the water, turn water to wine, or rise from the dead after hundreds of zombies came out of their graves and marched on Jerusalem. Nevertheless, of course, he was the most powerful personality who ever lived, grabbed the attention and devotion of twelve disciples, and changed the history of the world forever.

Ignoring for the nonce the contradictoriness of the entire argument, let us focus on the beginning claim: *Jesus existed but was too ordinary and obscure a person to attract attention.* How could one ever test such a claim? If you went back in your time machine to check on him, *ex hypothesi* you would not find him because he would not attract your attention! Moreover, most arguments alleging that "absence of evidence is not evidence of absence" actually involve an untestable presupposition such as this one.

Second: true science must eschew the informal fallacy of logic known as *ignotum per ignotius*—trying to explain the unknown in terms of the more unknown. True science must seek to explain the unknown in terms of the known—or at least the better known. Another way to put this is to say that science is *reductionistic*, seeking to reduce the unknown to terms of what is known.

Thus, Benjamin Franklin explained lightning in terms of electricity—something he had experimented with in the laboratory and field, something of which he had practical knowledge. The theologians of his day, however, explained lightning in terms of the wrath of Jehovah or punishment for sin—things of which no man or woman has ever had any knowledge, practical or otherwise.

Franklin's scientific method led to the salvation of every church steeple in the modern world, but no amount of theological reasoning has ever convincingly been shown to have saved a church from lightning. Nearly every church steeple in the world is protected by what the theologians used to call "Franklin's wicked iron points." This is reductionistic science at its finest.

Third: in science the *onus probandi* is crucially different from that governing jurisprudence or some other fields of human endeavor. In law, it is a general rule that the party who alleges the affirmative of any proposition shall prove it. The case becomes complicated, however, by the fact that there are many situations in which the law itself presumes the affirmative, and then the *onus probandi* lies with the party denying the fact. For example, the legitimacy of a child born in wedlock is presumed and the burden of proof falls upon those who argue against legitimacy.

In science, however, the burden of proof lies not so much with anyone alleging the affirmative of any proposition, but rather with those alleging the veridical existence of a physical entity, process, or event. The crucially important difference for us to note today is that for all claims of existence, science presumes the negative. It will ignore all affirmative arguments if they are not supported by evidence and facts.

Let me repeat: *for all claims of existence, science presumes the negative.* For us that means that the burden of proof lies not with those who deny the historicity of "Jesus of Nazareth," but rather with those who hold the traditional view that even if he might not have been a god, he was at the very least a man.

MY ARGUMENT

I shall argue that there is no compelling or convincing evidence to support the proposition that a man—carrying out all the bodily functions common to human beings generally—identifiable as Jesus of Nazareth was living in Palestine at the turn of the era. Moreover, I will maintain that there is irrefutable evidence against the proposition—even though it is not beholden upon me to prove the negative.

I shall argue that the historical existence of Jesus of Nazareth and his equally unknown and unattested disciples has always been merely assumed or loosely inferred from the writings of a handful of ancient authors. Only in the last few centuries have any scholars asked for genuine evidence of his historicity, and only in my own lifetime has anyone had the temerity to rest the burden of proof on those holding the traditional opinion—and to demand that evidence sufficient for proof be brought forward.

Having studied for nearly thirty years the evidence adduced to prove the historical reality of Jesus of Nazareth, I must tell you that I find absolutely no good reason to suppose he was any more historical than Mithra, Dionysus, Zeus, or Thor. Interestingly, the American founding father Thomas Paine (1737–1809) came to the same conclusion shortly before his death.

Euhemerus, I think, was wrong more often than he was right! Not only is there no evidence supporting Jesus' existence, there is compelling archaeological evidence weighing against it.

EVIDENCE OF ABSENCE

Earlier this year [2008], American Atheist Press published what I think is an extremely important book by an author named René Salm. Its title is *The Myth of Nazareth: The Invented Town of Jesus.*[1] It shows conclusively, I think, that the city now called Nazareth in the Galilee was not inhabited at the turn of the era when Jesus and his family should have been living there. Salm's reanalysis of the sparse archaeological evidence seems to me to be absolutely irrefutable and demonstrates that Jesus, if he existed, could not have come from Nazareth.

In 2003, my own book, *The Jesus the Jews Never Knew: Sepher Toldoth Yeshu and the Quest of the Historical Jesus in Jewish Sources,*[2] showed that the ancient Jews had never heard of "Jesus of Nazareth." Moreover, they had never heard of Nazareth either!

But Nazareth is not the only fictive place that figures in the Gospels' geographical setting. My essay in the *Journal of Higher Criticism*, "Capernaum—A Literary Invention,"[3] makes a strong case for the claim that the archaeological site K'far Nahum cannot be the biblical Capernaum and cannot be the place mentioned by Josephus—the only extrabiblical author alleged to have mentioned Capernaum.

A popular article of mine, "Where Jesus Never Walked" (available on the American Atheists' Web site, http://www.atheists.org), argues that Bethany, Bethpage, and Aenon are also fictional places. Even more startling was the report in 2006 by Israeli archaeologist Aviram Oshri that he could find no archaeological evidence to indicate that Bethlehem in Judaea was inhabited at the turn of the era![4]

Now if even just one of the above geographic claims is able to withstand the fierce criticism that is just now beginning, it will have to be concluded that the character "Jesus of Nazareth" was a literary invention.

QUESTIONS TO BE ANSWERED

Since science requires us to explain unknowns in terms of what is known, let us consider some astonishing unknowns, some questions that we must answer before we can answer questions of the historicity of Jesus.

(A) *When*, exactly, did Christianity begin? *Did* Christianity, in fact, have a beginning? Can we visualize the origin and early evolution of Christianity better as a tree, with a single trunk producing many branches, or as a multifilamentous braid, with the oldest threads appearing out of the mists of religious and philosophical antiquity?

Did these strands of tradition then twine together, pick up new threads and incorporate them as time went by? Did other threads then fray, branch, or break off the main braid from time to time? Did Christianity—like Mormonism—have a discrete, clearly defined beginning that we might trace to a single historical figure, or was it rootless like Hinduism or the ancient religions of Egypt and Mesopotamia?

If we cannot find compelling evidence that Christianity began, say, within the space of a specific decade in known history, should we not conclude that it did not have a discrete beginning but was, rather, a confluence of social movements that at some point in its evolution came to be tagged with the Christian label?

(B) *Where*, exactly, did Christianity begin? *Did* Christianity, in fact, start in a single place? Can we show, conclusively, that it began in Jerusalem or Galilee—as tradition would claim—or in Rome, or Alexandria, or Antioch, or Tarsus, or elsewhere in Asia Minor as some revisionists have claimed? Or did Christian-like movements coalesce out of the mythic milieu in all those places as well as in North Africa, Gaul, and the Greek mainland?

Did the Great Church form from the confluence of tributary streams flowing off a large cultural watershed, or did it, like the Nile in the Delta, form by reuniting some of its distributary streams into a smaller number of channels, finally to debouche into the sea of history?

(C) *How*, did Christianity begin? Did it begin as an open, exoteric movement with a kerygma broadcast publicly, or did it begin as an esoteric mystery cult? The Pauline Epistles—and various hints in the canonical Gospels—would indicate an esoteric origin, yet tradition would have us believe that that was not the case. At some point might Christianity have been both an esoteric cult and an exoteric church?

There are many other questions of importance that cannot be answered substantively enough to satisfy an unbelieving scientist. To list just a few:

(1) Was St. Paul historical?

(2) Did the "Crucifixion" take place on a hill near Jerusalem or at the celestial vernal equinox, the point where the ecliptic path of the sun *crosses* the celestial equator?

(3) Why were *two* fishes, the astrological symbol for Pisces, among the earliest symbols of Christianity?

(4) Was Euhemerus ever correct?

(5) What was the role of martyrs in the earliest church?

(6) Were the first Christians Jews or Gentiles?

(7) Did the New Testament authors borrow the word *Gospel* (ευαγγελιον, euangelion) from Augustus Caesar's use of the plural form, or did they reinvent the word later?

(8) Why was the New Testament originally written in Greek?

(9) What were the mysteries to which Paul alludes?

(10) *Why* were there mysteries?

(11) Were the Twelve Apostles/Disciples historical? The Virgin Mary? Joseph? The Twelve Pillars? St. Stephen?

(12) Why isn't Sepphoris mentioned in the New Testament?

(13) Why can we not identify convincingly the sites of Capernaum, Nazareth, Bethany, Bethpage, Aenon, etc.?

(14) Do we know who the authors of *any* New Testament books were?

(15) Why did Latin Christianity begin in North Africa instead of Rome?

(16) Do we know any document of the New Testament that is the product of a single author?

(17) Is a "high Christology" evolved or primitive: did Jesus become Christ, or did Christ become Jesus of Nazareth?

(18) Since the oldest attested use of the *chi-rho* cross was an abbreviation for Chronos/Kronos in a manuscript at Pompeii/Herculaneum of Artistotle's *Constitution of the City of Athens*,[5] how can we know if other early occurrences of this symbol were Christian or Chronian?

(19) When and where did the Christian liturgy begin? Did it resemble that of the Caesar cults?

(20) Is the Passion narrative history or a transcript of a passion play for a mystery cult?

(21) Why and how did the belief in a "Second Coming" come about? Was it in any way related to the Sibylline Oracle lines concerning the Second Coming of Nero?

(22) Why is Easter at the vernal equinox?

THE LESSON OF ISAAC NEWTON

As a scientist, I find it shocking that *not one* of these fundamental questions can yet be answered conclusively—despite centuries of scholarly toil, study, and publication. As a scientist, I not only want to know the answers to the questions just raised; I want to understand why so little progress has been made in trying to answer them since 1727, the year in which Sir Isaac Newton died.

As you know, Isaac Newton was an immensely brilliant mathematician and physicist who created the first unified, modern science. But you may not be aware that Newton was also a theologian and biblical scholar of immense—although peculiar—erudition. In fact, Newton published more pages on biblical "research" than on physical research. It is likely that he devoted more time and pages to elucidating biblical numerology and prophecy than to developing the calculus.

As I have just noted, Newton died in the year 1727. Since that time, the seed he planted in his great treatise *Philosophiae naturalis principia mathematica* has sprouted and grown into the magnificent tree of modern physics, a science that seems close to achieving a "Theory of

Everything"—a theory comprehending everything from the quantum reality of virtual and subatomic particles to the structure of the entire universe.

Every generation of physicists that has followed Newton has been able to stand upon his shoulders—and on the shoulders of succeeding generations leading up to it—in order to see farther into the unknown.

But what of his writings on biblical numerology and prophecy? What modern knowledge has been gained by adding to his writings in this area? Can we name any modern biblical scholar who has been able to build upon a foundation of Newton's religious writings to erect an edifice of greater understanding of the New Testament?

Why did Newton's physical science lead progressively to greater and greater understanding of our world? Why did his religious studies lead nowhere?[6] Why has there been steady progress in all of the sciences, but almost no progress at all in religious studies?

Why did science need to invent the wheel only once? Why does nearly every generation of religion scholars seem to have to reinvent their wheel? Why do scientists march steadily forward, when those in the humanities typically have to wander forty years in the wilderness before achieving any breakthrough in understanding—and that almost by accident in most cases? How, exactly, do you measure progress in the humanities any way?

I suggest the problem is that we have not even been trying to use the scientific method in the field of religion studies. Only since the time of Charles Darwin have religion in general and Christianity in particular become proper subjects for scientific study. Only rarely have studies of Christian origins attempted to be completely reductionist, to explain the unknown in terms of the known or the relatively certain.

After all, how does one find out what is already known in a particular area of the humanities—short of reading everything that has ever been written on the subject and evaluating it all? There has never been a database to which one could turn to discover what already is known, so that one might embark on a particular new investigation in order to discover new truth, say, in New Testament studies.

In fact, to speak of discovering "truth" in New Testament studies might possibly strike some veteran scholars as amusing. Why should that be? Why shouldn't it be as possible to discover truth in New Testament studies as in biochemistry?

BIOCHEMISTRY VERSUS
NEW TESTAMENT STUDIES

There are at least three reasons why it sounds odd or amusing to speak of discovering truth in New Testament studies.

First, it is a sad fact that too often New Testament studies have simply been exercises in Christian apologetics. No one expects truth to be discovered when our conclusions have been drawn before we have set to work! Second, there is the problem of tying a putative new truth with unassailable logic and evidence to reference points of demonstrated verity. What is there in New Testament studies that has been demonstrated so thoroughly that even an unbelieving scientist would agree that it is a fact or is "true"?

Third, there is the problem of knowing if one's discovery is in fact new. In less than a scholar's lifetime, how does one discover what has been discovered and reported—in all the languages used in scholarly discourse?

Consider, now, how different the situation is for a biochemist working for a pharmaceutical company and wanting to see if an interesting compound unexpectedly just discovered is really novel or might perhaps have been discovered long ago.

First, there is no such thing as biochemical apologetics.[7] So, our biochemist can assume that although the information that might be found in the biochemical literature might be wrong in the sense of faulty or mistaken, it is not at all likely to be a willful fabrication.

Second, in seeking new truth, a biochemist has at his or her disposal tools that make it possible in less than a week to find out *everything* that has ever been discovered and reported on any particular topic of biochemistry. Consider, for example, *Chemical Abstracts*—a huge journal that has been published since the year 1907.

Since at least 1967, nearly every chemical journal in the world—in all languages from Afrikaans to Azerbaijani and to Ukrainian and

beyond—has been sent to Columbus, Ohio, where a scientifically professional editorial staff has read it, summarized it in English, and
indexed all the chemical substances and concepts for the use of
chemists throughout the world. Moreover, for many years now *Chemical
Abstracts* has been available for searching online, and nearly everything
known about chemistry is retrievable at close to the speed of light.
Exhaustive searching is a routine procedure. Has any one of you ever
been able to do an *exhaustive* search of the entire world literature in
your field?

Third, a biochemist can find help in weighing the relative importance of the various pieces of information that an online search will
produce. It is possible to discover how many other scholars have cited
a particular paper—both approvingly and critically in the refereed literature. The wheel of criticism need be reinvented no more than the
wheel of discovery.

NEED FOR A DATABASE OF FACTS

It seems clear that the scientific study of religion will not move very far
into the humanities side of the research field until there exists an information system analogous to *Chemical Abstracts*, a system wherein everything known about religion has been identified, indexed, summarized,
referenced, and made available in a single *lingua franca*. For any topic, it
should be possible to learn what the primary sources are, where they are
located, and how to access them. Archaeology, history, chronology, neuro-
physiology of religious experience, sociology of religion, psychology of religion, linguistics, anthropology, comparative religious studies, bibliography—
all the areas relating to the scientific study of religion need to be included.
Perhaps it could be compiled as a cooperative, public effort—a *Wikireligia!*

It will be necessary to have instant access to all relevant primary-
source manuscripts, texts, and documents, both in the form of facsimile,
high-resolution images, and in the form of word-searchable text files.
The *Thesaurus Linguae Graecae* (TLG) and the *Thesaurus Linguae Latinae*
(TLL) are a step in this direction. However, although they contain the
texts of an enormous number of writings of importance to scholars of

religion, they do not contain specific files of important individual man-uscripts, so it is not possible yet to study the all-important variant read-ings so necessary for purposes of text criticism.

Moreover, they only cover Greek and Latin materials. As far as I am aware, there is no equivalent database for Hebrew, Coptic, or Ara-maic/Syriac, still less for Arabic, Ethiopic, Old Armenian, Old Geor-gian, Egyptian, Akkadian, Ugaritic, and Ebblaite. These are minimum requirements for a science seeking to investigate the origins of Judaism, Christianity, and Islam.

Of course, having access to all the relevant primary documents is a necessary but insufficient condition for producing a database from which a scientific theory of religion could be derived.

No single person could comprehend so large a database of primary sources, let alone evaluate it. It is imperative that one have access to the critical secondary literature as well. It is important to be able to see how other scholars have "digested" the various primary materials, and abstracts of secondary sources are invaluable for this purpose.

Making available all the relevant secondary books and articles will be a daunting project. However, we are living in the age of computers. Google is beginning to scan and digitize several of the great libraries of the world, and it would seem that a great amount of this secondary liter-ature will eventually be accessible on our laptops at the local coffeehouse.

But of course, all that material will need to be abstracted and made available. For half a century or so we have had *New Testament Abstracts* and *Old Testament Abstracts*, both of which are now accessible online. If somehow they could be linked to TLG and TLL, they would provide a solid core for our necessary database. But of course their scope and coverage would have to be greatly enlarged.

From a database such as this we could begin to assemble a database of facts—not just tendentious opinions—from which to create and test theories of Christian origins and other problems in the scientific study of religion.

Remember, science must explain the unknown in terms of what is known.

Remember also that in science the burden of proof rests with the person claiming the existence of a thing, a person, or a process. Proof requires evidence. Evidence requires facts. A database of religious facts is *sine qua non* for those seeking to understand and explain the origins of the Abrahamic religions.

But what, in our present state of confusion and controversy, can we all agree upon to use as the core of our database of facts? I think the answer is easy: chronology. Much of the needed chronology has already long ago been established: the dates of the Roman emperors, the dates of most of the Greek philosophers, the dates of important battles, numismatic sequences, etc. In addition to such "absolute" chronologies, however, we need to also include relative chronologies such as Greek, Hebrew, Latin, and Coptic paleographic sequences, ceramic sequences, architectural sequences, burial practice sequences, etc.

Onto a skeleton of such chronologies we must then affix another type of fact that we can all agree upon: the date of first- or last-known attestation of persons, places, or things of interest. When was Nazareth first mentioned outside the New Testament? By whom? How secure is our dating of the attestation? When are any of the Pauline Epistles first attested? When and where was Mithraism first commented on by a Christian? When did the Romans first notice the Christians? With such information we will be able to reconstruct credible trajectories in the evolution of religions.

As in science, it will be necessary to provide references (primary sources whenever possible) to support each fact, so that if studies begin to call into question the accuracy or correctness of particular facts, it will be possible to reevaluate the sources from which newly contested facts were derived. Like all sciences, our science of Christian origins must be self-correcting and progressively must become more and more reliable.

The addition of first-attestation information to our database of facts will enormously expand its size. It will reach daunting proportions within a year of serious teamwork by scholars. However, the overall size of the database will be invisible to scholars wishing to search it.

Simple computer word searches with elementary Boolean capability would allow one to discover—almost instantly—the first-known attestation of Marcion's existence, the first attestation of the *Testimonium Flavianum*, a canon first including the Apocalypse of John, the first use of the word "gospel" (ευαγγελιον, *euangelion*), the first use of the name "Jesus" as a word of power, all Greek manuscripts dated to the period 275–300 CE, and so forth.

More importantly, however, it will be possible quickly to update the entries retrieved as new discoveries make revision necessary. Such a database not only will rapidly increase in size; it will also quickly increase in reliability and utility.

RESOLVING DISPUTES

In the past, the disputes of biblical scholars almost never have come to resolution. I submit that this is largely because the various disputants rarely align their data and arguments to the same point of reference. Rarely do they engage each other on a common ground.

It is often claimed, for example, that the work of Arthur Drews was largely refuted and discredited. I do not, however, agree. I would argue instead that the few polemics published against him did not fully engage his database but rather used separate databases that were never tied in to the one used by Drews. After Drews died, mainline scholars agreed he had been refuted and quickly he was forgotten. Such has been the fate of most Christ-myth theorists for the last two centuries. I would argue that in almost all cases, Christ-myth disputes have been the equivalent of shadow boxing. The disputants rarely become objectively engaged with each other. Rather, they tilt against each other's shadows.

Such exercises in futility do not need to continue, however. We cannot expect apologists to agree to relate their hypotheses and theories to our database, but all genuine scholars should be willing and happy to do so. It is truth, after all, that we all seek. None of us wants to go through life believing things that are wrong or not understanding things we could have figured out had we allowed ourselves to be corrected by the facts. True scientists, such as Charles Darwin, *try to prove themselves wrong* as rigorously as possible—to the end that they may have the greatest possible confidence in their theories.

For a last time I shall remind you that we must always remember that in science it is not necessary to prove a negative. Science *assumes* the negative. If no one can provide convincing *positive* evidence that Jesus of Nazareth—or Jesus of Anyplace—once lived, we must then resort to the tried-and-tested, successful methodology of science to account for the origins of Christianity.

We must examine all the facts that are relevant to the question of how the various Christianities began, formulate a testable hypothesis to answer the question, and then do everything possible to disprove the hypothesis. Any hypotheses that survive rigorous tests can then be elevated to the rank of theory. In time, one of the rival theories—probably after many amendments and reformulations—will predominate and gain the scientific consensus.

Although the hypothesis that Jesus once walked the earth should be among the hypotheses advanced for testing, I am confident that no one will ever be able to present convincing, positive evidence for the historicity of Jesus of Nazareth. Consequently, I have given a lot of thought to alternative explanations that are compatible with a mythical or literary Jesus.

In answering the question, "How did Christianity begin?" I am confident that we will not need to assume the existence of Jesus. Like the mathematician Pierre-Simon de Laplace (1749–1827), when Napoleon asked him why he had not mentioned "*le bon Dieu*" in his *Traité de Mécanique Céleste* (1799–1825), we shall be able to reply, "*Je n'avais pas besoin de cette hypothèse-là*"—"I have had no need of that hypothesis."

METHODOLOGICAL MINIMALISM

It will justly be claimed that the methodology I am proposing is "minimalism." Indeed, it is. But that is because science itself is minimalistic in the sense that it must employ Occam's Razor at all times. "*Entia non sunt multiplicanda præter necessitatem*"—basic assumptions should not be multiplied beyond necessity. If we can explain adequately the origins of Christianity without postulating the quondam existence of a historical Jesus, we must be satisfied with such an explanation.

It may very well be the case that my own astral theory for the origins of Christianity—a theory hinging upon the precessional movement of the vernal equinox from Aries into Pisces at the turn of the era—may prove to be incorrect or require radical revision. But, like all scientific theories, my theory must be tested against a database of all that is known that is pertinent to our problem. It must be tested in a number of ways:

(0) Most importantly, *is my theory falsifiable* (testable)? Can one at least imagine a way it could be proven wrong? This is the zeroeth commandment of all science. Only propositions that can be tested—at least in the imagination—fall within the realm of science.

(1) Are any facts already known that are incompatible with my theory? If so, do they completely rule out my theory or merely require a minor revision of details?

(2) Are there any facts that clearly indicate my theory is probably true?

(3) How well does my theory fit available facts? Does it fit the facts better than other theories do?

(4) Does the theory have heuristic value? Does it help us discover new facts? Does it allow us to make useful predictions? Does it allow us to explain things hitherto inexplicable or mysterious?

We must resolve to make the study of religions a science. No longer can we afford to allow magical thinking to intrude into our investigations. No longer can we allow traditional modes of thinking to compromise our objectivity. No longer can we let ourselves substitute the world of wishes for the world of reality.

Religion is arguably the most powerful force on earth. We must understand it in order to guide it out of the valley of the shadow of death, that it might lead us into the green pastures of a sustainable life for our species.

Martin Luther once said, "Gott macht Kinder, der wird sie auch ernähren" (God makes children, and he feeds them too). But, like many popes who have agreed with him, he was wrong. He was not thinking scientifically. Children everywhere are starving. No illusion is going to feed them. Only science and a calm and unemotional objectivity will show us how to feed them or prevent the problem.

Illusions about the nature and origins of religion—like delusions concerning the place of humankind in a vast universe of galaxies—must be dissolved and sharper images must come into focus if our kind is to avoid the extinction that has been the fate of more than 99 percent of all the species that have ever traveled on this spaceship we call Earth.

The creation of a science of religion could start right here. Most of the facts we need for the database that I think we need are already available to us. It could—indeed, should—be here, instead of Tübingen, Oxford, or Harvard, that the foundation could be laid on which to build a genuine science of religious studies. The discovery of objective truths in the field of religion will be more lifesaving than the discovery of vaccination or penicillin in the field of medicine.

As we face the dangers and problems that threaten our survival, we must let the light of science shine into every pit of darkness. Time is running out. As the Persian poet Omar Khayyám once wrote: "The bird of time has but a little way to flutter—And the bird is on the wing." So, we must hurry. The development of a truly scientific study of religion can be delayed only at our peril.

"EVERY PLANT WHICH MY HEAVENLY FATHER HAS NOT PLANTED SHALL BE UPROOTED"

Robert Eisenman with Noelle Magana

W hat I would like to do in this essay is to show that the famous aphorism, "Every plant which my Heavenly Father has not planted shall be uprooted," attributed to Jesus in the Synoptics, which comes following a long diatribe condemning the Pharisees (to my mind a euphemism for the anti-Pauline "Party of the Circumcision") and famously referring to them as "Blind Guides," followed up by the equally famous "And the Blind shall lead the Blind and both shall fall into the Pit," was written by people who were aware of the Dead Sea Scrolls—in fact, more specifically, the First Column of the Cairo Damascus Document (CD), where the same metaphors or, shall we say, similes or allusions are used, albeit to 180-degree opposite effect.

Of course, everyone knows what the Damascus Document does later with the idea of the Pit. From my perspective, I do not believe all these correspondences are simply accidental and, in fact, right after CD talks about how "He [God] caused a Root of Planting to grow... and inherit the good things of this Earth," it goes on to talk about how "they were as blind men groping for the Way" when "He [God] raised up a Teacher of Righteousness to guide them in the Way of His heart." I do not think I need to say more but there is, of course, more to say as there always is.

As the Synoptics then unfold, the Jesus they are presenting then goes on with his "toilet bowl parable," which talks about how "a man is known not by what goes into his mouth but by that which goes forth from it." (I have shown in my recent New Testament Code, as might be known, that this is just a variation of what R. Yohanan b. Zacchai says about R. Eliezer b. Hyrcanus after the latter put cow dung in his mouth to give himself bad breath!—a neat little bit of refurbishment but, clearly, to reverse ideological effect. Again the keynote is always reversal. What once was a pro-Torah pronouncement is inverted à la Paulinism into an anti-Torah one.)

The final point is that Jesus is then made to conclude (or at least the narrator does) in all these Synoptic Parables that "He said this declaring all foods clean" (something Peter forgot when he had his "Tablecloth" vision in Acts). But never mind, the point is always the same—a neat 180-degree reversal from the position of Qumran. This is what I would like to show—that the authors of these materials not only knew the Qumran documents or at least some of them (most notably, the Damascus Document), but were reversing them in a systematically consistent manner.

The linguistic interdependence of the "Root of Planting" allusion of Matthew 15:1–20 and Mark 7:1–23 and much else in the depiction of Jesus' arguments with the "scribes and Pharisees from Jerusalem" should be clear. This is the case in Matthew 15:1. In Mark 7:1, this changes into the even more pregnant "the Pharisees" and the telltale "some of the scribes who had come from Jerusalem" (thus—note both the "coming" and the "some") and a euphemism, it would appear, evocative of Paul's interlocutors from "James," "Church," or "Assembly" in Jerusalem. In Matthew, Jesus rebukes the Pharisees as Blind Guides—in this instance, in a polemical exchange with his own disciples, following this up with the passage which is the title and subject of this essay:

> Every plant which my Heavenly Father has not planted shall be rooted up.
>
> (Mt 15:13)

It should be obvious that these are anti–"Jerusalem Church" aspersions, since they are usually followed by and tied to equally proverbial statements like "the First shall be Last and the Last shall be First" (Mt 19:30, 20:16 and pars.)—"the Last" having, patently, to do with Paul's new "Gentile Christian" communities and those, like him, making no insistence on seemingly picayune legal requirements for salvation. The inverse parallel to this—which as at Qumran, as we shall show further below, will also involve a "Guide" or "Maschil"[1]—will be present in the

Damascus Document's dramatic opening imprecation about how God caused

> a Root of Planting to grow [the parallel is here] from Israel and from Aaron to inherit His land and to prosper on the good things of His Earth.[2]

I say "patently," because Paul first made the allusion to being "last" in his 1 Corinthians 15:8 Jesus-sighting-order determinations—also, importantly enough, citing James, even albeit if defectively.[3]

> And last of all he appeared, as if to one born out of term [or "to an abortion"], also to me.

But "the First" is an extremely important expression at Qumran—especially meaningful in the Damascus Document—carrying with it the signification of "the Forefathers" or "the Ancestors." The sense is always "those who observed" or "gave the Torah," while "the Last"—aside from Paul's evocation of it regarding his own post-Resurrection appearance experience—usually has to do with "the Last Times" or "the Last Days" denoting the "present" or "Last Generation" as opposed to "the First."[4]

On the other hand in the Gospels, once again absolutely turning Qumran ideology on its head, "the Last" are "the simple" or "these little children"—completely representative of Paul's new "Gentile Christian Community" knowing or required to know little or nothing about such onerous legal requirements, yet still in a state of salvation, or, as it were, "in Jesus." The simile, symbolism, parable, or allegory—as the case may be—in all these allusions is not hard to figure out despite endless academic attempts at evasion or posturing to the contrary.

Furthermore, and even perhaps more germane, these polemics in Mark 7:1–23 and Matthew 15:1–20 actually evoke the famous Talmudic tractate, Pirke Abbot (The Traditions of the Fathers, which has a variation in the ARN—The Fathers According to Rabbi Nathan, here in Mark 7:3–5 and Matthew 15:2, "The Traditions of the Elders"). This designation "Elders" or "*Presbyteron*" is used at various junctures in the Gospels and the book of Acts and is the actual designation for James's

"Jerusalem Community" in both Acts 21:18 and the Pseudoclementine Homilies.[5]

In some of the most convoluted reasoning imaginable, these polemics invoke the Mosaic commandment, "Honor your father and your mother" (Mk 7:10/Mt 15:4) and, in doing so, leave no doubt that we are dealing with "the Fathers." Just as importantly in Mark 7:1–5 (and to some degree paralleled in Matthew 15:1–4 and 12), the Pharisees are invoked as well—three times in five lines. As just suggested above, this is an expression that often acts as a blind for those of the Jamesian persuasion within the early Church—as, for example, in Acts 15:5 at the renowned "Jerusalem Council" and the elusive "some who believed" of "the sect of the Pharisees" who provoked the council by their insistence on circumcision and "keeping the law of Moses" (thus).

The evocation of these same Pharisees is being used to attack those of the James school over the issue of "table fellowship with Gentiles" in these passages about Blind Guides from Mark and Matthew (an issue clearly being raised by Paul in Galatians 2:11–14). Moreover, there is the additional derivative attack, which now seems to us, if not bizarre, at least rather specious, on the Jewish people as a whole—in this case, plainly meant to include the Jerusalem Community of James, and others of similar mindset—that "eating with unwashed hands does not defile the man" (Mt 15:20/Mk 7:2–3). This attack derogates "washing one's hands before eating" to the level only of what is being called "a Tradition of Men" and "breaking the [obviously higher] Commandment of God." In the ad hominem logic being displayed in this patently pro-Pauline exposition, the meaning of this last would appear to be the Mosaic commandment and that of humanity generally "to honor your father and your mother" (Mk 7:8–9/Mt 15:3 and 15:19).

The argument appears to turn on the point that, since one's parents might have "eaten with unwashed hands," the commandment not to do so—which the Gospel Jesus is pictured as dismissing here merely as "a Tradition of the Elders" (meaning the allusion to "a Tradition of Men" above)—would be contradicting the higher commandment (the one he is terming "a Commandment of God") not to dishonor them! This appears to be the gist of an extremely tortured and, indeed, highly polemicized argument but, to judge by the time spent on it in Mark as well as Matthew, a clearly pivotal one as well. The writer sees it as a striking example of retrospective pro-Pauline polemics or "Paulinization" and, consequently, feels it to be a service to rescue "the historical Jesus" from this particular bit of tendentious and not very sophisticated, medically speaking, sophistry.

Both Mark 7:6–7 and Matthew 15:7–9 picture Jesus as using this passage to attack the "vanity" of those who "teach as their doctrines the Commandments of Men," meaning, "the Traditions of the Elders" just mentioned in Mark 7:5 and Matthew 15:2 above. Not only is this clearly an attack on what in Rabbinic parlance is called "oral tradition," but it turns around the parameters of Paul's debates with those of the Jamesian school or, if one prefers, inverts their arguments turning them back against themselves.[6] Again, the meaning both the Gospels of Mark and Matthew are clearly ascribing to their Jesus from the start here is that "hypocrites" of this kind, following "the Tradition of the Elders," are forcing people to wash their hands before eating, something that most people nowadays would consider as not only normal but hygienic; however, in Paul's inverted invective, something Paul (to say nothing about his alter ego, Jesus) would obviously consider quite reprehensible.

As in all of the previous episodes above, the denouement of this abolishing purity requirements/table fellowship episode in Mark 7 and Matthew 15, which further legitimatizes the Pauline Gentile Mission, once more has Jesus in 7:17 entering a "house" (as he does yet again in Mark 7:24). In Mark 7:17, this is typically "away from the multitude" to rebuke the disciples. In Matthew 15:15 there is no house[7] and the rebuke of "being yet without understanding" is as per usual—because of Galatians 2:11–14—only to Peter. Still, "the multitude" from Mark 7:17 (which probably should be read "the many" or "the *Rabim*"; the term—unlike "the Sons of Zadok"—usually applied to the rank and file at Qumran) are the ones already portrayed earlier in Mark 7:14 and Matthew 15:10 as the ones being addressed by Jesus on the subject of "pure foods," "unwashed hands," "Blind Guides," and "Uprooted Plants."

In both Gospels, Jesus' discourse begins with the words, "Hear and understand," which has direct links to and appears to play off the opening exhortations of the Damascus Document that read—and this very familiarly and, for that matter, not insignificantly—"Hear, all you who know Righteousness, and understand" (i.1) …

and now listen to me all who enter the Covenant ["the New Covenant in the Land of Damascus" demanding both "purity" and "separating the Holy from the profane"] and I will unstop your ears. (ii.2)[8]

But in Mark 7:16 in the midst of Jesus' attack on "the Tradition of the Elders" and "purifying all food" preceding this, the same ears metaphor from column 2 of the Damascus Document, just reproduced above, actually appears, to wit, "If anyone has ears, let him hear."

To go back to Matthew 15:16, there the rebuke about "being yet without understanding" is, as already remarked, directed at Peter alone and not at the disciples. Notwithstanding, prior to this, after "calling the Multitude" or "the Many to him" (15:10, reprised in Mark 7:14), Jesus does actually address the disciples in Matthew 15:12 as well. There the reproof he gives the disciples concerning staying away from the Pharisees and "leaving them alone" (in 16:6–12 later, "the leaven of the Pharisees" repeated multiple times)—which includes the "Blind Guides," "planting," and "uprooting" allusions we have just been calling attention to above—comes in the wake of his enunciation of the following famous doctrine:

> Not that which enters the mouth defiles the man, but that which proceeds out of the mouth, this defiles the man. [15:11—in Mark 7:15, this changes into the more prolix and obviously derivative, "There is nothing from without the man that going into him can defile him. Rather the things that proceed out of the man are those that defile him."]

This allusion to the Pharisees, the evocation of whom initiated the whole series of encounters right from the beginning in Mark 7:1 and Matthew 15:1 above, comes—as Matthew 15:12 now phrases it—because the disciples reported to Jesus that "the Pharisees were offended by what they heard him saying."[9] It must be reiterated that expressions like "the Pharisees," regardless of their overt meaning in any other context here or historically, have a covert meaning in these contexts as well. As we have been at pains to point out, they—like "the Scribes" ("some of the Scribes who came down from Jerusalem") coupled with them in Matthew 15:1 and Mark 7:1 above—are, in this context in the Gospels, stand-ins for "the James Community" in Jerusalem that not only insisted upon circumcision but (as it would appear) its legal consequences as well, such as purity regulations that, by implication, would have included measures of bodily hygiene like "washing their hands" that seem, in the picture Mark and Matthew are presenting, to so upset their Jesus here.[10]

It is also perhaps not without relevance that an expression like "Pharisees"—*Perushim* in Hebrew—carries with it, as well, the meaning of "splitting away" or "separating themselves from"—the implication being that, in some contexts, it can even be understood as "heretics," which, in fact, is one of the appositions Acts 15:5 applies to it. Nor should the reader overlook the fact that Matthew's picture of Jesus at this point, reproving the Pharisees, follows his exhortation to the Many/the *Rabim* in 15:10 to "hear and understand" (in Mark 7:14, "hear me all of you and understand")—a phrase, as we just saw, that has to be seen as comparable to CD i.1's "Now hear, all you who know Righteousness and understand the works of God."

Matthew 15:14 also pictures Jesus as calling these Pharisees "Blind Guides" (an allusion we shall presently show to be charged with significance) because of their complaints against his teaching that "eating with unclean hands does not defile the man" (15:20), as well as related matters concerning purity and dietary regulations, themselves having a bearing on the key issue in Galatians 2:11–14 above of "table fellowship with Gentiles."[11] It is at this point, in Matthew 15:14 too, that Jesus then cautions his disciples (none of this paralleled now in Mark or, for that matter, any other Gospel) to "leave them alone." It would be well to point out that even the line in Matthew 15:19, preceding 15:20 on "eating with unclean hands not defiling the man" just cited and echoed in Mark 7:21–23, enumerates "the things that proceed out of the mouth" (thereby, according to the discourse being attributed here to Jesus, "coming forth out of the heart" and, most famously, therefore "defiling the man") as: "Evil thoughts, murders, adulteries, fornications, thefts, lies, blasphemies—these are the things that defile the man" (Mark 7:22 adds "greedy desires, wickednesses, deceit, lustful desires, an evil eye, pride, and foolishness").

But this catalogue of "evil" inclinations almost precisely reprises one of the most famous passages in the Community Rule from Qumran as well, the "Two Ways": the "Ways of Darkness" and the "Ways of "Light." In this document, the "Spirit of Evil"/"Ungodliness" or "of Darkness" is depicted even more lengthily as

> greediness of soul, stumbling hands in the Service of Righteousness, Wickedness and Lying, pride and proudness of heart, duplicitousness and deceitfulness, cruelty, Evil temper [there is a lot of Paul in this— to say nothing of Mark 7:21–23 above], impatience, foolishness, and zeal for lustfulness [the opposite, of course, of proper zeal—"zeal for the Law" or "zeal for the Judgments of Righteousness," as it is expressed in the Hymns from Qumran],[12] works of Abomination in a spirit of fornication, and ways of uncleanness in the Service of pol- lution [now we are getting into it—as opposed to the proper "Service of Righteousness" of "true" Apostles above—all issues of "table ser- vice," for instance, aside), a Tongue full of blasphemies [the "Tongue" imagery of the Letter of James],[13] blindness of eye and dullness of ear [this, too, momentarily reappearing in the Gospel episode we shall now describe], stiffness of neck and hardness of heart [as will this] in order to walk in all the Ways of Darkness and Evil inclination.[14]

This is quite a catalogue, but the parallels with Matthew and Mark do not stop here. Even the allusion to "Blind Guides," to say nothing of "leave them alone," which Matthew depicts Jesus as advising vis-à-vis the Pharisees, actually seems to parody the pivotal character evoked at Qumran (in particular, in the Community Rule again, but also in the Hymns), the Maschil or Guide. He is defined, just like "the Teacher of Righteousness," as instructing the Many in the Ways of Righteousness.[15]

In the Community Rule this Maschil or Guide is pictured, inter alia, as "doing the will of God" (that is, "being a Doer," not "a Breaker," in the manner of the recommendations in James 1:22–25—nor should one forget, in this regard as well, all the "signs" or "miracles," Jesus is depicted as doing, in John 2:11, 2:23, 6:2, 6:14, etc.) and

> studying all the Wisdom that has been discovered from age to age, to separate [the language of "separation" again, just evoked above in the "leave them alone" allusion] and evaluate the Sons of the Righteous One [here, the usage really is "the Sons of the Righteous One" or "the

Zaddik," not the more usual Qumran and New Testament "Sons of Righteousness"—in Hebrew, *Zedek*, without the definite article] according to their spirit and fortify the Elect of the Age according to His will as He commanded and, thereby, to do His Judgment [once more the Jamesian emphasis on "doing"] on every man according to His spirit.[16]

This does begin to seem New Testament–like. Not only does it hark back to several New Testament themes, such as the "Two Spirits" and Paul's "knowing the things of man according to the spirit of man which is in him" of 1 Corinthians 2:11–15, but the Community Rule's description of the Guide then goes on to actually evoke two allusions, "clean hands" and "not arguing with the Sons of the Pit"—in other words, the "leave them alone" theme just encountered in passages from Matthew 15:14 and to a certain extent in Mark 7:8 above (the latter to be sure not quite in the same context). Perhaps even more strikingly, yet another allusion is evoked—the third, "the Pit," just remarked as well and an allusion known throughout the Dead Sea Scrolls, which we shall encounter in Jesus, further disparagement of these "Blind Guides" as we proceed:

[The Maschil shall allow] each man to draw near according to the cleanness of his hands [here, yet another allusion to "clean hands," should one choose to regard it] and his wisdom and, thus, shall be his love together with his hate. Nor should he admonish or argue with the Sons of the Pit [here again, yet another allusion to Jesus' directive to the disciples a propos of the Pharisees in Matthew 15:12–14, just highlighted above, to "leave them alone"].

Moreover, the Guide or Maschil is commanded in this pregnant, concluding exhortation from the Community Rule to rather

conceal the counsel of the Torah [that is, "the Law"] from the Men of Evil ["the Men of the Pit" or "Ungodly" above], confirming the Knowledge of the Truth and Righteous Judgment to the Elect of the Way ["the Elect" is, of course, a very widespread and important terminology at Qumran, as is "the Way"] ... comforting them with Knowledge, thereby guiding them in the Mysteries of the Marvelous

Truth…, that is, to walk in Perfection each with his neighbor. [This being, of course, nothing less than James's "Royal Law according to the Scripture"—"to love each man his neighbor as himself." It is often found in the Scrolls.]

Of perhaps even more significance, this leads directly into the Community Rule's second citation of Isaiah 40:3's "preparing a Straight Way in the wilderness" in as many columns:

For this is the time of the preparation of the Way in the wilderness. Therefore he [the "Maschil"—in Matthew above, Jesus' Blind Guide] should guide them in all that has been revealed that they should do in this Time [n.b., again, the pivotal emphasis on "doing"] to separate [here again too, the Nazirite-like directive to "come out from among them and be separate," just enunciated by Paul in 2 Corinthians 6:17 as well] from any man who has not turned aside his Way from all Evil [including, of course, from these "Sons of the Pit," just alluded to above as well].

To further demonstrate the interconnectedness of these kinds of usages, the denotation "the Sons of the Pit" is immediately reprised in these climactic passages from the Community Rule:

These are the rules of the Way for the Guide in these Times [presumably "the Last Times" of other Qumran documents and the Gospels]: Everlasting hatred for the Sons of the Pit in a spirit of secrecy, to leave them to their Riches [here the language of "the Pit" coupled with express allusions both to "Riches" and "leaving them alone"] and the suffering ['amal] of their hands, like the slave to his Ruler and the Meek before his Lord.

Not only do we have the "master" and "lord" vocabulary here but also, yet again, that of hands—this time in the sense of "that which their own hands have wrought"—the same hands presumably that were to remain unwashed when eating in Jesus' crucial "toilet bowl" homily in both Matthew and Mark above.[17] The conclusion of all this is quite extraordinary:

And he [both the Maschil and the rank and file] shall be as a man zealous for the Law, whose Time will be the Day of Vengeance [meaning, in this context, "the Last Judgment" but, as usual, without a touch of nonviolence], to do all His will in all the work of his hands ["hands" again]... delighting in all the words of His mouth [the "mouth" vocabulary of Jesus' "what comes into the mouth" or "goes forth from the mouth" above] and in all His Kingdom as He commanded.

The reader should pay particular attention to all these usages, but especially: "doing the will of God"; "separating the Sons of the Righteous One" and "not disputing with the Sons of the Pit," but "leaving them to their Riches" and "the works of their hands"; and "doing all His will in all the work of his (the Maschil's or the adept's) hands" and finally "delighting in all the words of His mouth."

It is now possible to return to Jesus' allusion to the Pharisees as Blind Guides in Matthew 15:14 with a little more insight. This is where we began and, it will be recalled, that it was in the run-up to this allusion that Jesus was pictured as evoking the "plant" or "planting" vocabulary in which we are so interested in this essay. It should also be observed that Paul uses this vocabulary, too, when he speaks of "God's plantation" or "growing place" and "God's building" in 1 Corinthians 3, concluding in 3:6: "I planted, Apollos watered, but God caused to grow." It should be clear that this is also playing off a similar vocabulary, i.e., the Messianic "plant" and "planting" imagery that permeates the literature of Qumran in general[18]—in particular, "the Root of Planting," with which the Damascus Document follows up its opening imprecation to "hear and understand" and the focus of our excursus here.

This reads, as we have partially seen above, as follows:

And in the Age of Wrath... He [God] visited them and caused a Root of Planting to grow [these are some of the same words that Paul used in 1 Corinthians 3:6–8 above] from Israel and Aaron to inherit His Land [Paul's "field" or "growing place" imagery in 1 Corinthians 3:9] and to prosper on the good things of His Earth.[19]

In Matthew 15:13–14, the preliminary characterization introducing Jesus' "Leave them alone, they are Blind Guides" reproof, alluding to the Pharisees, reads:

But he answered, saying, "Every plant which My Heavenly Father has not planted shall be uprooted."

Of course, we are QED here, the "uprooting" or "rooting up" language being exactly the same as "the Root of Planting" just encountered in the opening exhortation of this First Column of the Cairo Damascus Document—the "uprooting" playing off the "Root of Planting" that God "caused to grow"; and the "Planting" part of the "Root" imagery. Nor is this to say anything about Paul's parallel "Apollos planted, I watered, and God caused to grow," we just highlighted, which not only plays off but is an actual verbatim quotation of the remainder of this all-important preliminary metaphor in the Damascus Document. One cannot get a much closer fit than this and the Damascus Document's "the Root of Planting" to Matthew's "every plant which my Heavenly Father has not planted shall be uprooted."

Even so, the very next line in Matthew 15:14 continues the borrowing:

They are Blind Guides leading the Blind and, if the Blind lead the Blind, both will fall into the Pit.

First of all, one has in both subject and predicate here the image of the Maschil, just as in several of the passages quoted from the Community Rule above. Combined with this is the language and imagery of the Pit—in particular, "the Sons of the Pit" just underscored as well and used to attack all the enemies of the Community including, presumably, persons of the mindset of Paul.[20] One should also note that in Matthew 15:14, it is both "the Blind Guides" and "the Blind" they lead who will, metaphorically, fall into "the Pit"!

This is an extremely telling example of another process detectable in comparing these documents—one reverses the other, that is, someone using the very language of another person and turning it back on that other person to undermine him. Indeed at this point in Matthew, this whole allusion that on the surface seems innocuous enough actually plays off yet another, seemingly unrelated passage concerning regulations governing the Sabbath in the Damascus Document, most of which are counterindicated in the Gospels. In the process, Matthew 15:12–14 makes fun of and pictures its Jesus as having contempt for these too, i.e., if a man's "beast falls into a pit on the Sabbath, he shall not lift it out."[21]

More importantly, however, the borrowing does not stop even here, and this is nothing in comparison to the importance of the allusion to "being blind," which will now follow this pivotal passage about "God visiting them" and "causing a Root of Planting to grow" in the Damascus Document and link up directly with the allusion to the Pharisees as Blind Guides in the Gospel of Matthew. This occurs as follows and in the very next lines in this First Column of the Cairo Damascus Document. There, one comes upon, as we have already to some extent seen and parts of which we have already quoted above, the final linchpin of all this borrowing, ending with the very first introduction of the renowned "Righteous Teacher" himself—"the Guide of all Guides" as it were. It reads in its entirety, following right after the allusion to "God having visited them and caused a Root of Planting to grow" and the words "to inherit His Land and to prosper on the good things of His Earth":

And they were like blind men groping for the Way ["the Way in the wilderness" and the name for early Christianity in Palestine as recorded in Acts on three different occasions] for twenty years [the time elapsed, perhaps, between the death of whomever "the Messiah Jesus" is supposed to represent and the relevation of James].[22] And God considered their works, because they sought him with a whole heart [this language of "works" and "heart" that is pivotal throughout the Qumran corpus] and He raised up for them a Teacher of Righteousness to guide them in the Way of His heart [the "guiding" language here is a variation of that of "the Way," again combined with that of the "heart"].[23]

Of course, nothing could better illustrate the interconnectedness of all these imageries than the appearance of this allusion to "being like blind men" and how they were to be "guided by the Teacher of Righteousness" in "the Way" of God's "heart," following directly upon the one to "planting" the all-important Messianic "Root," which God then "caused to grow" (the "caused to grow" here using the exact same language of the Messianic "Branch of David" in other documents and contexts, one of which I had the privilege of helping to bring to light)[24] and preceding the equally pivotal introduction of the proverbial "Teacher of Righteousness." One could not get a tighter construction of the inter-relatedness of all these documents than this.

One final point that, perhaps, should be made: the reason for all this borrowing, parody, and sometimes even derogation has to have been that so original and impressive were these new ideas and usages, we now know from the discovery of the Dead Sea Scrolls, and so well versed were some of the original creators of some of this material from the Gospels (in this instance, particularly Matthew), to say nothing of the material in Paul, that they were unable to resist continually playing off them and reversing or inverting the actual original sense or meaning.

ON NOT FINDING THE HISTORICAL JESUS

R. Joseph Hoffmann

And he asked them, "*Who do you say that I am?*" (Mk 8:28)
And the scholars began to write.

The following comments are designed to reorient the question that has perplexed historians, theologians, and philosophers for centuries, but for quite different reasons. It seems self-evident to many people that it is "important" for there to have been a historical Jesus, and yet the reasons for his importance are not altogether clear from the sources available to reconstruct his life and thought.

Among the early Christians, a majority took his historicity for granted, either on the basis of hearsay and preaching by people who had claimed to know others who had known him (a process that leads to the formulation of "apostolic succession" in the second century), or from the Gospel accounts presumed to be written by eyewitnesses or associates of eyewitnesses from the earliest days of the Christian church. A significant minority of Christians—labeled docetists and Gnostics by the majority—had less interest in the historical Jesus, or none at all, preferring instead to focus on his "revelation" as an expression of the True God's nature and being. That there was no Jesus in the historical sense is implicit in Gnostic teaching, but submerged in the Gnostics' exaggerated claims of his supernality, while for the orthodox, Jesus' significance is determined precisely in the core belief that he had lived, died, and was raised from the dead at a particular point in history, "under Pontius Pilate." That there was neither a supernal, nonphysical Jesus nor a historical Jesus was not a question broached even by the pagan critics of the church, most of whom assumed that Jesus was a man of no significance to whom the unoriginal fables of Hellenistic mythology had been selectively attached.

In what follows, I want to consider the way in which the theological discussion of Jesus' importance, that is to say, the way in which his "reality" was apprehended, affects the consideration of his historical existence. It is my claim here that neither the sources we possess nor approaches to them developed over the last two centuries yield any resolution of the question of his actual existence and that the church's description of his reality has never depended primarily on the status of such a question.

*   *   *

To believe that something is real is to take a position towards its existence. To say that a chair is real is to say it occupies space, i.e., that it is physical and is accessible to the senses. Almost everybody will be happy with some form of that definition, with its focus on sensory apprehension. On the other hand, to say that love is real may be merely the expression of a feeling towards an object or person raised to the level of a category: The lover is certain his feeling is precipitated by the existence of something unseen, but nonetheless real, without the reality of which his feeling is inexplicable. While he may never have read Plato, he will point to the effects of love on his behavior, on creating a sense of well-being—and confusion—and on other results, such as marriage, family, harmony, even that most important of Greek ideals, happiness. Given the overriding evidence of these results, it may be hard to maintain the position that love is not "real." Plato's "ideas" (goodness, truth, beauty, justice, etc.) are categories presumed to exist quite independently of their very imperfect expressions in language, art, government, philosophy, poetry, and human conduct. But to complete the circle, even these imperfect expressions would not exist without the reality of the ideas. They are shadows, Porphyry argued, for example, of the unseen supernal realm that our mind longs to reach but can only attain in moments of philosophical ecstasy.

Hardheaded opponents of Plato's metaphysics, beginning with Aristotle—a long and distinguished train of experientialists—would limit the reality of things to those that cannot be doubted by the senses. Love is the reality of the heart in crisis. To the extent it has anything to do with sense, biology is its sufficient explanation.

What do we do with the reality of things that are not real in the sense a chair is real and not real in the sense some people believe love is real—things that possess a reality that is neither physical nor, in the strict sense metaphysical? To pose the question this way is slightly misleading because I am not asking about the existence of gnomes or paradise islands or lost plays of Shakespeare. Historical inquiry has its own ways of dealing with such questions, and each question will be answered using a slightly different technique. Archaeology and the context of reports concerning gnomes will come into play if anyone is interested in pursuing the habits of the denizen tinkers of Gnomeregan. Paradise islands may exist, but one, invented by Anselm's friend Guanilo, seems to have surpassed all others in beauty and splendor, such that its reality was only to be imagined and never experienced.

The idea of a perfect island that can never be visited on a yacht is a rich man's nightmare, of course, but it is also (merely) a semantic trick. No reality is at stake in postulating the imaginable. And in the case of a lost Shakespeare play—well, there is nothing mysterious about reports of lost works of literature, art, cities, animals, races, kingdoms. Some, like reports of the kingdom of Prester John, are probably unreliable. Some, like the existence of Troy, are probably partly reliable, and some, like reports of the Hanging Gardens of Babylon, are almost certainly reliable (to a point) though the most famous of Greek historians, Herodotus, does not mention their existence. The fact that an object, event, or person is "historical" does not mean its reality is untestable, but that its reality "behaves" differently and must be approached differently from the way we approach chairs and love. Like the chair, the historical reality once occupied space. But like love, or black holes (if not the same phenomenon) it can sometimes only be known from the objects and conditions that surround it.

Belief in God and belief in Jesus, thanks to the proclivities of Christian theology, seem to be the same sort of belief. A Christian who believes ardently in the Trinity might want to argue that the belief is a package deal: to believe in God is to believe in a particular orthodox formulation of God's being and essence, and in "orthodox" Christianity (however unfashionable the term) that formulation is the Nicene Creed. In the creed, Jesus Christ and God the Father (note the phrase) are "one in being" but different in person: not to believe in Jesus as the only begotten son of God is not to believe something vitally important about God himself. Indeed, you may as well be talking about Allah or Mazdayasna since you will not be talking about what Christians historically have believed to be the primary characteristic of God: fatherhood, and the eternal generation ("begetting," a process rather than a birth) of his son, Jesus Christ.

But in fact, the two beliefs are different. The existence of God can be argued theologically or philosophically. If theologically (using traditional language) the proofs are usually called "demonstrations" and include some of the classical arguments of the theistic tradition—such as Anselm's ontological argument or Thomas Aquinas's five "ways." It is convenient for philosophers to have these arguments because they don't have to go about inventing their own. They have normally simply taken aim at these rather good ones and subjected them to tests of their own devising, ranging from ethical tests to those that spring from schools of thought, such as philosophical naturalism. The existence of God is not a question for history, though the emergence and shape of particular beliefs about him are of considerable historical importance.

"Believing" in Jesus can be argued historically or theologically, but not philosophically. Historically, the existence of Jesus to be indubitable would need to be demonstrated in the same way the existence of any other human being can be shown. The standard of proof is fairly high, making allowance for the age in which the person lived or is thought to have lived. Normally we would expect records, reports, artifacts (bones are best), or the writings of people who mention Jesus in their reports of other events. For example, a chronicle of the Roman administration of Pontius Pilate in Palestine with a mention of the crucifixion of an outlaw named Yeshu, a Galilean, would be very helpful. But we do not possess such a record. Instead, we possess reports written by members of a religious group that had very specific and self-interested reasons for retelling his story. And the way in which it is told differs so markedly from the sorts of histories the Romans were writing in the second and third century CE that scholars have acknowledged for a long time the "problem" of deriving the historical Jesus from the Gospels—and even more the problem of deriving his existence from the letters of Paul or any other New Testament writings.

Having said this, I don't mean to suggest that the Gospels are "made up," that they are like Greek myths (though bits are) or that they possess no historical value. *The Iliad* is Greek myth, mainly made up, perhaps seven hundred years older than the earliest Gospel, and yet seems to point (however obscurely) to actual events that transpired six centuries before Homer immortalized them. Herodotus, who lived more than five centuries before the Gospels, is known to us primarily as a purveyor of history, but freely uses mythology and the supernatural without totally discrediting the stories he has to tell. The line between history and myth is not always clearly drawn in ancient accounts, even those that purport to be historical.

Why then, it can plausibly be asked, can we not assume the Gospels point to events that transpired within (say) a generation of their tellers' lifetimes, as many perfectly reputable scholars continue to think? And even given doubts about their historical particulars, a discussion that will occupy scholars for many years to come and probably without resolution, would it not be more unusual not to find the mythical and supernatural as part of their fabric than to find precisely the kind of documents we possess—especially coming from a class of writers who were not historians or literary craftsmen? What would a disinterested, journalistic appraisal—a "report"—of the life and teachings of Jesus look like given the literary genres available to such amateurs? Those who argue the case for the basic reliability of the Gospels usually make this minimalist case: that there is more reason to assume the Gospels reflect actual events transformed in the light of religious experience than to believe that they are the products of religious experience alone. From this minimal position, certain scholars—the indefatigable N. T. Wright is perhaps the most popular modern example—then go on to claim much more in terms of historical reliability.

*　　*　　*

The existence of Jesus can also be argued theologically. Paul does it this way by quoting (we assume) a hymn in Philippians 2:5–11. It locates Jesus in a cosmic timeframe that might be Gnostic except for the emphasis on his death and exaltation. The Eucharistic narratives and the sequence, the Passion story in the synoptic Gospels, create Jesus' historicity this way as well, by making him the centerpiece in an unfolding drama of betrayal and martyrdom. The Crucifixion story is as much a theological memoir as a historical one—or rather a peculiar blending of two interests, a kind of intersection between historical expectation and superhistorical completion. The earliest church writers, especially Ignatius of Antioch, saw Jesus not just as the fulfill-ment of prophecy but as the way in which prophecy acquires its meaning through the church. The increasingly elaborate theological framing of Jesus may distract from the fading image on the canvas, but it is the enthusiasm for ever-more detailed frames that kept the histor-ical figure from disappearing entirely.

These theological arguments are better described as constructions of the "reality" or necessity of the human Jesus and lead to various con-troversies that historians have left it to the theologians to sort through. In effect, this has created a kind of scholarly apartheid in which secular historians have treated the theological debates of the fourth and fifth century as the weird preoccupations of a bygone era, while (except among scholars who represent Anglican and Roman Catholic ortho-doxy) many contemporary theologians regard the debates in just the same way. The most liberal theology since the nineteenth century has found its justification in translating the idioms of patristic Christianity into more modern categories of thought, while since the late twentieth century it has been typical to construct challenges to the patristic system—theologies that regard the categories of the church fathers provisional, "sexist," outmoded, or irrelevant to contemporary dis-course. The theologian Daphne Hampson is one of a dozen theologians who have used the term *post-Christian* to describe the radical break with the past that the newer theologies purvey. Their interest in the histor-ical Jesus is (by far) secondary to the promotion of a critique of the church—which in many ways replaces Jesus as the fundamental histor-ical datum of their theology.

Yet these early debates that seem so distant from our concern and interest irreversibly colored the picture of the historical Jesus and created in his place the Byzantine cosmocrator who ruled the aeons, a king enthroned on high who would come again to judge the living and the dead. The doctrines of the one-personed, two-natured Christ, the hypostatic union (the doctrine that Jesus is both God and Man without confusion or separation of natures), would probably count as myth if they told a better story. But at all events the fully divine and human Jesus had become a theological necessity before the end of the second century and a confessional statement in the fourth. The historical presupposition, the man named Jesus, was buried in this controversy, if it had ever existed independently.

To accept the "reality" of Jesus after the fourth century is to accept the rather bizarre figure immortalized in the icons, the Jesus of the fertile Christian imagination. This Jesus is a myth cobbled together from other myths—imperial, soteriological, apocalyptic and messianic, priestly, Gnostic, Stoic with a healthy dash of Byzantine splendor tossed into the mix. To the extent that every Jesus is a composite of culture and theology, the Jesus of Nicaeo-Chalcedonian orthodoxy would have been quite impossible in a first- or second-century context, and for the same reasons—though his image is emblazoned on cathedral walls from London to St. Louis in tribute to the famous "original" in the Hagia Sophia in Constantinople—impossibly exotic to later generations. The rate of change in reframing the reality of Jesus between the Middle Ages, the Reformation, and since the Reformation is enough to suggest that theological definitions of reality relate more to love than to chairs; that is to say, they are impressions of interpretation rather than interpretations of fact.

* * *

Historically, then, the reality of Jesus cannot be indubitable because his existence does not meet the high standard of proof we set for other historical figures. That statement may seem naive to New Testament scholars who have staked their scholarly careers on tomes promising to uncover what Jesus really said or who Jesus really was. But in fact, their work, to a book, suffers from confusing love and chairs, feelings and facts.

I have no particular case in view: whether Jesus was a peasant farmer or a Galilean bandit, a magician or a preacher of wisdom is unknown and cannot be known. It cannot be known for the same reason that there can be no compromise between the Jesus of Byzantine orthodoxy and the Jesus of the Brethren of the Common Life, between the good shepherd and the King of Glory, a failed messiah and the Son of Man: images do not establish historicity but create scenarios of how a reality might have been, given certain conditions and ignoring or omitting others. Scholars who find it inconvenient for Jesus to have been an apocalyptic preacher, for example, will now argue that this is an insignificant part of his message. Scholars who find limited support for political agendas or social positions in the Gospels will turn to the "possibility" that the radical sayings of Jesus were buried by a power-hungry church, using the concealment of Gnostic sources as "proof" of such an enterprise. Defenders of older images will argue that theirs is the one provided in sources of irrefragable orthodoxy, without acknowledging that antiquity, far from establishing historicity, finds myth more compelling than fact. The most cynical approaches of all are those reductivist ones that purport to be recovering the historical Jesus from sayings, contexts, or scenarios argued to be more (or less) historical than the others associated with the tradition, thus permitting scholars to shape their reality on demand, constrained only by publishing schedules. Theology thus facilitates the re-creation in every generation of a Jesus who never existed for the benefit of women and men who find the Jesus who might have existed an embarrassment. That Jesus, like the Inquisitor's guest in *The Brothers Karamazov*, "We will not allow ... to come to us again."

JESUS TO CHRIST?

Many books on the subject of the historical Jesus employ what some have called the Jesus-to-Christ model of development. The assumption behind such approaches is that Christianity began with an event roughly equivalent to the birth and ministry of Jesus and following his death (whether expected or unanticipated), the development of a community that believed him risen from the dead. The added details need not be elaborate, but the basic model requires us to accept that as the community developed its confession during Paul's time—1 Corinthians 5:6 seems a good minimum—the things believed about Jesus also intensified, so that by the end of the first "generation" (a meaningless term invented by early twentieth-century New Testament scholars), Jesus had become a magnet for a hodgepodge of beliefs, ranging from the idea that he was a prophet to the belief that he was the messiah and God incarnate. The model appears to be commonsensical, on the analogy of Descartes' famous example of how a city develops pari passu from a village or how organic systems move from the simple to the complex.

But the model does not work well if the question in point is the reality of Jesus rather than how the church becomes more complex. The phenomena are not identical, and the use of a historically "minimal" Jesus as a *point d'appui* for the process through which Christian theology and structure evolves into a complex system would not bear comparison to developments in other religions, especially those—the majority—that do not depend on a historical "founder" or progenitor who is also its deity. Indeed, Christianity is almost unique and uniquely problematical in its assertion of a founder who is also its god.

In short, the "from Jesus to Christ" model is conceptually flawed because it sees ecclesiastical developments as representing a stratum in the aggregation of the Jesus tradition that is unavailable apart from the developments themselves—a recognition clear enough from the disregarded slogan of nineteenth-century radicals who professed that the search for the historical Jesus "leads to the door of the church."

In the case of the "Jesus question," there is no point at which the theological imagination does not shape the subject matter. Love comes before the chair, feelings and impressions before the "facts" have been put into place, and interpretation before detail. No matter what element of the Jesus tradition comes first, that element—as scholars for the most part today are willing to acknowledge—comes to us as an act in a religious drama, not as a scene in an ordinary life. Indeed, nothing is more unsupported by the sources than the standard liberal critical perspective that Jesus' death was unexpected, the Gospels an attempt to theologize away the embarrassment of the early church, and the residual parts of the tradition developed "backward" from the seminal moment—the catastrophe—of his mission. This "trauma theory" of Christian origins presumes a real death and the reactions of real persons who would have had religious and perhaps psychological or political reasons to conceal the failure of their leader or the disappointment of their hopes. But there is nothing in the tradition that requires a real death and very little apart from a few literary flourishes in Luke 24:21 that convey disappointment. Is it not just as plausible that the Passion narrative is a drama based on the binding of Isaac, whose death was equally "unexpected," but not in any historical sense? The need—the love—for this historical Jesus as a cipher or a principle of explanation is seductive, but in fact it is a very poor way of doing history. It does not give us a chair.

Flatly put, the Jesus tradition was ab origine either the story of the death and resurrection of a historical individual called Jesus, or it was belief in the story of a dying and rising god that caused a story to emerge, fleshed out in historical detail in the sources we call Gospels. Either way, it was belief in his extraordinary triumph over death and not the facts of his life that saved Jesus from obscurity. Either way, the movement from the "ordinary" to the "extraordinary" upon which the Jesus-to-Christ model depends is implausible.

There is simply no evidence that the early Christians were concerned about "whether" Jesus had really lived and died. They became Christians because of the Gospel, and the Gospel was a summary of "things believed" by the brethren. If there is one cold, hard, unavoidable historical datum that virtually everyone who studies the New Testament can agree on, it is that the early Christian community came into existence because of the preaching of the Gospel. The pluralized form of that datum in the form of written Gospels is the literary artifact of what they believed, not a factual record of events that transpired prior to the framing of the oral message. It may well be true that the beliefs of these communities were as varied as colored buttons for more than a century. But the Jesus they "proclaimed" (a good first-century verb) was part of a story, not a doctrine—a story they believed to be true. You can't go very far into the second century without seeing the story becoming clouded with doctrine and definition, however.

The church fathers and the Gnostics were really two sides of the same obscurantist process: the Gnostics needed a Jesus whose humanity was transparent or unreal, the church fathers needed a Jesus whose humanity was real but disposable. It is not surprising that the disposable won out over the unreal.

The Resurrection stories, as they lengthened, seemed to suggest that a kind of transformation took place in the hiatus between death and being raised from the dead. In other words, the historical (human) Jesus who rose from the dead won out over the Gnostic Jesus who does not, not because the Gnostic story is fabulous but because the familiar story was human—grounded in history. Paul seems to have caught on to the market value of this fact very early (1 Cor 15:4–8).

At any rate, if the question is asked why the story of Jesus needed to be historicized at all, the answer lay in the appeal of Paul's suggestion that Jesus Christ was crucified and died and was raised from the dead. That is enough to form the core of the tradition to which all other "historical" data are attached. It also to a large extent explains the democratic success of the Christian missionary preaching: Jesus and his followers were "ordinary"—the "yokels, slaves, and fishermen" of society, as they continued to be known from the time of Celsus down to the time of Julian the "apostate." They were not the elite (spiritual or moral) of Gnostic concern. What would become the orthodox Jesus, for all the shortcomings Christian belief would eventually embed in the church they attributed to his actions, was real, imitable, attractive. The Gnostic Jesus was austere and obscure: he spoke sentences that did not parse to followers whose teachings were barely comprehensible about rewards that were completely uncertain. The reality of Jesus is the reality of a historicized, rather than a historical Jesus, but one whose attraction was fundamentally linked to his this-worldly interests and existence as it was preached by his followers in language many seem to have found appealing.

HUMANITY AND HISTORICITY

The reality of Jesus is not important in the same way that a Roman emperor's existence is important—that is, as a simple *causa prius* to his being declared divine, or (for example) as a way of averaging human and divine qualities, as the ancient world was fond of doing with demigods and heroes. We tend to forget that men of the fourth century, confronted with defining the humanity of Jesus, still had the images and stories of Achilles, Dionysus, and Heracles in view. It was not, in any sense, a thoroughly Christian world, but a world still infused with the seductive images of demigods and their courtesans—the same world whose attractions Clement had anguished over a hundred years before Nicaea. Saving the savior from that kind of emulsion prompted some of the more intricate doctrines of the early period. The Jesus whose historicization had been a necessity in the missionary period had become a liability before the end of the second century, as the church grew more confident and demographically more stable: the image of a simple founder (or even as in the fourth Gospel a partly degnosticized one) was simply inconvenient. It was imperative for Jesus to be human, in the strict sense; but his historical portrait in the Gospels needed theology to help it along.

The preservation of the humanity of Jesus came at the expense of his historicity. In making sure he would not be confused with Caesar, Apollo, or Mithras, theologians focused on the *way* in which he was God and *how* God became man. At the end of the makeover, however, no first-century Jew remained to be seen. Even a spirit-struck Pentecostal preacher who has only the dimmest idea of what Chalcedon was all about calls on a "Jesus" who was born there—a man-god who can walk on water, heal the blind, and save from sin not because he is a healer or magician but because he is divine, God in the flesh.

The historical Jesus is important because he is a presupposition for the faith that millions of people have placed in nonhistorical consequences, and not only Christians. His status, if primarily significant to Christians, is also important, in different ways, to Jews, Muslims, and even unbelievers. Whether or not he really lived may not make much difference to believers, and may not be much good to nonbelievers whose interest in the question may be malignant or trivial. But in any case, I do not believe it is a question that will ever be answered.

The reality of Jesus comprises a range of questions that can no longer be resolved on the basis of the sources we possess, and anyone who thinks differently is either looking at other sources or is not especially good at reading the ones we have. Pending the discovery of authentically new sources—the "real" Nazareth, the "authentic" tomb of Jesus, a Roman report of his death—the recovery of Jesus after two thousand years of theological repair is impossible.

John Henry Newman died in 1890. He was buried in a wooden coffin in a damp site just outside Birmingham. To the disappointment of many, when he was exhumed as part of the normal process for canonization in October 2008, no human remains were to be found—only artifacts of wood, brass, and cloth. He was not reported missing. Despite a certain personal charm and a sizeable following, he was not pronounced risen from the grave. Had several of these followers pronounced him risen, others would have thought them mad. He had celebrated Mass on Christmas Day in 1899. He had died at the Birmingham Oratory, of pneumonia. He was buried in the grave of his lifelong friend, Ambrose St. John. Previously, they had shared a house. The pall over the coffin bore his cardinal's motto *Cor ad cor loquitur* (Heart speaks to heart). Inseparable in death as in life, a joint memorial stone was erected for the two men; the inscription bore words Newman had chosen: *Ex umbris et imaginibus in veritatem* (Out of shadows and phantasms into the truth).

Interpret his exit as you will, his disappearance was not miraculous.

We are considerably better off, of course, in the case of Newman. The grave site was known, and we have letters, diaries, treatises, biographies, the memories of friends and relatives—even his own instructions for burial. But that is because he was a man living in an age of documentation and moreover a man of some prominence and means. We have photographs, and well into the twentieth century, the recollections of people who had known him, corresponded with him, or heard him preach.

Everything we think we know historically about Jesus points in a more depressing direction: a man of no prominence, living in a widely illiterate age in a backward province even by Roman standards, with few friends who could have told his story. Yet the story is oddly similar—a remembrance of a life, wisdom, preaching, struggle, and death. One of the priests of the Birmingham Oratory, on being told that Newman was not to be found in his grave, replied calmly, "It's enough that he was here."

In the case of Jesus of Nazareth, we cannot say even that much.

ASSESSING THE EVIDENCE
Philosophical and Legal Perspectives

Ronald A. Lindsay

A general observation: before beginning any undertaking, it is usually useful to have not only a goal in mind, but at least a rough idea of the means of reaching that goal. It is reassuring to know that the first formal meeting of the Jesus Project is devoted to the critical issue of methodology, and in particular an evaluation of what constitutes evidence relevant to the Jesus tradition.

One may think it is presumptuous, if not arrogant, for someone who is a lawyer and philosopher to be discussing issues of evidence with specialists in religious studies. But precisely because I am a lawyer and philosopher, presumption and arrogance are expected of me and I do not want to disappoint.

In any event, law and philosophy do have something to contribute to the evidentiary questions being considered. Let us begin with the law. The law reminds us that evidence should not be confused with fact. There are many facts that would not be considered by the decision maker in a trial, whether a judge or jury, because the law deems them irrelevant. The fact that someone is wearing a yellow shirt at the time an agreement is executed may suggest that person has an underdeveloped aesthetic sensibility, but it is not germane to the question of whether the person has entered into a binding contract. Evidence represents facts that the law has determined are probative of whether an event with legal implications has occurred.

Here we immediately see one difference between the law and studies focusing on the historicity of Jesus. There are no generally accepted authoritative standards on what constitutes material evidence on the question of whether Jesus of Nazareth existed. (And, as religious scholars are aware, some would even dispute the existence of Nazareth itself.) Of course, scholars associated with the Jesus Project may attempt to develop standards that will help determine what constitutes such evidence. To say this represents a daunting challenge would be an understatement—one is tempted to say an understatement of biblical proportions.

In addition to this fundamental problem of the lack of generally accepted standards for what constitutes material evidence on the Jesus question, there is the not insignificant problem that arguably none of the assertions about Jesus that some regard as embodying factual claims would constitute legal evidence of his existence, even under the most expansive definitions of relevance. We need to consider where these factual claims are to be found. They are found in various documents, and none of the documents usually mined for information about Jesus, such as the various Gospels and Epistles and the works of Josephus, would be readily accepted as evidence in a court of law. Insofar as they attest to the existence of some sort of religious, cultural, or political leader called Jesus, they are all hearsay. The authors of the documents are not available for questioning, and, for the most part, we cannot look outside the documents themselves to determine the factual foundation, if any, for their assertions.

Some who have knowledge of the rules of evidence may protest that there is an "ancient documents" exception to the rule against hearsay. Indeed, there is a whole school of so-called juridical apologists going back to Simon Greenleaf (1874),[1] one of the founders of Harvard Law School, who have argued that the Gospels and other ancient documents referencing Jesus constitute admissible evidence concerning not only the existence of Jesus but of the events that transpired during Jesus' life—and death.[2] Ancient documents—which under the law in most Anglo-American jurisdictions are simply any documents more than thirty years old—are sometimes admitted into evidence. Typically, such documents are newspapers, deeds, or other contemporaneous records of the events they report. But a necessary precondition for their admission into evidence is that there is no suspicion concerning their authenticity. In other words, if a document purports to be the identification card of a member of the Ukrainian Police circa 1943, then before it is admitted into evidence, that document has to be established conclusively as authentic.[3]

To put it mildly, the authenticity of the documents that refer to Jesus is open to question. Among other problems, none of them qualify as contemporaneous records created by a person or persons with direct knowledge of the reported facts, and no proper chain of custody has been established for these documents. Indeed, there is no dispute that in most cases we do not have access to the original documents. What we have instead are copies of copies.

Furthermore, authenticity is one thing and reliability is another. You may possess a document that appears to be authentic that, nonetheless, is rejected as evidence that certain events took place because the document was not created by a disinterested person or is otherwise clouded with uncertainty or improbability. We may have an authentic document that is the original of a writing by Joseph Smith (the founder of Mormonism) in which Smith declares he was visited by Jesus, but this document would not be accepted by a court as proof that Jesus visited Smith. Authentic ancient documents are accepted as evidence only when they have indicia of reliability. Among those indicia is the fact that they were *not* created principally to help establish the truth of the claim currently being contested. An ID card for a Ukrainian policeman was created to show he was a Ukrainian policeman, not to show that the person who was a Ukrainian policeman in 1943 subsequently lied about that fact in order to gain illegal entry to the United States, and therefore, as the court of appeals ruled in *United States v. Koziy*, 728 F.2d 1314 (11th Cir. 1984), if established as authentic, the ID card should be admitted into evidence in the context of a deportation proceeding. Similarly, as the trial court found in *Fulmer v. Connors*, 665 F.Supp. 1472 (N.D. Ala. 1987), a payroll record from 1940 that indicates that Mr. X worked for a coal company should be admitted into evidence in a lawsuit by his widow, Ms. X, seeking retirement benefits in 1990 because the payroll record was not created with the intent of influencing the outcome of litigation over a pension that takes place more than fifty years in the future.

The only document referencing Jesus written anywhere near the time that Jesus allegedly lived that arguably was written for a purpose other than advocacy on behalf of Jesus are the histories of Josephus, but most scholars contend that the key passage in Josephus that refers to

Jesus is, in large part, an interpolation.[4] Accordingly, its reliability is in serious doubt.

Of course, there are numerous Gospels and Epistles referencing Jesus, but these documents are quite clearly not designed to be dispassionate biographies of Jesus, reporting to us the various details of his life. To the extent they serve any purpose other than telling an interesting story, they advocate—they attempt to persuade. Is there an analogue for such documents in the courtroom? Yes, as a matter of fact there is, but it is an analogue that suggests the Gospels and Epistles should not be regarded as evidence. The Gospels and Epistles are analogous to lawyers' arguments, and anyone who has ever been a juror—and actually paid attention to the instructions given by the court—will recall that the judge instructed the jurors that the lawyers' arguments are not evidence. They are attempts to characterize the evidence to their clients' advantage.

So what we have, at best, in the Gospels and Epistles might be characterized as the equivalent of lawyers' arguments. But in reality we do not even have that limited degree of reliability. First, it is doubtful that the Gospels represent the work of one author or even a committee of advocates. Instead, they represent a compilation of orally transmitted advocacy that likely had many contributors over extended periods of time. Moreover, the constraints that one normally finds placed on a lawyer's argument—namely, the fact that a lawyer cannot stretch or obscure the evidence too much, because the jury has just listened to the evidence, opposing counsel will point out any inconsistencies or fabrications, and the court may sanction counsel for remarks that are too tendentious or inflammatory—are entirely absent in the context of the Gospels. There was no penalty that we know of—at least initially—for those who contributed to the Gospels if they stretched the facts to persuade their audience of their story.

And what was their story? What were they trying to establish? This is yet another significant way in which the various Gospels differ from a lawyer's argument. When parties go to court, there is agreement at least on this much: there is a certain critical set of facts that need to be proved. For example, was there an offer and acceptance sufficient to create a contract? Did the employer's agent engage in sexually harassing conduct that was so pervasive and offensive that a reasonable person would conclude that a hostile work environment was created? Lawyers' arguments focus on a limited, circumscribed, judicially defined set of transactions and occurrences. But with the three dozen or so Gospels relating to Jesus, there is no consensus regarding what facts the Gospels are designed to establish. We have known now for some time that even the limited consensus exemplified by the synoptic Gospels is illusory—an illusion created by the suppression, ignorance of, or disappearance of other Gospels, such as the Gospel of Thomas or the Gospel of Judas, which advocate for quite a different Jesus than one finds portrayed in the synoptic Gospels. Effectively, we are presented with something resembling a collection of attorney's arguments from different and distinct cases that share a reference to a character named Jesus.

Is this shared reference to a character named Jesus at least sufficient to establish that there was a person who existed in what is now known as Israel or Palestine in the early years of the Common Era who was a leader and had a following of some sort? Before answering that question, we need to turn to philosophy.

In his *Philosophical Investigations*, Ludwig Wittgenstein offered some observations about the historicity of Moses. He remarked:

> Consider this example. If one says "Moses did not exist," this may mean several things. It may mean the Israelites did not have a *single* leader when they withdrew from Egypt—or: that their leader was not called Moses—or: there cannot have been anyone who accomplished all that the Bible relates of Moses—or: etc. etc. We may say, following Russell, the name Moses can be defined by means of various descriptions. For example, as "the man who led the Israelites through the wilderness," "the man who lived at that time and place and was called 'Moses,'" "the man who as a child was taken out of the Nile by the Pharaoh's daughter" and so on....
>
> But when I make a statement about Moses—am I always ready to substitute some *one* of these descriptions for "Moses"? I shall perhaps say: By "Moses" I understand the man who did what the Bible relates of Moses, or at any rate a good deal of it. But how much? Have I decided how much must be proved false for me to give up my proposition as false? Has the name "Moses" got a fixed and unequivocal use for me in all possible cases?[5]

We need to ask the same questions about Jesus that Wittgenstein posed about Moses. Wittgenstein's observations about Moses are, I submit, a little-appreciated reminder of the daunting difficulties facing any project that seeks to resolve the question whether a person with the legendary dimensions of someone such as Jesus actually existed. Wittgenstein's comments persuasively suggest that before we even arrive at the stage of trying to evaluate the evidence that might be relevant to the historicity of Jesus, we must first try to answer the question: what does it mean to say Jesus existed?

To help illustrate just one aspect of these difficulties, please consider the following statements:

1. The Gospel of Matthew says mostly false things about Jesus.
2. Many of the events related in the Gospel of Matthew did happen, but the deeds attributed to Jesus were actually performed by someone named Irving; the stories in the Gospel of Matthew simply accreted around Jesus through a mistake in transmission of the oral history.
3. Jesus never existed.

What is the difference in meaning among these statements? One might contend that there is a significant difference between Statement 1 and Statement 2 because Statement 2 indicates that the events most Christians care about did occur; they were "just" mistakenly attributed to Jesus instead of Irving. Discovery of such a fact would unsettle many, and necessitate a less than felicitous rewriting of our hymn books ("What a friend we have in Irving" simply does not seem as euphonious), but the critical transactions and occurrences related in the Gospels and Epistles would still be understood to be referring to *someone*.

But what about Statement 1 and Statement 3? Any difference? If 98 percent of the assertions about Jesus in the Gospel of Matthew are not accurate, is a statement to that effect substantively any different in meaning than a statement that Jesus never existed? For example, let us assume that the accurate statements in Matthew are that there was a person known as Jesus who was born in Galilee during the reign of Herod; that when he was an adult, this Jesus traveled about and had some unkind words to say about the Pharisees and Sadducees; that some persons liked what this fellow Jesus said; and that this Jesus suggested using a prayer such as the "Our Father." Everything else in Matthew is false. What is the difference then between making that assertion and saying that Jesus never existed?

Before answering this question, let us consider another figure of legendary dimensions, but someone in whom not as much emotion or metaphysical significance is invested. Let us consider Agamemnon. Specifically, let us consider these statements about Agamemnon:

1. The *Iliad* says mostly false things about Agamemnon.
2. Many of the events related in the *Iliad* did happen, but the deeds attributed to Agamemnon were actually performed by someone named Irving; the stories in the *Iliad* simply accreted around Agamemnon through a mistake in the transmission of the oral history.
3. Agamemnon never existed.

How much of what is set forth in the *Iliad* must be false before we are willing to assent to Statement 3? Does it matter if most of the events happened, but we have "Agamemnon's" name wrong? As indicated above, presumably not. But does it matter if there was no Achilles or no dispute over Briseis? Does it matter if there was no Menelaus or Helen? No Odysseus, Paris, Priam, or Hector? What is the essential core set of facts associated with Agamemnon? Is there such an essential core set of facts? If a coalition of armed forces from what we now call the Peloponnesus was led by a ruler of Mycenae and attacked a city or cities in northwest Asia Minor in the period somewhere between 1400 and 1200 BCE, is that sufficient to warrant the assertion that Agamemnon existed, but most of what the *Iliad* says about him and the Trojan War is false?

There is, of course, one major difference between questions regarding the existence of Agamemnon and questions regarding the existence of Jesus, and that is, despite the interest in and curiosity about the Trojan War and other possibly historical events alluded to in the *Iliad*, the *Aeneid*, and other works of classical literature, it ultimately matters little to us today whether there was an Agamemnon similar to the figure portrayed in the *Iliad*. Granted, investigations into the historical accuracy of the *Iliad* make for interesting archeological expeditions and related television specials on the Discovery Channel, but nothing much turns on the findings of those investigations. One's worldview, one's religious and ethical beliefs, are not dependent on whether someone similar to the Agamemnon of the *Iliad* existed. However, given the influence that Christianity has exerted throughout the course of history and continues to exert today, the question whether Jesus existed is of profound significance.

This critical difference between the significance of the historicity of Jesus and the significance of the historicity of Agamemnon suggests one way to specify more precisely what we mean to say when we claim "Jesus existed" or "Jesus did not exist." At this juncture, I must perform a necessary philosophical task and discuss briefly Saul Kripke's theory of rigid designation, also known as the theory of direct reference. Implicit in the foregoing discussion of the meaning of "Jesus" or "Agamemnon" is the thesis that there are certain descriptions associated with a particular individual. In other words, by "Agamemnon" we may mean to refer to the ruler who led a coalition of forces against a city-state in northwest Asia Minor circa 1300 BCE. Saul Kripke rejects the notion that there is descriptive content conveyed by a name, or to be more precise, a directly referring expression.[6] The intuition behind Kripke's position is that it is always possible that some event we associate with a person may not have happened. For example, Richard Nixon might not have won the 1968 presidential election; he might not have authorized the Watergate break-in; he might not have resigned the presidency. Our world is composed of contingencies. It is always possible that a certain event might not happen. Furthermore, and more important, whether a particular event happened does not affect the identity of individuals. Although it is true that Richard Nixon won the 1968 presidential election, Richard Nixon still would have been Richard Nixon had he lost the election. It is possible that those in attendance at the inaugural meeting of the Jesus Project might have decided not to attend—they would have missed a great program, but that decision would not have affected their personal identity.

For Kripke, the semantic content of the name that designates an individual is nothing more than the referent himself or herself. The name of an individual is a so-called rigid designator and it refers to that individual in all possible worlds—worlds, for example, in which Hubert Humphrey and not Richard Nixon won the 1968 election.

Evaluating Kripke's theory properly would require much discussion of transworld semantics, modal logic, and other abstruse metaphysical matters. Fortunately, for my purposes, we can be spared that discussion. I have referenced Kripke's theory only for the sake of philosophical completeness and to reassure the philosophically minded that in my discussions of the meaning of "Jesus" I am not overlooking an alternative way to understand the referents of names.

Whatever the validity of Kripke's theory in general, for figures with such critical significance as Jesus, there are certain essential descriptions that must be associated with that individual—*if* that individual is to retain his or her critical significance. For most individuals, it may be a metaphysical truth that no set of descriptions is necessarily associated with that individual, but for Jesus and some other extraordinary personages, either some descriptions must be associated with that individual or, for all intents and purposes, we might as well say this particular person never existed.

What set of facts must be true before we are prepared to give assent to the claim "Jesus never existed," or give assent to the claim "Jesus existed"? Permit me to suggest that arriving at a consensus on the key set of facts relevant to such claims is an indispensable part of any investigation of the historicity of Jesus. Concluding that some isolated assertions in the Gospels or Epistles are likely true, or likely false, will not help us in addressing the fundamental question. Do not confuse the trees with the forest. Moreover, arriving at this consensus fairly early in the process is important if an investigation is to achieve any credibility. Determining at the end of my inquiry into the historical evidence that certain facts are required to support the claim that Jesus existed risks branding the investigation as disingenuous, one designed to arrive at a predetermined conclusion.

To illustrate my point, let us assume that we have fairly firm evidence that there were no synagogues in Galilee during the time Jesus supposedly lived and, therefore, the statements in Matthew that Jesus

taught in the synagogues of Galilee is false (Mt 4:23). Can we then conclude that Jesus did not exist? Why? Why is the assertion that Jesus
taught in the synagogues of Galilee essential to the fundamental question of Jesus' existence? Obviously, it will not withstand intellectual
scrutiny to argue that if some of the assertions in the canonical Gospels
are false, they must all be false. Those who believe in biblical inerrancy
may be disturbed by evidence that some of the assertions in those
Gospels cannot be true, but an objective investigation of the Jesus question does not establish its credibility or importance by undercutting
Christian fundamentalists. Proof that there were no synagogues in
Galilee at the time Jesus is said to have lived is significant to the question whether Jesus existed *only* if we have previously established the
critical importance of this fact—but the task of sorting out essential
from nonessential descriptive statements is a task that remains to be
performed.

The importance of establishing what descriptions are essential to
Jesus may be shown by considering another figure of historical importance, but someone who, unlike Agamemnon, most believe actually
existed, namely, Socrates. Consider that no one regards Plato's dia-
logues as providing us with a verbatim transcript of the exchanges
between Socrates and his various interlocutors. Moreover, it is doubtful
whether Socrates actually had exchanges with some of the historical
figures around which Plato structured several of his works, such as Pro-
tagoras. In addition, the extant sources of information we have for
Socrates are relatively few in number, being effectively four, that is,
Plato, Aristophanes, Xenophon, and Aristotle.[7] One of these, Aristophanes, is explicitly fictional in nature. Indeed, given the paucity of
information about Socrates, some who have been fairly rigorous in their
assessment of the evidence for Jesus have speculated that we have
better historical support for Jesus than we do for Socrates.[8] Finally, the
character and interests of Socrates as found in Xenophon differ in various ways from the character and interests of Socrates as found in Plato.

Nonetheless, few, if any, doubt that Socrates actually existed, that
he was a person interested in moral questions, that he was a gadfly or a
crank (depending on one's perspective) and that he was condemned to
death. Moreover, we accept this even though, as indicated, the contem-

porary documents referring to Socrates are very few in number. One reason we accept the historical existence of Socrates is that there is some consensus about what the statement "Socrates existed" implies. It is, I submit, an essential part of the meaning of "Socrates" that this name is understood as referring to a person who lived in Athens in the fifth century BCE who had an interest in discussing ethical issues with others and who was condemned to death as a result of what he was accused of saying. And, with the exception of Aristophanes, what sources we do have seem reliable, in part, because they are in agreement on these core assertions. (It also helps, of course, that there is some record of the indictment against Socrates apart from the usual sources for his life—although the reliability of this evidence is not immune from dispute.)[9]

Is there a similar set of descriptive statements that constitute an essential part of the meaning of "Jesus"? I hope so, because otherwise it is difficult to understand how an inquiry into the historicity of Jesus will result in an intellectually defensible conclusion.

But don't look to me to provide you with the definitive set of descriptions essential to Jesus. My obligation as a philosopher was to present questions and difficulties, not to resolve them. And I have discharged that duty.

PAUL AS A WITNESS TO THE HISTORICAL JESUS

Gerd Lüdemann

INTRODUCTION

Paul of Tarsus is often hailed as one of the foremost disciples of Jesus of Nazareth, but such a claim is beset with historical difficulties. For one thing, Paul did not know Jesus personally; for another, Paul never calls himself a disciple of Jesus. Furthermore, Paul's theology, together with its theological, anthropological, and soteriological ideas, in no way represents a recapitulation of Jesus' preaching nor even a further development of it. It is especially significant that the apostle never adduces any of Jesus' citations of the Torah in support of his own teaching about it. In addition, the "Reign of God," a concept central to Jesus' message, is at best marginal for Paul. Conversely, Paul's repeated emphasis on "the righteousness of God" as a main thing of salvation has no parallel in Jesus' teaching. For Paul, God's righteousness is revealed in the Gospel "through faith for faith" (Rom 1:17).

It comes, therefore, as no surprise that according to some, Paul founded a new religion centered on the cult of Christ, one that has little in common with the religion of Jesus' disciples in Jerusalem and Galilee. This view, however, minimizes the fact that Paul considered the Christ who appeared to him near Damascus to be the same person as the Jesus who had appeared to Cephas and the Twelve and other members of the Jerusalem community. No doubt it was for this reason that three years after his conversion, Paul went to Jerusalem to visit Cephas. The reason was not to talk about the weather, as C. H. Dodd once quipped, but to seek assurance that "his" Christ could be identified with "their" Jesus.

Be that as it may, we find a clear disparity between the Jesus revealed by historical study and the Christ proclaimed by faith. A troublesome question therefore arises: Can Paul, whose seven genuine letters are likely the oldest Christian documents, serve as a reliable witness to the historical Jesus? Before we address that question, two definitions are overdue and a few ancillary questions need to be answered.

As for the definitions, a distinction has to be made between the historical Jesus and the earthly Jesus. The phrase "historical Jesus" is to be understood as the result of scholarly study of the Jesus texts, whereas the phrase "earthly Jesus" is to be understood as the birth, life, and death of Jesus. In light of these definitions, it makes no sense to speak of Paul's, Matthew's, Mark's, Luke's, or John's view of the historical Jesus. Rather, we should speak of their view of the earthly Jesus.

As for the ancillary questions, we first need to determine in what way Paul was concerned with the earthly Jesus. Of course, in order to answer this question, we must ask another: what did Paul mean when he identified Jesus as "Christ"? Furthermore, yet another question necessarily follows: what traditions about Jesus, if any, did Paul use in his letters and during his missionary activity?

After dealing with those questions we will have to present a systematic evaluation of Paul's relation to Jesus. Last but not least, we shall turn to our main question: does the evidence in Paul's letters show him to have been a reliable witness to the historical Jesus?

THE RISEN JESUS IS THE EARTHLY JESUS

For Paul, the "Risen Christ" was of primary, indeed overwhelming, importance. Paul was convinced that Christ had appeared to him near Damascus and called him to be an apostle. Moreover, Christ was present in the community of the saints who confessed him to be Lord, and would one day return on the clouds of heaven to establish his rule. Though when confessing Christ as the Lord, Paul is thinking in the first place of the Resurrected One, nevertheless he repeatedly uses this same title when speaking of Jesus between his birth and death. The following passages will serve to illustrate this:

To the married I give this ruling, not I but the Lord, that the wife must not separate from her husband ... and that the husband must not divorce his wife. (1 Cor 7:10–11)

The Lord gave charge for those who proclaim the gospel, that they should live by the gospel. (1 Cor 9:14)

The Lord Jesus on the night he was handed over took bread.... (1 Cor 11:23)

[The Jews] who killed the Lord Jesus and the prophets... (1 Thes 2:15)

God has raised the Lord and will also raise us. (1 Cor 6:14)

The cross of our Lord Jesus. (Gal 6:14)

the brothers of the Lord / ... James, the Lord's brother. (1 Cor 9:5 / Gal 1:19)

For you know the grace of our Lord Jesus Christ, that he, being rich, yet for your sakes became poor. (2 Cor 8:9)

Therefore one must conclude that in speaking of "God's Son, Christ Jesus whom we proclaimed among you" (2 Cor 1:19), Paul refers to both the man Jesus *and* the Risen Lord. One might go so far as to say that he repeatedly conflates the two. Clearly, the Jesus of Paul's proclamation included his human existence, his work, and his message. This is beyond any doubt when we consider Paul's emphasis on the birth of God's son (cf. Gal 4:4: "But when the time had fully come, God sent forth his Son, born of a woman, born under the law") and the heavenly preexistence of the divine son who was born of woman (see the below text from Philippians). Incidentally, it is worth noting that Gal 4:4 seems to exclude Paul's knowledge of the virgin birth tradition.

In referring to Jesus as "Lord," Paul has taken a title belonging to the Resurrected One and assigned it retroactively to the earthly Jesus, and then to the Preexistent One. And yet it was important to Paul that Jesus was born a Jew (Rom 1:3, 15:8) and lived under the Law (Gal 3:1).

This characteristic Pauline merger of personae is indisputable evidence that when Paul speaks of the Resurrected Lord, the man Jesus is at the same time in his mind, and that for Paul, the man Jesus and the preexistent and risen Lord are one and the same.

When the apostle uses Jesus as an example or refers to him as someone to emulate, he thinks of both the preexistent *and* the earthly Jesus (cf. Rom 15:2–3; 1 Cor 11:1; 2 Cor 8:9, 10:1; 1 Thes 1:6) who serves as the main figure in a cosmic drama. His sonship is to be seen in his obedient fulfillment of God's will. Jesus' obedience is the key quality adduced in the early hymn Paul records in Philippians 2:6–11, specifically in verses 7–8:

> [He] emptied himself, taking the form of a servant, being born in human likeness. And being found in human form he humbled himself and became obedient unto death, even unto death on the cross.

Even more striking, the apostle contrasts Jesus' obedience with Adam's disobedience:

> As through the disobedience of the one man the many were made sinners, so through obedience of the one the many will be made righteous. (Rom 5:19)

THE PROBLEM OF 2 CORINTHIANS 5:16

In view of these facts, it is strange that some have drawn the conclusion that the earthly Jesus was of no significance for Paul. They have amplified this by citing the statement in 2 Corinthians 5:16:

> Henceforth we know no one according to the flesh; if indeed we had known Christ according to the flesh, we no longer know him thus.

But this is clearly a misconstrual and a misapplication of 2 Cor 5:16, for here Paul is not denying interest in the earthly Jesus. He is not talking about "Christ in the flesh," but about knowing Christ "from a human point of view" (RSV). What Paul rejects is a this-worldly relation to Jesus. In short, while Paul is far from a systematic biographer, it is incorrect to say that the earthly Jesus did not matter to him.

As noted above, Paul seldom cites Jesus; but he occasionally alludes to sayings of Jesus or so attributes injunctions to him. This is eminently understandable when we recognize that while he presents Jesus as the authority (cf. 1 Cor 7:10), Paul can always claim for himself, as one commissioned by Christ, the mantle of present authority. Note, for example, 1 Cor 7:40: "But I think that I have the spirit of God."

DEATH AND RESURRECTION OF JESUS AS THE MAIN FOCUS IN PAUL

In short, Paul appeals to Jesus' life and teachings when doing so suits his agenda, but the unchanging focus of his proclamation is Jesus' death and Resurrection. For it is only through these that sin and death have been conquered, and God's plan of salvation at last actualized (Rom 8:3; cf. Col 1:22; 2:14–15). Herein rests the dynamic appeal of Paul's message, and hence he can unequivocally pronounce the crucified Christ as the essence of his Gospel: "But we preach Christ crucified, a stumbling block to Jews and folly to Gentiles" (1 Cor 1:23); "You foolish Galatians ...before whose eyes Jesus Christ has been proclaimed as crucified" (Gal 3:1). Since this now exalted man is of central importance to the apostle's proclamation, it seems strange indeed that the Epistles so seldom make reference to his life and teachings.

THE EXTENT AND THE ROLE OF JESUS' SAYINGS IN PAUL

Having concluded that Jesus' earthly ministry did figure into Paul's formulation of Christianity, we must, in keeping with our task description, determine the extent and the role of Jesus' teachings in Paul's thinking. I want to propose that the *first* step should be to analyze and evaluate those passages in which Paul explicitly refers to sayings of Jesus. In these, at any rate, there is a reasonable likelihood that Paul is quoting a saying that came down to him in the tradition as a word of the Lord. But then in a *second* step we should examine the possibility that the letters might contain allusions to or echoes of Jesus' sayings.

References to Sayings of Jesus

> To the married I give this ruling, not I but the Lord, that the wife must not separate from her husband, but if she does, let her remain single or else be reconciled to her husband, and that the husband must not divorce his wife. (1 Cor 7:10–11)

The prohibition of divorce has parallels in Mark 10:1–12 and Q (Mt 5:32/Lk 16:18). Note, however, that the earliest stratum of the tradition is reflected by Q, where only the husband's right to divorce his wife is presupposed. In both Mark and Paul, the wife has the right to initiate a divorce, a provision clearly derived from Greco-Roman law. And not only that, but Paul's is the earlier mention of this case; obviously, he has met women in his communities who availed themselves of a right familiar to their culture. In other words, although Paul quotes the Lord, the historical Jesus cannot possibly have spoken the words attributed to him because he had said nothing about women initiating a separation. Either Paul's prescription is a developed form of the saying or he has applied an earlier, less-developed saying to the situation in Corinth. The same can be said for the first evangelist, who in Matthew 5:32 (cf. Mt 19:9) uses the Q saying on divorce but, no doubt because of cases of fornication in his community, has Jesus allow divorce in such instances.

> The Lord ordered that those who proclaim the gospel earn their living by the gospel. (1 Cor 9:14)

Paul refers to the Lord here because he wants to build up a strong case for the support of missionaries even though it is a perquisite he personally renounces. So far is he from adopting these "words of the Lord" as a new tradition applying to himself that he had on purpose not accepted any support from the Corinthians. In 1 Corinthians 9 he adduces the following points in asserting the missionary's right to support: reason and common experience (verse 7), the Old Testament (verse 9), universal religious practice (verse 13), and the teaching of Jesus himself (verse 14). All these support the custom by which apostles and other ministers are maintained at the expense of the church built up by their ministry.

The saying suggests that Paul has in mind the one contained in Q: "the laborer deserves his food/his wages" (Mt 10:10/Lk 10:7). It presupposes a fully developed missionary movement and seems to be a group invention.

> For I received from the Lord what I also delivered to you, that the Lord Jesus on the night when he was handed over took bread, and when he had given thanks, he broke it, and said, "*This is my body which is for you. Do this in remembrance of me.*" In the same way he also took the cup, after supper, saying, "*This cup is the new covenant in my blood. Do this, as often as you drink it, in remembrance of me.*" (1 Cor 11:23–25)

One feature of worship service in the Greek-speaking community persecuted by Paul is certain: its focal point was the Lord's Supper, which was an integral part of the church's common meal. This was one reason for the severity of the crisis at Antioch, for when Jewish Christians withdrew from the common table, they left the communion table as well (Gal 2:11–13).

The name *Lord's Supper* has its single explicit New Testament attestation in Paul (1 Cor 11:20: *kyriakon deipnon*), a text probably written in the year 51. The name is clearly pre-Pauline, and like the later attested name *Lord's Day* (Rev 1:10) reflects a Christian communal concern, the cult of Christ.

The communion ritual that Paul originally taught the Corinthians —which he himself had received—appears in the tradition he passed on in 1 Corinthians 11:23–25. Note, however, that he claims to have received it from the Lord (verse 23). Yet, this can hardly mean that we are dealing here with a word of Jesus taken from a narrative nor that Paul heard these sentences spoken to him directly by the heavenly Jesus, for the apostle here employs the same terms that he uses in 1 Corinthians 15:3 (received–delivered). These were the same words Jewish scribes used to designate the reception and transmission of traditions. The phrase "from the Lord" thus indicates the ultimate source of the communion ritual in which the Lord is present. He himself has established the holy rite of eating and drinking.

The institution of the Lord's Supper as a cult observance occurs not only in 1 Corinthians 11:23–25 but also in Mark 14:22–25, Matthew 26:26–29, and Luke 22:15–20. The Synoptics, though, present the Lord's Supper as a Passover meal. This is an important departure from Paul, who in 1 Corinthians 5:7 accepts the interpretation of Jesus' death as a Passover sacrifice, but excludes that concept from the tradition of the Last Supper. Matthew has essentially taken over Mark's text, and Luke is dependent on Mark and the tradition found in Paul. That means that in order to get to the earliest texts about the Lord's Supper, we must start with Paul.

Paul reiterates the injunction (underlined in the above text) that this rite be performed on a regular basis. A liturgical origin is thus attested, and something more than remembering is indicated: this is a commemoration, an act in which the significance of a vital event of the past becomes a present reality. Indeed, we are dealing here with a foundational account of a sacred rite that derives from the events of the night in which Jesus was handed over, and this etiological legend explains the origin and meaning of a current practice in a community. That it contains or even reflects actual words of Jesus is highly doubtful. Can one seriously imagine a pious Jewish teacher of righteousness inviting his followers to partake, even symbolically, of his flesh and blood?

> If any one thinks himself to be a prophet or spiritual person, let him recognize that what I am writing to you is the command of the Lord [in some manuscripts, "comes from the Lord"]. (1 Cor 14:37)

There can be no doubt that some in Corinth thought themselves to be prophets or spiritual persons. Against their authority Paul insists that he has the mind of Christ and therefore the authority of Christ (cf. 1 Cor 7:25, 40). Thus the injunctions referred to in the above text cannot be taken to represent actual words of Jesus.

> *"My grace is sufficient for you, for my power is made sufficient in weakness."* (2 Cor 12:9)

Paul claims to have received these words directly from the Risen One in the course of an ecstatic experience.

> For not only has the word of the Lord sounded forth from you in Macedonia and Achaia, but your faith in God has gone forth everywhere, so that we need not say anything. (1 Thes 1:8)

Here, of course, the "word of the Lord" does not refer to a saying of Jesus but to the success of Paul's missionary efforts in Thessalonica.

> Jesus said, "*It is more blessed to give than to receive.*" (Acts 20:35)

This purported saying of Jesus is part of Luke's report of Paul's speech at Miletus to the church elders of Ephesus. It has a certain affinity to a Persian maxim reconstructed from Thucydides II, 97,4: "to give rather than receive." Another parallel appears in 1 Clement 2:1, but not as a saying of Jesus.

ALLUSIONS TO SAYINGS OF JESUS

> Bless those who persecute you; bless and do not curse them. (Rom 12:14)

This is a likely echo of Jesus' command in Matthew 5:44: "Love your enemies, and pray for those who persecute you." But Luke 6:27, the Q parallel to Matthew 5:44, shows that Romans 12:14 constitutes a more developed form of Jesus' command. In Luke 6:27 we read simply, "Love your enemies." It appears that Paul must have known a later version of Jesus' command to love one's enemies, a recension that included the reference to persecution like the Matthew version of Q.

> Never pay back evil for evil. (Rom 12:17)

This verse recalls Matthew 5:39: "Do not set yourself against the man who wrongs you." A common Jewish background for both sayings is the most likely explanation.

> Conquer evil with good. (Rom 12:21)

While finding no precise parallel in the synoptic Gospels, we naturally think of Jesus' advocacy of nonresistance (see Mt 5:39–42). Still, the fact of Paul's affinity for this repeated theme hardly justifies seeing this verse as an allusion to Jesus' words. The advice to conquer evil by doing good was a maxim in Judaism.

> Pay all of them their due—taxes to whom taxes are due, revenue to whom revenue is due, respect to whom respect is due, honor to whom honor is due. (Rom 13:7)

This verse bears some resemblance to Mark 12:17: "Give to Caesar what is Caesar's and to God what is God's." Since the second half is absent from Paul, however, a direct relation cannot be claimed.

> Owe nothing to anyone except to love one another; for he who loves another has fulfilled the law. The commandments—You shall not commit adultery, You shall not kill, You shall not steal, You shall not covet, or any other commandment—are summed up in this one: You must love your neighbor as yourself. Love does no wrong to a neighbor; that is why love is the essence of the law. (Rom 13:8–10)

This statement of the central importance of love might be taken as a reprise of Jesus' teaching as reported in the Synoptics (Mk 12:28–34; Mt 22:34–40; Lk 10:25–28). But their two-part commandment is apocopated in Romans 13 (cf. Gal 5:14) to the single injunction to love one's neighbor. To be sure, this does not involve a contradiction, but the difference in form argues against direct derivation from Jesus. Besides, parallels in the rabbinic literature indicate that Romans 13:8–10 is not a demonstrable case of Paul quoting Jesus.

> Why do you judge your brother? (Rom 14:10)

Naturally we hear in this verse an echo of "Do not judge lest you be judged" (Mt 7:1). But here again one can cite a number of parallels from the rabbinic literature. There is, for example, the famous saying of Hillel (early first century CE): "Do not judge your neighbor until you have gotten into his condition." When we note that the same injunction appears in Romans 2:1 and James 4:11, we recognize that it would be much safer to assume that all these passages are variations on a common Jewish theme.

> Let us no longer judge one another, but rather decide never to put a stumbling block or an obstacle in a brother's way. (Rom 14:13)

First of all, note that verse 13 is a clear echo of verse 10 ("Why do you judge your brother?"). Besides, the mere use of the "stumbling block" (*skandalon*), an image or motif that is similarly employed in synoptic sayings (Mk 9:42; Mt 18:7; Lk 17:1–2), is insufficient evidence that Paul here reflects these or similar Jesus traditions. More important, perhaps, the appearance of the symbolic stumbling block in Leviticus 19:14, Isaiah 57:14, and five times in Ezekiel (3:20, 7:19, 14:3, 4, 7) suggests that Paul may be using a much older tradition.

> As one who is in the Lord Jesus, I know and am convinced that nothing is unclean in itself; but it is unclean for any one who considers it unclean. (Rom 14:14)

This, of course, has a familiar ring: "There is nothing outside of a man that can defile him; but the things that come out of a man are what defile him" (Mk 7:15; cf. Mt 15:11). In this passage, however, Paul is dealing with a particular issue involving the Roman community, and the phrase "in the Lord Jesus" is not in any way an attribution, but simply a formula by which he avows his association with the risen Lord as a basis for the correctness of his opinion. The reason for the agreement of Romans 14:14 with Mark 7:15 is uncertain; at any rate, whether this pronouncement of Paul comes from Jesus remains an open question. (See also 1 Cor 8:4 as a possible background of Rom 14:14.)

> Therefore, who ever rejects this (God's call to holiness) rejects not human authority but God. (1 Thes 4:8)

Some try to read into this verse a reference to Luke 10:16: "Whoever hears you hears me, and who ever rejects me rejects the one who has sent me." Unfortunately, their primary evidence, namely, that the two passages contain the same verb, "reject" (*athetein*), is rather shaky support for the notion that Paul, who again and again asserts divinely ordained authority, may have derived the saying from Jesus.

You are yourselves taught by God to love one another. (1 Thes 4:9)

This has no direct synoptic parallel, but some have suggested that it shows a clear though unspecific affinity with the spirit of Jesus that, it is purported, Paul's thinking amply and consistently reflects. This lovely and indeed pious sentiment, however, falls far short of being evidence of derivation from a saying of Jesus.

> But we do not want you to be ignorant, brothers, concerning those who have fallen asleep, that you may not grieve as others who have no hope. For since we believe that Jesus died and rose again, even so, through Jesus, God will bring with him those who have fallen asleep.
> This we say to you in a word of the Lord, that we who are alive, who are left until the Lord's coming, shall by no means precede those who have fallen asleep. For the Lord himself will descend from heaven with a cry of command, with the archangel's call, and with the sound of the trumpet of God. And the dead in Christ will rise first; then we who are alive, who are left, shall be caught up together with them in the clouds to meet the Lord in the air; and so we shall always be with the Lord. (1 Thes 4:13–17)

The view that a saying of the Lord is contained in this section is supported primarily by verse 15 ("For this we say to you in a word of the Lord") which stands as an introduction to verses 15–17. This conclusion is not undisputed. Some contend that verse 15 is not the introduction of a direct quotation, but a reference to Jesus using prophetic modes of discourse (cf. Sir 48:3: "By the word of the Lord he [Elijah] shut up the sky and three times called down fire"). Moreover, it is not clear whether the postulated quotation is to be found in verse 15 or in verses 16–17. Linguistic analysis indicates that phrases untypical of Paul appear specifically in verses 16–17. Moreover, an awkward fit between the terminology and the redactional context supports the assumption of an independent tradition in verses 16–17. And whereas

Paul uses "those who have fallen asleep," for the dead in verse 13, verse 16 speaks of "the dead." Originally the saying in verses 16–17 may have referred to the descent of the "Son of Man," which Paul has replaced by "the Lord himself," in view of the understanding of the community in Thessalonica. The Pauline "in Christ" may also be an addition, as may also be verse 17 as a whole (cf. the we-style as in verse 15).

Some regard verses 16–17 as an authentic Jesus tradition, which was perhaps spoken by Jesus forecasting the persecution of his disciples (Mt 10:16–23). Their death will not put them at a disadvantage at the return of Jesus on the clouds of heaven. In terms of content, scholars have also discovered in verses 16–17 analogies to such sayings of Jesus as Matthew 10:39; 16:25, 28; 24:31, 34; 25:6; 26:64; Luke 13:30. However, none of these instances, including 1 Thessalonians 4:15–17, is really convincing. Since what are generally accepted as the authentic words of Jesus do not include the raising of the dead or his return on the clouds of heaven, to discover in these verses an oblique reference to Jesus' teachings requires a vivid imagination indeed.

Rather, in 1 Thessalonians 4:16–17 we seem to have a Jewish "miniature apocalypse" that has been put into the mouth of Jesus—like the Synoptic apocalypse in Mark 13. The imagery used in verses 16–17 recalls the ancient Near Eastern ceremonial reception of the king and works with similar motifs and ideas, many of which are to be found in Jewish apocalyptic. Along with the report of the Son of Man (4 Esra 13:13), reference can be made to the notion, also attested elsewhere, that the dead take part in the eschatological salvation (4 Ezra 7).

Paul inserts this Jewish miniature apocalypse—which, however, he presents as a saying of the exalted Lord—into a wider appeal (1 Thes 4:13–18) that he develops in view of the critical situation in Thessalonica. There the fate of members of the community who have already died is becoming a divisive issue. The death of some members of the community obviously led to hopelessness and mourning in the community—either because the notion of the resurrection of Christians was unknown in Thessalonica or because Paul's promise of salvation had been chronologically inaccurate or misunderstood. How can they attain the eschatological salvation at the return of Jesus if they have already died?

Paul attempts to combine the notion of the return of Jesus with faith in the Resurrection. After an exposition in verse 13, he makes use of the traditional creed of the death and Resurrection of Christ, through which he confirms that the dead Christians will also have future communion with Christ (verse 14). Since Jesus died and rose again, the dead, too, will have a share in paradise. This statement, which would seem to be new to the Christians in Thessalonica, is further explained by what we earlier argued was a Jewish miniature apocalypse avowed by Paul to be a saying of the Lord (verses 16–17). Verse 15 applies this in advance to those to whom Paul is writing and sums it up for them. The dead will not be at a disadvantage upon Christ's return, because through their resurrection they will be put in the same situation as the living, and in fact will lead the way to heaven. Both will experience communion with Christ as they meet the Lord in the air (verse 17). Verse 18 ("Therefore comfort one another with these words") serves as a concluding admonition.

The day of the Lord comes like a thief in the night. (1 Thes 5:2)

This uses the same image as the Q parallel in Matthew 24:43/Luke 12:39. (Cf. also Thomas 21:5; 2 Pt 3:10; Rv 3:3.) The images used reflect common Jewish tradition (cf. Jb 24:14; Hos 7:1) and cannot be used as an instance of Paul's dependency on a saying of Jesus.

When people say, "There is peace and security," then sudden destruction will come on them as the pangs that come on a woman with a child, and there will be no escape. (1 Thes 5:3)

The suddenness of God's coming in judgment at the end of the world is, to be sure, also an element in the traditions of Jesus' sayings (cf. Lk 12:39; 21:34), but there are also many similar passages in Jewish literature. Nothing in the present text justifies a reference to synoptic traditions.

So we must not sleep, as others do, but keep awake and sober. (1 Thes 5:6)

To be sure, we find in Matthew 24:42 an injunction purported to quote Jesus: "Therefore be awake, because you do not know on what day your Lord is coming" (cf. Mk 13:37; Lk 21:36). However, the attribution is highly dubious, especially inasmuch as admonitions to watchfulness and sobriety are frequent in Jewish literature.

You must live at peace among yourselves. (1 Thes 5:13)

This is very close to Mark 9:50: "Be at peace with one another." However, the phrase in Mark reflects the editorial work of the second evangelist and, apart from that, is simply too general to serve as evidence for Paul's dependency on a saying of Jesus.

See that none of you pays back evil for evil, but always seek to do good to one another and to all. (1 Thes 5:15)

See above on Rom. 12:17.

Rejoice always. (1 Thes 5:16)

This admonition is sometimes regarded as an echo of Luke 6:23 ("Rejoice in that day.... your reward is great in heaven") and Luke 10:20 ("Rejoice that your names are written in heaven"). Since both passages are of dubious authenticity, however, one must certainly exercise great imagination to see an allusion to Jesus' teachings here.

PRELIMINARY RESULT

First, two specific references to what Jesus has said make it certain that Paul was familiar with traditions about Jesus' teaching and knew certain specific elements of that teaching. However, it goes without saying that Jesus' ethic was ill suited to serve as a moral guide for the church in a Hellenistic society. This point receives unambiguous support in 1 Corinthians 7:25, where Paul expresses disappointment that "concerning those who are not married," no word of the Lord is available to him. Not only that observation, but also the apostle's care to distinguish his own opinion from the charge of the Lord (1 Cor 7:12), demonstrate both the value and importance Paul could ascribe to sayings of Jesus and his readiness to issue advice and commands on his own authority. But of Paul's familiarity with *some* traditions of Jesus' sayings in *some* form, there should be no doubt.

Second, one must nevertheless concede the infrequency of either explicit or implicit references to Jesus' teachings to be found in the Pauline letters. The argument that he could assume his readers' familiarity with these because he had already passed them on in his missionary preaching is not convincing. He could and does presume some familiarity with the Greek translation of the Scripture, the Septuagint, which was mediated to his converts either by himself or earlier by the local Jewish community. For this reason he repeatedly and specifically cites it in the course of his ethical teaching. Moreover, when Paul himself summarizes the content of his missionary preaching in Corinth (1 Cor 2:1–2; 15:3–5), there is no hint that a narration of Jesus' earthly life or a report of his earthly teachings was an essential part of it. The tradition about the Last Supper (1 Cor 11:23–25) is no exception, for it is an etiological legend that serves to endorse a liturgical practice in the various churches.

In the letter to the Romans, which cannot presuppose the apostle's missionary preaching and in which he attempts to summarize its main points, we find not a single direct citation of Jesus' teaching. One must record with some surprise the fact that Jesus' teachings seem to play a less vital role in Paul's religious and ethical instruction than does the Old Testament.

Third, not once does Paul refer to Jesus as a teacher, to his words as teaching, or to Christians as disciples. In this regard it is of the greatest significance that when Paul cites "sayings of Jesus," they are never so designated; rather, without a single exception, he attributes such sayings to "the Lord."

Fourth, the term *Law of Christ* should not be taken to mean a summary of Jesus' teaching; rather it designates the law of love. In other words, the phrases "under the law of Christ" (*ennomos Christou*) in 1 Corinthians 9:21 and "the law of Christ" in Galatians 6:2 cannot be used to support the hypothesis that Paul conceived of the traditional words of Jesus as constituting a new Torah or a Christian Halakah.

PAUL AS A WITNESS TO
THE HISTORICAL JESUS?

Paul thought that a person named Jesus had lived and that he now sat at the right hand of God in heaven. Yet he shows only a passing acquaintance with traditions related to his life and nowhere an independent acquaintance with them. In short, Paul cannot be considered a reliable witness to either the teachings, the life, or the historical existence of Jesus.

JESUS' APOCALYPTIC VISION AND THE PSYCHODYNAMICS OF DELUSION

J. Harold Ellens

INTRODUCTION

Albert Schweitzer seems to have been quite concerned about the question of whether Jesus was delusional.[1] He faced honestly the fact that the report on Jesus in the Gospels contends that he lived with a vivid concept of reality that would call his sanity into question.[2] This Jesus is not a historical person but a literary character in a story, though there may or may not be a real person behind that story. In the story, Jesus is depicted as believing that he heard otherworldly voices that the sane humans around him did not hear (Jn 12:28–29). He was sure those experiences were God speaking directly to him from a transcendent world. He became progressively certain that God was calling him to a tragic journey that would result in an apotheosis of exaltation to heavenly status (Mk 8:31ff). He envisioned that soon after this honorific exaltation, he would return as the unique agent of God to end history (Mk 13:26; Mt 10:23, 16:28). At that occasion, he claimed, he would give history its ultimate meaning by paying off the unrighteous with the extermination of evil; while his angelic agents would gather the righteous into a divine domain (Mt 13:41).

Schweitzer, and most biblical scholars a century ago, thought that this sounded a lot like psychosis. They were correct, of course. Few of them, however, were willing to leave the matter at that. There was another, admirable side to the person and work of Jesus of Nazareth, as depicted in the Gospels, which prompted them, as well as most thoughtful persons for the last twenty centuries, to examine carefully how one might understand this apparent psychosis while salvaging the admirable Jesus of the story. Schweitzer solved this problem to his own

213

satisfaction by opting for what he called a "thoroughgoing eschatology," with at least a sidelong glance to Jesus' apparent apocalyptic view of history. Nonetheless, Schweitzer left us with a most enigmatic and ambiguous conclusion:

> In the knowledge that he is the coming son of man, Jesus lays hold of the wheel of the world to set it moving on that last revolution which is to bring all ordinary history to a close. It refuses to turn, and he throws himself upon it. Then it does turn and crushes him. Instead of bringing in the eschatological conditions, he has destroyed them. The wheel rolls onward, and the mangled body of the one immeasurably great man who was strong enough to think of himself as the spiritual ruler of mankind and to bend history to his purpose, is hanging upon it still. That is his victory and his reign.[3]

He might have done better leaving off his last seven words, unless he means them in bitter irony! Actually, by a "thoroughgoing eschatology" Schweitzer meant that he believed Jesus was sane but lived out his life and ministry with a sense that history is under a divine imperative, standing every moment before the face of God, under the pressure of eternity. Moreover, though hesitant to call Jesus and the New Testament narratives apocalyptic, Schweitzer saw that Jesus expected that his eschatological worldview implied a final consummation in a history-ending divine act, one in which the exalted Jesus would definitively participate. Karl Barth confirmed this vision of Jesus and the New Testament in the second edition of his commentary on Romans when he made his now classic assertion, "Christianity that is not wholly and without exception eschatology has wholly and without exception nothing to do with Christ."[4]

However, we must ask whether this resolution of the problem can be trusted. Has Schweitzer done anything more than paste over Jesus' psychosis with an ancient, mythic ideology? What is the real state of affairs with Jesus of Nazareth? This is not a question about the Jesus of history but about the Jesus of the literary narrative. How are we to take the troubling biblical narratives on the one hand, and the incredible impact of this figure upon the last twenty centuries, on the other? The three or four quests for the historical Jesus that characterized nineteenth- and twentieth-century New Testament studies tried to entice that historic figure out of the underbrush, only to find themselves invariably mired in a rather large swamp. The difficulty with these quests lay in their attempt to pare away from the biblical figure anything that looked or smelled mythic, hoping thus to expose the historic. However, the further that quest progressed, the less of a believable or recognizable Jesus we had left.

One might argue, and even be forced to conclude, that the historical investigation has reduced Jesus so severely because he really was a historic person no greater or more significant than the quests for the historical Jesus have come to see him. If there were some way to confirm that as fact, the manner in which the quest has peeled away the dogma and myth from the character of the Jesus of scripture would clearly be of great service to us and to the truth. The difficulty arises, however, in the fact that each researcher in the quest for the historical Jesus has come away from the scholarly task with a different image of Jesus than that held by any of his or her colleagues. The quests have produced no consensus, and no Jesus that rings true to his story.

Many of the more noted scholars of the various quests of the historical Jesus have now written their stories in an attempt to reconstruct what they have discovered that supposed historical person to be like. Each of those books is remarkable and dishearteningly different from all the others. Each of those scholars has looked down the deep well of history and has seen what everyone sees in looking down any deep well—a reflection of their own faces. That has not helped us much in discerning whether Jesus ever existed and if he did, who he was or what he was really like. The same outcome will eventuate from our new Jesus Project if we are not at great pains to prevent that. In the end, the conclusions each of us draw and for which each of us argue will be shaped after the picture in our own inner selves and the assumptions about Jesus that we make from the outset. If we take an atheistic assumption, that faith position will determine what we see in our research. If we take an orthodox assumption, our outcome will be shaped by that faith perspective. It is going to be difficult to be objective and to avoid a radical reductionism regarding this figure, real or mythic, who has shaped the world for the last twenty centuries.

The figure that has become the end product of the various quests for Jesus is sufficiently diminished that he cannot carry the weight of the story developed about him. That is a fatal flaw in any historical quest. If one is to find out who the real historic person, Jesus of Nazareth, was, it is crucial to ask the question through the lens of what the story says, not through a lens that has pared away as much of the story as possible. That is, the story about Jesus, in which he is a leading character, is a story told by people who claimed they knew him, and for whom the story served a significant purpose. Assuming that those people were not psychotic, it must be understood at the outset that they told the story about Jesus in a fashion that seemed to them to ring true to what they thought they knew about him, and what they felt compelled to say about him.

That does not mean that the story they told was literally his story, but they could not have gotten away with telling a story that did not make some kind of sense in terms of the kind of person they believed they knew him to be or to have been. The story had to be the sort of story that could be carried by the character of the person whom they made the main character in the story. The residual Jesus of the historical quest cannot carry the weight of the story those early narrators claimed was his story. The Jesus of the quests is too diminished, too emasculated. The results of the historical quests are consequently not believable as a description of the man from Nazareth who actually existed at a specific point in time, and who has produced such a world-shaping force in history as did he. Nor is it believable as a description of the literary character in the story, if that is all he was or all we have to work with.

That is to say, while we know that stories serve ulterior purposes and are fashioned in the image and need of the persons telling them, there are certain things you simply cannot get away with in telling a story. For example, if you expected people to believe your story about the Wright brothers and their primitive flying machine, then, however romantically or heroically you told it, you could not say that they invented a space and time travel machine that they flew to Andromeda and back, writing a secret report of their escapade that the CIA has kept from us for nefarious reasons, and that this whole thing was really the basis for the story of Jules Verne about a trip to the moon. You could not get away with that for many reasons: Verne's story was written before the Wright brothers were born, the CIA did not exist until fifty years after the Wright brothers' flights, the technology available at the beginning of the twentieth century would not support space travel, and we still do not have time travel machines. However mythic the story, it must have certain plausible groundings in the characters and times it represents.

WHO IS THIS FELLOW?

As noted already, the Jesus with whom we have to deal on the pages of the New Testament is only a literary character in a story, not a person we can identify in history. Jesus as we know him is a character in a story narrated in the Gospels four decades after his death. In his story this character posits a worldview that is 1) radically visionary, 2) apocalyptic, and 3) eschatologically idealized. It is rooted in identifiable Second Temple Judaism sources and traditions, particularly regarding the Son of Man. As the ardors of his life ordeal intensify in the narrative, this character in the story raises the ante on his apocalyptic vision, so to speak. At first we encounter him proclaiming the impending arrival of a divine order in the world, as the Son of Man does in the biblical book of Ezekiel. From Mark 8 forward, he predicts a season of suffering for the cause, as do the Messianic figures at Qumran (War Scroll and Hodayot—Thanksgiving Hymns), connecting for the first time in Judaic tradition the messianic notions of Isaiah 53 with Isaiah 61.

As it becomes clear that he is irretrievably on a catastrophic collision course with the religious authorities, he envisions that he will be delivered from suffering and death by God, and become the exalted Son of Man as in Daniel 7:13ff. Under these circumstances his field forces on earth, Daniel's people of the holy ones of the Most High, will carry forward his mission of destroying the powers of this world and installing the reign of God.

Finally, in the courtroom of Caiaphas and Pilate, when all is obviously lost, he envisions himself as the Son of Man, who will reign in his own heavenly kingdom, and who will be seen again as the eschatological judge. As judge, he will return from heaven with "power and great glory," as the Son of Man in 1 Enoch 37–71. As this story progresses in the mind of the Jesus character, he progressively loses his poetic distance from the story and slips into the *dramatis persona* of the main character in the story. Thus, he finally achieves the delusional state in which he foresees his tragically painful demise as a triumph, until, of course, those bitter words of reality from the cross, "My God...why have you forsaken me?" Then "Jesus declared himself to have been finished off, and the head dropping, he gave up the spirit."[5]

It is important to unpack and illustrate the role of psychological process unfolding in the development of Jesus' Master Story, in the context of the Master Stories of Judaism and Christianity. This formative process is shaped by the memory and interpretation of key historical events that answer the main question driving the development of the faith, theology, and religion of Judaic and Christian tradition. The question driving the historic Israelite quest, and consequently the quest in which Jesus' story unfolded, was: how is God in history, and what does our history and experience, therefore, mean?

The biblical report on Jesus' answer to that question, in the context of the Israelite vision of history, became the story of the Jesus Movement and of early Christianity. The trajectory of development of rabbinic Judaism seems to have derived from the rational humanism of the Pharisees, while Christianity arose from the other Judaism, namely, the apocalyptic stream and the apocalyptic Jesus Movement that flowed from it. The consequence of these two different sources is the rise of twin religions, born from the same womb but having radically different psychological tones, styles, objectives, and rationales.[6]

Such narrative constructs, theological formulations, ritual processes, liturgies, and transcendental visions of reality as are fashioned in the Jesus story, are fixed upon by such a charismatic leader as Jesus or by a culture or community in large part because of the psychological need that these formulations and processes fill. They fill these needs by giving meaning, identity, and consolation to that person, community, and culture. These formulations and community visions derive their warrant from the degree to which they meet those individual and communal psychological needs.

This does not preclude the presence of genuine spiritual, transcendental, or transpersonal factors at work in these formulations. Indeed, quite the opposite! The theology and religion of any given community reflects the key formative psychological factors at work in the initial experience that gave rise to that particular theology and religion, such as the experience and memory of suffering, disempowerment, exile, massive loss, intuitive insight, theophany, theophany, or other real paranormal spiritual experiences. They also reflect the central psychological factors at work in the habitual ways in which the human psyche gives voice to such experiences, such as in the metaphors and mythos, or Master Story, in which the memories of the founding experience and person are preserved.

Of the numerous kinds of religious perspectives that have been shaped in important ways by psychological dynamics, one of the more interesting and pervasive in biblical and apocryphal literature is the apocalyptic tradition of postexilic Judaism. This apocalyptic tradition developed innovative ways of envisioning human encounters with the transcendent world and of conceptualizing the nature and presence of transcendental forces in the history and experience of human communities. These visionary perspectives are evident throughout the Bible. They are rooted mainly in the memory of the perceived divine interventions in the history of the believing community that George Ernest Wright called "The Mighty Acts of God;" particularly as those interventions are reflected in the theology of the Exodus tradition. It is this tradition that shapes much of the religious mainstream in the Hebrew Bible.[7] I believe that this Exodus tradition is essentially a psychological perspective and that it seeded the eschatological and apocalyptic formulations of postexilic Judaism, including that form of it which became Christianity.

THE CULTURAL, RELIGIOUS, AND PSYCHOLOGICAL CONTEXT OF JESUS' DELUSION

Judaism

As noted above, apocalypticism represents one of two trajectories of postexilic Judaism. The other one is the mainstream tradition of

Judaism that matured into the Pharisee-Sadducee and Talmudic traditions. This latter movement produced what we now know as rabbinic Judaism. Of course, it seems that there was a streak of apocalypticism in the thought of the Pharisees, but this seems to have been largely eliminated during the formulation of the Mishnah and the Talmudim.

On the other hand, the apocalyptic tradition led to cloistered and urban Essenism, as well as to the imagery of the preexistent and eschatologically exalted Son of Man tradition in Ezekiel, some of the Psalms, Daniel, and 1 Enoch. This tradition was adopted by Jesus and the Jesus Movement.[8] The psychodynamics of this apocalyptic Judaism trajectory reflect the way in which that community processed the loss experiences of the Babylonian exile, in a drive toward a persistence of hope. The achievement of such a hope was necessary for vindicating the transcendental (heavenly) integrity of the faith community in the face of its temporal mundane (earthly) devastation. It accomplished this through use of psychologically significant metaphors and models, and eschatological and apocalyptic figures and trajectories. These thus also came to inform later Christian theology. The main such apocalyptic figure was the Son of Man.

The Exodus tradition dominates the theology and psychology of the Hebrew Bible and became the primary grounding metaphor for both Jewish and Christian scriptures and worldviews. As a result, proto-apocalyptic ways of thinking about the God-human interface are evident throughout the Hebrew Bible and are rampant in the New Testament. Crucial psychological dynamics can be discerned as gathering continually increasing momentum throughout this long tradition of proto-apocalypticism from the Exodus to the Exile, and from the Exile to the Bar-Kochba collapse of Second Temple Judaism. By *psychological factors* I mean the full range of factors that have to do with the function of the human psyche: all of that which we normally describe as *psychology* and *spirituality*.

In my model, these two words are interchangeable, in the sense that both deal with the full range of the dynamics of the inner person, the self. So for something to be psychological does not reduce it from spiritual or transcendental or transpersonal, but merely means that the event or experience is processed and formulated in terms of how the psyche needs to experience it and how psychology needs to describe that experience. The psychological dimension of that process includes, of course, all the person-formative psychospiritual defensive dynamics and growth dynamics set in motion by any event or experience.

Such psychological factors in both the cultural setting and in the faith tradition of the biblical and postexilic communities of Judaism are strongly evident. They can be seen, for example, in the metaphors of transcendental deliverance that form the mainstream of the Exodus narrative and its pervasive tradition. We note them as clearly in the theology of the remnant and its suffering servant. These constitute the backdrop for the community's longing for an ultimate eschatological consummation, in which the cosmic conflict, in which God and the believing community are thought to be engaged, will be brought to resolution. Those psychological factors also become the warrant for the persistence or survival of both the hope and the existence of the ancient faith community itself.

Faced with the ultimate depression and confusion attendant upon the destruction of Israel and its exile in the era between 722 and 500 BCE, the persistence of hope and meaning and the psychological survival of the community and its members required a massive re-rationalization of the perceived role of the transcendental forces operating in the daily life and eschatological destiny of the faith community. Their memory and metaphors of the Exodus provided them with the ready-made storehouse of resources for that re-rationalization, and for the persistence of hope and meaning.

In this trajectory of Judaism that produced the Pharisee-Sadducee and rabbinic worldview, transcendental presence or intervention in this world was understood to come through the ministry of divine wisdom (*Hokma*). This personified divine wisdom was initially represented as the source of Israel's deliverance from bondage and the source of the Torah given on Mt. Sinai. However, by the time of the Talmudim (300–600 CE), the Torah itself was seen as the preexistent divine agent and the transcendent source of divine and human wisdom (*Hokma*). In this model, life and destiny are, therefore, a mundane quest for wisdom: rational and responsible godly living on earth in the here and now.

However, the apocalyptic tradition that developed from the

eschatological worldviews of Ezekiel, Daniel, and 1 Enoch produced the Enochic tradition, celebrated especially by the urban and cloistered (Qumran) Essene Sects, Gnostics, and the Jesus Movement. In these models also, transcendental and divine presence manifested itself in history through the presence of divine wisdom (*Hokma* and *Sophia*). In these innovative traditions, however, divine wisdom was manifested in the Son of Man; the Torah being less central and eventually irrelevant. The Gospels have Jesus declaring that in the Son of Man, one superior to Abraham, Moses, Solomon, and even the Torah and Temple is present in history.

It is interesting that in this apocalyptic tradition, also, divine Wisdom starts out as preexistent and transcendent, manifesting itself on earth in the Son of Man, rather than in Torah. However, as in rabbinic perspective, Torah became preexistent and heavenly, and thus the source of divine and human wisdom; so also in the end the Son of Man became transcendent and preexistent in the apocalyptic Christian tradition, especially in the Gospel of John. In both traditions the world was turned upside down and the product of wisdom became the divine source of wisdom. The Son of Man became the preexistent and divine source of the wisdom of both God and mankind.

The much-discussed character of this Son of Man had at least the following qualities. He was a prophetic figure with a divine call to an earthly ministry. He anticipated a transcendental exaltation, and a cataclysmic eschatological return. In that final *parousia*, the world would be judged, history ended, and a new age of the divine reign once and for all introduced. This would constitute and usher in the consummation of the transcendental and transpersonal destiny of humans. This was a re-rationalization of the devastating psychospiritual loss sustained by the community because of Jesus' unanticipated and premature death. That reframing produced a persistent Christian hope and an ultimate vindication of the apocalyptic faith community. Its heavenly destiny was guaranteed, even if its earthly existence was precarious or even terminal.

The psychodynamics of this kind of process involve the special experiences through which any given community and its individual members process and rationalize into an operational model the following kinds of typical experiences: (1) massive loss such as bondage in

Egypt, exile in Babylon, or the death of "him whom we thought would be the one to deliver Israel"; (2) meaninglessness resulting from a lack of a clear sense of God; (3) lack of a clear and consistent life of right-eousness and prosperity in the community; (4) depression resulting from diaspora and exile, despair of trying "to sing the Lord's songs in an alien land"; (5) anxiety, fear, guilt, and shame resulting from inter-nalizing the pain of these losses as humans typically do; and (6) efforts toward a persistence of hope against all hope, resulting, for example, in the Jesus Movement in the Easter Faith. To process these driving psy-chological needs, master them in an operational model, and vindicate the transcendental faith and the integrity of the faith community, these believers formulated apocalyptic metaphors, models, visions, and mythic ideations of a hopeful destiny. They created eschatological apocalyptic figures, trajectories, and consummations that became their faith visions and operational expectations.

Christianity

The enigma of Jesus, in this question of the psychodynamics of apoca-lyptic faith tradition, is focused by the tension we see between the Low Christology of the Synoptic Gospels, the Jesus story, and the High Christology of the (1) doxological hymns in Colossians 1:15–20 and Philippians 2:5–11, (2) Johannine transcendental theology, and (3) the second- and third-century Eucharistic theology of the church. The problem unfolds in the following picture.

The Son of Man sayings in the Gospels are generally understood to fall into four categories: Son of Man as earthly teacher and healer, Son of Man as suffering servant who dies, Son of Man who is exalted, and Son of Man returning on the clouds in judgment at the end of his-tory as eschatological judge. All of these sayings in the Gospels are always placed in the mouth and only in the mouth of Jesus, and he seldom uses or tolerates any other designation of himself. All four cat-egories are in Q, except exaltation, provided you grant that the "Son of Man hath not where to lay his head" is in the second category, that is, *logia* about the suffering Son of Man.

The *Sitz im Leben* for all the *logia* in the Gospels, except those that are obvious anachronisms, can be found comfortably and authentically in the literary narrative of the life and work of Jesus as depicted by the Synoptic Gospels. This is a vulnerable point in the argument because the same community that gives us the report of Jesus' Son of Man *logia* is the community that gives us the narrative presenting the *Sitz im Leben.* Therefore, the argument is persuasive only if the evidence for this model is internally consistent, in the end overwhelming, and verifiable on the basis of external evidence.

The second-century and later church did away completely with the biblical meanings of the Son of Man title or phrase, never hung any doctrine or celebrated truth on it, and never identified with it in any way in its celebration of Jesus. Therefore, it is hard to believe that they would have claimed that this was his self-designation, unless they could not avoid it because it really was his phrase and self-identity in the core story, wherever that came from. It is internally consistent to assume or acknowledge that this really is the self-designation of the original Jesus in that core story, and that it represents a definitional notion he is described as having about his person and role.

It seems likely, given the above, that the concept of the Son of Man progressed and developed in the unfolding of the narrative of his self-consciousness over time so that it came to include all four categories of *logia.* The first phase was that of a man with a ministry of teaching and healing on earth proclaiming the kingdom of God, as did Ezekiel in his role as Son of Man. The second was that of a man in this ministry suffering and dying as Isaiah's Suffering Servant. The third was that of a man being exalted by God to transcendent status, as Daniel's Son of Man. The fourth was that of a man accorded an apocalyptic and eschatological role as heavenly judge, who descends at the end of history in a *parousia* of a new age, as promised by and for the Son of Man in 1 Enoch.

The first phase could have been the psychological result of Jesus' spiritual consciousness from his early years, focused by the drama of his Baptism. He obviously had a special sense of vocation to proclaim the kingdom of God. This sense of urgency and his consistent antinomianism throughout the narrative of his life and work may be explained, as does Donald Capps, by his having been treated from childhood as an illegitimate child. This would have involved living with the denigration of his mother by the community, and may explain why the story is crafted with the absence of his father.

The narrative in the Gospels suggests that Jesus achieved significant clarity during his retreat in the wilderness immediately after his Baptism. During the temptations in the wilderness, as the story goes, he dissociated himself from the Son of David messianism of the Jerusalem religious authorities, expanding (or reducing) his messianic identity to that of the Son of Man traditions. It is clear from the narrative of the temptations that he struggled with messianic ideas of nearly megalomaniacal proportions: solving the world's problems by feeding the poor with stones turned to bread, captivating humankind with the spectacular psychological manipulation of miraculously jumping harmlessly from the temple parapet, and bowing down to the secular powers so as to become the new Alexander the Great.

The story has him apparently moving psychologically to the second phase, the suffering, dying, and exalted Son of Man, after the failure of the first mission of the disciples and the abandonment by the multitudes. Then he is depicted as becoming aware of the fact that he was on a collision course with the authorities in Jerusalem. This seems to be a scenario lurking behind the language of Mark 8:27–33.

Assuming this model to be warranted, he can be seen to have moved psychologically to an apocalyptic and eschatological notion of his role and destiny when he realized that his cause was destined to fail. The only way to save himself and his cause, ideologically, would have been to envision himself drawn up into the transcendent status of divine vindication, from which he would descend to bring in the kingdom after all, end history, initiate a new divine era, and demonstrate that he was right and all his detractors were wrong after all.

This description of the Jesus story is vulnerable to criticism, of course, because it is impossible to sequence chronologically with any precision the four categories of *logia* in the story of Jesus' development. It is difficult to create a narrative sequence that is consistent and has an inherent logical and structural coherence.

If this model is taken as our hypothesis, for the sake of testing it against the data, it must be said at least that neither the Son of Man *logia* nor the exalted eschatology in the Pauline and Deutero-Pauline literature in Colossians and Philippians are merely products of liturgical enthusiasm but reflect a thoughtfully crafted theological worldview present in the Jesus Movement and in the very early church.

If this was the authors' design for Jesus' psychological and theological worldview, and therefore for his self-concept as the main character in the story, progressively developing through all the four categories, where would he have gotten such a worldview? Why did it produce such a Low Christology in the Synoptic Son of Man sayings and such a High Christology in the Pauline and Johannine literature, as well as in the theology of the second- and third-century church?

According to Boccaccini's *Beyond the Essene Hypothesis*, just such a worldview was available in Enochic Essene Judaism in its various forms. A review of his entire argument is genuinely worthwhile to the student or scholar with special interest in this issue.[9]

According to the rubrics of Occam's Razor, this model hypothesis manages the data better than any of the others available and, therefore, it is imperative to take it seriously. This would imply that inherent to the developing self-concept of the literary character Jesus, conceived in the context of Ezekiel, Daniel 7:13, the Dead Sea Scrolls, and 1 Enoch 37–71, there were seeds and warrants for the church's subsequent High Christology.

THE HISTORICAL QUEST

Much scholarly energy, time, and money has been invested over the last fifty years to distill from history enough evidence regarding Jesus of Nazareth to discern to what extent this suggested model is historically accurate. A great deal of good has come of this passionate pursuit. However, in the end, the result seems to have produced a much diminished Jesus, literary or historical.

Relevant Judaic Traditions

The Son of Man was well known in Judaic tradition by the first century CE and thus could be used as a stock-in-trade concept available to

Mark and the other crafters of the story in which Jesus is the main character. It had identifiable roots and meanings in that tradition. As indicated above, the first prominent appearance of the title is in the prophecy of Ezekiel, where it is used ninety-three times. Each time, the expression is a formula with which God addressed Ezekiel as a mortal ("So it was that the word of Yahweh came to me, 'Son of Man'" [6:1–2]). Each of the ninety-three times, God called him to prophesy the impending arrival of divine intervention in history and proclaim the advent of God's kingdom on earth.

The second prominent appearance is in Daniel 7–9 in which "one like a Son of Man" (7:13) is exalted to heavenly status, with power and dominion over the earth. This power and dominion is delegated to and exercised by the Son of Man's proxies on earth, who are called the "people of the holy ones of the Most High" (7:27).

The third significant occurrence of the title Son of Man is in Enoch, in an apocalyptic and eschatological section of that prophecy in which is promised the dramatic advent of the exalted Son of Man as the judge of the earth at the end of time. In 1 Enoch a human being, namely, Enoch himself, is designated as the Son of Man (71:14), exalted to heavenly status, and given his eschatological role. The fourth prominent appearance of a figure with the characteristics Jesus associates with the title Son of Man is in the Thanksgiving Hymns and the War Scroll from Qumran. In those Dead Sea Scrolls, the royal messiah is described as suffering and dying. An argument may also be made for the presence of a virtual Son of Man in 11Q13 Melchizedek, in which the messianic figure expends himself for the salvation of the people of God but does not die.

In the Jesus story of the Synoptic Gospels, these images of the Son of Man-Messiah appear as progressive stages in Jesus' self-concept development. This is also true in the Gospel of John, except that the end of the story as John tells it has Jesus adding a fifth prominent use or construct for the title and for Jesus' identity and vocation. In John's second-century narrative, Jesus is depicted as dissociating himself as Son of Man from the role of eschatological judge and prosecutor. In John's Gospel, the meaning of the term *Son of Man* moves from heavenly messiah and eschatological judge to divine savior. It is in the context of the relevant Judaic pre-Gospel traditions of a progression of

Son of Man images that the meaning and use of the term *Son of Man*, as it is placed in the mouth of Jesus, the Jew, must be sought. Only then can we discern what the self-concept of this literary character is intended by his story to be.[10]

THE PROGRESSION OF IMAGES I: EZEKIEL *REDIVIVUS*

Marvin A. Sweeney, and before him, Margaret S. Odell[11] gave us real assistance here. Odell argued persuasively that the key figure in the drama of the biblical book of Ezekiel is both priest and prophet; and that the story of his call to be a prophet is developed on the framework of the ritual for the ordination of priests in Leviticus 8–9 as well as in Numbers 4 and 8. This fact illustrates that in Ezekiel's life and vocation, his call represents a transition in his identity from the primary vocation of priest to the primary vocation of prophet, though in gaining the latter he does not lose the former. His prophetic role is a new type of unfolding of his priesthood in a setting in which the temple, the holy city, the holy land, and the holy people are defiled; and thus the authentic priestly rituals can no longer be carried out there.

In *Ezekiel: Zadokite Priest and Visionary Prophet of the Exile*, Sweeney builds upon Odell's argument. He outlines the correspondence in categories of ritual elements in the Levitical ordination of priests and in the story of Ezekiel's prophetic call. Sweeney points out that the entire book of Ezekiel is a progression of the ritual elements of Levitical ordination (Lv 8–9). Careful comparison demonstrates that the Jesus story contains these same ordination-ritual elements, giving strong indication that, at one level, those telling the story in which Jesus is the main character consciously crafted the story in terms of Jesus' Ezekiel-like priestly ordination. In the biblical book of Ezekiel, this ordination process leads to the priest, addressed by God as the Son of Man, being called and ordained as a prophet of the coming reign of God. The ritual factors in Levitical ordination of priests, the progressive phases in Ezekiel's development as prophet, and their counterparts in the Jesus story are as follows.

Factor One: Ordination at Age Thirty

Levitical priestly ordinands were initiated into the vocation at age thirty and continued for a career, retiring at age fifty (Num 4:3, 23, 30); Ezekiel began his career at age thirty, and his book closes the odyssey when he is age fifty [Ez 1:1]. Jesus' ministry began at approximately age thirty, in keeping with the prescription for Levitical priests and the precedent in Ezekiel. This aligns the Jesus of the Gospel narratives with the first notable Son of Man in Judaic tradition.

Factor Two: Ingesting the Divine Gift

Levitical priest ordinands ate the ram of ordination (Lv 8:31). Ezekiel ate the scroll given him by Yahweh (Ez 2:8–3:3), that is, both the Levitical ordinands and Ezekiel digested the sacred gift from God, thereby presumably being equipped for service and thereby receiving the required divine illumination. It is not obvious that Jesus' official call status began with ingesting and digesting a sacred gift from God that equipped him for service. However, two aspects of the biblical record are suggestive and noteworthy here.

First, Mark says that immediately after his Baptism, Jesus was driven by the divine spirit into the wilderness where, for forty days, he was deprived of sustenance except for that which "the angels ministered to him." The forty days of consuming angelic food were the transforming experience that led to Jesus' illumination regarding his call, as was the digestion of the scroll for Ezekiel and the consecrated ram for the Levitical priest candidates. The sustenance provided by angelic ministration to Jesus in the wilderness was the counterpart of the eating of the sacred gift by the priestly ordinands and by Ezekiel.

Second, the author of the Apocalypse of John noticed this paradigmatic correspondence between Jesus as the Son of Man and Ezekiel as the Son of Man of Levitical certification. That author noticed the key role of ingesting the divine gift of illumination, the ram or scroll, for in the Johannine Apocalypse, John, the surrogate (1:19) of the one like the Son of Man (1:13) is instructed to eat the scroll proffered by the angel (10:8–11), and the eating and its aftertaste are described in language that is exactly like that in Ezekiel. Moreover, that same surrogate for the Son of Man in the Apocalypse is then instructed to measure the holy city and temple (Rv 11), as Ezekiel is instructed in preparation for the renewed creation (new heaven and earth—Rv 21:1), a new holy city (the new Jerusalem, coming down out of heaven from God—Rv 21:2), and a new temple ("Its temple is the Lord God the Almighty and the Lamb"—Rv 21:22). Clearly the allusion to Ezekiel and the Levitical paradigm is too striking to ignore regarding Jesus as Son of Man in the Gospel narratives.

Factor Three: Spiritual Retreat

Levitical priest ordinands sat in seclusion for seven days (Lv 8:33). Ezekiel sat in silence among his people for seven days (Ez 3:15). Seven is the first symbolic number to appear in the Hebrew Bible, being the timeframe of creation. The primary symbolic timeframe in the Jesus story is the forty days of silence or seclusion in the wilderness, which initiated Jesus' career as the Son of Man. Jesus' symbolic time is not seven days but corresponds, instead, to the second most prominent paradigmatic time symbol in the Hebrew Bible, namely, the number forty. There is undoubtedly a conscious relationship between Jesus' forty days in the wilderness receiving the heavenly illumination, and Moses' forty days on Sinai in the wilderness receiving the Torah. The Son of Man in Christian tradition corresponds exactly to the Torah in Rabbinic tradition.

This cannot be unrelated to the forty years of Moses' preparation in the wilderness before his commission to lead the Exodus, and the forty years of the Israelite preparation for their vocation. During this period of sacred time, they were called to the vocation of being the unique and paradigmatic people of the covenant, who were to inherit the divine domain of the Promised Land. The shift from seven to forty cannot be accidental or insignificant, within the structure of the paradigm, in view of the impending declaration by Jesus that, as Son of Man, he is greater than the Torah, Jonah, Abraham, Moses, and Solomon (Mt 12). Nor does it violate the Levitical model since the outcome is a corresponding symbolic sacred time of preparation for vocation.

Factor Four: Atoning for the Sins of the Multitude

Levitical priest ordinands make atonement for the guilt of the people (Ezekiel bears the guilt of the people although he does not make a formal sacrifice of atonement). Both Ezekiel and Levitical priest candidates symbolically bear the guilt of the people and make symbolic sacrificial atonement in order to purify the temple, city, people, land, and all creation, anticipating God's renewal of all these sacred aspects of the believing community's life. So Jesus, as Son of Man, is represented in the Gospels as destined to proclaim the impending reign of God, and be sacrificed "for the sins of many." Frequent references are made in the Gospels to the suffering, death, and exaltation of the Son of Man. This is particularly evident in the references to Jesus, as Son of Man, being lifted up, "as Moses lifted up the serpent in the wilderness." Paul speaks of this as the act that will redeem all creation (Rom 8:22 and 1 Cor 15).

These references are clearly not intended merely as references to Jesus' crucifixion but rather to the fact that he is depicted, as Son of Man, to be the symbolic agent of the healing of the people. He will be brought to the attention of the world of needy humans, as was Moses' brass serpent, and as was Ezekiel. Only in the later reflections of the post-Easter church's theology was this notion associated with the crucifixion. Sweeney tells us that Ezekiel is the agent of both the guilt and the atonement of Israel, as he "portrays the destruction of the Jerusalem Temple as a sacrifice that is designed to purify Jerusalem, the nation of Israel, and creation at large." This same symbolic purification is undoubtedly what Jesus intended in the "cleansing of the temple" (Mt 21). Donald Capps, Paula Fredriksen, and others refer to Jesus' aggression in the temple as a symbolic destruction of the temple, as a mode of its purification, and as a purification of the world.[12]

Factor Five: The Theophany

Levitical priest ordinands were admitted to the sanctuary to see the glory of Yahweh (Lv 9:23). Ezekiel saw the glory of Yahweh as God prepared the destruction of Jerusalem and its temple (Ez 8–11). Ezekiel and the priest candidates experienced a theophany when they were admitted to the sanctuary of the temple. They saw the *Kabod*. Jesus' call to ministry started with such a theophany: "In those days Jesus came from Nazareth of Galilee and was baptized by John in the Jordan. Immediately coming up out of the water, he saw the heavens opened and the Spirit descending upon him like a dove; and a voice came from heaven, saying, '*Thou art my beloved Son; with thee I am well pleased*'" (Mk 1:9–11).

Factor Six: Proclaiming the Kingdom of God

In Ezekiel's time, with temple, holy city, and holy land defiled by foreign invasion and the consequent violation of the sacred places, Ezekiel lived in a foreign place without access to the site of priestly service. He was reduced to living his life in the kind of work and rituals that made *him* impure as well. He ate ordinary food, dressed in ordinary ways, carried out ordinary forms of hygiene, and so was called Son of Man each time God addressed him. In this context the term must have meant "ordinary mortal." According to the story, God called him as an ordinary mortal, despite his priestly identity and heritage, and commissioned him as a prophet to proclaim the advent of God's reign, his kingdom. Ezekiel, as son of Adam (human being), has to live in an ordinary way in the ordinary world, defiled and impure, waiting for the renewal of the temple, city, land, and people, when God arrives, intervenes, and brings in his reign.

Ezekiel's prophetic role, calling for the renewal of God's domain, people, and reign, fulfills his priestly role as the agent of atonement and redemption. Jesus, likewise, as Son of Adam/Man, perceives himself called to the prophetic role of proclaiming the advent of the kingdom of God. The story places Jesus in the same role and mode as Ezekiel, commissioned to bring in God's reign, and fulfilling his task as agent of the world's renewal and redemption.

Factor Seven: Predicting Destruction of the Holy Places

In reference to factor four above, although Ezekiel did not offer a sacrifice of atonement for the people, despite the fact that this is an important requirement in the ritual of the priest ordinands, Sweeney points out that Ezekiel does, indeed, offer a sacrifice as atonement insofar as he portrays the destruction of the Jerusalem Temple as a sacrifice that is designed to purify Jerusalem, the nation of Israel, and creation at large. This results not only in a transformation of Ezekiel's role as both priest and prophet but in a transformation of all creation as the Jerusalem Temple, the holy center of creation, is destroyed and replaced with a new temple that signals the beginning of a new creation in the aftermath of the Babylonian exile.[13]

While Ezekiel predicts the destruction of the city and temple when God intervenes for the purification of the temple, city, land, and people, Jesus predicts the destruction of the city and temple and then carries out a symbolic purifying destruction of the temple and its ritual. Moreover, he does this with the conscious awareness that he is thereby precipitating the final conflict with the religious authorities who will fulfill his apocalyptic vision of the suffering, dying, and exalted Son of Man. Capps teased out the details of this psychodynamic action of cleansing the temple.[14] Jesus claimed symbolically that his exaltation was the effectual purification of all the sacred aspects of the believing community: *"Destroy this temple and I will rebuild it in three days"* (Jn 2:19). The story has Jesus clearly envisioning that this symbolic act of cleansing the temple, thus precipitating his own death, would lead to the advent of the divine rule on earth. He promised that it would come in the first generation and that it would be attended by the appearance of the Son of Man reentering the drama on earth by appearing on the clouds of heaven with all the holy angels in the glory of his father, as eschatological judge (Synoptic Gospels) or as savior John's Gospel. This is to be the denouement of the dramatic Jesus story.

So we have here the depiction of a priestly prophet, whose career can be described in terms of these seven ritual factors. This figure is known as and answers to the title Son of Man. It cannot be accidental that the key turning points in Jesus' career correspond precisely to the Levitical paradigm of ordination that shaped Ezekiel's call to the identity and role of Son of Man. The authors of the Jesus story clearly had Ezekiel and the Levitical paradigm in mind. Therefore, it is obvious that one clear Judaic tradition, written into the Jesus story, is that of the

Son of Man image in Ezekiel, a human prophet proclaiming that God's kingdom is in the process of breaking in upon this mundane world.

It is surprising that no one has developed this clear correlation between the Son of Man model in the Gospel narratives, the model in Ezekiel, and the Levitical ordination ritual. Obviously, the first identifiable meaning of *Son of Man* that the Jesus story intends to associate with the literary character of Jesus is that of a human priest/prophet like Ezekiel, who is called to proclaim the impending advent of the reign of God.

However, we have a problem here. Where did the notion come from that having been called as an Ezekiel-type human prophet to proclaim the reign of God on earth, Jesus, as the Son of Man, would move on to envision himself as the suffering and dying Messiah who would eventually find his deliverance and triumphal destiny as an exalted heavenly figure? How could the authors write that into the story and get away with it? Where did they acquire the notion that he would actually *become* the redeeming sacrifice (Mk 8:31) rather than, as Ezekiel had done, symbolically narrate the purifying atonement in the form of the story of the impending destruction and renewal of the temple and the city? Why do they portray him as going further and talking about a second, third, and fourth phase of the Son of Man odyssey, namely, suffering, dying at the hands of the gentiles, being exalted of God, and returning as the eschatological judge? That is certainly not the Son of Man in Ezekiel. It is the Messiah of a later Judaic tradition, namely, that of the suffering Messiah of Qumran, combined with the Son of Man of Daniel.

THE PROGRESSION OF IMAGES II: THE SUFFERING MESSIAH OF QUMRAN

To the great astonishment of some scholars, there is no Son of Man at Qumran. That is, the title *Son of Man* is not employed in the rich literature of the Qumran Essene sect. However, some references in the Dead Sea Scrolls seem to offer evidence of a figure and a messianic concept notably similar to Son of Man sayings in the Gospels. This suggests that those Dead Sea Scrolls, which are dated between 400 BCE and 50 BCE, may well have been the sources of the messianic images in the minds of the Gospel writers. They imported those messianic images into the concept of the Son of Man with which Jesus, the literary character, was identified in the literary drama of those Gospels.

The Rule of the Qumran Community and the Synoptic Son of Man

Heinz E. Tödt found, in the *Rule of the Community* (*Serekh ha-Yahad*),[15] IV 25 and IX 11, references to the actions of a messianic figure like the one in the Son of Man sayings of Matthew 19:28 and as Tödt simply noted that the only setting in the Gospels, in which the Qumran notion of a messianic human who moves toward an apotheosis as eschatological judge arises, is in the Son of Man *logia*. Tödt points out that in the Markan passage, Son of Man and Messiah are joined. Caiaphas asked Jesus, "Are you the Messiah, the Son of the Blessed?" Jesus' reply was direct: "Again the high priest asked him and said to him, 'Are you the Christ, the son of the Blessed?' Jesus said, *'I am; and you will see the Son of Man sitting at the right hand of power, and coming with the clouds of heaven.'*" At Qumran and in the Synoptic Gospels, the messianic man is divinely appointed to function as judge, in the sense of separating the righteous from the condemned unrighteous in the eschaton.

The Qumran reference with which Tödt joins this Markan pericope concerns the hope for the endurance of the righteous, "until the prophet comes, and the Messiahs of Aaron and Israel."[16] Tödt claims that this hope for multiple messiahs is refined into a unified messianic hope by the time of the Gospel writers. In the form of the Enochic Essenism that became the Jesus Movement, this unified hope centered in the messianic Son of Man, as it had in the Royal Messiah at Qumran. In the literary drama of the Gospels, Jesus announces that this Son of Man is the figure who is to suffer at the hands of evil men and die, in direct correspondence with the Qumran expectation regarding the Messiah. Thus Tödt sees a relationship of concepts between the Royal Messiah of Qumran and the Jesus character of the narratives; a virtual Son of Man of Qumran and a literal Son of Man in the Gospels. Both are suffering and dying messiahs. The Qumran Community does not refer to this figure as the Son of Man but clearly has in mind the same messianic figure as the one for which the Jesus Movement employed that title, Son of Man, and claimed that it was Jesus' own self-concept.

The War Scroll and the Synoptic Son of Man

George W. E. Nickelsburg developed at length the relationship between Daniel 7 and the Parables of Enoch, with particular emphasis upon the judicial role of the messianic figure.[17] While he distinguished between the judicial role of Michael in Daniel 10 and 12 and the nonjudicial role of the one like a Son of Man in Daniel 7, he nonetheless points out that heavenly enthronement of the one like a Son of Man will involve Israel's earthly supremacy over all the nations. This supremacy is reminiscent of the messianic destiny of Israel in Isaiah 61. While Nickelsburg is in error in supposing that the Son of Man in Daniel is enthroned at any point, he is correct in pointing out that it is this supremacy of the messianic figure or people that one finds in 1QM XVII:8. Here we read that God will exalt "the dominion of Israel over all flesh."

In Daniel 7, the one like the Son of Man is exalted to heavenly status while both he and his minions on earth, the people of the holy ones of the Most High, are exalted over all mundane kingdoms and powers. Thus the one like the Son of Man becomes the heavenly epitome of the people of the holy ones of the Most High who are on earth, and they become the earthly epitome of the exalted and heavenly Son of Man. In 1 Enoch 69:26–29, however, the Son of Man combines the role of enthronement and judgment, as does the Son of Man in the Synoptic Gospels. The Enochic scene is straightforward. The hosts of heaven witness the exaltation and judgment carried out by the Son of Man. Nickelsburg invites us to hear clearly the strains of the overture played in the Parables of Enoch, which will become the theme of the sonata developed in the Gospels:

> And there was great joy amongst them,
> And they blessed and glorified and extolled,
> Because the name of that Son of Man had been revealed to them
> And he sat on the throne of his glory,
> And the command of the judgment was given unto the Son of Man
> And he caused the sinners to pass away

And be destroyed from off the face of the earth,
(*or,* he shall never pass away or perish from the face of the earth)

And those who have led the world astray
Shall be bound with chains,
And their ruinous assembly shall be imprisoned
And their works shall vanish from the face of the earth.
And from henceforth there shall be nothing corruptible
For that Son of Man has appeared,
And has seated himself on the throne of his glory,
And all evil shall pass away from before his face,
And the word of that Son of Man shall go forth
And be strong before the Lord of Spirits.

Nickelsburg clearly intimates in his superb article the mutuality of language and concept of this great variety of literatures of Second Temple Judaism associated with the Son of Man as exalted heavenly figure and eschatological judge. One can hardly miss the correlative, if not the literarily genealogical, relationship between these Qumran documents and the Synoptic Gospels. The implication of Nickelsburg's work is that Tödt's references to the messianic expectation and eschatological judgment at Qumran in the *Rule of the Community* is a correlate of the Son of Man ideology in the Parables of Enoch. Thus, while the Dead Sea Scrolls do not name or title a Son of Man, they present the same messianic theology of eschatological judgment that is presented more concretely in 1 Enoch 37–71 (not present at Qumran) where it is given the name, title, and messianic character of the Son of Man. Moreover, it is precisely this Son of Man in 1 Enoch 37–71 and the messianic Suffering Servant–Son of Man in the Jesus story that is the Suffering Servant–Royal Messiah at Qumran.

The Son of Man and the Suffering Servant at Qumran

Israel Knohl[18] has described, at considerably greater length than Tödt and Nickelsburg, his argument for a significant messianic figure(s) in the Dead Sea Scrolls associated in nature and role with the Suffering Servant motif and with eschatological judgment. Knohl is at pains to draw out the implication of his citations from the scrolls even further in relationship to the nature and role of the Son of Man in the Gospel. Knohl finds a surprising Suffering Servant–Messiah who appears in the text of two or three Dead Sea Scrolls and is attested by four or five separate copies.[19]

Knohl cites 4QH^e (4Q427) fragment 7, 1QH^a column XXVI; and 4Q491 fragment 11, column I. As the H indicates in the first three references these are all from the Hodayot. They are hymns from the Thanksgiving Scroll series. These all belong to the first version of the hymns. The fourth citation is 4Q491 from the *War Scroll* and is a second version of the hymns.[20] The main evidence for the first version is found in two rather substantial fragments of 4QH^e. The relevant text in the first fragment speaks of the messianic figure as beloved of the king who, from the context, seems clearly to be God. This messianic figure, whom God loves, is described as dwelling among the holy ones, though rejected by humanity. The first term, regarding his exaltation by the king, certainly rings with the sounds of Psalms 2, 8, and 110; the second, depicting heavenly transcendence, echoes the strains of Daniel 7–9; and the third, introducing suffering and rejection, seems reminiscent of Isaiah 53. If these references seem a bit tenuous, they are confirmed by the second fragment, which speaks of the messianic figure being despised and enduring evil.

The fragmentary nature of 4QH^e is, of course, troublesome. However, we are fortunate to be able to flesh out virtually the entire document by comparative analysis of all other texts in version one, where "parallel expressions are sometimes preserved in a more complete form."[21] Moreover, parallels also exist in version two for most of the relevant citations. For example, 1QH^a speaks of the messianic figure expressing "gentleness to the poor" but being "oppressed" (fragment 16, column III). Similar confirmation is evident for the expressions of divine exaltation of the messianic figure, his assignment to dwell with the angels and the holy ones, his glory, and his role as judge. Knohl reconstructs this section of the first version of the first hymn as follows:

> I shall be reckoned with the angels,
> My dwelling is in the holy council.
> Who...has been despised like me.

And who has been rejected of men like me?
And who compares to me in enduring evil?
No teaching compares to my teaching
For I sit...in heaven.
Who is like me among the angels?
Who would cut off my words?
Who could measure the flow of my lips?
Who can associate with me,
Thus compare with my judgment?
I am the beloved of the king,
A companion of the holy ones...
And to my glory none can compare.

The second version of Hymn 1 has very similar language, as one would expect. Here again we have the messianic figure on an eternal heavenly throne of power. Three times over he is declared to be assigned to the angelic council. None can compare with his glory except the sons of the king. No one has been so exalted. He sits in heaven and none can accompany him to this unique majestic place. The holy council is his dwelling place. He has been despised, has borne incomparable afflictions, has endured incomparable evil—and he has been glorified. No one is like him, no teaching like his teaching. No one can associate with him or compare with his exercise of judgment.

Hymn 2, version 1, is preserved in 4QH^a 7 columns I an II, but this hymn is an exaltation of God and a celebration of his redemptive exaltation of redeemed humans. "Proclaim and say: Great is God who acts wonderfully, for he casts down the haughty spirit so that there is no remnant and lifts up the poor from the dust to the eternal height and to the clouds he magnifies him in stature, and he is with the heavenly beings in the assembly of the community." The second version of Hymn 2 is preserved in a mere fragment (11, column I of 4Q491) but refers to the exaltation of God's Messiah to the heavenly realm with the angels, and to his being accorded heavenly power.

Of course, as suggested above, it is difficult to miss the specific correspondence between the language of suffering, exaltation, and judgment associated with the Messiah in these messianic hymns and the language of the Son of Man *logia* of the Synoptic Gospels. Indeed, references to this messianic figure fit all three of Bultmann's categories of Son of Man *logia*, as discussed below, but Knohl is particularly interested in category two, the suffering Messiah. It is also obvious how dependent both literary sources, Knohl's Qumran references and the *logia*, are upon Psalms 8:4–6 and 110:1, Isaiah 53:1–12, Daniel 7:13–14 and 26–27, and 1 Enoch 37–71 (particularly 69). The latter is surprising, since 1 Enoch 37–71, as an identifiable text, seems to be totally absent from the Qumran library, as noted above.

What is very suggestive about the associations made in this discussion thus far is the degree to which the messianic figure referred to in Daniel, in the Similitudes (Parables) of Enoch, and in the gospels of the New Testament, is like the Messiah of Qumran (the Hodayot, War Scroll, and Rule of the Community). Thus the important point here lies in that evidence which strongly relates the suffering messianic figure at Qumran with the similar suffering messianic figure of the Synoptic Gospels known as the Son of Man, though the community of Qumran did not employ that title. So there is a remarkable correspondence of language, concept, and content between the Suffering Servant at Qumran and the suffering and dying Messiah Son of Man in the Synoptic Gospels; and between the ultimate heavenly exaltation and enthronement as judge of the Suffering Servant in both traditions.[22]

Who Is the Suffering Messiah at Qumran?

John J. Collins argues that the identity of the speaker in the Qumran hymn is not the Teacher of Righteousness nor a composite figure representing the righteous community, Daniel's people of the holy ones of the Most High; but rather an individual author whose identity is a mystery.[23] Knohl argues on the basis of a conjunction of references in the *Oracle of Hystaspes*, the biblical book of Revelation, the *Assumption of Moses*, and Roman history that the two messianic leaders killed in the streets of Jerusalem in 4 BCE by the Romans under Caesar Augustus were the Royal and the Priestly Messiahs for whom the Qumran Community had been looking; and that one of these was the speaker in the messianic Hymns of Thanksgiving. Since the speaker refers to being exalted to a throne, Knohl concludes it was the Royal Messiah who gave us the hymns:

As the two messianic leaders were killed in 4 BCE they surely were active in the period previous to that year, that is, during the reign of King Herod (37–4 BCE)....All four copies of the messianic hymns were written precisely at that period. One can, therefore, assume that one of the two Messiahs killed in 4 BCE was the hero of the messianic hymns from Qumran. The hero of the hymns did not have any priestly attributes; on the other hand, he spoke of sitting on a "throne of power" and mentioned a crown. From this we may deduce he was the royal Messiah.[24]

By order of the authorities, the two slain religious figures were left unburied in the city streets for three days, after which they disappeared, leading their disciples to believe that they had risen to life and ascended to heaven, as the Royal Messiah in the hymns promised. As the messianic figure in the hymns had appropriated to himself the character and role of the Suffering Servant of Isaiah, so also had he appropriated to himself the exaltation of Isaiah 52:13, "Behold, my servant shall prosper, he shall be exalted and lifted up, and shall be very high." At the time of the murder of the messianic figures, his disciples took the abusive neglect of his body in the streets as a reason to appropriate to him also Isaiah 53:9 and 12:

> They made his grave with the wicked and with a rich man in his death, although he had done no violence, and there was no deceit in his mouth....Therefore I will divide him a portion with the great, and he shall divide the spoil with the strong, because he poured out his soul to death, and was numbered with the transgressors; yet he bore the sin of many, and made intercession for the transgressors.

It was a short leap, in the minds of the disciples of the Qumran Messiahs, from this Isaianic notion, to fashioning an association between the disappearance of the corpse and resurrection and ascension to the heavenly enthronement, which the author of the Thanksgiving Hymns had anticipated and promised.

Knohl sees the outcome of this historic event in Roman history to have been of great significance and relevance to the Qumran Community and its literature.

Thus after the Messiah's death his believers created a "catastrophic" ideology. The rejection of the Messiah, his humiliation, and his death were thought to have been foretold in the Scriptures and to be necessary stages in the process of redemption. The disciples [of the Qumran Messiahs] believed that the humiliated and pierced Messiah had been resurrected after three days and that he was due to reappear on earth as redeemer, victor, and judge.

Daniel prophesied that the fourth beast would be destroyed and the kingdom would be given to the "Son of Man," whom Daniel described as sitting on a heavenly throne and as coming in the clouds of heaven. The disciples and followers of the Qumranic Messiah believed that he had been resurrected after three days and had risen to heaven in a cloud. He now sat in heaven as he had described himself in his vision—on a "throne of power in the angelic council." Eventually he would return, descending from above with the clouds of heaven, surrounded by angels. The time would then have come for the overthrow of the fourth beast—Rome—and the Messiah would thus fulfill Daniel's vision of the "son of man."[25]

Knohl points out that this is the first time in Israelite history that the notion of catastrophic messianism is introduced, in which "the humiliation, rejection, and death of the Messiah were regarded as an inseparable part of the redemptive process" and of his exaltation, enthronement, and ultimate apotheosis as divine judge.[26]

Why the Suffering Servant and Messianic Judge, Not the Son of Man at Qumran?

The enigma in all of this lies in one question: why do the Qumran texts not employ the Enochic term *Son of Man* to refer to their messianic eschatological judge, or to their suffering, dying, exalted, and enthroned Messiah, in the manner in which the Synoptic Gospels refer to him? The Qumran Community's model of the suffering and dying Messiah who was to become the Eschatological Judge lay close in time, concept, geography, and sociopolitical setting, to the Son of Man *logia* of the Synoptic Gospels. Both communities depended heavily upon the Enochic tradition. The Son of Man figure was prominent under that title in that Enochic tradition. The Daniel narrative about heavenly exaltation of the Son of Man similarly shaped both the Qumranic and Jesus Movement expectations. Why is the suffering messianic eschatological judge of Qumran not called by the standard title? It seems likely that the writers saw the connection between Jesus and the Qumran model of the suffering, dying, and exalted Messiah, and had good reason to integrate those characteristics into their model of Jesus' self-concept as Son of Man. Why the difference between the two apocalyptic communities?

In his erudite and incisive chapter on the "The Schism between Qumran and Enochic Judaism," Gabriele Boccaccini emphasizes that there are two types of documents in the Dead Sea Scrolls: those common to Essenes both within and outside of Qumran and those unique to Qumran.[27] The former are pre-sectarian or extra-sectarian and remained normative for the urban Essenes, while the latter are sectarian in character and chronology, and exclusive to Qumran. Thus, prior to the cloistering of the Qumran Essenes, the Halakhic Letter, Dream Visions, Jubilees, the Temple Scroll, the Proto-Epistle of Enoch, and the Damascus Document (CD) were theologically determinative in the thought systems and practice of all Essene communities. CD states that God calls his righteous people to separate themselves from the world and declares, surprisingly, that God has not elected all of Israel, but only a remnant, to salvation.

However, like the other documents listed, CD provides for a certain degree of free will exercised by humans and sub-divine heavenly beings. Thus the strict supralapsarian determinism of the sectarian documents at Qumran was not standard in Essenism before and outside of Qumran. That Qumranic doctrine of determinism, Boccaccini argues, made no room for any freedom of will on the part of humans, or of the "fallen angels" who were seen as the source of evil in the world. Moreover, the Parables of Enoch, which elaborate the Danielic tradition of the exalted Son of Man, since they were not present at Qumran, must have been an addition to the Essene literature outside of Qumran among the urban Essenes. They must have been produced after the cloistering of the sectarian community. This is a critical fact in the argument because the Parables (Similitudes) clearly speak against the Qumranic notion of supralapsarian determinism, as do other facets of 1 Enoch:

The Epistle of Enoch does not simply lack specific Qumranic elements, it has specific anti-Qumranic elements. The most obvious is 1 En 98:4. The passage explicitly condemns those who state that since human beings are victims of a corrupted universe, they are not responsible for the sins they commit, and they blame others (God or the evil angels) for having exported "sin" into the world. "I have sworn unto you, sinners: In the same manner that a mountain has never turned into a servant, nor shall a hill (ever) become a maidservant or a woman; likewise, neither has sin been exported into the world. It is the people who have themselves invented it. And those who commit it shall come under a great curse" (98:4).[28]

In the sectarian documents unique to Qumran, evil is transcendent and supralapsarian in both source and remedy: a state of affairs preset by God from the beginning by election of some to righteousness and others to damnation. In the urban Essene movement, salvation from evil is accomplished by a divine salvific intervention, for which a Son of Man, like the one in Daniel, would be an adequate resource, when he descends as judge to separate the righteous from the unrighteous. Boccaccini points out that the cosmic tragedy, induced by fallen angels (Sons of God who cavorted with the daughters of men, Gn 6), requires more than a human or angelic savior since in order to subdue the evil powers, such a judge or redeemer must have power superior to that of those angels who brought evil into the world. The exaltation of the Son of Man to the heavenly enthronement, in the Enochic tradition outside Qumran, places the Son of Man above the angels in power and glory. Thus, in Enochic literature outside Qumran, the Son of Man is empowered by God to bring the ultimate resolution to life, history, and evil, at his advent as eschatological judge. The Parables of Enoch were part of the urban Essene theological tradition, not the tradition of Qumran.

Among the Essenes outside Qumran, one can willfully choose a righteous life: "The boundaries between the chosen and the wicked remain permeable. The door to salvation, which the Damascus Document kept open only for a limited period of time and which the sectarian documents [at Qumran] barred from the beginning for those who have not been chosen by God, will be open until the very last moment."[29]

The most distinctive quality of this extra-Qumranic Essene model lies in the fact that humans can contribute to their legitimate inclusion in the community of the elect by willfully conducting their lives as the righteous ones, the people of the holy ones of the Most High. There is no possibility of such human action in will or deed at Qumran. There, all is preset from eternity. God has preset the destiny of the elect and the reprobate. There is no room for one's volitional choice to live in complicity with evil or in identification with the righteousness of God, as one of the people of the holy ones of the Most High. One has only one's preset destiny. So at Qumran there is no place for a Son of Man, as redemptive messianic figure or as messianic eschatological judge. God is the only judge, and he made the final judgment by a supralapsarian act at the time that he decided to create the world and humanity in it. Both salvation and judgment, therefore, are already past. They will not come at the end of time. There is no role for the Son of Man:

> The Qumran community did not become less apocalyptic, if we consider its roots and worldview; but it certainly became less Enochic the further it parted from the parallel development of mainstream Enochic Judaism since the first century BCE. Therefore, the decreasing influence of Enochic literature on the sectarian texts is by no means surprising; it is the logical consequence of the schism between Qumran and Enochic Judaism.[30]

Why the Suffering Messiah at Qumran?

Knohl offers an intriguing rationale in his "Sherlock Holmes" narrative. He asserts that the Royal Messiah who produced the messianic hymns at Qumran was promoting a notion that ran counter to the orthodox doctrine of the community. His idea of a suffering Messiah, who would redeem and preserve the community of the righteous, was an attempt to recover a pre-sectarian biblical doctrine. He associated the suffering Messiah as exalted judge with Psalms 2, 8, and 110; Daniel 7; and Isaiah 52:13 and 53.

His doctrine was heretical at Qumran. This caused the unusual condition of the manuscripts of the hymns as we have them. Knohl suggests that normal aging, decay, or environmental conditions were not the cause of these manuscripts' being in fragments. Other manuscripts were discovered in fragments in the caves at Qumran because their clay containers had been menaced, damaged, or destroyed. The main manuscript of this edition of the hymns was found in its jar, undisturbed, but carefully and intentionally torn into rather large pieces and then stored.[31]

Knohl judges that this tells us an important story. This edition of the manuscripts was suppressed at Qumran. It was torn into pieces with careful intentionality. The pieces were preserved by one of the heretical messiah's devotees, who carefully and surreptitiously placed these pieces in the clay jars in the caves, along with the rest of the library. It would have been impossible to employ the term *Son of Man* at Qumran. It had neither credence nor currency and would have made the heresy extremely obvious and unnecessarily offensive, "sticking it into the face of the authorities" of the esoteric supralapsarian community. This scenario, despite its speculative quality, is possible. Whether one can declare that it is probable requires further evidence confirming that there was the type of heretical movement at Qumran that Knohl proposes as the key to his argument.

If this speculative theory is true, in a suppressed text of the Dead Sea Scrolls library three key factors conspire to form a single historical datum that is eminently relevant to Jesus as he was fashioned into the Son of Man character in the Gospels. First, we have at Qumran a messianic figure who speaks of his role as that of proclaiming the kingdom of God, Bultmann's first category of Son of Man *logia* in the Gospels. Second, Qumran presents a messianic figure who is suffering, dying, and then exalted by God to the status of a heavenly figure, Bultmann's second category. Finally, the Hodayot and the War Scroll present a Messiah who takes up the role of eschatological judge, Bultmann's third category. Thus we have at Qumran a *virtual* Son of Man, like the *literal* Son of Man in the Jesus Movement, and its gospel narratives.

If Knohl's argument holds water, Jesus, the literary character who traverses the pages of the canonical Gospels, internalized as the second phase of his personal identity development an Essene concept of a suffering and dying Messiah (Mt 12:40, 17:12, 17:22) that had already existed for some time in a heretical form of Qumran Essenism; and Jesus, as literary character, is depicted as having identified with the Son of Man of 1 Enoch, Daniel, and Ezekiel.

THE PROGRESSION OF IMAGES III: DANIEL'S VISION

The Exalted Son of Man in Daniel is remarkable in many ways. Daniel reports a vision in which "one like a Son of Man was introduced to the Ancient of Days in heaven." Scholars generally agree that the term *Son of Man* in 7:13 means a human being or mortal, as in Ezekiel. He is called and presented before God.[32] Contrary to events in Ezekiel, this man is accorded a place of high honor next to God himself. He is given power, dominion, judgment, and responsibility to bring down the evil kingdoms and empires operating on earth. The Son of Man in this model functions as a political and military chief of staff to the Most High, hence his permanent status in heaven at the throne of God. However, through his mundane field forces, he carries out operations on earth to accomplish the objectives of his mandate. His power, dominion, judgment, and responsibility are delegated to the people of the holy ones of the Most High, his action agents or field forces who subdue evil and bring in the divine reign on earth.

It seems quite clear that Jesus had just this picture in the back of his mind when he spoke to Nathanael in John 1:51, declaring that Nathanael and the multitude would see heaven opened and the angels ascending and descending upon the Son of Man. With assiduous intentionality, Jesus is identified here as the Son of Man Messiah and not the Son of David Messiah, making clear and certain that he is the Son of Man of heavenly status. Obviously Jesus' third stage of self-image development as Son of Man depends upon Daniel. In the Gospel stories he is of the human and mortal. He is also a heavenly being whose divinity and transcendent destiny has already been described (Jn 1:1–3). His presence on earth belies his heavenly status and proper locus.[33]

At this point Jesus is described as the exalted Son of Man, despite the impending season of suffering on earth. He has come to believe that Daniel prophesied of him. Though the mission of the disciples to proclaim the advent of the kingdom of God has failed, and the multitudes have left in despair and disinterest, from his impending heavenly status, after suffering and exaltation, he will direct the field operations on earth that will bring in the reign of God. He has failed to do it on earth because he has been opposed by the religious and political authorities, but he will triumph and those who opposed him and killed him will be surprised in the end to see the tables turned.

Obviously the Jesus in the story is moving to an increasingly apocalyptic perspective of himself and his understanding of what it means for him to be the Son of Man. He began as a human being like Ezekiel, proclaiming the coming of God's reign on earth. By Mark 8, and the failure of the first naïve mission of kingdom proclamation, he moved the apocalyptic metaphor up a few notches, announcing his impending suffering and death at the hands of wicked men. This is a move from Ezekiel to the Qumran Essenes' suffering Messiah of the Hodayot, the Serekh ha-Yahad, and the War Scroll.

Almost within the same breath, the horizon is raised again. We hear the promise that the Son of Man will be mightily exalted as the Son of Man of Daniel. The apocalyptic vision has enlarged and become both cosmic and transcendental. The mundane and heavenly worlds of the apocalyptic vision are coalescing in the exaltation of the messianic Son of Man to his status as divinely ordained chief of staff of kingdom operations. In this exalted role, he will join earth and heaven in the endeavor to bring in God's kingdom. He will recruit the hosts of heaven and the people of the holy ones of the Most High on earth for this grand and inevitably victorious offensive. They will see heaven open and the angels ascending and descending upon the Son of Man (Jn 1:51).

THE PROGRESSION OF IMAGES IV: 1 ENOCH 37–71

Scholars of the Son of Man issue have long associated this title, given to Jesus by the gospel writers, with the passage in Daniel just discussed. Recently, however, more attention has been given to the relationship between the Son of Man in the Parables of Enoch and Jesus as Son of Man in the Synoptic Gospels. The Parables, with their articulate, apocalyptic Essene perspective, offer an essential component for interpreting the distinctive way the Synoptic Gospels elaborate the fourth stage in the development of the Jesus Son of Man motif.

Clearly Jesus, as a literary character, came on the scene as an Ezekiel-like prophet, proclaiming the advent of God's reign on earth. The narrative soon thereafter presents Jesus as the Suffering Servant of Qumran, as establishing the divine reign on earth. Relatively quickly in the Gospel story, we see Jesus emphasizing, as his vision of himself, the exalted Son of Man of Daniel. The second and third phases of Jesus' self-image development arise as a result of the failure of the mission to bring in the divine reign. Obviously, the Gospel narratives present Jesus' as (1) sensing his mission running into trouble, as (2) becoming increasingly aware of a collision course with the authorities, and as (3) perceiving that a catastrophic impasse is more and more inevitable. His response at each point was to move his self-concept increasingly toward a mythic and magical destiny. The self-image of the confident man proclaiming the divine reign shifted to that of the suffering Messiah, who then became the divinely exalted and vindicated Son of Man in this Gospel scenario.

The fourth phase seems to have become full-blown when he finally found himself standing before Caiaphas and Pilate. There he raises the mythic imagination of the apocalyptic vision one step higher. Before Caiaphas, he envisions himself as the Son of Man of 1 Enoch who leaves his transcendent "enthronement" and returns to earth on the clouds of heaven as the Eschatological Judge. Before Pilate, he declares that the kingdom he was trying to establish on earth is a kingdom that he at long-last realizes is not of this world: "Jesus answered, *'My kingdom is not of this world; if my kingship were of this world, my servants would fight so that I might not be handed over to the Jews; but my kingdom is not of the world'*" (Jn 18:36). It is transcendental and has a spiritual component that resides in the inner selves of those with allegiance to him ("*The kingdom of God is within and among you*" [Lk 17:21]).

As Jesus moved further toward the impasse with the authorities, it dawned on him that he had set himself on a totally destructive trajectory of hopeless defeat. The only hope for salvaging himself, his reputation, and his project was to move it to a divine, magical, transcendent, and spiritualized plane. The model of the Son of Man in Daniel gave him such a transcendental Son of Man. God had exalted and commissioned that one to bring in the divine reign on earth, and to do it from his remote heavenly locus. The Son of Man in 1 Enoch reinforced that model. So the Jesus of the story perceived that he could not lose, even if defeated and killed on earth, so long as it was certain that God's purposes guaranteed his ultimate exaltation; particularly when it meant that all those who opposed the Son of Man on earth would be shown up for the ultimately defeated scoundrels that they really were.

So it should not be a surprise to us that this fourth phase of the progression of images should be the apocalyptic eschatological picture from 1 Enoch. The Son of Man of the Parables of Enoch offered a model of the Son of Man being manifested in his heavenly status, and setting things right in God's domain, as the Judge at the eschaton. Enoch 38:3ff uses the term *the Righteous One* as a designation of the Son of Man and prophesies that when "the secrets of the Righteous One are revealed, he shall judge the sinners." In 1 Enoch 61:8ff, the Son of Man is referred to as the Elect One, a frequently recurring title for him in the Parables of Enoch. God, the Lord of the Spirits,

> placed the Elect One on the throne of glory; and he shall judge all the works of the holy ones in heaven above, weighing in the balance their deeds. And when he shall lift up his countenance in order to judge the secret ways of theirs, by the word of the name of the Lord of the Spirits, and their conduct, by the method of the righteous judgment of the Lord of the Spirits, then they shall all speak with one voice, blessing, glorifying, extolling, sanctifying the name of the Lord of the Spirits.

The consequences of this judgment by the Son of Man are explicated where we read, "Open your eyes and lift up your eyebrows, if you are able to recognize the Elect One!" The narrative continues, describing the day of judgment for the kings, governors, high officials, and landlords:

> One half portion of them shall glance at the other half; they shall be terrified and dejected; and pain shall seize them when they see that Son of Man sitting on the throne of his glory. On that day, all the kings, the governors, the high officials, and those who rule the earth shall fall down before him on their faces, and worship and raise their

hopes in that Son of Man; they shall beg and plead for mercy at his feet. But the Lord of the Spirits himself will cause them to be frantic, so that they shall rush and depart from his presence. So he will deliver them to the angels for punishments in order that vengeance shall be executed on them, oppressors of his children and his elect ones.

The consummation of the judgment by the Son of Man is going to be joy in heaven. In 69:27ff, Enoch tells us of the Son of Man who executes the judgment of God upon the earth at the end of time, exterminating all evil and evil ones, gathering the righteous of God into the community of God's reign, and causing blessing, glorifying, and extolling to be offered the Lord of the Spirits. This is "on account of the fact that the name of that (Son of) Man was revealed to them. Thenceforth nothing that is corruptible shall be found; for that Son of Man has appeared and has seated himself upon the throne of his glory; and all evil shall disappear from before his face."

One can imagine the enormous renewal of hope and meaning the literary character, Jesus, is represented as experiencing in his own sense of self, as he stood condemned before Caiaphas, and yet was able to internalize this triumphal vision of 1 Enoch and of his own destiny as the Son of Man and Eschatological Judge. He would return on the clouds of heaven, with all the holy angels, in the power and great glory of God, finally vindicated and prepared to exterminate his adversaries. This triumphalist vision holds up for him all the way to the very last minutes on the cross. At that last moment he loses his grip on his delusional drama and is thrust painfully into reality—the reality of his death.

So the Jesus of the dramatic Gospel narrative is characterized by the Synoptic Gospel authors as building his own role and self-image, as he progressed along the explorative pilgrimage of his life. He was doing life, and fashioning its shape, right in the middle of the action of living. This was the journey of living out what he increasingly perceived to be his divinely ordered destiny. So Jesus, the Jew, identified himself as the Son of Man of Judaic tradition. He began his ministry believing he was, like Ezekiel, a human Son of Man called to a prophetic role of proclaiming the impending advent of the reign of God on earth. When his mission failed, he ratcheted up his self-image as Son of Man a number of notches to the role of the Suffering Servant-Messiah from the Qumran heresy of the Hodayot and the War Scroll, foreseeing the impasse with the Jewish religious authorities for which he seemed to be headed.

As the trajectory of his conflict with the power people in Jerusalem and with the audiences in Galilee progressed toward open opposition, Jesus realized this collision course would lead to his death. Nonetheless, he developed the transcendental vision that God would vindicate him by exaltation to a heavenly status similar to that of the Son of Man in Daniel. In the final moments of his life, when he was inescapably a prisoner of the Jewish and Roman authorities, he escalated his vision of what it meant to be the Son of Man to the point of seeing himself in the role of Eschatological Judge who would return on the clouds of heaven on the last day and gather the righteous, exterminating the wicked. As this progress became increasingly lethal, Jesus, as literary character in this drama, moved along in a composite Son of Man mythology, until he was captivated and captured by it.

There is great psychological strength and empowerment in such a mythic vision of one's destiny, in the face of the vicissitudes, failures, and irresolvable impasses of life. The psychology of projection makes it possible for a person in a difficult moment in life's travail to identify with an idealized figure or mentor to such a degree as to internalize the person and identity of that heroic figure. Capps refers to this as the process in which a person like Jesus develops into a fictive character through fashioning his Master Story by identification with a heroic and somewhat mythic figure.[34] Surely it is the inebriating power of this transcendent vision of self as the Son of Man that empowered Jesus in his dramatic role.

It gave him the strength and narcissistic confidence to violate the temple and disrupt the legal enterprise of the money changers, a perfectly innocent business of great help to pilgrims from the provinces. He is depicted as carrying out this violation of the temple, consciously and intentionally, in the face of his inevitable defeat by the authorities in Jerusalem. He did it boldly in the face of the fact that he was throwing down the gauntlet in a final form of provocation that he knew would precipitate his death.

Earlier in Galilee his brothers tried to provoke him to go up to the feast in Jerusalem. He insisted that he would not go to the Passover that year because of the hostility of the authorities (Jn 7:1–9; Mt 20:17–19). After a few days of reflection, the brothers having gone on ahead, he suddenly changed his mind. With determination, he "steadfastly set his face to go to Jerusalem" (Lk 9:5; Jn 7:10). Arriving there, he apparently decided that what he was to do he would do quickly, moving toward his heavenly exaltation as a Danielac Son of Man. So he precipitated his death by violating the holy places.

This gives meaning to his remark to Judas at the Last Supper, "*What you must do, do quickly.*" It also affords some credence to the notion in the Gospel of Judas that he and Jesus had a private scheme to quickly effect Jesus' exaltation by provoking the authorities to take him. Apparently Judas thought this would provoke the rise of a popular revolution, while Jesus had already moved to the vision of a heavenly exaltation. Judas was surprised and lethally disappointed by Jesus' nonresistance in Gethsemane and by his passive complicity in the legal actions against him.

CONCLUSION

Jesus progressively identified himself with the lead character in his own apocalyptic drama and then lost his footing; lost all poetic distance from his role. He internalized that lead figure as his own real self, completing in his own person the development of the character in the story. By this point in the drama, Jesus had moved sure-footedly into the delusion of his mythic Son of Man drama. How pathetic and heart wrenching, therefore, the words of graphic reality bursting upon him finally, at the end: "*My God, my God, why have you forsaken me?*" It is no wonder that by the beginning of the second century, this tragic vision of the Son of Man had been revised by the Fourth Gospel to eliminate the notion of the triumphalistic Eschatological Judge. John turned Jesus, as Son of Man, into the Suffering Servant-Redeemer. John's Heavenly Messiah became the Divine Savior?

After rehearsing in detail how the sources developed the Jesus character in their dramatic narratives, it is necessary to ask what it might have been about the historical Jesus, if there was one at all, that made it possible to generate such a remarkable literary work around him as the main character. The thing that has functioned throughout history as the source of consolation and hope for perplexed humanity is not the historical Jesus, but the literary character of Jesus that we have in the Gospels. This literary character is sufficiently developed to carry the enormous symbolic drama of transcendent idealism, personal endurance, consummate faith, religious certitude, vibrant human spirituality, and triumphal hope, with which we have loaded him. The myth is both the medium and message.

By those meanings he has carried the human community through prosperity and adversity, triumph and tragedy, pleasure and pain, through life and death. This notion of him has sustained an innumerable multitude of believers in the Christian gospel of divine grace. What was it about him that could generate such a resilient force for good, despite his obviously delusional sense of reality and his endgame of triumphalistic tragedy?

Schweitzer's resort to a thoroughgoing eschatology was an escape from the bite of that delusional reality. He effected that slight of hand by shifting Jesus' delusional vision from his reality regarding this mundane world to a supernaturalized world of reality in some transcendental world to come. Charles R. Joy informs us that the insights that constituted the core of Schweitzer's conclusions came to him during military maneuvers in Germany and "changed the whole course of Schweitzer's thinking, and in so doing changed the whole course of modern theology."[35] He reported Schweitzer as declaring, "When I reached home after the maneuvers, entirely new horizons had opened themselves to me. Of this I was certain: that Jesus had announced no kingdom that was to be founded and realized in the natural world by himself and the believers, but one that was to be expected as coming with the almost immediate dawn of a supernatural age."[36]

Joy continues his observation regarding Schweitzer's new-found convictions and Christological perspective: "He himself was sure that Jesus was completely sane. That Jesus existed, that he shared the Messianic ideas of late Judaism, that he who was really a descendant of David had come to believe that in the world to come he was destined to be the Messiah, are in no rational sense evidences of mental disease."[37]

The authentic warrant for any religion is: "Will it bury your child?"

For twenty centuries the mythic drama of Jesus of Nazareth empowered tragically grieving parents to stand at the brink of an empty grave and gently lower their lost child into it—and have some meaning left in life. It empowered them to survive, go on, love again, live again, and hope again. That mythic drama also empowered civilizations, generating the grandest idealism and the most majestic creations of beauty. It was not the historical Jesus who did that. It was the literary character of Jesus, from the narrative drama of the Gospels and from the confessional myths and transcendental vision made of it.

What did the man, if there was a man, behind that story have that made that drama and its myth so vitalizing? That the myth is powerful and empowering is no mystery. We see and know it in operational practicality every day. But what was it about that historic Son of Man (*bar enosh, ben Adam*), real or imagined, behind the literary character that made it possible for him to generate and carry the transcendental weight and power of that myth? That will forever be the most intriguing question and the most unsolvable mystery.

THE CANONICAL-HISTORICAL JESUS

R. Joseph Hoffmann

With the thunderous exception of the canonical version of Luke's Gospel, the historicity of Jesus is not a question for the New Testament writers. I suggest that his historical existence cannot be established and cannot be confuted on the basis of the literary remains we possess from the late first and early second century. The radical myth school of the nineteenth century that advocated nonhistoricity and the view that serious scholarship is no longer interested in the question mark the extremes. However, the question that dominates early Christian discussion, the question through which the question of the historicity of Jesus emerges in later discussion, is fundamentally theological: the question of his humanity.

My argument in this modest essay is that while we cannot know for certain very much about a historical Jesus, not even for certain whether he existed, we can reconstruct fairly exactly the theological conditions under which his historical existence became indispensable for Christian theology. This being so, the question of the selection of books that were useful in the pitched battles between two views of Jesus—call them spiritual and earthly—is central, not anterior, to the question we call historicity.

When we think of the chronology of events that led to the development of the New Testament, we usually think of the canon in its final position. The making of the church's book is regarded as the last act, so to speak, in the compilation of letters, short stories, an apocalypse, and Gospels that make up the collection. The way scholars and theologians have traditionally spoken about the canon suggests that it has almost nothing to do with the subject matter of the whole, but that its wholeness determines the permissible limits of the subject matter.

That it is, in some sense, an executive decision imposed on unruly members. If Jesus is the protagonist of the Gospels, the saving presence that inspires Paul's letters, the heavenly king of Revelation, he is, in some strange way, missing from the concept of a canon. That is because a canon is a selection of books thought to be authoritative and complete. In Greek the word implies a hard and inflexible instrument used for writing, and its closest Latin equivalent is *regula*, from which we get words like ruler and rule—a standard against which other things must be judged. The canon as it is traditionally understood regulates what can be regarded as trustworthy, or to use a term manufactured by the church fathers, apostolic.

*   *   *

The theory that has dominated New Testament scholarship until relatively recently has run something like this. The historical Jesus was enshrined in memories about his life, words, and work. This would have happened before his death and the process would have accelerated following his death, especially if his death was interpreted as a martyrdom, or otherwise thought to have significant consequences.

Of these memories (without prejudice to their historicity), the event of his Resurrection was the most prominent, for obvious reasons. The memory, embedded in oral traditions about Jesus, was not fixed and final; it moved from mouth to ear, community to community. It became affixed to local traditions—the Jesus of Rome was not in every detail the Jesus of Antioch or Anatolia. The Jesus of Mark is not the Jesus of the Fourth Gospel. Scholars for the last century have described the variance in these memories as trajectories or lines of tradition rather than as a single tradition arising from a single source. Various Jesus quests and other Jesus projects have made it their business to bring the trajectories as close as possible to a defining event, and this defining event is assumed to be historical.

In time, recorders of the traditions arose. We think they worked in the service of a movement (communities of believers), not as simple biographers, and that their work was closely attached to preaching and propaganda. They recorded things Jesus was said to have said, and said to have done. Their words were not coherent biographies, but more of the order of *aides memoires* or collections of sayings, reminiscences. They were not, as far as we can determine, transcriptional—that is, based on direct knowledge, though later, for apologetic reasons, the concept of witness and successions of witnesses becomes prominent. The assured authority these writings lacked at the point of their composition is imposed by later writers in debates about what constitutes right belief or orthodoxy.

Some early communities seem to have possessed a class of prophets—women and men believed to be able to recall the words of Jesus on a number of topics, ranging from divorce to paying taxes to the unimportance of worldly goods and duties towards neighbors and enemies. Other strands envisioned Jesus pronouncing on the end of days and God's judgment. Others envisioned him as a teacher of aphoristic wisdom and a revealer sent by God to preach, essentially, a message about his heavenly origins. This last strand tended to portray Jesus as a relatively obscure figure whose sayings were mysterious and limited to a kind of spiritual elite, as in the Fourth Gospel. But even in the so-called Synoptic Gospels, this strand is present with the role of the elite being played by apostles whose minds have been clouded by earthly concerns. Since the mid-twentieth century it has been convenient if not exact to call this strand "Gnostic." Gnosticism was not one thing, however, but many things; even Irenaeus, who made bashing Gnostics a fine art, compares them to weeds.

To be brief, however: at some point at the end of the first century and continuing well into the second, Gospels appear, as do letters from missionaries, apocalypses both Christian and adopted, books of oracles, stories of the apostles and their miraculous feats. (One of the remarkable things about this development is the sheer increase of letters ascribed to "the apostles" and women followers of Jesus' day, some seventy-five years and more after the death of Jesus.) As in the study of secular literature, scholars recognize these variant literary forms as genres or types, each type serving a slightly different confessional purpose but all tending to support the interests of Christian communities in knowing who Jesus was, what he said, what he had come to do.

Different communities said different things, however. The most heavily Gnosticized of them, while not denying the historical Jesus, possessed a theology of such Pythagorean complexity that it sometimes verges on what Joseph Fitzmyer once described as "crazy." The ones we recognize as "orthodox" or canonical, for the most part, are familiar if unresolved blends of the historical and supernatural, the pedagogical and the mysterious: words about the poor, or advice about adultery, stand next to stories about raising a widow's son from the dead, and being transfigured alongside Moses and Elijah. The effect of this blending was to create a god-man of uncertain proportions. How human was he? How divine? The literature itself did not provide the percentages, the definitions, but the questions nagged and would finally result in official decisions about the divinity and humanity of Jesus in the fourth and fifth century.

*   *   *

Between the second and the fourth century, however, is the making of the New Testament. And this is where the canon—the process of winnowing and selection—comes in. It is important to remember, as we look at the canon, that no one who wove the web of sayings and deeds into the form we call Gospel wrote with the intention of having his work anthologized. Think back to those literature survey courses you may have taken in college—Shakespeare wrote what he wrote; he did not design it to be included as a unit in the section before the Metaphysical poets and Restoration Drama. "Mark" likewise wrote what he wrote; his editors edited what they edited, and the canon makers chose what they chose.

The canon gives an *impression* of consensus, evangelical uniformity, as if a vote had been taken, with all members present, to certify that what is written is their contribution to the "authorized version" of Jesus. This is of course the impression the proponents of canonicity (though not with one voice or at one time) wished to convey when they linked the canon to the defense of a growing body of doctrine, or teaching about Jesus, and the origins of that doctrine to another idea, belief in apostolicity.

To oversimplify this process: certain beliefs about Jesus, including above all the matter of his humanity and divinity, were at the center of second- and third-century discussion. This discussion does not take the form of theological point and counterpoint in its earliest phases. In its earliest phases, it must go back to the way the Jesus story spread, or was understood, in places like Antioch, Ephesus, Rome, and Sinope, or was communicated by missionaries like Paul, whose references to the historical Jesus, if there are any, are not prominent.

What we possess are documentary traces of the discussion before it becomes an official debate by early church leaders, who will make each other orthodox and heretical in the course of the argument. In its formative stages, including the composition of the individual New Testament books, Christianity did not seek uniformity of doctrine because the shapers of the Jesus tradition did not imagine their works would be forced into alignment.

The idea of a fourfold or tetramorph Gospel goes back to ancient harmonies like Tatian's and are still being produced for use in Sunday schools, like McGarvey's 1914 *Fourfold Gospel*, "Resulting in a complete chronological life of Christ, divided into titled sections and sub-divisions, with comments injected in the text." It is too much to say that individual writers thought they had a monopoly on the whole story—an author of John's Gospel, for example, expressly puts his story forward as a collection, a partial one—or that individual writers wrote in order to produce a final version, though an editor of the Gospel called Luke writes with an intention to sequentialize versions of the sources he knows. In terms of other kinds of New Testament literature, Paul may have had a canonical intention, but the collecting and canonizing of his letters and the creation of new ones is an event of the early second century, of a Paul devotee known to history as a heretic—Marcion—not of his lifetime.

The canon does not arise as a spontaneous development, any more than Christian orthodoxy emerges as a single deposit in a bank account—to use an image from the second century. The canon is the regulation of sources that supported a growing consensus about who Jesus was, or rather, what was to be believed about him. If not a majority, then a significant, well-organized, and powerful minority of voices found his complete and total humanity a nonnegotiable criterion for believing the right thing about him. They found their support for this view in a fairly small number of sources that they believed dated from apostolic times.

My argument here is that it is impossible to discuss the historicity of Jesus simply on the basis of the individual sources available in the church's selection of books, or by parsing their contents, and equally difficult to advance the argument much further on the basis of Gnostic and apocryphal sources that did not make the final cut. I am certainly not saying that research into the sayings of Jesus and attempts to construct a prototype Gospel are useless. But the endeavor is bound to be incomplete unless the theological motives for defending a fully historical Jesus are brought into the picture. The early church, the framers of the canon especially, were not interested in a historical Jesus per se but in a fully human Jesus. Indeed, it is partly their concern and stress on this overt humanness with no accompanying mitigation of other claims—e.g., that he ascended into heaven, calmed seas, rose from the dead—that fuels speculation about whether such a man can have existed historically at all. The canon is not the proof of his historicity therefore, but the earliest theological matrix out of which suspicions about it arise. In any consideration of the historical Jesus therefore, the following propositions about the canonical and human Jesus need to be weighed.

1. The Gospels make no explicit argument for the historicity of Jesus. In the Gospels, his historical existence is assumed. In the letters of Paul—while I agree that Paul is profoundly silent on many of the historical markers—it is in the background. In late letters, such as 1 John, acknowledgement that Jesus has come in the flesh is made decisive—those who deny it are antichrist (4:3). I regard Galatians 4:4–5 as completely unhelpful as a "proof" of Paul's conviction as to the existence of an earthly, flesh and blood, Jesus: "But when the time had fully come, God sent his Son, born of a woman, born under law, to redeem those under law, that we might receive the full rights of sons. (ὅτε δὲ ἦλθεν τὸ πλήρωμα τοῦ χρόνου ἐξαπέστειλεν ὁ θεὸς τὸν υἱὸν αὐτοῦ, γενόμενον ἐκ γυναῖκος, γενόμενον ὑπὸ νόμον, ἵνα τοὺς ὑπὸ νόμον ἐξαγοράσῃ ἵνα τὴν υἱοθεσίαν ἀπολάβωμεν.)"

2. If there is a litmus test for the "physical historical" Jesus in the Gospels, it is the Crucifixion. Secondarily it is his bodily Resurrection—

which may sound odd, but in a significant way qualifies the *kind* of human existence his believers thought he possessed. In time, stories of virgin birth, fabulous details, and genealogy are appended to complete the story. The birth stories, however, are designed to illustrate Jesus' exceptionality, even to correct the impressions of his human ordinariness. Any indifferent reading of the nativity accounts of Matthew and Luke sees them as epiphany stories whose closest analogies are accounts of the birth of Hermes in the Homeric "hymn," or of Augustus' in the account of Atia's pregnancy. That miraculous components from biblical sources are intertwined with these allusions is equally plain.

3. I believe that by the early second century, a certain comfort level concerning the humanity of Jesus was being achieved among significant teachers—the names we now group under designations such as apostolic fathers, the apologists, heresiologists—men like Polycarp, Ignatius, Justin, Irenaeus, and Tertullian. At the risk of being outrageous, I would add Marcion to the list even though he was not destined to become a church father but rather an arch-heretic. They had settled on the idea that Jesus was "truly" or "wholly" human. In the Nicene Creed it would run, "was incarnate by the Holy Spirit of the virgin Mary, and was made man; and was crucified also for us under Pontius Pilate; He suffered and was buried. (εκ Πνεύματος 'Αγίου καί Μαρίας τής Παρθένου καί ενανθρωπήσαντα. Σταυρωθέντα τε υπέρ ημών επί Ποντίου Πιλάτου καί παθόντα καί ταφέντα.)"

4. Beginning with Polycarp—that is, prior to 155 or so—the practice of proof-texting or citing scriptural passages to teach doctrine and win arguments becomes a standard method in Christian theology. This presupposes a process of selection of sources useful to root out teaching thought to be false or, to use the word that becomes fashionable by the end of the century, heretical. The canon therefore arises in the process of these debates with false teachers.

5. The key element in this process—which is not always explicit, that is, not a simple list of books decreed to be canonical such as the so-called Muratorian fragment or the decree of Pope Gelasius in the fifth century—is to affirm against the teachings of docetists and assorted Gnostic groups that Jesus of Nazareth has come in the flesh (truly born and truly died). This is the doctrinal motive of canon formation. It also

establishes once and for all the conjunction between canonicity, historicity, and humanity—three ideas now so closely interwoven theologically that they cannot easily be separated phenomenologically.

6. But there is a second motive: with the exception of Luke's belated construction of an apostolic college in the book of Acts, the apostles do not fare well in the Gospels. To be kind, they are slow-witted students. Without exploring the many interesting guesses about this characterization, early Christian writers like Irenaeus and Tertullian were obsessed with their rehabilitation—especially since teachers like Marcion preferred to leave them in the mud or at the bottom of their class. The true reasons for this characterization had been lost by the second century, indeed even by Luke's day, though there is ample reason to believe it was not historical accuracy but pedagogical necessity that sealed their reputation in Mark's Gospel. By the time Irenaeus writes his treatise against the heresies at the end of the second century, the idea of a continuous tradition of truth, transmitted by faithful, inerrant followers, and a faithful passing down of teaching from apostle to later teachers (John to Polycarp and Anicetus, for example) has become standard. Canonicity has been tied to apostolicity.

7. Irenaeus is really the first to make this motive explicit around the year 180, though an earlier church leader (how much earlier is hard to decide) named Papias hints at something of the same logic. Actually Papias is remembered by the historian Eusebius as a man with limited intellectual powers (3.39.13), but the germ of an idea of unbroken tradition extending from Jesus to the apostles to the presbyters is present in his journalistic approach to sources. His criterion is oral tradition handed down to presbyters; in fact, he says he doesn't put much stock in "books" and rejects the voluminous falsehoods they contain—whatever that may mean—but prizes the living "voice of truth." Papias's reference to "books" is odd, and even what he says about what he *says* he knows, for example, about Gospels like Mark and Matthew, is improbable.

However that may be, Irenaeus exploits the idea of unbroken male succession to offer a fourfold attestation of truth, corresponding he says (3.11.8) to the four principal churches, the four winds, and the four corners of the earth. "It is impossible that the Gospels should be greater or fewer in number than four."

Irenaeus argues tradition as a *natural* principle: using his predecessors' assumptions, he finds denial of the humanity of Jesus the benchmark of false teaching and in a famous scene depicts his own teacher Polycarp as rejecting Marcion in a bathhouse in Ephesus, calling him the first born of Satan (AH 3.3.4). The key to overcoming the spiritualized Jesus of Gnosticism was to insist on an unbroken tradition that required his material, physical existence. An earthly, fully historical savior is the presupposition of the historical process he uses as the basis of his argument.

The *historical* Jesus is therefore not inherent in any Gospel, nor even in the canon, but in a process. That process was slow to develop and developed in response to specific threats, the teachings of men and women who rejected a mundane understanding of salvation and the role of Jesus in the process. The historical Jesus was not necessitated by the Gospel, but by the need for an authoritative teacher who selects and commissions other teachers, and in a self-referential way, who are able to select those books where the approved story is told.

NOTES

PREFACE: OF ROCKS, HARD PLACES, AND JESUS FATIGUE

1. Adolf von Harnack, *What Is Christianity?* trans. Thomas Bailey Sanders (Philadelphia: Fortress Press, 1986), p. 191.

2. http://www.secularhumanism.org/index.php?section=library&page=hoffmann_27_3.

3. R. Joseph Hoffmann, introduction, G. A. Wells, *The Jesus Legend* (Chicago: Open Court, 1996), p. xi.

4. William Dever, "What Remains of the House That Albright Built?" *Biblical Archaeologist* 56, no. 1 (March 1993): 464.

AN ALTERNATIVE Q AND THE QUEST OF THE EARTHLY JESUS

1. Dennis R. MacDonald, *The Homeric Epics and the Gospel of Mark* (New Haven, CT: Yale University Press, 2000).

2. John P. Meier, *A Marginal Jew: Rethinking the Historical Jesus* (New York: Doubleday, 1991), 1.167–95.

3. Ibid., 1.183.

4. Ibid., 1.174.

5. See Meier's sage and detailed treatment of this passage in *Marginal Jew*, 2.56–62.

6. Meier, *Marginal Jew*, 1.61. The ellipses are mine; I omit some content from Meier's reconstruction that also reeks of a Christian scribe.

7. I suspect that Josephus's treatment was much longer, in keeping with his more expansive treatments of religious turmoil during Pilate's administration of Judea according to the larger context (*A.J.* 18.55–89).

8. It is tempting to link the oracle against Jerusalem in *Logoi* 9 with such

an event, even though there is no mention of James, and even though it was considered an oracle of Jesus presented decades earlier.

9:20	"*O Jerusalem, Jerusalem, who kills the prophets*	13:34
	and stones those sent to her!	
	How often I wanted to gather your children together,	
	as a hen gathers her nestlings under «her» wings,	
	and you were not willing!	
9:21	*Look, your house is forsaken!"*	13:35

9. The closest verses probably are 13:2 and 9–10 (17:24 and 17:34–35).

10. Meier, *Marginal Jew*, 1.168.

11. Some scholars would propose that embarrassing too would have been the charge that Jesus cast out demons by Beelzebul (8:23 [11:15]), but one can easily imagine that the author created it in a polemic against "this evil generation."

12. Meier, *Marginal Jew*, 1.171.

13. Ibid., 1.172.

14. According to Paul, "the kingdom of God [is present] not in word but in power" (1 Cor 4:20).

15. In Gal 5:19–21, Paul lists vices and ends the list with the statement, "those who commit such acts will not inherit the kingdom of God." See also 1 Cor 6:9–10 and 15:50.

16. Meier, *Marginal Jew*, 1.176.

17. Ibid., 1.177.

JESUS AND THE BROTHERS: THE THEOLOGY OF THE IMPERFECT UNION

1. Marcus Borg, *Meeting Jesus Again for the First Time: The Historical Jesus and the Heart of Contemporary Faith* (New York: HarperCollins, 1994), p. 59.

2. John Crossan, *Birth of Christianity* (New York: HarperCollins, 1999), p. 212.

POPULAR MYTHOLOGY IN THE EARLY EMPIRE AND THE MULTIPLICITY OF JESUS TRADITIONS

1. Raymond E. Brown, *The Birth of the Messiah* (New York: Doubleday, 1993); Edwin D. Freed, *The Stories of Jesus' Birth. A Critical Introduction* (Sheffield, UK: Sheffield Academic Press, 2001); Gerd Lüdemann, *Virgin Birth? The Real Story of Mary and Her Son Jesus* (London: SCM, 1997).

2. Stanley E. Porter, *The Criteria for Authenticity in Historical-Jesus Research: Previous Discussion and New Proposals* (London: T&T Clark, 2000); Bernard Brandon Scott, ed., *Finding the Historical Jesus: Rules of Evidence* (Santa Rosa, CA: Polebridge, 2008); Gerd Theissen and Dagmar Winter, *The Quest for the Plausible Jesus: The Question of Criteria* (Louisville, KY: Westminster John Knox, 2002).

3. Justin J. Meggitt, "Sources: Use, Abuse and Neglect," in *Christianity at Corinth: The Scholarly Quest for the Corinthian Church*, ed. D. Horrell and E. Adams, pp. 241–53 (London: Westminster John Knox Press, 2004).

4. Justin J. Meggitt, "Magic and Early Christianity: Consumption and Competition," in *The Meanings of Magic: From the Bible to Buffalo Bill*, ed. A. Wygrant, pp. 89–116 (New York: Berghahn Books, 2006).

5. Justin J. Meggitt, "The Madness of King Jesus: Why Was Jesus Put to Death, but His Followers Were Not?" *Journal for the Study of the New Testament* 29, no. 4 (2007): 379–413.

6. Justin J. Meggitt, "Taking the Emperor's Clothes Seriously: The New Testament and the Roman Emperor," in *The Quest for Wisdom: Essays in Honour of Philip Budd*, ed. C. Joynes, pp. 143–70 (Cambridge: Orchard Academic, 2002).

7. Justin J. Meggitt, *Paul, Poverty and Survival* (Edinburgh: T&T Clark, 1998).

8. E. P. Thompson, *The Making of the English Working Class* (London: Victor Gollanz, 1963), p. 12.

9. See, for example, John R. Clarke, *Art in the Lives of Ordinary Romans: Visual Representation and Non-elite Viewers in Italy, 100 B.C.–A.D. 315* (Berkeley: University of California Press, 2003); W. Hansen, *Anthology of Greek Popular Literature* (Bloomington: Indiana University Press, 1998); Nicholas Horsfall, *The Culture of the Roman Plebs* (London: Duckworth, 2003); Ardle Mac Mahon and Jennifer Price, eds., *Roman Working Lives and Urban Living* (Oxford: Oxbow Books, 2005); Teresa Morgan, *Popular Morality in the Early Roman Empire* (Cambridge: Cambridge University Press, 2007).

10. K. R. Bradley, *Slaves and Masters in the Roman Empire: A Study in Social Control* (Oxford: Oxford University Press, 1984), pp. 150–53; see also Niklas

Holzberg, "The Fabulist, the Scholars, and the Discourse: Aesop Studies Today," *International Journal of the Classical Tradition* 6 (1999): 236–42; Leslie Kurke, "Aesop and the Contestation of Delphic Authority," in *The Cultures within Ancient Greek Culture: Contact, Conflict, Collaboration*, ed. C. Dougherty and L. Kurke, pp. 77–100 (Cambridge: Cambridge University Press, 2003); Lawrence M. Wills, "The Aesop Tradition," in *The Historical Jesus in Context*, ed. Amy-Jill Levine, Dale C. Allison, John Dominic Crossan, pp. 222–37 (Princeton, NJ: Princeton University Press, 2006).

11. David Braund and S. D. Kryzhitskiy, eds., *Classical Olbia and the Scythian World: From the Sixth Century BC to the Second Century AD*, Proceedings of the British Academy, 142 (Oxford: Oxford University Press/British Academy, 2007).

12. Catherine Hezser, *Jewish Literacy in Roman Palestine: Texts and Studies in Ancient Judaism* (Tübingen: Mohr-Siebeck, 2001), p. 71.

13. D. R. MacDonald, *Christianizing Homer: The Odyssey, Plato and the Acts of Andrew* (Oxford: Oxford University Press, 1994), p. 17.

14. Joseph Farrell, "Roman Homer," in *The Cambridge Companion to Homer*, ed. Robert Fowler, pp. 254–71 (Cambridge: Cambridge University Press, 2004).

15. Papyri Graecae Magicae (PGM) IV.2145–2240; Daniel Ogden, *Magic, Witchcraft and Ghosts in the Greek and Roman Worlds: A Sourcebook* (Oxford: Oxford University Press, 2002), pp. 270–72.

16. P. Lond. 121 (PGM VII); Peter Parsons, *City of the Sharp-Nosed Fish: Greek Lives in Roman Egypt* (London: Weidenfeld & Nicolson, 2007), p. 190.

17. Horsfall, *Culture of the Roman Plebs*, p. 56.

18. See Guido Schepens and Kris Delcroix, "Ancient Paradoxography: Origins, Evolution, Production and Consumption," in *La letteratura di consumo nel mondo greco-latino*, ed. Oronzo Pecere and Antonio Stramaglia, pp. 343–460 (Cassino, Italy: Universite degli Studi di Cassino, 1996); Hansen, *Anthology of Greek Popular Literature*.

19. Anna Clark, "Gods in Pompeian Graffiti," in *Ancient Graffiti in Context*, ed. Jennifer Baird and Claire Taylor (New York: Routledge, forthcoming).

20. Jörg Rüpke, *Religion of the Romans* (Cambridge: Polity, 2007), p. 126.

21. Bettina Bergmann, "The Roman House as Memory Theater: The House of the Tragic Poet in Pompeii," *Art Bulletin* 76, no. 2 (1994): 225–56; Bettina Bergmann, "Greek Masterpieces and Roman Recreative Fictions," *Harvard Studies in Classical Philology* 97 (1995): 79–120.

22. James Deetz, *In Small Things Forgotten: An Archaeology of Early American Life*, 2nd ed. (New York: Doubleday, 1996).

23. J. J. O'Hara, "Fragment of a Homer-Hypothesis with No Gods," *Zeitschrift für Papyrologie und Epigraphik* 56 (1984): 1–9.

24. David Castriota, *Myth, Ethos, and Actuality* (Madison: Wisconsin University Press, 1992), p. 78; see Maria Pretzler, "Pausanias and Oral Tradition," *Classical Quarterly* 55, no. 1 (2005): 241.

25. G. Comotti, *Music in Greek and Roman Culture* (Baltimore: Johns Hopkins University Press, 1989); J. G. Landels, *Music in Ancient Greece and Rome* (London: Routledge, 1999); Paul Veyne, *Did the Greeks Believe in Their Myths? An Essay on the Constitutive Imagination* (Chicago: Chicago University Press, 1983), pp. 139–40.

26. Kathleen M. Coleman, "Fatal Charades: Roman Executions Staged as Mythological Enactments," *Journal of Roman Studies* 80 (1990): 44–73.

27. M. Bonaria, ed., *Mimorum Romanorum Fragmenta* (Geneva: Institutio di Filologia Classica, 1955).

28. Geoffrey S. Sumi, "Impersonating the Dead: Mimes at Roman Funerals," *American Journal of Philology* 123 (2002): 559–85.

29. Peter Brown, *The Cult of the Saints: Its Rise and Function in Latin Christianity* (Chicago: Chicago University Press, 1981), pp. 12–22; see also A. Momigliano, "Popular Religious Beliefs and the Late Roman Historians," *Studies in Church History* 8 (1971): 1–18.

30. Jas Elsner, Review of *Religion in Roman Egypt: Assimilation and Resistance* by David Frankfurter, *Classical Philology* 95, no. 1 (2000): 104.

31. David Frankfurter, *Religion in Roman Egypt: Assimilation and Resistance* (Princeton, NJ: Princeton University Press, 1998).

32. William G. Doty, *Mythography: The Study of Myths and Rituals* (Tuscaloosa: University of Alabama Press, 1986).

33. Rüpke, *Religion of the Romans*, p. 127.

34. Kenneth Dowden, *On the Uses of Greek Myth* (London: Routledge, 1992), p. 7.

35. T. P. Wiseman, *The Myths of Rome* (Exeter, UK: University of Exeter Press, 2004), pp. 10–11.

36. Fritz Graf, "Myth," in *Religions of the Ancient World*, ed. Sarah Illes Johnston, pp. 45–58 (Cambridge, MA: Harvard University Press, 2004), p. 45.

37. Keith Roberts, *Religion in Sociological Perspective* (London: Wadsworth, 1995), p. 91.

38. See Stephen H. Travis, "Form Criticism," in *New Testament Interpretation: Essays on Principles and Methods*, ed. I. Howard Marshall, pp. 153–64 (Carlisle, UK: Paternoster Press, 1977).

39. Graf, "Myth," p. 54.

40. James F. Kay, "Myth or Narrative? Bultmann's 'New Testament and Mythology' Turns Fifty," *Theology Today* 48 (1991): 328.

41. Burton L. Mack, *The Christian Myth: Origins, Logic and Legacy* (London: Continuum, 2003), p. 17.

42. E.g., Ron Cameron and Merrill P. Miller, ed., *Redescribing Christian Origins* (Atlanta: Society of Biblical Literature, 2004).

43. John Gould, "On Making Sense of Greek Religion," in *Greek Religion and Society*, ed. P. E. Easterling and J. V. Muir, pp. 1–33 (Cambridge: Cambridge University Press, 1985), p. 8.

44. Phiroze Vasunia, "Hellenism and Empire: Reading Edward Said," *Parallax* 9, no. 4 (2003): 88–97.

45. Wiseman, *Myths of Rome*, p. 11.

46. Ibid.

47. Frankfurter, *Religion in Roman Egypt.*

48. See Lynn E. Roller, *In Search of God the Mother: The Cult of Anatolian Cybele* (Berkeley: University of California Press, 1999).

49. See James Aitken, "Hengel's *Judentum und Hellenismus*," *Journal of Biblical Literature* 123, no. 2 (2004): 331–41.

50. Philip Alexander, "Hellenism and Hellenization as Problematic Historiographical Categories," in *Paul Beyond the Judaism/Hellenism Divide*, ed. Troels Engberg-Pedersen, pp. 63–80 (Louisville, KY: Westminster John Knox, 2001), p. 79.

51. Jacob Neusner, *Development of a Legend: Studies on the Traditions Concerning Yohanan ben Zakkai* (Leiden: E. J. Brill, 1970).

52. E.g., Baba Metzia 59b, Menahot 29b; Eliezer Segal, "'The Few Contained the Many': Rabbinic Perspectives on the Miraculous and the Impossible," *Journal of Jewish Studies* 54 (2003): 273–82.

53. David E. Aune, "Prolegomena to the Study of Oral Tradition in the Hellenistic World," in *Jesus and the Oral Gospel Tradition*, ed. H. Wansbrough, (Sheffield, UK: Sheffield Academic Press, 1991), p. 98.

54. Luc Brisson, *How Philosophers Saved Myths: Allegorical Interpretation and Classical Mythology* (Chicago: University of Chicago Press: 2004).

55. J. Pépin, "Euhemerism of the Christian Authors," in *Mythologies*, ed. Yves Bonnefoy, pp. 666–71 (Chicago: Chicago University Press, 1991).

56. Veyne, *Did the Greeks Believe in Their Myths?* p. 45.

57. David Noy, *Foreigners at Rome: Citizens and Strangers* (London: Duckworth, 2000), p. 185.

58. Veyne, *Did the Greeks Believe in Their Myths?* p. 27.

59. Ibid., p. 1.

60. Ibid., p. 42.

61. Ibid.

62. Aune, "Prolegomena," p. 83.

63. John J. Winkler, *Auctor and Actor: A Narratological Reading of Apuleius'* The Golden Ass (Berkeley: University of California Press, 1985), p. 237; Alex Scobie, "Storytellers, Storytelling, and the Novel in Graeco-Roman Society," *Rhenisches Museum für Philologie* 122 (1979): 229–59.

64. See Aune, "Prolegomena," pp. 69–71.

65. Horsfall, *Culture of the Roman Plebs*, pp. 48–63.

66. S. F. Bonner, *Education in Ancient Rome* (London: Routledge, 1977), p. 212.

67. Theresa Morgan, *Literate Education in thhe Hellenistic and Roman Worlds* (Cambridge: Cambridge University Press, 1998).

68. Eva Canterella, *Pandora's Daughters: The Role and Status of Women in Greek and Roman Antiquity* (Baltimore: Johns Hopkins University Press, 1987), p. 134.

69. Veyne, *Did the Greeks Believe in Their Myths?* p. 43.

70. Notably in the otherwise exemplary work of Aune, "Prolegomena"; though see Scobie, "Storytellers."

71. Joanna Dewey, "The Survival of Mark's Gospel: A Good Story?" *Journal of Biblical Literature* 123 (2004): 495–507; Holly E. Hearon, *The Mary Magdalene Tradition: Witness and Counter-Witness in Early Christian Communities* (Collegeville, MN: Michael Glazier, 2004), pp. 37–73, 320–36.

72. Birger Gerhardsson, *Tradition and Transmission in Early Christianity* (Lund: Gleerup, 1964); Birger Gerhardsson, *The Reliability of the Gospel Tradition* (Peabody: Hendrickson, 2001); Werner H. Kelber, *The Oral and the Written Gospel: The Hermeneutics of Speaking and Writing in the Synoptic Tradition, Mark, Paul, and Q* (Philadelphia: Fortress, 1987); James D. G. Dunn, *Christianity in the Making: Vol. 1, Jesus Remembered* (Grand Rapids, MI: Eerdmans, 2003); James D. G. Dunn, *Unity and Diversity in the New Testament: An Inquiry into the Character of Earliest Christianity*, 2nd ed. (London: SCM, 1990).

73. J. N. D. Kelly, *A Commentary on the Epistles of Peter and Jude* (Grand Rapids, MI: Baker, 1969), p. 316.

74. Jerome H. Neyrey, "The Form and Background of the Polemic in 2 Peter," *Journal of Biblical Literature* 99 (1980): 409–12.

75. Alistair Logan, *The Gnostics: Identifying an Ancient Christian Cult* (London: Continuum, 2005), p. 2.

76. Helmut Koester, "GNOMAI DIAPHOROI: The Origin and Nature of Diversification in the History of Early Christianity," *Harvard Theological Review* 58 (1965): 279–318.

77. Daniel J. Harrington, "The Reception of Walter Bauer's 'Orthodoxy and Heresy in Earliest Christianity' during the Last Decade," *Harvard Theological Review* 73, no. 1, (1980): 296.

78. John Dominic Crossan, *The Birth of Christianity: Discovering What Hap-

pened in the Years Immediately After the Execution of Jesus (Edinburgh: T&T Clark, 1998); Mack, *The Christian Myth*.

79. Robert M. Price, *Deconstructing Jesus* (Amherst, NY: Prometheus Books, 2000), p. 149.

80. David Seeley, "Jesus' Death in Q," *New Testament Studies* 38 (1992): 222–34.

81. Price, *Deconstructing Jesus*, p. 266.

82. See Austin Farrer, "On Dispensing with Q," in *Studies in the Gospels*, ed. D. Nineham, pp. 55–86 (Oxford: Basil Blackwell, 1955); Mark Goodacre, *Goulder and the Gospels* (Sheffield, UK: Sheffield Academic Press, 1996); Mark Goodacre, *The Case Against Q: Studies in Markan Priority and the Synoptic Problem* (Harrisburg, PA: Trinity Press International, 2002); Mark Goodacre and Nicholas Perrin, eds., *Questioning Q* (London: SPCK, 2004); M. Goulder, *Luke: A New Paradigm*, 2 vols. (Sheffield, UK: JSOT Press, 1989); M. Goulder, "Is Q a Juggernaut?" *Journal of Biblical Literature* 115 (1996): 667–81.

83. Stephen Carlson, *The Gospel Hoax: Morton Smith's Invention of Secret Mark* (Waco, TX: Baylor University Press, 2005); Peter Jeffery, *The Secret Gospel of Mark Unveiled: Imagined Rituals of Sex, Death, and Madness in a Biblical Forgery* (New Haven, CT: Yale University Press, 2006); cf. Scott G. Brown, *Mark's Other Gospel: Rethinking Morton Smith's Controversial Discovery* (Waterloo, ON: Wilfrid Laurier University Press, 2005).

84. See Dennis E. Smith, "What Do We Really Know about the Jerusalem Church? Christian Origins in Jerusalem According to Acts and Paul," in *Redescribing Christian Origins*, ed. Ron Cameron and Merrill P. Miller, pp. 237–52 (Atlanta: Society of Biblical Literature, 2004); Merrill P. Miller, "'Beginning from Jerusalem...': Re-examining Canon and Consensus," *Journal of Higher Criticism* 2, no. 1 (1995): 3–30; Merrill P. Miller, "Antioch, Paul, and Jerusalem: Diaspora Myths of Origins in the Homeland," in *Redescribing Christian Origins*, ed. Ron Cameron and Merrill P. Miller, pp. 177–235 (Atlanta: Society of Biblical Literature, 2004).

85. Melanie J. Wright, "Re-viewing My Son the Fanatic after 7/7; or Roots, Routes, and Rhizomes," in *The Religious Roots of Contemporary European Identity*, ed. Lucia Faltin and Melanie J. Wright, pp. 29–39 (London: Continuum, 2007), p. 38.

86. Gilles Deleuze and Félix Guattari, *A Thousand Plateaus: Capitalism and Schizophrenia* (Minneapolis: University of Minnesota Press, 1987).

87. Price, *Deconstructing Jesus*, p. 149.

88. Kenneth E. Bailey, "Informal Controlled Oral Tradition and the Synoptic Gospels," *Asia Journal of Theology* 5, no. 1, (1991): 34–54; Kenneth E. Bailey, "Middle Eastern Oral Tradition and the Synoptic Gospels," *Expository*

Times 106, no. 12 (1995): 363–67; Richard Bauckham, *Jesus and the Eyewitnesses: The Gospels as Eyewitness Testimony* (Cambridge: Eerdmans, 2006); Thorleif Boman, *Die Jesus-Überlieferung im Lichte der neueren Volkskunde* (Göttingen: Vandenhoeck & Ruprecht, 1967); Samuel Byrskog, *Story as History, History as Story: The Gospel Tradition in the Context of Ancient Oral History* (Leiden: Brill, 2002); Dunn, *Christianity in the Making*; Gerhardsson, *Tradition and Transmission*; Gerhardsson, *Reliability of the Gospel Tradition*; Kelber, *The Oral and the Written Gospel.*

89. Bauckham, *Jesus and the Eyewitnesses*, p. 8.

90. Dunn, *Christianity in the Making*, p. 240.

91. Emilio Gabba, "True History and False History in Classical Antiquity," *Journal of Roman Studies* 71 (1981): 53. This reference was not included in the bibliographical listings.

92. A. M. Honoré, "A Statistical Study of the Synoptic Problem," *Novum Testamentum* 10 (1968): 95–147.

93. Anne M. O'Leary, *Matthew's Judaization of Mark Examined in the Context of the Use of Sources in Graeco-Roman Antiquity* (London: Continuum, 2006).

94. Justin J. Meggitt, "The Psycho-Social Context of Jesus' Miracles," in *Jesus and Healing*, ed. Fraser Watts (Cambridge: Cambridge University Press, forthcoming); Meggitt, "Magic and Early Christianity."

95. Meggitt, "Magic and Early Christianity," p. 114; Gerd Theissen, *The Gospels in Context: Social and Political History in the Synoptic Tradition* (Minneapolis: Fortress Press, 1991), p. 103.

96. Meggitt, "The Psycho-Social Context of Jesus' Miracles"; Meggitt, "Magic and Early Christianity."

97. Meggitt, "The Madness of King Jesus."

98. E. P. Sanders, *Jesus and Judaism* (London: SCM, 1985), p. 11.

BAYES'S THEOREM FOR BEGINNERS: FORMAL LOGIC AND ITS RELEVANCE TO HISTORICAL METHOD

1. For examples, criticisms, and bibliography, see Christopher Tuckett, "Sources and Methods," in *The Cambridge Companion to Jesus*, ed. Markus Bockmuehl, pp. 121–37 (Cambridge: Cambridge University Press, 2001).

2. Stanley Porter, *The Criteria for Authenticity in Historical-Jesus Research: Previous Discussion and New Proposals* (Sheffield, UK: Sheffield Academic Press, 2000).

3. Hector Avalos, *The End of Biblical Studies* (Amherst, NY: Prometheus Books, 2007), pp. 203–209.

4. Cf. e.g., Stanley Porter, "The Criterion of Greek Language and Its Context: A Further Response," *Journal for the Study of the Historical Jesus* 4, no. 1 (2006): 69–74, in response to Michael F. Bird, "The Criterion of Greek Language and Context: A Response to Stanley E. Porter," *Journal for the Study of the Historical Jesus* 4, no. 1 (2006): 55–67.

5. E.g., Dale Allison, "The Historians' Jesus and the Church," in *Seeking the Identity of Jesus: A Pilgrimage*, ed. Beverly Roberts Gaventa and Richard B. Hays, pp. 79–95 (Grand Rapids, MI: William B. Eerdmans, 2008).

6. Gerd Theissen and Dagmar Winter, *The Quest for the Plausible Jesus: The Question of Criteria* (Louisville, KY: John Knox Press, 2002).

7. Though see C. Behan McCullagh, *Justifying Historical Descriptions* (Cambridge: Cambridge University Press, 1984), pp. 45–73.

8. Porter, *Criteria for Authenticity*, p. 115, quoting remarks by Theissen.

9. Mary Rose D'Angelo, "Abba and Father: Imperial Theology in the Contexts of Jesus and the Gospels," in *The Historical Jesus in Context*, ed. Amy-Jill Levine, Dale C. Allison Jr., and John Dominic Crossan, pp. 64–78 (Princeton, NJ: Princeton University Press, 2006).

10. E.g., Richard Carrier, "The Spiritual Body of Christ and the Legend of the Empty Tomb," in *The Empty Tomb: Jesus Beyond the Grave*, ed. Robert Price and Jeffery Jay Lowder, pp. 105–231 (Amherst, NY: Prometheus Books, 2005), pp. 107–10.

11. Eliezer Yudkowsky, "An Intuitive Explanation of Bayesian Reasoning (Bayes's Theorem for the Curious and Bewildered: An Excruciatingly Gentle Introduction)," http://yudkowsky.net/rational/bayes (accessed December 3, 2005).

12. Douglas Hunter, *Political [and] Military Applications of Bayesian Analysis: Methodological Issues* (Boulder, CO: Westview Press, 1984).

13. E.T. Jaynes and G. Larry Bretthorst, *Probability Theory: The Logic of Science* (Cambridge: Cambridge University Press, 2003); Luc Bovens and Stephan Hartmann, *Bayesian Epistemology* (Oxford: Oxford University Press, 2003); Richard Swinburne, ed., *Bayes's Theorem* (Oxford: Oxford University Press, 2002); Timothy McGrew, "Bayesian Reasoning: An Annotated Bibliography," http://homepages.wmich.edu/~mcgrew/bayes.htm (accessed December 3, 2005).

14. Richard Carrier, "Bayes's Theorem for Beginners: Formal Logic and Its Relevance to Historical Method—Adjunct Materials and Tutorial." Archived December 10, 2008, http://www.richardcarrier.info/Carrier Dec08.pdf.

15. Richard Carrier, *Sense and Goodness without God: A Defense of Metaphysical Naturalism* (Bloomington, IN: AuthorHouse, 2005), pp. 57, 227–52.

16. Carrier, "The Spiritual Body of Christ," pp. 168–82.

17. Per Carrier, *Sense and Goodness without God*, pp. 40–42, 219–20.

THE ABHORRENT VOID: THE RAPID ATTRIBUTION OF FICTIVE SAYINGS AND STORIES TO A MYTHIC JESUS

1. C. H. Dodd, "About the Gospels," radio broadcast, 1949, quoted in F. F. Bruce, *Tradition: Old and New* (Grand Rapids: Zondervan, 1970), p. 41.

2. Everett F. Harrison, "Tradition of the Sayings of Jesus: A Crux Interpretum," in *Towards a Theology for the Future*, ed. Clark H. Pinnock and David F. Wells, p. 44 (Carol Stream: Creation House, 1971).

3. As Don Imus's character, the Reverend Billy Saul Hargis, once tried to do!

4. Raymond E. Brown, *The Gospel of John: Introduction, Translation, and Notes*, Anchor Bible 29 (Garden City: Doubleday, 1966), vol. 1, comments on Jn 2:1–11.

5. Ignaz Goldziher, *Hadith and the New Testament* (London: SPCK, 1902).

6. Paul-Louis Couchoud, *The Creation of Christ: An Outline of the Beginnings of Christianity*, trans. C. Bradlaugh Bonner (London: Watts, 1939), p. 182. Of course, many nonmythicist Gospel critics recognize the same thing, but they do not seem to notice the oddity that the Christ-mythicist Couchoud noticed: why would such a wholesale borrowing be necessary if there really had been a great teacher at the start of the thing?

7. Cf. Jn 14:26; 16:12–15.

8. Cf. Lk 10:16; 21:14–15.

9. Ignaz Goldziher, *Introduction to Islamic Theology and Law*, Modern Classics in Near Eastern Studies, trans. Andras and Ruth Hamori (Princeton, NJ: Princeton University Press, 1981), pp. 43–44.

10. The Herod story, that of the Slaughter of the Innocents, is most easily explained as copied from Josephus's account of Moses' nativity, while the link with the historical Pilate is ruined by the gross improbability of the ruthless Roman bending over backwards to free Jesus, even letting a known killer of Romans go free in his place. It is just not believable as history. See S. G. F. Brandon, *Jesus and the Zealots: A Study of the Political Factor in Primitive Christianity* (New York: Scribner's, 1967), pp. 3–5.

11. Cf. Rom 3:8.

12. See the stories in which Jesus repudiates his relatives, a polemic against the leadership of the heirs, e.g., Mk 3:20–21, 31–35; John 7:5; or endorses them,

Mk 6:3's official list of his caliph-successors; cf. Thomas saying 12. Pro-Paul in Mk 9:38–40; anti-Paul in Mt 5:17–19; 7:21–23.

13. Muhammad Zubayr Siddiqi, *Hadith Literature: Its Origin, Development and Special Features* (Cambridge: Islamic Texts Society, 1993), p. 32.

14. Ibid, pp. 33–34.

15. E.g., pro-fasting in Mt 6:16–17, Mk 2:20, Thomas saying 27; anti-fasting in Mk 2:21–22, Thomas saying 14.

16. E.g., mission only to Jews in Mt 10:5, or to all nations in Mt 28:19.

17. Ram Swarup, *Understanding the Hadith: The Sacred Traditions of Islam* (Amherst, NY: Prometheus Books, 2002), pp. 6–7.

18. Joseph Schacht, "A Reevaluation of Islamic Traditions," in *The Quest for the Historical Muhammad,* ed. and trans. Ibn Warraq, p. 361 (Amherst, NY: Prometheus Books, 2000).

19. E.g., I. Howard Marshall, *I Believe in the Historical Jesus,* I Believe Series no. 5 (Grand Rapids, MI: Eerdmans, 1977), pp. 195–96.

20. Harald Riesenfeld, *The Gospel Tradition,* trans. Margaret Rowley and Robert Kraft (Philadelphia: Fortress Press, 1970); Birger Gerhardsson, *Memory and Manuscript: Oral Tradition and Written Transmission in Rabbinic Judaism and Early Christianity,* Acta Seminarii Neotestamentici Upsaliensis XXII, trans. Eric J. Sharpe (Lund: C. W. K. Gleerup and Ejnar Munksgaard, 1961); Birger Gerhardsson, *The Reliability of the Gospel Tradition* (Peabody, MA: Hendrickson, 2001).

21. Jacob Neusner, *The Peripatetic Saying: The Problem of the Thrice-Told Tale in Talmudic Literature,* Brown Judaic Studies 89 (Chico, CA: Scholars Press, 1985).

22. Majella Franzmann, *Jesus in the Nag Hammadi Writings* (Edinburgh: T. & T. Clark, 1996), pp. 1–18.

23. Margaret Barker, *The Risen Lord: The Jesus of History as the Christ of Faith* (Philadelphia: Trinity Press International, 1996), pp. 98–110.

24. F. F. Bruce, *The New Testament Documents: Are They Reliable?* 5th ed. (London: Inter-Varsity Fellowship, 1960), p. 33, quoted in John Warwick Montgomery, *History & Christianity* (Downers Grove, IL: InterVarsity Press, 1974), p. 39.

25. Elizabeth Claire Prophet (as Jesus Christ), *Watch with Me* (Gardiner, MT: Summit Lighthouse, 1965).

26. Helen Schucman, *A Course in Miracles* (Glen Ellen, CA: Foundation for Inner Peace, 1975).

JESUS' DISPUTE IN THE TEMPLE AND THE ORIGIN OF THE EUCHARIST

1. As I have shown at length, Jesus is called "rabbi" more than any other title in the Gospels, and his characteristic activities correspond well to those of other rabbis of his period: Bruce Chilton, *Rabbi Jesus: An Intimate Biography* (New York: Doubleday, 2000).

2. See Bruce Chilton, *Pure Kingdom: Jesus' Vision of God*, Studying the Historical Jesus 1 (Grand Rapids, MI: Eerdmans, 1996).

3. Josephus, *Jewish War* 2.197, 409; *Against Apion* 2.77; Philo, *Embassy to Gaius*, 157, 317.

4. Mishnah tractate Shekalim 1:1, 3; Josephus, *Jewish War* 7.218; *Antiquities of the Jews* 18.312.

5. See Bruce Chilton, "A Coin of Three Realms: Matthew 17:24–27," in *The Bible in Three Dimensions: Essays in Celebration of Forty Years of Biblical Studies in the University of Sheffield*, Journal for the Study of the Old Testament, Supplement 87, ed. D. J. A. Clines, S. E. Fowl, and S. E. Porter, pp. 269–82 (Sheffield: JSOT, 1990).

6. *Antiquities* 13.372–73.

7. *Antiquities* 17.149–67.

8. See Bruce Chilton, *The Temple of Jesus: His Sacrificial Program Within a Cultural History of Sacrifice* (University Park: Pennsylvania State University Press, 1992).

9. Babylonian Talmud tractate Beza 20a, b; Tosephta Chagigah 2:11; Jerusalem Talmud tractate Chagigah 2:3 and Beza 2:4.

10. Shabbat 15a; Sanhedrin 41a; Avodah Zarah 8b.

11. Josephus, *Antiquities* 15.417.

12. For a full exegetical discussion, see Bruce Chilton, *A Feast of Meanings: Eucharistic Theologies from Jesus through Johannine Circles*, Supplements to Novum Testamentum 72 (Leiden: Brill, 1994).

13. Josephus, *Jewish War* 2.409.

14. See Bruce Chilton, "The So-Called Trial Before the Sanhedrin," *Forum* 1.1 [new series] (1998): 163–80.

THE AUTHORIZED VERSION OF HIS BIRTH AND DEATH

1. David Trobisch, *The First Edition of the New Testament* (Oxford: Oxford University Press, 2000).

PROLEGOMENON TO A SCIENCE OF CHRISTIAN ORIGINS

1. René Salm, *The Myth of Nazareth: The Invented Town of Jesus* (Cranford, NJ: American Atheist Press, 2008), pp. xvi, 375.

2. Frank R. Zindler, *The Jesus the Jews Never Knew:* Sepher Toldoth Yeshu *and the Quest of the Historical Jesus in Jewish Sources* (Cranford, NJ: American Atheist Press, 2003), pp. xvii, 524.

3. Frank R. Zindler, "Capernaum—A Literary Invention," *Journal of Higher Criticism* 12, no. 2 (Fall 2006): 1–27.

4. Aviram Oshri, "Where Was Jesus Born?" *Archaeology* (November/December 2005): 42–45.

5. Edward Maunde Thompson, *An Introduction to Greek and Latin Palaeography* (Oxford: Clarendon Press, 1912), pp. 78, 79, 81.

6. It is true that Newton did show in *An Historical Account of Two Notable Corruptions of Scripture* (1754) that the *Comma Johanneum* in 1 John 5:7 was a corruption originally lacking "the Father, the Word, and the Holy Ghost," and that 1 Timothy 3:16 had been altered by substituting "God" for "he." However, these discoveries involved a completely different type of investigation than did most of his religious writings.

1 Jn 5:7—For there are three that bear record in heaven, *the Father, the Word, and the Holy Ghost:* and these three are one.

1 Timothy 3:16—And without controversy great is the mystery of godliness: *God* was manifest in the flesh, justified in the Spirit, seen of angels, preached unto the Gentiles, believed on in the world, received up into glory.

7. It may be admitted that in rare cases the safety of a product may be overestimated due to pressure from company executives who are more worried about the fiscal bottom line than about medical truth. Even so, such apolo-

getics is never successful for very long because in its very nature science is a self-correcting system, and apologetically fraudulent findings almost always are exposed by research in other laboratories.

"EVERY PLANT WHICH MY HEAVENLY FATHER HAS NOT PLANTED SHALL BE UPROOTED"

1. See below or *New Testament Code* (London: Watkins, 2006), pp. 289–97 and, for example, CDI.10–12, XII.20–1, XIII.22, 1QSIII.13, IX.12, IX. 21, etc.

2. CDI.7–8. This is followed by the note about "being like Blind Men," "seeking Him with a whole heart," and God "raising up for them a Teacher of Righteousness to guide them in the Way of His heart," i.e., "the Guide." There is also the first note here about God "visiting them"—see *New Testament Code*, pp. 601–29.

3. The defect here, which was first recognized by A. Von Harnack in "Die Verklarungsgeschichte Jesu, der Gericht des Paulus (I. Kor. 15.3ff.) under die Beiden Christusvisionen des Petrus," *Sitzungsberichte der Preussischen Akademia* 1922: 62–80, has to do with two versions of the sighting order in 1 Corinthians 15:6–7: "first to the Twelve" (there were only supposed to be "Eleven" at the time) and "then to James, then all the Apostles" (a redundancy)—the latter obviously being the authentic tradition.

4. For "the First" at Qumran, which usually represents "the Forefathers who received the Torah," see CDI.16 "the Last" or "Last Generation"/"Last Times" is already making its appearance here in I.11–12, but see also I.4, III.10, IV.6–9, VI.2, VIII.16–17, 1QpHabII.7, VII.2–12, IX.4–5, etc.

5. See, for instance, the Epistle of Peter to James 5.1 introducing the Homilies.

6. Cf. how Paul does this allegorically in Galatians 4:21–31 or in 1 Corinthians 6:12 (also about "food" and "the belly")—10:29: "All things are for me lawful"; and my conclusion on p. 997 of *New Testament Code*.

7. It should be appreciated, however, that in Matthew 15:24 the "house" does reappear, but now it becomes "not being sent except to the lost sheep of the house of Israel. "One should also note that in Matthew 15:13–14 the language of falling into a pit" also occurs, as does "uprooting plants," both of which will also recur, as we shall see, in CDI.7 and XI.13.

8. This is recapitulated in CDII.14–15, but now the exhortation includes "uncovering your eyes that you may see and understand the works of God... in order that you may walk in Perfection in all His ways and not follow after the thoughts of a sinful imagination or fornicating eyes."

9. The reader should appreciate, it would be easy to read here, "what they heard Paul saying"—as, for example, "John Mark" evidently was in Acts 13:13 and 15:38 when he "withdrew from them in Pamphylia." In these allusions in Acts, it becomes clear that "Mark's desertion" of the team (as Paul would have it) to report what was transpiring back to Jerusalem was not an amicable one; but clearly involved a good deal of ill will—and this in the usually more accurate "We document." Here, since Mark 7:1 had already used the verb "come" to describe the usual "coming down from Jerusalem, while Matthew 15:1 had rather expressed this as: "then come to Jesus from Jerusalem Pharisees and Scribes" (forgetting both the "some" and the "down"); to avoid redundancy Mark must now use the basically meaningless phraseology "there gathered unto him the Pharisees and some of the scribes"—n.b., how Mark has added here the usual "some" to complete the implication of the "some from James coming" down from Jerusalem of Paul in Galatians 2:12 and elsewhere in the Gospels as earlier in Mark 14:4 or Luke 19:39 or John 9:40.

10. Even the allusion in Mark 7:21–23 (in this instance, the most prolix Gospel) to the heart's "evil thoughts, murder, adulteries, fornications, thefts, false witness, railings" as "defiling the man" recalls the Community Rule's depiction of "the Spirit of Unrighteousness" or "of Evil" as: "greediness of soul, stumbling hands in the service of Righteousness (cf. Paul in 2 Corinthians 11:15), Wickedness and Lying, pride and proudness of heart, duplicitousness and deceitfulness, cruelty, ill-temper, impatience, much folly, and zeal for lustfulness, works of abomination in a spirit of fornication, and Ways of Uncleanness in the service of pollution, a Tongue full of blasphemies, blindness of eye and dullness of ear, stiffness of neck and hardness of heart in order to walk in all the Ways of Darkness and Evil inclination" in 1QSIV.9–11; cf. Matthew 15:19 and below.

11. That the issue is "table fellowship with Gentiles" is just strengthened by all these allusions to "blindness" (as in John 9:13–41 above), "Blind Guides," and "hypocrites"/"hypocrisy." At Qumran, as reiterated variously in the Damascus Document, the position is "doing according to the precise letter of the Torah" and "setting up the Holy Things according to their precise specifications" (IV.8, VI.20, XX.6, etc.), whereas in Paul and the New Testament following him, it is "not to separate Holy from profane" (Acts 10:14–5) and "all things are for me lawful . . . eat everything sold in the butcher shop, in no way inquiring because of conscience" (Paul's favorite euphemism for "the Law"— 1 Corinthians 10:23–25).

12. The reference is to 1QSIV.4 on "the Two Spirits." The parallel kind of expressions in Hymns are to be found in II.15, V.24, IX.3 and 23, XIV.13–14, etc.

13. See James 3:4–8.

14. This is the second part of "the Two Spirits" in the Community Rule—"the Spirit of Righteousness" or "Cleanliness"—1QSIV.9–11.

15. Cf. CDI.11–12, XII.20–21, XIII.22–3, 1QHIII.13, IX.12–26, 1QHXII.11, etc.

16. 1QSIX.12–14.

17. Furthermore, the implication of the whole simile embodied in this passage, would appear to involve "the Judgment Day," since the Hebrew *camal* —as in the all-important Isaiah 53:11 proof-text and the Qumran Habakkuk Pesher, seemingly like the Gospels dependent upon it—is eschatological and also part of the vocabulary here. One can see this *camal* in 1QpHabVIII.2–3's interpretation of Habakkuk 2:4: "the Righteous shall live by his Faith."

18. In the incredible hymn at the end of the Community Rule in 1QSX–XI, the Council is even pictured as "joined to the Sons of Heaven" and described as "an Eternal Planting" or "Plantation" (XI.8–9, but also see VIII.4–9: "With the existence of these in Israel, the Council of the Community will be established upon Truth like an Eternal Plantation, a House of Holiness for Israel . . . a Tested Rampart, a Precious Cornerstone, the foundation of which will not shake or sway in their place . . . a House of Perfection and Truth in Israel"). This is not to mention the "God causing a Root of Planting to grow" itself of the Damascus Document, which will also be directly parodied not only in Paul, but here in the Synoptics as well.

19. CDI.5–8.

20. This "Pit" language is very important and, as we shall see, is duplicated in Matthew 15:14, however tendentiously. Probably the best example of it is to be found in CDVI. 12–14, including the "Nazirite" language of "keeping away from" and "separation," as well as Acts 21:30's "barring the door," introducing the definition of "the New Covenant in the Land of Damascus" in VI.16–18; but also see XIII.14 and XIV.2 and 1QSIX.16–21 above.

21. CDXI.13–14.

22. There is some evidence that "Jesus" (whoever he may have been) came in 19–21 CE. This comes in Eusebius's citation from what he considers to be the fraudulent *Acti Pilati*, which places the crucifixion in that year (E.H. 1.9.3–4); but Tacitus, too (*Annals* 2.85), places the expulsion of the Jews from Rome under Tiberius in most peculiar and suspicious circumstances in this period as well, not later as in Josephus's version of similar events—see James the Brother of Jesus, pp. 66 and 863–64. In this manner, the mysterious "twenty years" in CDI.10 evaporates. Furthermore, this would explain why Paul, who is supposed to be functioning ca. 37 CE onwards, knows so little about the

"Christ Jesus" (the eyewitness testimony of whom is almost nil) he is talking about. If there is a "Historical Jesus"—aside from the Samaritan one—this is probably the best way of understanding him.

23. CDII.9–11.

24. See, for instance, the document Prof. Wise and myself discovered (4Q285—we called it "The Messianic Leader"), which identifies "the Root of Jesse" with "the Branch of David" and, in turn, "the Nasi ha-cEdah"/"the Leader of the Assembly" or "Church." This Messianic Leader, of course, then reappears in documents like 4QFlorI.11–13 and CDVII.16–20, above, not to mention the interpretation of "the Shiloh Prophecy" of Genesis 49:10 in 4Q252 or so-called "Genesis Pesher"—see Robert Eisenman and Michael Wise, *Dead Sea Scrolls Uncovered* (New York: Penguin Books, 1992), pp. 24–29 and 77–89, and *New Testament Code*, pp. 349–55, 638–56, and 674–75.

ASSESSING THE EVIDENCE: PHILOSOPHICAL AND LEGAL PERSPECTIVES

1. Simon Greenleaf, *The Testimony of the Evangelists Examined by the Rules of Evidence Administered in Courts of Justice* (Grand Rapids, MI: Baker Book House, 1984 [1874]).

2. R. Clifford, *Leading Lawyers' Case for the Resurrection* (Edmonton: Canadian Institute for Law, Theology and Public Policy, 1996).

3. A discussion of the relevant federal rules of evidence, 803(16) and 901(b)(8), may be found in S. Saltzburg and K. R. Redden, *Federal Rules of Evidence Manual*, 4th ed. (Charlottesville, VA: Michie Company, 1986).

4. J. D. Crossan, *The Historical Jesus: The Life of a Mediterranean Jewish Peasant* (San Francisco: Harper, 1991).

5. L. Wittgenstein, *Philosophical Investigations*, 3rd ed., trans. G. E. M. Anscombe (New York: Macmillan, 1968), § 79.

6. S. Kripke, *Naming and Necessity* (Cambridge, MA: Harvard University Press, 1980).

7. W. K. C. Guthrie, *A History of Greek Philosophy: The Fifth-Century Enlightenment* (Cambridge: Cambridge University Press, 1969).

8. A. Schweitzer, *The Quest of the Historical Jesus: A Critical Study of Its Progress from Reimarus to Wrede*, 3rd ed., trans. W. Montgomery (London: A. & C. Black, 1956), p. 6.

9. See Guthrie, *History of Greek Philosophy*, p. 382.

JESUS' APOCALYPTIC VISION AND THE
PSYCHODYNAMICS OF DELUSION

1. Albert Schweitzer, *The Psychiatric Study of Jesus: Exposition and Critique*, trans C. R. Joy (Boston: Beacon, 1948 [1913]).

2. Albert Schweitzer, *The Quest for the Historical Jesus: A Critical Study of Its Progress from Reimarus to Wrede*, trans. W. Montgomery (New York: Macmillan, 1968 [1907]).

3. Schweitzer, *Psychiatric Study of Jesus*, flyleaf preceding the Prefatory Note.

4. Karl Barth, *The Epistle to the Romans* (London: Oxford University Press, 1933), p. 314.

5. Throughout this paper, translations of biblical texts are my own.

6. Alan Segal, *Rebecca's Children: Judaism and Christianity in the Roman World* (Cambridge, MA: Harvard University Press, 1986).

7. G. Ernest Wright and Reginald H. Fuller, *The Book of the Acts of God: Christian Scholarship Interprets the Bible* (Garden City, NY: Doubleday, 1957).

8. Gabriele Boccaccini, *Beyond the Essene Hypothesis: The Parting of the Ways between Qumran and Enochic Judaism* (Grand Rapids, MI: Eerdmans, 1998).

9. Ibid.

10. The following paradigm of the Progression of Images was previously published in a somewhat different and less developed form in J. Harold Ellens, *Jesus as the Son of Man, the Literary Character: A Progression of Images*, Occasional Papers 45 (Claremont, CA: Institute for Antiquity and Christianity of the Claremont Graduate University, 2003).

11. Margaret S. Odell, "You Are What You Eat: Ezekiel and the Scroll," *JBL* 117 (1998): 229–48.

12. Donald Capps, *Jesus: A Psychological Biography* (St. Louis: Chalice Press, 2000). See also Paula Fredriksen, *From Jesus to Christ: The Origins of the New Testament Images of Jesus*, 2nd ed. (New Haven, CT: Yale University Press, 2000).

13. Marvin A. Sweeney, *Ezekiel: Zadokite Priest and Visionary Prophet of the Exile*, Occasional Papers 41 (Claremont, CA: Institute for Antiquity and Christianity of the Claremont Graduate University, 2001), pp. 5–6.

14. Capps, *Jesus: A Psychological Biography*.

15. Florentino García Martínez, *The Dead Sea Scrolls Translated: The Qumran Texts in English*, 2nd ed. (Grand Rapids, MI: Eerdmans, 1996), pp. 7 and 13–14.

16. Ibid., pp. 13–14. This same description of the redemptive messianic figure is expressed in 11Q13(Mel).

17. George W. E. Nickelsburg, "Son of Man," in *Anchor Bible Dictionary (ABD)*, ed. David Noel Freedman (New York: Doubleday, 1992), 6:138.

18. Israel Knohl, *The Messiah before Jesus: The Suffering Servant of the Dead Sea Scrolls*, trans. D. Maisel (Berkeley: University of California Press, 2000).

19. Ibid.

20. Ibid., pp. 75ff.

21. Ibid., p. 76.

22. Boccaccini, *Beyond the Essene Hypothesis*, pp. 137–38 and 147–48.

23. John J. Collins, *Apocalypticism in the Dead Sea Scrolls* (New York: Routledge, 1997), p. 147.

24. Knohl, *Messiah before Jesus*, p. 42.

25. Ibid., pp. 45–46.

26. Ibid., p. 3.

27. Boccaccini, *Beyond the Essene Hypothesis*, pp. 119–62.

28. Ibid., p. 134.

29. Ibid., pp. 137–38 and 147–48.

30. Ibid., p. 149.

31. Unfortunately, it has not been possible for me to examine the manuscripts and fragments themselves, but only the available photographs. On the face of it there seems to be some cogency to Knohl's claim regarding the state of the manuscripts as a result of their being intentionally torn—as well as intentionally preserved. However, in a personal conversation with James C. Charlesworth over a superb Italian dinner at the Villa Villoresi in Florence during the first Enoch Seminar at the International Conference on Second Temple Judaism (19–23 June 2001), that notable Dead Sea Scrolls scholar stated that he believes it is likely that the fragmentary character of the remains of these hymnic manuscripts is a result of the same process of deterioration from age, exposure, and vermin that caused the fragmentation of other Dead Sea scrolls. Moreover, he does not think highly of Israel Knohl's argument.

32. Philip B. Munoa III, in a lecture delivered in 1995 at the University of Michigan, Department of Near Eastern Studies, argued on the basis of the *Testament of Abraham* that the Ancient of Days in Daniel 7 is Adam in a transcendent state. This thesis was published in more elaborated form in *Four Powers in Heaven: The Interpretation of Daniel 7 in the Testament of Abraham*, *JSPSup* 28 (Sheffield, UK: Sheffield Academic Press, 1998).

33. Notice the shift to the plural verb in John 1:51, in contrast with the singular verb in 1:48 and 1:50.

34. Donald Capps (2004), "Beyond Schweitzer and the Psychiatrists: Jesus as Fictive Personality," in *Psychology and the Bible, A New Way to Read the Scrip-*

tures, ed. J. Harold Ellens and Wayne G. Rollins (Westport, CT: Praeger, 2004), pp. 89–124. See also Donald Capps (2004), "Jay Haley's Psychological Portrait of Jesus: A Power Tactician," in Ellens and Rollins, *Psychology and the Bible*, pp. 125–62; Donald Capps (2004), "Erik Erikson's Psychological Portrait of Jesus: Jesus as Numinous Presence," in Ellens and Rollins, *Psychology and the Bible*, pp. 163–208; Donald Capps, *Jesus: A Psychological Biography* (St. Louis: Chalice Press, 2000); and Donald Capps (2004), "A Psychobiography of Jesus," in Ellens and Rollins, *Psychology and the Bible*, pp. 59–70.

35. Charles R. Joy, Introduction, "Schweitzer's Conception of Jesus," in Schweitzer, *Psychiatric Study of Jesus*, p. 21.

37. Ibid., p. 25.